S0-BOI-483

the Gardeners' Community Cookbook

SMITH & HAWKEN

the Gardeners' Community Cookbook

Compiled and written by

VICTORIA WISE

Photography by ALISON MIKSCH

WORKMAN PUBLISHING • NEW YORK

Published simultaneously in Canada by Thomas Allen & Son Limited.

Library of Congress Cataloging-in-Publication Data

Wise, Victoria.
The gardeners' community cookbook / compiled and written by Victoria Wise.
p. cm.
ISBN 0-7611-1743-1 (pbk.)
ISBN 0-7611-1772-5 (hc.)
1. Cookery, American. I. Title. II. Title: At head of title: Smith & Hawken. III. Smith & Hawken.

TX715.W78393 1999
641.5973 21—dc21 99-043491

Design by Paul Hanson and Elizabeth Johnsboen

Workman Publishing Company
708 Broadway, New York, NY 10003-9555
www.workmanweb.com

Manufactured in the U.S.A.

First printing September 1999
10 9 8 7 6 5 4 3 2 1

Most of all, everyone who submitted a recipe for inclusion in this book must be heartily thanked. It was heartwarming to receive the wonderful stories of how people love their gardens and were moved to share their own recipes and those from their family archives.

The recipe testers must not only be thanked but given a double bow. With so many recipes, I could not have gotten the job done without them. Each, whose cooking and gardening credentials are of the highest degree, furrowed a row in the middle of busy schedules to join the community spirit of this project. For their special participation, their avid love of gardening and cooking, and their expertise, I thank Arayah Jenanyan, Penny Brogden, Karen Frerichs, Fernando Brito, and Jenan Wise.

I also thank my professional associates from around the country who happily joined in with *gratis* contributions because of their love of gardens, cooking, garden cookbooks, and worthwhile community projects such as Second Harvest. They include: Bruce Aidells, Rose Levy Beranbaum, Jan Birnbaum, Deborah and Jerry Budrick, Ruth Rogers Clausen, Barbara Damrosch, Gail Deferrari and Julia McClasky, Shaun Doty, Janet Fletcher, Beth Hensperger, Richard Hirshen, Susanna Hoffman, Ken Hom, Gary Jenanyan, Barbara Kafka, Thomas Keller, Kevin Kennedy, Deborah Krasner, Sheila Lukins, Deborah Madison, Alice Medrich, Mark Miller, Diana Murphy, Cindy Pawlcyn, James "Chooch" Potenziani, Dori Sanders, Lindsey Shere, Sandy Sonnenfelt, Mike Tierney, Emilie Tolley, Patricia Unterman, Alice Waters, and Paula Wolfert. In addition, I thank Paul Rude, who patiently suffers every bug and botanical question I bring to him, and Susan Derecskey, whose vast knowledge and eagle eye I rely upon.

This book would not have come to be without the collaboration of Smith & Hawken, in particular Kathy Tierney and Deborah Bishop; Workman Publishing, in particular Peter Workman, Sally Kovalchick, Paul Hanson, and Elizabeth Johnsboen; my agent, Martha Casselman; and Bonnie Dahan, who had a lot to do with putting together the group.

Finally, I cannot end my accolades without a special bow to my husband, Rick Wise, who somehow manages to allow my preoccupations and distractions when I am in the throes of writing a book and, better than that, actually enjoys the process and the resulting finished dishes that often are what we have for dinner.

Under the aegis of them all, I have had the opportunity to compile, edit, and write the entries for this cookbook. Doing so has been a true joy. The community, sharing, and participation that came from every corner of the country and beyond have widened my horizons and gladdened my days.

Good cooking comes from good growing
Good growing comes from loving the earth
Good dishes come from tending your pot
as you do your plot

—VICTORIA WISE

Contents

“You grow for yourself and you pass
over the fence to your neighbor.
How do you quantify the benefit of knitting
a family or a neighborhood together?”

—RICHARD DOSS

The Gardeners' Community Cookbook began simply enough—with a small stack of three-by-five cards and an envelope of handwritten pages. Like a bountiful garden, the collection grew to abundance as gardeners and cooks enthusiastically and generously contributed their tips, tricks, and a treasure trove of recipes for the sheer pleasure of participating in the project. From those seeds and that exuberance, this book took form and the persona of a community emerged. Unlike the traditional, over-the-fence or right-around-the-corner passing along, however, in this electronic age the "seeds" and sharing came from a neighborhood that extends to every state, Puerto Rico, and a few foreign countries. Spanning all occupations and places of residence—rural, urban, and suburban, north, south, east, and west—the contributors by and large work in jobs that are not cooking or gardening. Yet they are intent to make room in their lives for honing their gardening and cooking skills as they indulge their love of those activities.

As I reviewed the mounting mail, it was clear that inspiration for garden cooking can be found anywhere there is seasonal provender. It could be a very handy kitchen garden, a mountain meadow, a stairwell full of pots, a farmers' market. It was also clear that the genuine pleasure found in such places leads naturally to the desire to share the produce and creative ways to "fix" it. A modest pound of beans and a handful of fresh herbs might turn into a fine dish for the family's evening meal. A flat of strawberries at an irresistible price may call forth visions of ruby-red jam, enough to use as gifts for the holiday season. A summer garden full of edible flowers can lead to morning muffins with flower petal butter for bed-and-breakfast guests.

As a gardener, professional and home cook, and cookbook writer, I marveled over the host of uses the same ingredient can be put to according to individuals, to regions of the country, to ethnic background, to the time of year and what the harvest is: Zucchinis fixed in so many innovative and delicious ways that you won't mind having them every day or, should that nonetheless become tiresome, ways to make zucchini keepers. The same with tomatoes—from dozens of recipes for using them fresh in salads, appetizers, pies, soups, and vegetable side dishes to preserving them in relishes, chutneys, and reliable old put-bys.

Testing and selecting from the huge number of recipe offerings, many more than could be included in this volume, has in turn kindled my imagination and provided much food for thought. As I plant my tomatoes, I hear the advice on how nicely to keep away the tomato plant pests. As I ponder an abundance of peppers, I recall the recipe for turning them into a relish to perk up otherwise ordinary fare. When I consider an easy, not-too-much-work pasta sauce, I remember the formula of a contributor's grandmother who brought her cherished recipe with her from the old country. A tip on how properly to stir a drink and an old-fashioned way of finely puréeing have made my writing more fun as I learned that a stir stick used to be called a muddler and a fine sieve used to be called a dilver.

Perhaps best of all is that in crafting this book I have been part of a vivacious community of gardeners and cooks. Their passionate, creative, humorous, and universally earth-friendly approach to gardening and cooking has sparked my own enthusiasm as it revealed a remarkable blend of American pass-along heritage with a celebration of the ever-new garden.

From its beginning more than twenty years ago as a purveyor of finely turned garden tools that make you want to get out and work in the garden, Smith & Hawken has sprouted a community of gardeners who want to share. *The Gardeners' Community Cookbook* continues the tradition in a collection of garden recipes that, in true pass-along spirit, gives back by donating a share of the proceeds from the sales of this book to Second Harvest, the largest food bank in the country.

VICTORIA WISE, *Oakland, California*

starters:

appetizers and beverages with a spark from the garden

Finger food, small bites, served buffet-style, from passed-around trays, or individual small plates like Greek mezes or Spanish tapas—appetizers invite sharing food in an informal way. They are meant to assuage hunger and welcome guests to the table. That might mean a big display if the occasion is a fancy cocktail party or holiday spread. It might also mean an assortment of this and that to nibble and munch. In this chapter are appetizers to fit all occasions and a selection of beverages to accompany them or to enjoy on their own.

"Boild" Peanuts

Makes 1 pound

"My first recollection of boiled peanuts is from my early childhood in Macon (rhymes with bacon), Georgia, where I grew up. My father, an avid baseball fan, was a pitcher for the Mercer University Bears and an enthusiastic rooter for the Macon Peaches. That's where I met the peanuts—they and Coca-Cola were the concession-stand fare. The peanuts were sold in little brown paper bags that tended to be a bit soggy but must have been unusually strong because I don't ever remember them tearing. The fans would eat the peanuts and throw the empty shells on the stadium floor. Even when there wasn't a game going on, the beloved snack was available at makeshift stands along the road that wound through our peanut-farm country. One of my favorite purchase points was a stand advertising its ware on a hand-inscribed wooden board: 'boild' peanuts. I loved those peanuts then, and I love them now." As an adult, however, he finds that the shells on the floor aren't as much fun; it's the peanuts that count.

KEITH FULLINGTON (OAKLAND, CA, VIA MACON, GA)

Peanuts: The New World Nut That's Really a Legume

Both its common names, peanut and groundnut, well describe the now widespread, indigenous American edible *Arachis hypogaea.* The name familiar here, peanut, comes from both its taste (nutty) and its true botanical family, Leguminosae, which includes flowers (lupine), ground covers (red clover), and trees (Chinese redbud), as well as other edibles (beans and peas). Its other designation, groundnut, describes the taste and also the way this legume grows, underground. Originating in South America, the peanut traveled north as far as Mexico and Haiti, then took a right turn and appeared in East Africa. When inhabitants there were forced to relocate to colonial plantations in the southern United States, the peanut wound up again in the New World, this time in North America. From its humble origin as slave food, the cultivated peanut gained clout in the nineteenth century when it replaced cotton destroyed by the boll weevil as the major southern crop. It continued its journey, eventually showing up as highly popular in the kitchens of Europe, Asia, and most of the rest of the world.

3 tablespoons salt
3 quarts water
1 pound raw peanuts in the shell

1. Place all the ingredients in a large pot and bring to a boil. Remove from the heat, cover the pot, and set aside to soak for 1 to 2 hours.

2. Return the pot to the heat and bring to a boil again. Adjust the heat to maintain a brisk simmer and cook, covered, for 3 to 3½ hours, or until the shells are pinchable without cracking and the peanuts are almost mealy. Drain and serve while still warm and a bit moist.

Note: The boiled peanuts can be stored in the refrigerator—at room temperature they will mold eventually—for up to 2 weeks. Briefly reheat them in boiling water before serving.

Rosemary-Roasted Walnuts

MAKES 2 CUPS

"Sometimes the easiest of preparations, calling for few ingredients and little fuss, can turn out to be what everyone goes for at the cocktail buffet. Such are these walnuts. Not merely toasted, they are tossed with paprika and fresh rosemary and roasted until the nuts become crisp and studded with the rosemary spikes. It's an inspired simplicity. For larger parties or to have some to save, the recipe can be doubled or tripled, as long as you make sure to spread the nuts in a single layer so each piece gets roasted golden all around. More important, the walnuts must be fresh from the current season; older nuts will taste stale."

~ SANDY TRUCKNER, GREENSBURG GARDEN CENTER (GREENSBURG, PA)

1 pound walnut halves
2 tablespoons olive oil
2 tablespoons butter, melted
3 tablespoons fresh rosemary leaves
2 teaspoons hot paprika
½ to 1 teaspoon salt

1. Preheat the oven to 325° F.

2. Place all the ingredients in a bowl and toss to mix. Spread on a baking sheet large enough to hold the nuts in a single layer. Bake for 20 to 25 minutes, stirring once or twice, or until the nuts are golden but not browned and the scent of rosemary fills the room.

3. Remove and cool. Serve right away or at room temperature. May be stored in an airtight container for up to 2 weeks.

OLIVES OF ONE KIND AND ANOTHER

The recipe for Andalusian-Style Marinated Olives calls for Ascolano or Sicilian Queen olives because these work well without overpowering the flavors of the Andalusian seasonings. However, another kind of mildly brine-cured, green to light-brown olive can be substituted. Choices include picholine, Atalanti, Naphlion, French cracked, and many others your local market may import or purchase domestically under a number of other delightful, if somewhat mysterious, names.

Andalusian-Style Marinated Olives

MAKES ABOUT 6 CUPS

Sandy Sonnenfelt is Prepared Food Coordinator of Oakland's renowned Pasta Shop—fresh pasta manufacturer and delicatessen par excellence. Her marinated olives, soaked in olive oil with whole almonds and Andalusian herbs, are the best ever, anywhere, mari-

nated olives. One fragrant whiff can transport you to the sun-blest mountains and plains of Andalusia in southernmost Spain, a region where Mediterranean, North African, and Middle Eastern ingredients happily meet at table on a regular basis.

SANDY SONNENFELT (OAKLAND, CA)

4 cups Ascolano, Sicilian Queen, or other Mediterranean-style green olives (see page 3)
1 cup blanched whole almonds, toasted until golden brown
2 tablespoons chopped garlic
1 tablespoon coriander seed, cracked
1½ teaspoons fennel seed
½ teaspoon ground cumin
2 bay leaves, fresh is nice
½ teaspoon crushed red pepper
1 tablespoon kosher or pickling salt
1 teaspoon cracked black pepper
Chopped zest of 1 lemon
1 cup fresh lemon juice
2 cups sherry wine vinegar
¼ cup extra virgin olive oil, preferably Spanish

Combine all the ingredients in a bowl. Let stand for 24 hours at room temperature before using. Will keep, covered, in the refrigerator indefinitely.

Olives from Tree to Table: A Real Alchemy

For olives, the path from grove to table must have been a long one. The fruit of the olive tree cannot be eaten out of hand. In its natural state it is unpalatable, and anyone curious enough to test this proposition with a bite of uncured olive knows how literally true it is. Yet, somehow such innate curiosity led to the discovery that pressed, the olive yields a true prize, its oil; and cured to remove its bitter, acrid glucoside, the fruit becomes not only edible but prized for the table. That must have been early on because at least since Biblical times the olive has been cultivated, and its oil and fruit have been an important part of cooking in many cuisines around the world.

Kumquat Appetizers

Makes 50 pieces

"Kumquats are prized as ornamental plants for their dark green leaves and brightly colored fruit. Though the flesh is quite tart, the rind is usually tender and sweet. Three kumquat trees on our terrace provide a bountiful supply of the small, oval, orange-colored citrus fruit to use for this unusual delicacy."

SHARON BLUMBERG (FRESNO, CA)

25 kumquats
8 ounces quality cream cheese, at room temperature
2 teaspoons Triple Sec or other orange liqueur
2 teaspoons sugar
½ cup roasted, salted pistachio nuts, finely chopped
Kumquat leaves for garnish (optional)

1. Cut the kumquats in half lengthwise and scoop out the pulp. Reserve the pulp and juices for another use and set the shells aside.

2. Beat the cream cheese together with the liqueur and sugar until smooth and a little fluffy. Fill a pastry bag fitted with a ¼- to ½-inch tip with the cheese mixture. Pipe the mixture into the shells, mounding slightly.

3. Spread the pistachios on a plate. Dip the cream cheese side of each filled half into the nuts and arrange on a serving platter, nut side up, as you go. Lightly cover with plastic wrap, without pressing down on the mounds. Chill until the cheese is slightly firm.

4. Garnish the platter with sprigs of kumquat leaves, if using, and serve.

Deviled New Potatoes

MAKES 20 HALVES

"Not only is this recipe a great use of fresh produce, it's a new use for the deviled-egg platter!" So, pull out that white elephant (or is it a treasure?) you've been meaning to take to the Antiques Roadshow or sell at the flea market and have new fun with it.

VICKIE SCHLICK (BLACK EARTH, WI)

10 small red new potatoes, scrubbed (about 1½ pounds)
1 rib celery, trimmed and finely chopped
1 small carrot, scraped and finely chopped
1 green onion (scallion), trimmed and finely chopped
1 tablespoon finely chopped sweet pickle
1 tablespoon finely chopped fresh dill
½ teaspoon salt
½ teaspoon black pepper
½ cup mayonnaise (see page 64)
½ cup sour cream
Paprika, preferably Hungarian hot, for garnish

1. Bring a medium pot of water to boil. Drop in the potatoes and cook briskly over medium heat until tender but still holding their shape, about 15 minutes. Drain and set aside to cool.

2. When cool, cut the potatoes in half and gently scoop out the centers, leaving the shells intact. Place the scooped-out centers in a large bowl and set the shells aside.

3. Mash the potato centers with a fork. Add the celery, carrot, green onion, pickle, dill, salt, pepper, mayonnaise, and sour cream, and blend until thoroughly mixed but still a little chunky.

4. Spoon a bit of the potato mixture into each of the potato shells, enough to mound above the rim without spilling over. Put the filled shells in the wells of a deviled-egg platter or arrange them on another kind of serving platter, making sure they are upright.

5. To serve, sprinkle the top of each potato half with a good pinch of paprika and set on the table.

Notes

• If the potato mixture in Step 3 seems too dry, thin it out with a little bit of milk.

• The hot paprika garnish is what makes the stuffed potatoes deviled. If you'd care for a milder taste, substitute mild paprika instead or use chopped fresh dill or chopped fresh parsley for the splash of color.

TOOLS *of the* TRADE

Old-Fashioned Service Ware Used in New Ways

There's no need to banish the fancy or specialized serviceware of yesteryear to the attic. With a gardener's resourcefulness and a cook's creativity, such objects can be reborn so that they are useful in modern, less formal ways.

DEVILED-EGG PLATTER: For deviled potatoes or filled wonton cups.

CRYSTAL PLATE FOR PICKLES AND OLIVES: For that still, plus dips.

GRAPE SCISSORS: For that still, and also as pruners for boutonnières.

ICE CUBE TONGS: For olives or lemon wedges served in a bowl.

GRAVY BOAT: For salsas.

GRAVY LADLE: For berry compote.

SILVER OR PORCELAIN CREAM-AND-SUGAR SERVICE: For miniature flower arrangements to decorate the table.

VINEGAR AND OIL CRUETS: Also for flowers to decorate the table.

NUTCRACKERS: For cracking crab shells.

FISH KNIVES: For cutting cheese and scooping it onto a cracker.

SALT CELLARS: For candle holders.

Eggplant Polpettes

MAKES ABOUT 20 POLPETTES

Since both contributors offered very similar recipes—with individual variations, of course—we melded them into one. Traditionally either an informal appetizer or a "meatball" for pasta sauce, the polpettes are usually eaten hot off the press or dropped directly into the sauce that will blanket the pasta. In the modern interpretation here, they are whisked to the appetizer table with a bowl of dipping sauce and offered up for the cocktail crowd.

GERI FORD (METAIRIE, LA) AND ELIZABETH SPARANO (MARION, IA)

1 medium eggplant, peeled and cut into 1-inch cubes (about 1 pound)
3 tablespoons grated Parmesan cheese
1 large clove garlic, pressed
¾ cup coarse bread crumbs, preferably homemade (see page 76)
1 large egg, beaten
½ teaspoon salt
Fine bread crumbs, preferably homemade (see page 76) for coating the polpettes
Olive oil, for frying
A selection of dipping sauces (see box below)

1. Bring a medium pot of water to boil, add the eggplant, and cook over medium heat until very tender, 5 to 7 minutes. Drain, press out some of the liquid, and mash in a food processor.

2. Transfer to a bowl and mix in the Parmesan, garlic, coarse bread crumbs, egg, and salt. Refrigerate for at least 2 hours.

3. Spread a layer of fine bread crumbs on a plate. Form the eggplant mixture into walnut-size balls and roll each in the crumbs.

4. Heat ¼ inch of oil in a heavy skillet. Cooking in batches, fry as many of the

Sauce Suggestions for Eggplant Polpettes

There is plenty of choice for the dipping sauce to accompany the polpettes. You can pick one to accent the cuisine theme for the occasion or offer an international array for the sheer fun of it.

GREEK: Yogurt with dill or mint and garlic or a dish of top-quality olive oil infused with finely chopped spring garlic and lemon zest.

INDIAN: Cilantro pesto (without nuts), page 309, or mango chutney.

ITALIAN: Any pesto (with nuts) or smooth tomato sauce.

MEXICAN: Salsa, any of the moister, not too chunky ones, such as Connecticut Salsa (page 298) or Oregon Salsa (page 306), or thickened cream mixed with avocado purée and cilantro.

PAN-ASIAN: Soy sauce spiked with jalapeños, cilantro, and sesame oil, or hot mustard or wasabi paste dissolved in a pool of rice vinegar.

PACIFIC RIM: Soy sauce seasoned with fish sauce and lemon grass or thick coconut milk infused with grated fresh ginger.

polpettes as will fit without crowding. Transfer to paper towels. Add more oil to the skillet if necessary and continue until all the polpettes are fried.

5. Arrange on a serving platter and serve right away, accompanied with a selection of sauces.

Variations

• Add an herb, such as chopped basil, parsley, or mint leaves.

• Add a nut, such as finely ground walnuts, almonds, or peanuts, in place of half of the coarse bread crumbs.

Deep-Fried Cheese-Filled Jalapeño Tidbits

MAKES 24 PIECES

For anyone with a penchant for melted cheese and a love of spicy flavors, these tidbits are the ticket. A modest amount of cheese is packed into a jalapeño chili half, coated with bread crumbs, and fried just enough to soften the cheese and still keep the jalapeño al dente.

HELEN RUSSOM (HOLLY SPRINGS, MS)

12 jalapeños
½ cup coarsely grated melting cheese, such as sharp white cheddar, Monterey Jack, or queso cotija
1 large egg, beaten
1 cup fine bread crumbs, preferably homemade (see page 76)
Vegetable oil, for frying

1. Cut the tops off the jalapeños, halve them lengthwise, and remove the seeds. Pack cheese into each half. Coat the filled halves in egg and then bread crumbs and transfer to a plate. Set aside to air-dry for 10 to 20 minutes.

2. Pour ½ inch of oil into a heavy skillet and heat until beginning to smoke. Fry as many of the pieces as will fit in a single uncrowded layer, turning once, until the jalapeño shells are golden but still al dente and the cheese is creamy, about 45 seconds on each side. Transfer to paper towels to drain and continue with another batch, adjusting the heat as necessary, until all the jalapeños are fried.

3. Serve right away, while still warm.

Deep-Frying

For deep-frying it is important to lift the goods out of the oil with a tool that allows the excess oil to drip back into the pan. The following tools work well for Asian, Mediterranean, American, or any deep-fried dish.

Long-handled kitchen tongs

Chopsticks

Forks: Use both a long-handled, two-tined kitchen fork and a four-tined table fork to work together. Dip the kitchen fork into the hot oil and lift up the piece using the table fork to hold it without slipping.

Slotted spoon or wire skimmer: Use in conjunction with a wooden spoon, as in the double-fork technique.

Have ready a set-up that allows some of the oil to drain away once individual batches are out of the oil. For this you can use:

Cloth towels: Perhaps the most effective medium for absorbing oil and also the least damaging to the environment. The towels need to be washed soon after using, or the oil will turn rancid.

Paper towels: The best solution to draining fried foods on a disposable material. Also the most expensive.

Brown paper bags, opened out: The old-fashioned way, and a good one, except that bags are not as absorbent as paper towels.

A plate large enough to hold each batch in one layer: First hold the fried food out of the oil to allow the excess oil to drain back into the pan, then tilt the plate a little so any remaining oil can flow to one side. This method results in a bit greasier dish.

In addition, you will need:

Cloth pot holders or terry kitchen towels: Thick ones, for grasping pot handles or metal-handled instruments when they're hot enough to burn your hands.

Baking soda: A large box within easy reach for dousing any flames that might flare up.

Greek-Style Zucchini Pancake Appetizers

MAKES ABOUT EIGHT 3-INCH PANCAKES

Around the Mediterranean, these might be called zucchini croquettes, one among the boundless variety of fried vegetable delights served in village tavernas and at tables set outdoors to provide a seat and a sip. Here, they're called appetizer pancakes, and they perfectly suit a patio brunch or before-dinner taste treat. Finely grated carrot, wilted shredded cabbage, mashed potato, peas, lentils, or chickpeas can also be turned into croquettes.

KATHY HEYE (FREEPORT, ME)

3 cups grated zucchini, skins and all
½ teaspoon salt
2 large eggs, beaten
3 tablespoons all-purpose flour
1 cup crumbled feta cheese
Butter, for frying
Garnishes, such as yogurt or sour cream, fresh or dried oregano leaves, lemon slices, salsa

1. Toss the zucchini with the salt and let stand in a colander for 1 hour at room temperature to sweat out the moisture.

2. When ready to cook, squeeze the zucchini with your hands to get rid of excess moisture without wringing it dry. Place in a medium bowl, add the eggs, flour, and feta, and mix well.

3. Melt about 1 tablespoon of butter in a heavy sauté pan or griddle, enough to coat the bottom generously. Fry the zucchini mixture in small pancake-size amounts over medium-low heat until dark golden on both sides, about 5 minutes altogether. Transfer to paper towels to drain and continue with another batch until all the pancakes are fried.

4. Arrange the pancakes on a serving platter and garnish as desired.

Note: A shot of ouzo, Limoncello (page 42), or Mint Liqueur (page 41) might also be welcome.

To Peel or Not to Peel Your Cucurbits

Melons and winter squashes are always divested of their skins in one way or another before eating. Cucumbers require a bit of decision making. Are the skins tough and bitter? better to pare them away. Thin and sweet? might as well leave them for color. With zucchini—either you like them peeled to pare away the dirt and get to their sweet pulp or you prefer to scrub them and retain the peel for a more robust texture. It may not matter in the end, however, because usually zucchinis are cooked to a softness where the peels are hardly noticeable, if at all.

Fried Squash Blossoms

MAKES ABOUT 16 FRIED BLOSSOMS

"We admit, our families love this recipe so much that we now cultivate zucchini just for the blossoms and use both the male and female for the dish. If you want a good squash harvest, though, pick only the male blossoms. You can tell them apart by checking the stems: The female stems show evidence of fruit; the male stem is elongated. Once picked and cleaned, the flowers may be wrapped in paper towels and stored in the refrigerator for one day but will not last longer than that, so pick daily as you need them." Fried blossoms have become so popular that nurserymen have developed a squash hybrid that puts its energy into flowering; the fruit is rudimentary. Any summer squash blossom will do, as will the flowers of cucumber or melon, but the squash blossoms are more delicate.

MICKEY CLEMENT (HUNTINGTON BAY, NY) AND NINA ROBERTSON (MARBLEHEAD, MA)

16 summer squash blossoms
¾ cup water
½ cup all-purpose flour, sifted
Olive oil, for frying
Salt

1. To prepare the blossoms, pick in the morning of the day the flower is in full bloom. Cut off the green stems but leave any tiny fruits attached. (If male, remove the pistle.) Carefully wash, drain on paper towels, and set aside to dry.

2. Pour the water into a shallow bowl. Slowly whisk in the flour until the mixture is smooth and the consistency of a runny mayonnaise.

3. Pour ¾ inch of oil into a heavy sauté pan and heat until a bit of batter dropped in the oil rises immediately to the top. Dip as many blossoms as will fit in the pan without crowding into the batter and fry until barely golden on both sides, about 1 minute. Transfer to paper towels to drain and continue until all the blossoms are fried. Sprinkle lightly with salt and serve right away while still crisp.

A Very Versatile Batter

Light and delicate as a summer breeze off the Adriatic, this Italian-style batter can be used to coat many vegetables besides zucchini flowers. Try:

MUSHROOMS, stemmed and thinly sliced.

ZUCCHINI OR OTHER SUMMER SQUASH, thinly sliced lengthwise, crosswise, or on the diagonal.

BABY ARTICHOKES, well-trimmed and halved.

ONION RINGS, not too thin.

FENNEL, very thinly sliced.

BABY OKRA, whole, only very small ones.

EGGPLANT, thin rounds.

HERBS, such as large basil leaves or tops of parsley sprigs.

LEMON, thinly sliced into rounds and gently squeezed.

Asparagus Stalks Cradled in Endive Leaves

MAKES ABOUT 24 APPETIZERS

"Many years ago we bought an adobe house in Corrales, New Mexico. It was a very special place. The kitchen had a raised fireplace just the right height to warm your backside, and while doing so you could look out the backdoor window and contemplate, well, whatever. Along came spring, and we made a discovery. In the ditch we had been viewing not as a garden, just as a southwestern view, suddenly there were little green shoots springing up. Our children were intrigued with the progress of this rising vegetation and checked it out every day. Before long, we realized we had wild asparagus, in abundance. We picked and used and picked some more and shared with the neighbors and ate asparagus until the end of the season. One of our favorite treasures still from this time is an hors d'oeuvres platter of asparagus stalks in Belgian endive leaves with a bowl of lemon-mustard vinaigrette for a dipping sauce. Be sure to offer cocktail napkins as you pass around the platter so guests have a way to dab at any drips from the dip."

~ JACQUELINE SMALLY (LOS OSOS, CA, VIA NEW MEXICO)

"The earth laughs at him who calls a place his own."

—Hindustani saying

24 asparagus stalks, tough bottoms trimmed off
24 large Belgian endive leaves, rinsed, patted dry, spread on paper towels, and chilled
2 teaspoons Dijon mustard
2 tablespoons white wine vinegar or fresh lemon juice
¼ cup olive oil

1. Bring a large pot of water to boil. Drop in the asparagus and cook until the stalks are just barely bendable, 3 to 5 minutes. Drain, rinse with cool water, and set aside to drip dry.

2. Arrange the endive leaves attractively on a serving platter. Place an asparagus stalk in the center of each endive leaf. Set aside until ready to serve.

3. When ready to serve, whisk together the mustard, vinegar, and oil in a small serving bowl. Set the bowl in the center of the platter so the guests can wrap an endive leaf around an asparagus stalk and dip in the vinaigrette. Serve.

Cheese-Filled Asparagus Roll Canapés

MAKES 3 DOZEN

These attractive canapés are a nostalgia dish reminiscent of Forties-style cocktail party fare. Not exactly diet food nor cholesterol free, they are nonetheless seductive. The cream cheese must be best quality from a deli or cheese counter. And though the bread should also be above ordinary, buy it presliced—it's too hard to slice thin enough at home.

SHIRLEY ORFANELLA (QUARRYVILLE, PA)

12 stalks asparagus, preferably fat ones
4 ounces quality cream cheese, softened
2 ounces blue cheese
1 small egg
12 very thin slices good-quality white bread
8 tablespoons (1 stick) butter, melted

1. Trim the tough ends off the asparagus, leaving the stalks long enough to reach end to end on the bread slices. Cook the asparagus in boiling water until barely bendable and still bright green, 5 to 10 minutes, depending on the size of the stalks. Drain and set aside.

2. Combine the cream cheese, blue cheese, and egg in a small bowl. Trim the crusts off the bread and flatten the slices with a rolling pin or the palm of your hand. Spread each slice with the cheese mixture, place an asparagus stalk on top of the cheese at the edge of the slice, and roll up to enclose the asparagus. Dip the roll in melted butter and then lay them on an ungreased cookie sheet as you go.

3. Place the cookie sheet in the freezer for 15 minutes, or until the rolls are almost frozen.

4. Preheat the oven to 400° F.

5. Cut each roll into thirds and bake for 15 minutes, turning once, until golden and toasty. Serve while still warm.

Locating Asparagus

Asparagus is a perennial that requires three years to mature to full production. Then it will continue to offer up its shoots every spring for 20 years or more. So, when planning an asparagus bed, choose a spot where the plants can remain undisturbed for many years rather than a vegetable garden or flower bed that gets turned and replanted annually. Another consideration is to situate an asparagus bed where its foliage can be seen. The tall, lacy, fernlike branches, which may be cut for floral arrangements, also make a graceful backdrop for flowers outdoors.

Herb-Marinated Feta Cheese

MAKES 2 CUPS

"As an avid gardener, I have been trying every remedy conceivable to counter the foraging of deer in my unfenced yard. Although I have only been partially successful, I have found that they steer away from plants with pungent odors. Herbs! Although planting herbs in among things they like solves no problems, they do not eat the herbs themselves. Hence, I am cooking more and more with fresh herbs, as in this recipe that I have found I can make for a fraction of the cost of buying it in a specialty food store. It makes a great spread on toast rounds or garnish in the center of a Caesar salad or mixed vegetable toss." Such spirit, humor, flexibility, and resourcefulness might lead one to grow some herbs just to season a block of feta.

SYLVIA BELL (HUNTSVILLE, TX)

⅔ cup olive oil
1 heaping teaspoon green or red peppercorns
2 cloves garlic, slivered
2 tablespoons shredded fresh basil leaves
2 tablespoons fresh thyme leaves
2 tablespoons fresh oregano leaves
3 bay leaves, preferably fresh
½ pound feta cheese, cut into ¾-inch cubes

Place the oil, peppercorns, garlic, basil, thyme, oregano, and bay in a quart jar. Cap and shake well. Add the feta, taking care not to crumble it, cap again, and gently turn to mix. Let stand at room temperature for several hours, turning the jar several times. Use right away or store, covered, in the refrigerator. Bring to room temperature before serving. Keeps indefinitely.

CREAM CHEESE CONSIDERATIONS

For cheese spreads and dips, take the trouble to scout out a deli or cheese store that offers a cream cheese with naturally soft texture and a taste that lets you know it's cheese.

Garlic-Herb Cheese Spread

MAKES ABOUT 1½ CUPS

"I am an artist who gains great inspiration from her garden. I love to paint, grow things, and cook for my friends. Each year I have a large vegetable garden and a number of flower gardens with rock walls and brook and trout pond too, all on one-and-a-half acres in

New Hampshire. I think my garlic and herb cheese spread is better than store-bought, and I offer the recipe so that anyone, even without a basket of homegrown garlic and herbs can simulate with a selection from the farmers' market." Accompany the spread with crackers and toast either purchased from the bakery or homemade (see pages 19–25).

DEBORAH BRUMFIELD (WALPOLE, NH)

"Garlic is as good as ten mothers.

—Les Blank

***8 ounces quality cream cheese, softened** (see page 14)*
8 tablespoons (1 stick) butter, softened
2 cloves garlic, fresh as possible, crushed
1 teaspoon chopped fresh oregano leaves
1 teaspoon chopped fresh marjoram leaves
1 teaspoon chopped fresh basil leaves

1. Combine all the ingredients in a medium bowl and beat with an electric mixer until blended into a spreadable consistency. Cover and refrigerate overnight or up to several days for the flavors to blend and mellow.

2. When ready to serve, bring the spread to room temperature. Mound on a platter and serve.

Garden Garlic and Its What-Alls?

Like almost no other plant in the world (with the possible exception of ginger), garlic is considered and used as vegetable, cooked seasoning, fresh herb, and medicine. What the season is determines the best use of this versatile allium that is good from top to bottom.

SPRING AND SUMMER. Snip garlic leaves and flowers while they are still green and fresh enough to rise high and still tender enough to chop for a salad, cheese spread, fresh soup, or any dish that might invite a change from the more predictable scallion or chive garnish. If you have enough of a garlic crop to afford two harvests, one in spring and another in fall, pull up some while their bulbs have barely developed and the cloves are milder than late summer garlic. The whole bulbs at this point make a special seasoning for a spring lamb stew, poussin or quail marinade, or stir-fry dish. For the dedicated gardener cook who is willing to spend time peeling the minuscule cloves, a handful of them sprinkled into a pan of just-done sautéed carrots, turned once and served up with a generous garnish of chopped chervil, will change everyone's mind forever about what glorious heights a humble root can achieve.

FALL AND WINTER. When the leaves have browned and bowed to the ground, they announce, "That's it for this year." If you pull them while the tops are still supple, you can plait a garlic braid and hang it to air-dry the bulbs and adorn your kitchen both. The bulbs, fully developed, are just right for roasting or grilling whole, or peeling. Chop the garlic into any and every dish that could "use some garlic," braise it whole in a cold-weather beef stew, stuff it into the cavity of a roasting chicken, or just plain taste, as they do in Gilroy, California, each August or September to the tune of drum rolls, big bands, and huge crowds.

Radish and Chive Canapés

Makes about 1 cup

For a casual get-together, this uncomplicated radish and chive spread can be mounded in the center of a platter and surrounded with pumpernickel triangles and small rye bread rounds so the guests can gather to spread their own canapés as they converse. For a more formal party, you can assemble the canapés in the kitchen and have fun creating designer toppings with paper-thin radish rounds, watercress tips, and a length or two of chive. The contributor advises that the spread "tastes best with first of the season radishes, the big red ones, and they must be dried well or the spread will be runny."

SUSAN KORONOWSKI
(DUNCANSVILLE, PA)

Radishes: The Lore, Lure, and Love of Simple Growing

If you've ever grown them, you know the enthusiasm radishes can elicit. Just by being, they bring forth certain stories.

Lore: Companion Planting. True or false, radishes are said to be a companion plant to many other vegetables, especially carrots, lettuce, peas, and beans. When planted at the same time, the radishes pop up first, hearken spring, and mark the spot where the other seedlings are barely emerging. That way, the gardener, in a moment of inattention, doesn't step on the new sprouts while going about other garden business. Moreover, it is said radishes and beans in particular like each other in a way that's good for their mutual growing. Perhaps there's a scientific explanation for this—maybe they keep each other's predators at bay. This part is surely true: They thrive together in the garden as it grows.

Lure: Here and Now. Radishes are a quick fix for children and beginning gardeners who become entranced with seeing something planted sprout up almost right away, much before other vegetables come to fruition. Radishes also entice the cook, who might plant them in a pot just outside the kitchen door to have a fresh, tangy, red spring garden garnish for the plate.

Love: Thanks for the Memories. Just as radishes allow the almost immediate satisfaction of watching something grow, they also provide long-term pleasure. Set beside slices of brown bread and a pot of sweet butter, radishes can engender memorable pleasure and pride in having grown your own food, no matter how simple.

8 ounces quality cream cheese, softened
1 tablespoon butter, softened
½ to ¾ cup finely chopped red radishes
½ cup chopped fresh chives (see Note below)
Salt
Pumpernickel triangles and/or small cocktail rye bread rounds
Thinly sliced radish rounds, watercress tips, and/or whole chives, for garnish (optional)

1. In a medium bowl, beat together the cheese and butter until fluffy. Lightly squeeze the chopped radishes to press out extra moisture and add to the bowl. Add the chopped chives and mix well. Season with salt to taste, cover, and refrigerate until firm but still spreadable, at least 1 hour or up to overnight.

2. When ready to serve, mound the cheese mixture on a serving platter. If using, arrange a ring of radish rounds, watercress tips, and whole chives around the cheese. Surround with a border of overlapping pumpernickel and rye bread slices around the edge of the platter and serve.

Note: If you don't have enough chives to make half a cup, top the measure with minced green onion (scallion) or garlic green.

Herb-Vegetable Spread for Tea Sandwiches

MAKES 1 HEAPING CUP

Densely polka-dotted with garden colors, this spread is also chock-full of garden flavors. In traditional tea sandwich style, the recipe calls for cutting the bread into "fingers" after smoothing on the spread. However, since many country-style loaves come in odd shapes, you can improvise and settle for irregular forms that taste just as good. Serve with a tiny dish of freshly cracked black pepper and a tall pitcher of iced flavored tea (page 37) or berry lemonade (page 39).

KATHERINE LOAFMAN
(WINSTON-SALEM, NC)

8 ounces quality cream cheese, softened
¼ cup mayonnaise
1 tablespoon finely chopped celery rib
2 tablespoons finely chopped green bell pepper
2 tablespoons coarsely grated carrot
1 to 2 teaspoons finely chopped chives or green onion (scallion) tops
1 tablespoon finely chopped fresh parsley leaves
½ teaspoon minced fresh dill
1 teaspoon chopped fresh thyme leaves
Salt
Thinly sliced country-style bread

Herb Potpourris: Fresh or Dried?

There are many esteemed herb and spice blends that rely on dried herbs; Herbes de Provence (page 180), Pickling Spices (page 316), Cajun Spice (page 189), Curry Powder (page 95), and Ras el Hanout (page 369) are five in this book. However, for cheese spreads, whatever the combination called for, the herbs must be fresh so that they meld softly into the cheese and don't remain unpleasantly dry. If you don't have the exact herbs called for, improvise your own fresh potpourri, choosing from parsley, sage, rosemary, thyme, tarragon, oregano, marjoram, basil, and mint.

You can also go a bit afield and chop in some of the lesser-used, more exotic herbs, such as burnet, lemon balm, hyssop, or one of the scented geraniums. Go easy with these, though; they can be quite overpowering.

If you find yourself completely bereft of fresh herbs, use dried herbs, rehydrating them in a little warm butter or water before mixing into the cheese.

1. In a small bowl, whisk together the cream cheese and mayonnaise until creamy. Add the remaining ingredients except the bread and mix well. Cover and refrigerate until set but still spreadable, at least 3 hours or up to overnight.

2. Just before serving, spread the mix over the bread slices. Trim the crusts and cut into fingers or any other shape that works. Serve right away.

Note: The bread can be trimmed of crust and set aside for up to several hours, uncovered, at room temperature. Not longer than that, though, or it might become too dry.

Sherried Mushroom Cheese Pâté

MAKES ABOUT 2 CUPS

Flavored with a good sherry, a handful of fresh herbs, and a mix of plain and fancy mushrooms, ordinary cream cheese becomes sumptuous. Shaped in a mold and presented unmolded, it becomes fancy enough to be called pâté.

CATHY GARNER (CORDOVA, TN)

2 tablespoons butter
1 pound fresh mushrooms, preferably a combination of fancy mushrooms and plain button mushrooms, wiped clean, stemmed, and thinly sliced
2 small cloves garlic, minced
8 ounces quality cream cheese, softened
¼ cup medium-dry sherry, such as Amontillado
1 tablespoon chopped fresh tarragon leaves
1 tablespoon chopped fresh marjoram leaves
1 tablespoon chopped fresh thyme leaves
½ teaspoon chopped fresh rosemary leaves
1 teaspoon black pepper
Salt
Fresh herb sprigs, for garnish
Assorted crackers

1. Melt the butter in a saucepan over medium heat. Stir in the mushrooms and garlic and sauté until the liquid is evaporated, about 5 minutes. Remove from the heat and cool to room temperature.

2. Line a 2- to 3-cup mold with plastic wrap. Set aside.

3. Transfer the mushrooms and garlic to a food processor. Add the cream cheese, sherry, chopped tarragon, marjoram, thyme, rosemary, and the pepper and blend until smooth. Blend in salt to taste and scoop the mixture into the lined mold. Cover with plastic wrap and refrigerate until well set, at least overnight.

4. When ready to serve, peel the plastic wrap cover off the top of the mold. Invert the mold onto a serving plate, prodding it a bit to loosen and release it onto the plate. Peel away the plastic wrap lining. Garnish the plate with herb sprigs and serve, accompanied by a basket of assorted crackers.

Sherried Mushrooms: A Classic Combo

There are some classic combinations in cooking that are so linked that it's hard to resist their magnetic attraction to each other no matter the form of the dish: tomatoes and basil, cheese and bread, berries and cream. Mushrooms and sherry with herbs, especially tarragon or thyme, is another such "natural." For instance, without the cream cheese, the sautéed mushrooms can be used to top steak or polenta for a kind of chunky sauce or spread on a plate lined with lettuce for a warm salad. They can also be used to fill a savory pie.

TO MAKE MUSHROOM PIE: Sauté the mushrooms and garlic as directed in the recipe at left, adding the sherry and herbs while sautéing. Stir in a splash of lemon juice, perhaps a dash of paprika, and a sprinkle of flour to thicken the mixture. Let it cool. Fill a prebaked 9-inch pie crust (page 170) with the mushroom mixture, cover with a top crust, and bake in a hot (425° F.) oven until golden on top, 30 to 35 minutes. Cool enough to slice, then cut into whatever size portions you'd like.

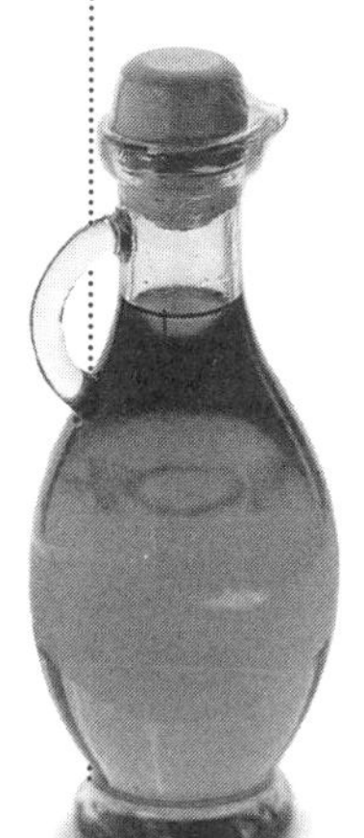

Basic Bruschetta

The toasts known as bruschetta were originally used to dip into the new season's olive oil. They served much like an edible spoon for tasting and assessing the current pressing. Eventually they became popular in Italian working-class trattorias where the fare, though frugal, had to be tasty nonetheless, and so the wood-fire grilled toasts were rubbed with freshly cut garlic before being drizzled with olive oil. And thus bruschetta flowed into the mainstream. It holds its place there to this day with an ever-expanding repertoire of toppings. Following are some creative bruschetta concoctions. But first, the basics.

When preparing bruschetta, remember that this is not an effete nibble. One is a good two or three bites, so for an appetizer one or two per person will do.

TO MAKE 8 BASIC BRUSCHETTA: Cut Italian or French country-style bread, preferably day-old, into ¾-inch-thick, 3- to 4-inch-long slices. Toast on both sides over a charcoal fire or under the broiler until barely golden and still supple, not hard. While still warm, rub one side of each slice with the cut side of a lightly crushed garlic clove half. (One half will do for 2 or 3 slices.) Place the toasts garlicked side up on a platter and drizzle each slice with 1 to 1½ teaspoons of the best olive oil you have.

You can serve the basic bruschetta as is, accompanied with a glass of hearty red wine. Or you can embellish away, keeping in mind that the toppings are the garnish, not the substance of the dish.

Tomato Bruschetta

Not surprisingly, one of the first bruschetta variations that comes to mind is tomato, so much so that many people think of bruschetta as garlic–olive oil toast with to-mato. Once on the path of such a combination, it's almost inevitable to include a bit of herb. Then, as garden cooks will have it, a bit of this or that fresh from the garden is added as a special touch. Tomato bruschetta topping variations contributed from around the country include:

FROM ELIZABETH FLORES (GOLF, IL): *Roma tomatoes, seeded and diced, mixed with olive oil and balsamic vinegar, sprinkled with shredded basil over the top.*

FROM KELLY DEGMAN (BROOKFIELD, IL): *A salad-y mix of garden-warm tomatoes, red onion, green pepper, basil, balsamic vinegar, and olive oil, sprinkled with chopped parsley over the top.*

FROM MARY PAT BLAYLOCK (HUNT VALLEY, MD): *A toss of chopped vegetables—tomatoes, black olives, green olives, red onion, parsley, lemon juice, and crushed garlic.*

FROM MADELINE SEARS (REHOBOTH, MA): *A mix of diced vegetables—tomatoes, cucumber, red onion—and minced oregano, basil, and garlic, seasoned with cracked black pepper.*

FROM SUSAN CORRADO-GOLDBERG (PALM HARBOR, FL): *A mix of chopped tomatoes, garlic, basil, Italian parsley, oregano, salt, and freshly ground black pepper mounded on the bruschetta and baked together for 10 minutes.*

Bruschetta with Roasted Pepper Salad

MAKES ABOUT 1 CUP, ENOUGH TO TOP ABOUT 12 BRUSCHETTA

"In September, we have an abundance of green peppers in our northwest Indiana garden. Roasted and peeled, they make a sweeter pepper, and then we can use them in a number of ways." Cut into strips and combined with quartered tomatoes, garlic, and onion, they make a salad to scoop into a butter-lettuce leaf. With all the vegetables cut a little finer, they turn into a condiment topping for sandwiches or bruschetta.

LILLIAN HISKES (CROWN POINT, IN)

1 large green bell pepper, roasted, peeled, seeded, and cut into thin strips (see page 99)
½ small tomato, peeled, seeded, and cut into thin strips
¼ small red onion, halved and thinly sliced
1 clove garlic, finely chopped
1 tablespoon olive oil
Salt and pepper
12 bruschetta toasts (see page 20)

1. In a medium bowl, toss together all the ingredients except the toasts. Set aside to marinate for 30 minutes.

2. When ready to serve, top each toast with a spoonful of the pepper salad. Serve right away, before the toasts become soggy.

THE PRIMARY PALETTE OF THE SUMMER GARDEN

Green is first, early and continuing.
Red is later, more short-lived, but profusive at season's end.
Yellow abounds early to later and peaks in between.
So does Blue, especially in aromatic flowers of herb plants that butterflies and bumblebees like, too.

Bruschetta with Braised Red Onions

MAKES 8 BRUSCHETTA

Cookbook author (Fresh from the Farmers' Market) *and award-winning writer for the San Francisco* Chronicle *food section, Janet Fletcher regularly puts her vivid, vegetable-oriented imagination into creating bruschetta variations. This one, with a splash of red wine vinegar to brighten the color and another of balsamic vinegar to deepen the flavor, is among her favorites. The braised onions alone are an excellent side garnish for a plate of roast beef.*

JANET FLETCHER (NAPA, CA)

2 tablespoons olive oil
2 ounces pancetta, minced (see box below)
1 pound red onions, halved and thinly sliced
2 large cloves garlic, minced
1 teaspoon minced fresh thyme
1 teaspoon red wine vinegar
Salt and pepper
1 tablespoon balsamic vinegar
8 bruschetta toasts (see page 20)
1 tablespoon minced fresh Italian parsley leaves

1. Combine the oil and pancetta in a nonreactive skillet. Cook over moderate heat until the pancetta begins to crisp, about 3 minutes.

2. Add the onions, garlic, thyme, red wine vinegar, and salt and pepper to taste and toss to mix. Cover the skillet and continue cooking over medium heat until the onions are soft and sweet, about 15 minutes. Stir occasionally to make sure the onions don't burn.

3. Remove from the heat, uncover, and set aside for 5 minutes, then stir in the balsamic vinegar.

4. Top each bruschetta with a generous amount of the onion mixture, sprinkle the parsley over the top, and serve.

About Pancetta

Pancetta is like bacon, but distinctly less salty, more peppery, and sweeter than American-style bacon. It is also used differently. Pancetta is meant to enrich a tomato sauce, encircle a filet mignon, gird a quail for grilling. Sometimes, as here, it is used to add a certain sine qua non to braised vegetables. Many gourmet food shops, especially Italian delis, carry pancetta. Very thin sliced bacon is an acceptable substitute.

Mexican Bruschetta

MAKES ENOUGH TO TOP 6 BRUSCHETTA

Besides grilled corn bread or sourdough bread, the chili-tomato mix can top a polenta square or toasted tortilla. It also offers a way to perk up a plain poached chicken breast. The roasted jalapeños add memorable flavor, but you can seed and chop fresh jalapenos and include them without the roasting step. You can also use canned roasted chilies. They are milder than jalapeños but provide a true taste of chili.

GAIL VINES, FLIPS WINE BAR & TRATTORIA (OKLAHOMA CITY, OK)

1 teaspoon olive oil
½ small onion, thinly sliced
4 large jalapeños, roasted, seeded, and finely chopped
2 small tomatoes, chopped into ¼-inch pieces
½ teaspoon salt
6 (2-inch) squares corn bread (see box below) or 6 (3-inch) lengths of sourdough baguette
Olive oil, for brushing the bread
½ cup coarsely grated hard cheese, such as queso cotija, aged Jack, or aged Asiago
6 to 12 tender sprigs of cilantro

1. Heat the teaspoon of olive oil in a medium sauté pan. Stir in the onion and jalapeños and cook until wilted, 5 to 6 minutes. Transfer to a medium bowl and stir in the tomato and salt. Keep warm.

2. Brush the corn bread with olive oil and grill or broil until lightly toasted.

3. While still warm, spread the tomato mixture over the bread. Sprinkle cheese over the top and garnish each piece with 1 or 2 sprigs of cilantro. Serve right away.

Keeping the Bread in Corn Bread

It's true, there are many corn bread mixes on grocery-store shelves. They are popular for the same reason as are cake mixes and whatever else can save the modern cook time gathering and measuring. But, when it comes to corn bread for grilling, it's easy enough to return to the roots. Stir up a batch using the recipe for corn muffins on page 361, but use only 1 tablespoon sugar, and bake as directed. Leave the muffins to stale a day or two until they're dry enough to toast or grill without falling apart. Or make polenta (see pages 175–176), leave to dry as with the corn bread, and carry on in the same way.

Once you have your corn bread or polenta squares, besides topping them with a salsa, you can also heat them in a toaster oven and slather them with butter, Southwest style. If they're for breakfast, a garnish of jam might be added, but that would be very modern indeed. Or you can crumble the dried corn bread into a glass of milk and sop it up, cowboy style. It's kind of an American Southwest take on the bread soups that serve as similar modest fare on the other side of the world.

Crostini

Snappy like bruschetta, but more canapé size, crostini serve the same appetizer need: At day's end, when liquid refreshment and a bite to eat are what's wanted, a couple of them, or three or four, will fill the bill.

KEEPING CROSTINI
The crostini should be topped the same day, while still fresh and sweet tasting.

TO MAKE CROSTINI TOASTS: Start with good bread, such as baguette or country-style Italian bread. Slice the bread about ½ inch thick. If the slices are larger than 2 inches wide, cut them in half—crostini are small. Traditionally the crusts are removed, but some prefer to leave them on. Fry the bread slices in oil until light golden and drain on paper towels. Or toast the slices until light golden, then brush them with oil on one side.

CROSTINI TOPPINGS: Crostini toppings can be almost anything as long as the elements fit neatly on the toasts and aren't layered too high—crostini are not a Dagwood sandwich. Possibilities include:

A thin spread of chicken liver or duck liver mousse, with or without garnish.

A transparent slice of ahi tuna topped with a few shreds of shiso leaf (perilla).

A paste of minced parsley, garlic, and lemon zest moistened with olive oil, topped with an anchovy fillet.

A spread of the best sweet cream cheese, whipped and thinned with cream and garnished with:

- Crispy minced pancetta and a small sprinkle of parsley.
- Two slivers of smoked salmon and the tiniest sprig of dill or tender watercress.
- Any edible flower petal (page 361).
- A thin sliver or two of sun-dried tomato topped with whole cilantro leaves.
- A spoonful of caviar, any kind from beluga to salmon to golden to *tobiko* (flying fish).

Among the multitude of other toppings a gardener cook might devise, following is one that is quite special.

Crostini with Fava Bean Paste

MAKES 2 CUPS

"A week ago, my fava beans were almost three feet tall, standing erect and orderly, tidily contained in their corner of the garden. This week, after wind and rain, they are drunkenly slewing about in every direction, leaning on their neighbors, imposing their weight on the green garlic and spring lettuce, beginning to elbow back up to the sun. I have been picking them as fast as I can, but I know I will inevitably fall behind. The small pods I've gathered so far have all gone into what I consider their finest use: barely blanched, then cooled and stirred with small chunks of sheep's milk cheese, some fresh thyme, and good olive oil. But now, as the pods expand, I think of what to do with cooked favas. Here is one idea, for a special occasion." Use the paste to spread on French bread toasts (crostini) or fill raviolis.

~ MICHAEL DURPHY (FAIRFAX, CA)

2 cups shelled fresh fava beans
1½ tablespoons bread crumbs (see page 76)
½ tablespoon chopped lemon basil (see right)
¼ cup olive oil
¼ teaspoon salt

1. Bring a pot of water to a boil. Add the fava beans and simmer for 10 minutes, or until soft enough to mash. Drain, cool, and peel the beans.

2. Mash the beans together with the remaining ingredients to make a chunky paste. Use right away or store in the refrigerator for up to overnight.

LEMONY HERB OPTIONS

Lemon basil adds a "wonderful, idiosyncratic" taste, as our contributor puts it, to the fava bean paste. If it's not available, substitute Italian basil mixed with a little lemon balm or a few strands of lemon zest.

JB's Softshell Crab BLT

MAKES 24 APPETIZER SANDWICHES

Chef Jan Birnbaum's softshell crab BLT is built upon familiar ingredients, but in his version they appear in most extravagant forms: arugula for the lettuce, special sourdough bread for the toast, the very best smoked bacon, perfect end-of-summer tomatoes. As if that weren't enough, he tops it with a softshell crab. There's more still: the Creole aïoli not only is a spiced-up version of regular mayo but is also, in garden style, herbed-up. Altogether, this is a BLT raised to heights until now unexplored. Chef Birnbaum, a native of New Orleans and author of All I Ever Wanted to Do Is Cook, *cut his restaurant teeth at the knee of Paul Prudhomme. He continues the pass-along spirit, suggesting that his old-yet-new BLT recipe makes "great passed hors d'oeuvres. Serve with frosty beverages by the pool or on a picnic."*

JAN BIRNBAUM, CHEF/OWNER CATAHOULA RESTAURANT (CALISTOGA, CA) AND SAZERAC RESTAURANT (SEATTLE, WA)

8 tablespoons kosher salt
2 tablespoons freshly ground black pepper
1 teaspoon white pepper
2 teaspoons cayenne
2 teaspoons ground cumin
1 teaspoon ground coriander
1 teaspoon mustard powder
1 tablespoon hot paprika
6 softshell crabs, cleaned
1 cup buttermilk
1 cup Creole Aïoli (recipe follows)
12 slices sourdough French or Italian bread
2 tablespoons olive oil
12 slices smoked bacon
1½ cups all-purpose flour
1½ cups cornmeal
Vegetable oil, for frying
24 thin slices juicy tomatoes
2 cups arugula leaves
6 large leaves of soft lettuce, such as Bibb, red leaf, or red oak

1. Prepare a grill or preheat the broiler.

2. Combine the salt, black pepper, white pepper, cayenne, cumin, coriander, mustard, and paprika to make a seasoning mix.

3. Place the crabs in one layer in a deep dish and toss them with half of the seasoning mix and the buttermilk. Set aside to soak in the refrigerator for 30 minutes or up to 1 hour.

4. Prepare the aïoli.

5. Brush both sides of each bread slice with olive oil and sprinkle generously with the remaining seasoning mix. Place the bread on the grill rack or in the broiler and lightly toast, turning once. Remove and set aside.

6. Grill or broil the bacon, moving it frequently to avoid flare-ups, until crisp. Remove to paper towels to drain and set aside.

TOOLS *of the* TRADE

The Serrated Bread Knife, Inside and Out

A serrated bread knife is a relatively inexpensive implement that comes in handy more ways than one:

- It is the best and safest way to slice bread.
- It is a gem for cutting tomatoes into neat, not raggedy, slices.
- It sections sandwiches into enviously trim, canapé-size diamonds.
- It makes a lightweight small saw for the garden. Use it for cuttings or casual thinning of intermediate-size canes, stalks, and branches that are a bit too large and tough for a hand clipper but not so much so as to require a sturdy pruning saw.

7. Mix together the flour and cornmeal. Lift the crabs out of the buttermilk, shaking them a bit to dry. Dredge the crabs in the flour-cornmeal mixture, patting them to help the flour stick on the outside and lifting the "wing flaps" of the crabs to get the mixture well underneath.

8. Heat about 1 inch of oil in a heavy skillet or sauté pan. Fry the crabs, in batches so as not to crowd the pan, until lightly golden on both sides. Remove them to paper towels as you go.

9. To assemble, spread 1 side of each toasted bread with the aïoli. On six of the slices, stack first 4 tomato slices, 2 pieces of bacon, arugula, a lettuce leaf, and a crab. Top each stack with a bread slice. Secure each stack with sandwich picks or toothpicks pushed into its four corners. With a serrated bread knife, cut the sandwiches diagonally into quarters. Gently remove the picks and serve right away while the crab is still crispy.

Note: Chef Birnbaum advises that you can grill the crabs, but they turn out more crisp with frying. That's the way he goes.

Creole Aïoli

MAKES 1 CUP

1 large egg yolk
1 tablespoon fresh lemon juice
2 teaspoons prepared mustard, preferably Creole-style
½ teaspoon Tabasco-style hot sauce
1 teaspoon Worcestershire sauce
2 cloves garlic, minced
1 tablespoon paprika
½ teaspoon salt
½ teaspoon white pepper
1 cup peanut oil
1 tablespoon cider vinegar
Warm water, as needed
1 teaspoon minced fresh oregano leaves
1 teaspoon minced fresh basil leaves
1 teaspoon whole fresh thyme leaves

1. Combine the egg yolk, lemon juice, mustard, hot sauce, Worcestershire, garlic, paprika, salt, and pepper in a food processor and swirl together for 15 seconds.

2. With the machine running, add the oil in a slow, steady stream. (If necessary, stop the machine and use a rubber spatula to wipe the ingredients that cling to the sides of the bowl back into the center.) When all the oil is incorporated, swirl in the vinegar and just enough warm water to achieve a medium-stiff, still spreadable mayonnaise consistency.

3. Pulse in the oregano, basil, and thyme and use right away or refrigerate, covered, for up to 5 days.

A Trio of *Amuses Gueules*

Alice Waters has a decided talent for, among other things, composing a plate of offerings that appeal to the visual, olfactory, and taste senses all at once. Viewing some just picked baby carrots alongside some freshly dug potatoes, she might decide to pair them on an appetizer plate of small tastes. A third taste is added, olives, another natural for before-dinner munching. Each element gets individual attention and the outcome is olives in a classic Niçoise olive tapenade, carrots with Moroccan seasoning, and potatoes in a spread enriched with salt cod. It's a trio of amuses gueules in the Mediterranean style but with Alice's own flair.

ALICE WATERS, FOUNDER OF CHEZ PANISSE RESTAURANT (BERKELEY, CA)

ANCHOVY DETAILS
Salt-packed anchovies are the joy of anchovy lovers because they maintain a firm texture and taste of anchovy. Quality oil-packed anchovies, the kind that come in small tins, also do just fine.

Alice's Tapenade

MAKES 2½ CUPS

2 cups Niçoise olives, pitted (see Note below)
2 salt-packed anchovies, well rinsed, filleted, and coarsely chopped
1 clove garlic, peeled and smashed
2 tablespoons capers, rinsed and drained
2 teaspoons fresh lemon juice
6 tablespoons olive oil
Crostini (see page 24), rubbed with garlic
Whole small basil leaves, for garnish (optional)

1. Place the olives, anchovies, garlic, and capers in a food processor and chop into a coarse paste. Add the lemon juice and oil and continue processing until thoroughly mixed without puréeing. The olives should be minced but still recognizable as olives.

2. Spread the tapenade on the crostini, garnish each with a basil leaf, if using, and serve. The tapenade will keep, covered, in the refrigerator for up to 1 month.

Note: Niçoise olives are available in bulk in delis and sometimes in jars in upscale supermarkets. If you can't find them, you can substitute another mild, not oil-cured, not already-seasoned, olive.

The Ever-Abiding Olive Tree

In the course of cultivation through the centuries, the olive tree has undergone a transformation from a shrublike plant native to the sunny, dry regions of the eastern Mediterranean to the stately trees of modern olive groves to the singular beauty that might serve as focus in a warm-climate garden. Oddly, there's more. Horticulturists, admiring the tree for its elegant shape rather than for its yield, have created a hybrid *Olea europaea* that bears no fruit at all, the better to keep a mess-free lawn and driveway! It's lovely to look at and provides soft, filigreed sunlight.

Alice's Moroccan Carrots

MAKES ABOUT 1½ CUPS

18 to 24 baby carrots with ¼-inch stem attached, scrubbed and halved lengthwise
1 clove garlic, crushed
Pinch of salt
¼ teaspoon ground cumin
¼ teaspoon paprika, hot or mild
⅛ teaspoon ground cinnamon
Pinch of cayenne
2½ tablespoons fresh lemon juice
¼ cup olive oil
1 tablespoon chopped fresh parsley leaves

1. Combine the carrots, garlic, and pinch of salt in a large sauté pan. Add water to cover, bring to a boil, and simmer briskly over medium heat until tender, 3 to 4 minutes. Drain and cool to room temperature.

2. Transfer the carrots to a nonreactive dish large enough to hold them without overlapping too much. Toss with the cumin, paprika, cinnamon, and cayenne. Add the lemon juice, oil, and parsley, toss again, and set aside to marinate for at least 1 hour. May be refrigerated for up to 3 days, holding out the parsley until just before serving.

Alice's Potato and Salt Cod Spread

MAKES 2 CUPS

½ pound dried salt cod
Water or milk (see Notes below)
1 medium red potato
¼ cup half-and-half, warm
1 small clove garlic, minced but not pressed
1 tablespoon red wine vinegar
2 tablespoons olive oil
Salt and pepper
Crostini (see page 24), rubbed with garlic
Chopped parsley, for garnish

1. Rinse the salt cod and soak it, refrigerated, in water to cover for 24 to 48 hours, changing the water 2 or 3 times, until the cod is pliable, no longer dry and stiff, and mostly desalted.

HAND OR MACHINE?
A potato masher is a good tool for blending together the cod and potato for the salt cod spread. A food processor can also be used if you keep a quick and gentle hand on the button, pulsing to blend without puréeing the mixture.

2. Drain and place the cod in a medium pot with milk to cover. Bring to a boil, reduce the heat, and simmer until soft, 5 to 10 minutes. Drain and let cool enough to handle. Flake the flesh, removing any bones or skin.

3. While the cod cooks, peel and boil the potato until soft. Drain and, while still warm, mash using a food mill, a ricer, or potato masher.

4. Combine the flaked cod, mashed potato, half-and-half, and garlic in a large bowl. Mix thoroughly, breaking up the cod even further, until the mixture is somewhat, but not quite, smooth. Add the vinegar, oil, and salt and pepper to taste (see Notes below) and continue mixing and mashing until the mixture is amalgamated and the texture is smooth but not puréed like mashed potatoes.

5. While still at room temperature, spread generously on crostini toasts, sprinkle with parsley, and serve. Will keep for up to 3 days in the refrigerator. Bring to room temperature and whip to restore its fluffiness before serving.

Notes

• Rather than water you can use milk. Some say it helps to desalt and sweeten the cod even more.

• The amount of salt depends on two things: the saltiness of the cod after soaking and the palate of the cook. The pepper is also up to the cook; white pepper is nice, not only for its more discreet color, but also for its milder, nuttier flavor.

Egg Rolls with Sweet-and-Sour Dipping Sauce

MAKES 10 EGG ROLLS

"You could say we are farmers who cook, but we also have a certified kitchen on the farm, so we could be called cooks who farm. We specialize in heirlooms, European and Asian vegetables, herbs, and cut flowers to supply small gourmet restaurants, groceries, and the Highlands Farmers' Market in Louisville. This is one of the three most requested recipes we hand out when people tour our gardens over the course of the growing season."

CAROL CASSEDY, WHITESTONE ORGANIC FARM (BAGDAD, KY)

½ cup Sweet-and-Sour Dipping Sauce (recipe follows)
¾ pound bok choy or other Asian greens of the choy family, finely chopped, washed, and patted or spun dry
3 spring onions, trimmed and finely chopped
1 large clove garlic, minced
2 tablespoons minced cilantro leaves
½ tablespoon ground ginger
2 tablespoons soy sauce
10 egg roll wrappers
Vegetable oil, for deep-frying

1. Prepare the dipping sauce and set aside.

2. Place the bok choy, spring onions, garlic, cilantro, and ginger in a bowl and toss to mix. Add the soy sauce and toss again. Set aside.

3. To form the egg rolls, place a wrapper on the counter. Spread about 2 tablespoons of the greens mixture in the center. Roll up the wrapper, envelope style, and, if necessary, seal the final fold with a little water to keep the envelope from springing open. Continue with the remaining wrappers until you have 10 egg rolls. Set aside.

4. Pour ¾ inch of oil into a wok or heavy skillet and heat until smoking. Place as many egg rolls in the wok as will fit without crowding and fry, turning once, until lightly browned and crispy, about 1 minute. Lift the rolls out of the oil and transfer to paper towels to drain. Continue with another batch until all the rolls are fried.

5. Serve right away, accompanied by the dipping sauce.

Notes

• The filling mixture can be made up to several hours in advance. Keep in mind that the vegetables wilt and release liquid as they stand. If they are set aside for several hours, drain away the accumulated liquid before filling the wrappers.

• Egg roll wrappers are available in the refrigerated produce section of most supermarkets.

• The rolls may be wrapped and set aside for up to several hours before deep-frying. Longer than that and they get soggy.

"The guests are met, the feast is set: May'st hear the merry din"

—Samuel Taylor Coleridge, *The Rime of the Ancient Mariner*

Good Company for Egg Rolls

Surrounded with a table of condiments, egg rolls can serve as the centerpiece for an enticing buffet. For such party times, you can offer all or some of the following in addition to or in place of sweet-and-sour sauce:

Fruit chutney, such as:
• Cockholder Plum (page 342)
• Fragrant Pear (page 341)
• Green Tomato (page 344)

Pesto, such as:
• Cilantro (page 309)
• Arugula Lover's (page 309)
• Winter (page 310)
• Sun-Dried Tomato (page 311)

Soy sauce
Chinese chili pepper oil
Rice vinegar
Hot mustard paste (see page 33)
Cilantro leaves

Sweet-and-Sour Dipping Sauce

Makes 1¼ cups

1 cup ketchup
⅓ cup (packed) dark brown sugar
⅓ cup granulated sugar
½ tablespoon ground ginger
½ teaspoon ground cinnamon
Pinch of ground nutmeg

1. Place all the ingredients in a heavy saucepan. Bring to a boil over medium heat, stirring constantly to prevent scorching.

2. Reduce the heat to low and simmer, partially covered, for 15 minutes, until the consistency is slightly sticky and the spices no longer taste raw.

3. Remove and cool. Use right away or store, covered, in the refrigerator for up to 6 weeks.

Sweet-and-Sour Dipping Sauce in Barbecue Style

Well-spiced and almost spreadable, Sweet-and-Sour Dipping Sauce can do double duty as a basting sauce for barbecue chicken or ribs, either pork or beef. As a barbecue sauce, it's terrific as it is, or you can style it further with additional seasonings, such as:

- Mustard, prepared, powdered, or as seeds, for a somewhat sharper flavor.
- A splash of red wine vinegar, for a tarter taste.
- A splash of strong coffee, for a southern taste.
- Celery seed, especially good with chicken.
- Fennel seed, especially good with pork ribs.
- Crushed red pepper, especially good with beef ribs.

Asian-Style Harvest Salsa in Baked Wonton Cups

Makes 3 cups, enough to fill 18 wonton cups

"In San Diego, summer is announced by the arrival of vine-ripened tomatoes and the presence of yellowfin tuna in our local waters. This recipe was created to accompany the tuna that my fisherman husband proudly brings home. I grow beefsteak and cherry tomatoes, among other varieties, and turn them into a salsa combined with an ear of my precious white corn, roasted for extra sweetness, cilantro, chives, and basil. Together in a

baked wonton cup, summer brims over in a crisp taste experience." Not only that, the wonton cups lend themselves to many another sweet or savory filling at a moment's notice (see box on page 34).

STELLA FONG (POWAY, CA)

18 Baked Wonton Cups (recipe follows)
1 ear of white corn
2 teaspoons sesame oil
6 shiitake mushrooms, fresh, or dried and soaked in warm water, then squeezed dry
1 tablespoon olive oil
3 cloves garlic, minced
1 tablespoon soy sauce
½ cup finely chopped tomato
2 tablespoons chopped cilantro leaves
1 tablespoon thinly shredded fresh basil leaves
2 tablespoons finely chopped chives or green onion (scallion) tops
¼ teaspoon grated fresh ginger
1 tablespoon rice vinegar
½ teaspoon Chinese garlic sauce (optional, see Note below)
Salt

1. Prepare the wonton cups and set aside.

2. Preheat the broiler.

3. Rub the corn all around with 1 teaspoon of the sesame oil. Place under the broiler and roast, turning 4 times, until golden and toasty all around, 5 to 8 minutes. Cool and scrape the kernels into a bowl. Set aside.

4. Trim off the mushroom stems and cut the caps into thin slices.

5. Heat the olive oil in a skillet. Add the garlic and mushrooms and sauté until both are soft but not browned, 2 to 3 minutes. Stir in the soy sauce and remove from the heat right away. Cool, then transfer to the bowl with the corn.

6. Add the remaining ingredients to the mushrooms and stir gently to mix.

7. Spoon a generous 2 tablespoons of salsa into each wonton cup. Arrange the filled cups on a buffet platter and serve. Will stay fresh and crispy for up to 3 hours at room temperature.

Note: If there is extra salsa, you can use it as garnish around the plate of cups.

Hot Mustard Paste

When you know how easy it is to stir up, there's no mystery to having a small saucer of freshly mixed mustard paste on the table, just as they do in Chinese restaurants.

TO MAKE, place 1 tablespoon of mustard powder on a saucer. With a fork or tiny whisk, slowly mix in 1½ tablespoons water until the powder is dissolved and the paste is smooth. Serve right away or within 30 minutes, before the paste thickens.

Baked Wonton Cups

MAKES 18 CUPS

Vegetable oil, for coating the wrappers

18 wonton or gyoza (pot-sticker) wrappers (see box at left)

Baked Wonton or Gyoza Cups: Crisp Money in the Bank

Crisp cups of baked wonton or gyoza wrappers are a boon to anyone who enjoys entertaining. Wonton wrappers are square; gyoza (pot-sticker) wrappers are round. They're the same dough and pretty much the same size except for this shape difference. The wonton wrappers need to have their corners trimmed in order to form a cup when pressed into the muffin tin. The round pot-sticker wrappers fit easily and neatly without trimming. You can improvise with larger egg roll wrappers. Cut them into quarters and use the same way.

Both wonton and gyoza wrappers are available in Asian groceries as well as most supermarkets these days. You can bake up a package and have them ready to fill with practically any tidbit on hand. Some filling suggestions are:

- Salsa (pages 298–307)
- Sautéed mushrooms, finely chopped (pages 237 and 238)
- Chicken salad (page 77)
- Minced shrimp or crab salad
- Leftover bits of lamb or beef stew
- Green Tomato Chutney (page 344)
- Marmalade (pages 349–351)
- Lemon Curd (page 351)

1. Preheat the oven to 350°F.

2. Lightly grease 18 muffin wells with vegetable oil. Place 1 wrapper in each well and gently press down to the bottom without breaking the wrapper. Lightly oil the insides of the wrappers.

3. Bake until barely golden, about 8 minutes. Lift the cups out of the wells and set aside to cool slightly. Fill right away or cool completely and store in an airtight container for up to 1 month.

thirst quenchers

Depending on the time of day and your inclination, a thirst quencher can take on many forms. Lemonades and coolers suit a midday break on the porch; warm tea is for a quiet moment; a liqueur or mint julep might be for sipping at a sidewalk café table, watching the day's end; a vegetable tomato juice can be a pick-me-up anytime. Following are recipes for each, with an eye to the garden, of course.

Homemade Vegetable Juice

MAKES 8 TO 10 QUARTS,
DEPENDING ON THE JUICINESS OF THE TOMATOES

"This makes an excellent start to chili and to vegetable or other soups, or enjoy it chilled as juice." With a less copious harvest of tomatoes, you can reduce the recipe by half with equal success. If you can resist drinking it up on the spot, use some for gazpacho (see page 124).

ANGELA BENSON (BLOOMINGTON, IN)

25 pounds tomatoes, cut into large (1½-inch) chunks
6 to 8 celery ribs, trimmed and coarsely chopped
¼ cup coarsely chopped fresh parsley leaves
3 large garlic cloves, coarsely chopped
3 medium onions, coarsely chopped
4 tablespoons salt
¼ cup sugar, or to taste

1. Place all the ingredients in a large nonreactive pot. Bring to a boil, reduce the heat to maintain a simmer, and partially cover the pot. Simmer for 30 minutes, checking and stirring once or twice to make sure the tomatoes are not sticking to the bottom, until the tomatoes are free floating and completely disintegrated. Remove and cool enough to handle.

2. Purée the mixture in a juicer or through a food mill. Divide among quart jars and store in the refrigerator for up to several weeks. For longer keeping, freeze or process in a hot-water bath (page 315) for shelf storage.

TOOLS *of the* TRADE

The Juicer

A juicer is an awesome machine. Besides washing the produce and peeling fruits like bananas or pineapples, little else is required from the cook except to start the motor and watch as it rapidly churns out purées and smooth juices of every sort. Carrot, tomato, and mixed vegetable juices were the popular pours in the Seventies and Eighties. In the Nineties, fruit smoothies have risen to prominence and brought the juicer from home to the marketplace, with shops standing ready to whir your selection into a refreshing and healthful beverage. Make mine with raspberry, blackberry, and wheat grass.

It's in the Water

In most places and most situations, tap water suffices for daily use. In fact, in areas where fluoride is added to tap water, you may find your dentist or pediatrician recommending it over any kind of bottled water because growing teeth need fluoride to form a strong armor against decay. On the other hand, for the thirst quenchers in this book, spring water is called for because of its clearer taste. To complicate matters, even spring waters vary. The following list, compiled with the expertise of Jerry Budrick, founder of the former Aquador Water company, should help sort through the choices.

STILL WATERS

SPRING WATER: From one of a number of select natural springs variously advertised as purer, better-tasting, more healthful, and so on. Besides taste, part of the appeal of spring water is its mineral content, which must be less than 500 parts per million.

MINERAL WATER: Also from a natural spring, but with more mineral content, no fewer than 500 parts per million.

DISTILLED OR PURIFIED WATER: Both are waters that have had their minerals removed, though by different processes. Distilled water is purified by vaporization; purified water is demineralized by filtration. Initially, the waters for both distilled and purified water may be from a natural spring, a well, or the tap. Either of these is the type of water preferred for tea and many homemade liqueurs.

BUBBLY WATERS

SPARKLING WATER: Mineral or spring water that has been artificially carbonated. As with still spring water, the selling point is the source spring; the carbonation does not affect the taste, only the texture.

SODA WATER: Water that is either naturally or artificially carbonated. The mineral baths at Baden Baden are one of the most famous examples of naturally carbonated water. Artificially carbonated ordinary or well water, such as club soda, is by and large twice as bubbly as natural sparkling waters.

SPRITZ: Spring, distilled, or tap water that is artificially carbonated on the spot by passing it through a CO_2 cartridge attached to a canister holding the water as for "cream" soda or gin fizz. Its taste is distinctly different from bottled bubbly waters because those are chilled before being carbonated so that the water accepts more CO_2 and the result is a more unified infusion.

Kay Allen's Mint Cooler

MAKES 4 QUARTS

"My mother, Kay Allen, made this cooler during World War II, and her original notes indicate that only half a cup of sugar was used, due to rationing. I still grow mint in my garden for this tea, but even an apartment dweller with a small pot of mint on the balcony could make this refreshing drink. The method may seem impossible at first, but it does work to dissolve the sugar and blend the ingredients." She adds that in less lean times, she has upped the sugar. Our recipe testers were divided on which version they preferred; it's a matter of whether you like your cooler more or less sweet. Any tea or tea blend will work for the mint cooler as long as it is full-bodied yet not so strong as to overpower the fresh flavors of mint and lemon. Especially good are mango tea, blackberry tea, and orange pekoe tea. Whichever the choice, for the best brew, the tea should be loose leaf, not powdered and not bagged.

~ NANCY FOSTER (CATONSVILLE, MD)

½ to 1 cup sugar, to taste
4 to 6 heaping tablespoons loose tea leaves
1½ cups (packed) fresh mint leaves
4 large lemons, scrubbed and coarsely chopped
4 quarts distilled water

1. Put the sugar, tea, mint, and lemons in a large heatproof bowl. Using a potato masher, wooden spoon, or kitchen mallet, mash the ingredients until the lemons are thoroughly juiced and the sugar is dissolved.

2. Bring the water to a boil. Add the water to the bowl and set aside to steep for 5 minutes, no longer or the tea will become bitter.

3. Strain the mixture through a muslin- or cheesecloth-lined sieve set over a clean container. Let cool, then cover and refrigerate before serving. Will keep in the refrigerator, covered, for up to 1 week.

TEA OR TISANE?

The meanings of some words can be the same or just a little bit different. Tea, for instance, means a brew of dark or green leaves or bark, always dried, often caffeinated, sometimes not. Tisane means an infusion of either dried or fresh leaves, never caffeinated. Both teas and tisanes are reputed to have curative and restorative powers. If nothing else, taking a moment to brew a cup or pot of tea can't help but help.

Lemon Verbena Tisane

MAKES 1 CUP OF TEA

Bonnie Dahan, author of Wise Concoctions, Natural Elixirs and Tonics for Health and Energy, *has long centered her creativity around the joy and restorative power of gardens. At the end of a jam-packed day, she often picks a handful of lemon verbena leaves from her own garden and makes a soothing tisane to reknit frayed nerves and take a moment's rest. She advises, "Stress is not simply a state of mind; it is also a physical condition, and both these aspects of life are brought into balance with a calming cup of lemon verbena tea. Refreshing and crisp, tart yet softened with hints of tarragon and fennel, it's a tisane you can enjoy anytime for its taste alone."*

BONNIE DAHAN (SAN ANSELMO, CA)

4 large fresh lemon verbena leaves, sliced crosswise into 5 or 6 pieces, or ½ teaspoon dried lemon verbena (see Note below)

1 cup distilled water

1. Place the leaves in a cup or mug.

2. Bring the water to a boil, turn off the heat, and say yes, slowly, 5 times. Pour the water over the leaves, cover the cup, and leave to steep for 5 minutes.

3. After 5 minutes, not much longer, lift off the cover, taking care in case it's become hot, and set it aside. Sit back and wait until the steam has escaped, so you don't burn yourself. When the tea and its container are just cool enough for you to hold the cup cradled in your hands, lean forward, take in its aroma, and have a sip.

Note: Dried lemon verbena is available in health-food stores.

Brewing and Steeping Tea

No matter what kind of tea—leaf, flower, herb, even a tea bag in a cup—there's a way to coax the best out of the brew. Whether for hot tea now or for iced tea later:

- If making hot tea, warm the container with hot water.
- Have the tea in the container.
- Have the water at a bare rest after boiling. Pour over the tea and set aside to steep for 5 minutes, no longer. This way you avoid bitter or cloudy tea.
- Serve while very warm but not burning hot, accompanied by a tea strainer. Or, strain right away and cool. Add to your cooler mix or pour over ice and serve as iced tea on its own.

Strawberry Lemonade Concentrate

MAKES ABOUT 7 QUARTS

"Strawberries are usual garden fare in Arkansas. Though we must rely on the farmers' market for our supply, we 'harvest' from there to make this family favorite." The recipe makes a lot, and that's somewhat the point. As long as you're at it and it's the season, make enough to store in the refrigerator for a few weeks or in the freezer for longer.

~ SANDRA THOMPSON (WHITE HALL, AR)

4 quarts strawberries, hulled
4 cups fresh lemon juice (about 16 lemons)
6 cups sugar
Sparkling water

1. Purée the strawberries in a blender or food processor. Transfer to a large nonreactive pot and add the lemon juice, sugar, and 3 quarts of water. Set the pot over medium heat and bring to 165°F. (do not boil), stirring occasionally. Skim off the foam and cool completely. Transfer to individual containers and store in the refrigerator for up to 1 week or freeze longer.

2. To serve, mix 1 part concentrate with 2 parts sparkling water.

SUGAR REFINEMENTS
For ades, coolers, and sorbets, use superfine sugar. Its very fine crystals dissolve more readily than granulated sugar and without the clouding that can occur with unheated powdered sugar.

Raspberry Meyer Lemonade Syrup

MAKES ABOUT 5 CUPS SYRUP

"This recipe came into my life one summer when my husband, his father, and his uncles were building a deck in the 90°F. heat. As I loitered around, I discovered Aunt Geri's Meyer lemon tree overflowing with lemons, so I decided to make lemonade. Over the years, I have altered that original offering by adding black raspberries from my yard or sometimes red raspberries from the farmers' market. Sometimes I need to substitute Eureka lemons for the Meyers. To this day, whenever I make it, in whatever new incarnation, I have a sweet memory of that summer day in the backyard with the family."

~ JULIET PRATT (DANVILLE, CA)

8 Meyer or 6 Eureka lemons, well scrubbed
2¼ cups sugar
1 pint black or red raspberries
Water, still or bubbly

1. With a vegetable peeler, remove the zest from three of the Meyer lemons or two of the Eurekas.

2. Combine the zest, sugar, and 1 cup of water in a nonreactive saucepan. Bring to a boil over medium heat, then simmer briskly for 5 minutes without stirring. Remove from the heat and cool to room temperature.

3. Juice all the lemons and stir the juice into the cooled sugar mixture. Add the raspberries, pressing them with the back of a spoon until mashed but not puréed.

4. To serve, fill a 12-ounce glass with ice cubes or crushed ice. Add ⅓ to ½ cup of the raspberry-lemon syrup and fill to the top with carbonated or still water, as desired. The syrup may be stored in the refrigerator for up to 1 week or frozen for longer keeping.

Ade Alternatives

FRUIT: In place of strawberry or raspberry, use another fruit purée, such as:

Any blackberry—boysen, marion, olallie, logan, tay
Blueberry
Huckleberry
Watermelon
Melon—cantaloupe, honeydew, Persian, cassava or Crenshaw—thinned with water
Tropical fruit, such as guava, mango, or pineapple

GARNISHES: In place of the usual citrus twist or fruit skewer, visit the herb garden for the final fillip and pick a sprig of:

Spearmint or peppermint
Lemon verbena
Fennel
Borage
Burnet
Any scented culinary geranium

Carter's Mint Julep

MAKES 1 MINT JULEP

"I was first introduced to the mint julep by Carter, my father-in-law. Anyone who savored his mint julep remarked at how great a drink it is. Among my fondest memories are the evenings the family spent in good conversation on the porch, the breezeless summer heat chilled by Carter's refreshment. I have tasted others' mint juleps and none compare. Carter always said it was in the curly mint, his own garden crop having come from mint cuttings from his mother's garden begun a century ago and transplanted to each new home. Eventually, I was given a cutting and it's now thriving in my garden, ready to be introduced to our guests in the same way it was to me." Curly spearmint is occasionally

available in nurseries and garden shops, but lacking a plant or cutting of such, our recipe testers had to settle for ordinary garden-variety mint. All agreed it was quite a pleasing mint julep anyway.

∾ WILLIAM MASETH, JR. (BALTIMORE, MD)

2 tall sprigs spearmint, preferably curly
1 heaping teaspoon sugar
3 ounces bourbon
Crushed ice

1. Pull the leaves off the mint sprigs, leaving the top portion of one sprig for garnish. Wash the leaves, put them in an 8-ounce mint julep cup or beaker, and crush them with a muddler (stir stick) or pestle.

2. Add the sugar and ½ ounce of the bourbon and mix. Fill the container one-third full with crushed ice and pour 1½ ounces bourbon over the ice. Mix. Fill the container with crushed ice and add the remaining bourbon. Top with a final layer of ice, garnish with a mint sprig, and serve with a straw.

Mint Liqueur

MAKES 1¼ QUARTS

Minty and sweet but not as syrupy as crème de menthe, this homemade liqueur is a mild aperitif to serve over ice. "Decanted into decorative bottles, it makes a lovely hostess gift at holiday time."

∾ CLIONE STEWART (CARY, IL)

1½ cups (packed) fresh mint leaves
Rind of 1 lemon, very coarsely chopped *(see page 287)*
4 whole cloves
¾ cup sugar
2 cups 80- to 100-proof vodka
3 cups distilled water

1. Combine all the ingredients in a large jar with a tight-fitting lid and stir to dissolve the sugar. Cap the jar and set aside at room temperature for 1 month, shaking the jar every day or two.

2. Strain and transfer to a decanter or wine bottle. Cork and store indefinitely.

Limoncello de Malibu

MAKES 1½ QUARTS

"My husband and I had just finished shooting a movie together, Leap of Faith, *and after wrapping, escaped to Capri, Italy. While there, we discovered an ambrosial liqueur called limoncello, which is served after dinner in every restaurant and kitchen on the island. Getting the recipe became our quest: no one would part with the formula, no how. Defeated, we brought home a few bottles and meted out thimblefuls for the next two years. But the lemon trees in the backyard beckoned, so we experimented. Eventually, we arrived at a recipe that comes close to the magical elixir we discovered on Capri. Serve it on lots of ice and watch out—limoncello goes down easy, then turns your legs to rubber!"*

JANUS CERCONE AND MICHAEL MANHEIM (MALIBU, CA)

THE HOMEOPATHY OF GINGER
Take it as a powder to prevent seasickness, car sickness, and morning sickness. Steep it with parsley for a tea to alleviate bladder distress.

6 large thick-skinned lemons, scrubbed
4 cups 100-proof vodka
1⅔ cups sugar
2⅔ cups spring or distilled water

1. Peel the zest off the lemons with a vegetable peeler, reserving the rest of the fruit for another use. Place the zest in a 1-gallon jar or bottle fitted with a lid. Pour in the vodka and cap the jar. Set aside in a dark, cool place for at least 3 weeks, giving the jar a shake from time to time.

2. Combine the sugar and water in a large pot and bring to a boil. Simmer briskly for 5 minutes, until slightly thickened. Remove from the heat, cool completely, and add to the jar with the vodka (see Note below). Recap the jar and again set it aside in a dark, cool place for at least 1 month or up to 6 weeks before using.

3. To serve, pour a small amount of the limoncello over ice and enjoy. The limoncello will keep indefinitely.

Note: You can remove the lemon zest or not before adding the sugar syrup to the vodka. With the zest left in, the limoncello has more of a citrus bite.

salads:

fresh concoctions for all seasons

"Salat: Take persel, sawg, garlec (etc.) . . . waische hem clene and myng hem wel with rawe oile, lay on vynegar and salt, and serve it forth."

—OLD ENGLISH DEFINITION, *OXFORD ENGLISH DICTIONARY*

It seems that the essentials in the venerable old English recipe were aromatics, fresh herbs and vinegar, plus oil. Still, the "etc." implies other ingredient possibilities, such as lettuce or another green leaf that's good to eat uncooked. As the salad evolved, even more ingredients like beets, diced carrot, and peas were added, and there the plot thickens because the salad now includes cooked elements. So it rested for many a year until the salad met the New World, where such amazements as tomatoes, strawberries, and potatoes began to appear on salad plates. Today, salad means cold or warm, fresh or cooked compositions, most often mainly vegetables but sometimes with meat, poultry, or fish bits. The recipes in this chapter offer some of each, all with a special spark from the garden.

For the Garde-Manger

In classic European kitchens the garde-manger is the person in charge of the pantry. That means, among other things, the salads, which are freshly assembled from already prepared ingredients and then beautifully arranged on salad plates. That might entail something as seemingly simple as tossing together some greens with a dressing or something more involved, like layering ingredients in just the perfect and pretty way, then drizzling the dressing over the top. In either case, it's the care taken that turns out a fresh salad. Tools to have for salad making are:

A LARGE BOWL for combining the ingredients for mixed salads. Wood is far and away the nicest material for a salad bowl—there are some who claim a truly divine tossed salad cannot be had without one. A glazed ceramic or sturdy glass bowl will do but these do not have the benefit of becoming seasoned with age and thereby imbued with the spirit of salad over time, as a wooden bowl does. Most important is to have the bowl large so that the ingredients may be tossed freely to coat with the dressing without bruising.

SALAD TOSSERS can be just about any two instruments working together to mix the salad. Spoon and fork or two spoons are the standard. For the home cook, two (clean) hands do the job in a most sensitive way.

A LARGE PLATTER with a lip or slightly raised edge so that the dressing and other juices don't spill over the side. This is crucial for assembling salads that, for taste and appearance both, are to be presented in layers with the dressing drizzled over the top and served from the bottom up without tossing. The same effect can be accomplished on individual plates, but for a more spectacular centerpiece and less formality than individual plates, the large platter comes in very handy.

VINEGAR AND OIL are the next most important "tools" for the salad maker. How they are added to the salad is another topic that elicits many an opinion. The oil first, then the vinegar so the vinegar doesn't wilt or pickle the ingredients? The vinegar first, ever so lightly, so it barely kisses the ingredients before being modified with a coat of the oil? Whisk them together and add at once so there's no discussion? Whichever your preference, there are choices to be made first.

The vinegar: Cider to malt, white wine to red, rice to balsamic, the range of vinegars to choose from could make a section on its own. The recipes in this chapter explore a broad selection of vinegar flavors and give more than a basic rundown of vinegar possibilities.

The oil: For the salads in this book, vegetable oil, olive oil, or extra virgin olive oil are called for, per the contributors' instructions.

PEPPER: In addition, pepper is crucial to salad perfection. Why else would the waiter approach your table with a tower of pepper and ask if you'd like some freshly ground onto your salad? At home you can use a more modest tool to grind pepper just before using. It does make a difference.

The Queen of Salads

SERVES 4

With a mesclun mix of tender greens and a delicate dressing of olive oil with a touch of vinegar and a whiff of fresh herb, there's almost nothing more to be desired from a salad. If you'd like to crown the queen, however, cherry or pear tomatoes, a few shreds of thinly sliced onion, a sprinkle of toasted chopped walnuts and crumbled blue cheese do the trick. Be sure to add the nuts and cheese at the end, over the top, without tossing in or they will weigh too heavily on the feather-light greens.

KIMBERLY JENNINGS (BARRINGTON, IL)

4 cups mesclun mix of salad greens (see box below)
1 cup red or yellow pear or cherry tomatoes, cut in half
4 thin slices red onion, separated into rings
1 tablespoon coarsely chopped walnuts, toasted (see Note below and page 135)
1 tablespoon crumbled Roquefort or other good blue cheese
⅓ cup Mesclun Salad Dressing (recipe follows)

1. Place the greens, tomatoes, and onion in a large salad bowl and toss lightly. Sprinkle the walnuts and cheese over the top.

2. Just before serving, drizzle the dressing over all and serve right away without tossing again.

Note: Toasting the walnuts for this salad is an important step. Otherwise, they won't be crunchy enough to counterpoint the delicate lettuces and soft, crumbled cheese.

Mesclun Means What?

Mesclun, from the French countryside, or from Italy, where it's called *misticanza,* is a salad mix of tender young lettuce leaves or other greens, preferably picked fresh from your own backyard or patio pot. Unlike the full-grown heads of Romaine treasured for their hearts, unlike the broad, cup-like leaves of butterhead or Boston lettuce, mesclun mixes are of baby leaves. The specialness of a mesclun mix comes not from any particular formula, but from its variety. Any gardener who enjoys broadcasting seeds and the pleasure of watching them sprout can think of mesclun as a palette of vari-colored greens and tastes from which to select a personal mix for the salad bowl.

OTHER MESCLUN MEDLEYS

- *Replace the tomatoes with thin slices of slightly underripe pear.*
- *Replace the walnuts with a few ribbons of thinly sliced ham or prosciutto or a sprinkle of crumbled crisp-fried pancetta.*
- *Replace the blue cheese with shaved Parmesan or crumbled mild goat cheese.*

Mesclun Salad Dressing

MAKES ⅓ CUP

2 tablespoons aged sherry or red wine vinegar
¼ cup extra virgin olive oil
1 tablespoon finely chopped fresh oregano leaves
Salt and freshly ground black pepper

Combine all the ingredients in a pint jar and shake to mix. Use right away.

Belgian Endive Salad with Homegrown Dressing

SERVES 2 TO 4

Barbara Damrosch is a garden writer (The Garden Primer) *and television show personality ("Gardening Naturally"). Naturally, she has a few tricks up her sleeve or, in this case, under the sink. "When I serve Belgian endive solo, not mixed with other greens, I like to use a dressing punched up with herb and spice flavorings from our garden. I use parsley we grow all winter under a floating row cover inside an unheated plastic greenhouse. The thyme and oregano are picked in summer and dried on screens. The paprika is from red bell peppers we grow, dry on the shelf above our woodstove, and then pulverize by whirring them in a blender." With all that, who needs a complicated recipe? It's more than plenty on its own and, also, it's the essence of garden-to-table dining satisfaction.*

BARBARA DAMROSCH (HARBOR SIDE, ME)

8 heads Belgian endive
¾ cup Homegrown Dressing (recipe follows)

1. Trim off the base of the endives and separate the leaves. If necessary, rinse the leaves and pat them dry. Place the leaves in a bowl or on a serving platter.

2. When ready to serve, pour the dressing over the leaves, mix ever so gently to coat, and serve.

Homegrown Dressing

MAKES ¾ CUP

2 tablespoons white wine vinegar
8 tablespoons extra virgin olive oil
2 tablespoons sweet paprika
1 tablespoon grainy mustard
2 tablespoons finely chopped fresh parsley
1 teaspoon dried thyme
1 teaspoon dried oregano
1 garlic clove, pressed
½ teaspoon salt
½ teaspoon freshly ground black pepper

Place all the ingredients in a small glass jar, cap, and shake to mix. Use right away or store at room temperature for up to 5 days; the flavors improve with time.

A Secret Winter Garden: The Story of Forcing Endive Indoors

"Forcing Belgian endive in winter is like having a secret garden; ours is hidden under the kitchen sink. In our Maine garden, the magical process begins on June first, when we sow the seeds in the outdoor vegetable plot. Except for weeding and occasional watering, the crop is all but ignored until the last two weeks of October, when it's pulled up, roots and all. We trim off the tall, bitter-tasting tops, leaving only an inch of foliage, and snip off the root tips to a uniform 8 or 9 inches long. Then we pot them in 2-gallon plastic buckets filled with damp sand, a dozen or so roots per bucket, and keep them in our cool, dark root cellar. (At this point, any cold but not freezing place will do, as long as it's dark.)

"To force the roots to fruition, we bring a bucketful up into the warmth of the kitchen, add water to the sand, and put the bucket in the cupboard under the sink. As new shoots appear, any amount of light will make them turn bitter, so we invert a 5-gallon black plastic bucket over the smaller one to maintain the darkness. The little white *chicons,* crisp and tender, are ready for harvesting at 3 or 4 inches.

"When one bucket is fully harvested, we bring up the next. And so, we are able to enjoy fresh, crunchy Belgian endive salad all winter long. Whenever we're in the grocery store, we note the price of those tiny white heads climb and climb and smile as we think about our delicious secret garden."

—BARBARA DAMROSCH

Arugula Farm Salad

SERVES 2 TO 4

"I lived for a number of years on a farm outside Pittsburgh where we had an arugula bed. One spring, when the Vidalia onions were plentiful, I invented this salad. We have made interesting variations since, but this original is the best. You can add salt and pepper if you like, but the salad tends to have plenty of flavor without them."

ROBIN CONNORS (PITTSBURGH, PA)

Arugula

Also known as rocket or *roquette,* depending on the language you are speaking, arugula is a tall-growing, hearty green that will reseed itself throughout the garden without regard for any taming border lines the gardener has established. But that's okay. It doesn't really crowd out anything and its purple-veined, creamy white flowers can be cut to accent many a bouquet. For kitchen use, its nutty, peppery leaves are prized for adding bite to pesto sauces or serving as greens for a salad that boasts the strength of spring.

3 cups (packed) arugula leaves, whole if small, torn if large, washed and spun dry
½ cup crumbled feta cheese
½ medium Vidalia or other sweet onion, thinly sliced
½ cup pine nuts, lightly toasted (see page 135)
¼ cup olive oil

Spread the arugula on a serving platter. Sprinkle the feta over the leaves. Strew the onion slices over the feta. Sprinkle the pine nuts over the onions. Drizzle the oil over the top and serve without tossing.

Wilted Dandelion Salad

SERVES 4

"Several years ago, I lived in a small beach cottage on the headlands of Lake Erie. Besides the herbs, day lilies, and a few vegetables from my small garden in the sun, I also enjoyed the wild strawberries and dandelions I gathered there." The pairing of dandelion with bacon is a classic one, especially delicious with tender wild dandelions gathered in the spring. Though dandelions are often available in produce markets, those are by and large too tough and bitter for salads and are better used for cooked greens. To simulate the feel and taste of a freshly foraged salad without a field or forest nearby, use watercress in place of the dandelion.

PATRICIA WILKS (CONCORD, OH)

6 cups dandelion leaves or watercress sprigs, tender tops only, washed and spun dry
1 hard-cooked egg
Salt and pepper
4 slices bacon
2 tablespoons tart vinegar, such as Raspberry-Lemon Balm Infused Vinegar (see box below)
1 to 2 tablespoons olive oil

1. Place the dandelions in a salad bowl. Coarsely cut the egg and add to the greens. Lightly sprinkle with salt and pepper to taste.

2. Cut the bacon crosswise into ¼-inch-wide pieces and sauté until crisp. Remove the pieces from the pan with a slotted spoon and add to the greens. Sprinkle on the vinegar and toss gently. While still warm, pour the bacon grease over the greens, add oil to taste, and toss gently again. Serve right away.

Note: If preparing the salad ingredients in advance, do not add the dressing. Just before serving the salad, add the vinegar, and reheat and add the bacon grease.

Raspberry-Lemon Balm Infused Vinegar

MAKES ABOUT 1 CUP

"When I relocated to an apartment after years of large yards with plenty of space for a garden, I faced the challenge of finding plants that grow well in patio containers. I have always been fond of growing herbs for use in the kitchen, and in my new location, with its southern exposure balcony, patio containers of herbs proved to be just the right start for my new garden. A few of my favorite patio herbs are cilantro, basil, rosemary, parsley, thyme, and lemon balm. Together with raspberries, the lemon balm makes a quick infused vinegar that's excellent as a dressing for vegetable salads and egg dishes."

ROSE ANN KOFFLER (WEST HOLLYWOOD, CA)

1 cup distilled white vinegar
1 cup red raspberries
3 sprigs of lemon balm

1. Combine the vinegar and raspberries in a small, nonreactive saucepan. Bring to a boil over medium heat and simmer for 2 minutes.

2. Pour the vinegar mixture through a fine mesh strainer lined with a double layer of cheesecloth set over a small bowl. When the liquid has drained off, press the sediment remaining in the cloth into the bowl.

3. Place the lemon balm sprigs in a pint jar and pour in the strained vinegar mixture. When completely cooled, remove the sprigs and use right away or cover and store in the refrigerator indefinitely.

LIQUID SPICE *Worcestershire sauce has a long-term place in the American pantry as* the *ready-to-hand dash of spice. Based on tamarind and anchovy, its unique blend of all natural ingredients lends a flavor boost to many a soup, stew, marinade, and salad dressing that might otherwise be a rather bland dish. By the same token, however, it should be used in judicious amounts, as its flavor is not subtle.*

Spinach and Strawberry Salad

SERVES 4 TO 6

"This recipe belongs to my mother, a gracious Southern hostess. We always grew spinach and strawberries and enjoyed the salad seasonally—a bounty from our garden."

SCOTT PRICE (LOUISVILLE, KY)

1 pound fresh spinach leaves, stems removed, washed and spun dry
2 cups fresh strawberries, hulled and halved
¾ cup Kentucky Salad Dressing (recipe follows)

Place the spinach and strawberries in a large salad bowl. Pour in the dressing and toss gently to mix. Serve right away.

Kentucky Salad Dressing

MAKES ¾ CUP

¼ cup vegetable or olive oil
¼ cup cider vinegar
¼ to ½ cup sugar, to taste
½ tablespoon minced onion
2 tablespoons sesame seeds
1 tablespoon poppy seeds
Dash of Worcestershire sauce (optional)

Place the oil, vinegar, ¼ cup of sugar, the onion, sesame seeds, poppy seeds, and Worcestershire sauce, if using, in a food processor and mix until homogenized. Taste and add additional sugar if needed. Use right away or store in the refrigerator for up to overnight.

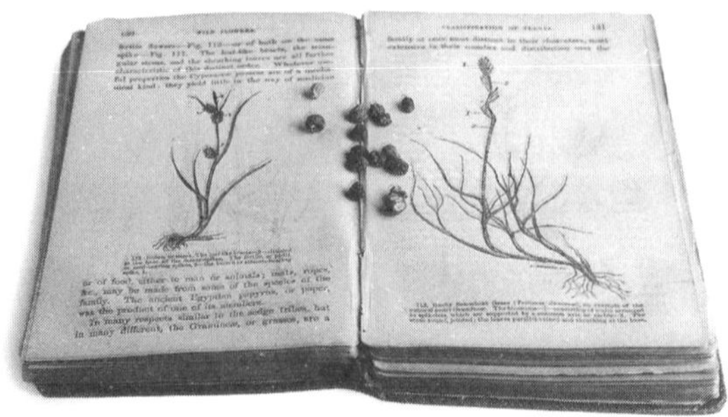

Spring Spinach Salad with Pear, Raspberry, and Chicken

SERVES 6 TO 8

"When the greens come you must enjoy them before they bolt or go bitter. This is a salad that makes use of the spinach while it's still fresh and tender and there's enough of it to serve as the base of a light meal. It's delicious with a loaf of crusty bread."
MARIAN CHRISTENSEN (HOLLADAY, UT)

3 cups small spinach leaves, washed and spun dry
¼ cup crumbled feta cheese
¼ cup pine nuts, lightly toasted (see page 135)
2 boneless, skinless chicken breasts, cooked and cubed (see Note below)
½ cup Sweet-and-Tart Vinaigrette (recipe follows)
1 ripe but still firm pear, halved, cored, and thinly sliced
½ cup raspberries

Place the spinach, feta, nuts, and chicken in a large salad bowl. Add half the dressing and gently toss to mix. Arrange the pear slices and raspberries over the top and pour the remaining dressing over all. Serve without tossing again.

Note: Thinly sliced smoked chicken may be substituted for the cooked chicken. Or for a lighter, side-dish salad, omit the chicken altogether.

Sweet-and-Tart Vinaigrette

MAKES ABOUT ½ CUP

2 tablespoons minced red onion
2 tablespoons sugar
¼ teaspoon mustard powder
½ teaspoon salt
3 tablespoons red wine vinegar
⅓ cup vegetable oil, such as canola

Combine all the ingredients in a pint jar and shake to mix. Use right away or refrigerate for up to 2 weeks.

"Outside in the yard is a big orchard on both sides of the gates, of four acres, and a hedge runs along each side of it, and there tall leafy trees have grown, pears and pomegranates . . . pear upon pear grows old and apple upon apple, grapes upon grapes and fig upon fig."

—Homer,
The Odyssey

Multicolor Mediterranean Salad with Sun-Dried Tomato Dressing

SERVES 4

TO STALE BREAD
If a recipe that sparks an appetite calls for stale bread but you don't have any stale bread on hand, you can rush the process with a fresh loaf: First cut it into the size pieces you need. Place the pieces in a paper (not plastic) bag and set aside at room temperature for a day. More quickly or, more important, if you live in a humid climate, spread the pieces on a baking sheet, place in a 300°F. oven, and bake until dried out.

"I must confess. When improvising from the garden, I don't measure much and oftentimes use whatever's on hand. These proportions should be close, though." And so they were. The salad, from a garden in Tennessee, is a gustable picture of a Mediterranean lunch under the shade of an olive tree. To suit your own Mediterranean harvest, you can innovate with what's on hand: the cucumbers can be green, not yellow; the tomatoes can be yellow, not red; the onion can be white; the spinach can be sorrel (more tart) or rocket (more peppery).

ALISON KROHN (NASHVILLE, TN)

4 lemon cucumbers, cut into ½-inch cubes
2 yellow banana chili peppers or other mild chili pepper, such as Anaheim, seeded and thinly sliced
1 medium bell pepper, preferably yellow, seeded and chopped into ¼-inch chunks
1 medium red onion, chopped into ¼-inch chunks
8 ounces tomatoes, preferably plum, seeded and chopped into ½-inch chunks
2 cups coarsely torn spinach leaves
1½ cups ¼-inch cubes stale French bread (see left)
⅔ cup Sun-Dried Tomato Dressing (recipe follows)
12 Mediterranean-style black olives, such as oil-cured or kalamata
¼ cup crumbled feta cheese
1 teaspoon freshly ground black pepper

1. Place the cucumbers, chili and bell peppers, onion, tomatoes, spinach, and bread in a large bowl and toss to mix.

2. When ready to serve, pour in the dressing and toss again. Top with the olives, feta, and black pepper and serve right away.

Sun-Dried Tomato Dressing

Makes about ⅔ cup

1 teaspoon finely chopped fresh rosemary leaves
2 tablespoons finely chopped fresh oregano or marjoram leaves
3 cloves garlic, minced or pressed
⅓ cup olive oil
1 dried tomato, not oil packed, finely chopped (see page 337)
¼ cup balsamic vinegar

1. Place the rosemary, oregano, garlic, and olive oil in a small bowl and set aside to steep for 3 to 4 hours.

2. Add the sun-dried tomato and vinegar, whisk to mix, and use right away or store in the refrigerator, covered, for up to 3 days.

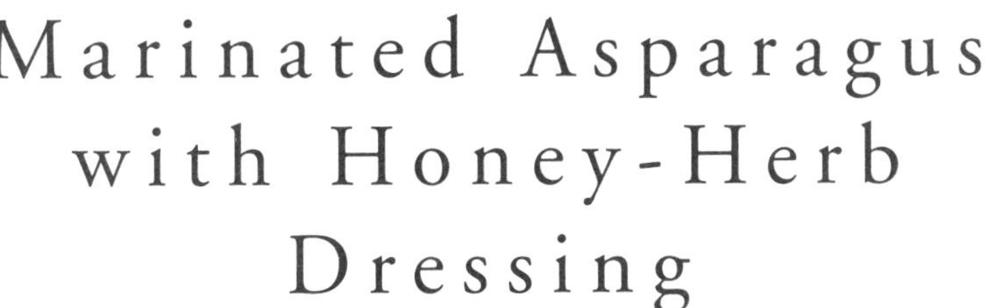

TOOL TINES

One is a prong and can also be a skewer.
Two become tines and make a tuning fork or a meat fork.
Three tines make table forks in all sizes or a garden claw for loosening soil.
Four tines also make table forks—and garden rakes, too, though those are better with eight.

Marinated Asparagus with Honey-Herb Dressing

Serves 4

"I developed this recipe one afternoon when my husband's nephew was joining us for dinner. It has become a favorite we call Sean's salad." Once you've had a taste, it's easy to understand how it could be appealing to all ages: The touch of honey heightens the natural sweetness of asparagus and red bell pepper and, at the same time, softens the bite of red onion. On a bed of red leaf lettuce, the composition is also pretty. A good-quality light vinegar and an aromatic honey are essential to the success of the dressing.

JANE WILLARD (HILLSBORO, OR)

8 ounces asparagus tips, steamed 2 minutes
1 medium red bell pepper, seeded and thinly sliced
1 medium red onion, thinly sliced and separated into rings
¾ cup Honey-Herb Dressing (recipe follows)
1 head red leaf lettuce, torn into bits, washed, and spun dry

1. Place the asparagus, bell pepper, and onion in a shallow dish. Pour the dressing over the vegetables and let stand at room temperature for 30 minutes.

2. To serve, combine the dressed vegetables and lettuce in a serving bowl and toss gently.

Herbed Vinegar

Makes 4 cups

"This mix sounds really goofy, but it makes an amazingly gentle and pleasant-tasting vinegar."

AVIS MAY (MEDFORD, OR)

1 tablespoon chopped shallot
1 tablespoon chopped fresh chives
1 tablespoon chopped fresh mint leaves
1 tablespoon dried summer savory
3 small bay leaves
2-inch piece of cinnamon stick
¼ teaspoon grated nutmeg
1 tablespoon brown sugar
1 teaspoon salt
4 cups distilled white vinegar

1. Combine all the ingredients except the vinegar in a quart bottle that has a tight-fitting cork or gasket-sealed lid.

2. Heat the vinegar to boiling and pour into the bottle. Cool to room temperature, then cork securely. Let stand at room temperature for 10 days, shaking the bottle once a day.

3. Strain into a clean bottle and store at room temperature. Use as needed. Keeps for up to 6 months.

Honey-Herb Dressing

Makes about ¾ cup

¼ cup Herbed Vinegar (see recipe at left)
½ cup olive oil
1 tablespoon honey
1 clove garlic, minced or pressed
1 tablespoon chopped fresh basil leaves
Freshly ground black pepper

Combine all the ingredients in a small bowl and whisk to mix. Use right away or store in the refrigerator up to overnight.

Turnip Slaw

Serves 4 to 6

"I'm 82 years old. I've cooked all my life, love cooking, and I'm still cooking. I'm sending this family recipe, which I doubt has ever been printed in any cookbook. It was passed to my family from a farm family in the Southwest fifty years ago. I am passing it on to you because I'm pleased that some of the proceeds from this book will go to charity, especially to help the children."

BONNIE LAY (MODESTO, CA)

1 pound small turnips, peeled and coarsely grated
8 ounces carrots, scrubbed or peeled and coarsely grated
½ medium green bell pepper, seeded, membranes removed, and very thinly sliced into strips
¾ cup very thinly sliced celery, including some of the tops
¼ cup finely chopped fresh chives or green onion (scallion) tops
¼ teaspoon salt
¼ cup cider vinegar
Butterhead lettuce leaves (optional)
⅔ cup crumbled Roquefort or other crumbling blue cheese

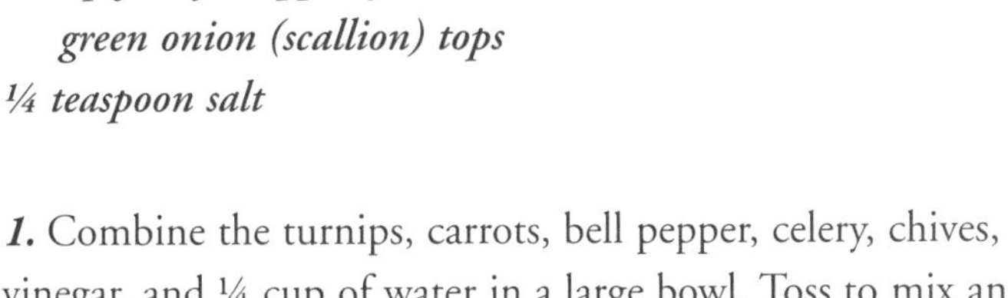

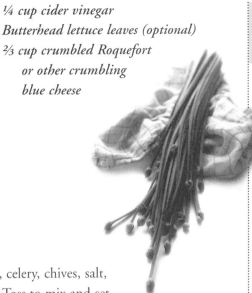

1. Combine the turnips, carrots, bell pepper, celery, chives, salt, vinegar, and ¼ cup of water in a large bowl. Toss to mix and set aside to wilt slightly for 30 minutes.

2. Arrange the lettuce leaves, if using, on individual plates or a serving platter. Toss the vegetables to mix again and mound on the lettuce leaves. Sprinkle the cheese over the top and serve.

Notes

• To grate the turnips and carrot for this recipe, a food processor fitted with the julienne blade works fine, and quickly. Otherwise, use the largest holes of a hand grater; it doesn't take that much longer.

• Another color bell pepper may be used in place of the green.

• The slaw, without its cheese garnish, can be stored in the refrigerator for up to 2 days. As time goes by, however, it becomes more of a pickled slaw than a fresh and crunchy slaw.

Slaws to Savor

Dutch slang for salad, *slaw* first meant the form of the salad—sliced vegetable. Later it came to mean cabbage salad. At some point, slaw came to be called coleslaw because cabbage, the main vegetable used this way, is called cole. So, *cole* refers not to the salad's temperature, but to what it's made of.

One of cabbage's cousins, turnip root, carries the same crunchy, moist brassica flavor, and it, too, makes an excellent slaw. An orange vegetable, like carrot, adds a festive color.

In fact, another brassica cousin, red radish, could happily join this company, adding a sprightly note.

Green bell pepper slices provide the verdance that is needed to create a vivid color composition. Altogether they make up an impressive heap of slawed vegetables; crowned with good blue cheese, they make an occasion of it.

Slaw Supreme with Fennel, Artichoke, and Radicchio

SERVES 6

Chef Doty of the Mumbo Jumbo Restaurant in Atlanta, Georgia, clearly is inspired by fresh vegetables. As he smiles and puts his professional hand to a basketful of them, we can feel the heat of the day alleviated. A bowl of finely cut summer vegetables, ever so lightly dressed, appears. The dish invites a cool drink and a refreshing bite to eat under an umbrella on the patio, or maybe in the air-conditioned indoors.

~ SHAUN DOTY (ATLANTA, GA)

1 baby artichoke, thorny tips cut off, outside leaves removed down to the tender light green ones
1 summer squash, preferably yellow for color, trimmed and cut into very fine julienne strips
1 young fennel bulb, trimmed and cut into very fine julienne strips
1 small head radicchio, halved, cored, and shredded lengthwise
¼ cup whole Italian flat-leaf parsley leaves
½ cup fresh sprouts, such as alfalfa, sunflower, or pea
¼ cup shaved Parmesan cheese
3 tablespoons extra virgin olive oil
2 tablespoons fresh lemon juice
1 tablespoon red wine vinegar
Sea salt and mixed peppercorns

Combine all the vegetables in a large bowl. Sprinkle on the oil and toss gently. Sprinkle on the lemon juice and vinegar and gently toss again. Crumble the Parmesan over the top and serve accompanied by a cellar of the salt and a grinder of pepper for each to sprinkle on as desired.

Fennel: An All-Around Garden-to-Table Plant

Fennel started as a weed with a rudimentary bulb; in the wild its roots, foliage, and flowers are more important for serving the plant's purposes as erosion deterrent and food for welcome bugs. The kitchen garden fennel has been cultivated to produce an enlarged bulb, the part preferred by humans, who also enjoy eating it. The Italians slice it thinly crosswise, douse it with a good bath of lemon juice, add a pinch of salt, set it aside to wilt for a short while, and serve it for an appetizer or side salad. The French cut it lengthwise, braise it in a bit of stock enriched with cream at the last minute, and serve it as a warm vegetable. Other Mediterranean cooks slice and fry or grill it and serve it with a lemon wedge to squeeze on. More to the north, fennel is added chopped to fish soups and stews or puréed with potatoes and served garnished with chives, cracked black pepper, and fennel fronds. Americans, especially in the new cooking, have adopted all these uses and added gratins, casseroles, and slaws that include fennel.

Fennel seeds have a story of their own. Cooks everywhere employ them as a spice (that's what makes sweet Italian sausage sweet). Gardeners everywhere let them blow in the wind, the better to have fennel forever.

Mango and Radish Salad

Serves 4

"One day at the farmers' market, the mangoes called me. Multihued, red, orange, and green, they were ready to eat but still firm. Perfect for slicing. The garden was alive with ready-to-pick radishes, and there was an inviting red onion on my kitchen counter, plus a bunch of green grapes that needed attention. 'Hah!' I said, 'salad.' Color combinations are as important to me in cooking as flavor combinations, and this salad satisfied both. Together on the plate, I had a picture created from a bright and sunny palette and a delightfully fresh taste."

BARBARA HAUGELAND (PITTSBURGH, PA)

1 medium red onion, quartered and very thinly sliced
½ teaspoon salt
2 ripe but still firm mangos, peeled and sliced (see page 81)
12 radishes, preferably multicolored, trimmed and quartered
12 green grapes, halved lengthwise
½ cup cilantro sprigs
⅓ cup Lime-Ginger Salad Dressing (recipe follows)

1. Place the onion in a small bowl, sprinkle with the salt, and set aside to wilt for 15 minutes.

2. Arrange the mango slices, radish quarters, and grape halves on a serving dish. Strew the wilted onions and cilantro sprigs over the top and pour the dressing over all. Serve right away.

Lime-Ginger Salad Dressing

Makes ⅓ cup

3 tablespoons fresh lime juice
2 tablespoons olive oil
½ teaspoon grated fresh ginger
⅛ teaspoon black pepper
⅛ teaspoon salt

Mix together all the ingredients in a small bowl. Use right away or set aside for up to several hours, but not too much longer or the dressing will lose its fresh aroma and bright flavor.

Tomato and Peach Summer Salad with Tarragon Vinaigrette

SERVES 6

Curiosity piqued, this is one of the first recipes we tested because it seemed such an intriguing combination. The contributor succinctly notes, "I created it for my family and friends using the herbs from my garden. It's refreshing, colorful, and delicious!" We found it so, and a good conversation piece besides! Though she makes her own tarragon vinegar from her garden tarragon, she assures us that "any good-quality store-bought tarragon vinegar would be fine, too." We also found the tarragon vinaigrette an excellent dressing for many other salads and a good light sauce for grilled chicken or fish.

LIZ GOODROE (GERMANTOWN, MD)

SALAD TO SALSA

To turn the tomato and peach salad into a salsa, especially good with roast pork, coarsely chop the tomatoes and peaches, toss with the tarragon leaves, and moisten with just a little dressing.

4 large tomatoes, sliced into ⅛-inch-thick rounds (about 1½ pounds)
3 large ripe but still firm peaches, peeled and cut into ⅛-inch wedges (about 1¼ pounds) (see Note below)
2 teaspoons fresh tarragon leaves
½ cup Tarragon Vinaigrette (recipe follows)

1. Lay out the tomatoes and peaches on a serving platter and sprinkle the tarragon leaves over the top.

2. Pour the vinaigrette over all. Chill for at least 1 hour, then serve.

Note: For neat slicing, freestone peaches—varieties that are easy to separate from the pit—are best. For coarse slicing or chopping (see left), any tasty type will do.

Tarragon Vinaigrette

MAKES ABOUT ½ CUP

3 tablespoons light white vinegar, such as rice vinegar
2 teaspoons fresh tarragon leaves
6 tablespoons olive or vegetable oil
Pinch of salt
Tiny pinch of white pepper

1. Place the vinegar and tarragon leaves in a small bowl and set aside to steep for 30 minutes.

2. Add the oil, and salt and pepper to the vinegar and tarragon mixture and whisk together. Use right away or set aside at room temperature for up to 2 days.

Creamy Cucumber Aspic on a Bed of Lettuce

SERVES 12

"This recipe is adapted from the famous Mrs. Beeton, whose cookbook was a favorite in the Victorian era. Since the aspic must be made ahead of time in order to set, the hostess can whisk it from refrigerator to table in a minute. It can be poured into a plain or fancy mold. I have often used a tube pan so that, when unmolded, the center hole can be filled with flowers, such as violets or nasturtiums, set in a shot glass."

DOROTHY SNOWMAN (BETHLEHEM, CT)

3 medium cucumbers, peeled, seeded, and coarsely chopped (1½ to 2 pounds)
1 green onion (scallion), trimmed and coarsely chopped
1 large celery rib, trimmed and coarsely chopped
¼ cup chopped fresh parsley leaves
½ cup cottage cheese
1½ cups chicken broth (see page 86) or water
3 envelopes plain gelatin
¾ cup plain yogurt
¼ cup mayonnaise (see page 64)
1 tablespoon fresh lemon juice
Salt
Oil, for greasing the mold
Whole lettuce leaves, washed and dried, for lining the serving platter

COAXING AN ASPIC TO THE PARTY
If an aspic or jelled mousse does not slip easily from its mold onto the serving platter, warm the bottom of the mold with a hot rag or a brief dip in a bowl of hot water, taking care not to over-warm or you will have a melted-down top after it slips onto the plate.

1. Purée the cucumbers, scallion, celery, parsley, cottage cheese, and 1 cup of the chicken broth in a blender or food processor. Transfer to a mixing bowl and set aside.

2. Place the remaining ½ cup chicken broth in a small saucepan or microwave bowl. Sprinkle the gelatin over the top, stir to mix, and heat, without boiling, just until the gelatin dissolves, about 30 seconds on the stove, 20 seconds in the microwave. Add the gelatin mixture to the cucumber mixture and whisk to smooth.

3. Whisk together the yogurt and mayonnaise until smooth, then whisk into the cucumber mixture. Add the lemon juice and salt to taste.

4. Lightly oil a 1½-quart mold. Pour the cucumber mixture into the mold, cover, and place in the refrigerator until set, at least 4 hours, up to overnight.

5. When ready to serve, cover the bottom of a serving platter with the lettuce leaves. Invert the mold over the platter so that the aspic falls free onto the leaves. Garnish as described in the headnote and serve.

Different Ways to Put the Jiggle in the Dish

In Mrs. Beeton's time molded appetizer and salad sides were quite popular, and one such often appeared as a centerpiece for a large party or buffet table. The featured ingredient could be a purée of beets or tomato or cucumber or a mixture of finely chopped fruits or vegetables, the latter with or without an additional enhancement of poultry or seafood bits. The liquid for suspending the purée or bits could be based on vegetable stock, tomato juice, or, more fancily, jellied veal stock. As long as the composition turned out firm enough to unmold for the presentation, the cook's imagination was given free reign. Perhaps that's why mousses, aspics, and jellied dishes appear in many cuisines around the world, from American to European to Japanese, to name a few. Following are the ways cooks have found to put the jiggle in the dish:

WITH GELATIN: an animal-based product; readily available and most widely used in American cooking today.

WITH ISINGLASS: a fish-based product; probably most widely used in Mrs. Beeton's day.

WITH AGAR-AGAR: a sea vegetable-based product; popular in Asian and other vegetarian cuisines.

Anne's Black Bean, Corn, and Cactus New World Salad

SERVES 6 TO 8

"This recipe was inspired by the wonderful corn and tomatoes I enjoyed as a child in the Minnesota countryside." Over time, the salad expanded to include black beans. Cactus strips added the exact "out-West" touch required for its West Coast rendering.

ANNE BEAVERSON (SEATTLE, WA)

2 cups cooked black beans
4 to 5 cups fresh corn kernels, blanched and drained
1 cup cherry tomatoes, halved
¼ cup diced fresh cactus (see box at right)
¾ cup chopped fresh cilantro leaves
⅔ cup Spicy Vinaigrette Dressing (recipe follows)
Whole lettuce leaves, washed and spun dry
24 tortilla chips

1. Place the beans, corn, tomatoes, cactus, cilantro, and vinaigrette in a large bowl and toss to mix. Chill for at least 2 hours or up to four.

2. Arrange the lettuce leaves on a serving platter or individual plates. Spoon the salad over the top. Stand the tortilla chips upright in the center of the salad and serve.

Culinary Cactus

Both the fruit and the paddles of the prickly pear cactus are protected by prickly thorns that cover it top to bottom like the quills on a porcupine. Still, intrepid humans who like the paddles for cooking garner this cactus for the kitchen. Its fruit adds a brilliant carmine color, not to be duplicated, to jams and jellies. The paddles, or *nopales,* add an indescribable taste and texture to salads and soups that take their theme from the Southwest, either of the Americas, or the Mediterranean. Okra, a similar glutinous green, comes close, but it doesn't elicit the same sense of arid climates, uncultivated wildness, and untended gardens that cactus paddles do.

To collect the paddles or fruit of the nopal, you have to wear impenetrable gloves and keep them on while removing the thorns and prickles. Not that the thorns and prickles are poisonous—you wouldn't die from them in your skin—but they will cause several moments of misery as you realize that you have been stung and can't get out all the stingers because they're so tiny and there are so many. Produce markets often carry fresh paddles or fruit with the thorns and prickles already removed. Cactus paddle, diced and ready to go, is also available in cans.

Spicy Vinaigrette Dressing

Makes about ⅔ cup

2 tablespoons balsamic vinegar
3 tablespoons red wine vinegar
¼ cup olive oil
2 cloves garlic, minced or pressed
Dried oregano and toasted cumin seeds, pulverized
1 teaspoon black pepper
⅛ to ¼ teaspoon cayenne, to taste
1 teaspoon salt

Combine all the ingredients in a bowl, stir to mix, and use right away or refrigerate for up to overnight.

Warm Honey-Mustard Tofu Salad

Serves 4 to 6

"When, as a college student, I needed an inexpensive, healthful one-plate meal that was not pasta or rice I concocted this dish. It has become my most widely requested garden recipe. Even if you haven't cared for tofu before, try this and I guarantee it will change your mind. And don't be shy or light-handed with the herbs." The recipe testers agreed with the claim about suddenly liking tofu and add that the surprise is how the tofu melds with the honey and mustard to make a smooth dressing that silkily coats the lettuce and vegetables. After college days, the salad may be more suitable as a side dish for supper, but it is balanced and filling enough to serve as the main course for a light luncheon.

MATTHEW MARQUIS (CINCINNATI, OH)

About Tofu, Cotton to Silken

Tofu, or soybean curd, comes in two basic types, cotton and silken. Cotton is the older style, more like the original Chinese tofu. As its name suggests, it is sturdy, and it holds up well with grilled or sautéed preparations where the tofu should remain in whole pieces. Silken tofu, on the other hand, is more delicate and lighter on the tongue, more suitable for summer fare, such as the traditional Japanese dish of iced tofu, or for thickening sauces and dressings.

Both cotton and silken tofu come in three textures: extra firm, firm, and soft. For salad dressings, as in the warm tofu salad, firm silken tofu is the appropriate choice. All kinds of tofu are available in many supermarkets these days. You can find the various kinds in the refrigerator section of most supermarkets, packaged in water to keep the curd fresh and moist. You can also find tofu in modern aseptic packages in the produce section. The aseptic packages have the advantage of being longer keeping. The water-packed tofu, whether opened or not, should be used within four days for optimum freshness. Whether water-packed or aseptically packed, tofu is a fresh, not preserved, product and should be refrigerated after opening.

1 large head butterhead, Boston, or Bibb lettuce, washed and spun dry
2 tablespoons olive oil
1 pound firm silken tofu, cut into ½-inch cubes (see box at left)
1 medium green bell pepper, stemmed, seeded, and thinly sliced
1 small red onion, thinly sliced
⅓ cup mixed chopped fresh herbs, such as basil, oregano, thyme, sage, marjoram, and cilantro
Freshly ground black pepper
2½ tablespoons honey, preferably clover honey
2 tablespoons Dijon mustard

1. Place the lettuce leaves in a large serving bowl or platter and set aside.

2. Heat the oil in a large heavy skillet until beginning to smoke. Add the tofu cubes and cook on medium-high heat until beginning to brown, about 3 minutes.

Add the green pepper and onion and stir to mix. Continue cooking until the pepper is well wilted, about 3 minutes.

3. Turn off the heat, leaving the pan on the burner. Add the herbs, black pepper to taste, honey, and mustard and stir vigorously to combine. While still warm, spoon the mixture over the lettuce leaves and serve right away.

Peas and Cheese Salad

SERVES 6

Peas and cheese salad (sometimes peas and peanuts) is culinarily interesting because it seems to have nestled into the heartland of America, in particular Michigan and Minnesota, without showing up too much elsewhere. Our contributor's version is also particularly interesting. While some older recipes call for canned or, later, frozen peas, she unequivocally exclaims, "We never tire of this salad and can eat it as long as we have fresh peas!" She offers an uncomplicated interpretation of an old-fashioned favorite that satisfies in a fresh-from-the-garden way. One of the American sharp white cheddars now available takes the dish to a new era.

KATHY JOHNSON (DULUTH, MN)

2 cups English peas (about 2 pounds pea pods)
1 cup finely diced celery
½ cup finely diced, not grated, firm cheese (see page 64)
½ cup finely chopped sweet pickles, such as bread and butters or sweet gherkins
½ tablespoon grated onion (see box at right)
½ cup Mayonnaise (recipe follows)
¼ teaspoon salt
⅛ teaspoon black pepper
6 large soft-leaf lettuce leaves, rinsed and patted dry

1. Bring a pot of water to boil. Drop in the peas, bring to a boil again, and drain right away. Shake dry, transfer to a bowl, and refrigerate until chilled.

TOOLS *of the* TRADE

Hand Graters

Grated onion is yet another "old-fashioned" aspect of the Peas and Cheese Salad. It means grated through the fine or medium (not large) holes of a hand grater so that you get onion juice, not onion pieces. The outcome can't be duplicated by hand mincing or finely chopping in the food processor. Since it's a little "risky" for the fingers and care must be taken not to nick them and since the yield is small for the oomph involved, you may be tempted to resort to the bottled stuff. Don't. It will ruin your dish. Instead, take the time to use:

AN ONION GRATER, a metal box fitted with a lid with very fine holes; also good for grating ginger.

A STANDARD METAL HAND GRATER, small or medium holes.

A WOODEN GINGER GRATER, looks like a miniature scrub board for a washtub but with sharp metal or wooden prongs.

2. Add the celery, cheese, pickles, onion, mayonnaise, salt, and pepper to the chilled peas and stir to mix.

3. Arrange the lettuce leaves on a serving platter or individual plates. Spoon the pea salad into the leaves and serve.

Real American Cheese

Despite the poor reputation that American cheese has suffered because of those commonly available commercially, there were always so-called farmhouse cheeses to be found off the main roads. Fortunately for all, such honest, real cheeses have become so popular that most supermarkets carry at least a minimal selection. For a genuine classic like Peas and Cheese Salad, the cheese does make the difference. Any of the excellent aged sharp cheddars from Oregon or Vermont or aged cow's milk cheeses from Wisconsin would be a good choice and add far more character to the salad than a prosaic mild cheese.

Mayonnaise

MAKES 1¼ CUPS

While there are more and more good commercial mayonnaises on the market, none compares to homemade. As a dipping sauce for vegetables or seafood or for aïoli, homemade mayonnaise is essential. For mixed vegetable and chicken salads, it elevates the fare to a cut above the ordinary. With a food processor, you can turn out mayonnaise in a snap, but care must be taken not to overprocess, or the oil, especially olive oil, will become too heated and turn bitter.

2 egg yolks
1 teaspoon Dijon mustard
1 teaspoon fresh lemon juice
⅛ teaspoon salt
1 cup olive or peanut oil, or a mixture
1 tablespoon or more very hot water

1. In a medium bowl or food processor, whisk the egg yolks to thicken a bit. Add the mustard, lemon juice, and salt and whisk until blended into the yolks.

2. Whisking all the while, slowly add the oil, starting with drops and working up to tablespoon amounts until you have half the oil incorporated. Continue whisking as you add the remaining oil, in larger amounts now, until the mixture is saturated and turning stiff.

3. Stir in 1 tablespoon of the hot water to thin and set the mixture so it doesn't separate. Stir in enough more hot water to make the mayonnaise the consistency you'd like. Use right away or store in the refrigerator for up to 1 week.

Warm Roasted Beet Salad

SERVES 6 TO 8

"I love this dish in the fall when the beets are ready and I'm on my second crop of arugula." Oven-roasting is, some say, the way to turn out the sweetest beets. Also, when the weather is cooling and the sun descending earlier in the day, the kitchen gets heated while you wrap a scarf around your neck and go to the garden to pick the greens for the salad plate.

~ KRISTEN DILL (TAKOMA PARK, MD)

1 pound mixed red and yellow beets, topped and rinsed
2 cups arugula leaves, washed and spun dry
3 tablespoons fresh orange juice
1 tablespoon rice wine vinegar
1½ tablespoons olive oil
Salt and pepper

1. Preheat the oven to 400° F.

2. Place the beets in a baking dish and sprinkle with a little water. Cover and cook in the oven until fork tender, about 1 hour. Remove and cool enough to handle.

3. While still warm but not piping hot, slip the skins off the beets, then slice them into thin rounds.

4. Transfer the beet rounds to a salad bowl, add the arugula, orange juice, vinegar, and olive oil, and toss to mix. Add salt and pepper to taste, toss again, and serve.

BEET LEAVES AS SALAD GREENS
Young beet leaves, the tiny ones that appear at the top of the root, make a delightful addition to a salad of mixed baby greens. They are aslo a natural choice for a warm beet salad.

Red Root Salad

SERVES 4 TO 6

"Out of respect for their ability to ruin my clothes I never cooked fresh beets until I was fifty,. But beets are full of iron and they come with fine tops that can go into the stockpot. Most of all, they have a good, deep flavor and a solid texture that is not hinted at by the canned variety. So, I said to myself, 'Just wear an old apron and handle them carefully so the juice doesn't stain your wooden cutting board or clothes as you prepare them.'" When you peel fresh beets, your hands will surely be stained magenta red, but it's not a permanent dye. Like that of cherries or pomegranates or henna, the red will wash

away shortly. Besides, the phosphorescent red/orange of the salad, brilliant enough to light up a rock concert, is reason enough to risk a stain of its color.

~ JEANNE DESY (COLUMBUS, OH)

3 medium carrots, peeled and thinly sliced
3 cloves garlic, smashed
1 tablespoon shredded orange zest
⅓ cup chicken or vegetable broth (see pages 86–87), or water
2 medium beets, cooked, peeled, halved, and sliced thin
1½ tablespoons balsamic vinegar
1 teaspoon peanut oil
Salt and pepper
Whole lettuce leaves, washed and spun dry
4 green onions (scallions), trimmed and thinly sliced on the diagonal

1. Place the carrots, garlic, orange zest, and broth in a small saucepan. Bring to a boil, reduce the heat, and simmer until the carrots are wilted but still crunchy, about 4 minutes. Drain, discarding the garlic and zest, and chill the carrots.

2. Just before serving, combine the carrots, beets, vinegar, and peanut oil in a bowl and gently toss to mix. Season to taste with salt and pepper and toss again.

3. Make a bed of lettuce leaves on a large serving platter and spoon the root mixture on top of the lettuce. Sprinkle the green onion slices over all and serve.

Toppers for Beet Bottoms

Perhaps it's their irresistible color. Or their indescribable taste. Or just their friendly variability. But there's no doubt beets have inspired nurserymen and hybridizers to the extent that we now have beets and their relative, chard, in every color of the rainbow for garden, cooking, and decorating. You can take advantage of such botanical generosity and embolden any beet dish, root or leaf, warm or cool, with garnishes of:

- *Quail eggs, hard-cooked and halved*
- *Egg yolk, sieved*
- *Green peppercorns, cracked but not pulverized*
- *Orange zest, cut into thin ribbons*
- *Beet greens, tender leaves only, very thinly shredded*
- *Cilantro sprigs*
- *Tarragon leaves*
- *Baby mizuna leaves*

Classic Potato Salad

SERVES 4 TO 6

Once a cook turns to the garden, there's no telling what will come up, even in the potato salad. Here, a lover of herbs and their lore has suited the classic to include many sparks from her garden.

~ SARAH PANTANO (LOMBARD, IL)

1 medium onion, thinly sliced
Apple cider vinegar
1 tablespoon finely chopped fresh basil leaves
1 tablespoon finely chopped fresh summer savory leaves
1 tablespoon finely chopped fresh marjoram leaves
1 cup mayonnaise (see page 64)
4 medium potatoes, red, white, or russet, peeled or not, cooked and cooled (see box below)
2 hard-cooked eggs, coarsely chopped
Big pinch of celery seeds (optional)
Salt and pepper

1. Place the onion in a small bowl and add vinegar to cover. Set aside.

2. Mix together the basil, savory, marjoram, and mayonnaise in a medium bowl. Set aside.

3. Slice or dice the potatoes, and place them, with the eggs, in a large bowl. Sprinkle with the celery seeds, if using, and salt and pepper to taste. Drain the onions, squeeze out the extra liquid, and add them to the bowl with the potatoes. Stir in the mayonnaise mixture and serve right away or refrigerate for up to overnight.

Other Potato Salad Classics: Variations Galore

Classic potato salad includes potatoes and some other ingredients mixed together with mayonnaise. That's the base. After that, the discussion can go on over picnic and party tables for years as to what ought to be included. Makers of classic potato salad have been known to include:

VEGETABLES, such as capers, pickles (sweet or dill), green olives (black ones discolor the salad), celery, bell pepper, green onions, green beans

HERBS, such as dill, parsley, lovage

SEEDS, such as ustard seed, caraway seed

MEATS, such as salami (finely chopped), bacon fried crisp and crumbled

And a very special seasoning trick: a soupçon of Dijon mustard tossed in while the potatoes are still warm so that the mustard coats the potatoes with a film of spunky seasoning but leaves plenty of room for other flavors.

Herbed Potato and Sausage Salad

SERVES 4 TO 6

Whether it was Mom's offering for every picnic your family ever had, or the one served every year at the Fourth of July church social, or the special new version you made up to stand on your own when it was your turn to show and tell with the potato salad, the dish has achieved status as a sacred childhood food memory. Skipping straight ahead to the late twentieth century, the contributor offers her own current version of an old love. "Sometimes I add lovage and omit the chervil, but I always use the tarragon. This potato salad is a good light meal served with a crusty loaf and chilled dry rosé." Indeed, it is a divine potato salad and, with its fresh herbs, one that gardeners might exclaim over.

GLORIA DRUMMOND (BAILEYS HARBOR, WI)

1½ pounds small red potatoes, quartered
2½ tablespoons olive oil
1 clove garlic, minced
2 medium red onions, chopped into ¼-inch dice
8 ounces kielbasa, thinly sliced
3 celery ribs, trimmed and sliced ¼ inch thick
1½ tablespoons balsamic vinegar
1½ tablespoons red wine vinegar
1 tablespoon fresh tarragon leaves
1 tablespoon fresh thyme leaves
1 tablespoon fresh chervil leaves
¼ teaspoon crushed red pepper
½ teaspoon salt
1 small tomato, seeded, patted dry, and finely chopped

1. Place the potatoes in a medium pot and add water to cover by 1 inch. Bring to a boil and cook until the potatoes are tender but still hold their shape, about 10 minutes. Drain and set aside to drip dry.

2. Heat the oil in a skillet. Stir in the garlic, onions, and sausage and sauté until the onion wilts, about 4 minutes.

3. Transfer to a large bowl and add the potatoes and remaining ingredients except the tomato. Toss gently and serve right away or chill first. Stir in the tomato just before serving.

Potato Salad Considerations

As there are opinions and traditions about what to put *in* the salad once the potatoes are ready, there are at least as many ideas about what potatoes to start with and how to prepare them. You can use white, red, yellow, blue, or russet potatoes, depending on your preference and what's available in your garden or farmers' market. Each and all can turn into a delightful potato salad if you keep in mind their individual personalities.

Russet potatoes are mealier and will make a creamier potato salad, an advantage or disadvantage according to your taste, whereas the waxy-type red or white potatoes hold their shape even after cooking. The newly available yellow (Yukon Golds), purple (Peruvian blues), and fingerlings all should be used either whole, halved, or diced but without peeling. And, whatever potatoes you are using, keep in mind that they should be cooled completely to room temperature but not chilled before peeling, dicing, or dressing.

tomatoes: the ruby jewel of the americas

When the seafaring, gold-seeking explorers of the fifteenth and sixteenth centuries crossed the oceans and stumbled onto America, they unearthed a treasure chest of edibles. Its amazing contents included culinary prizes the likes of which had never been seen in the Old World: corn, potatoes, squashes, capsicum peppers, pineapple, avocado, chocolate, vanilla, almost every bean, and tomatoes. Though not always welcome for many reasons, the newly arrived wayfarers did nonetheless bring along their own comestibles: rice, wheat, cows, domestic pigs, chickens and their eggs, never before seen in the New World.

It was a grand time in the history of cuisine as gardeners and cooks from both sides of the Atlantic, with total disregard for political boundaries, shared what each had to offer. Out of the intercontinental exchanges of those two centuries, the tomato emerged as the most adored of all the New World culinary plants. In farmlands, home gardens, patio pots, boxes on balconies, the almost-weed that began as a free-running vine now not only thrives but is earnestly attended for both commercial and domestic uses in almost every corner of the world. With a luster undiminished by time, the tomato shines brighter than ever and remains the edible ruby jewel of the Americas.

HOW TO HAVE YOUR TOMATOES RISE AND SHINE

Growing Tips Gleaned from the East Coast to the West

Each year my wife and I have an ardent, almost ritual discussion about the tomatoes: when to plant, when and how much to water, and until when. We never disagree about choosing as many of the new varieties as we can fit into the garden; we do disagree about what worked best last year because we don't keep complete notes. As a tomato gardener with years of experience raising tomatoes from New Jersey to France to California, I have found my technique prevails for practical reasons: our backyard crop yields enough truly superb tomatoes to fill our kitchen with plenty to share around. Whatever the zone and its weather changes for the present season, the steps I follow are:

DECIDE TO AND *DO* PLANT SEEDLINGS as soon as danger of frost is over. That means, before the soil has warmed, in spite of some recommendations to the contrary. It could be anywhere from March to June, depending on your zone. Putting the seedlings in the ground at this time allows them to take hold of the earth and delve their roots into the ground in a way that is natural for them and allows their strong growth.

CHOOSE A LOCATION that receives some gentle sun now and will have more intense sun later in the season. For plot gardeners, that might take a bit of assessing and knowing the light pattern of your yard. For pot gardeners, it's a bit more flexible because the pot can be moved around the garden to follow the sun through the growing season.

PLANT SEEDLINGS ALMOST NECK DEEP. This may seem difficult, but keep in mind, tomatoes are one of the few plants that thrive from this treatment. Some gardeners suggest another method: Lay the plants on their sides in a planting trench and almost, but not completely, cover them with good dirt; leave at least one tender sprig exposed above the top. I prefer the former technique, but either way, once in the ground, water the plants well.

CONTINUE TO WATER gently for several weeks, until the weather is warm and the plants rise upright. If the night temperature drops during this time, protect the seedlings with a loose tarp of plastic to keep them from shivering.

WHEN EARLY FLOWERS FORM, pinch them all off. Hard as it is, this is a very important step for ensuring that the plants at this stage grow with their energy directed to the roots and stems and so ultimately produce fruit to capacity. Do this for several weeks until the weather is truly warm from midmorning to midafternoon.

REDUCE THE WATER. As the plants grow and develop from toddler to teenager stage, their thirst needs diminish. It's hard to do, especially when you notice their leaves wilt a bit. Take heart. If there seems to be true wilt distress, the next A.M. give them a small drink, just enough to revive them.

REMAIN STAUNCH. Now is when the plants are meant, for their biological destiny, to call upon their stored energy to fruit, engender the next generation, and, in the process, make the sweetest, not watery, vine-ripened, tomatoes for you.

—RICK WISE (OAKLAND, CA)

Sweet-and-Sour Basil Tomatoes

SERVES 4 TO 6

In an out-of-the-ordinary tomatoes and basil preparation, the tomatoes are sprinkled with brown sugar and vinegar to accent both the sweet and the sour aspects of their natural taste. It's also important to keep the marinating time short so they don't become pickled.

BILLIE HENNINGER (CANANDAIGUA, NY)

1 pound tomatoes, any color
2 to 3 teaspoons brown sugar
2 to 3 teaspoons balsamic vinegar
1½ to 2 tablespoons olive oil
2 to 3 tablespoons shredded fresh basil leaves
1 tablespoon chopped fresh chives

Slice the tomatoes as thick or as thin as you like and arrange them on a serving platter. Sprinkle on the brown sugar, then the vinegar. Drizzle the olive oil over the top. Sprinkle on the basil and chives. Set aside to marinate for 5 to 10 minutes, then serve.

A Different Kind of Scarecrow

"My neighbors were leaving on vacation and asked me to pick all the ripe tomatoes from their garden while they were away. Late one evening, at dusk, I remembered that I had not gathered the tomatoes that day. I took my bowl and started to walk down the rows of tomatoes in the garden. I reached for a tomato and screamed and ran all the way home to tell my husband there were snakes hanging from the tomato vines. He whooped with laughter and confessed he forgot to let me know the neighbor had tied rubber snakes to all the tomato stakes, the better to scare away the marauding birds." The contributor completes the story with a note that, after calming herself, she returned to the garden. Dauntless, she was intent on having the tomatoes, got some, and decided that she might use the hanging snake trick herself sometime.

—BEVERLY TUDOR (PORT NECHES, TX)

Tomatoes Layered with Egg Salad

SERVES 4

Eggs and tomatoes are natural table companions. No less an expert than Julia Child included a recipe for a cold dish of tomatoes stuffed with scrambled eggs in her first volume of Mastering the Art of French Cooking. *The following American version is from the era when ladies took lunch in the tearooms of large department stores as a break from shopping. All that's changed since then is that the tearoom may be your patio or dining room.*

FREDA MARKS (LANCASTER, PA)

BLANCHING TOMATOES

To blanch tomatoes for peeling, plunge them into a hot water bath for a minimal amount of time so they do not begin to cook and soften. The idea is to have a fresh tomato, but peeled.

4 large tomatoes, peeled (see left)
Salt
2 hard-cooked eggs, coarsely chopped
1 celery rib, finely chopped
2 tablespoons finely chopped green bell pepper
3 tablespoons finely chopped onion
2 tablespoons mayonnaise (see page 64)
¼ teaspoon Dijon mustard
¼ teaspoon cider vinegar
¼ teaspoon salt
Hot sauce, to taste
Salt and pepper
8 lettuce cups, such as Boston lettuce, or 4 cups assorted baby lettuce or watercress leaves

1. Slice each tomato into 3 rounds. Place the rounds in one layer on a paper towel-lined plate, sprinkle lightly with salt, and refrigerate to chill and drain a bit.

2. Place all the remaining ingredients except for the lettuce cups in a medium bowl, season with salt and pepper to taste, and mix together with a fork, breaking up the eggs a bit more without mashing them.

3. Place the lettuce on 4 individual plates, arranging two whole leaves to form cups or spreading baby leaves across the plate. Place a tomato round over the lettuce. Spread some of the egg salad over the top, cover with another tomato round, and continue with another layer, ending up with a tomato round. Serve right away.

Note: Combine the egg salad ingredients just before serving so that the vegetables don't make the mix too moist as they release their juices while standing. If you need to prepare in advance, have all the elements ready and put them together at the last minute—it's a quick toss.

Egg Salad Options

Once a staple of school lunches and teatime treats, egg salad has fallen into disrepute, mainly for health reasons: eggs, too much cholesterol; mayonnaise, not good for you; too many calories everywhere. When a hankering for a taste leads you to a bite or two, accent the positives.

First and foremost, start with healthful, better-tasting, hormone-free eggs that are fresh, fresh, fresh. Not only do they taste better, good eggs provide protein and other essential nutrients that are required for growth. Once that's settled, you can:

- Replace the mayonnaise with a touch of olive oil to assuage the cholesterol worry.
- Add an herb, such as parsley, tarragon, or lovage leaves, to perk the color and broaden the taste.
- Add chopped capers, also to perk up and widen the taste.
- Garnish with a slice of anchovy fillet.
- Skip the tomatoes altogether, spread the egg salad on slices of good, hearty bread, and garnish liberally with freshly ground black pepper.

Chèvre-Filled Squash Blossoms on Tomato Concassé

Serves 6

"I often offer this dish on a hot summer's day when we lunch on the deck overlooking my historic Calistoga gardens. It delights guests and is a favorite of mine too because I can easily pick from among dozens of herbs for the filling and concassé. It also allows me to ignore the prolific giant squash and consider them nothing more than the seed pods for next year's squash blossoms! The blossoms are easiest to stuff if you pick them in the morning, before the afternoon heat closes the petals. You can use blossoms from both summer and winter squashes, such as pumpkin, so long as they are tender." The tomato concassé also serves as a fresh pasta sauce or a side dish for seafood.

LINDA-MARIE LOEB, LAZY SUSAN RANCH (CALISTOGA, CA)

12 squash blossoms
4½ cups Tomato Concassé (recipe follows), chilled
8 ounces mild chèvre
1 large egg, beaten
3 to 4 tablespoons chopped fresh herbs, such as a blend of marjoram and oregano or a mix of savory, chives, and parsley
1½ teaspoons freshly ground white pepper or chopped pink peppercorns
1 teaspoon salt
4 cups arugula leaves, washed and spun dry
Nasturtium, purple society garlic, or other edible flowers, for garnish

1. Gently rinse the squash blossoms and pat them dry. If some have baby squash attached, carefully slice them lengthwise, keeping them attached to the blossoms. Set aside in a cool place until ready to use, up to 1 hour, or refrigerate for up to 3 hours.

2. Prepare the concassé and refrigerate to chill.

3. In a small bowl, blend the cheese, egg, herbs, pepper, and salt until smooth. Fill each blossom with about 1 tablespoon of the cheese mixture and gently close the petals around the filling. Place the stuffed blossoms in a single layer in a steam basket and set aside momentarily.

HOW TO DIVIDE A RAW EGG IN HALF

Often it is desirable to make only half a recipe. For instance, perhaps you have only six squash blossoms to stuff. What to do when the filling calls for a whole egg? Beat the egg until yolk and white are well mixed, measure the amount, and use only half of it. Save the other half for another time, another dish, or add it to the compost pile.

TOMATO GROWING TIP

"When planting tomatoes, wrap their stems with newspaper to keep cut worms away."

—SHEILA WEBB, PLAIN CITY, OH

4. Spread the arugula on individual serving plates. Spoon the concassé over the arugula, leaving a bit of green showing around the edge. Set aside.

5. Fill a pan large enough to hold the basket with 1 inch of water and bring to a boil. Place the basket in the pan, making sure it rests above the water. Cover and steam just until the cheese begins to melt, about 1 minute. (Steam in batches if the basket is too small to hold all the blossoms in a single layer.) Carefully remove the blossoms with a slotted spoon and place them on top of the concassé on the individual plates. Garnish with the flowers and serve right away.

Note: The contrast between the warm fried blossoms and the chilled concassé is interesting but if there isn't time to chill the concassé, you can serve it right out of the pan while still warm.

Tomato Concassé

MAKES ABOUT 4½ CUPS

2 tablespoons olive oil
2 large shallots, finely chopped
3 pounds fleshy tomatoes, preferably a mix of red and yellow, peeled, seeded, and coarsely chopped into ½-inch pieces
2 tablespoons shredded fresh basil leaves
2 tablespoons cilantro leaves

1. Heat the oil in a large sauté pan, stir in the shallots, and cook over medium heat just until turning translucent, about 1 minute.

2. Stir in the tomatoes, basil, and cilantro and continue cooking until warmed through and slightly wilted, 1 to 2 minutes more. Remove and use warm or chilled.

The Concassé Cut

In culinary use, *concassé* is the French word for food that has been cut into large pieces. For instance, sole concassé means the fillets have been cut into 2- to 3-inch pieces. When applied to vegetables, the term means coarsely chopped. Tomato concassé, in particular, is quite popular on restaurant menus these days, where it appears listed as an element in a dish or enhanced in one way or another as the dish itself, as in the preparation here. For concassé, the tomatoes may be peeled or not. Peeled, they make a more professional presentation and are more pleasant to eat.

Panzanella

Serves 4 to 6

An avowed "fanatic about tomatoes and a devotee of Italian cooking because of its emphasis on fresh ingredients presented directly and without complication, I offer this recipe that satisfies both of those tastes." With the help of garden tomatoes and fresh basil, it also turns stale bread into a fresh salad.

LOUISE ROBACK (VALATIE, NY)

6 cups cubed stale bread (see page 76)
6 cups ¾-inch chunks tomatoes
4 large cloves garlic, minced
2 tablespoons chopped fresh oregano leaves
½ cup roughly torn fresh basil leaves
2 tablespoons red wine vinegar
½ cup olive oil
Salt and pepper
½ cup pitted olives, niçoise, gaeta, or oil-cured (optional)

1. Place the bread in a large salad bowl. Add the tomatoes, garlic, oregano, and basil and toss to mix. Pour in the vinegar and oil and toss again. Season with salt and pepper to taste and set aside at room temperature for 15 minutes so flavors can blend.

2. Add the olives, if using, toss again, and serve.

Note: The bread for panzanella should be country style, with a coarse crumb. Otherwise the salad will soggy.

Other Herbs for Tomatoes

Tomatoes are an almost universal receiver of herb embellishment. In case you haven't thought beyond basil and parsley, try: chive, dill, fennel, lovage, marjoram, mint (especially dried; a particularly delicious Greek and Southern Italian herb and tomato combination), oregano, rosemary, tarragon, and spring onion or newly sprouted garlic or their flowers.

In addition, with proviso:

CHERVIL, as long as there is enough of it to stand up to the natural front-and-center presence of tomato.

BORAGE, as long as it is finely chopped so its fuzzy leaves aren't unpleasantly tongue tickling.

GREEK BAY, as long as it's a fresh and tender leaf finely chopped and the tomatoes are to be cooked a bit.

FRESH TO STALE, OLD TO NEW

Cooks' Tricks with Extra Bread

Ever since people learned to turn wheat into bread, there must always have been the problem of what to do with the leftovers. Bakers certainly lamented when their fare languished, remaining unsold at the end of a not-busy day. Cooks, not wanting to waste food, must also have bemoaned the extra. Thus came about bread crumbs and croutons and dishes such as bread soups, bread salads, and bread puddings. Originally, the main ingredient was stale bread, but some of the ways became cherished. Beyond thrift, they were established as exemplars of the home hearth, its warmth, its nourishment, its promise of tomorrow.

For keeping beyond the day-old uses, you can slice the stale bread while it's still not too dry to cut without cracking, then toast the slices slightly to dry them out a bit more. This way, they can be used right away or stored in an airtight container for many months.

Brush the slices with olive oil and retoast them to make croutons or crostini. Turn them into homemade bread crumbs to suit the need of the dish:

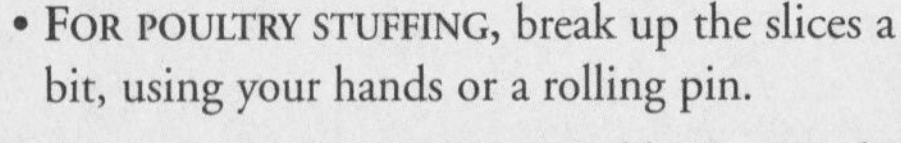

- **FOR POULTRY STUFFING**, break up the slices a bit, using your hands or a rolling pin.
- **FOR THICKENING SOUPS**, sprinkling over salads, or topping casseroles, use a rolling pin to crush them coarsely.
- **FOR COATING FRIED FOODS**, from meatballs and polpettes to chicken and fish, pulverize them into fine crumbs with a food processor or a rolling pin and elbow grease.

Herbed Chicken Salad with Whole Wheat Biscuits

SERVES 4

"The slightly sweet biscuits with their pronounced whole wheat flavor make a good contrast to the savory herbs and mildly tart yogurt dressing in the chicken salad." The chicken is best if cooked and chilled slightly but not overnight; the biscuits are best if served while still fresh and warm. A side of lightly dressed leafy herbs adds color and a crisp foil for the soft texture of the chicken and biscuits.

SANDY MURPHY (DENVER, PA)

1 tablespoon olive oil
3 large or 4 small boneless, skinless chicken breast halves (about 1¼ pounds)
12 Whole Wheat Biscuits, warm (recipe follows)
¼ cup plain yogurt
⅓ cup mayonnaise (see page 64)
1 teaspoon Dijon mustard
¼ cup chopped fresh basil leaves
2 tablespoons chopped fresh parsley leaves
3 green onions (scallions), trimmed and thinly sliced
¼ teaspoon salt
2 cups Herb Leaf Salad (optional, see page 78)

1. Heat the oil in a skillet and sauté the chicken breasts over medium-high heat, turning once, until cooked through, about 10 minutes. Remove and cool the breasts, then place in the refrigerator to chill slightly.

2. While the chicken breasts are chilling, make the biscuits.

3. When ready to serve, tear the chicken into large pieces. Combine the yogurt, mayonnaise, mustard, basil, parsley, green onions, and salt in a large bowl. Whisk to mix, then stir in the chicken.

4. Arrange the chicken on individual plates or a large platter. Surround with the Herb Leaf Salad, if using, and serve, accompanied by a basket of the warm biscuits.

TELLING TIME NATURALLY WITH FLOWERS

"Flowers have their own clocks. Some open in the morning, some wait till evening. They all know when their pollinators will come."

—BARBARA DEUTSCH, SAN FRANCISCO, CA

Whole Wheat Biscuits

MAKES 12 BISCUITS

½ cup all-purpose flour
½ cup whole wheat flour
1½ teaspoons baking powder
¼ teaspoon baking soda
1½ teaspoons sugar
¼ teaspoon salt
2 tablespoons olive oil
⅓ cup milk
Extra all-purpose flour, for kneading

1. Preheat the oven to 400°F. Lightly grease a baking sheet.

2. Sift the dry ingredients into a large bowl. Stir together the oil and milk and add gradually to the dry ingredients to make a soft dough. Transfer the dough to a lightly floured surface and, with floured hands, knead for 6 turns.

3. Roll out the dough to 1 inch thick. Cut into approximately 3-inch circles with a biscuit cutter, wide-mouth glass, or knife.

4. Transfer the circles to the baking sheet and bake until golden, about 12 minutes. Serve right away or soon, while still warm.

Note: If necessary, you can store the biscuits in plastic bags overnight and reheat in the oven just before serving.

Herb Leaf Salad

MAKES 2 CUPS

Sometimes when a composition needs a brisk, slightly sharp counterpoint to bring its other components into balance, leafy herbs modestly dressed precisely suits what's called for. Not meant to be a separate dish, it's to serve on the side of the plate as a garnish. The vinegar and oil amounts are minuscule, it's true, but don't be tempted to overdress the salad; its power is in its simplicity.

2 cups mixed herb leaves, such as cilantro, parsley, chive, wild onion, or a mix, tender parts only, washed and spun dry
¼ teaspoon salt
1 teaspoon fruity vinegar, such as cider, sherry, or Raspberry-Lemon Balm Infused Vinegar (see page 49)
1 teaspoon olive oil

Place the herbs in a bowl. Sprinkle on the salt, then the vinegar, and toss. Drizzle the olive oil over the top and serve right away.

Grilled Chicken Salad with Roasted Red Bell Pepper Dressing

Serves 4

Hearty greens and large pieces of smoky grilled chicken can both stand up to a forceful dressing, like the one here. The dressing plays a dual role: It acts as a binding for what might otherwise be just a plate of chicken and greens, and it provides an extra vegetable element, a cooked one, in the salad.

~ PHILIP BARBER (MINNEAPOLIS, MN)

3 large or 4 small boneless, skinless chicken breast halves (about 1¼ pounds)
2 tablespoons olive oil
4 cups hearty salad greens, such as arugula, watercress, or frisée
⅓ cup oil-cured olives, pitted (see page 131)
1 cup Roasted Red Bell Pepper Dressing (recipe follows)

1. Prepare a charcoal fire.

2. Brush the chicken on both sides with olive oil and grill, turning once, until done but still moist, about 10 minutes. Set aside to cool, then slice diagonally into ¼- to ½-inch-wide strips.

3. Spread the greens on a large serving platter. Arrange the chicken and olives over the top. Spoon half of the dressing over all and serve right away, accompanied by the remaining dressing on the side.

GRILL ROASTING PEPPERS

If you already have a charcoal fire going for other parts of the meal, you might as well go ahead and roast bell peppers that are to be peeled right on top of the grill over the coals rather than in the oven. Not only does this save heating the oven, it also gains extra use from the coals. In other words, a thrifty technique.

Roasted Red Bell Pepper Dressing

Makes 1 cup

1 medium red bell pepper, roasted, peeled, and seeded (see box on page 99)
12 to 15 cloves roasted garlic, pulp squeezed from the skin (see pages 83 and 132)
2 tablespoons coarsely chopped fresh basil leaves
¼ cup olive oil
2 tablespoons balsamic vinegar
Salt and pepper

Place all the ingredients in a food processor and blend until puréed as fine as possible. Use right away or store in the refrigerator for up to 2 days. After that the flavor fades.

PINEAPPLE
Juicy, sweet, fragrant tropical fruit insists on attention: a stop to savor the day, a moment of thirst-quenching relaxation . . . Pineapple in particular stands out as an exemplar of such moments to the extent that the philosopher David Hume devoted several lines to extolling the wonder of pineapples in his otherwise heavy-headed Treatise on Human Reason. *An entire island in the Hawaiian chain, Lanai, is devoted to growing pineapples, and the fruit itself has become an icon of hospitality—from doorstep to kitchen to table, pineapple means welcome around the world.*

Smoked Chicken Salad with Tropical Fruit and Basil-Malt Vinegar Dressing

SERVES 6

When it comes to chicken salad, it's hard to imagine too many to choose from. When it comes to summer and a chicken salad that completely escapes the heat, this one is at the top of the list. Only the sweet potato needs cooking, and that can be done early in the day before it's too hot. The dressing, made doubly dulcet with sweet basil plus a good boost of confectioners' sugar, together with the deep brown, toasty-tasting malt vinegar, is not only delicious but saves the cook from seeming too, too lazy because, even though there's almost no cooking involved, there's still a garden's worth of surprises.

JANET ENRIGHT (LOS ANGELES, CA)

1 smoked chicken (about 3½ pounds)
1 pound sweet potato, peeled and cut into ¼-inch dice
6 cups soft-leaf lettuce, such as curly leaf, red leaf, oak leaf, or any other leaf lettuce from your garden
½ red bell pepper, finely chopped
½ green bell pepper, finely chopped
3 green onions (scallions), trimmed and thinly sliced
1 Hass avocado, peeled, pitted, and sliced (see box on page 81)
1 slightly ripe but still firm mango, peeled and cut into thin slices (see box on page 81)
1½ cups Basil-Malt Vinegar Dressing (recipe follows)

1. Tear the chicken into bite-size pieces, removing the skin and bones. Set aside.

2. Bring a pot of water to boil, add the sweet potato, and cook over medium-high heat until fork tender but not yet mashable, 10 to 12 minutes. Drain in a colander and set aside to cool and drip dry.

3. To assemble the salad, spread the lettuce on the bottom of 6 individual plates or on a large serving platter. Arrange the chicken on top of the lettuce. Distribute the sweet potato, bell peppers, and green onions over the chicken. Place the mango and avocado slices around the chickens. Pour the dressing over the top and serve right away.

Note: Instead of mango, you can use slices of grapefruit, melon, or pineapple (see page 80).

Basil-Malt Vinegar Dressing

MAKES ABOUT 1½ CUPS

½ packed cup fresh basil leaves
1½ teaspoons mustard powder
½ cup confectioners' sugar
1 teaspoon cracked black pepper
½ teaspoon salt
½ cup malt vinegar
1 cup olive oil

Place all the ingredients in a food processor and process until well blended. Use right away. Or store in the refrigerator for up to 5 days, whisking to smooth before serving.

TRICKS *of the* TRADE

Peeling and Pitting Avocados and Mangos

When it comes to avocados and mangos, it's no easy matter to inveigle the fruit onto the plate in neat slices. If the fruit is to be finely chopped or puréed, of course, it doesn't matter how you get at it as long as you do. For slices that should appear somewhat professionally pretty on the plate, here's how:

FOR MANGOS: First, slice off the stem end. Next, cut through the peel lengthwise at quarter intervals, then pull the peel away. Finally, slice through the pulp, cutting through to the pit, to form whatever size pieces you would like to end up with: long, thick or thin slices or chunky dice.

FOR AVOCADOS: Cut through the skin all the way to the pit, dividing the avocado almost in half lengthwise. Using your hands, twist the halves in opposite directions so they come apart. The pit will probably remain in one of the halves. Next, pull away the skin and slice or cut the pulp as desired. If the half that still has the pit doesn't release easily with a gentle prod, slice or dice the pulp first and then cut it away from the pit as neatly as you can.

salad dressings to mix and match

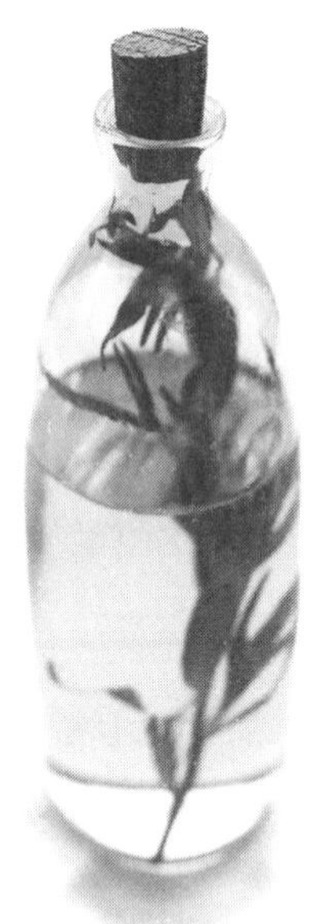

Just as each gardener has a special notion of what to plant and how to grow the vegetables, each cook has a notion of how to prepare and dress them for the table. Below are two recipes that, even though not attached to any particular dish, lend themselves to multiple ways for adorning garden goods followed by a list of the salad dressings offered in this book.

A FESTIVAL OF GARLIC
Purple garlic
Elephant garlic
Ecru cloves
Purple cloves

So desirable are they all, Gilroy, California, where much garlic is grown, proudly proclaims itself the Garlic Capital and holds a fair each summer to celebrate its prolific crop in every incarnation including garlic ice cream.

Roasted Garlic Dressing

MAKES 1¼ CUPS

"Quite often, on my days off, I enjoy roasting garlic just to fill the house with its fragrance, which sends me straight to heaven. This creamy dressing is wonderful over mixed field greens tossed with romaine and Parmesan or sparingly spread over grilled swordfish."

BRAD BARBOUR (BOSTON, MA)

24 to 30 Oil-Roasted Garlic Cloves (recipe follows)
1 cup olive oil
1 tablespoon balsamic vinegar
1 tablespoon fresh oregano leaves
1 tablespoon chopped fresh basil leaves
½ tablespoon fresh thyme leaves
½ teaspoon salt
¾ teaspoon black pepper

Combine all the ingredients in a food processor and mix until creamy, 2 to 3 minutes. Use right away or store in the refrigerator for up to 1 week.

Oil-Roasted Garlic Cloves

MAKES 24 TO 30 CLOVES

2 large heads garlic, 24 to 30 cloves

¼ cup olive oil

1. Preheat the oven to 400°F.

2. Separate and peel the garlic cloves. Place them in a baking dish with the oil. Cover the dish and bake for 30 to 40 minutes, until lightly golden and soft.

3. Lift the garlic out of the oil and use right away. Or cool and refrigerate in the oil for up to 1 week.

Note: For another way to roast garlic, see page 132.

"The herb garden must have plenty of sun but, in locating it, consideration should be given to its nearness to the kitchen. This will save many steps. Furthermore, in dry weather, most of the plants will have to be watered, and under all circumstances these precious little plants should be grown under the caring hands and eyes of the home gardener."

—Leonid de Sounin, *The Magic of Herbs*

Herb Gardener's All-Purpose Dressing

MAKES ABOUT 3 CUPS

"All the herbs in this dressing are grown in planters on my terraced apartment in New York. The recipe makes a lot, but it is so versatile—as salad dressing, pasta sauce, marinade, or dip—there never seems to be enough."

ADRIENNE ADRIAN (NORTH WOODMERE, NY)

½ small onion, chopped
2 tablespoons coarsely chopped garlic
1 medium red bell pepper, roasted, peeled, seeded, and chopped *(see page 99)*
¼ cup fresh parsley leaves, preferably curly leaf
¼ cup chopped fresh basil leaves
1½ tablespoons fresh tarragon leaves
¼ cup Dijon mustard
1½ teaspoons sugar
2 teaspoons salt
1½ teaspoons black pepper
¼ cup balsamic vinegar
¼ cup red wine vinegar
1½ cups vegetable or olive oil

Place all the ingredients except the oil in a food processor and blend for 1 minute. Slowly add the oil and continue blending until well mixed. Use right away or store in the refrigerator for up to 1 week.

Index of Salad Dressings

Whether to cool a warm day or warm a cool day, every salad needs dressing. In this book are the following salad dressings:

soups:

soothing garden goodness in a bowl

Homemade soups signify loving care. They are labor intensive, obliging the cook to expend some effort in preparing the ingredients; time intensive, requiring slow cooking to simmer into goodness; and space intensive, often calling for a large pot, which takes up lots of room on the stovetop. Yet soup is a first thought when the heart needs warming, the spirit needs nurturing, and the stomach needs filling. As long as one is at such an important task, it might as well be a very good soup; this begins with the broth. When the soup ingredients are delightfully fresh and aromatic enough to create a flavorful broth as they simmer, water may be not only an acceptable but a desirable way to begin so the brew stays light and, important for some, stays vegetarian. When the vegetable and herb ingredients are themselves relying on the soup for freshening, as long as the broth is tasty, the cook can't miss. In this chapter are soups that meet all needs: spring light, summer fresh, autumn full, winter hearty.

No-Bother Chicken Broth

Making stock—poultry, beef, or veal—is one of the arts of classic European cuisine. More than the soup itself, the stock requires huge amounts of ingredients, at least a day's time, and that's not to mention the size of the pot necessary to produce one. There's not much way around this rigamarole for meat stocks. But for poultry, especially chicken, a more modest broth is often preferable not only for its ease of making but also for its lighter taste. These days, you can take advantage of store-bought products—in particular, one of the low-sodium, truly chicken-tasting, aseptic-packaged offerings available in many grocery stores. But they're not as good as homemade, and homemade is a way to use what might otherwise be wasted, namely, the wing tips, backbones, and giblets. Here's how:

1. Rinse and place the wing tips, backbones, and giblets (not the liver) from cut-up chickens, along with any other chicken pieces you would like to turn into broth in a pot. Include the skin and fat trim; it will flavor the broth and can be skimmed off later. Add water to cover by 1 inch and bring to a boil over medium, not high, heat. Reduce the heat so the liquid is barely bubbling and cook, uncovered, for 1 hour and 15 minutes.

2. Remove from the heat, cool enough to handle, and strain into a bowl or storage container. Set aside to cool to room temperature. Either skim the fat off the top and use right away or refrigerate.

Note: Though a chicken or two won't yield restaurant amounts of broth, you can stockpile small amounts in the freezer until there's enough for that big pot of soup. You can also store it in the refrigerator for up to two weeks, as long as the layer of congealed fat on top of the broth, which acts as a natural sealant, is not broken.

TOOLS *of the* TRADE

The Soup Pot

Soup making, by its nature, involves cooking for more than one, usually for four to six, and sometimes more if you are preparing enough to freeze. That means the pot needs to be:

LARGE, at least five-quart capacity, in order to hold all the ingredients freely floating in the liquid, not all jammed together.

NONREACTIVE, so both the color and the flavor stay bright and clear. Aluminum or cast-iron pots do not make good soup pots because they will taint both color and flavor if there is any acidic element in the brew, like tomato, many leafy greens, lemon, vinegar, or wine, to name a few.

SOMEWHAT HEAVY, NOT FLIMSY, so an even distribution of heat can be maintained throughout the cooking, starting from any initial sautéing all the way through to long simmering.

FITTED WITH A COVER, not necessarily tight-fitting, that can completely cover the pot when it's necessary to hold in all the moisture or partially cover the pot when it's desirable to simmer while allowing a bit of moisture to escape for reducing the liquid.

Vegetable Broth

While there are excellent chicken broths to purchase when you don't have the time or inclination to make your own, the story is not the same with vegetable broths. Honest and pure as they might come, none compares to what you might easily simmer up at home with some quickly chopped vegetables plus parings and trim. For when your soup needs a little boost from the starting broth and the broth should be vegetable:

1. Combine 1½ pounds coarsely chopped tomatoes; an onion, unpeeled and quartered; 2 or more cloves garlic; 2 celery ribs, including tops, cut up a bit; 2 carrots, scrubbed and cut up a bit; 2 good handfuls of shredded greens, such as chard, spinach, or kale; another handful of fresh parsley; a bay leaf; and a good pinch of salt to bring out the flavors. To these basics, you can add some chunks of summer squash or other herbs, such as cilantro, thyme, oregano, or marjoram. Place all these ingredients in a large pot and add 4 quarts water. Bring to a boil over medium heat (this will take some time), reduce the heat to a simmer, and partially cover. Cook for 1 to 1½ hours, until the broth is well colored and no longer watery looking.

2. Cool, strain, and use right away or refrigerate for up to 5 days. May be frozen for longer.

Some notes to keep in mind

- First and foremost, don't hold back on the amount of vegetables when putting together the stock. As with chicken broth, the mix should include enough solid ingredients barely to float in the water, not so many as to crowd the pot and not so few as to get lost in it.
- Rice, potato, lentils, and such ingredients are not a good addition to the stock as it simmers. They will cloud it. Also, bell pepper of any color is not a good addition because it takes over to the detriment of other tastes.
- As with any stock, keep an eye on the pot and don't let it boil full-tilt or you will have a murky, not clear, broth.
- For vegetable broth as well as chicken broth, the time should be kept short. About 1 to 1½ hours is sufficient to render the most flavor and have the broth remain fresh-tasting.

Around the World with Vegetable Broth

The vegetable broth can be varied to match the cuisine and style of cooking you have in mind. Simple additions to take the flavor in a specific direction are:

LATIN AMERICAN: chili pepper, fresh or dried, as much as you would like

JAPANESE: daikon, kelp, shiitake mushroom, ginger, bean sprouts, no tomato

PACIFIC RIM: lemongrass, coconut milk, galanga (a relative of ginger)

RUSSIAN: parsnip, parsley root, cabbage

INDIAN: cumin seed, coriander seed, cardamom pod

Chive Soup

SERVES 4 TO 6

The short ingredient list and straightforward method for preparing this soup from "a gardener who cooks, a cook who gardens, a caterer, a restaurateur, a husband, and father of teenage boys" belie its rich and deep flavors. Similar to a vichyssoise, the soup here leans away from the potato element and toward the onion flavor, provided by a generous use of chives in place of the traditional soup's leeks. If your garden or pocketbook can't provide the lavish amount of chives called for, you can substitute half the measure with young green onion (scallion) tops. If using green onion tops, cook them in the pot with the potatoes for the last five minutes before proceeding with the recipe. Delicate chives need no precooking.

JAMES A. KINION (FINCASTLE, VA)

1½ pounds russet potatoes, peeled and cut into 1-inch chunks
2 cups chicken broth *(see page 86)*
¾ teaspoon salt
8 ounces fresh chives, cut into 1-inch pieces
2½ to 3 cups milk
1 cup heavy (whipping) cream
Chive flowers, for garnish (optional)

The Chivalry of Chives

Chives are a friendly plant for doorstep gardeners. In a pot on the stoop, they will proliferate and supply as long as they have full, but not burning-hot, sun and you keep them well watered. Unlike most other alliums whose destiny is to develop into bulbs underground, chives do best with regular moisture. They also seem to like a haircut, so you can snip away their tops for kitchen use, right down to a crewcut and, in doing so, actually encourage them to sprout right back up.

1. Place the potatoes, broth, and salt in a medium pot and bring to a boil over medium-high heat. Reduce the heat, cover the pot, and simmer for 20 minutes, or until the potatoes have collapsed. Remove from the heat and cool enough to handle.

2. With a food processor or a food mill, purée the potato mixture along with the chives and 2 cups of the milk until the chives are chopped as fine as possible. Transfer the purée to a clean pot or microwave bowl.

3. Stir in the cream and enough extra milk, ½ to 1 cup, to make a soup of the consistency you like (see Note below). Reheat the soup on the stovetop or in the microwave until beginning to bubble without boiling, about 4 minutes either way.

4. Serve right away while hot, or cool and chill. Garnish with the chive flowers, if using, just before serving.

Note: When adding the milk in Step 3, keep in mind that if the soup is served cold, it will thicken as it chills.

Leek Soup

Serves 4 to 6

"We live on a typical 100 by 60-foot plot on Long Island, New York, and our small backyard garden yields a variety of produce throughout the growing season, including leeks, onions, garlic, parsley, and thyme for my garden-based leek soup."

A. PENNY CRONIN (GARDEN CITY, NY)

2 tablespoons olive oil
3 medium leeks, white part only, thinly sliced, well washed, and drained (about 9 ounces)
½ small onion, finely chopped
4 medium cloves garlic, minced
6 cups chicken broth (see page 86) or water
2 pounds russet potatoes, peeled and coarsely chopped
¼ teaspoon fresh thyme leaves or ⅛ teaspoon dried thyme
1 small bay leaf
1 tablespoon chopped fresh parsley leaves
1 teaspoon salt
1 teaspoon black pepper
1 cup milk (optional)
⅛ teaspoon mace (optional)

1. Heat the oil in a heavy pot. Stir in the leeks, onion, and garlic and sauté over medium heat until the leeks are tender, about 10 minutes.

2. Add the broth, potatoes, thyme, bay leaf, parsley, salt, and pepper and bring to a boil. Reduce the heat, cover the pot, and simmer until the potatoes are tender, 25 minutes. Cool enough to handle, remove the bay leaf, then purée in a food processor or through a food mill.

3. Return the soup to a clean pot and stir in the milk, if using. Gently reheat, sprinkle with mace, if using, and serve.

Note: The soup may also be served chunky style, in which case, don't bother puréeing it; just mash with a wire whisk

How to Make Your Leeks Leap from House to Garden to Kitchen

"I start my leek seeds indoors 10 to 12 weeks before planting them in my garden. I transplant them into larger containers to allow more growth. I then harden them off in my cold frame before setting them into the ground. As soon as the weather permits, I dig a 6-inch trench and plant my now ¼- to ½-inch-thick leeks.

"Throughout the summer, I pile dirt around each plant. This excludes light and bleaches more of the stem. This is important, as this white part is the only part that is used in most recipes.

"Leeks can be left in the garden very late into fall and even through winter. But because my garden gets plowed up at the end of the season, I harvest all the leeks, thinly slice six at a time, and freeze them in a small freezer bag.

"Between teaching and running our farm household, having these mild onions sliced and ready in my freezer sure makes planning a light meal all that much easier."

—CATHY SLADEK (IOWA CITY, IA)

or potato masher and continue with the recipe, adding the milk or mace as you like. Remember to remove the bay leaf before ladling out.

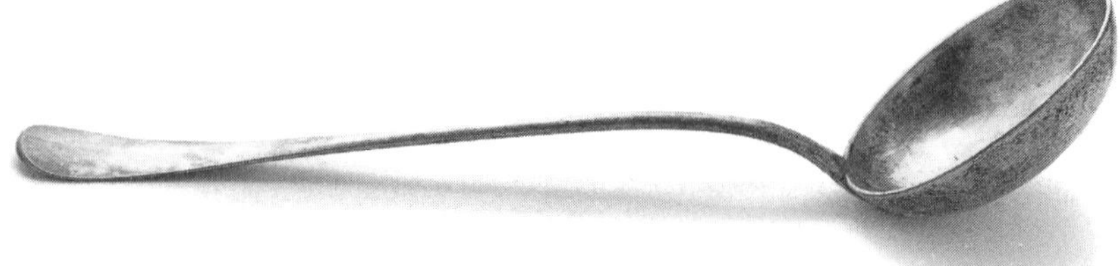

Fresh Pea Soup

SERVES 4 TO 6

"I serve this soup during the peak pea-harvesting time. Besides the dill, mint is a good herb to choose for the final seasoning." A plethora of peas is a momentary passing in the spring garden, best taken advantage of while they last. Dill or mint, each also spring greens, are almost not needed unless you have them right there. The basket of peas, enough to turn into a soup, is glory enough by itself.

SHERYL LOZIER, SUMMER PAST FARMS (FLINN SPRINGS,CA)

4 tablespoons (½ stick) butter
1 medium carrot, scraped and finely chopped
1 medium or 2 small (½ pound) leeks, trimmed, thinly sliced, and washed
3 cups shredded lettuce, such as Romaine or curly leaf lettuce
½ teaspoon sugar
5 cups shelled English peas
3 cups chicken broth (see page 86)
1 teaspoon salt
½ cup heavy (whipping) cream
¼ cup chopped fresh dill

1. Melt 3 tablespoons of the butter in a large soup pot. Add the carrot and leeks and sauté until tender, about 10 minutes. Stir in the lettuce and sugar and cook over low heat until the lettuce is wilted, about 5 minutes.

2. Add the peas, broth, 2 cups of water, and salt. Bring to a boil, reduce the heat, and simmer for 10 minutes, until the peas are mashable. Purée and return the mixture to the pot. Stir in the cream, dill, and remaining 1 tablespoon butter. Reheat briefly and serve.

The Many Ways Peas Please

- Greenery for the garden fence.
- Flowers in spring.
- Sprouts for the salad.
- Pods for the vegetable stock.
- Green morsels floating in the soup bowl.
- Green morsels in the rice bowl.
- Dried and split for winter soup.

Heavenly Carrot Soup

Serves 3 to 4

The secret of this soup is "the cooking method and the fact that coriander and carrots do special things for each other. Hot, cold, or even at room temperature, the combination is heavenly and the color is dazzling."

SUSAN RIHERD (SANTA FE, NM)

4 tablespoons (½ stick) butter
1 small onion, finely chopped
1 pound carrots, scraped and finely chopped
½ cup white wine
1½ teaspoons ground coriander
4 cups chicken broth (see page 86)
½ teaspoon salt
¼ teaspoon black pepper
Sprigs of cilantro, for garnish (optional)

1. Melt the butter in a large soup pot. Stir in the onion and sauté for 5 minutes, until slightly wilted. Add the carrots, wine, and coriander. Cover the pot and cook over low heat for 30 minutes, stirring occasionally, until the carrots are mashably soft. Remove from the heat and cool enough to handle.

2. Purée the carrot mixture, along with 1 cup of the broth, in a food processor or through a food mill. Return the purée to the pot and stir in the salt, pepper, and remaining 3 cups of broth. Reheat and serve right away if serving warm, or cool and chill if serving cold. Garnish with the cilantro, if using, just before serving.

CARROTS THROUGH THEIR AGES
Tiny and tender, middle-size and munchable, old and gnarly, carrots in all their stages are provender for the table.

Cream of Carrot Soup

Serves 3 to 4

In this soup, down-to-earth carrots, cooked until they practically purée on their own, thickened with a butter and flour roux, and enriched with heavy cream, are elevated far above their original lowly station.

NAN STRICKLAND AND SALLY CHATMAN (FAYETTEVILLE, NY)

3 tablespoons butter
2 to 2½ pounds carrots, scraped and thinly sliced
¼ teaspoon sugar
2 tablespoons all-purpose flour
¼ cup milk
¼ cup chicken broth (see page 86)
½ teaspoon salt
¼ teaspoon black or white pepper
½ cup heavy (whipping) cream
Fresh herb sprigs, such as chervil, fennel, or parsley, for garnish (optional)

What About the Carrot Tops?

Carrots are a member of the Umbelliferae family, easily identifiable by their feathery foliage that not only marks the spot where the root is growing underground but also looks pretty. Though it might be tempting to cut the tops for kitchen use, resist because it is through them the root collects the above-ground nutrients needed to continue growing underground. In any case, unless the plant is very young, still a seedling, the greens are really not very tasty, actually somewhat bitter. So, when the grocer offers to twist off the tops, you might as well go ahead and say okay because the roots store better without them. You can, however, bring the greens home to feed the compost bin or your pet rabbit. Or, you can leave the foliage intact and fill a tall glass vase with a bouquet of carrots, the whole plant, tops and roots both, for a party table decoration.

1. Melt 1 tablespoon of the butter in a large sauté pan. Add the carrots, sugar, and 1½ cups water, partially cover the pan, and cook over medium heat for 30 minutes, or until the carrots are tender. Set aside.

2. Melt the remaining 2 tablespoons butter in a large soup pot. Whisk in the flour and stir over medium heat, without browning, until smooth, about 1 minute. Whisk in the milk and broth and continue stirring until smooth. Add the carrots and their pan liquid, the salt, and pepper. Bring to a boil, then simmer until the carrots are fork mashable, 30 to 40 minutes. Remove from the heat and cool enough to handle.

3. Purée the carrot mixture in a food processor or through a food mill. Return to the pot, stir in the cream, and gently reheat. Serve warm, garnished with the herb sprigs, if using.

Cheddar Chowder

SERVES 4

In a soup evocative of Welsh rarebit, diced carrots, celery, onion, and potato float in a broth thickened with cheddar cheese and white sauce. The diced vegetables, in recognizable size, make it chowder; the cheddar white sauce makes it divine.

JUDY MORRIS (JACKSONVILLE, AR)

½ cup diced carrots
½ cup diced celery
¼ cup diced onion
2 cups diced potatoes
1 teaspoon salt
1 teaspoon white pepper
2 cups Basic White Sauce (recipe follows)
2 cups shredded sharp cheddar cheese, preferably orange
1 cup finely diced ham (optional)
Garlic-Parmesan Crackers (see page 109) or sourdough bread

1. Place the carrots, celery, onion, and 2 cups of water in a large pot and bring to a boil. Add the potatoes, salt, and pepper and cook over medium-high heat until the vegetables are tender but not mushy, 10 to 15 minutes.

2. Stir in the sauce and cheese, reduce the heat to low, and continue to cook, without boiling, until the cheese melts and the soup is warmed through. Serve right away, garnished with the ham, if using, and accompanied by the crackers.

Basic White Sauce

MAKES 2 CUPS

4 tablespoons (½ stick) butter
2 cups milk
¼ cup all-purpose flour

1. Melt the butter in a saucepan over medium heat. Whisk in the flour and stir until the mixture is smooth, about 1 minute. Slowly whisk in the milk and continue stirring over medium heat, taking care not to boil the mixture, just until thickened, about 5 minutes.

2. Remove from the heat and use right away or at room temperature. Or cool and store in the refrigerator for up to 1 week. Reheat before using and thin with a little milk if necessary.

Note: You can make it in the microwave using a microwave bowl and following the same procedure.

White Sauce: Variations on an Old-Fashoned Favorite

Once home cooks routinely made white sauce, also called béchamel, without even having to look up the recipe. Though such a lush sauce doesn't fit into the modern "eat slim" philosophy, at least not on a daily basis, there are dishes for which it remains essential: savory soufflés, casseroles like moussaka, many homey cream soups. You can further enhance a white sauce, depending on how it is to be used, with:

SPICES: Allspice, curry powder, ground ginger, mustard powder, nutmeg, paprika.

CHEESE: Usually cheddar, but almost any other melting cheese makes a delicious variation.

CHOPPED HARD-COOKED EGG: Especially for creamed spinach.

STOCK OR WHITE WINE: In place of the milk, sometimes also with a cream enrichment, especially for saucing fish or poultry in the classic French manner.

Beautiful Beet Soup

SERVES 4

You can easily turn what the contributor calls soup into what Russian or Jewish cooks might call borscht by omitting the half-and-half and skipping the purée step to leave the vegetables in separate pieces. Either soup or borscht, it is undeniably beautiful and an elegant way to begin a meal.

IRENE BRENNEMAN (KALONA, IA)

¾ pound trimmed beets
¾ pound russet potatoes, peeled and cut into 1-inch chunks
½ small onion, finely chopped
¼ cup (packed) chopped fresh dill
2 cups chicken broth (see page 86)
⅔ cup half-and-half
2 tablespoons fresh lemon juice
Salt and pepper
8 fresh mint leaves
Sour cream or yogurt, for garnish
4 thin slices lemon, for garnish (optional)

1. Place the beets and 4 cups of water in a pot and bring to a boil. Adjust the heat to maintain a brisk simmer and cook until fork tender all the way through, 30 to 50 minutes depending on the size and age of the beets. Drain through a colander set over a bowl, reserving the liquid. Set both the beets and liquid aside to cool.

2. When the beets are cool enough to handle, peel and cut them into 1-inch chunks. Set aside.

3. Meanwhile, place the potatoes, onion, dill, and broth in a pot and bring to a boil. Adjust the heat to maintain a gentle simmer and cook until the potatoes are fork mashable, about 20 minutes. Remove from the heat and set aside to cool without draining.

4. Transfer the potato mixture, including the liquid, the drained beets, and 1½ cups of the reserved beet cooking liquid, to a food processor. Blend until smooth. Stir in the half-and-half, lemon juice, and salt and pepper to taste.

5. Serve hot or chilled, garnishing each bowl with 2 mint leaves, a dollop of sour cream, and a lemon slice, if using.

Beet Bounty

Any gardener's cookbook probably has several beet recipes. Beets in salad, beets on the side, beets in soup, beets in the brownies (see page 397) even! Why? Because it's easy to nurture them in a relatively small space. They can be pulled for spring to early summer delicacies or remain happily in the ground until the gardener is ready to harvest them for fall to winter dishes. Once pulled, they keep indoors without demanding immediate attention, as long as they are kept cool and dark. From ground to fridge, beets are there for the cook to make use of their nutritious, sweet, earthy flavor.

Curried Zucchini Soup

SERVES 6

"I consider vegetable gardening a remarkable journey from barren soil to seeds to seedlings to lush plants and finally to the beloved vegetables and the sharing they invite. My friends look forward to my August harvest with one exception, the zucchini. I have helped ease the pain of insisting that they take several by offering also a recipe that calls for plenty of this prolific vegetable. One of my favorites is the following soup."

PAULA RYAN (NEW CANAAN, CT)

2 tablespoons margarine
2 pounds zucchini, trimmed and coarsely chopped
1 medium onion, coarsely chopped
2 cloves garlic, minced or pressed
1 teaspoon curry powder
½ teaspoon salt
1 teaspoon white pepper
4 cups chicken broth (see page 86)
½ cup milk

1. Melt the margarine in a large, heavy soup pot. Stir in the zucchini, onion, and garlic and sauté until the vegetables are soft, about 10 minutes. Stir in the curry powder, salt, pepper, and 2 cups of the broth. Remove from the heat and cool enough to handle.

2. Purée the mixture in a food processor or through a food mill and return to the pot. Stir in remaining 2 cups of broth and the milk. Reheat over medium heat without boiling, then serve.

Curry Powder: A Bright Entry in the Parade of Spice Blends

Curry powder does not come ready for action. In fact, it may not include the curry leaf itself, an esoteric ingredient of southern Indian cooking. Rather, it includes a selection of spices: turmeric, red pepper, black pepper, coriander, cumin, fenugreek, and mustard seeds, all pounded into a powder and mixed together. You might try your hand at making up a curry powder. But for practical purposes, a packet from an Indian grocery or other food boutique that specializes in fresh spices and spice blends can probably supply a mix with that characteristic golden-yellow-brown color and that unique flavor that here does much to brighten zucchini.

SEARCHING FOR PRODUCE: FINDING A COMMUNITY

"Efforts to seek out really good produce are always repaid by the pleasure it gives. I've found unexpected sources of good ingredients that weren't apparent at first—the chili man from New Mexico who sets up his stand and roaster in the fall, the local arboretum for herbs, a network of women who bring down wonderful fruit from Utah in the summer, the generosity of avid gardeners who grow enough to share. . . ."

—Deborah Madison, *The Savory Way*

summer's end, winter's glory

When the last of the tender-skinned, soft-pulp summer squashes have been gone long enough to be missed, the cook turns to their thicker-skinned fellows, the winter squashes, to fill the niche. Unlike summer squashes that easily go from garden to pot, the beauty and prize of the winter squash must be pried from within. Once revealed, the earthy pulp suggests new dishes for the new season: different colors, different textures, warm and warming soups.

Curried Butternut Squash Bisque

SERVES 6 TO 8

"Butternut squash has been a staple of hearty New England fare for centuries. This elegant and delicious bisque proves its staying power. Baking the squash whole intensifies its aromatic, sweet flavor and makes peeling and seeding a snap." For other ways to cook winter squash, see page 139.

EDIE SCHUMANN RAVENELLE (CENTERVILLE, MA)

1 medium butternut squash (about 1¾ pounds)
1 tablespoon butter
¾ cup finely chopped onion
1 clove garlic, minced
1 large cooking apple, such as Cortland or McIntosh, peeled, cored, and chopped into ¼-inch pieces
1 teaspoon curry powder
¼ teaspoon grated nutmeg
2 tablespoons all-purpose flour
4 cups chicken broth (see page 86)
1 tablespoon tomato paste
½ cup half-and-half
1 tablespoon minced fresh sage leaves or ½ teaspoon dried sage
Salt and pepper
Whole sage leaves, for garnish

1. Preheat the oven to 350°F.

2. Wrap the squash in aluminum foil and bake for 1½ hours, or until squeezable to the center. Remove and cool enough to handle, then seed, and scoop out the pulp. Set aside.

3. Melt the butter in a large soup pot. Add the onion, garlic, and apple and cook over low heat until soft, about 10 minutes. Add the curry, nutmeg, and flour and stir until the flour disappears.

4. With a food processor or a food mill, purée the onion-and-apple mixture along with the squash and 1 cup of the broth. Return the purée to the pot and stir in the tomato paste, half-and-half, minced sage, remaining 3 cups of broth, and salt and pepper to taste. Heat over medium heat, stirring constantly, until beginning to boil.

5. Serve right away, garnished with the whole sage leaves.

Bisque from Home to Haute and Home Again

Bisque began its culinary history as a smooth and richly flavored but not extravagant soup based on shellfish, poultry, or hearty, mealy vegetables such as potato, carrot, or butternut squash. As bisque history evolved, restaurant chefs took over the task of preparing such dishes, and the poultry and vegetable bases were dropped in favor of the fancier shellfish, in particular, crayfish or lobster. From the second half of the 1800s until well into the 1900s, bisque on the menu meant the shellfish version, a pricey treat of European haute cuisine. Bisque in American cooking today appears in its original, homier rendition, often with a vegetable base, and our tables once again sport a puréed butternut squash soup with the old and new—again—nomer "bisque."

Butternut Squash Soup Swirled with Red Bell Pepper Purée

Serves 4

"I developed this soup on one of those cold and rainy days that keep the gardener in the house. Serve it with fresh bread and it's sure to ward off the chill of the first winter's frost." The only hard part is deciding which herb or flower to use for garnish. To keep the green, another fresh herb of spunkier flavor, such as chive or burnet, might be sprinkled

over the top of the soup. Or a contrasting color could be edible flowers: purple pansy petals, bold orange-yellow petals of tuberous begonia, nasturtium, the last of the marigolds, or the newly blossomed chrysanthemums.

RONALD JUBIN (WATCHUNG, NJ)

2 tablespoons butter
½ cup finely diced celery
½ cup finely diced onion
1 medium butternut squash, peeled, seeded, and cut into 1-inch cubes (about 1½ pounds)
4 cups chicken broth (see page 86)
Salt and white pepper
2 large red bell peppers, roasted, peeled, and seeded (see page 99)
4 sprigs of parsley, for garnish

1. Melt the butter in a large saucepan. Add the celery and onion and cook over low heat until the onion is translucent, about 10 minutes. Take care not to brown the vegetables.

2. Add the squash and chicken broth and bring to a boil. Simmer for 15 minutes, until the squash is mashable. Remove and let cool enough to handle.

3. Transfer the mixture to a food processor and blend until smooth. Return to the saucepan, stir in salt and white pepper to taste, and keep warm over very low heat.

4. Rinse the food processor bowl and purée the roasted peppers and their juices into a smooth paste. Transfer to a small saucepan or microwave bowl. Stir in ¼ cup of water, whisk to mix, and heat briefly.

5. To serve, divide the soup among 4 large soup bowls. Spoon a big dollop of the roasted pepper purée into each bowl and swirl it around with a toothpick or knife to create a design over the top of the soup. Garnish each bowl with a parsley sprig and serve right away while still warm.

Climbing Vines

Climbing vines provide interest for any gardener who has a fence that needs decorating. For the gardener who also likes cooking and flowers, vines that yield edibles and house bouquets are doubly or triply interesting. Here are some climbing vines to suit all:

PASSION VINE: Flowers to die for; fruit, if that's the variety you have (some passion vines are for flowers only); butterflies to delight the day.

PEAS: Both sweet pea edibles (English and snap to snow varieties) and decorative peas (lovely to look at and bring in for bouquets, but don't eat them).

HOPS: An old-fashioned fence covering, but very invasive; the gardener must pay attention to pulling out its shoots, as with raspberry or blackberry, to prevent it from going too far. Its flowers are used for making beer and also for attracting red admiral butterflies to its thistlelike leaves, which nestle their eggs and protect them from predators.

HONEYSUCKLE: A fence climber that will run rampant without close and frequent pruning. In return, it offers fragrant flowers that attract pollinators to the garden and provides much happiness to children who are young enough to take pleasure in a very small sip of the sweet, edible nectar from the center of its flowers.

GRAPES: Any kind (see box on page 206).

In addition, tomatoes and all the squashes, winter and summer both, can serve as momentary verdure for the gardener who cares to take the trouble to trellis them.

Roasting Bell Peppers for Peeling

Bell peppers of any color or size have wended their way into every cuisine they have met. Sometimes they are preferred for their garden-fresh crispness, seeded and sliced for appetizer garnishes, salads, or last-minute additions to sautéed dishes. They are also prized for their pulp, which, when peeled, can be turned into many other additions to the table. Here's the way to roast bell peppers for peeling:

Place the peppers:

- Right in the center of a hot charcoal fire.
- In the middle of a hot oven.
- Under a well-heated broiler.
- Over a stovetop gas burner.

Leave them there, turning frequently as necessary, until they become blackened on the outside but not burned to the center. This takes 15 to 25 minutes, depending on the size of the peppers and the heat of the fire.

When the peppers are charred all around and their skins loosening away from the pulp, you can choose from another set of options. Remove the peppers and place them:

- In a brown paper bag: close the bag to continue the steaming process.
- In a bowl of cold water: let the peppers rest until cool enough to handle. Some cooks like to have ice cubes in the water to hasten the cooling.
- On the counter: cover with a towel, or hot pads, or anything else that's handy enough to hold in the steam.

Whichever cooling-down way you choose, let the peppers rest for at least 20 minutes or up to several hours, until the skins are cool and soft enough to pull away easily. Then:

- Peel the peppers with your hands, using a paring knife to help scrape away any peel that doesn't come off easily.
- Pull off the stems and cut or pull open the peeled peppers lengthwise.
- Scrape away the seeds and inner membranes, being sure to save the juices.
- Use right away or transfer the peeled peppers and their juices to a bowl and store in the refrigerator for up to one week.

Butternut Squash Soup with Fried Sage Leaves

Serves 6

Deborah Madison was the founding chef of Greens Restaurant in San Francisco, where her creative melding of Zen Buddhist moderation and gentility with lusty cooking and bold flavors led to an astounding redefinition of vegetarian cuisine. Continuing in that down-to-earth style, she authored The Greens Cookbook *(with Edward Espe Brown),* The Savory Way, *and* Vegetarian Cooking for Everyone, *in which a version of this soup appears. She now resides in New Mexico, where, she says, "my garden isn't large enough to grow rambling vegetables, but I'm quick to buy from our farmers when they arrive in the fall with their beautiful tan butternut squashes. While any winter squash can be used in this soup, I always find butternut the easiest to work with, as well as one of the sweetest and richest tasting. Halving and baking it first speeds things along, and it can be done well in advance. Winter squash soups don't require a stock, but a quick stock using the scooped out seeds and squash skins is so easy and so flavorful that I generally make one."*

DEBORAH MADISON (SANTA FE, NM)

ABOUT FRIED SAGE LEAVES
The fried sage leaves are so enticing, so easy to snatch up for a crunchy, quick nibble, they should be guarded from all kitchen loiterers and passersby or there won't be any left for garnishing the soup (that goes for the cook, too). Or make three times as many and serve a small plate of them on the side, in the kitchen or at the table. In any case, don't make them too far in advance; they are best savored within the hour.

One 3-pound butternut squash
Olive oil, for coating the squash halves
6 cloves garlic, not peeled
¼ cup olive oil
18 whole fresh sage leaves
2 medium onions, finely chopped
2 tablespoons chopped fresh sage
½ teaspoon fresh thyme leaves or ¼ teaspoon dried thyme
¼ cup chopped fresh parsley leaves
2 quarts Quick Stock for Winter Squash Soup (see box on page 101) or water
Salt (see Notes below)
½ cup diced fontina cheese or other Italian-style melting cheese
Freshly ground black pepper

1. Preheat the oven to 375°F.

2. Cut the squash in half lengthwise and scoop out and reserve the seeds. Lightly grease the squash halves with olive oil. Place them, cut side down on a baking sheet and tuck the garlic cloves underneath the cavities. Bake until tender when pressed with a finger and glazed on the bottom, 40 to 60 minutes. Remove and let cool enough to handle.

3. Scoop out the pulp, reserving the skins, and place it in a medium bowl. Peel the garlic cloves and put them into the bowl with the squash pulp. Add any juices that have collected on the baking sheet.

4. Heat the ¼ cup olive oil in a sauté pan. Drop in the whole sage leaves and fry briefly until speckled and darkened, about 1 minute. Remove to a paper towel to drain and set aside.

5. Transfer the oil to a deep and wide soup pot. Add the onions, chopped sage, thyme, and parsley and cook over medium heat until the onions have begun to brown around the edges, about 12 minutes.

6. Add the squash and garlic, stock, and salt to taste and bring to a boil. Lower the heat, partially cover, and simmer gently for 25 minutes, until thickened but still liquid.

7. Remove from the heat and, when no longer bubbling, purée in a food processor or through a food mill gently. Reheat and ladle into bowls. Distribute the cheese among the bowls (it will sink and melt into the soup). Garnish each bowl with fried sage leaves, add freshly ground black pepper to taste, and serve.

Notes

• If you are using the quick stock, the soup probably will not need any extra salt. If you are using water, add 1½ teaspoons salt to boost the flavor.

• The soup can be served straightaway without puréeing. It will not be as svelte, but it will have an equally appealing texture that hovers between silken and chunky.

Quick Stock for Winter Squash Soup

The seeds and skin of any winter squash, not only butternut, can be turned into a quick and delicate yet flavorful soup stock. (If you do not use the seeds and skin for quick stock, be sure to recycle them for compost.)

Simmer 10 cups water with the squash skin and seeds, half a sliced onion, any tiny cloves from the center of a garlic bulb, parsley stems, and 2 teaspoons salt. Bring to a boil, simmer for 25 to 30 minutes, and strain.

—DEBORAH MADISON

Homemade Tomato Soup

SERVES 4 TO 6

"You can make the recipe through the purée stage and freeze that part until you want to make the soup." Defrosted and warmed, the purée can serve as a fine tomato soup without the final butter and cream enrichment. Or you can extend the creaminess with Crème Fraîche (page 382) in place of the whipping cream. Creamed or not, the soup serves as a fresh, homemade replacement in any recipe that calls for canned tomato soup.

JANET HOLDEN (MANCHESTER, IA)

1 tablespoon oil
8 tablespoons (1 stick) butter
1 large onion, thinly sliced
3 pounds fresh tomatoes, peeled, seeded, and coarsely chopped, including juices, or an equal amount of already peeled, winterized tomatoes (see pages 336–337), including juices
2 tablespoons fresh thyme leaves or 1 teaspoon dried thyme
1 tablespoon fresh basil leaves or 1 teaspoon dried basil
1 teaspoon salt
¼ teaspoon black pepper
4 cups vegetable broth (page 87)
¼ cup all-purpose flour
1 cup heavy (whipping) cream
1 or 2 pinches of sugar (optional, see box below)
Herbed Croutons, for garnish (see box on page 103)

1. Place the oil and 4 tablespoons of the butter in a large heavy soup pot and heat until the butter melts. Add the onion and sauté over medium heat until soft, about 8 minutes.

2. Add the tomatoes, thyme, basil, salt, and pepper and stir to mix. Bring to a boil and cook over medium heat until the tomatoes have collapsed, 6 to 8 minutes.

3. While the tomatoes cook, heat ½ cup of the broth until beginning to boil. Whisk in the flour to make a smooth paste.

4. Add the flour paste and the remaining broth to the pot and bring to a boil. Simmer for 5 minutes, stirring frequently, until the flour is cooked. Remove and cool enough to handle.

5. Purée the mixture in a food processor or food mill. Return to the soup pot and stir in the cream, the remaining 4 tablespoons of butter, and the sugar, if using. Heat the soup without boiling and serve right away, garnished with the croutons.

TRICKS *of the* TRADE

To Sweeten or Not to Sweeten the Tomatoes

When the tomatoes have sweetened on the vine under the full burst of late summer sun, there is no need for sugar. With earlier, more tart tomatoes, you may want to add a pinch or two of sugar to soften the acidity of the fruit and boost the tomato flavor. Or if you have a hankering for homemade tomato soup after the vines are long gone and canned tomatoes are all that's available, follow the advice of many a grandmother cook who would want to have tomatoes in the dish, in or out of season: Rather than live without them; add a good pinch of sugar.

Sandra's Moroccan Tomato Soup

Serves 4

"Our vegetable garden was putting out produce like The Little Shop of Horrors *last summer. This soup helped use up some of the excess in a delicious way." The special touch of adding North African spices, cumin and turmeric, to tomato soup takes tomatoes to another place where they are warmly welcomed. Another special touch is adding the fresh cilantro during the cooking stage.* *See box on page 104 for more on that topic.*

MEREDITH PHILLIPS (PALO ALTO, CA)

1 tablespoon olive oil
1 large onion, finely chopped
5 cloves garlic, coarsely chopped
2 pounds tomatoes, coarsely chopped
2 to 3 teaspoons minced fresh chili pepper, to taste
3 cups vegetable broth (see page 87)
1 teaspoon cumin powder
½ teaspoon turmeric
1 teaspoon salt
¼ teaspoon black pepper
½ cup chopped fresh cilantro leaves
2 tablespoons fresh lemon juice (optional)

1. Heat the oil in a large heavy pot. Add the onion and garlic and cook over medium heat until wilted, about 5 minutes. Add the tomatoes and chili and continue cooking, stirring from time to time, until the tomatoes are collapsing, about 10 minutes.

2. Stir the stock, cumin, turmeric, salt, pepper, and cilantro into the pot. Cover and simmer for 15 minutes, or until the tomatoes are very soft. Remove from the heat, uncover, and let cool enough to handle.

3. Purée the soup through a food mill or press it through a sieve set over a bowl. Reheat briefly. Stir in the lemon juice, if using, and serve.

Herbed Croutons

The trick with making fried croutons is to have the oil hot enough to sizzle the cubes golden very quickly but not so hot as to burn them. You can tailor the herb to the dish the croutons will garnish, but actually any of the selections below will do. You can also sprinkle the cubes with Parmesan cheese when tossing with the herbs. Or add some garlic slices to the oil while frying.

Olive oil, for frying
2 cups ½-inch cubes bread cut from hearty country-style or good-quality French bread
1 tablespoon chopped fresh thyme, oregano, rosemary, or marjoram leaves or 1½ teaspoons dried herbs

1. Pour ½ inch olive oil into a large heavy sauté pan. Heat until a cube of bread sizzles when dropped into the oil. Add all the cubes and fry, stirring and turning frequently, until golden all around, about 5 minutes. With a wire strainer or slotted spoon, transfer the cubes to paper towels.

2. Sprinkle the herbs over the cubes and toss to coat. Serve right away or within several hours.

Fresh and Creamy Tomato Soup

SERVES 3 TO 4

As though there were ever too many tomato soup recipes, especially in summer when there are sometimes too many tomatoes, this one is particularly appealing because, as the contributor exults, "You can have this fresh tomato soup steaming on your table about half an hour after you pick the tomatoes!"

VALERIE VALENTINE (PACIFIC PALISADES, CA)

2 pounds tomatoes, coarsely chopped, juices reserved
1 large russet potato, peeled and chopped into ¼-inch pieces
2 teaspoons sugar
1 teaspoon salt
¼ teaspoon black pepper
8 to 10 fresh basil leaves
1 cup chicken broth (see page 86)
½ cup sour cream
Watercress sprigs or fresh mint leaves, for garnish
Extra sour cream, for garnish (optional)

1. Put the tomatoes and their juices, the potato, sugar, salt, pepper, and basil in a large, heavy pot. Bring to a boil, reduce the heat to medium-low, and simmer, stirring from time to time, until the potato is soft, about 20 minutes.

2. Add the broth to the pot, bring to a boil, and simmer for 5 minutes more, until the tomatoes and potato are collapsing. Remove from the heat and set aside until cool enough to handle.

3. Purée the mixture with a food mill or press through a sieve (see box on page 105) and return to the pot.

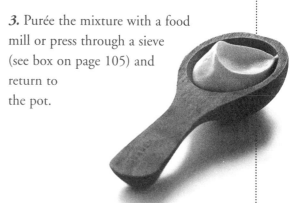

In the Pot or on the Side: Culinary Refinements for Basil and Cilantro

Of all the culinary herbs, basil and cilantro stand out as two that ought to be used fresh rather than dried. On the other hand, there are exceptions. Sometimes basil may be collected and dried for winter use, before it withers in the cold, and then used to imbue a soup or sauce with its special perfume. This works if the basil is freshly dried. Sometimes fresh cilantro, especially in Moroccan or Mexican dishes, may be added to contribute an extra punch to a dish before the cooking is finished. This works if it is stirred in only briefly so that its ephemeral presence doesn't evaporate into the air.

4. When ready to serve, combine the sour cream and 1 cup of the puree in a small bowl. Whisk to smooth, then stir into the pot. Reheat without boiling and serve right away, garnished with watercress and dollops of extra sour cream, if using.

Variations

- Use cilantro or parsley in place of the basil.
- Use vegetable broth (page 87) in place of the chicken broth.
- Use plain yogurt or heavy (whipping) cream in place of the sour cream.

TOOLS *of the* TRADE

The Right Stuff for Puréeing

When the recipe calls for puréeing a soup, a sauce, or a jam, a Foley food mill remains the best tool for home use. It requires a bit of a balancing act as you steady the food mill over the bowl with one hand and turn the crank with the other, but the strings, seeds, and skins of vegetables and fruits are stripped away in one step. If your kitchen equipment doesn't include a food mill, you can achieve the same result with an extra step and a little extra elbow grease. First, strain the cooked vegetables or fruit, reserving any liquid, and mince them as fine as possible in a food processor or with a chef's knife. Then press the mixture, along with the reserved juices, through a fine sieve set over a bowl and continue with the recipe.

Parslied Dumpling Soup

SERVES 4 TO 6

"Almost every gardener has parsley. Here's a great recipe for dumplings that is greatly improved when you add fresh parsley!"

KATE WHARTON (ACTON, MA)

1 cup all-purpose flour
2 teaspoons baking powder
¼ teaspoon salt
⅛ teaspoon black pepper
1½ tablespoons butter, melted
¼ cup (packed) chopped fresh parsley leaves
1 small egg, lightly beaten with enough milk to make ½ cup
3 quarts chicken broth (see page 86) or vegetable broth (see page 87)
Extra chopped parsley, for garnish

1. Place the flour, baking powder, salt, and pepper in a large bowl. Stir with a fork to blend well. Add the butter, parsley, and egg mixture and mix into a sticky dough.

2. Pour the broth into a large pot and bring to a boil.

3. Drop tablespoonfuls of the dough into the hot broth and cook over medium-high heat for 7 minutes, until the dumplings are floating to the top. Lower the heat, cover the pot, and continue simmering for 7 minutes more, until light and fluffy and cooked all the way through.

4. Ladle some broth and dumplings into individual bowls and serve right away, garnished with more parsley.

Other Dumpling Thoughts

Such flavorful and fluffy dumplings might inspire more dumpling fancies. For instance:

FOR THE HERB: Substitute cilantro for the parsley or add a pinch of rosemary along with the parsley.

FOR THE SPICE: Substitute cayenne for the black pepper.

FOR COOKING THE DUMPLINGS: Flavor the broth with ancho chili for a Mexican flair, or season it with dill for a Swedish touch.

Pioneer Potato Soup with Humble Cupboard Egg Dumplings

SERVES 4 TO 6

"This recipe is from my grandmother, a homesteader in North Dakota." Supping upon it, you can imagine yourself warmly nestled inside the house as the wind whistles and howls across that isolated landscape. It's comfort food, created out of sparse cupboards stocked with little more than dry ingredients. Still, it was a recipe to keep and pass down through the generations even as travel led to more verdant pastures, or to town with more fully stocked grocery shelves. Eventually, in such places, fresh chives and cheddar cheese could be found to brighten and enrich the soup.

LAURA CHANT (PERKASIE, PA)

3 medium potatoes, scrubbed and cut into ½-inch pieces
2 medium carrots, scraped and coarsely chopped
Humble Cupboard Egg Dumplings (recipe follows)
2 cups milk, warmed
1½ teaspoons salt
¼ teaspoon black pepper
1 tablespoon chopped fresh chives
¼ cup shredded sharp cheddar cheese

1. Place the potatoes and carrots in a large pot and cover with water by 2 inches. Bring to a boil and cook over medium-high heat until the potatoes are tender but still hold their shape, about 10 minutes.

2. Prepare the dumpling batter.

3. Drop teaspoonfuls of the dumpling batter into the pot and continue cooking until the dumplings rise to the top, about 5 minutes.

4. Drain off all but 2 cups of the cooking water, leaving the ingredients in the pot. Add the milk, salt, and pepper to the pot and return to the stove. Stir over medium-low heat just until warmed through. Sprinkle the chives and cheese over the top and serve right away, before the dumplings toughen.

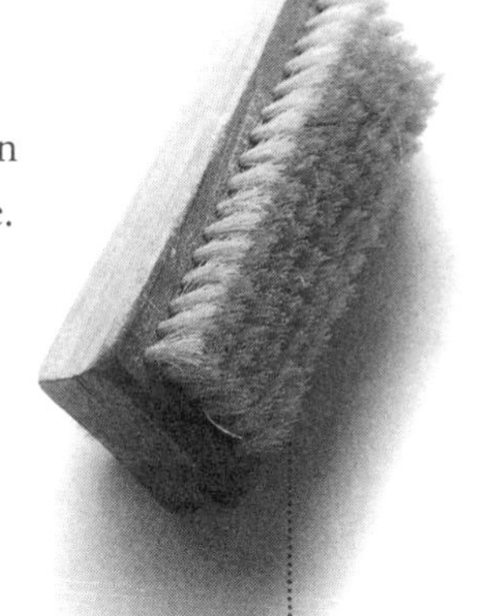

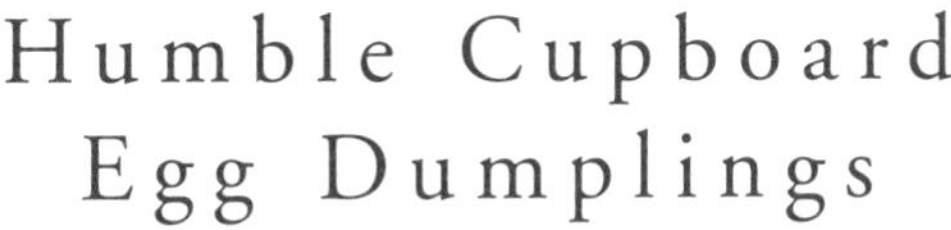

Humble Cupboard Egg Dumplings

Makes about fifteen 1-inch dumplings

1 large egg
¼ teaspoon celery seed
¼ teaspoon dried basil
¼ teaspoon salt
⅛ teaspoon black pepper
½ cup all-purpose flour

Crack the egg into a small bowl and lightly beat. Add the spices and ¼ cup of the flour and blend with a fork. A little at a time, mix in the remaining ¼ cup of flour until you have a stiff ball of dough that sticks to the fork. Use right away, while still soft and moist.

FOR THE BIRDS

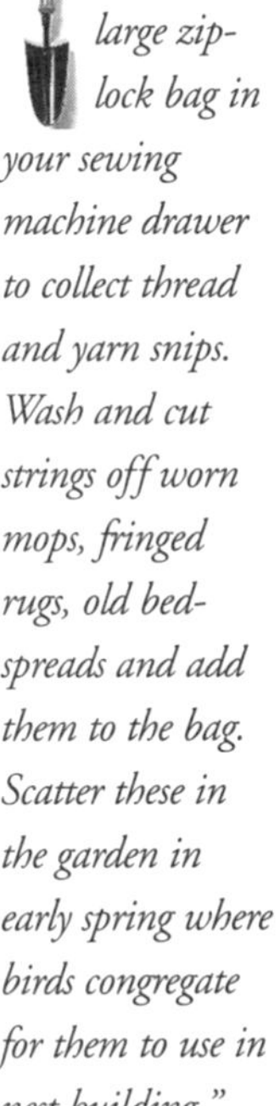

"Keep a large zip-lock bag in your sewing machine drawer to collect thread and yarn snips. Wash and cut strings off worn mops, fringed rugs, old bed-spreads and add them to the bag. Scatter these in the garden in early spring where birds congregate for them to use in nest building."

—Judy Morris, Jacksonville, AR

Garlic Lover's White Bean Soup

Serves 6 to 8

"When you are trapped indoors on a bleak winter day, an obvious thing to do is cook, and the obvious thing to cook is a soup that simmers on its own while filling the house with warmth and a heavenly aroma. Dry-roasting the garlic adds tremendous flavor but little effort and keeps the soup fat-free. If you are lucky enough to have leftovers,

you can freeze them for a day when the sun keeps you outdoors and all you desire from the kitchen is instant gratification."

❧ SUSAN BRINKLEY (EMINENCE, MO)

COOKING DRIED BEANS
Red, white, or black, large or small, garbanzos or turtles, beans should cook without added salt until the last half hour. Adding salt to the cooking water at the beginning turns beans irreparably tough.

2 cups Great Northern beans, soaked overnight, drained, and rinsed
1 teaspoon chopped fresh rosemary leaves or ½ teaspoon dried rosemary
1 teaspoon fresh thyme leaves or ½ teaspoon dried thyme
¼ teaspoon fennel seeds
1 large bay leaf
1 small turnip, peeled and diced into ¼-inch pieces
1 small potato, peeled and diced into ¼-inch pieces
1 medium yellow onion, coarsely chopped
2 medium carrots, scrubbed and diced into ¼-inch pieces
¼ cup (packed) fresh parsley leaves, coarsely chopped
10 to 15 large cloves garlic, not peeled
1 teaspoon salt
½ teaspoon black pepper
Fresh parsley sprigs, for garnish
Garlic-Parmesan Crackers (recipe follows) or other toasts and crackers, to accompany

1. Place the beans, 3 quarts of water, rosemary, thyme, fennel seeds, and bay leaf in a large soup pot. Bring to a boil, reduce the heat, and simmer briskly, uncovered, for 1 hour, until the beans are half-tender.

2. Add the turnips, potato, onion, carrots, and parsley to the pot, along with 1 to 2 cups extra water, enough to keep the vegetables barely free-floating. Continue simmering slowly for 1 hour more, until the vegetables are soft and the mixture is soupy. Remove from the heat and let cool enough to handle.

3. While the soup simmers, heat the oven to 350°F. Place the garlic in a small oven-proof dish, sprinkle with water to moisten, and roast for 30 minutes, until soft. Remove and let cool, then peel and set aside.

4. Remove the bay leaf. Swirl half of the soup and the garlic in a food processor until still slightly chunky but not smooth. Return to the pot with the remaining half of the soup. Stir in the salt and pepper and heat until beginning to simmer. Cook gently, stirring occasionally, until the beans are completely tender, 15 to 20 minutes more.

5. Serve right away, garnished with the parsley sprigs and accompanied by a basket of the crackers.

Garlic-Parmesan Crackers

MAKES FORTY TO FORTY-FIVE 1½-INCH SQUARE CRACKERS

"Once you've tried homemade crackers, it's hard to go back to store-bought, especially when you realize how easy they are to make." The fresh garlic, minced with salt to take away the sting, gives the crackers "an unexpected—but not overpowering—bite." Salt sprinkled over the top turns them into a more traditional saltine-type cracker, but they are plenty flavorful without it. Either way, this is a cracker for all occasions, from appetizer dipper to soup accompaniment to crunchy munch on their own.

SUSAN BRINKLEY (EMINENCE, MO)

2 cloves garlic
¼ teaspoon salt
1 cup all-purpose flour
½ teaspoon baking powder
½ cup grated Parmesan cheese
1½ tablespoons cold butter, cut into small pieces
⅔ to ¾ cup milk, as needed
Extra flour, for rolling out the dough
Salt, for sprinkling on top of the crackers (optional)

1. Preheat the oven to 375°F.

2. Place the garlic and salt on a cutting board and mince together.

3. Place the flour, baking powder, Parmesan, butter, and garlic in a medium bowl. With a pastry blender, fork, or your fingers, blend until the mixture resembles fine crumbs. Add the milk and continue blending until you have a dough you can gather into a ball.

4. Divide the dough in half. Transfer one half to a floured surface and roll it out into a 12 by 10-inch rectangle about 1/16 inch thick. Lightly prick the dough with a fork, then cut it into 1½-inch squares or any other desired shapes. Transfer the squares to an ungreased baking sheet and set aside. Continue with the remaining half of the dough.

5. Sprinkle the tops of the crackers with salt, if using. Bake until light golden brown, 18 to 20 minutes. Remove and transfer to a wire rack to cool and crisp up. Serve or store in an airtight container for up to several weeks.

CRISPING CRACKERS

If you are storing crackers over time, whether they are homemade or store-bought, they inevitably sog a bit from air moisture. It's easy enough to restore them to their crunchy selves by recrisping them for a few minutes in a hot oven before serving.

Lara's Okra Soup

SERVES 8

"This dish came about because of my daughter Lara's request that we grow okra in the garden. It did so well, we suddenly were faced with the problem of having to do something with it. The recipe had its basis in an old okra pilaf recipe that gave us the main ingredients of okra, corn, and tomatoes. We added stock because we wanted a soup; we added green beans because we had tons of them. Over time, my husband added the bacon, my daughter added the garlic and herbs, and I added the wine. It was truly a family effort that kept evolving until we got it right. My son's contribution is to eat it."

DIANNE MILLER (MILFORD, OH)

Tomatoes: The Belle of the Ball; What's the Dress?

Don't forget, since tomatoes were originally a scrappy vine that not only survived but thrived on its own without benefit of human intervention or attention, too much tender loving care from the gardener could weaken the true mission of the plant, which is to continue its own existence in the world. For gardeners, the plant's mission is also to have good fruit. Overfussing the tomatoes may be a bit like outfitting for the ball and expecting that things will turn out fine because of the dress. Tomatoes don't need a bush of fine foliage. They're perfectly happy at home in the garden, showing off their finery not with their foliage but with their ruby fruit.

6 ounces bacon, diced
8 ounces okra, trimmed and cut crosswise into 1-inch lengths
2 large ears corn, shaved and scraped (see page 122)
8 ounces green beans, trimmed and cut crosswise into 1-inch lengths
2 pounds fresh tomatoes or 4 cups winterized tomatoes (see pages 336–337), coarsely chopped into ¼-inch pieces, juices reserved
1 large onion, quartered and thinly sliced
2 cloves garlic, finely chopped
½ cup red wine
1 tablespoon shredded fresh basil leaves
½ teaspoon fresh thyme leaves
2 tablespoons chopped fresh parsley leaves
½ teaspoon crushed red pepper, or to taste
¼ teaspoon black pepper
½ teaspoon salt

1. Place the bacon in a large, heavy pot and cook over medium heat, stirring frequently, until crisp, 10 to 12 minutes.

2. Add the remaining ingredients, stir to mix, and bring to a boil. Reduce the heat, partially cover the pot, and simmer for 30 minutes, or until the green beans are soft. Serve right away.

Southern Summer Soup with Toasted Parmesan Bread

Serves 3 to 4

"My neighbor has a garden in which he leaves me three rows to plant whatever I choose. This year I put in zucchini, yellow summer squash, and okra. What fun it is to watch it grow, bloom, and produce."

BEVERLY LONERGAN (WESTON, MO)

1 tablespoon olive oil
2 ribs celery, trimmed, cut lengthwise, and thinly sliced
1 medium carrot, scraped and cut into ½-inch pieces
½ medium onion, cut into ½-inch pieces
1 medium zucchini, trimmed and cut into ½-inch pieces
1 medium yellow squash, trimmed and cut into ½-inch pieces
6 small okra, trimmed and cut into ½-inch rounds (about 2 ounces)
½ teaspoon salt
¼ cup (packed) shredded fresh basil leaves
3 cups chicken broth (see page 86)
Toasted Parmesan Bread (recipe follows)

1. Heat the oil in a large soup pot. Add the celery, carrot, and onion and sauté over medium heat for 5 minutes, until slightly wilted.

2. Add the zucchini, yellow squash, okra, salt, and basil and continue sautéing for 5 minutes more, or until the okra releases its juices. Stir in the broth, bring to a boil, and simmer for 5 minutes, or until the vegetables are cooked al dente.

3. Serve right away, accompanied with the toasted bread.

TRICKS *of the* TRADE

Techniques for Ensuring Fresh and Sparkly Soup in Summer

Any soup that contains chicken broth needs attentive handling, especially in summer, and especially in the South, where the days can be very humid, though the caution applies to northern hot days also. To ensure a fresh and sparkly soup:

- Serve right after cooking, before the summer humidity slackens the flavor and turns the soup sour.
- If storing the soup for a later meal, allow it to cool, uncovered, completely to room temperature. Then place it, still uncovered, in the refrigerator until it is chilled through. At that point, you can cover the soup and keep it refrigerated for a day or two.

Toasted Parmesan Bread

SERVES 6 TO 8

1 loaf Italian bread
Olive oil
Parmesan cheese

1. Preheat the oven to 400°F.

2. Cut the bread in half lengthwise. Brush the cut side of each half with oil, enough to coat the surface without saturating the bread. Sprinkle as much Parmesan as you would like over the top and bake until golden and toasty, 10 to 12 minutes.

3. Cut the toasted halves crosswise into 1- to 2-inch-wide sections and serve right away, while still warm.

ABOUT THE BEANS IN MINESTRONE
Cannellini beans are called for in this recipe because they are traditional for minestrone, but the contributor adds that you can use whatever cooked beans you have. Dried beans, when cooked, ferment very rapidly, especially in hot, humid weather. So, even though the minestrone does not have chicken broth for an ingredient, it warrants the same care as described in the box on page 111.

Gardener's Catchall Minestrone

SERVES 6 TO 8

Minestrones come in as many colors and flavors as the families and individual cooks of Italy and America. Each is special. This one, from Arizona, comes with the explanation of the soup's flexible nature: "If you have to leave something out, it won't matter. If you want to add something more, like Italian green beans or tomatoes, don't hesitate." All in all, a generous soup both in spirit and quantity. With grated Parmesan cheese on the side and a loaf of warm bread, it makes dinner for eight.

PATRICIA DORSEY (SIERRA VISTA, AZ)

Oil, for greasing the sauté pan
1 pound ground beef
½ medium onion, not chopped
1 bay leaf
½ cup fresh parsley leaves
¼ cup chopped celery leaves
2 teaspoons salt
¼ cup olive oil
¼ pound bacon, chopped
1 medium onion, finely chopped
2 ribs celery, finely chopped
1 clove garlic, finely chopped
8 ounces sweet Italian sausage, cut crosswise into ½-inch rounds
4 carrots, scraped and finely chopped
4 medium potatoes, cut into ¼-inch dice
4 medium zucchini, cut into ¼-inch dice
1 cup cooked dried beans, preferably cannellini (see page 112)
1 small head cabbage, preferably savoy, cored and finely shredded (about 1 pound)
1 small bunch escarole, finely shredded
1 cup uncooked orzo pasta, anellini rings, or partially cooked rice
¼ teaspoon cayenne

1. Lightly grease a large sauté pan and brown the beef, stirring with a fork to crumble the meat, about 5 minutes. Add the unchopped onion, bay leaf, parsley leaves, celery leaves, 1 teaspoon of the salt, and 6 cups of water. Bring to a boil, reduce the heat, and simmer for 30 minutes. Drain into a large bowl, reserving the liquid for broth and discarding the solid ingredients.

2. Meanwhile, heat the ¼ cup olive oil in a large soup pot. Add the bacon, chopped onion, celery, and garlic and sauté until all the ingredients are wilted, about 8 minutes. Add the sausage, carrots, potatoes, zucchini, beans, cabbage, escarole, and reserved broth. Bring to a boil, reduce the heat, and simmer for 30 minutes, or until the vegetables are soft.

3. Add the pasta and 2 to 3 cups more water if necessary so there is enough liquid to cover the ingredients well. Bring to a boil, then simmer for 5 minutes more, until the pasta is done. Stir in the remaining teaspoon of the salt and cayenne and serve right away.

Zucchini Growing Tips

"When growing zucchini, be careful not to use insecticides, if ever, during the time when those friendly little bees are pollinating the blossoms; otherwise, you'll have no fruit. Also, inspect your plants frequently for any small holes in the stems and an accumulation of the granular matter called frass; both are signs of the presence of the squash vine borer. If you have a borer, all is not lost. Slit the stem lengthwise, just above the entry hole, remove the borer, and close up the incision with mud."

—ROBERT HEVER (COLUMBIA, MD)

Whatever's-Ready-to-Harvest Soup

SERVES 6

"This soup is in honor of my mom, who ran a very healthy and ecologically minded kitchen from the time I was a little girl. Mom never wasted little bits of veggies. Instead, she bagged them, and when the bag was full, she put them to good use in a soup floating with small pieces of garden goodness." The recipe, with its shiitake mushrooms and European herbs in a broth infused with soy sauce, suggests a model for a free-wheeling, East meets West delight of warmth in a bowl.

JILAN GLORFIELD (SANTA CRUZ, CA)

"Soup of the evening, beautiful soup."

—Lewis Carroll, *Alice's Adventures in Wonderland*

7 dried shiitake mushrooms
2 tablespoons olive oil
2 large leeks, trimmed, finely chopped, and washed
1 large onion, finely chopped
2 shallots, finely chopped
6 cloves garlic, finely chopped
1 teaspoon salt
2 carrots, scraped and finely chopped
2 celery ribs, trimmed and finely chopped
1 cup fresh corn kernels
1 tablespoon chopped fresh parsley leaves
1½ teaspoons chopped fresh thyme leaves
1 teaspoon chopped fresh sage leaves
1½ teaspoons soy sauce
2 scallions, trimmed and sliced into thin rounds

1. Place the shiitakes and 5 cups of tepid water in a bowl and set aside until softened, at least 15 minutes or up to 1 hour.

2. Heat the oil in a large soup pot. Stir in the leeks, onion, shallots, garlic, and salt and sauté over medium heat until almost caramelized, about 10 minutes.

3. Strain the mushroom water into the pot. Remove and discard the stems from the shiitakes and slice the caps into ½-inch-wide strips. Add to the pot. Add the carrots, celery, corn, parsley, thyme, sage, soy sauce and enough extra water to cover the vegetables by ½ inch. Bring to a boil, reduce the heat, and simmer until the carrots are barely tender, about 8 minutes.

4. Sprinkle the scallions over the top and serve right away.

Herbed Tortellini Soup

SERVES 4

"We grow about twenty kinds of culinary herbs and I use them almost daily. When summer is over, I dry the herbs and prepare my own herb mixes." With a preponderance of herbs over vegetables, this delightfully different, Italian-style tortellini soup certainly takes its spark from the contributors' garden bounty.

❧ WAYNE AND SUSAN SCHMOYER, (ANNVILLE, PA)

2 tablespoons olive oil
2 cloves garlic
1 pound tomatoes or an equal amount winterized tomatoes (see pages 336–337), coarsely chopped, juices reserved
1 cup tomato sauce (see page 293)
2 tablespoons chopped fresh parsley or 2 teaspoons dried parsley
1 tablespoon chopped fresh oregano leaves or 1 teaspoon dried oregano
1 teaspoon chopped fresh thyme leaves or ½ teaspoon dried thyme
1 tablespoon chopped fresh basil leaves or 1 teaspoon dried basil
¼ teaspoon chopped fresh rosemary or ⅛ teaspoon dried rosemary
¼ teaspoon chopped fresh sage or ⅛ teaspoon dried sage
2 teaspoons sugar (optional, see page 102)
⅛ teaspoon salt
1½ cups chicken broth (see page 86) or vegetable broth (see page 87)
8 ounces fresh or frozen tortellini (see Note below)
½ small bunch spinach leaves, shredded into 1-inch-wide strips, washed and drained (4 to 5 ounces)
Grated Parmesan cheese, for garnish (optional)

1. Heat the oil in a large soup pot. Add the garlic and sauté until tender but not browned, about 4 minutes. Add the tomatoes, tomato sauce, herbs, sugar, if using, salt, broth, and 6 cups of water. Bring to a boil, reduce the heat, and simmer, covered, for 30 minutes, or until the tomatoes are soft and the flavors are blended.

Praise for the Homegrown

Of the hundreds of recipes reviewed for this volume, a significant portion of them had something to say about tomatoes. Of all the comments, not one, even from contributors who announced themselves as into the seventh and eighth generations of their lives, suggested that he or she had grown tomatoes a few times but decided it wasn't worth the bother because they're just as good from the store. Each one rose to praise the homegrown tomato.

2. Raise the heat and bring to a boil again. Add the tortellini and cook until tender, 8 to 12 minutes depending on the type used.

3. Stir in the spinach and cook until wilted but still bright green, about 1 minute. Serve right away, garnished with the Parmesan, if using.

Note: You can also use dried tortellini. In that case, parboil the pasta for 10 minutes before adding to the soup so that it is properly al dente and the soup is not overcooked.

Dried Herbs: The Gardener Cook's Change Pouch

Anyone who grows herbs probably loves them. Watching them bolt at the end of the season, or wither into nothingness when the weather turns too cold to support their basically warm-weather being signals time for action. This is doubly so if the herb tender is also a cook who continues to rely on their sapor and boost all year round. There are three basic ways to preserve fresh herbs for later use.

The most traditional way is to tie together a bunch—a decorative string or ribbon is nice—and hang the bundle, tops down, in an airy place to dry slowly. The advantage of this method is that the herb bundle can also provide adornment for any wall it's hung on and also aroma in any room it's placed. This works well for herbs that are being preserved for their leaves.

For herbs being dried for their seeds, such as cilantro or fennel, the sheaves of herbs should be bagged, also top down, so that when the seeds drop they are collected. Unfortunately, this method detracts from the decorative value, but it is the only way to go, practically speaking.

In a step away from tradition and practicality, the artful gardener cook might adorn an entire wall in the kitchen or dining room with an arrangement of beautiful rice paper bags, each filled with an upside-down bouquet of herbs drying either for their leaves or seeds, stems and roots exposed over the top.

The completely efficiency-oriented cook might turn to the microwave. With this modern kitchen helpmate, a spread of herbs, whether being collected for their leaves or their seeds, dries in a thrice. You do still need to cull the leaves or seeds from their stems.

Beef-Barley Soup a New Way

SERVES 6

Food columnist (New York Times, Vogue, Family Circle) *and award-winning cookbook author (*The Microwave Gourmet, Food for Friends, Soup: A Way of Life*) Barbara Kafka hardly needs an introduction. Her culinary writings are known and admired in households around the nation. For this volume, she offers a barley soup "rich with stock and meat and enlivened by a mere whisper of orange, capable of being a meal." Besides barley, it includes earthy mushrooms, fresh herbs, and a garden ingredient you might not have thought of—parsley root.*

BARBARA KAFKA (NEW YORK, NY)

8 cups beef stock (see box on page 118)
1 pound beef stew meat, cut into ¾-inch pieces
½ cup pearl barley
2 sprigs of fresh thyme or ¼ teaspoon dried thyme
2 sprigs of fresh oregano or ⅛ teaspoon dried oregano
1 tablespoon unsalted butter
1 medium onion, coarsely chopped
2 cloves garlic, finely chopped
8 ounces mushrooms, preferably shiitakes, stemmed, wiped clean, and caps cut into 1-inch pieces
8 ounces parsley root, trimmed, peeled, and cut into ½-inch rounds, or 4 ounces parsnips, prepared the same way (see box at right)
2 sprigs of parsley, if using parsnips
2 tablespoons kosher salt
Freshly ground black pepper
1½ teaspoons chopped fresh thyme leaves or ¼ teaspoon dried thyme
1½ teaspoons chopped fresh oregano leaves or ¼ teaspoon dried oregano
2 tablespoons fresh orange juice

1. In a large saucepan, bring the stock to a boil. Add the beef pieces and poach gently until the meat is tender, about 45 minutes. Remove the beef pieces to a plate and set aside to cool.

Parsley Root: An Almost Forgotten Vegetable

Though roots of ordinary parsley plants are too bitter to eat, a varietal called Hamburg parsley, is cultivated especially for its root. In the late middle ages, the root was candied and used for medicinal purposes. Culinarily, it is used in European and Russian dishes much like parsnip, which it vaguely resembles in taste, though parsley root is milder. The Dutch braise it like young carrots; the Germans use it to broaden the flavor in potato soup; the Russians routinely include it in borscht; and, in Polish cooking, it is deemed essential in barley soup. Like carrots or turnips, parsley root is easy to grow in a well-prepared bed with deep, rich soil and good drainage. You can occasionally find it in produce stores or Asian markets.

2. Add the barley and thyme and oregano sprigs and bring to a boil. Lower the heat and simmer, partially covered, for 1 hour, until the barley is tender.

3. While the barley is cooking, melt the butter in a small frying pan over medium heat. Stir in the onion and cook, stirring frequently, for 10 minutes, until golden. Stir in the garlic and mushrooms and continue cooking and stirring for 10 minutes more. Add ½ cup water and cook until the water has evaporated, about 5 minutes. Set aside. Also bring a pot of water to boil, add the parsley root or parsnips, and cook for 3 minutes. Drain and set aside.

4. Remove the thyme and oregano sprigs from the pot with the barley, add the mushroom mixture, and simmer for 15 minutes. Add the beef pieces and the parsley root. Heat to the boiling point.

5. Stir in the salt and pepper, chopped fresh thyme and oregano, and orange juice. Leave on the heat a moment, then ladle into wide bowls and serve.

Note: If using dried herbs instead of chopped fresh herbs, add them in Step 4 after the soup has simmered for 10 minutes.

TRICKS *of the* TRADE

Quick and Easy Beef Broth

Classic restaurant-style beef stocks require costly ingredients and large amounts of them just to have a yield of a quart or two. They also require many steps that must be executed over several days' time. For those reasons, the recipes in this book by and large do not call for beef broth or stock. However, there is a little trick suggested in the minestrone recipe (Step 1) on page 113 that will yield a light beef broth from inexpensive ingredients and in less than an hour. It doesn't have to be for the minestrone alone. You can use the same technique and ingredients for other recipes that call for beef broth. Just follow the instructions through Step 1. You can use the broth right away or cool then chill it overnight. That way, the fat will rise to the top and you can lift it off to wind up with a clear broth.

Rich Seafood Brew in Rosemary Broth

Serves 2

"I created this recipe when I was in the mood for a warm soup with rosemary and chicken broth. I love to use fresh herbs and tomatoes from my garden," and this is "the perfect soup to complement them both." The "rich" part of the title comes from the other ingredients, a mix of fish, shellfish, and asparagus. The recipe is given for two, but if you care to expand it for more, it's "sure to impress and delight any guests."

MARY GRUENWALD (CINCINNATI, OH)

½ pound salmon fillet, skinned and cut into 4 pieces
6 mussels or oysters in the shell, scrubbed
6 medium shrimp, peeled and deveined, tails left attached
6 sea scallops
1 large lime, cut in half
1½ cups chicken broth (see page 86)
2 tablespoons butter or margarine
¼ teaspoon finely chopped fresh rosemary or pinch of dried rosemary
½ teaspoon fresh thyme leaves or ¼ teaspoon dried thyme
Pinch of black pepper
Pinch of cayenne
2 Roma tomatoes, cut into ¼-inch dice
12 medium asparagus stalks, top 4 inches only (about 6 ounces)

1. Rinse the salmon, mussels, shrimp, and scallops in a colander. Squeeze the lime over the seafood, toss to coat, and set aside.

2. Place the broth in a wide saucepan or stovetop casserole and bring to a boil. Add the butter, rosemary, thyme, pepper, cayenne, and tomatoes and stir to mix. Add the asparagus and cook over high heat until the asparagus is bright green, 2 minutes.

3. Add the seafood in 2 batches, starting with the salmon and mussels. Cover the pot and cook for 3 minutes over high heat. Carefully lift the cover, toss in the shrimp and scallops, replace the cover, and continue cooking for 3 minutes more, or until the mussels are open, the shrimp is pink, and the scallops are firm but still tender. Dish into soup bowls, being sure to divide everything evenly, including the juices. Serve right away.

Fish in Broth: An Offering from the Sea to the Table

Wherever there are coastal waters with plentiful fish, some sort of seafood soup or stew has been created. All rise out of what once seemed the ever-supplying seas with a natural harvest that could never be depleted. Originally devised to make use of the catch of the day and feed the fisherman's family, such dishes were often so good they came to be expected, even hallowed. Thus bouillabaisse, cioppino, kakavia, bourride, and billi-bi became honored dishes around the world. Over time, the list lengthened as other waters far beyond the Mediterranean, Aegean, and Baltic seas engendered further culinary relishes: clam chowder, conch chowder, oyster gumbo, and mixed seafood in rosemary broth.

Seafood and Tomato Stew

Serves 8

"I have sent my family's favorite soup recipe. We always have it with our Christmas Eve dinner, but it is great any time of the year." Of course, if you are serving the dish not for the winter holidays but in the spring when the herbs are growing anew, you can substitute fresh herbs for the dried.

LUANNE PELLOTTA (FAIRMONT, WV)

6 slices bacon, diced
1 small onion, cut into ¼-inch pieces
1 clove garlic, minced
1 large celery rib, trimmed and cut on the diagonal into ¼-inch-wide slices
½ small green bell pepper, stemmed, seeded, and chopped into ¼-inch pieces
2 cups winterized tomatoes (see pages 336–337), coarsely chopped, juices reserved
1½ pounds potatoes, peeled and cut into ½-inch dice
¼ teaspoon dried oregano leaves
½ teaspoon dried basil leaves
1 teaspoon salt
½ teaspoon black pepper
1 cup tomato sauce (see page 293)
1 pound cod fillets, cut into bite-size pieces
1 pound sea scallops
1 pound small shrimp, peeled and deveined
2 tablespoons chopped fresh parsley leaves, for garnish

1. Fry the bacon in a large, nonreactive soup pot until limp but not crisp, about 2 minutes. Pour off any excess fat, add the onion, garlic, celery, and bell pepper, and sauté over medium heat until translucent, 6 to 8 minutes.

2. Add the tomatoes, potatoes, oregano, basil, salt, pepper, tomato sauce, and 2 cups of water. Bring to a boil, cover, and simmer for 20 minutes, or until the potatoes are tender.

3. Add the cod, scallops, and shrimp, cover again, and continue to simmer briskly until the fish is done, 6 to 8 minutes more. Serve right away, garnished with the parsley.

Potatoes: England's Happiness Increased, or a Sure and Easie Remedy against all succeeding Dear Years; by a Plantation of the Roots called Potatoes.

—J. Forster, 1664 book title, culled from the *Oxford English Dictionary*

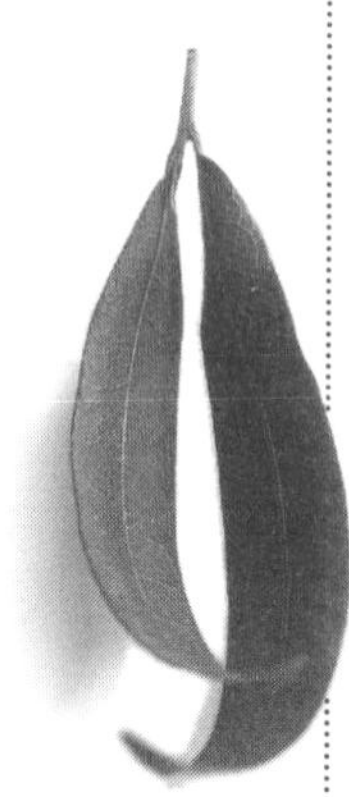

Mustangg's Island Fish Stew

SERVES 4 TO 6

In a felicitous confluence of land and sea, ingredients from both come together in a lively fish stew that befits the location of close-by-the-coast Houston, Texas. The contributor suggests serving the stew ladled over small macaroni. A bed of steamed rice or a side of warm bread makes an equally good accompaniment.

BECKY KARL (HOUSTON, TX)

1 tablespoon olive oil
1 large onion, cut into ¼-inch pieces
2 cloves garlic, minced
1 medium carrot, scraped and cut into ¼-inch pieces
2 small bell peppers, preferably one red and one green, stemmed, seeded, and cut into ¼-inch pieces
2 pounds tomatoes, coarsely chopped, juices reserved
2 tablespoons chopped fresh parsley
1 tablespoon chopped fresh oregano
1 tablespoon chopped fresh basil
1 small bay leaf, preferably fresh *(see box below)*
2 cups chicken broth *(see page 86)*
Salt and pepper
1½ pounds fresh cod fillets, cut into 1-inch pieces

1. Heat the oil in a large, nonreactive soup pot until beginning to smoke. Add the onion, garlic, carrot, and peppers and sauté over medium-high heat for 10 minutes, or until wilted but still crisp.

2. Add the tomatoes and their juices, the parsley, oregano, basil, bay leaf, broth, and salt and pepper to taste. Bring to a boil, reduce the heat to maintain a gentle simmer, and cook for 10 minutes, or until the tomatoes are soft. Add the cod and continue simmering for 20 minutes, until the cod pieces are cooked through but not falling into flakes.

3. Remove the bay leaf and serve right away.

The Lovely Laurel

From Greece to California and throughout the kitchens of the European world, bay leaves have been deemed a seasoning par excellence. In Greece and around the Mediterra-nean, bay laurel (*Laurus nobilis*) grows mainly as shrub, with plants twelve to forty feet high; in California a different variety (*Umbellularia californica*) scents the air and provides shade wherever established out-doors. Bay can also be grown indoors, as long as it has lots of filtered light and plenty of circulating air (no air condition-ing). Indoors or out, the laurel tree offers its branches to twine into an honorific laurel crown for the head of a winner or an aromatic wreath to grace the hearth of the home. Its berries can be crushed and added to paraffin and molded into fragrant candles.

Bay leaves, fresh or dried, add a vivacious herbal aroma to any dish that includes them. The difference between fresh and dried bay is not remarkable, except the fresh leaf retains more of its natural oil and so is somewhat more pungent. Whether fresh or dried, bay leaves should be used with restraint in cooking. Too much renders the dish medicinal tasting; one or two small leaves will do for most dishes. Unless finely chopped or crumbled, remove the leaves from the dish before serving.

Summer Thyme Salmon and Corn Chowder

SERVES 3 TO 4

In this quick-to-assemble-and-cook summer chowder, there's a low-fat cooking method to be learned: Adding salt while sautéing leeks brings out their juices, so they wilt without browning in a very modest amount of oil. It's a technique you can apply to many a dish or chowder variation,.

ELLEN BURR (TRURO, MA)

1 tablespoon olive oil
3 to 4 slender leeks, trimmed, finely chopped, and washed (about 4 ounces)
1 teaspoon salt
1 pound Yukon Gold potatoes, peeled and cut into ⅛-inch cubes (see Notes below)
1 small fresh bay leaf or ½ small dried leaf
1 large sprig fresh thyme or ¼ teaspoon dried thyme
1 small red chili pepper, fresh or dried, stemmed and seeded, or ¼ teaspoon crushed red pepper
1 pound salmon fillet, skinned and cut into 1½-inch chunks
4 ounces soft chèvre cheese, at room temperature
1½ cups scraped fresh corn (see box below)
½ teaspoon fresh thyme leaves, for garnish (optional, see Notes below)
Hot paprika, for garnish

1. Heat the oil in a large soup pot. Stir in the leeks, sprinkle with the salt, and sauté over medium heat for 5 minutes, or until wilted but not browned.

2. Add the potatoes and 4 cups water, bring to a boil, and simmer for 10 minutes, or until the potatoes are almost tender. Add the bay leaf, thyme sprig, chili pepper, and salmon. Bring to a boil, then simmer for 3 minutes, until the salmon becomes opaque.

3. Whisk together the chèvre and ½ cup of the cooking liquid to smooth the

Corn off the Cob

To remove corn from the cob, American cooks have long used a method called scraping. That means not just cutting the kernels free but also grating the cob across a corn scraper set over a bowl to catch the starchy juices as they are released from the cob. The fresh and milky sweetness of the juices is an essential part of the recipe.

FOR 1½ CUPS SCRAPED CORN:

Shuck and remove the silks from 2 medium ears fresh corn. Cut the kernels off the cobs without slicing too deeply and set the kernels aside. With a hand grater held over a bowl, grate the cobs down to the inner core to release the milky juices. Add the kernels to the bowl and set aside without refrigerating. Use within an hour so the kernels and juices don't become starchy.

cheese. Stir into the pot, add the scraped corn, and continue simmering for 1 minute, or until the salmon is cooked through.

4. Remove the bay leaf, thyme sprig, and chili pepper. Serve right away, garnished with the thyme leaves and a dash of paprika sprinkled over the top.

Notes

• Yukon Gold potatoes, with their butter-yellow color and firm texture, are particularly suitable for this chowder.

• If you've used crushed red pepper, don't fuss with removing the flakes before serving the chowder.

• The optional thyme garnish adds a touch of green and an additional pungency to the chowder. If you don't have fresh thyme, either omit it or substitute parsley—dried thyme won't do.

Twin Weather Sorrel Soup

SERVES 6

"I have had a patch of French sorrel for over five years. I put the leaves on my sandwiches and in my salads, but my favorite recipe is this one." On a spring day that has turned chilly by suppertime, or for those who prefer warm soup no matter the weather, the cooling step can be skipped and the soup gently reheated before serving.

MERCY INGRAHAM
(HULMEVILLE, PA)

A Song to Sorrel

Sorrel, often described as lemony spinach, comes in two varieties: garden sorrel (*Rumex acetosa*), native throughout Europe and Eurasia, and French sorrel (*Rumex scutatus*), native to a more particular region of central Europe. Both garden sorrel, larger and more robust in flavor, and French sorrel, its more diminutive cousin, delight gardener and cook. Gardeners love it because it's a hardy, almost undauntable perennial that reappears after the harshest winter. It even survives a spring digging where its gnarled and sturdy roots, sequestered underground and protected from the zealous gardener, waiting to send forth a verdant patch of green that announces the new season is here. Cooks also love sorrel because its delicate tang is culinarily intriguing—is it herb, salad green, or leafy vegetable? All uses suit it and it suits gardener and cook.

3 tablespoons vegetable oil
1 medium onion, finely chopped
4 cups (packed) fresh sorrel leaves, washed
10 cups chicken broth (see page 86)
1½ pounds potatoes, peeled and coarsely chopped
2 tablespoons fresh lemon juice
¼ teaspoon cayenne
¼ teaspoon black pepper
1 teaspoon salt
1 cup half-and-half
Paper-thin lemon slices, for garnish

1. Heat the oil in a heavy pot over medium-high heat. Add the onion and sauté until transparent and soft, 10 minutes. Stir in the sorrel leaves and continue sautéing until wilted, about 2 minutes.

2. Add the broth, potatoes, lemon juice, cayenne, pepper, and salt and bring to a boil. Reduce the heat, cover the pot, and simmer until the potatoes have collapsed, about 45 minutes. Cool enough to handle, then purée. Cover and refrigerate until chilled.

3. Stir in the half-and-half and serve, garnished with the lemon slices.

GAZPACHO IN ANDALUSIA
In its land of origin, Andalusian gazpacho is meant to be a revivifying, cool taste to relieve the summer heat. To this end, the gazpacho is always well chilled, as are the serving bowls. In addition, many cooks float ice cubes in the soup for a final chill.

Gazpacho Scented with Mint

SERVES 6 TO 8

Thomas Keller, owner and chef of the French Laundry Restaurant in Yountville, California, has established an elegant country-style dining spot at the top of the two-lane highway that wends through the Napa Valley wine country. For this volume, he offers a recipe that shows how a disarmingly simple dish like gazpacho can become refined with a creative touch, in this case refreshing mint. With a restaurant-style flourish, he arranges the condiments in large, individual soup bowls and ladles the soup around them. For home serving, the condiments can be set on the table for each person to add according to taste. Fried bread cubes or plain crostini are a traditional accompaniment.

THOMAS KELLER (YOUNTVILLE, CA)

Mint by Many Another Name

The mint family, botanically known as the Labiatae, contains a huge number of herbs and shrubs, among them many medicinal herbs and potherbs that often go by another name. Spearmint and peppermint are obvious ones. A baker's dozen of relatives includes:

Basil	Marjoram	Sage	Wood betony
Bergamot	Oregano	Savory	Yerba buena
Lavender	Perilla	Thyme	
Lemon balm	Rosemary		

1 medium white onion
1 medium green bell pepper
2 medium cucumbers, peeled
2 large tomatoes (about ¾ pound)
¼ cup (packed) fresh mint leaves
1 tablespoon minced garlic
¼ cup tomato paste
Juice of 1 lemon (about 2 tablespoons)
¼ cup distilled white vinegar
¾ cup extra virgin olive oil
2 quarts tomato juice
Gazpacho condiments (suggestions follow)

1. Roughly chop the onion, green pepper, cucumbers, tomatoes, and mint leaves and place in a bowl. Add the garlic, tomato paste, lemon juice, vinegar, olive oil, and tomato juice. Stir to mix, cover, and marinate in the refrigerator overnight.

2. The next day, pass the mixture through a food mill or process, in a food processor, then press through a China cap (see box at right) or a fine sieve. Return to the refrigerator and prepare the condiments.

3. To serve, place a generous amount of each garnish in large individual soup bowls. Ladle the soup around the condiments and serve right away, while still cold.

TOOLS *of the* TRADE

The China Cap

The China cap, called a *chinois* in French, is a cone-shaped, very fine-meshed sieve. It's a tool that requires a serious commitment to puréeing a mixture as fine as possible. That means it's not a tool for quick puréeing. For those who would like to spend time pushing and coaxing the ingredients through a China cap using the long wooden pestle designed for the job, the reward is a silken purée free of pith, pit, or peel.

Gazpacho Condiments

MAKES AS MUCH AS YOU WANT

Mince equal amounts of red onion, green bell pepper, and cucumber, keeping them separate. Dice an equal amount of tomato. Shred a big handful of mint leaves. To serve, place on individual small plates and set on the table, or add a spoonful of each to each bowl before ladling in the gazpacho.

Icy Cold Summer Soup

Serves 6

The languid, hot days of late summer invite a bowl of icy cold summer soup. Like a gazpacho, this soup reflects the brilliance of the sun. The size of the vegetables is pretty much up to the energy of the cook—finely cut is very nice, but on very hot days, a little chunkier will do.

SHARON DALTON (WATERFORD, CA)

Soup Seasoning Cubes

Makes 1 standard ice tray full, 14 cubes

Soup seasoning cubes are for the storehouse, the freezer storehouse, in this case. They allow one "to keep from losing those little pieces of garden produce that can add extra flavor later to another dish. The proportions to be used are individual to each gardener and/or cook." You can have a great good time mixing and matching combinations of vegetables and herbs: Make cubes of bell peppers and garlic to drop into a summer gazpacho. Make cubes of carrot, onion, and thyme to liven a winter stew. Make cubes of basil, parsley, and scallion to season a delicate spring soup. ANN HINKHOUSE (WEST LIBERTY, IA)

1 cup minced sturdy vegetables and herbs, such as bell peppers, carrots, garlic, onions, scallions, parsley, thyme, and oregano

1. Pack about 1 tablespoon of the mixture you have chosen into each compartment of an ice tray. Add enough water to each compartment so that the water floats a little above the ingredients without overflowing. Freeze until solid.

2. To use, drop however many cubes you'd like into a pot of soup just as it finishes cooking and allow the cubes to melt. Continue cooking until the vegetables from the cubes are softened and the soup is warm again. Or garnish a bowl of cold soup with a cube and stir and watch as it melts.

Note: To make more of the cubes to store up, remove the frozen cubes, pack in plastic freezer bags, and continue with another batch. The frozen cubes will keep in the freezer for up to 6 months.

1 cup finely shredded green cabbage
¼ each yellow, red, and green bell pepper, stemmed, seeded, and thinly sliced
1 cucumber, peeled, seeded, and thinly sliced
1 celery rib, trimmed and sliced very thin
½ small red onion, finely chopped
1 green onion (scallions), trimmed and thinly sliced
2 radishes, trimmed and sliced into thin rounds
1 medium tomatoes, cut into ¼-inch dice
8 cups Homemade Vegetable Juice (see page 35)
Sour cream or plain yogurt, for garnish (optional)

1. Combine all the ingredients except the sour cream in a large bowl. Stir to mix, cover, and refrigerate for several hours.

2. Serve chilled, with a bowl of sour cream on the side, if desired.

Note: In place of the Homemade Vegetable Juice, you can substitute a good-quality commercial tomato juice and add a cube or two of soup seasoning cubes (see box at left).

pasta aplenty:

noodles with a flourish

Pasta dishes have become a kind of fusion cooking we don't even think of as new anymore. The ingredients—noodles of every sort from the Old World and Asia, vegetables from the Old World, New World, and Asia, all—have become so familiar and the possibilities for innovation so vast that pasta is now part of virtually everyone's home cooking. From Newark to Atlanta and Waukegan to Telluride, Tacoma, and Taos, the noodle triggers the cook's imagination in an almost unbounded set of variations as it offers its ease of preparation. An advantage for family cooking is that you can almost always "hold the sauce" for those who don't care for tonight's rendition.

The recipes call for the pasta suggested by the contributor. However, feel free to choose the shape according to what you have on hand and what you like best—as long as you keep in mind that fine pasta, such as angel hair strands, will faint away under a hearty blanket of pumpkin alfredo sauce and sturdy noodles, such as penne, will overpower a delicate clam and white wine broth.

Pasta Leonardo

Serves 4

"Good fortune sent me to study architecture in Venice, Italy, in the fall of 1992. I had the honor of cooking with my late professor, Leonardo Ricci, one of Italy's most incredible modernist architects. My first day in Venice, I found myself shopping the markets for ingredients that would be used to create this simple, but unforgettable dish. This was my introduction to the Italian celebration of eating. Purity in ingredients, power in flavor. I now reside in Portland, Oregon, where I garden bounties of freshness. With each tomato that's picked, a gentle reminder of that Venetian experience filters through the air. To eat from the earth, to celebrate. To love, to remember."

~ KIRSTA JACOBS (PORTLAND, OR)

½ cup olive oil
4 to 6 Roma tomatoes, thinly sliced (1 pound)
2 small zucchini, thinly sliced
2 teaspons chopped fresh oregano leaves or 1 teaspoon dried oregano
1 tablespoon shredded fresh basil leaves or 2 teaspoons dried basil
½ teaspoon crushed red pepper
½ teaspoon salt
1 cup grated Parmesan cheese
¾ pound fusilli, cooked, drained, and set aside in a warm place (see box at left)

1. Pour the olive oil into a deep sauté pan large enough to hold the tomato and zucchini slices in one overlapping layer. Arrange the slices in the pan and sprinkle evenly with the oregano, basil, red pep-

Pasta Cooking Basics

Whatever the shape or size of noodle you are preparing, and whether it is fresh or dried, there are some guidelines always to follow, and some from which to choose.

ALL AGREE

- Perfectly cooked pasta requires plenty of water if it's to plump properly. That means, about 4 quarts of water per pound of pasta.
- Once the pasta begins to wilt in the water, stir, stir, stir until the noodles have softened enough not to stick to each other or to the bottom of the pot.
- Once the water has returned to a boil, lower the heat just enough to maintain a steady and brisk boil without boiling over.
- When done, the pasta should be drained ever so briefly and returned to the pot or mixing bowl with water still clinging to it.
- Pasta for salads should be cooked slightly softer, that is, less al dente, than for warm dishes so that the noodles can absorb the dressing.

CONTROVERSY SURROUNDS WHETHER OR NOT TO

- Add salt to the cooking water so the pasta is seasoned as it cooks. Some say this step adds unnecessary sodium, and salt to taste can be added at the saucing stage.
- Add olive oil to the water to keep the noodles from sticking together. Some say this is a waste of precious oil; it's the stirring that keeps pasta from sticking during cooking, and a light oil coating after cooking will do the same job if holding the pasta aside for a while.
- Hold over pasta for reheating. Some say the noodles must be served warm or dressed for salad right away. Others say, with a light oil coating and a splash or two of water, noodles reheat beautifully in the microwave.

per, salt, and ½ cup of the cheese. Simmer for 20 minutes over low heat, until the vegetables are soft.

2. Place the pasta in a serving bowl and spread the vegetables evenly over the top, dribbling the oil and juices from the pan over all. Serve right away, accompanied by the remaining Parmesan on the side.

Garden Lore, Garden Tips, Sweet 100s, and Roses, Too

Tomatoes, hardy as they are, are nonetheless susceptible to unfriendly invasion from bugs, bacteria, and viruses. Sweet 100 cherry tomatoes, which practically insist on staying low to the ground no matter how the gardener may attempt to elevate them for their own good, are prone to disease and injury caused by lack of aeration and excess moisture from the dew below. Other tactics are required to lend them a helping hand. One such is the following.

"I am 82⅓ years old and love to garden. I am looking forward to spring when I can be out to plant again. Here is a garden tip: To prevent tomato virus, mix 2 teaspoons skim milk to one gallon water and spray over the plants."

Enthusiastic as all gardeners are, she goes on to offer a tip for keeping rose pests at bay: "Hang a couple of bars of Dial soap nearby."

—GERTRUDE LORIG (MCGREGOR, IA)

Other gardeners offer similar tips with certain quirky twists. Some say to make the milk spray a buttermilk one for roses. Others say to use the soap trick as a water solution to spray on the tomatoes. Some say to add garlic to any solution meant for pest control. Where lore ends, science begins, and what ultimately works is not yet completely defined. It is clear that, insofar as keeping the earth well is the value, a homeopathic solution is desirable. Most gardeners agree, and thus arise garden lore, garden tips, and some garden prose poetry, to boot.

Linguine with Sweet 100 Tomatoes, Basil, and Cream

SERVES 4 TO 6

In recent years, the Sweet 100 variety of cherry tomato has become wildly popular both for growing and eating. Prolific in the garden, one plant offers up enough of its tiny fruit for humans and other creatures alike to share directly off the vine. Sweet on the palate, it's a cultivar that also pleases the cook inclined to gather a basketful for a quick, creamy pasta sauce "that manages to taste fresh but rich at the same time."

BRENDA WINDLE (MENLO PARK, CA)

2 tablespoons butter
2 to 3 cloves garlic, finely chopped
4 cups Sweet 100 cherry tomatoes, rinsed and left whole (see Notes below)
½ cup heavy (whipping) cream
½ cup (packed) shredded fresh basil leaves
¼ teaspoon salt
¼ teaspoon black pepper
¾ pound fresh linguine or fettucine (see Notes below), cooked, drained, and set aside in a warm place (see box on page 128)
½ cup grated Parmesan cheese

1. Melt the butter in a large nonreactive sauté pan. Add the garlic and sauté over medium-high heat until wilted but not browned, about 1 minute.

2. Add the tomatoes and sauté until softened, about 2 minutes. Stir in the cream, bring to a boil, and simmer briskly until slightly thickened, 1 to 2 minutes.

3. Stir in the basil, salt, and pepper. Pour over the pasta and serve right away, accompanied by the Parmesan on the side.

Notes

• If Sweet 100s are not available, other cherry tomatoes, from the miniature pear tomato varieties to the slightly larger, more available cherry-size cherry tomatoes, may be used. If using the latter, cut them in half so they rapidly melt into the sauce without overcooking.

• The softness of fresh noodles makes a supreme underpinning for this quick and uncomplicated saucing. Dried noodles can, of course, be substituted, as long as they are of the strandy linguine or fettuccine type.

TOOLS *of the* TRADE

The Pasta Pot

For those who think a day is not done without a bowl of pasta, the pot for cooking the pasta is of prime importance. It must be large, voluminous enough to allow the pasta to cook at a fast clip without crowding so the individual noodles or other shapes don't clump together as they roil about. More specifically, the pot should be a pot, meaning not a large sauté pan or stovetop casserole because even though those might hold a good measure of liquid, they don't provide the depth of water required for tender noodles.

It doesn't matter to the pasta if the pot is not so fancy. It can be one of those big aluminum vessels, familiar to many kitchens of the Fifties and Sixties. Though they are not good to use for tomatoes, spinach, or any other dish that includes a reactive ingredient such as lemon or wine, they remain just dandy for boiling up a lot of spaghetti for a crowd.

Fusilli with Olives and Tomatoes

SERVES 4

"In families, the usual procedure when one receives a recipe, most of the time it is passed along from mother to daughter. Well, in this case, my daughter passed this recipe along to me. It uses my delicious ripe tomatoes from my garden, and my lush basil that I grow for all my cooking."

DOROTHY SZALAY (BAYSIDE, NY)

1 pound tomatoes, coarsely chopped into ¼-inch pieces
1 cup black olives, preferably oil-cured, pitted but not chopped (see box at right)
1 clove garlic, minced
1 cup shredded fresh basil leaves
½ cup olive oil
1 teaspoon salt
½ teaspoon black pepper
¾ pound fusilli
½ cup grated Parmesan cheese

1. Place the tomatoes, olives, garlic, basil, oil, salt, and pepper in a large serving bowl. Stir gently to mix and set aside.

2. Cook the pasta al dente according to the package instructions. Drain and immediately transfer to the bowl with the tomato mixture without shaking dry. Gently stir to mix and serve right away, accompanied by the Parmesan on the side.

TRICKS *of the* TRADE

Pitting Olives; Peeling Chestnuts

As with all magic, when the secret is revealed to you, you become the magician. Of course, it's usually a matter of trickiness. A bonus of this trick is that it can also be employed for peeling chestnuts. When a recipe calls for fresh chestnuts that do not need to be whole and you are not willing to take the time or finger-numbing effort to prepare them, turn again to that handy mallet for aid.

FOR OLIVES: Spread however many olives you need to pit on a counter. Using a wooden mallet or light hammer, tap them, one by one, just strongly enough to break open the fruit without splintering the pit. With your fingers, pull the flesh away from the pit—it should come off pretty much in halves. Continue until you have enough for the recipe. Or, go on until you have enough pitted olives to stockpile in the fridge. They keep pretty much indefinitely, and you don't have to pay the price for store-bought pitted ones.

FOR CHESTNUTS: Make a small slit through the peel with the point of a paring knife; anywhere it's easy to insert the knife is fine. Blanch the chestnuts as usual for 10 minutes in briskly boiling water. Drain and tap away, strongly enough to crack open the peel without smashing the nut to pieces. The peel and inside skin should be easily removable. If the skin is still recalcitrant, drop the chestnut back into the hot water for a few minutes and try again.

Fresh Tomato and Roasted Garlic Pasta

SERVES 6

"Living in California gives us the opportunity to grow many things in our garden, and sometimes even year-round. This seems to be the case with garlic and herbs. Then come spring the tomatoes go in. While they are all fresh we enjoy this recipe that just sort of grew in the kitchen as the tomatoes, basil, and garlic grew in the garden." The dish is also good cold for picnics or a pasta salad.

~ WES AND DIANE MORRILL (SALINAS, CA)

6 to 8 whole heads Roasted Garlic (see box below)
6 medium tomatoes, coarsely chopped
1 tablespoon salt
¾ to 1 teaspoon freshly ground black pepper
1 cup coarsely chopped fresh basil leaves
½ cup olive oil
1 pound fresh or ¾ pound dried pasta, any form cooked, drained, and set aside in a warm place (see box on page 128)
½ cup grated Parmesan cheese

1. Roast and peel the garlic and set aside.

2. Place the tomatoes, salt, and pepper in a medium bowl, toss to mix, and set aside for 15 minutes or up to 1 hour.

3. Add the garlic, basil, and oil to the tomatoes and toss.

4. Place the pasta in a serving bowl and add the tomato mixture. Sprinkle the Parmesan over the top and either toss to mix or serve as is.

Roasted Garlic

The advantage of roasting garlic is that the pulp is easily squeezed out of the cooked heads without having to peel each clove. While a glazed clay garlic cooker is a charming pot to use, it's not necessary; heavy-duty aluminum foil works as well. For ½ cup roasted garlic pulp:

Preheat the oven to 400°F. or prepare a charcoal fire. Cut the tops (stem, not root, end) off 6 to 8 whole garlic heads. Peel away the outside paper from the heads and place 3 to 6 heads on a length of heavy-duty aluminum foil. Drizzle the heads with enough olive oil to moisten them without floating them. Wrap the heads in the foil and place in the oven or on the grill rack. Roast for 45 minutes to 1 hour. To test the timing, carefully open one of the packages, taking care to avoid escaping steam, and pinch one of the heads. If it squeezes easily, it's done; if not, rewrap and leave a few minutes more. When done, remove the packages and cool enough to handle. To use, slit open the skins and squeeze out the pulp.

For another method of roasting garlic, see page 83.

Pasta with Red Bell Pepper Sauce

SERVES 4 TO 6

"Mature red bell peppers taste like an entirely different vegetable than the green bell peppers, much sweeter. It requires a great deal of patience waiting for the green peppers to turn into the red beauties." The implication is, the wait is worth it when you have enough to make this pasta sauce, which is also delicious over rice or baked potato.

RITA HUWE (ROCKFORD, IL)

2 tablespoons olive oil
1 large onion, finely chopped
2 garlic cloves, finely chopped
8 medium red bell peppers, finely chopped (about 4 pounds)
½ teaspoon sugar
1 teaspoon salt
¼ teaspoon black pepper
1 tablespoon chopped fresh basil leaves
1 tablespoon chopped fresh oregano leaves
½ cup white wine or water
¾ pound spaghetti or other pasta, cooked, drained, and set aside in a warm place (see box on page 128)

1. Heat the oil in a large sauté pan. Add the onions and garlic and sauté over medium heat until softened, 8 to 10 minutes.

2. Add the bell peppers, sugar, salt, and pepper and stir to mix. Cook over medium heat until the peppers are soft, about 10 minutes. Stir in the basil and oregano and continue cooking 1 minute more, until the herbs are wilted. Remove and cool enough to handle.

3. Purée the mixture in a food processor until as smooth as possible. Return to the pan and stir in enough wine or water, up to ½ cup, to thin the mixture to a saucy rather than paste consistency. Reheat over low heat, pour over the pasta, and serve right away.

Sautéed Red Bell Peppers

For those who love red bell peppers and can't get enough of them, the sauce recipe can be modified to serve as a vegetable side or salad.

Rather than chopping the peppers, cut them into ¼- to ½-inch-wide strips. Begin with 4 tablespoons oil and follow the recipe through Step 2, allowing a little more time if necessary to soften the peppers. Serve warm, at room temperature, or chilled. If serving as a salad, a generous amount of capers (at least 2 tablespoons) stirred in and a good sprinkle of parsley on top make an even more distinctive dish.

Pasta with Asparagus, Sugar Snap Peas, and Parmesan Cheese

SERVES 4

"I am a lifelong gardener from a family of lifelong gardeners. I grow herbs and lettuces in tubs, plus I have a large garden on a hill above my home that I call the Patch. There I grow strawberries, asparagus, gooseberries, blackberries, and other crops that the deer do not care for—squash, broccoli, tomatoes. I have another smaller garden right on the shore of the lake where I grow beans, peas, peppers, tomatillos, beets, eggplant, some herbs, and sunflowers. The deer's favorites are beans and sunflowers, but they can't get at them here because it's about ten feet from the water. This recipe is my hands-down favorite and I eat it once a week at least in summer."

DONA PIERCE (LAKE SHORE, MN)

1 pound asparagus, cut into ½-inch lengths
8 ounces sugar snap or snow peas, tips snapped off
8 ounces bow-tie pasta
3 tablespoons olive oil
½ cup grated Parmesan cheese
Salt and pepper

1. Bring a large pot of water to boil. Add the asparagus and cook over high heat for 2 minutes. Add the peas and cook for 2 minutes more, until the vegetables are al dente and still bright green. With a slotted spoon, transfer the asparagus and peas to a bowl and set aside in a warm place.

2. Bring the water back to the boil, add the pasta, and cook until al dente. Drain the pasta and transfer to a serving bowl. Add the olive oil, asparagus and peas, and Parmesan. Season with salt and pepper to taste and serve right away.

Deer Be Gone

Deer are the survivors of the four-footed mammals. Why? Because, like humans, they can adapt to many, many menus so long as, for them, the dishes are vegetarian. What's a gardener to do?

FENCES: As long as they are more than 6 feet high, fences will protect the garden from deer feasting on your plants.

DOGS: As long as the dog is ready at the patrol and available for night duty, this is a good way to keep the deer away from any yard.

UNCOMPANIONABLE PLANTING: As long as the gardener is satisfied with plants that the deer eschew, the deer will go find their meal elsewhere. Such plants for kitchen use include: broccoli and many of its brassica relatives; squash and many of its relatives, such as cucumbers and melons; and, lo and behold, tomatoes.

LOCATION: As long as the garden is in a place deer do not populate (hard to find) or one they can't get to, such as the waterside "south-forty" the contributor describes (also hard to find), no problem.

Cheese Tortellini with Garlic and Spinach

Serves 4

"My father-in-law (L.J.) became known for his garlic and would bestow it upon anyone he thought of as especially kind or thoughtful. Garlic flourished, indeed grew rampant, in L.J.'s garden, and whenever he mowed, the scent of garlic would carry on the breeze down Virginia Street, through the alleys, over the smell of the afternoon creosote and the freshly cut grass. The dogs with twitching noses held high would be the first to catch the perfume and bark fiercely. We would spread out hundreds of his precious bulbs to dry and braid into wreaths. We would all smell of his garlic, and with our breath we exhaled the fine odor of the harvest. Here is a recipe we recommend to lovers of the stinking rose."

ANTON HATFIELD-NICHOLSON
(MIFFLINTOWN, PA)

8 ounces cheese tortellini
⅓ cup to ½ cup pine nuts, toasted (see box at right)
1 small bunch spinach leaves, torn or coarsely chopped, washed, and drained, (about 8 ounces)
4 cloves garlic, minced
3 tablespoons olive oil
½ cup grated Parmesan cheese

1. Place the nuts, spinach, garlic, and olive oil in a large serving bowl. Set aside.

2. Cook the tortellini according to the package instructions. Drain and transfer to the bowl. Toss, sprinkle the Parmesan over the top, and serve.

Toasting Nuts

From pine nuts to peanuts to almonds, pecans, and walnuts, a light toasting brings out the aroma, restores the freshness, and adds a pleasing crunch to nuts. There are several ways to accomplish this, and the timing is the same for whichever method you are using, 3 to 4 minutes, depending on the amount.

On the stovetop: Spread the nuts in an ungreased skillet and stir over medium-high heat.

In the oven or toaster oven: Spread the nuts on an ovenproof sheet and cook at 375°F., stirring once.

In the microwave: Spread the nuts on a microwave dish and cook on high.

FRESH MOZZARELLA

Buffalo to Bovine and Tomatoes In Between

If you've ever wondered how buffalo, usually associated with the American Great Plains, and mozzarella, decidedly evocative of Italian cooking, got together in a ball of fresh cheese, it's because the name actually refers to the origin of its best rendition, water-buffalo milk. So far, nowhere else is mozzarella made with the milk of water buffalo, which feed on the grasses of the hills around Salerno in Italy. It is available in specialty cheese shops. Don't faint over the price, though; it's air-shipped fresh from the Italian farm to your door, or close by, within two days, so it's doubly expensive. For a comparable fresh mozzarella, you can buy an honest and good domestic product made from cow's milk. Buffalo or bovine, balls of fresh mozzarella, still moist in their whey brine, are far preferable to any product that comes wrapped in plastic, not exactly bone dry, but no longer malleable.

Fresh mozzarella is a sensual ingredient. As you hold it, you might fantasize sculpting forms for table decorations. More practically, you might decide to dice it into bits to stir into a pasta sauce. Or you might also go for an unbeatable, never tiresome, uncomplicated combination Italian cooks thought up ages ago: sliced tomatoes and fresh mozzarella under an umbrella of whole basil leaves moistened with drops of olive oil (see inset).

Tomatoes, Fresh Mozzarella, and Basil on a Plate

Nicely slice a ball of mozzarella into ¼-inch thick rounds. Arrange the rounds on a platter alternately with rounds of the best tomatoes you can garner. Place a whole basil leaf over each cheese and tomato duo. At the last minute before serving, drizzle some extra good, fine olive oil over all and present the platter.

There's a special note here: Hold the vinegar and salt that usually season tomatoes. To meet the elegant simplicity of the dish, serve these on the side, the vinegar in a cruet, the salt in a cellar.

Summer Pasta with Mozzarella Cheese

SERVES 4 TO 6

"Rhode Island is a state with a strong Italian heritage that very much influences the gardening and food culture. This recipe has many variations but always starts with home-grown tomatoes and freshly picked basil." It's true, such fresh pasta concoctions hail from the Northeast, where many Italian families settled, planted gardens, and kept on cooking "even if they do not have a real garden." Here the variation is that the traditional summer pasta includes chicken broth as part of the liquid for saucing the noodles.

NOREEN SHAWCROSS (EAST GREENWICH, RI)

6 medium tomatoes, coarsely chopped
6 cloves garlic, minced
½ cup shredded fresh basil leaves
8 ounces fresh mozzarella cheese (see page 136)
½ cup olive oil
¼ cup chicken broth (see page 86)
1 teaspoon salt
¾ pound thin pasta, such as angel hair or linguine
½ cup grated Parmesan cheese
1 teaspoon black pepper

1. Place the tomatoes, garlic, basil, mozzarella, oil, broth, and salt in a large serving bowl. Stir to mix and set aside at room temperature for at least 1 hour.

2. Cook the pasta until al dente. Drain briefly and add to the bowl with the tomato mixture. Add the Parmesan and pepper and toss to mix. Serve right away while the pasta is still warm.

BASIL VERSUS MARJORAM

The choice between basil and marjoram is truly a matter of taste. Both are aromatic and both impart a Mediterranean flavor to the pasta. Basil is softer leaved and softer on the palate. Marjoram, even though the leaves are smaller, is a bit tougher in both ways.

Pasta Autunno

SERVES 4

"In our area, the Blue Ridge Mountains of Virginia, spring can be too hot and humid to grow broccoli and greens successfully. But fall is long and gradual, with cool dry nights and sunny days, and as long as the gardener provides water, these crops thrive during September and October. This dish takes advantage of the fact that these green vegetables peak

at the same time that the peppers ripen, the carrots planted in July are ready, and the garlic harvested in June is still at full flavor. Some years, sunflower seeds are dried and ready."

~ ELAINE EMERSON (ROSELAND, VA)

4 tablespoons olive oil
4 cloves garlic, minced
3 green onions (scallions), trimmed and thinly sliced
2 mildly hot chili peppers, such as Hungarian wax peppers, seeded and minced
2 or 3 small carrots, scraped and thinly sliced
2 cups thinly sliced broccoli florets
A generous handful of delicately textured but strongly flavored baby greens, such as arugula, mizuna, chicory, or turnip washed and drained (about 1 cup)
½ cup grated Gruyère or fontina cheese
1 tablespoon chopped fresh basil leaves or 1 teaspoon chopped fresh marjoram leaves
¾ pound spaghetti, fettuccine, or linguine, cooked, drained, and set aside in a warm place (see box on page 128)
¼ cup grated Parmesan cheese
2 slices bacon or pancetta, fried crisp and crumbled, for garnish (optional)
2 tablespoons oven-roasted sunflower seeds, for garnish (optional)

1. Heat 2 tablespoons of the olive oil in a large heavy skillet. Add the garlic, green onions, and chilies and sauté over medium heat until wilted, about 1½ minutes.

2. Add the remaining 2 tablespoons olive oil, the carrots, and broccoli. Continue cooking, stirring from time to time, until the vegetables are well wilted, about 8 minutes. Remove the pan from the heat. Spread the greens over the top and leave aside without stirring.

3. Sprinkle the Gruyère and basil or marjoram over the pasta. Spoon the vegetable mix over the top, add the Parmesan, and toss gently. Sprinkle a garnish over the top, if using, and serve.

The Garden at Any Time: Some Joys It Unfolds

A meander without aim.

A lackadaisical pull at weeds.

A look-see at what's there and what needs doing.

A place to expend energy in deep digging.

A place to sit and watch the birds, bees, and butterflies do their work to keep the whole thing going.

Tortellini with Pumpkin Alfredo

SERVES 4

When pumpkins have disappeared from the market after their short, fall-to-early-winter season, other hearty winter squashes, such as butternut, Kabocha, or acorn, may be substituted for this new-style traditional pasta dish.

MIMI FINDLAY, MIMI'S OCEAN GRILL (MAHONE BAY, NOVA SCOTIA, CANADA)

1½ cups cooked fresh pumpkin or other winter squash pulp (see box below)
8 tablespoons (1 stick) butter
1 shallot, minced
1 small leek, trimmed, halved lengthwise, thinly sliced, and washed
½ cup chicken broth (see page 86)
1½ cups heavy (whipping) cream
½ cup white wine
1 tablespoon fresh lemon juice
½ cup quality cream cheese
2 tablespoons finely chopped fresh sage leaves
½ teaspoon finely chopped fresh thyme leaves or ¼ teaspoon dried thyme
⅛ teaspoon ground nutmeg
½ teaspoon white pepper
1 teaspoon salt
1 tablespoon brandy
¾ pound fresh tortellini or other fresh stuffed pasta, cooked, drained, and set aside in a warm place (see box on page 128)
¼ cup hazelnuts, toasted (see box on page 135) and coarsely chopped
½ cup grated Parmesan cheese

1. Mash the pumpkin pulp in a food processor or with a fork and set aside.

2. Melt the butter in a large pot. Add the

Getting to the Heart of the Matter with Winter Squash

Under their tough and almost impenetrable shells, winter squashes yield a surprisingly sweet and tender pulp. Their softness can be got out in a number of ways.

BY BAKING: Wrap the squash in foil and bake in a preheated 350°F. oven until squeezable all the way through when pressed, 1½ to 2 hours. Remove and cool, then unwrap the foil. Cut the squash in half and spoon out the seeds. Scoop out the pulp and mash or cut up as needed. This method works best for winter squashes of 2 to 3 pounds.

If the squash is tender enough to cut through it without endangering your hands, save baking time this way: Halve the squash and scoop out the seeds. Place the halves, cut side down, on a baking dish. Add 1 inch of water to the dish and bake for about 1 hour, until soft all the way through.

BY BOILING OR STEAMING: If the squash is quite young and tender enough, halve it, scoop out the seeds, and pare away the skin. Boil or steam until tender, about 30 minutes.

BY MICROWAVING: Cut the squash in half. Place the halves, cut side down, in a microwave dish. Generously sprinkle with water to moisten well, cover with a microwave dish (partially is okay), and microwave for 30 minutes. Let rest for 5 to 10 minutes more, until cool enough to handle.

shallot and leek and sauté over medium-high heat until wilted, 2 to 3 minutes. Whisk in the broth, cream, wine, and lemon juice. Bring to a boil and cook over high heat for 2 to 3 minutes, until slightly thickened.

3. Add the cream cheese, sage, thyme, nutmeg, pepper, salt, brandy, and pumpkin purée. Bring to a boil, whisking to smooth, and remove from the heat.

4. Add the tortellini and gently mix. Sprinkle the hazelnuts over the top and serve, accompanied by the Parmesan on the side.

Pasta and Fresh Greens

SERVES 4

"Special thanks to Granny Vella, who introduced me to the idea of greens being served with pasta. You may choose to serve the pasta and greens either on a platter or in a soup bowl with the cooking liquid. Either way,, you must top the dish with the best Romano cheese available to you."

MELINDA HOLLINGSWORTH (BIRMINGHAM, AL)

2 pounds fresh greens, coarsely chopped, washed, and drained (see box below)
2 tablespoons minced garlic
8 cups chicken broth (see page 86)
¾ pound spaghetti, linguine, or fettuccine
½ cup grated Romano cheese

Eyeing the Greens

Greens suitable for pasta include chard, dandelion, kale, spinach, escarole, and Asian greens, such as tat soi or mitsu. Depending on the variety and age of the greens, the cooking time to tenderize the leaves before adding to the pasta will vary from three minutes for soft greens like spinach or baby tat soi to ten minutes for sturdier greens like dandelion or escarole. The only way to know for sure is the way of a gardener cook: keep an eye on the pot as you do on your plot.

1. Place the greens, garlic, and broth in a large pot. Bring to a boil over high heat, then simmer until the greens are tender, 3 to 10 minutes, depending on the greens. Remove from the heat but do not drain. Set aside in a warm place.

2. Cook the pasta until al dente. Drain briefly and transfer to a platter or large bowl. Ladle the greens along with a bit of their cooking liquid over the pasta. If you are serving the dish as a platter pasta, toss together the greens and pasta, top with the cheese, and serve. If you are serving the dish in a bowl as more of a soup, pour the rest of the pot liquid over the pasta and greens. Sprinkle the cheese over the top, and serve without tossing.

Soba Noodles with Swiss Chard, Ginger, and Pine Nuts

SERVES 4

"We started growing Swiss chard because it did well in containers that could be placed in sunny areas of our mostly shady yard. Now that we have a sunny garden, we use chard, both green and red, as a border plant for the beauty of its lush leaves. Also, it gives us a continuous supply of delicious, succulent leaves for much of the year and so has found its way into many of our recipes. This one is a favorite because it's nutritious, can be thrown together at the last minute, and always satisfies." It can be added that the chard seasoned with this blend of Mediterranean and Asian ingredients becomes a simple dish turned special and different enough to serve for company fare.

THELMA SNYDER (SOMERS POINT, NJ)

1 tablespoon olive oil
2 cloves garlic, minced
2 teaspoons chopped fresh ginger
¾ pound Swiss chard, cut crosswise into ½-inch strips, washed and drained (see box on page 140)
2 tablespoons soy sauce
8 ounces soba noodles (see Note below)
2 tablespoons pine nuts, toasted (see box on page 135)
Freshly ground black pepper
Crushed red pepper
½ cup grated Parmesan cheese (optional)

POT LIQUOR
The "pot liquor" called for in recipes is the vitamin-rich liquid flavored by the foods that have been cooked in it—the juices left in the pot. Though not alcoholic, pot liquor is nonetheless an elixir. It is cherished by cooks everywhere, who use it on beans, braised meats, and noodles that want a bit of moistening broth and extra taste just before serving.

1. Heat the oil in a large sauté pan. Add the garlic and ginger and stir over medium heat until beginning to brown, about 2 minutes. Add the chard and soy sauce and stir to mix. Cover the pan and continue cooking until the chard is wilted and tender, about 20 minutes.

2. Meanwhile, bring a large pot of water to boil. Add the noodles and cook until tender, about 3 minutes. Drain, reserving ½ cup of the cooking liquid. Stir the reserved liquid into the chard and divide the noodles among 4 bowls.

3. Spoon the chard and pot liquor (see page 141) over the noodles. Sprinkle the pine nuts, black pepper to taste, and a good pinch of crushed red pepper over the noodles. Serve right away, accompanied by the Parmesan cheese, if using.

Note: Soba noodles are available in Asian markets and in the international section of many supermarkets. Pasta shells also work for this recipe.

Vermicelli 101: Soba Noodles Unraveled

Soba noodles are thin buckwheat noodles, similar to Western-style vermicelli. Though both are long, thin noodles, the differences are considerable nonetheless.

Color: Soba are buff colored rather than creamy white like vermicelli.

Taste: Soba noodles, which are made from buckwheat, not a true grass have a more grassy taste than wheat vermicelli, which are made from a true grass.

Texture: When cooked al dente, soba noodles remain firm enough to use for cold noodle compositions whereas vermicelli are better used warm (choose another, less delicate noodle for pasta salad). Despite such differences, a harmony can be gathered out of the seeming cacophony, as in this recipe.

Linguine with Baby Clams in White Wine Sauce

Serves 4

"I often prepare meals late at night. I am certain that my neighbors are very curious about my nocturnal sojourns as I venture barefoot, scissors in one hand, a trug in the other, with my snake flashlight coiled about my neck. Linguine with baby clams, sparkled with fresh herbs, is one of my favorite quick meals from such garden forays. And, when the meal is done, the clam shells can be put back into the garden, hollow down, to keep out the weeds."

Deborah Jacobsen (Verona, NJ)

3 tablespoons olive oil
6 cloves garlic, minced or pressed
2 tablespoons chopped fresh chives
1 tablespoon chopped fresh parsley leaves, preferably Italian flat leaf
1 teaspoon chopped fresh basil leaves
1 bay leaf, preferably fresh
1 teaspoon fresh thyme leaves, especially lemon thyme
½ teaspoon chopped fresh dill
2 tablespoons butter
1 cup clam broth
1 cup white wine
2 dozen baby (Manila) clams, rinsed
¾ pound linguine, cooked, drained, and set aside in a warm place (see box on page 128)
½ cup grated Parmesan cheese

1. Heat the olive oil in a large nonreactive pot or sauté pan. Add the garlic and stir over medium heat until wilted, about 2 minutes. Add the herbs, butter, clam broth, and wine. Bring to a boil, reduce the heat, and simmer briskly for 10 minutes, or until the wine is no longer raw.

2. Add the clams, cover the pot, and cook over medium-high heat until the clams open, 5 to 10 minutes.

3. Place the linguine in a large serving bowl. Pour the clams, including the broth and herbs, over the top. Serve right away, accompanied by the Parmesan cheese

Note: Don't forget to accompany the dish with a bowl for collecting the empty shells, which will be recycled to the garden.

Clams Now and Later

Clam shells are not a good candidate for the compost bin. Tempting as it might be to add them, resist because they are animal matter that will beckon other animals not welcome in the pile. However, you can recycle them another way:

Faux-age the shells, either by drying them in the sun or in a microwave oven.

When they're dry as a bone, smash them with a hefty hammer, hard enough to break them into small pieces, small as time might have done on its own.

Then take the pieces to the garden and spread them on the ground of a bed that is momentarily resting between seasons.

When it's time to turn that bed for the next planting, shovel the shells into the earth and let the whole matter lie for the time you would for turning under any fallow crop.

Come time to plant, the shells will have added to the soil both their humus-building shards and their minerals.

Rotelle Pasta with Sautéed Shrimp and Nasturtium Seeds

SERVES 4 TO 6

"My favorite suppers are those inspired by a late-afternoon contemplation of my vegetable garden, a sort of instant cuisine. This is a fall recipe using Roma tomatoes fresh off the vine, leeks fattened up in their ranks, the last of the tarragon (a change from basil), and a handful of seeds from still-flowering nasturtiums."

WANDA MCCADDON (KENSINGTON, CA)

4 tablespoons olive oil
¾ pound large raw shrimp, rinsed, shells and tails left on
2 medium leeks, trimmed, coarsely chopped, and washed
6 cloves garlic, finely chopped
1½ pounds vine-ripened tomatoes, peeled and very coarsely chopped
2 teaspoons coarsely chopped fresh tarragon leaves
½ cup nasturtium seeds, rinsed (see Note below)
¼ teaspoon salt
¼ teaspoon black pepper
8 ounces rotelle, cooked, drained, and set aside in a warm place (see box on page 128)

1. Heat 2 tablespoons of the oil in a large nonreactive pot or sauté pan. Add the shrimp and sauté over medium-high heat until barely pink, about 2 minutes. Transfer the shrimp to a plate, leaving the oil in the pan.

2. Add the remaining 2 tablespoons oil, the leeks, and garlic and sauté over medium heat until well wilted but not browned, about 6 minutes. Transfer the leeks and garlic to the plate with the shrimp.

3. Add the tomatoes to the pan, raise the heat, and cook over medium-high heat until the liquid is reduced and the tomatoes are soft, about 8 minutes.

About Nasturtiums

If you're a gardener who has nasturtiums, you may occasionally have been tempted to call them "nasty-turtiums." While they're a delight for the cook, proliferating leaves for salads, flowers for garnishing, and bouquets for the table, once established, nasturtiums just won't quit. That means work and a little heartache for the gardener who must yank them out from time to time to make room for other plants. In the process, the hearty seeds spill around and about, easily germinate, and in the blink of an eye, they're new plants again. But, it's true, they are pretty plants and provide foliage and color at times when it seems not much else does. And the seeds, if you have the patience to collect them, can be used fresh in pasta dishes like the one here or pickled (see page 327).

4. Stir in the tarragon, nasturtium seeds, salt, and pepper. Add the shrimp, leeks, garlic, and any collected juices. Bring to a boil to reheat, then spoon over the warm pasta. Serve right away.

Note: You can substitute 2 tablespoons bottled capers, preferably large ones, for the nasturtium seeds.

Angel Hair Pasta with Grilled Shrimp

SERVES 4

"Out of our English-style vegetable garden, tomatoes are our most abundant crop. By the end of summer, we've always made new friends thanks to the overabundance of tomatoes given away in nicely arranged baskets. This grilled shrimp and tomato basil pasta is just one of the many meals we prepare at home with our own share of fresh tomatoes."

DENNIS COOK (MARIETTA, GA)

20 medium-size raw shrimp, shelled and deveined with tails left attached (about ¾ pound)
2 tablespoons olive oil, plus extra for coating the shrimp
5 cloves garlic, coarsely chopped
4 medium tomatoes, cut into ½-inch dice
3 tablespoons coarsely chopped fresh basil
1 teaspoon salt
¼ teaspoon black pepper
¾ pound angel hair pasta, cooked, drained, and set aside in a warm place (see box on page 128)

1. Prepare a charcoal fire.

2. Skewer the shrimp and brush with olive oil. When the fire is ready, place the shrimp on the grill and cook, turning once, until barely pink and firm to the touch, 3 to 4 minutes. Remove from the grill and take the shrimp off the skewers. Set aside in a warm place.

3. Place the 2 tablespoons olive oil and garlic in a large nonreactive sauté pan. Sauté for 1 minute, until the garlic wilts. Add the tomatoes and basil, cover the pan, and cook over low heat for 8 minutes until the tomatoes are soft. Stir in the salt and pepper and set aside in a warm place.

"No man but feels more of a man in the world if he have a bit of ground he can call his own. However small it is on the surface, it is four thousand feet deep; and that is a very handsome property."

—Charles Dudley Warner, *My Summer in a Garden*

4. Spread the pasta on a serving platter. Pour the tomato mixture over the top and arrange the shrimp over all. Serve right away.

Note: Instead of grilling the shrimp, you can sauté them in a little olive oil. The timing is the same.

Fettuccine Via d'Oro with Chicken, Mushrooms, and Basil Cream

Serves 4

Caffè Via d'Oro is situated in the heart of Sutter Creek, California, in the center of Amador County's gold country. Just as the charm of the town has established it as a destination for tourists following the gold rush trail, the restaurant has become a destination where dishes such as this chicken fettuccine can be enjoyed. The owners share the recipe here, plus a few professional tips (see box on page 147).

DEBORAH AND JERRY BUDRICK, OWNERS, CAFFÈ VIA D'ORO (SUTTER CREEK, CA)

"Basil, the Good Herb that from the window Blesses both the House and the Dishes."

—Greek saying

1 cup (packed) fresh basil leaves
3 cloves garlic, peeled and left whole
2 tablespoons pine nuts
⅓ cup plus 1 tablespoon olive oil
4 boneless, skinless chicken breast halves
Flour, for dredging the breasts
½ cup white wine
1 tablespoon chopped garlic
6 ounces mushrooms, stemmed and thinly sliced (½ to ¾ cup)
8 baby artichokes, trimmed to the hearts, cooked, and halved
2 cups heavy (whipping) cream
½ cup grated romano cheese
Salt and pepper
¾ pound fettuccine, cooked, drained, and set aside in a warm place (see box on page 128)
8 (¼-inch-wide) strips roasted red bell pepper, for garnish

1. Combine the basil, garlic cloves, pine nuts, and ⅓ cup of olive oil in a food processor and purée as smooth as possible. Set aside.

2. One at a time, place a chicken breast between 2 sheets of wax paper or plastic wrap and pound until evenly ¼ inch thick. Dredge the breasts in flour to coat each side.

3. Heat the remaining 1 tablespoon oil in a large sauté pan over high heat. Add the chicken breasts and brown on one side, about 2 minutes. Turn the breasts over, stir in the wine and chopped garlic, and add the mushrooms, artichoke hearts, basil mixture, and cream. Stir to distribute the ingredients evenly around the pan and bring to a boil. Simmer until the cream is thickened enough to coat a spoon, about 4 minutes. Turn off the heat.

4. Transfer the breasts to a cutting board and slice them into ½-inch-wide strips. Stir half of the cheese into the cream mixture and season with salt and pepper to taste.

5. Spread the fettuccine on a serving platter or on individual plates. Arrange the breast strips over the top and pour the sauce and other ingredients over. Sprinkle with the remaining cheese and garnish with the pepper strips. Serve right away.

It's in the Timing: Sauté Tips from the Pros

The sauté station in a restaurant is a study in rapid, coordinated activity with no wasted effort. Every move counts as the sauté cook almost literally throws together a dish over high heat in a matter of minutes. This means preparation. Each ingredient is measured out and set beside the stove, ready for its quick flash in the pan. It also means each element of the recipe that requires any ahead-of-time preparation—such as puréeing the basil with the pine nuts and oil, or precooking the roasted pepper strips or artichokes—be readied well in advance. In other words, the only thing left for the last minute is the sautéing.

—DEBORAH AND JERRY BURDICK

Arizona Pasta with Chicken, Lime, and Cilantro

SERVES 4

"Arizona Pasta is extremely simple and quick (something I appreciate during the summer when my husband and I are usually in the yard or garden until dark or sometimes after dark). I love cilantro and we can grow it easily in our garden at 6,300 feet where the nights stay relatively cool all summer. And don't all of us want another way to utilize the ever-abundant summer squash (something my father had the habit of saying was 'real good the first 40 days')! The recipe is wide open to variation, and is just as tasty when made without the chicken."

SARAH MCENANEY (PAYSON, AZ)

2 tablespoons butter or olive oil
1 to 2 large cloves garlic, minced
2 small summer squash, such as zucchini, crookneck, or pattypan, trimmed and julienned
1 cup heavy (whipping) cream
1 large red bell pepper, roasted, peeled, seeded, and julienned (see box on page 99)
2 tablespoons fresh lime juice
1 teaspoon minced lime zest
½ cup chopped cilantro leaves
1½ teaspoons salt
½ teaspoon black pepper
¾ pound boneless, skinless chicken breast, cooked (preferably grilled) and cut into ¼-inch-wide strips
¾ pound fettuccine or linguine, cooked, drained, and set aside in a warm place (see box on page 128)
½ cup grated Parmesan or Asiago cheese

1. Heat the butter in a large skillet. Add the garlic and squash and cook over medium heat until slightly softened, about 3 minutes.

2. Add the cream and bring to a boil. Stir in the bell pepper, lime juice, lime zest, cilantro, salt, pepper, and chicken. Continue cooking until heated through, about 1 minute.

3. Add the pasta, toss to mix, and serve right away, accompanied by the Parmesan on the side.

CUTTING YOUR CUCURBITS

All of the cucurbits—winter and summer squashes, melons, cucumbers, and so on—have very prickly leaves and stems. When gathering the fruit or flowers, wear gloves to protect your hands. Also, to save stress on the plant, cut the fruit and flowers off the vine with scissors; pinching or twisting them off will break the brittle stems and result in a smaller crop later on.

three pasta dishes especially for company

Sometimes, when company's coming and pasta is on the menu, rather than a quick toss, a more elaborate assemblage is called for. A pasta torta, a layered lasagne, a grand gnocchi roll, all require several steps and loving hands-on work. They are pasta ways to welcome special company to the table.

Pasta and Vegetable Torta

Serves 8 to 12

"This is a marvelous dish that my grandmother used to make; I presume it came from her native Tuscany." Resplendent with garden-fresh vegetables, it's also rich with cheese, eggs, cream, and olive oil. In other words, an indulgence. Recipe testers were so enticed by the look, aroma, and promise of having this dish on the table, a number of friends were invited for an impromptu dinner of it. All the better to make an occasion and thereby justify the indulgence.

DONALD J. FREDIANI (SAN FRANCISCO, CA)

¾ pound fresh or dried tagliarini or other favorite strandy pasta
3 tablespoons olive oil
1 medium carrot, finely chopped
2 small summer squash, trimmed and finely chopped
1 medium red bell pepper, stemmed, seeded, and finely chopped
4 green onions (scallions), trimmed and sliced into thin rounds
2 cloves garlic, minced or crushed
1 teaspoon salt
½ teaspoon black pepper
3 large eggs
2 cups heavy (whipping) cream
1 cup grated Parmesan cheese

1. Bring a large pot of water to a boil. Add the pasta and cook until limp but not done. Drain and set aside without bothering to keep warm.

2. Preheat the oven to 350°F.

3. Heat the oil in a large sauté pan. Add the vegetables, salt, and pepper and stir to mix. Sauté over medium-high heat, stirring often, until the vegetables are slightly soft, about 5 minutes. Remove from the heat and set aside.

Torta Tectonics

Constructing a vegetable torta does not call for rocket science, but there are some considerations to keep in mind.

The torta is basically a custard pie.

The custard needs all its eggs to rise high and light and not collapse into a pasta pancake. It also needs all its cream for the richness of the dish.

The custard is the lift that transports the vegetables from the bottom to other, higher realms of the torta. But it's a fragile lift, one that can't take too heavy a weight at a time. That means the vegetables should be kept to the same total cup amount as in the recipe, about three cups.

With that in mind, you can vary the vegetables as long as you choose from a list of not-too-watery ones, which would sog the custard, and cut them into small pieces so they don't weigh it down. For instance, depending on the season and your inclination, try:

- finely diced bits of green bean, asparagus, mushroom, potato, yam, turnip, rutabaga, celery root
- ribbons of shredded kale, arugula, dandelion, or watercress
- other colors of bell pepper, as well as different kinds of squash, also finely cut

4. Crack the eggs into a large bowl. Whisk in the cream and cheese. Add the pasta and vegetables and stir to mix. Pour the mixture into an ungreased 10 by 8-inch baking dish and bake for 40 minutes, until the top is slightly springy when pressed.

5. Cut the torta into squares, 8 to 12 depending on the number of people and whether serving as a first course or a main course. Serve right away.

Sweet Potato, Caramelized Onion, and Butternut Squash Lasagne

SERVES 8

"This recipe makes a wonderful use of the fall harvest and puts a delicious spin on a favorite classic." The contributor is clearly a spin meister with a new lasagne vision. Sweet potatoes are decidedly sweet, as are caramelized onions and roasted butternut squash.

~ JAMES HICKEY (MANCHESTER, MA)

1 pound lasagne noodles
Extra olive oil for coating the pasta, brushing the potatoes, and greasing the dish
2 medium sweet potatoes, peeled and sliced into ¼-inch-thick rounds (1½ pounds)
2 tablespoons butter
2 tablespoons olive oil
3 medium Spanish or other sweet onions, sliced into ¼-inch-thick rings
1 teaspoon sugar
1 large egg, lightly beaten
3 tablespoons chopped fresh basil leaves or 2 teaspoons dried basil
1 tablespoon chopped fresh oregano leaves or 1 teaspoon dried oregano
2 cloves garlic, minced
1 teaspoon salt
3 cups ricotta cheese
½ cup mixed grated Parmesan and Romano cheeses
½ pound butternut squash, cooked and mashed (see box on page 139)
1 pound mozzarella cheese, preferably fresh (see page 136), thinly sliced
Freshly ground black pepper

RAINBOW SPUDS
Red Potato
White Potato
Blue Potato
Yellow Potato
Sweet Potato
Yam
And more.

All are good for you.

1. Cook the pasta until al dente, drain, and coat with enough oil to keep the noodles from sticking. Set aside.

2. Preheat the oven to 475°F.

3. Spread the sweet potatoes in one layer on a baking sheet. Drizzle a little oil (about ¼ teaspoon) over the potatoes and turn to coat both sides. Bake for 15 minutes, until cooked and lightly golden. Remove and set aside. Reduce the oven heat to 375°F.

4. Melt the butter along with the 2 tablespoons oil in a large skillet. Stir in the onions and sugar and sauté over medium heat for 20 minutes, until soft and beginning to turn golden. Set aside.

5. Place the egg, basil, oregano, garlic, and salt in a large bowl and whisk together. Add the ricotta and grated cheeses and whisk to smooth. Add the squash and mix to blend well. Set aside.

6. To assemble the lasagne, lightly oil a 13 by 9-inch deep baking pan. Line the bottom with a layer of noodles. Spread some of the cheese and squash mixture over the noodles. Add a layer of sweet potatoes, then a layer of the onions. Top with a layer of mozzarella and sprinkle with black pepper to taste. Continue until all the ingredients are used and the top is a layer of onions lightly covered with mozzarella.

7. Bake for 1½ hours, or until bubbly and golden across the top. Remove and cool for 5 minutes. Cut into squares and serve.

Note: To take the dish in a more savory direction, you can substitute other potatoes, such as russets or Yukon Golds, roasted in the same way.

Lasagne-Making Tips

Making lasagne is a labor of love. It's also a kind of culinary architecture project. For ease, it's best to break down the steps and have ready the various building blocks required for each layer. Following is a game plan for putting together a lasagne no matter what you are using to fill the layers:

1. Prepare the sauce(s) and set aside.

2. Prepare the cooked ingredients and set aside.

3. Cook and oil the noodles so they don't stick together and set aside to cool.

4. Prep the other uncooked ingredients and have them ready in separate piles.

When assembled, the lasagne can be baked right away or set aside for a few hours without refrigeration. If you need to refrigerate the dish overnight, allow time to bring it back to room temperature before baking.

Spinach-Filled Gnocchi Rolls with Sweet Butter and Basil

Serves 8 to 10

Chooch, as he is always called, never James, was the chef at Berkeley, California's famed delicatessen Pig-by-the-Tail until it closed in 1986. Among his countless glorious creations, these gnocchi rolls were outstanding and one of the most popular. When they were announced on the menu for the next Friday, customers would arrive early or phone in to reserve theirs for the weekend's company. Chooch, always the generous chef, would graciously step away from the stoves for a minute to answer questions about how exactly to finish cooking them at home (the gnocchi were "fresh take-out"). To serve such a spectacular dish with the fillip it deserves, go Italian style and present the Parmesan in a block accompanied by a cheese shaver so the diners have truly freshly grated cheese.

~ JAMES ("CHOOCH") POTENZIANI (RICHMOND, CA)

1 pound spinach, coarsely chopped, washed, and drained
¾ cup ricotta cheese, drained
½ cup grated Parmesan cheese
½ teaspoon freshly grated nutmeg
¼ teaspoon black pepper
Salt
Potato Gnocchi Dough (recipe follows)
½ cup shredded fresh basil leaves
16 tablespoons (2 sticks) sweet butter, melted, skimmed, and kept warm
1½ cups shaved Parmesan (see headnote)

1. Place the spinach, still moist, in a large nonreactive pot and stir over medium heat until wilted, about 5 minutes. Drain again and set aside until cool enough to handle.

2. Squeeze dry the spinach, wrap it in a cloth towel, and squeeze dry again. Purée the spinach in a food processor or mince with a chef's knife. Combine with the ricotta, grated Parmesan, nutmeg, pepper, and salt to taste. Set aside.

3. Prepare the gnocchi dough. When ready to use, divide into 6 balls. On a floured board, roll each out into a 6-inch circle about ¼ inch thick. Spread ¼ cup of the spinach mixture down the center and roll up the dough, enclosing the filling. Wrap each roll in cheesecloth and tie the ends with kitchen string. Set aside briefly until ready to cook or refrigerate up to overnight.

4. Bring a large pot of water to a boil. Drop in the gnocchi rolls and simmer briskly over medium-high heat for 20 minutes, until the dough is cooked through. Transfer to a colander and let drip dry for 10 minutes.

5. To serve, unwrap and cut each gnocchi into 6 rounds. Arrange the rounds on a serving platter, cut sides up, sprinkle the basil over the top, and pour the butter over. Serve right away, accompanied by the shaved Parmesan on the side.

Note: It is important to drain the ricotta cheese and squeeze the spinach well so that the filling will be as dry as possible.

"Sweet butter can only come from the udder of a sweet cow that has been sweetly milked."

—Old farm saying

Potato Gnocchi Dough

MAKES ENOUGH FOR 6 LARGE GNOCCHI ROLLS

2 pounds russet potatoes, scrubbed
2 cups all-purpose flour
1½ teaspoons salt
2 egg yolks
2 tablespoons butter, melted

1. Cook the potatoes in a large pot of water until done enough to pierce easily to the centers, 30 to 40 minutes, depending on the size. Drain and set aside until cool enough to handle.

2. Peel the potatoes and place them in a large ungreased skillet. Dry over low heat, turning frequently, for 30 minutes, until a skin forms. Set aside to cool again.

3. Peel away the dry skin. Rice the potatoes into a large bowl (or place them in a bowl and mash with a fork or potato masher). Add the flour and salt and make a well in the center. Drop the egg yolks into the well and, with your hands, work the yolks together with the dry ingredients. Work the butter into the dough a little at a time.

4. Knead the dough on a floured surface for 10 minutes. Set aside to rest for 30 minutes. Use right away, or wrap in plastic wrap and store in the refrigerator for up to overnight. Bring to room temperature before using.

Butter: Its Ways and Means

There's probably not a way to settle once and for all the controversy over sweet (or unsalted) versus salted butter. For table use, sweet butter, the more freshly churned the better, is undeniably the choice. For pastry cooks, sweet butter is almost always preferred. It has the disadvantage that after a while, five days or so, it becomes rancid tasting. That means, if you truly prefer sweet butter, you should use it within a week or store it in the freezer. For cooks who work more with savory dishes, salted butter is fine. It has the advantage that the salt keeps it fresher for longer and so it doesn't require so much attention and sniffing to test its acceptability each day.

The gnocchi recipe exhibits both butter considerations: Salted butter for the dough does quite well; sweet butter is essential for the basil-butter sauce.

pasta salad

Pasta, not hot for the first course or the dinner but cold or room temperature for, well, whatever potato and macaroni salads are for. What a concept. But it turns out that pasta salads are now so popular, they are almost de rigueur for picnics, buffet tables, student cafés, and deli takeout. Following is a special selection of contributors' recipes for new wave pasta salads and two of the good old, still-loved macaroni salads, all with a spark from the garden and a graceful touch.

"Don't hang noodles on my ears."

—Russian saying

Tomato, Basil, and Arugula Pasta Salad

SERVES 4

"This is a favorite recipe of our family and friends—perfect for a hot summer evening when the tomatoes are ripe, the basil is taking over the garden, the arugula is not to be ignored, and the cook wants an easy few minutes in the kitchen."

GLORIA DOUGHERTY (LAKE BLUFF, IL)

4 large tomatoes, cut into ½-inch dice
3 cloves garlic, minced or pressed
1 cup (packed) arugula leaves
3 tablespoons shredded fresh basil leaves
¼ teaspoon crushed red pepper
2½ tablespoons balsamic vinegar
⅓ cup olive oil
Salt and pepper
½ pound penne
½ cup grated Parmesan cheese

1. Toss the tomatoes, garlic, arugula, basil, crushed red pepper, vinegar, oil, and salt and pepper to taste in a large serving bowl. Set aside to marinate at room temperature for at least 1 hour or up to 3 hours.

2. Cook the penne al dente, drain briefly, and add to the tomato mixture. Add the cheese. Toss and serve without chilling.

Pasta Salad with Linguine, Tomatoes, and Brie

Serves 4

Brie cheese is a new darling of the American table. Easily meltable, its creamy unguence flows beyond the buffet into a divine pairing with tomatoes for an unchilled pasta salad. In case anyone wants more cheese, there's Parmesan called for to sprinkle on the top.

DONA HERRING (BLOOMFIELD HILLS, MI)

6 large tomatoes, peeled and coarsely chopped into ½-inch pieces
1½ cups shredded fresh basil leaves
4 cloves garlic, minced
1 pound Brie cheese, rind removed, cheese coarsely cut or torn into 1-inch pieces
½ cup olive oil
1 teaspoon salt
½ teaspoon black pepper
¾ pound linguine
½ cup grated Parmesan cheese

1. Place the tomatoes, basil, garlic, Brie, oil, salt, and pepper in a large serving bowl. Toss to mix and set aside at room temperature for at least 2 hours or up to 3 hours.

2. When ready to serve, cook the linguine to the al dente stage. Drain briefly, add to the tomato mixture, and toss gently. Sprinkle the Parmesan over the top and serve right away.

FRESH GREEN BEANS

Haricots Verts
Romano
Blue Lake
Kentucky
Yellow wax
Purple
Scarlet Runners

The flowers of all are beautiful and the flavor and texture of each are distinctive.

Pasta Salad with Herbs, Green Beans, and Feta

SERVES 6 TO 8

Small, whole green beans and whole cherry tomatoes make this salad a pretty picture. But at the end of summer, when the green beans have got away from rigorous daily picking and grown a bit large, cut them into two-inch lengths before cooking; and if the cherry tomatoes are on the large side, cut them in half for easier eating.

ANN PILCHER (JAMESVILLE, NY)

¾ pound small green beans
¾ pound pasta, preferably fusilli
⅔ cup olive oil
¼ cup red wine vinegar
1 large clove garlic, minced or pressed
1 teaspoon Dijon mustard
Salt and pepper
1½ cups cherry tomatoes, stemmed (about 8 ounces)
⅓ cup black olives, preferably oil-cured, pitted and cut in half (see box on page 131)
2 tablespoons finely chopped fresh basil leaves
2 tablespoons chopped fresh chives
2 teaspoons minced fresh oregano leaves
⅔ cup crumbled feta cheese

1. Bring a large pot of water to boil. Add the green beans and cook over high heat until slightly softened but still bright green, 3 to 4 minutes. With a slotted spoon, remove the beans to a colander and set aside.

2. Bring the water in the pot back to a boil. Add the pasta and cook until slightly softer than al dente. Drain in the same colander with the green beans, shake to dry a bit, and transfer the beans and pasta to a serving bowl. Set aside.

3. Meanwhile, whisk together the oil, vinegar, garlic, mustard, and salt and pepper to taste to make the dressing.

4. Add the tomatoes, olives, herbs, cheese, and dressing to the beans and pasta. Toss to mix and serve right away.

Dauber's Pasta Salad with Fresh Basil and Parsley Dressing

Serves 6 to 8

"This is a recipe that evolved from my overzealous planting of basil and parsley. By midsummer, having lots and lots of 'stuff,' I needed to find a way to use both of my favorite herbs. I dug out an old recipe, modified it, and created my favorite pasta salad. As my husband loves it and now helps me every spring plant extra basil and parsley for more dressing, I suppose you could call it Dauber's Pasta Salad."

ANN AND DAUBER FEYEN (WILLIAMSTON, MI)

1 pound rotini or other short chunky pasta, such as bow-ties, penne, or rigatoni, cooked and drained
1 cup cooked chickpeas (see Note below)
2 medium tomatoes, finely chopped
¾ cup Fresh Basil and Parsley Dressing (recipe follows)
3 to 4 green onions (scallions), trimmed and minced (see right)

Place the pasta in a large bowl. Add the chickpeas, tomatoes, and dressing and toss to mix. Sprinkle the green onions over the top and serve.

Note: Chickpeas add a special Mediterranean touch to this pasta salad. If you don't care to take the trouble of cooking up a batch, you can use ready-to-go canned chickpeas. The low sodium, organic products now available closely resemble cooked-from-scratch chickpeas.

Fresh Basil and Parsley Dressing

Makes ¾ cup

1 cup (packed) fresh basil leaves
1 cup fresh parsley leaves
2 to 3 cloves garlic, to taste
3 teaspoons sugar
¼ cup red wine vinegar
½ cup vegetable oil
¼ cup grated sharp Italian cheese, such as Parmesan, Romano, or Asiago

Place all the ingredients in a food processor and blend thoroughly. Use right away or store in the refrigerator for up to several hours, but no longer, or the freshness will be lost.

SPRING ONIONS

Green onions, spring onions, and scallions have some botanical differences, but for garnishing they all do the job in a fresh and sprightly way.

Pasta Salad Fresca à la Smith & Hawken

SERVES 4 TO 6

"My husband, Tim, was the warehouse manager at the Smith & Hawken Berkeley store during his college years. I loved picking him up so I could spend a few minutes drooling over the beautiful plants. Our first acquisition was a 4-inch pot of lemon marjoram and we soon added thyme, oregano, and a number of mints to our little patio garden. Every time we moved, we schlepped our potted (mobile) herb garden with us. When we finally bought a house, the grandest moment was 'de-potting' and placing our edible favorites in the ground. That's when we knew we were home. This salad captures the delicate flavors of lemon marjoram and basil and is ready in a snap."

ALEXANDRA EISLER (KENSINGTON, CA)

5 cloves garlic, coarsely cut
1 teaspoon salt
1 pound mixed ripe fresh tomatoes, such as golden cherries, Sweet 100 cherry tomatoes, and other heirloom types you have available, cut into ½-inch pieces
½ cup coarsely chopped lemon basil leaves
¼ cup coarsely chopped lemon marjoram leaves
½ teaspoon sugar
2 teaspoons black pepper
⅓ cup olive oil
1 pound fresh bow-tie pasta or ¾ pound dried bow-tie pasta (see box below)
¼ cup pine nuts, lightly toasted (optional, see box on page 135)

1. Place the garlic and salt on a cutting board and chop together until the garlic is minced. Transfer to a large serving bowl, add the tomatoes, lemon basil, lemon marjoram, sugar, pepper, and oil, and toss to mix. Set aside.

2. When ready to serve, cook the pasta until al dente, or a little softer if using dried pasta. Drain and add to the tomato mixture. Add the pine nuts, if using, and toss gently to mix. Serve right away at room temperature, but do not refrigerate.

How to Tie a Fresh and Perky Pasta Bow

Although fresh bow-tie pasta (farfalle) is nigh on to impossible to find ready-made, it's easy enough to make your own if you have a market that sells fresh pasta. Simply purchase 1 pound of fresh pasta, requesting that it be cut into 2-inch-wide ribbons. To make the bow-ties, place a ribbon on the counter, cut into 2-inch squares (a serrated pastry cutter makes nice edges, but it's not necessary), and pinch each square into a bow-tie. Transfer the bow-ties to a lightly floured plate, turn to coat, and set aside until ready to cook. Will keep for 30 minutes or so.

Garden Macaroni Salad

Serves 8 to 10

Here, macaroni salad, an established, almost essential offering in American delis and on summer picnic buffets, takes on fresh meaning when made with garden ingredients.

❧ CONNIE SMITH (KERNERSVILLE, NC)

8 ounces elbow macaroni, cooked, drained, and cooled to room temperature (see box on page 128)
1 teaspoon salt
1 medium cucumber, seeded (see Note below), and cut into ¼-inch dice
2 large celery ribs, trimmed and cut into ¼-inch dice
½ small green bell pepper, stemmed, seeded, and cut into ¼-inch dice
2 green onions (scallions), trimmed and minced
1 medium tomato, cut into ¼-inch dice, juices set aside for another dish (see Note below)
½ teaspoon black pepper
¾ cup mayonnaise (see page 64)
¼ teaspoon minced fresh basil leaves

Place all the ingredients in a large bowl and toss to mix. Cover and chill in the refrigerator for at least 2 hours or up to 2 days. Serve cold.

Note: It's important to seed the cucumber and also to leave aside the tomato juices after dicing. Otherwise, the salad will be too watery.

Picnic-Time Macaroni Salad with Boiled Dressing

Serves 6 to 8

"I've enjoyed gardening for over 40 years. I am enclosing a recipe for a picnic, cookout, or summer family meal." The classic boiled dressing can also be used to sauce a chicken, potato salad, or blanched vegetables such as broccoli or asparagus.

❧ MARION HICHWA (WEST REDDING, CT)

4 ounces macaroni, cooked and drained
3 large hard-cooked eggs
½ cup finely chopped onion
½ cup finely chopped celery
½ cup finely chopped green bell pepper
1 medium carrot, scraped and coarsely grated
2 tablespoons chopped fresh parsley leaves
Salt and pepper
⅔ cup Boiled Dressing (recipe follows)

Place all the ingredients except the dressing in a medium bowl and toss gently to mix. Pour the dressing into the bowl and toss again. Cover with plastic wrap and chill. Serve cold.

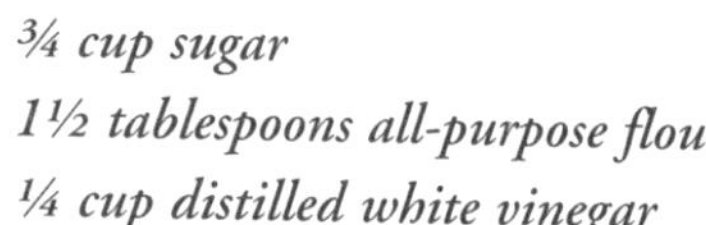

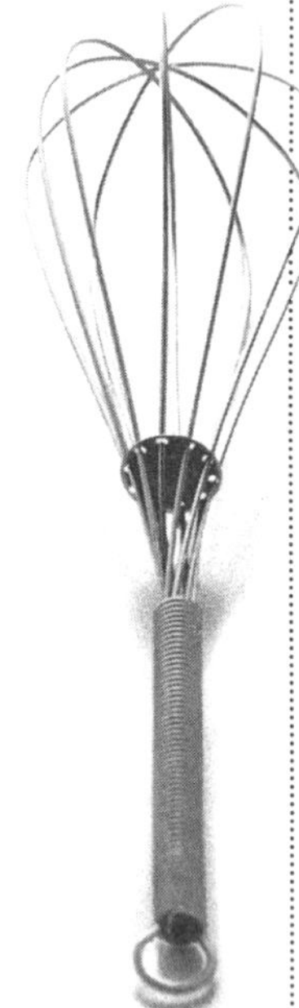

Boiled Dressing

MAKES 1¼ CUPS

¾ cup sugar
1½ tablespoons all-purpose flour
¼ cup distilled white vinegar
¾ cup water
1½ tablespoons Dijon mustard
½ cup mayonnaise

1. Whisk together the sugar, flour, vinegar, and water in a small saucepan. Bring to a boil and, still whisking, cook over medium to medium-high heat until translucent and thick but still fluid, about 2 minutes. Remove from the heat and set aside to cool.

2. Add the mustard and mayonnaise and whisk until smooth. Use right away or store in the refrigerator for up to 1 week.

main dishes:

the garden path to a nourishing meal

A basket of sparkling fresh zucchini and tomatoes turned into either a meal tart or a tomato-topped frittata accompanied with grilled zucchini rafts. The leaves from the run-amok kale sautéed to round out a dish of grain noodles. Roses in full bloom rethought as seasoning and garnish for a chicken breast dish. A warming lamb stew for company prompted by too many pumpkins in the garden patch. A quick seafood sauté triggered by tender new potatoes, tiny artichokes, and a fish fillet so fresh it still wafts of the sea. Delight after refreshing, well-seasoned delight, the recipes in this chapter demonstrate how gardeners and cooks create main dishes based on what the garden provides and the exuberance and inspiration elicited by those provisions.

Handy Gadgets for the Gardener Cook

In the haste of modern life, many of the previously standard, small kitchen tools to aid in freshly prepared food have been relegated to the back of the drawer, if not to a box in the basement. But these gadgets could be reconsidered for modern times. Such objects include:

APPLE CORER: Though seldom needed these days because whole, cored apples are seldom called for, it is nonetheless a good instrument for reaming summer squash to be stuffed whole for an entree.

CHERRY PITTER: While you may think you will never need one, when that certain cherry pie or cherry jam calls you, there's no easier way to remove the cherry pits.

CORN SCRAPER: Still useful, especially if you prepare lots of dishes that call for corn off the cob (see page 122).

EGG SLICER: Truly old-fashioned because the egg slices that, de rigueur, garnished many a salad are out of favor. Still, it's a fascinating gadget and works for neatly slicing beets as well as hard-boiled eggs.

GARLIC PRESS: Many say only mincing garlic with a chef's knife will do; don't believe it. Sometimes a press is better to release more juices.

HAND GRATER: There's no way any instrument, including the food processor and all its many blades, can replace it. Better to keep this one in the cupboard, not on the antique shelf.

LEMON ZESTER: This one you can put away and switch to a vegetable peeler to remove the zest, then cut or chop it into the size you'd like for the dish.

MALLETS: A hammer-like metal mallet with a wide, flat head, one side smooth for pounding chicken breasts or veal scallopini and the other pronged for cubing steak. These days, the pronged side is not so called for, but the flat side is still a good instrument for flattening chicken breasts.

A small wooden mallet, easier on the torque of the wrist and elbow and generally lighter to hand, also works for all pounding needs. It is especially useful for pitting olives (see page 131).

MELON BALLER: As with a cherry pitter and apple corer, you might think you would never use it, but when you are putting together a fruit salad for a summer party or carving potato balls for a fancy winter stew, you'll be happy to have one.

PASTRY BLENDER: Not that necessary for pastry dough, which can just as well be put together with your hands, but very useful as a substitute for a potato ricer.

POTATO RICER: There's no better way to get fluffy mashed potatoes.

PUMPKIN KNIFE: There is no better tool for carving pumpkins safely. If you are preparing a pumpkin for supper (page 139), use a pumpkin knife. For Halloween, if you have many pumpkin carvers, have one pumpkin knife per person.

VEGETABLE PEELER: Supremely handy for lemon zest as well as for potatoes and other vegetables.

Squash Blossom and Baby Squash Frittata with Asiago Cheese

SERVES 2

"We tend a special garden at our ranch/bed-and-breakfast inn in the Reno–Carson City area of Nevada. Watered from a running desert spring that feeds our pond, it's on the site that once was used by truck farmers to grow their crops and then transport the produce up Deadman's Canyon and Jumbo Grade to feed the miners on the Comstock. That was during the mining boom in Virginia City. Today still, the garden flourishes. We plant early varieties of each vegetable and always keep tarps at the ready for unseasonal frosty nights—freezing temperatures and snow flurries can occur any month of the year. We manage to have tomatoes, corn, and lots of other warm-weather fresh produce for the seasonal table at our bed-and-breakfast inn." Especially compelling are the brilliant yellow squash blossoms that entice the gardener to pluck a few and hie to the kitchen to stir up a frittata featuring them. For other delightful ways to use squash blossoms, see pages 11 and 73.

DAVID AND MUFFY VHAY, DEER RUN RANCH BED AND BREAKFAST (CARSON CITY, NV)

4 large eggs
1 tablespoon milk
1 tablespoon chopped fresh parsley leaves
2 tablespoons butter
2 green onions (scallions), trimmed and thinly sliced
2 baby yellow or green summer squash, trimmed and thinly sliced
6 to 8 squash blossoms, rinsed, patted dry, and quartered
¼ cup coarsely grated aged Asiago cheese

1. Preheat the broiler.

2. In a medium bowl, beat together the eggs, milk, and parsley. Set aside.

3. Heat the butter in a nonstick sauté pan suitable for the oven. Add the green onions and squash and sauté over medium heat just until soft, about 2 minutes.

4. Stir in the squash blossoms, then immediately add the egg mixture. Gently stir to mix and continue cooking over medium heat until almost set, about 3 minutes.

5. Sprinkle the cheese over the top and transfer to the broiler. Broil until lightly puffed and golden on top, about 30 seconds. Serve right away.

Sweet Spring Frittata

SERVES 4 AS AN ENTREE, MORE AS AN APPETIZER

"In the spring when the farmers' markets abound with tiny baby artichokes, Yukon Gold potatoes, and tender, sweet onions, I always whip up this frittata. It gets its fragrant aroma from the fresh rosemary and parsley plucked from my herb garden."

TARA PALEN (FLUSHING, NY)

Fun with Frittatas

A frittata is basically a baked omelet. As with any omelet, the ingredients can be varied with any of the herbs, vegetables, cheeses, or other elements that naturally go with eggs. Remembering to keep the herbs well chopped and the size of the other bits small, in addition to the ingredients called for in the frittata recipes in this book, try:

FOR THE HERB: Cilantro, dill, fennel frond, mint, nutmeg geranium, tarragon.

FOR THE VEGETABLE: Asparagus, cactus pads, chard, garlic or onion flower, mushroom, especially chanterelles or porcini, okra, shallot, spinach, spring garlic, sprouts (bean, pea, onion, radish, or sunflower).

FOR THE CHEESE: Aged gouda, aged Jack, dry ricotta, feta, kefalotyri, manchego, Prince de Claverolle, queso asadero, sharp white cheddar.

FOR THE MEAT: Bacon or pancetta, cooked crisp; ham; sausage, cooked.

Unlike an omelet, a frittata, standing higher and cooked longer, allows more leeway in the cooking method. Here's how to suit frittata cooking to your equipment:

You can adjust any of the frittata recipes for however many you are serving. Be sure to adjust the pan size so the frittata turns out puffy and tender, not hard and flat as a pancake. For an 8-egg frittata, enough to serve 4 to 6, use a large pan; for a 4-egg frittata, enough to serve 2 to 3, use a medium-size pan; for a 2-egg frittata, enough for yourself alone or 2 very modest eaters, use a small pan.

No matter the size, either a nonstick or lightly greased nonreactive pan that can move from stovetop to oven or broiler is essential. That means the handle of the pan must be heatproof. If the only pan you have is plastic- or wood-handled, wrap it in two layers of heavy-duty foil and choose the stovetop-to-broiler method for cooking the frittata (see below).

For the cooking of the frittata, some like to bake all the way; others like to start the cooking on the stovetop and finish off under the broiler. There's not much difference in the outcome except the moment under the broiler results in a browner top.

However you've flavored and cooked your frittata, keep in mind its other serving possibilities. Frittatas are also delicious at room temperature or even chilled. Slice ribbon-thin and use to garnish rice dishes. Or slice into small wedges and decorate with a bit of sauce for an appetizer. Fun sauce accompaniments include:

- a dab of any of the pestos (see pages 308–312).
- a smidgen of any of the tomato sauces (see pages 293–296).

2 tablespoons olive oil
¾ pound Yukon Gold potatoes, sliced ¼ inch thick
6 baby artichokes, dark green outside leaves pulled off, tops cut off down to the light green, and quartered
2 small sweet onions, such as Vidalia, Maui, or Walla Walla
2 large cloves garlic, coarsely chopped
5 large eggs
¼ cup grated Parmesan cheese
¼ cup grated Monterey Jack cheese
1 tablespoon minced fresh rosemary leaves
⅓ cup finely chopped fresh Italian parsley leaves
1 teaspoon salt
½ teaspoon black pepper

1. Preheat the oven to 375°F.

2. Heat the oil in a 9- to 10-inch ovenproof skillet. Add the potatoes, turn to coat, and sauté over medium-high heat until lightly browned, about 10 minutes. Add the artichokes, onions, garlic, and 3 tablespoons water and stir to mix. Cover the pan and cook over medium heat until the artichokes are tender, about 8 minutes.

3. Meanwhile, lightly beat the eggs in a medium bowl. Beat in the cheeses, rosemary, parsley, salt, and pepper.

4. Pour the egg mixture over the vegetables in the skillet and continue to cook, shaking from time to time, until the bottom is lightly browned, about 10 minutes. Transfer the skillet to the oven and bake until the top is lightly golden and set but not hard, 8 to 10 minutes more. Serve right away or at room temperature.

Tomato-Topped Summer Frittata

Serves 6

"The first year I moved to Ashland, Oregon, located in the sun-blessed Rogue Valley, I was overwhelmed with the bountiful baskets of bright red and yellow, large, small, and pear-shaped tomatoes. Since I own and operate a small bed-and-breakfast inn, the main meal I cook is breakfast. Putting together the gorgeous tomatoes and breakfast turned into my favorite offering: this tomato frittata. It's easy to make, is a beautiful presentation, and tastes delicious." The recipe testers add that it brings summer sun to the table, whether at breakfast, lunch, or dinner time.

~ NANCY JACOBSEN, ASHLAND VILLAGE INN (ASHLAND, OREGON)

8 large eggs
1 tablespoon cold water
Pinch of salt
Pinch of black pepper
3 tablespoons butter
½ cup finely chopped onion
½ cup finely chopped bell pepper, red, green, or yellow
3 medium tomatoes, sliced ⅛ inch thick (about ¾ pound)
½ cup grated romano cheese

1. Preheat the broiler.

2. Crack the eggs into a bowl, add the water, salt, and pepper, and whisk until mixed. Set aside.

3. Melt the butter in a large nonstick ovenproof skillet. Stir in the onion and pepper and sauté over medium heat until beginning to brown, 3 to 4 minutes.

4. Add the eggs and stir gently to mix. Continue cooking over medium heat until the eggs begin to set around the edges and bottom. Gently push the edges into the center while softly swirling the pan so that the uncooked portion flows under the more cooked center. Continue cooking until the eggs are almost set all the way through but still moist across the top, 2 to 3 minutes.

5. Arrange the tomato slices over the top and sprinkle with the cheese. Transfer the skillet to the broiler and cook until the cheese melts and the top is golden, 1 to 2 minutes.

6. To serve, cut into wedges. For a more elegant presentation, slide the whole frittata onto a serving platter and slice at the table.

BROWNING ONION AND BELL PEPPER THE ITALIAN WAY
First browning the onion and pepper until golden is an Italian way to add depth of flavor in an otherwise quickly cooked dish. It's an important step for the outcome, and one that brings frittata back to its ethnic origin.

Frittata al Giuseppe

SERVES 5 TO 6

"The desire to send along this recipe was a combination of my love of indoor gardening and my passion for Italian food. I have limited space in my studio, so I decided to raise herbs. Six of my favorites, basil, rosemary, sage, thyme, sweet marjoram, and Italian parsley, are included in a simple, open-faced baked omelet that showcases the rewards of my garden." As a side treat to accompany the frittata, the contributor offers a tiny tale about each of the herbs included *(see box on page 167).*

JOSEPH ALVARADO (CHICAGO, IL)

2 tablespoons olive oil
1 medium leek, white part only, thinly sliced, washed, and dried
1 tablespoon minced garlic
8 large eggs
Salt and pepper
½ cup grated Parmesan cheese
½ cup chopped prosciutto
1 cup mixed chopped fresh basil, rosemary, sage, thyme, sweet marjoram, and Italian parsley, leaves only (see Note below)

1. Preheat the oven to 350°F.

2. Heat the oil in a 10-inch nonstick ovenproof skillet. Add the leek and garlic and cook over medium heat until wilted, about 3 minutes.

3. Crack the eggs into a bowl and beat until blended. Add the remaining ingredients and stir to mix. Pour the mixture into the pan with the leek and garlic and stir to mix. Place the pan in the oven and bake until puffed and no longer runny on top, about 20 minutes. Slice into wedges and serve.

Note: When mixing the herbs, it's best to go light with the rosemary and sweet marjoram, as both are assertive herbs that drown out other flavors and tend to taste medicinal when too much is used.

Guiseppe's Herb Lore

Basil: The ancient Greeks and Romans believed that basil would not germinate unless the seeds were cursed at while being sown.

Rosemary: It is claimed that rosemary is good for digestion and stimulates the circulation.

Sage: Years ago, sage was mainly used as a remedy for coughs, colds, and fever.

Thyme: Throughout history thyme has been associated with strength and happiness.

Sweet marjoram: Dried and ground marjoram was once popular as snuff.

Parsley: Besides its other good qualities, parsley is rich in vitamin C.

Garlic: Though thought of as a vegetable today, garlic was originally believed to be a strengthening herb.

New Mexico Chard Enchiladas

Serves 4

"Our El Rancho Nido de las Golondrinas is a certified organic farm where we grow a variety of produce for farmers' markets and restaurants in Albuquerque and Santa Fe. This recipe is an adaptation of the enchiladas I grew up eating in northern New Mexico,

where we layer, instead of roll, our enchiladas. They're especially delicious with blue-corn tortillas. To make them authentically New Mexican, serve with a fried egg on top!"

CECILIA ROSACKER-McCORD (LEMITAR, NM)

4 medium tomatoes, coarsely chopped (about 1 pound)
3 cloves garlic, coarsely chopped
½ medium onion, coarsely chopped
6 dried New Mexico chilies, stemmed, seeded, and torn into coarse pieces
1 to 2 cups hot water
2 tablespoons vegetable oil
1 medium onion, finely chopped
3 cloves garlic, finely chopped
1 bunch Swiss chard, tough stems removed, leaves coarsely chopped, washed, and dried (about ¾ pound)
12 corn tortillas, preferably blue corn
1½ cups grated Jack or cheddar cheese
4 fried eggs (optional)

1. Preheat the oven to 350°F.

2. Place the tomatoes, coarsely chopped garlic, coarsely chopped onion, dried chilies, and 1 cup of hot water in a food processor. Blend until as smooth as possible, adding a little more water if necessary to make a liquid paste. Set aside.

3. Heat the oil in a large sauté pan. Add the finely chopped onion and garlic and sauté over medium heat until golden, 6 to 8 minutes. Add the chard and stir over medium-high heat until well wilted but not soft, about 2 minutes. Stir in the tomato purée and cook until thickened, 8 to 10 minutes.

4. Place 4 tortillas without overlapping on a jelly-roll pan. Spread each with enough sauce to cover. Sprinkle grated cheese over the sauce. Top with another tortilla, spread with sauce, and sprinkle with cheese. Continue layering until you have 4 stacks 3 layers high, with sauce and cheese on the top.

5. Place in the oven and bake until the cheese on top is melted, about 5 minutes. Serve right away, topped with a fried egg on each enchilada, if you'd like.

Tomato-Chili Purée: An Easy Entry to Mexican and Southwestern Cuisine

The tomato-chili purée in the New Mexico Chard Enchiladas recipe is a concoction with wide applications in Mexican and Southwestern cooking. As is, it enriches the broth for many soups. It gets cooked into a reduction that becomes the foundation for many of the more elaborate sauces in those cuisines, most notably red mole. As is again, it automatically turns itself into the sauce for moistening enchiladas. With the aid of a food processor, the purée can be whipped up in a snap. It can be refrigerated for up to 4 days.

Tri-Color Sweet Pepper Quiche

SERVES 4 TO 6

In an exuberant accolade to Smith & Hawken, this contributor exclaims: "I am the owner of a landscape design firm in San Francisco. You are a great resource for us. Your products have a wonderful way of blending the beautiful with the practical, which is exactly what our designs strive for."

HEATHER HARDCASTLE, BREAKING GROUND LANDSCAPES (SAN FRANCISCO, CA)

One 10-inch Easy Tart Crust (recipe follows)
4 tablespoons olive oil
3 medium bell peppers, preferably one each of red, yellow, and orange, stemmed, seeded, and thinly sliced into ⅛-inch-wide strips
¼ cup dry white wine or water
Salt
1 cup (loosely packed) fresh basil leaves
2 tablespoons grated Parmesan cheese
2 whole eggs plus 2 egg yolks
1 cup half-and-half
½ cup heavy (whipping) cream
1 cup grated provolone cheese
½ cup pitted and chopped kalamata olives (optional)

1. Prebake the tart crust as directed on page 170 and set aside.

2. Preheat the oven to 400°F.

3. Heat 2 tablespoons of the olive oil in a large sauté pan. Add the peppers and sauté over medium-high heat, stirring occasionally, until the peppers are well wilted but not browned, about 10 minutes.

4. Lower the heat to medium and stir in the wine and a pinch of salt. Continue cooking until the peppers are soft but not browned, about 15 minutes more.

5. While the peppers cook, put the basil, Parmesan cheese, and remaining 2 tablespoons of oil in a food processor or blender and purée as fine as possible. Set aside.

6. Whisk together the eggs and yolks in a bowl. Add the half-and-half, heavy cream, and about ½ teaspoon salt and whisk to smooth.

7. To assemble the quiche, spread the basil purée across the bottom of the crust. Top with half of the provolone, then all of the peppers. Dot the olives, if using, over the peppers. Spread the remaining provolone over the peppers and pour in the egg and cream mixture.

8. Bake for 40 to 45 minutes, or until a knife inserted in the center comes out clean and the edges of the crust are very golden. Remove and let rest for 10 minutes, then serve.

Easy Tart Crust

MAKES ONE 10- TO 12-INCH TART CRUST

1½ cups all-purpose flour
¼ teaspoon salt
8 tablespoons (1 stick) butter, at room temperature
2 to 2½ tablespoons water

1. Place the flour and salt in the bowl of a food processor. Cut in the butter and pulse several times until the mixture resembles coarse meal. Continue to pulse while adding the water 1 tablespoon at a time until the dough adheres to itself when pinched.

2. Gather the dough into a ball and set the ball on a sheet of plastic wrap. Cover with another sheet of plastic wrap and roll the dough into an 11- to 13-inch circle. Remove the top sheet and turn the dough into a 10- to 12-inch tart or pie pan, pushing gently into the corners and up the sides. Place in the refrigerator to chill before baking, up to overnight. If chilling overnight, remove from the refrigerator 30 minutes before baking.

Note: The dough can also be mixed by hand. You will need slightly more water with this method.

Prebaking the Crust for Quiches and Savory Pies

For quiches and savory pies that have a moist filling and short cooking time, the crust should be prebaked until golden so the pie turns out with a crispy, not soggy, bottom. To prebake a pie crust:

1. Have the rolled-out crust slightly chilled.

2. Preheat the oven to 425°F.

3. With a fork, prick all across the bottom of the crust and bake until beginning to puff up on the bottom, about 12 minutes.

4. Gently prick the bottom again to allow steam to escape. If the sides are beginning to collapse, press them up with the fork. Bake for 10 to 12 minutes more, until the crust is golden on the bottom and around the edges.

5. Remove and continue with the recipe, either right away or after the crust has cooled a bit but not longer than 1 or 2 hours and never chilled.

Sweet Onion Tart

SERVES 4 TO 6

"Spring always makes people in New England think of less heavy foods. This onion tart, delicious with a mixed salad and a glass of white wine, leads you to enjoy the season" and have a full meal in a light way. Cut into small wedges, the tart is also a delightful addition to an appetizer plate or buffet table. In keeping with the fresh spirit of the occasion, make your own pie crust from the selection on pages 413–418.

~ RITA McDONOUGH (MANCHESTER, NH)

One 10- to 12-inch Easy Tart Crust (page 170), preferably in a removable bottom tart pan, prebaked
2 tablespoons olive or vegetable oil
1½ pounds sweet onions halved and thinly sliced (see box at right)
2 large eggs
1 cup heavy (whipping) cream
⅛ teaspoon ground nutmeg
¼ teaspoon salt
⅛ teaspoon black pepper

About Sweet Onions

There are some who consider onions, that is, sweet onions, as good as apples for eating out of hand or, better yet, for slicing to top well-buttered bread. Lost as such a butter-frosted, onion-garnished bread delight may be in our modern, weight-conscious world, the thought and taste of bread, butter, and onions should not be lost. To have the treat in a more streamlined way, butter the bread ever so thinly, then pile on the sweet onions. Onions that will do for such a basic treat and for a sweet onion tart are Vidalias, Mauis, Walla Wallas, and Mayan Sweets.

Almost any other globe onion, white, red, or yellow, pulled directly from the garden and sliced right away, also works well. These are better if sprinkled with a little salt and allowed to sit for 15 minutes to mellow any inherent sharpness.

1. Prepare the tart crust and set aside.

2. Preheat the oven to 325°F.

3. Heat the oil in a large sauté pan. Stir in the onions and sauté over medium to low heat until very soft and beginning to caramelize, about 20 minutes. Remove and set aside.

4. Whisk together the eggs, cream, nutmeg, salt, and pepper in a small bowl.

5. To assemble the tart, spread the onions across the crust. Pour in the egg-and-cream mixture. Without stirring, place in the oven and bake for 35 to 40 minutes, or until the top is golden and a toothpick inserted in the center comes out clean.

6. Remove and cool slightly, then serve right away or at room temperature.

PICNIC PIES

If you're taking a pie to a picnic, it should be transportable, that is, sturdy enough to take the ride without collapsing and not in need of a refrigerator to keep it fresh for a few hours. Good choices include Sweet Onion Tart (page 171); Tomato, Basil, and Cheese Pie (page 172); Tomato-Zucchini Tart (page 173); and Kale Pie (page 174).

Tomato, Basil, and Cheese Pie

SERVES 4 TO 6

As the contributor exclaims, "This recipe is simply delicious. It's our favorite late-August dish here at Peace & Plenty Farm." Combining cottage cheese and fresh basil with what is essentially a savory custard works marvelously to provide a cushy filling for the fresh tomato slices that complete the dish.

ANN MORGAN CAMPBELL, PEACE & PLENTY FARM (LANGLEY, WA)

One 10-inch Easy Tart Crust (see page 170), prebaked
3 large tomatoes, sliced ⅜ inch thick (1½ pounds)
Salt
1 cup (firmly packed) fresh basil leaves
½ cup small-curd cottage cheese
2 large eggs
½ cup coarsely grated or chopped mozzarella cheese
½ cup grated Parmesan cheese
Oil, for brushing tomatoes on top of the pie

1. Prepare the tart crust and set aside.

2. Preheat the oven to 375°F.

3. Lightly sprinkle the tomato slices with salt on both sides. Set the slices on paper towels to absorb the liquid as the slices drain. Set aside.

4. Place the basil, cottage cheese, and eggs in a food processor and blend until well combined. Add the mozzarella, Parmesan, and ½ teaspoon salt and continue blending until well mixed.

5. To assemble the pie, pat the tomato slices dry and line the bottom of the pie shell with the end pieces. Spoon the cheese mixture over them and spread to smooth. Arrange the remaining tomato slices in one overlapping layer over the top of the cheese mixture. Brush the top layer of tomato slices with a little oil and place the pie in the oven.

6. Bake until the edges of the crust are crispy and golden and the cheese mixture is firm enough that a knife inserted in the center of the pie comes out clean, 50 to 60 minutes. Remove and let cool for about 15 minutes before slicing. Serve warm, at room temperature, or cover and store in the refrigerator and serve the next day.

Tomato-Zucchini Tart in Potato Crust

SERVES 4 TO 6

Here is an innovative way to respark your interest in putting to good use all that crop of tomatoes and zucchini at the end of summer. A potato crust, essentially a potato pancake baked in a pie tin, serves to underpin the layers of vegetables and cheese. The zucchini slices, tucked within the layers, remain pleasingly al dente but cooked enough to absorb the garden flavors surrounding them.

BONNIE BERGSTROM (WEST DES MOINES, IA)

One 10-inch Potato Crust, prebaked (recipe follows)
2½ cups grated white cheddar, Swiss, or provolone cheese
2 medium zucchini, trimmed and thinly sliced (8 to 10 ounces)
2 large tomatoes, thinly sliced (1 pound)
½ small onion, finely chopped
1 tablespoon chopped fresh basil leaves or 1 teaspoon dried basil
1 tablespoon chopped fresh oregano leaves or 1 teaspoon dried oregano

1. Prepare the crust and bake while preparing the filling.

2. Spread the bottom of the crust with one-third of the cheese. Place a layer of zucchini slices over the cheese, overlapping them to cover well. Next, arrange a slightly overlapping layer of tomato slices over the zucchini. Lightly sprinkle the tomatoes with another third of the cheese. Continue with a second layer in the same order, ending up with tomatoes.

3. Sprinkle the top layer of tomatoes with the onion, basil, and oregano. Finally, spread the remaining third of the cheese over the top. Bake for 45 minutes, or until the top is golden. Serve right away.

Note: Although the pie is best hot out of the oven, you can hold it for a while if you're willing to sacrifice the crispiness of the bottom crust. To do so, cut out a small wedge and transfer it to a small plate (that's the cook's treat). Prop up the pie tin with a spoon or saucer, setting it so that the juices releasing from the tomatoes converge at the point where you've removed the slice. Drain off the collected juices and serve.

Fresh Facts for Zucchini: Storage and Preparation

"If you're using zucchini in a custard or egg batter, salt and set the pieces in a colander to drain for 30 minutes. This removes the excess liquid that would turn the dish watery.

"For salads and stuffed zucchini dishes, very briefly blanch the vegetable first. This process cooks the zucchini slightly to bring out its flavor while leaving it crisp.

"To keep zucchini fresh for a few days, refrigerate it in a plastic bag. Left out, it will wilt."

—CATHERINE ZAJAC (LITIZ, PA)

KALE

Kale is a leafy member of the huge brassica family that includes cabbages and mustard greens, among dozens of others. Kale is easy to grow. Plant some in a sunny to partly shady part of the garden or in a large pot set in a place that receives the same kind of light. Water regularly, but don't drown it. Pick the small, tender leaves for salads; harvest the larger leaves for cooking and use as you would spinach or chard. Make kale pie.

Potato Crust

MAKES ONE 10-INCH PIE CRUST

2 cups grated raw russet or Idaho potato, squeezed as dry as possible (see Notes below)
1 small onion, very finely chopped
1 egg, lightly beaten
¼ cup all-purpose flour
½ teaspoon salt
Vegetable oil, for greasing the pie tin

1. Preheat the oven to 375°F.

2. Combine the potato, onion, egg, flour, and salt in a medium bowl, and mix well. Oil a 10-inch pie pan and transfer the mixture to it, spreading evenly across the bottom and up the sides, as for a pastry crust.

3. Bake until well browned around the edges, about 30 minutes. Remove, fill, and bake right away.

Notes

• Russet (Idaho) potatoes are essential for this crust. The waxy red or white potatoes will not crisp properly.

• It's important to go directly from the making and baking of the crust to the filling and baking of the pie. Otherwise, the bottom becomes soggy and tough.

Kale Pie

MAKES ONE 10-INCH PIE

Not exactly a quiche, nor a soufflé, nor a spanakopita, this dish brings together all those cooking classics in one good pie, here doubly good from its healthful, tasty kale leaves (see left).

MADGE KHO (SOMERVILLE, MA)

One 10-inch Easy Tart Crust (see page 170), prebaked
4 cups coarsely chopped kale leaves, washed and drained (about 8 ounces)
1 tablespoon olive or other vegetable oil
2 small onions, finely chopped
3 cloves garlic, minced
2 large eggs
1 cup crumbled feta cheese
½ cup half-and-half
½ teaspoon salt (optional)

1. Prepare the tart crust and set aside.

2. Preheat the oven to 375°F.

3. Bring a large pot of water to a boil. Add the kale, stir to submerge the leaves, and cook over high heat until wilted and somewhat tender but still bright green, about 3 minutes. Drain and set aside to drip dry.

4. Heat the oil in a medium sauté pan. Add the onions and garlic and sauté over medium heat, stirring frequently, until beginning to turn golden, about 6 minutes. Remove from the heat and set aside.

5. Break the eggs into a large bowl and lightly beat. Add the feta, half-and-half, kale, onion mixture, salt, if using. Stir to mix and pour into the prebaked crust. Bake until the center of the pie is firm and lightly golden across the top, 40 to 45 minutes. Remove and allow to cool 10 to 15 minutes. Serve while still warm, or let cool longer and serve at room temperature.

Polenta-Crowned Kale Casserole

Serves 4 to 6

Under a soft polenta crust, the sturdy texture and sweet flavor of kale shine forth. The mushrooms in the casserole make for a heartier dish if you are serving this for a main course. For a lighter side dish, the mushrooms may be omitted.

BETTY ANN BEAUCHAMP (RESCUE, CA)

2 tablespoons olive oil
3 cloves garlic, finely chopped
1 medium onion, finely chopped
2 ounces shiitake or portobello mushrooms, stemmed and thinly sliced
1 to 1½ pounds kale, tough stems removed, leaves coarsely chopped, rinsed, and drained
3 medium tomatoes, coarsely chopped (¾ pound)
1½ teaspoons salt
1 cup polenta or cornmeal
½ cup grated Parmesan cheese

POLENTA ON ITS OWN

Steps 4 and 5 on page 176 give you a perfect, creamy polenta. You can serve it on its own, perhaps with the cheese stirred in; top it with any fresh vegetable sauce; dollop it around poultry or game dishes; or have a lovely breakfast of corn porridge.

1. Preheat the oven to 350°F.

2. Heat the oil in a large sauté pan. Add the garlic, onion, and mushrooms and stir to mix. Add the kale, tomatoes, and ½ teaspoon of the salt. Without stirring, cover the pan and cook over medium heat until the kale is wilted well below the top of the pan, about 5 minutes.

3. Stir to mix the kale with the other ingredients in the pan, cover again, and continue cooking for 5 minutes more, or until the kale is well wilted. Transfer the mixture to a large baking dish or ovenproof casserole and set aside.

4. Meanwhile, bring 4 cups of water to a boil in a medium saucepan. Place the polenta, the remaining 1 teaspoon salt, and another cup of water in a medium bowl and whisk to smooth.

5. Pour the polenta mixture into the boiling water and whisk to mix. Reduce the heat to medium to maintain a simmer and cook, stirring often, until the polenta is thick and stirs easily away from the sides of the pan with bubbles rising from the center as you stir, about 20 minutes (see box at left).

6. Pour the polenta over the vegetables in the casserole, spreading evenly. Bake for 30 minutes, or until the polenta forms a crust and shows a few golden specks across the top. Sprinkle the cheese over the top and serve right away.

Polenta in the Microwave

Polenta may also be prepared in a microwave oven. Combine the polenta, salt, and 3 cups of water in a large microwave bowl. Microwave, uncovered, on high for 3 minutes, until beginning to thicken. Stir and continue microwaving, uncovered, on high for 3 to 5 minutes more, until as stiff as you want, keeping in mind that polenta thickens as it cools.

Warm-Weather Potato Casserole with Tomatoes and Summer Herbs

SERVES 6 TO 8

For those who love old-fashioned scalloped potatoes, here's a new-fashioned, dressed-up version. With its cheeses and ample seasonings, it's a dish robust enough to serve as a main course. Accompany it with a salad for a lazy summer lunch in the yard or a light supper after a day's gardening. Waxy type potatoes, either red or white, are preferable for this casserole because they hold their shape in the cooking, whereas russets collapse.

LINDA BERGSTEINSSON (PALO ALTO, CA)

2 tablespoons olive oil
4 tablespoons (½ stick) butter
2 medium onions, thinly sliced
2 cloves garlic, minced or pressed
8 medium tomatoes, peeled, seeded, and chopped into ¼-inch pieces (2 pounds)
2 tablespoons chopped fresh parsley leaves
2 teaspoons chopped fresh basil leaves or ½ teaspoon dried basil
1 teaspoon chopped fresh oregano leaves or ¼ teaspoon dried oregano
1½ teaspoons salt
½ teaspoon black pepper
2½ pounds white or red potatoes, peeled and sliced ⅛ inch thick
1 cup grated Swiss cheese
2 tablespoons grated Parmesan cheese

1. Preheat the oven to 325°F. Lightly grease a 13 by 9-inch ovenproof casserole.

2. Heat the oil and 2 tablespoons of the butter in a large sauté pan. Add the onions and garlic and sauté over medium heat until the onions are transparent, about 8 minutes.

3. Stir in the tomatoes, parsley, basil, oregano, salt, and pepper and remove from the heat without further cooking.

4. Spread one-third of the onion-tomato mixture in the bottom of the casserole. Arrange half the potato slices over that, followed by half the Swiss cheese and Parmesan. Repeat, finishing with the last third of the onion-tomato mixture. Dot the top with the remaining 2 tablespoons of butter.

5. Bake for 1½ hours, or until the potatoes are very tender. Serve right away or cool slightly first.

Note: Don't be tempted to rush the baking time. As with all scalloped potato dishes, it takes that long for the potatoes to soften and combine with the other seasonings.

The Glory of Growing Plenty: A Grand Story from a Backyard Gardener

"As a novice gardener, I always plant my basil and tomatoes together, and I'm very impressed with the size of the caterpillars that enjoy my tomato plants almost as much as I do. Fortunately, there is usually enough for all of us, and I can make tomato and basil salad to my heart's content."

—SARAH STEINHOUR (MASON, MI)

Crookneck Custard Casserole

Serves 4

"My late grandmother instilled in me a love for gardening. 'Othermother,' as we called her, lived to be 98 and missed very few days of inspecting her garden. Instead of scolding me when I picked flowers, she encouraged my wonder and delight in the flowers' beauty and taught me how colors, sizes, and textures complement each other in little bouquets. She also delighted in teaching me to recognize when produce was ripe and ready to pick. In her vegetable garden there was always yellow crookneck squash. I would like to share one of Othermother's recipes for using it. When I prepare it (which is often), it brings back wonderful memories of a truly wonderful lady."

BEBE BEASLEY WILLIAMS (COLUMBIA, AL)

8 to 10 medium crookneck squash, trimmed and sliced into ½-inch-thick rounds (2 pounds)
2 large eggs, lightly beaten
4 tablespoons (½ stick) butter, melted
½ cup milk
1 small onion, finely chopped
2 tablespoons finely chopped fresh parsley leaves
2 tablespoons sugar
1 teaspoon salt
¼ teaspoon black pepper
1 cup coarse bread crumbs, preferably homemade (see page 76)
1 cup grated melting cheese, such as white cheddar or Gruyère
2 strips bacon, sliced crosswise into 1-inch-wide sections, cooked crisp, and crumbled (see box at left)

1. Preheat the oven to 350°F. Lightly grease a 12 by 8-inch ovenproof casserole.

2. Bring a large pot of water to a boil. Add the squash and cook over medium-high heat until barely wilted, about 2 minutes. Drain and set aside.

3. Combine the eggs, butter, milk, onion, parsley, sugar, salt, and pepper in a large

Bacon Byways

It's easy enough to crisp bacon for topping salads, adding to a sauce, or crumbling onto casseroles. Here are two ways to have the real thing.

QUICK AND EASY: Place a paper towel on a large microwave plate. Arrange the bacon slices over the towel in one layer. Cover the bacon with another paper towel. Microwave on high for 2 to 5 minutes, depending on the thickness of the bacon and the number of pieces, until crispy. Check every 30 seconds or so after the first 2 minutes to make sure the bacon is crisping without burning. Remove, cool, and crumble as needed.

SLOW AND STEADY: Place the bacon slices in a heavy skillet and sauté on medium-high heat, turning occasionally, until cooked and browned all the way through. It will take 15 to 25 minutes, depending on the thickness and amount of bacon. Transfer to a paper towel to drain and cool. Crumble as needed.

bowl. Add the squash and mix. Transfer the mixture to the casserole. Sprinkle the bread crumbs, cheddar, and crumbled bacon over the top. Bake for 35 minutes, or until the top is golden and crunchy. Serve right away.

Farmers' Market Casserole with Bread-Cube Topping

SERVES 6

"I have a small vegetable garden along with a variety of herbs. This casserole is a wonderful way to take advantage of its produce, different varieties each year, my own small farmers' market." The generous splash of white wine adds a touch of elegance to the staples of the summer garden, and the homemade buttery bread cubes, along with the cheese, bring the various vegetables together in a delectable dish that is substantial enough for an entree.

~ MARY ANN ECKSTROM (CHICAGO, IL)

1½ pounds potatoes, any kind, peeled and sliced ⅛ inch thick
1 large onion, thinly sliced
2 medium zucchini, cut into ¼-inch pieces (½ pound)
3 large tomatoes, cut into ¼-inch pieces (1½ pounds)
2 carrots, scraped and thinly sliced
1 tablespoon fresh thyme leaves
1 teaspoon chopped fresh marjoram leaves
1 teaspoon salt
¼ teaspoon black pepper
¾ cup dry white wine
3 tablespoons butter
1 cup small (¼-inch) fresh bread cubes
2 cups grated sharp cheddar cheese

1. Preheat the oven to 375°F.

2. Layer the vegetables in an ungreased 11 by 8-inch casserole in the order listed, sprinkling each layer with thyme, marjoram, salt, and pepper as you go. Pour the wine over all, cover with foil, and bake for 1 hour, or until the carrots are almost tender and the juices are bubbling nicely.

3. Melt the butter in a small sauté pan over medium heat. Add the bread cubes and stir until they absorb the butter, about 1 minute. Remove and set aside.

4. Uncover the casserole and spread the cheese, then the bread cubes, over the top. Continue baking, uncovered, until the cheese melts and the bread cubes are browned, 15 to 20 minutes. Serve right away.

Gratin of Potato and Summer Squash with Herbes de Provence

SERVES 4

Though there are dozens of ways to combine squash and other vegetables in a casserole, here the Provençal herb seasoning and unpeeled red potato for color contrast make this gratin stand out from the ordinary. It's a dish suitable for a potluck picnic, luncheon, or light vegetarian supper.

MICHELE DUNCAN (EDMONDS, WA)

¼ cup olive oil
2 cloves garlic, peeled
3 medium zucchini or yellow squash, sliced ⅛ inch thick (about ¾ pound)
1 pound red potatoes, scrubbed and sliced ⅛ inch thick
1 large onion, thinly sliced
2 teaspoons herbes de Provence (see box below)
1 teaspoon salt
¼ teaspoon black pepper
¼ cup grated Parmesan cheese

1. Preheat the oven to 350°F. Lightly grease a 12 by 9-inch baking dish.

2. Combine the oil and garlic in a small pot and simmer together for 2 minutes. Set aside for 15 minutes for the garlic to infuse the oil. Remove and discard the garlic.

3. In the baking dish, make 2 layers of the zucchini, potatoes, and onion, sprinkling each layer with the herbes de Provence, salt, and pepper. Top with the cheese and drizzle the oil over.

4. Cover the dish with foil and bake for 1 hour, or until the potatoes are tender. Let stand for 10 minutes, then serve right away or at room temperature.

Herbes de Provence

Herbes de Provence is a mix of herbs typical of the Provençal landscape: rosemary, thyme, sage, summer savory, bay, lavender flowers, and fennel seed. You can find the mix packaged in charming small crocks in gourmet food shops. But, if you have some or all of the same herbs in your garden, you can dry them and make a mix ever so much more flavorful and aromatic. Use the above herbs in the ratio of one to one of each except the fennel seed and lavender—use less or they will predominate.

Eggplant Sandwich Casserole

Serves 4

"After 38 years of marriage, I wanted to try cooking. My wife finally let me into the kitchen because these are so-o-o good. The beauty of the dish is that because the eggplant rounds are layered like sandwiches, the servings can be individually spooned out." What more need be said? Except the contributor did have more to say, in the form of a garden story; see box below.

GARY BLAZIS (MARSTONS MILLS, MA)

3 medium globe eggplants, trimmed but not peeled, sliced into ½-inch-thick rounds
Coarse salt
Olive oil, for browning the eggplant
1 cup tomato sauce (see page 293)
1 cup coarsely grated mozzarella cheese
¼ cup grated Parmesan or romano cheese
⅓ cup coarse bread crumbs, preferably homemade (see page 76)

1. Generously sprinkle both sides of the eggplant slices with salt. Set aside in one layer to sweat and wilt for at least 1 hour. Rinse and pat dry each piece and set aside.

2. Preheat the oven to 350°F. Lightly grease a 13 by 9-inch baking dish.

3. Heat ⅛ inch of oil in a large frying pan until beginning to smoke. Add as many eggplant slices as will fit in one uncrowded layer and fry over medium-high heat until soft and golden brown on both sides, about 6 minutes altogether. Transfer to a plate and continue with another round, adding more oil as needed, until all the slices are browned.

4. Arrange half the eggplant slices in the baking dish, overlapping if necessary. Spread half the tomato sauce over the slices, then sprinkle all the mozzarella over the top. Make another layer with the remaining half of the eggplant slices and cover with the remaining sauce. Top with the Parmesan and then the bread crumbs.

Living with the World: A Modern Tale

"My very first garden after retirement was to be the perfect garden I had always dreamed of. When the outdoor stage was set and all my favorite vegetables planted, I stood back and admired my work. The next morning, lo and behold, all the leafy vegetables were gone. I imagined all the critters giggling with glee from their hidden bushes as they'd watched me create their new 'gourmet restaurant.' The next step was a wire fence. The problem was not solved. Some little creatures still dug under the fencing to dine in style! However, we figured, if they are that determined, so be it. We plant enough so there's plenty for all of us."

—GARY BLAZIS

5. Bake for 25 to 30 minutes, or until the juices are bubbling up and the bread crumbs are nicely browned. Serve right away or at room temperature.

Note: If you don't happen to have homemade bread crumbs on hand, you can substitute crumbled cracker crumbs (see page 244). You can also omit the crumb topping altogether, but that sacrifices the crunch that adds punch to the dish.

FRIED EGGPLANT SANDWICHES
For those who are passionate about eggplant, beyond a casserole, a gratinée, and a rollatine, there is an eggplant sandwich. To make one, slice the eggplant, dust the slices with flour, then dip them in beaten egg. Fry in hot oil until golden and crisp, turning once. Serve the slices sandwiched in bread, with or without mayonnaise, as you prefer.

Eggplant-Tomato Gratin

SERVES 8

In a lively variation on the theme of eggplant Parmesan, a mix of wilted onions, raw tomatoes, and chopped fresh herbs replace the more traditional cooked tomato sauce. Olives and capers tucked in with the tomatoes verify the Mediterranean origin of this newly classic dish.

DEBRA ABBOTT (DALLAS, TX)

Olive oil
3 medium globe eggplants, peeled and sliced into ½-inch-thick rounds
2 medium onions, sliced ¼ inch thick
2 large cloves garlic, finely chopped
4 large tomatoes, peeled, coarsely chopped, and drained (about 2 pounds)
¼ cup mixed chopped fresh herb leaves, such as oregano, basil, parsley, and/or thyme
8 kalamata olives, pitted and chopped
2 tablespoons capers, rinsed and coarsely chopped if large, left whole if small
¼ teaspoon black pepper
Salt
2 cups coarsely grated mozzarella cheese
½ cup grated Parmesan cheese
1 cup coarse bread crumbs, probably homemade (see page 76), browned in 2 tablespoons butter

1. Preheat the oven to 350°F. Lightly grease a 13 by 9-inch baking dish.

2. Generously grease a large skillet with the oil and heat until beginning to smoke. Add as many eggplant slices as will fit without crowding and sauté, turning once, until golden on both sides, about 6 minutes altogether. Transfer to a plate and continue with another round, adding more oil as necessary, until all the slices are browned.

3. In the same skillet, add enough oil to make about 3 tablespoons. Stir in the onions and garlic and cook over medium heat until wilted but not browned, about 8 minutes. Remove from the heat and stir in the tomatoes, herbs, olives, capers, and pepper. Taste and add salt if needed. Set aside.

4. Arrange half the eggplant slices in the baking dish, overlapping if necessary. Spread half the onion-and-tomato mixture over the slices. Sprinkle half the mozzarella and half the Parmesan over the onion-and-tomato mixture. Make another layer in the same way, ending with cheese. Top with the bread crumbs.

5. Bake for 40 minutes, or until the cheese is very bubbly and the bread crumbs are quite browned. Remove and let cool slightly, then slice and serve.

Eggplant Rollatine Camille

SERVES 4

"The eggplants from our garden are always a favorite with vegetarians. This recipe was developed in an effort to accompany the homemade cheese ravioli with a dish that would accommodate our non-meat-eating friends, in Italian style." Eggplant rollatine can also provide a main dish for anyone who would like to dine lightly, not so much with the whole huzzah, but still with buon gusto. Along with a fresh salad and an honest loaf, they make a generous dinner in Italian, and garden, style.

CAMILLE DILISSIO (MORRISVILLE, PA)

1 large globe eggplant, trimmed, peeled, and cut lengthwise into ¼-inch-slices (see Notes below)
1½ teaspoons coarse salt (see box on page 184)
¾ cup olive oil
1 large shallot, finely chopped
1 large clove garlic, finely chopped
8 ounces fresh mushrooms, stems trimmed, caps wiped, and finely chopped (see Notes below)
¼ teaspoon black pepper
½ cup dry white wine
¾ cup grated Parmesan cheese
¾ cup coarse bread crumbs, preferably homemade (see page 76)
½ cup tomato sauce (see page 293)
⅓ cup shredded mozzarella cheese

1. Sprinkle both sides of the eggplant slices with salt and leave aside in one layer for 30 minutes, until sweating and slightly wilted. Rinse and pat dry the slices and set aside.

2. Preheat the oven to 350°F.

3. Heat ¼ cup of the oil in a large sauté pan. Add as many eggplant slices as will fit in one layer and sauté over medium heat until lightly browned on both sides, about 2 minutes altogether. Transfer the slices to paper towels to drain. Continue with another round, adding more oil as necessary, until all the slices are browned.

4. Add the shallot and garlic to the pan and sauté over medium heat until beginning to brown, about 3 minutes. Stir in the mushrooms and pepper and continue cooking until the liquid has evaporated but the mushrooms are still moist, 3 to 5 minutes.

5. Turn up the heat to medium-high and, when the ingredients in the pan are sizzling, add the wine. Stir to mix and continue cooking for 5 minutes more, until the alcohol has burned off. Remove from the heat and stir in the Parmesan and bread crumbs. Set aside.

6. Coat the bottom of a 13 by 9-inch nonreactive baking dish with a thin layer of the tomato sauce.

7. Spread a ¼-inch-thick layer of the mushroom mixture over each eggplant slice. Roll up each and place in the baking dish. When all the slices are filled, rolled, and arranged in one layer in the dish, spread the remaining tomato sauce over the top. Sprinkle on the mozzarella and bake until the cheese has melted and the sauce is bubbly, 15 to 20 minutes.

8. Remove and let cool for 5 minutes, then serve while hot.

Notes

• It's important to have a very large eggplant for this dish so that the slices are long and broad enough to fill and roll up.

• The fancier the mushrooms, the more flavorful the filling. Commercial mushrooms also work to provide a whiff of forest in this already well-seasoned dish.

Salt Savvy

Salt in the form of coarse crystals is the salt of choice for purposes such as wilting eggplants, dry-curing meats, or salt-baking because it does the job without dissolving into the flesh and is easy to rinse off. You can find it as *gros sel,* packaged in convenient-size cylindrical boxes imported from France, available in most upscale supermarkets.

Rock salt, an American pantry staple when homemade ice cream was a part of summer and salting the sidewalk a part of winter, will also do, though its larger crystals should be crushed a bit for this particular use. The taste difference is subtle, though apparent to salt aficionados: *gros sel* is a sea salt, more refined and softer in taste than rock salt, which is a mined salt and a bit harsher in flavor.

In addition, lately chefs have become attracted to the salt "blossoms" harvested off the coast of Normandy. It's true that those salt crystals are softly, saltily divine. They are also expensive.

Garden Celebration Risotto with Basil-Walnut Pesto

Serves 2

"This risotto is a fresh, light way to use several of the different summer vegetables your garden is offering in one dish. It's the perfect thing if, like me, you have a small garden that gives you just a few of each vegetable at each picking." Since California enjoys a long growing season with many microclimates—even in one backyard—you might well find carrots still in the ground and squash burgeoning before the asparagus and peas disappear for the summer. If your growing region is more seasonally limited, follow the contributor's advice and use what you have to celebrate the garden pickings. "It's delicious with any combination of vegetables except tomatoes, and you can serve those surplus tomatoes sliced fresh on the side."

JUDY WARREN (LOS ANGELES, CA)

8 ounces carrots, trimmed, scraped, and cut into ¼-inch-thick rounds
8 thin asparagus stalks, cut into ½-inch lengths
½ cup shelled peas
2 small summer squash, trimmed and cut into ½-inch dice
4 cups chicken broth (see page 86)
1 tablespoon olive oil
1 medium leek, trimmed, finely chopped, washed, and drained
1 heaping cup Arborio or good-quality pearl rice
¼ cup Basil-Walnut Pesto (recipe follows)
2 cups finely shredded spinach leaves, washed and drained
½ teaspoon salt
½ cup freshly grated Parmesan cheese (optional)

"But for one grain of rice, I would be hungry tonight."

—Japanese saying

1. Bring a medium pot of water to a boil. Drop in the carrots and cook over high heat until almost soft, about 3 minutes. Add the asparagus, peas, and squash. Bring to a boil again and cook until the asparagus and peas are blanched, about 1 minute more. Drain in a colander, rinse under cool water, and set aside to drip dry.

2. Heat the broth in a saucepan without letting it boil. Set off the heat on the back of the stovetop to keep warm.

3. Heat the oil in a large, nonreactive pot. Add the leek and sauté over low heat until beginning to turn golden but not browned. Add the rice and stir to mix and coat with the oil. Raise the heat to medium, add ½ cup of the warm broth, and stir until the broth is absorbed but the rice is still moist.

4. Add another ½ cup of the broth and continue stirring until most of the liquid is absorbed. Repeat the process, stirring gently but constantly and adjusting the heat to maintain a low simmer, until the broth is used up and the rice is tender and creamy but still al dente. The process takes about 25 minutes.

5. Prepare the pesto and set aside.

6. Add the spinach and salt to the risotto and stir until wilted, about 1 more minute. Stir in the other vegetables and top with the pesto. Serve right away, accompanied by the Parmesan on the side, if using.

Note: The pesto makes the risotto a meal-in-one. If you would like to simplify and serve the risotto as a side dish, the pesto topping may be omitted. As a side dish, it serves 4.

Confetti of Rice

Used to be there was one kind of rice. Sometimes it was special, for instance, cooked from scratch, but basically, Americans have not esteemed rice as have other cultures that feature it as part of their daily fare—the Japanese, Chinese, Indians, Middle Easterners, and Persians. At their tables, rice appears daily, if not twice a day, and so it's not surprising that over time, distinctions and preferences have been defined and special dishes created. Fortunately, with the globalization of cooking and ever-curious chefs and food purveyors at the forefront of that trend, rice has achieved a position of honor in American cuisine. In the process, a world of flavors and textures has been revealed. We now can sample from:

LONG-GRAIN RICE
- Basmati
- Jasmine

SHORT-GRAIN/PEARL RICE
- Arborio
- New Rice

BROWN RICE (Short and Long Grain)

RED RICE

WILD RICE

Basil-Walnut Pesto

MAKES 1¼ CUPS

1 cup walnut halves or pieces, toasted (see page 135)
1 to 2 cloves garlic, to taste
2 cups fresh basil leaves
½ cup grated Parmesan or Asiago cheese
½ cup olive oil
¼ teaspoon salt (optional)

Pulverize the walnuts and garlic together in a blender or food processor. Add the remaining ingredients and process into a smooth paste. Use right away or store in the refrigerator for up to 3 days. May be frozen for longer storage.

Shrimp Delight

Serves 4 to 6

"We love our seafood and new ways to enjoy it. Shrimp is a year-round bargain in the Atlanta region. These facts combine well with our garden produce. Cherry tomatoes ripen early and herbs are always available. Since we grow our own salad ingredients especially for Greek salad, feta cheese is in the fridge. And that is how this quick casserole came to be. Put it together from what's fresh and on hand." The dish is pretty and flavorful without the optional garnishes, but they do add extra sparkle on top.

NELLIE NICHOLS (MARIETTA, GA)

1 cup orzo pasta
24 large raw shrimp, shelled and deveined, tails left attached (1 to 1½ pounds)
2 tablespoons olive oil
2 large red bell peppers, stemmed, seeded, and cut into ¼-inch-wide strips
2 large shallots, finely chopped
1 large clove garlic, minced
1 teaspoon salt
¼ teaspoon black pepper
1 basket cherry tomatoes, halved (about 8 ounces)
⅔ cup crumbled feta cheese
¼ cup finely chopped fresh chervil
¼ cup dry vermouth
1 tablespoon chopped basil or parsley leaves (optional)
Freshly ground black pepper (optional)

1. Preheat the oven to 350°F. Lightly grease a 2-quart casserole dish.

2. Bring a medium pot of water to boil. Add the orzo and cook over medium-high heat until slightly underdone, about 8 minutes. Drain and set aside.

3. Heat an ungreased cast-iron skillet or nonstick sauté pan until beginning to smoke. Add the shrimp and stir over high heat until barely beginning to turn pink, about 1 minute. Transfer to a bowl and set aside.

4. Heat the oil in the same pan, stir in the peppers, and sauté over medium-high heat until barely limp, about 4 minutes. Add the shallots, garlic, salt, and pepper and continue cooking, stirring often, until the shallots are translucent, about 4 minutes more.

5. Spread all the orzo in the bottom of the casserole. Top with half the pepper mixture, then half the tomatoes, half the shrimp, half the cheese, half the chervil, and half the vermouth. Make another layer in the same way. Cover with foil and bake for 15 minutes. The shrimp should be barely opaque; if not, cook 5 minutes more.

6. Remove and serve right away, garnished with the basil and/or freshly ground black pepper, if desired.

CHERRY TOMATO POLITESSE

When serving cherry tomatoes as a fruit treat, like cherries, whole is fine. For salads and garnishes they should be halved so that biting into one doesn't cause a spurt of juice into a neighbor diner's eye or onto your own shirt.

Jambalaya

SERVES 6

"I probably get my passion for cooking from my mom and dad. I have vivid memories of growing up in Louisiana, watching my parents in the kitchen. On Saturday mornings, we'd pick fresh vegetables, wash them, and prepare scrumptious Cajun dishes. This is my dad's recipe for jambalaya, the real thing straight from the Cajun country."

PHILIP TOUPS (ARLINGTON, VA)

4 tablespoons (½ stick) butter or vegetable oil
4 tablespoons all-purpose flour
1 large bell pepper, stemmed, seeded, and chopped
3 celery ribs, preferably tender ones from the middle of the head, trimmed and chopped
2 medium onions, chopped
1 to 2 cloves garlic, chopped
2 medium tomatoes, chopped (about 8 ounces)
6 cups water
3 cups raw long-grain white rice
2 boneless, skinless chicken breasts, cut into ½-inch pieces
1 link andouille sausage, sliced ¼ inch thick (see Note below)
8 ounces raw shrimp, shelled and deveined
1½ tablespoons Cajun Spice (see box on page 189)
¼ cup mixed chopped green onion (scallion) and fresh parsley leaves

1. Place the butter in a large nonreactive pot and melt over low heat. Raise the heat slightly, add the flour, and stir constantly until the mixture is a golden-brown, moist roux, about 10 minutes.

2. Stir in the bell pepper, celery, onions, and garlic. Cover the pot and cook over medium heat, stirring often, until the vegetables are wilted, about 10 minutes. Add the tomatoes, cover the pot again, and continue cooking until the tomatoes wilt, about 10 minutes.

3. Add the remaining ingredients and stir to mix. Bring to a boil, lower the heat, and cook, stirring often and adjusting the

Gumbo Filé: A Song Revisited

Jambalaya may trigger a memory, even an enthusiastic outburst of a phrase or two from the popular Fifties song that went something like: "Jambalaya, and a coffee [or was it crawfish?] pie, and a feelay gumbo, for tonight I'm gonna see my ma cher-a-mio. Son of a gun, have big fun, on the bayoooou." But what was the filé? The answer is simple. It's a powdered herb ground from the leaves of the sassafras tree, which grows from the Gulf of Mexico up to Ohio. As a seasoning in Cajun and Creole cooking, filé powder serves a dual role: It's both a flavor addition and a thickening agent, though it's not used in jambalaya. For soup or stewy-type dishes, such as gumbos, its thickening power is accented. For roasted birds and the like, its flavoring attribute is the highlight and it's used as a rub, plain or mixed with other dried herbs. In either use, filé is added in small amounts.

heat as necessary, until the rice is cooked al dente, about 25 minutes. Serve right away.

Note: You can substitute another smoked sausage, such as kielbasa, for the andouille.

Variations

- Use rabbit in place of the chicken.
- Use oysters in place of or in addition to the shrimp.
- Omit the seafood and use only the sausage, or omit the sausage and use only the seafood.
- Sprinkle a little freshly chopped parsley over the top for added color.

Cajun Spice

Various premixed Cajun spice blends are now widely marketed. All include essentially the same ingredients, with variations, of course. Following is a basic Cajun spice blend you can mix together in a moment. It's important that all the herbs, especially the bay leaf, be quite dried—so they can be crumbled almost to a powder—and that the mustard be in the form of powder, not wet, to keep the mix a spice blend rather than a seasoning paste. For about ¼ cup, mix together:

6 small dried bay leaves, stem and leaf spines removed, leaves pulverized
1 teaspoon finely crumbled dried thyme
1 teaspoon finely crumbled dried sage or dried oregano
½ teaspoon powder mustard
½ teaspoon cayenne
1 teaspoon finely ground white pepper
1 teaspoon finely ground black pepper
2 teaspoons salt

Use right away or transfer to a small jar, cap tightly, and store in the cupboard for up to 6 months.

In addition, according to the dish, ground cumin or crumbled dried basil leaves might be added.

Spoonbread with Crabmeat and Southern Greens

Serves 4 to 6

The spoonbread, rich to begin with, becomes extravagant when enhanced with crabmeat. To do justice to the dish, and justify the expense, the crabmeat must be very fresh, practically still wiggling in its shell. Otherwise, substitute shrimp or omit the shellfish altogether; the spoonbread with greens can stand on its own as an entrée or serve as a side dish for roasts, chicken, pork, or beef.

MARY HUNTZ (ATLANTA, GA)

2 ears corn, kernels cut off and cob scraped (see page 122)
⅓ cup heavy (whipping) cream
3 tablespoons butter
½ teaspoon sugar
½ teaspoon salt
⅛ teaspoon cayenne (optional)
½ cup cornmeal, preferably stone ground
6 ounces crabmeat
3 eggs, lightly beaten
1 cup milk
½ teaspoon baking powder
8 cups coarsely chopped, washed, and drained turnip, mustard, or collard greens, leaves only (about 2 pounds)
2 slices bacon, cut into 1-inch pieces
½ teaspoon salt
½ teaspoon black pepper

CREAMED CORN
The corn and cream put together as in Step 2 make a delightful, fresh creamed corn, far superior to canned or frozen.

1. Preheat the oven to 375°F. Lightly grease a 1-quart casserole dish.

2. Place the corn and cream in a small saucepan and bring to a boil. Reduce the heat to a simmer and cook for 2 to 3 minutes, until slightly thickened. Set aside.

3. Combine ¾ cup of water, the butter, sugar, salt, and cayenne, if using, in a medium saucepan. Bring to a boil and stir in the cornmeal right away. Continue boiling for 1 minute, stirring constantly, until thickened. Remove from the heat and stir in the crabmeat and creamed corn.

Harvesting the Gulf Waters

The waters of the Gulf of Mexico stretch from Florida all along the coasts of Georgia, Alabama, Mississippi, Louisiana, Texas, and on down to Mexico. Like the Mediterranean, these salt waters provide a nature-given, briny farmland with a bounty of fish and shellfish for the table. Some of the prized delights cooks of the region have long put to creative use include:

SHELLFISH

- Blue crab, harvested both in its hardshell stage and its softshell stage.
- Gulf shrimp, several species, including brown shrimp, pink shrimp, white shrimp, and rock shrimp, all some of the tastiest in the world.
- Gulf oysters, which match in flavor those harvested out of the Atlantic from the North Sea to the Bay of Fundy and up and down the Pacific from Tamales Bay to Vancouver Island.

FISH

- Pompano, a specialty of the Gulf waters, most often cooked in parchment or a brown bag with seasonings.
- Redfish, especially famous at table as Louisiana blackened redfish.
- Flounder, in particular southern flounder, which serves an all-purpose duty as a tasty white-fleshed chunk in any fish stew.
- Grouper, in particular red grouper, enjoyed in chowders and stews or deep-fried.

In addition, venturing farther away from the Gulf and into the waters around the Florida Keys, game fish, such as tilefish and the big prize, marlin, are sometimes available not only for the sportsman, but for the cook. Within easier catching distance, conch, a sea snail comparable to abalone supplies tasty morsels for chowders, fritters, and conch salad, a kind of seviche.

4. Mix together the eggs, milk, and baking powder. Slowly add the mixture to the cornmeal-and-crab mixture, stirring until well blended. Pour into the casserole dish and bake for 45 to 50 minutes, or until a knife inserted in the center comes out clean.

5. While the spoonbread is baking, prepare the greens. Sauté the bacon in a large pot or sauté pan over high heat until crisp, about 5 minutes. Remove the bacon to paper toweling and set aside. Add the greens to the pan, stirring and pressing them down until they are wilted enough to fit into the pan. Add about ¼ cup of water, enough to keep the greens moist, and simmer until tender, 8 to 10 minutes. Stir in the salt and pepper and set aside in a warm place until ready to serve.

6. To serve, spoon the spoonbread onto a large serving platter or individual plates. Arrange the greens around the perimeter and crumble the bacon over the top. Serve right away.

Spoonbread: An Uncertain History

Pudding, creamy baked polenta, grits soufflé, or fluffy porridge, however spoonbread is described, it evokes southern cooking. It takes its name more from the spoon part (its consistency is definitely spoonable) than from the bread part (it's definitely not sliceable). Its origin is not entirely clear—was it a dish of Native Americans or one introduced by the new Southerners, who adapted to corn in all its ways? In any case, what started as soft, baked "bread" evolved to higher heights until, in modern times, the spoonbread is customarily leavened by beaten egg whites. Along the way, the plain original also took on refinements such as the inclusion of whole corn kernels, whole hominy, and, as here, crab!

Tuscan-Style Petrale Sole with Tiny Potatoes and Baby Artichokes

SERVES 4

Patricia Unterman, owner of Hayes St. Grill, food columnist for the San Francisco Examiner, *and restaurant guide author, and chef Toni More combine delicate petrale sole with equally delicate baby artichokes and tiny fingerling potatoes in a land-meets-sea dish that practically sparkles off the plate. In an inspired yet uncomplicated way, the composition showcases each ingredient and brings them together in an easily home do-able dish that is undeniably professional.*

PATRICIA UNTERMAN, OWNER, AND TONI MORE, CHEF, HAYES ST. GRILL (SAN FRANCISCO, CA)

16 baby artichokes, dark green outside leaves pulled off and tops cut off down to the light green
16 to 24 very small, creamer-size potatoes, preferably fingerlings, scrubbed
¼ cup plus 2 tablespoons olive oil
1½ pounds petrale sole fillets
Flour seasoned with salt and pepper, for coating the fish
1 teaspoon minced garlic
1½ cups chicken broth (see Note below)
2 teaspoons fresh lemon juice
1 teaspoon finely chopped fresh rosemary
1 teaspoon finely chopped fresh flat-leaf parsley leaves
Salt and pepper
½ tablespoon finely shredded lemon zest, for garnish (optional)

1. Bring a medium pot of water to boil. Drop in the artichokes and cook at a brisk simmer until tender but still al dente, about 10 minutes. Remove the artichokes with a wire strainer and transfer them to a colander to cool. When cool enough to handle, cut them in half lengthwise and set aside.

2. Bring the water to a boil again, drop in the potatoes, and simmer briskly until tender all the way through but still holding their shape, 10 to 15 minutes, depending on the size of the potatoes. Drain in a colander and set aside to drip dry.

3. Heat 2 tablespoons of the olive oil in a large sauté pan. Coat both sides of the petrale fillets with the seasoned flour and place as many fillets in the pan as will fit without crowding. Sauté over medium-high heat, turning once, until barely flakable and still moist, 4 to 6 minutes altogether, depending on the thickness of the fillets.

TIPS *of the* TRADE

What If Here There Aren't Any?

While Patty waxes enthusiastic about the regional perfection of this dish, she also recognizes possibilities from other regions. To paraphrase her, yes, it's in the combination of particular ingredients, but it's mainly the fresh integrity of the ingredients that lifts a dish above the ordinary. Substitutions that will turn out an equally fine though not specifically coast-of-California dish include:

PETRALE, QUEEN OF SOLES: If petrale sole fillets are not available, red snapper, halibut, flounder, or another delicately flavored fish may be substituted, as long as it is pristinely fresh and not fatty.

BABY ARTICHOKES: By the same token, the artichokes must be very small and fresh; brined in cans or marinated in jars won't do. Better to substitute larger artichokes and peel away the outer leaves almost to the hearts.

FINGERLINGS, CREAM OF THE CREAMERS: With the potatoes, there's a little more leeway. In place of the fingerlings, use small creamers of Yukon Gold, White Rose, Red Sun, or Yellow Finn.

Transfer to a serving platter and continue with another round if necessary. When all the fish are fried, set aside in a warm place.

4. Turn the heat up to high, stir in the garlic, and cook 1 minute. Add the broth, artichokes, and potatoes to the pan and boil to reduce the volume by half, 3 to 5 minutes. Stir in the lemon juice, rosemary, parsley and remaining ¼ cup of oil. Season with salt and pepper to taste and continue boiling for 2 more minutes, until the sauce is still brothy but no longer raw.

5. Spoon the artichokes, potatoes, and sauce over the petrale and serve right away, garnished with the lemon zest, if using.

Note: Chef More emphasizes that if you are not using homemade chicken broth (page 86), for this dish it is essential to purchase a low-sodium product that is light in flavor.

Steamed Scallops Supreme

Serves 4 as a main course, 8 as an appetizer

You can tell from the list of places Ken Hom comes from or goes to that he is not only an esteemed chef but also a well-traveled one. Aside from the numerous cookbooks he has written, his BBC television series on Chinese cuisine, with its accompanying volume of recipes, has been one of the bestsellers of all time. Through it all, Ken maintains a balance that straddles many worlds and, in his works, brings together recipes and cooking notions spanning East to West. For this book, he offers a recipe that gleams both in the pot and on the plate. As he describes it: "Fresh scallops are sweet and rich. Perhaps one of the best methods featuring their qualities is the Chinese method of steaming. Using hot wet vapors, this technique brings out the succulent texture of the scallops without overcooking them. Their briny seafood taste and flavors are emphasized. And the bonus is that it is very simple to prepare and takes literally minutes to cook—ideal for a quick and easy, healthful meal. Also, I think it makes an ideal opener for any dinner party." Clearly, Chef Hom is a generous host. The recipe is enough for four for a meal; for an appetizer you can serve eight.

~ KEN HOM (BERKELEY, CA; HONG KONG; LONDON; CATUS, FRANCE)

THISTLES

Artichokes, as all thistles, flower into blossoms desirable to flying creatures and interior decorators, too.

1 pound sea scallops, with roe if possible (see Note below)
2 small fresh red chilies, seeded and chopped
2 teaspoons finely chopped fresh ginger
1 tablespoon rice wine or dry sherry
1 tablespoon light soy sauce
¼ teaspoon salt
¼ teaspoon freshly ground black pepper
3 tablespoons trimmed and finely chopped green onions (scallions)

1. Place the scallops in a single layer on a heatproof platter. Evenly distribute the chilies, ginger, rice wine, soy sauce, salt, pepper, and green onion slices over the top. Set aside at room temperature for a few minutes or refrigerate if holding longer.

2. Set up a wok steamer with a basket large enough to hold the platter of seafood (see box below). Fill the steamer with 2 inches of water and bring to a boil.

3. Taking care to avoid the rising steam, set the scallop platter on the steamer rack. Reduce the heat to low and cover the wok. Steam gently until the scallops are translucent on the outside, still pink inside, and firm, not flaccid, to the touch, about 15 minutes. Remove and serve at once.

Note: Though difficult to find, scallops with roe make for an especially fine dish.

Variations: The steamed scallops, complete and satisfying on their own, also invite embellishment. For a more complex dish, you can:

- Include chunks of a delicate white fish, such as sea bass, escolar, or snapper.
- Add a few very thin slivers of ham or prosciutto.
- Add finely julienned vegetables, such as leek, carrot, or zucchini.
- Garnish the platter with cilantro sprigs.

Other Ways to Steam Seafood

If your *batterie de cuisine* does not include a wok steamer large enough to hold a serving-size platter, you can improvise with a roasting pan with a fitted lid and bricks or other heat-proof objects that will hold the platter up out of the water.

YOU CAN ALSO STEAM THE SCALLOPS IN THE MICROWAVE: Set up the platter as described in Step 1. When ready to cook, cover loosely with a microwave-safe plate and microwave on high for 6 minutes. Remove and let rest for 2 minutes before serving.

LEMON

The Love and Care of a Warm-Climate Tree That Fruits in Cool Weather

and How to Keep the Ants Away

Though the lemon tree has many personal requirements to fruit into glory, it is basically weather and water hardy. As long as there is not serious freezing or long-term drought, it will survive to bloom again through many a travail. Whether yours is one of the sturdier varieties, such as Lisbon or Eureka, or a more particular kind, such as Meyer, with proper care you can have two crops a year. Here are some care tips:

FOOD: Feed once a year in spring with a high-nitrogen fertilizer.

WATER: Keep the lemon tree well watered with regular deep watering that reaches down to its roots in a circle as wide as its bough span. That means a biweekly ground soak, especially in zones that are hot and dry in summer.

PROTECTION: Lemon trees grow in warmth and come to fruition in coolness. If you live where snow covers the ground for weeks at a time, forget having one unless it is in a container and can be brought indoors in winter. If you live somewhere in between, you can protect the tree against temporary heat waves by watering more frequently. You can protect against temporary frost by providing a tarp or other kind of plastic blanket over the tree when the weather gets below freezing for a day or two.

In addition, lemon trees are particularly susceptible to ant and aphid infestation; the ants find lemon branches and leaves a good nursery for the aphids they raise to "milk." It's an interesting symbiotic relationship. The ants need the aphids for the sweet treat they provide to the ants in the form of a sugary syrup that is a by-product of the sap the aphids suck from the tree. The aphids welcome the ants' presence because they keep at bay the natural predators of aphids. But while the ants want the aphids, you do not. Neither ants nor aphids are harmful to mature fruit, merely pesky, and they can easily be washed away. However, the aphids can cause problems for the tree and for immature fruit. To prevent eventual damage to the tree:

Clip or prune all the lemon branches that touch another plant or object, providing a path to the soil, and pull out any grass or weeds around its base. This is because the ants will use any path, even an aerial one, to reach the tree. To stop the ants, you must be draconian, even if that means trimming away some of the branches of the lemon tree's contiguous neighbor.

Use Tanglefoot around the base. This is a marvelously sticky, spreadable gum that stops the ants in their path. Take care as you spread it around the trunk: It's not toxic and doesn't irritate the skin, but it is gummy and hard to get off your hands and clothes.

Once rid of the protecting ants, the aphid population will diminish. Regular hosing down of foliage with a forceful stream of water will wash away any that are left.

chicken, herbs, and lemon

Whether the bird is sautéed, oven-roasted, or grilled; served whole or in pieces; quickly rubbed with seasonings or marinated for a while, herb lovers share a high regard for the combination of chicken and herbs. They are also fond of adding lemon in many forms—slices for stuffing inside the cavity or under the skin, wedges for baking and grilling alongside, juice to squeeze over, zest for garnishing. Following are recipes that spotlight chicken and herbs, often with lemon, too, in many mouth-watering forms.

CHICKENS IN CULINARY HISTORY
Nary a pullet scratched around Western barnyards until the West discovered China and its domestic chickens.

Lemon Chicken with Sage

SERVES AS MANY AS YOU'D LIKE

In this recipe for chicken with herbs and lemon, sage is the herb of choice, overnight marinating is the method of choice, and wedges are the lemon cut of choice. Notes from the contributor suggest that this version of chicken and herbs is "best when grilled along with lemon quarters. It's even good at room temperature." It's a crowd-friendly dish that you can use for a family crowd of any size or to accommodate a gang of friends.

~ R. R. MILIUNAS (BLOOMFIELD HILLS, MI)

Chicken breasts, legs, or thighs, skin on
3 sage leaves per piece of chicken
4 large garlic cloves, per pound of chicken, slivered
Coarse salt
Black pepper, preferably freshly ground
1 whole lemon, per pound of chicken, quartered

1. Wash and pat dry the chicken parts. Rub the outside of each piece with sage, then tuck the leaves under the skin.

2. In a large bowl, layer the chicken parts with the garlic, a generous sprinkling of salt, ample pepper, and the lemon quarters, juice first squeezed over the layer as you go. Cover and marinate in the refrigerator for at least 12 hours or up to 24, turning occasionally.

3. When ready to cook, remove from the refrigerator and allow to come to room temperature. Bake, grill, or sauté the chicken and lemon quarters. Serve right away or at room temperature.

Lemon Chicken with Tarragon

Serves 6

"Several years ago, I decided I wanted to try my hand at an herb garden. I picked up sage, tarragon, oregano, parsley, and dill. I planted them in a close cluster because I like the lush look as quick as I can get it. It worked, and with the abundance of tarragon, I experimented with my favorite chicken dishes until I hit upon this recipe. It's become a Lancaster family standard."

PAULETTE LANCASTER
(CARMEL, IN)

6 boneless, skinless chicken breast halves (about 1½ pounds)
4 tablespoons (½ stick) butter or margarine
3 tablespoons Dijon mustard
3 tablespoons fresh lemon juice
½ tablespoon finely chopped fresh tarragon
½ teaspoon salt
¼ teaspoon black pepper
6 saltine crackers, finely crushed (see page 244)
⅓ cup grated Parmesan cheese

Tender Tarragon, Full of Flavor

Though you may not think so, tarragon is a perennial. When the weather gets cold, it shrinks down to its bottom-most stems. As the cold season goes on, it becomes barely visible and you might despair that it's gone forever. But take heart; it is actually waiting in the protection of the earth to spring forth again as soon as it's warm enough. This is a delicate transition time for the tarragon and gardener both. The tarragon, still barely visible, may not be noticed by the gardener, who, avid to turn the soil for the summer planting, may inadvertently dig it up in the process.

There are two kinds of tarragon to choose from. Russian tarragon is more winter-hardy but far less flavorful, though its leaves are large and pretty. For the kitchen, French tarragon is the cultivar of choice. Be restrained when using French tarragon; it has a rather aggressive flavor that can easily become overbearing.

1. Preheat the oven to 425°F.

2. Place the chicken in a lightly greased baking pan large enough to hold the pieces in one uncrowded layer.

3. Melt the butter in a small saucepan. Stir in the mustard, lemon juice, tarragon, salt, and pepper and pour the mixture over the chicken.

4. Mix together the crushed crackers and cheese and sprinkle over the chicken. Bake until the chicken is cooked through and the topping is golden, about 35 minutes. Serve right away.

Chicken and Chives

SERVES 4

"The chives I use originally came from my parents' garden in Connecticut many years ago. I have the chive plants in a large pot I put outdoors each spring and take into the garage for the winter. The chives love this routine so much they provide ample cuttings for summer through fall." A gentle and slender allium, chive adds a whisper of onion flavor to the chicken and also provides color in the sprightly sauce.

DORIS ZINNO (SANDWICH, MA)

4 large boneless chicken breast halves (see Note below)
½ teaspoon salt
½ teaspoon black pepper
¼ cup olive oil
2 tablespoons butter or margarine
2 tablespoons fresh lemon juice
¼ cup chicken broth (see page 86)
2 tablespoons brandy
2 tablespoons Dijon mustard
½ cup finely chopped chives
3 tablespoons chopped fresh parsley leaves

1. Place the chicken breasts, one at a time, between 2 sheets of wax paper or plastic wrap and lightly pound with a mallet or hammer until ¼ inch thick. Sprinkle with the salt and pepper and set aside.

2. Heat the oil and butter together in a large sauté pan until the butter begins to foam. Add the chicken breasts, arranging them in one layer. Cook over medium-high heat, turning once, until the centers are still moist but no longer pink, no more than 8 minutes altogether. Transfer the breasts to a serving platter and set aside in a warm place.

3. Add the remaining ingredients and stir to mix. Cook over medium heat for 1 minute more, until the mixture looks glossy and bubbles are breaking from the bottom of the pan. Pour over the breasts and serve right away.

Note: If you prefer, you can remove the skin from the chicken breasts before pounding them.

ROSES FOR THE KITCHEN *Whether scenting the sauce or infusing a jelly, roses from the red spectrum provide the best flavor, aroma, and color for cooking. And, of course, only use roses from pesticide-free, not chemically sprayed, bushes. To prepare the petals, pick the flowers when they are open and most fragrant. Pluck the petals off the hips, and if there are ants, brush them off or gently rinse and pat dry the petals. The petals will keep in a plastic bag in the refrigerator for up to 2 days.*

Rose Petal Chicken Breasts

SERVES 2 TO 4

"My mother was most content when working in her flower gardens, but she was also an outstanding cook. When I was a child, she first introduced me to her homemade violet pancake syrup, and from that day forward, I was hooked on both gardening and cooking. As an adult, I continue to experiment with many edible flowers. Roses are my favorite."

ELENA MARCHESO MORENO (MCLEAN, VA)

4 boneless, skinless chicken breast halves (about 1 pound) (see Notes below)
Salt and pepper
2 tablespoons butter
1 tablespoon peeled and minced fresh ginger
1 small clove garlic, minced or pressed
¼ cup dry sherry
1 teaspoon rose water (see Notes below)
1 teaspoon honey
2 tablespoons chopped fresh chives
1 cup strongly scented rose petals (see right), left whole if small or slivered if large

1. Put each half breast between 2 sheets of wax paper or plastic wrap and pound lightly to make ¼-inch-thick pieces. Remove the paper, lightly sprinkle with salt and pepper, and set aside.

2. Melt the butter in a sauté pan large enough to hold the breasts in one uncrowded layer. Add the ginger and garlic and sauté over low heat until wilted, about 1 minute. Raise the heat to medium and add the breasts. Sauté, turning once, until the breasts are golden on both sides, 6 to 8 minutes altogether. Transfer the breasts to a serving platter and set aside in a warm place.

3. Raise the heat to medium-high and stir in the sherry, rose water, and honey. Cook until bubbling, about 1 minute. Stir in the chives and rose petals. Pour over the breasts and serve right away.

Notes

- You can also use unpounded boneless, skinless breasts, or skinless thigh and leg pieces, for that matter. The sautéing time is longer, about 13 minutes.
- Rose water is available in Middle Eastern grocery stores and supermarkets that cater to an international clientele. It can be omitted if not available.

Chicken Provençal

SERVES 4 TO 6

*The contributor, a caterer, culinary career counselor, and cookbook author (*I Knew You Were Coming So I Baked a Cake*) offers a quick-to-make dish that will appeal to any busy cook. With its bouquet of fresh herbs and vegetables, it also appeals to any gardener.*

CAROL DURST (NEW YORK, NY)

1 cup dried tomatoes (see page 337), cut into ½-inch pieces
¼ to ½ cup olive oil
6 boneless chicken breast halves, cut into 1-inch cubes (about 2¼ pounds)
4 large shallots, cut into rings, or 1 medium red onion, cut into 1-inch cubes
1 pound assorted red, yellow, and green bell peppers, stemmed, seeded, and cut into 1-inch pieces
3 cloves garlic, minced
1 tablespoon fresh thyme leaves
1 tablespoon chopped fresh oregano leaves
1 tablespoon chopped fresh rosemary leaves
2 tablespoons chopped fresh basil leaves
½ cup chicken broth (see page 86) or white wine
1 teaspoon salt
⅛ teaspoon black pepper

1. Place the dried tomato pieces in a small bowl, cover with warm water, and set aside to soak for 5 minutes. Drain before using.

2. Heat 2 tablespoons of the oil in a large sauté pan. Add as many chicken cubes as will fit in one uncrowded layer and sauté over high heat until browned all around and cooked through, about 3 minutes. Transfer the chicken to a plate and continue with another batch, adding more oil as needed, until all the chicken is cooked.

3. Stir the shallots into the pan and sauté until nicely browned, about 4 minutes. Transfer the shallots to the plate with the chicken.

4. Add the peppers to the pan and sauté until wilted but still a little crunchy, about 5 minutes. Transfer the peppers to the platter.

5. Add the garlic, herbs, and tomatoes to the pan and stir to mix. Add the broth and stir to scrape the browned bits from the bottom of the pan. Return the chicken and vegetables, along with any collected juices, to the pan. Season with the salt and pepper, stir to mix, and serve right away.

Note: One cup seeded, diced, and drained fresh tomatoes may be substituted for the dried tomatoes.

Herb Chicken Cacciatore

SERVES 4

"My grandmother, a devoted gardener, now over 100 years old, still loves her fresh flowers, vegetables, and herbs. This recipe, which comes straight from Rome where she was born, has been a family favorite ever since I can remember. With its touch of sherry and fresh herbs, it's a nice change from the typical cacciatore recipes."

LARAINE WARD (VERO BEACH, FL)

½ cup olive oil
4 large boneless chicken breast halves
½ medium onion, finely chopped
2 cloves garlic, minced or pressed
2 celery ribs, including leaves, finely chopped
6 large fresh basil leaves, coarsely chopped
½ cup chicken broth (see page 86)
½ teaspoon salt
⅛ teaspoon black pepper
3 large tomatoes, peeled, seeded, and cut into 1-inch chunks (1½ pounds)
⅔ cup Amontillado or other medium-dry sherry
2 tablespoons red wine vinegar
2 large green olives, pitted and chopped
2 anchovy fillets, chopped
2 teaspoons chopped fresh rosemary leaves
Whole fresh basil leaves, for garnish
4 lemon wedges, for garnish

CELERY AS AN HERB

Often recipes call for celery ribs trimmed and cut in one way or another—sliced, diced, chopped, and so on. Often the recipe also says to include the celery tops. The tender but forthrightly flavored leaves add an herb element that is different from the vegetable element of the ribs. In fact, celery as an herb is often desired on its own, so a recipe may call for only celery tops. Celery as an herb is a potherb, quite to the point in a soup, stew, or other concoction that is to be cooked. It is too strident to replace, for instance, parsley as a garnishing herb.

1. Heat the oil in a large sauté pan. Add the chicken and sauté over medium-high heat until brown on both sides, about 8 minutes. Transfer to a plate and set aside.

2. Stir the onion, garlic, celery, chopped basil, broth, salt, and pepper into the pan. Return the chicken to the pan and cook over medium heat for 10 minutes, or until almost done but still a little pink in the center. Add the tomatoes, sherry, vinegar, olives, anchovies, and rosemary and stir to mix. Cook, making sure the sauce covers the chicken, for 10 minutes more, or until the chicken is cooked through.

3. Serve right away, garnished with the whole basil leaves and lemon wedges.

About Those Breasts

For anyone trying to keep to a low-fat diet, skinless chicken breasts are a good selection. But how to get them? You could cut the breasts off a whole chicken and reserve the rest for another dish. More handily, there are chicken breast halves, wrapped three or six to a package. They come as breast pieces with bone and skin; boneless with the skin; or boneless already skinned. Then to the ultimate ease, you can purchase boneless, skinless breasts already cut up and ready to stir-fry. Of course, as the pieces become smaller the price rises. As the sage advised, "You pays your money and you takes your choice."

Herb-Stuffed Whole Grilled Chicken

Serves 4

"I seemed to have had an overabundance of marjoram growing in my garden last year. Rather than cut it and relegate it to the compost pile, I took it to the kitchen to dry for the winter. A chicken thawing on the kitchen counter and the large basket of marjoram inspired the following recipe. I have since tried the dish with other herbs I have in abundance (rosemary, thyme, oregano) and it has continued to be an easy success."

SALLY WILLIAMS (POTOMAC, MD)

1 lemon, quartered
1 large fryer (3¾ to 4½ pounds) or small roasting chicken, rinsed and patted dry (4½ to 5 pounds)
1 small onion, quartered
1 cup (packed) fresh herb sprigs, such as marjoram, rosemary, thyme, or oregano
Salt and pepper

1. Prepare a charcoal fire in a barbecue grill fitted with a cover (see Note below).

2. Squeeze the lemon over the outside of the chicken, then stuff the remains of the quarters into the cavity, along with the onion and herbs. Lock the wings behind and tie the legs together with string. Sprinkle the outside liberally with salt and pepper.

3. Divide the charcoal into 2 piles with a space between them that is wide enough to position the chicken so that it is not directly over the coals. Place the chicken on the grill rack between the piles, cover, and cook for 1 hour and 15 minutes, or until an instant-read meat thermometer inserted in the thigh registers 180°F.

4. Remove from the grill and allow to rest for 15 minutes for the juices to settle. Cut the chicken into pieces, discard the stuffing, and serve.

Note: If you don't have a grill with a cover, you can improvise with a tent made of a double layer of heavy-duty aluminum foil. Or you can roast the chicken in a covered casserole in a 375°F. oven. Uncover the casserole for the last 15 minutes so the top and wings can brown. The total timing is the same.

Safe Poultry Practice

The practice of rinsing poultry inside and out with cold water is one conscientious cooks always follow. Whether the bird is to be cooked whole or in pieces, with or without the skin, the step ensures sanitation and adds a certain perk to the flesh before the chicken goes into the pot. Be sure to pat dry the inside and outside of whole birds or all around the pieces of cut-up poultry so the flesh can cook without steaming.

It's also important to clean knives and cutting boards that have been used for poultry preparation with a generous amount of soap and hot water. Also, rinse them from time to time with a light solution of water and bleach.

Peg's Oven-Roasted Chicken

Serves 4 to 6

"After experimenting to perfect the roast chicken, I have devised a chicken sure to please in a recipe that melds the earth with fowl. The herbs add their individual flavors to the inherently bland chicken. The paprika acts like 'sandpaper' and keeps the oil from sliding off the chicken. The salt 'crisps' the skin. And cooking the chicken upside down for the first 45 minutes draws the fat into the breast meat to keep it succulent."

MARGARET HOSKY (WASHINGTON, DC)

3 tablespoons olive oil
½ tablespoon sweet paprika
3 large cloves garlic, minced or pressed
1 roasting chicken (4½ to 6 pounds)
6 large sprigs of fresh herbs, such as tarragon, basil, oregano, or thyme, or a mixture
Salt
Freshly ground pepper, preferably a mixture of white and black

1. Preheat the oven to 375°F.

2. Heat the oil in a small saucepan. Add the paprika and garlic and simmer for 1 minute, until the garlic is very golden and the mixture smells toasted. Set aside to cool.

3. Place the chicken in a roasting pan and stuff the cavity with the herbs. Pour the oil mixture over the outside of the chicken and turn to coat thoroughly. Liberally salt and pepper all around and set the chicken, breast side down, in the pan (see Note below).

4. Place in the oven and roast, uncovered, for 45 minutes. Turn the chicken breast side up and continue roasting for 1 to 1½ hours more, depending on the size of the chicken, or until the juices run clear, not pink, and the legs move easily away from the thighs.

5. Remove and allow to rest for 15 minutes for the juices to settle. Carve the chicken or cut it into sections, as you wish, and serve.

Note: If you prefer, you can set the chicken on a rack in the pan. This method serves to keep the chicken above the rendering fat as it cooks, resulting in a lower-fat dish.

THE FLAVORS OF THAILAND

Lemongrass
Kafir lime leaves
Young ginger
Fresh chilies
Cilantro
Garlic
Thai basil
Tamarind
Turmeric
Shallots
Coconut milk
Fish sauce
Soy Sauce

Thai-Style Turkey Sausage Wrapped in Grape Leaves

MAKES 2 DOZEN SAUSAGE PACKETS

"We garden in an urban organic community garden in Philadelphia. We have the good fortune to have a Concord grape vine climbing over our garden fence—the grapes

are good, but I relish the leaves. We have also established lemongrass, originally garnered from a neighborhood Thai grocery store. I had the idea that if I combined the lemongrass with Thai seasonings in a turkey sausage wrapped in grape leaves . . . hummmm. This is my recipe developed from that inspiration." The ground turkey, bland on its own, takes on a lift when infused with the Thai seasonings and wrapped in the subtly tart grape leaves. The resulting sausage packets are especially good grilled over a hardwood fire or terrific sautéed indoors. They can also be arranged on a platter, warm or cooled, and garnished with a sprinkling of lemon zest, a shower of edible flower petals, or a few fine slivers of lemongrass to shine on a buffet table.

CHRISTINE HIBBARD (PHILADELPHIA, PA)

24 fresh grape leaves, stems cut off (see Notes below)
1 pound ground turkey
4 to 5 stalks young lemongrass, trimmed and minced
1 to 3 Thai or other small green chili peppers, to taste, stemmed and finely chopped
1 medium onion, finely chopped
2 tablespoons brown sugar
2 to 3 tablespoons fish sauce (see Notes below)
Olive oil

1. Bring a large pot of water to boil. Blanch the grape leaves, 5 or 6 at a time, for 30 seconds. With a strainer, lift them out of the water and transfer to a tea towel. Gently, so as not to tear them, spread out the leaves and set aside. Continue with another round until all the leaves are blanched.

2. Combine the turkey, lemongrass, chilies, onion, brown sugar, and fish sauce in a medium bowl. Mix well and set aside at room temperature if using within 30 minutes or refrigerate if making in advance.

3. Spread the grape leaves out on a counter, smooth side down, veined side up. Place 1 to 2 tablespoons of the turkey mixture in the center of each leaf. Roll up burrito-style, beginning with the stem side for the first fold, to make a

About Growing and Harvesting Lemongrass

As a true grass, which it is, lemongrass can fulfill its botanical destiny almost anywhere that there's a bit of sun, wet, fertile soil, and some water from above. In a less than ideal situation, its leaves and stalks may become tough as it strives to maintain itself and expand. For kitchen use, however, you want the lemongrass to be pandered to so that its stems, the part of the plant used for cooking, remain supple and tender. That means, since it is a grass, it needs plenty of water and the kind of nutrient-rich, wet soil you might find a bit inland from a marsh edge. In a mild-climate garden, these conditions can be simulated with regular watering, daily when it's hot, and fertilizing attention if the soil is not nutrient rich on its own. If the climate is cold in the winter, this almost tropical plant can be lifted out of the ground with some of its soil, placed in a deep bucket, and brought indoors until next spring. Remember to keep the soil moist even in this dormant stage.

small envelope enclosing the sausage. Transfer the envelopes to a plate as you go. If making in advance, set aside in the refrigerator.

4. When ready to cook, prepare a charcoal fire.

5. Lightly coat the sausages with olive oil and grill, turning once or twice, until firm and slightly charred, about 7 minutes. If cooking the sausages indoors, heat an ungreased, heavy skillet until beginning to smoke. Add the lightly oiled sausages and cook over medium-high heat as above. The timing is the same.

Notes

• Jarred grape leaves, either home-brined or store-bought, also work for wrapping the sausages. If using those, use a double layer because they are softer and don't hold up as well as the freshly blanched leaves during cooking.

• Fish sauce is available in Asian grocery stores, supermarkets that cater to an international clientele, and health-food stores.

The Goodness of Grapes

Growing grapes is about more than fruit for the summer table or wine for the year. Each season has its own special offering from the sturdy, ancient grapevine.

WINTER: The vines, bare of foliage, create a dry arrangement on their trellises, over their arbors, in their carefully tended fields.

SPRING: The vines leaf out and begin to bud, signaling the next season of the year. As the leaves develop, the small tender ones can be clipped for the meal, where they'll be used fresh: shredded and sprinkled over pilafs and spring lamb dishes, whole wrapped around tender quail to keep the birds moist on the grill, or, if there are enough, as a leafy embellishment around or under any other spring offering the cook has conjured up. A few of the delicate tendrils can also be taken and used for special garnishing.

SUMMER: When the vines are beginning to sag under the weight of the fruit, it's time for pruning back a little. Cuttings can be used to ornament the table for a summer meal in a garden way. If there are any still tender leaves (there probably are) they can be clipped, wilted in salt water, and stored in the fridge until it's time for stuffed grape leaves. It's also time to pluck the larger leaves before they become bitter, wilt them in salt water too, and add them to the jars of pickles being put by for later. The grape leaves, it is said, keep the pickles crisp.

FALL: When the grapes are harvested, the fruit of the grapevine provides many delights and delectables: wine, juice, jam, fresh in a rabbit casserole, dried into raisins. A bit later, when the vines are pruned for the final time before winter, the canes can be bundled and/or decoratively stacked by the hearth, waiting to perfume next summer's barbecues.

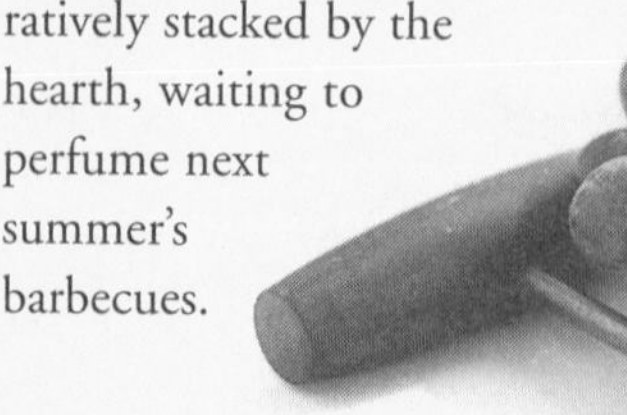

PICNICS

The Joy of Sharing Food

"For me picnics and eating outdoors were the beginning of a lifelong association with food as the focus of happy social events. I grew up in the New Mexico desert, where the outdoors was not exactly what most would call a garden. There were plenty of beef cattle grazing on what they could find to fatten themselves for market, tumbleweed rolling about, maybe a stubby cactus or two. That was my father's ranch on the range in Estancia, New Mexico. Closer to the house, chickens scratched about in the dusty yard and, maybe, there was a small potager plot outside the kitchen door for growing vegetables. Hardly an Eden, this desert; nonetheless, for me it was a place of joy that provided some of my best food memories.

"Though we actually lived in Albuquerque and had caretakers to tend the livestock on the ranch, regular visits to check up on things were part of our routine. We would drive there, sometimes with other relatives in tow, and have a grand meal with the caretakers. It was always fried chicken, prepared by the women while the men toured the land on horseback. The children played with the farm animals and rousted about being kids in what seemed to us a garden because it was so free.

"At dinner time, in the afternoon but after 3:00 P.M. to avoid the heat of the day and also to have all the business done, a large canvas cloth or sheet was spread on the ground and everyone gathered 'round to eat. There was always enough for each to have more than enough of his or her favorite pieces because they (the women) made so much. When served up, to my child's eye, it looked like a chicken mountain. Newspapers were our plates and our hands were the silverware.

"That land eventually was turned to soybean farming. I eventually turned to lusher landscapes where I was able to grow more water-loving greenery. Mint for nibbling upon as I walk my smaller garden and always parsley for kitchen bouquets are my favorites. To this day, my choice for a family celebration is to have a picnic, preferably with fried chicken, these days more healthfully 'oven-fried' and herb garnished, of course."

—RUTH JENANYAN
(SUTTER CREEK, CA)

Grilled Duck in a Jar

SERVES 6 TO 8

A member of Berkeley's renowned Cheeseboard Collective and a longtime associate of this writer, Arayah Jenanyan was the primary tester for the recipes in this book. She offers a special one here, one that exhibits her unique way of blending art and precision into gentle sharing. "I like to grow things in large bunches. As the plants grow, first you get the beautiful greens, then the flowers, then the vegetables themselves, as though the garden were a living bouquet developing into good food. When it's time to celebrate the beauty, I throw a backyard barbecue. The idea to layer the duck pieces and herbs in a jar came to me when, admiring the beauty of the duck with its garden-inspired rub, I thought it was a picture that ought to be displayed, and I remembered that jar. Not only is it a practical way to season the pieces thoroughly; it also becomes part of the party amusement. The guests can't help but chuckle at the sight of a jar full of herb-garnished duck parts waiting for the grill. You can also pull the same trick with rabbit, chicken, quail, and game hens. Especially festive is to have also a jar of garden vegetables marinating beside the duck jar. Two such jars make you rich."

ARAYAH JENANYAN (BERKELEY, CA)

TOOLS *of the* TRADE

When the Container Is the Inspiration

If you've ever marveled at an amphora standing sentry outside the door of a Mediterranean house, waiting to collect rain water when the olives are not in season, ready to hold the olive harvest as the tiny fruit spend their time in the brine to be cured for the kitchen; if you've ever admired a huge pottery crock that stands ready for the season's sauerkraut or a huge glass jar waiting to be filled with the season's pickles, you can understand the gardener cook's powerful impulse to fill the container with garden beauty. And when olives, sauerkraut, or pickles are not on your agenda for this fall, the crock or jar can cradle more immediate, smaller beauties, like an armful of tall cuttings to keep fresh for the moment, or a miniature steeple of duck quarters marinating as they await the grill. Somehow, its largesse inspires the reseeing that is the art of the gardener cook.

2 ducks, cut into 6 pieces each
12 sprigs of fresh thyme
12 fresh sage leaves
8 bay leaves
12 juniper berries, crushed
1 tablespoon black peppercorns
1 tablespoon coarse sea salt
Grilled Veggies in a Jar
(optional, see box on page 209)

1. Layer the ducks in a large glass jar or bowl, sprinkling each layer with the seasonings as you go. Refrigerate for 12 to 24 hours.

2. When ready to cook, prepare a charcoal fire in a grill fitted with a lid and let it burn until white hot with no flames.

3. Remove the duck from the refrigerator, lift out the pieces, and brush off the salt, leaving as much of the other seasonings as you can. Return the duck pieces to the jar and set it by the grill until the fire is ready.

4. Place the duck pieces on the grill rack directly over the coals and put the grill lid down. Cook for 20 to 25 minutes, turning once or twice, or until golden all around and cooked through. Serve right away or at room temperature.

Grilled Veggies in a Jar

Fill a large jar with an assortment of garden vegetables, such as summer squash, onion, any kind of pepper, whole heads of garlic, eggplant, leeks. Leave the vegetables whole if small or cut in half if large. Add:

12 sprigs of fresh thyme
12 sprigs of fresh parsley
10 garlic cloves, cut in half
1 teaspoon black pepper
2 tablespoons balsamic or red wine vinegar or juice of 1 lemon
¼ cup olive oil

Mix and set aside to marinate at least 30 minutes or up to 3 hours.

Place the veggies around the edges of the grill rack to cook while the duck cooks.

when it's meat tonight

Gardener cooks, in general, do not feature meat for the main meal of the day. So when it's time for meat, it is an occasion. Following is a somewhat eclectic set of recipes culled from around the nation for ways gardener cooks satisfy a taste for meat concomitant with that for fresh-from-the-outdoors produce. The section also includes a bouquet of marinade and rub recipes to choose from for seasoning whatever meat, poultry, or fish is on the menu. From the long-cooked to the quickly turned, each is very special.

An Ice Candle Centerpiece for the Garden Table

While those gorgeous, intricately carved ice sculptures for decorating haute cuisine banquets held in grand halls may be a bit out of reach for the average gardener host, a more modest but equally lovely ice candle for the center of a festive meal is quite easy to pull off with aplomb.

ALANA DUGGINS (KERNERSVILLE, NC)

TO MAKE ONE ICE CANDLE, YOU WILL NEED:

An empty paper milk or juice carton
A pillar candle, at least 1 inch in diameter, preferably 6 or more inches high
Foliage, fresh flowers, herbs, other garden cuttings that are colorful and seasonal
Water
Room in the freezer

1. Cut the top off the carton, rinse it out, and pat it dry. Place the candle in the carton. Arrange whatever garden cuttings you have chosen around the lower half or third of the candle, making sure the pretty side faces outward, not toward the candle. Very slowly, so as not to disturb the arrangement, pour enough water into the carton to barely cover the arrangement. Place in the freezer until frozen solid. Continue with another layer or two, freezing each as you go, building up until the ice is as high as it can be and still have the wick and ½ inch of the candle free.'

2. To use, tear away the carton and place the candle in a decorative bowl or deep dish to catch water as the candle burns and the ice melts. Light and enjoy; the candle burns slowly and will last for several hours.

Notes

• The carton can be ½-gallon size, quart size, round, or rectangular, as long as it's made of paper that can be peeled away when the candle is "done" and as long as it's tall enough to accommodate the height of the candle almost to its wick.

• The candle can be as tall or short as you'd like, but keep in mind that the taller, the more decorations can be installed as you build up the layers.

• The contributor suggests that "at Thanksgiving, fall leaves and pepper berries are nice. At Christmas, holly berries and rose petals look pretty. Ivy and eucalyptus, small flowers, and fresh fruit slices always work well."

• The clearer the water, the clearer the ice. So, if the water out of the tap is murky, use purchased spring water for the candle.

• You can build the ice candle in just two rounds or in four; it depends on your patience for the process of freezing in between each layer and on your artistic vision—for some, less is more; for others, the more the better.

• When choosing the dish in which to display the candle, keep in mind that, though the water catches most of it, there will probably be a bit of wax to scrape away when the candle has burned down. In other words, you may not want to set the ice candle on your finest bone china.

Broiled Lamb Chops with Garden Vegetables and Fiddlehead Ferns

SERVES 3 TO 4

"In the spring, I am a gardener who cooks; in the winter, I'm a cook who gardens. I created this dish last spring. It's quick, uses one pan, and I was back in the garden in no time flat." The pairing of lamb and fiddlehead ferns is a natural one. Not that you would find sheep in the forest or ferns in the meadow, or either in the garden, still they make good seasonal companions on the plate.

MARTHA BRADSHAW (BRANFORD, CT)

- *1 fresh sage leaf, coarsely chopped*
- *½ teaspoon chopped fresh thyme leaves*
- *½ teaspoon chopped fresh rosemary leaves*
- *2 tablespoons olive oil*
- *2 tablespoons fresh lemon juice*
- *1 clove garlic, crushed*
- *4 well-trimmed loin lamb chops*
- *8 creamer-size potatoes, any kind, scrubbed and parboiled until pierceable*
- *16 baby carrots, tops removed, scraped, and halved lengthwise*
- *4 spring globe onions, each about 2-inches in diameter, quartered lengthwise*
- *16 fiddlehead ferns, washed (see page 212)*
- *Salt and pepper*

1. Combine the sage, thyme, rosemary, oil, lemon juice, and garlic in a nonreactive dish. Add the chops, turn to coat, and set aside to marinate for 30 minutes, not longer or the meat will be overmarinated.

2. When ready to cook, preheat the broiler.

3. Line a cookie sheet with heavy-duty aluminum foil. Place the chops, potatoes, carrots, onions, and ferns on the foil and moisten

Story Updated

Once upon a time when lamb, like chicken eggs and suckling pig, was a salutation to spring, the beginning of the growing year, its presence on the table was reserved for that time and the celebrations that surrounded the season. These days, when chickens have been encouraged, even prodded, with grow lights and warmth into laying in the middle of winter and lambs have become a meat to have year-round—who knows what happened to all the mutton?—the story of spring meats has all but vanished from the collective consciousness. (Kid goat and suckling pig remain seasonal, probably from lack of demand.) Dishes like this one bring together the field, forest, and garden of the season to remind us of the inherent satisfaction of cooking with what's naturally there just now.

with some of the marinade liquid. Place under the broiler and broil for 15 to 20 minutes, turning and stirring once, until the meat is done as you like it.

4. Transfer to a serving platter, season with salt and pepper to taste, and serve.

FIDDLEHEADS AND HOW TO GET THEM
Those in the know forage for fiddleheads, the young, unfurled fern sprouts, of edible ferns. Their taste is reminiscent of asparagus, but with overtones of the forest garden in which they grow. You can find them in gourmet greengrocers from late March to the end of April. Early asparagus is a fine substitute.

Lamb-in-a-Pumpkin Supper

SERVES 8

"When my sons were in preschool and growing their own pumpkins, I devised this recipe to accommodate the plethora of their fall harvest. It is certain to be a surprising and entertaining meal, as well as a delicious one. You can also make the dish with your favorite meatball recipe made with ground lamb in place of the lamb cubes." If you miss the short pumpkin season, you can substitute butternut or acorn squash; one of these will hold about one-third of the lamb stew. Or you can plan ahead and put aside a pumpkin or two. Stored in a cool, dry place, they will keep for about three months.

ELIZABETH LEGENHAUSEN (TIMONIUM, MD)

1 medium pumpkin (6 to 8 pounds)
¼ cup vegetable or olive oil
3 pounds lean lamb stew meat, cut into 1-inch pieces
4 cloves garlic, minced
1 large onion, not too finely chopped
¼ cup all-purpose flour
1 cup light beef broth (see Note below)
¼ cup brandy
4 cups coarsely chopped fresh or canned tomatoes and their juices
1 teaspoon chili powder
1 teaspoon ground cinnamon
1 tablespoon brown sugar
1 teaspoon salt
½ teaspoon black pepper
Roasted Pumpkin Seeds, for garnish (optional, see box on page 213)

1. Using a pumpkin knife (see box on page 162), cut off the top of the pumpkin as for preparing a jack-o'-lantern. Scoop out the seeds and connecting membrane and set aside. With a melon baller or sturdy spoon, remove the flesh, leaving enough of a wall to keep the shell intact. Place the pumpkin shell and its lid on a baking sheet and set aside. Set the pulp aside separately.

2. Heat the oil in a large nonreactive pot until beginning to smoke. Brown the lamb over medium-high heat in batches so that the pieces are not crowded in the pan. Transfer to a bowl as you go.

3. When all the lamb is browned, add the garlic, onion, and pumpkin flesh to the pot and sauté until the onion is translucent, about 5 minutes. Add the flour and stir over medium heat until the flour is beginning to cook, about 2 minutes. Pour in the broth and brandy, stirring to deglaze the bottom of the pot.

4. Add the remaining ingredients, except for the pumpkin seeds and the lamb, along with any collected juices, and bring to a boil. Reduce the heat to very low, partially cover the pot, and simmer gently for 1 hour, until the sauce is thickened and the lamb is almost tender.

5. While the lamb is simmering, preheat the oven to 350°F.

6. Ladle the lamb mixture into the pumpkin shell and top with the pumpkin lid. Bake for 35 to 45 minutes, or until the outside of the pumpkin is golden and the lamb is very tender. Transfer the pumpkin and its contents to a platter and serve, garnished with the pumpkin seeds, if using.

Note: A good-quality low-sodium commercial beef broth is suitable for the stew. For a quick homemade one, see page 118.

Roasted Pumpkin or Winter Squash Seeds

The seeds of all winter squashes, including pumpkins, are suitable for roasting. To do so, separate the seeds from their connecting fibers—this takes a bit of patience, especially with pumpkin seeds, but the reward is worth it. Rinse and pat dry the seeds and spread them on a baking sheet or microwave dish. Place in a 325°F. oven for 30 minutes or microwave on high for 5 minutes. Toss with barely enough oil to coat to prevent sticking and continue baking for 30 minutes more or microwave for 5 minutes more, until golden and crunchy. Sprinkle lightly with salt and use right away or store in an airtight container for up to several weeks.

Lamb Shanks Slow-Baked with Garlic, Rosemary, and Mint

Serves 4

"I came to appreciate the succulent taste of lamb at an early age. My mother, understanding my affection for this food, always served thick, meaty lamb chops the night I returned home for the holidays, either from school or, later, from jobs in faraway places. Eventually I married Idaho rancher John Peavey and left urban life to raise sheep at his three-generations-old Flat Top Sheep Ranch Co. in the remote regions of the Pioneer Mountains. In the landscape of rolling sagebrush hillsides, wide meadows, basalt rocks, and

forested mountain foothills reachable only by dirt roads, I began to follow the cycles of the seasons as I learned that they are the cycle of life for our animals. After eighteen years at our ranch, I have gathered many family recipes for lamb dishes and developed new ones. Hardy lamb shanks are my favorite. It's a simple dinner that has at its heart garden mint, rosemary, and garlic."

DIANE PEAVEY, FLAT TOP SHEEP RANCH (PIONEER MOUNTAINS, ID)

Idaho Mountain Gardens

"Cooking with herbs is one of the satisfying experiences at our ranch headquarters. At an altitude of 6,000 feet, gardening can be tricky. Often fragile crops are destroyed by late spring frosts in July or early fall frosts in August. So, I plant selectively for short seasons and depend on herbs, lettuces, and leafy vegetables that grow quickly and on hardy root vegetables that withstand bursts of cold. Occasionally I rejoice when a summer squash makes it to my table."

—DIANE PEAVEY

Others who enjoy the altitude and pristine, unspoiled landscape of the Idaho mountains have learned to get the best out of mountain gardening and create pleasures for the table from what is there to be had. Bringing a chocolate moose to town is a story all will enjoy:

"Fifteen years ago, I decided to open a restaurant in Ketchum, Idaho, specializing in chocolate desserts. Creating the name, The Chocolate Moose, was the perfect way to incorporate a strong association with my signature product (chocolate) and a majestic representative of the mountains of southern Idaho—the moose. Although we have a short growing season, a small amount of work in the garden yields fresh herbs, edible flowers, and fruits and vegetables that lend a grandness to my salads, savory breads, dishes of our local apples, and especially, decorations for my pièce de résistance, chocolate cake."

—MARY JONES, DBA THE CHOCOLATE MOOSE (KETCHUM, ID)

4 whole lamb shanks (3 pounds)
4 cloves garlic, sliced
Four 2-inch sprigs of fresh rosemary or 1 tablespoon chopped dried rosemary leaves
1 cup red wine
Salt and pepper
½ cup coarsely chopped fresh mint leaves

1. Preheat the oven to 250°F.

2. Place the shanks in a ceramic or glazed-clay baking dish. Make several slits in the meat and insert the garlic and rosemary sprigs. If using dried rosemary, rub it on the outside of the shanks.

3. Pour the wine over the meat. Pour ¼ cup of water into the bottom of the baking dish. Generously salt and pepper the shanks and sprinkle the mint over the top.

4. Cover with a fitted lid or foil and bake for 5 to 6 hours, until the meat is falling away from the bone. At the end, add more water or wine if needed to keep from burning on the bottom.

5. Remove and let rest for a few minutes while the juices settle, then serve.

Beef Medallions with Mustard-Tarragon Glaze and Mustard Flowers

SERVES 4

"As a professional cook, I like to create dishes that bring together kitchen expertise and love of the outdoors. This is one such." The combination of tarragon and mustard in a sauce for a hearty, no-holds-barred portion of meat stands up to the occasion in a fancy dish suited for home cooking when you feel like pampering your guests.

RICHARD HIRSHEN (MILL VALLEY, CA)

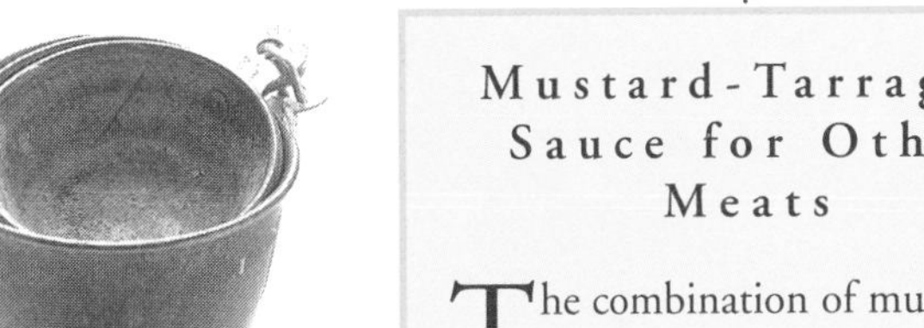

Four 4-ounce medallions of filet mignon
¼ cup olive oil
4 large sprigs of tarragon
1 tablespoon cracked black pepper
2 cups chicken broth (see page 86)
¼ cup Dijon mustard
½ tablespoon whole tarragon leaves
Mustard flowers, for garnish (see box at right)

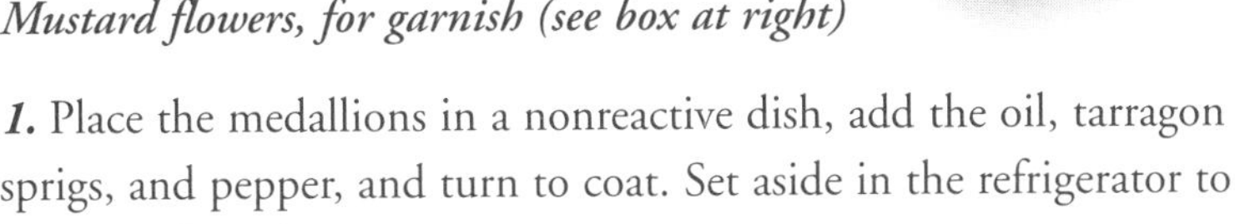

1. Place the medallions in a nonreactive dish, add the oil, tarragon sprigs, and pepper, and turn to coat. Set aside in the refrigerator to marinate for 2 hours.

2. While the meat marinates, pour the broth into a small saucepan and cook over medium heat at a brisk simmer until reduced to ½ cup. Remove from the heat and set aside in a warm place.

3. When ready to cook, bring the meat to room temperature. Have ready the mustard and tarragon leaves.

4. Lift the meat out of the marinade. Without patting dry, grill or broil it to the desired doneness. Place on a serving platter and set aside in a warm place for the juices to settle as you finish the sauce.

5. Reheat the reduced broth until beginning to boil, add the mustard, and whisk until smooth. Stir in the tarragon leaves and pour the sauce over the medallions. Scatter the mustard flowers over the platter and serve.

Mustard-Tarragon Sauce for Other Meats

The combination of mustard and tarragon in a white wine or light broth reduction is a classic and versatile quick meat sauce. You can vary the meat with lamb or pork chops. You can use dried as well as fresh tarragon. The garnish is flexible as well. Though mustard flowers add a double zing to the flavor of the dish, another edible flower in the yellow/orange range, for instance, nasturtium, chrysanthemum, or calendula petals, will serve to bedeck the plate in a bright and colorful way.

Flatiron Pot Roast with Pearl Onions and Fava Beans

Though many may think of pot roast as a slapped-together, long-cooked, forget-about-it-till-it's-done oven dish, in its perfection it is more like an opera production. When it comes to the table, if the production has been properly mounted and stage-managed, the roast will appear on the table, front and center, with an incomparable presence and a chorus of enticing vegetables around it. Chef McClasky's rendition of pot roast is ready to meet the Met.

JULIA McCLASKY, CHEF, AND GAIL DEFFERARI, OWNER, UNIVERSAL CAFE (SAN FRANCISCO, CA)

PEPPERCORNS RETHOUGHT: FROM CRUNCHY TO SOFT BERRY

There's no need to remove each and every peppercorn that may cling to the meat when you remove it from the pot. The peppercorns, actually berries of the Piper nigrum *vine, become soft again during the long cooking and provide a pleasing burst of pepper flavor when you bite into one.*

FOR THE FIRST ACT:
Salt and pepper
2 flatiron steaks (about 2½ pounds each) (see box on page 217)
Olive oil, for coating the skillet
2 carrots, scraped and coarsely chopped
2 celery ribs, coarsely chopped
1 onion, coarsely chopped
2 leeks, trimmed, coarsely chopped, well washed, and drained
4 cloves garlic, minced
1½ cups white wine
6 medium tomatoes, peeled, seeded, and chopped (about 1½ pounds), or 1 can (14-ounce) tomatoes, drained and chopped
6 sprigs of fresh thyme
2 tablespoons whole black peppercorns
4 to 6 cups chicken broth (see page 86)

FOR THE SECOND ACT:
1 pound carrots, scraped and cut into 4 by ½-inch batons or ½-inch ovals
2 cups peeled and diced parsnip
1 pound pearl onions, peeled (see Note below)
1 cup shelled fresh fava beans, peeled (see Note below)

FOR THE THIRD ACT:
Mashed potatoes (see page 274) or spoonbread (see page 189)
Chopped chives, for garnish

1. Preheat the oven to 350°F.

2. Generously salt and pepper both sides of each steak. Coat the bottom of an ovenproof casserole large enough to hold the meat in one layer with olive oil. Set over high heat. When the oil is very hot, add the meat and sear on both sides, 3 to 4 minutes altogether. Remove to a plate and set aside.

3. Reduce the heat to medium-high and add the chopped carrots, celery, onion, leeks, and garlic. Cook until the vegetables are browned but not scorched, about 5 minutes. Add the wine and simmer 1 or 2 minutes. Add the tomatoes, thyme, peppercorns, and 4 cups of broth. Bring to a boil, then return the meat to the pot. Add more broth to cover the meat if necessary and bring to a boil again. Cover the pot and place it in the oven.

4. Bake until the meat is fork tender but not falling apart, 2 to 2½ hours.

5. While the meat cooks, bring a pot of salted water to a boil. Parboil the carrot batons, parsnips, pearl onions, and fava beans separately (see Note below). Drain and rinse in cold water as you go along. Set the vegetables aside.

6. When the meat is done, remove it to a platter and keep it warm. Strain the cooking juices into a bowl and let sit a few minutes for the fat to rise to the top.

7. Skim off the fat from the juices and pour them into a clean pot. Add the parboiled vegetables. Bring to a boil, then simmer for 15 minutes (see Note below).

8. Carve the meat into long ½-inch-thick slices. Rewarm the meat slices in the juices in the pot just before serving.

9. To serve, mound some mashed potatoes on one side of individual shallow soup bowls or deep dinner plates. Arrange slices of meat across the potatoes. Arrange the vegetables around the meat, spoon pan juices over all, garnish with chopped chives, and serve right away.

Note: The easiest way to peel the pearl onions and fava beans is to hardboil them first and then peel. If you use this method, skip parboiling them a second time as in Step 5.

Flatiron Pot Roast: A Cut Above

Flatiron steak used to be readily available. Every Jewish mother and every Yankee grandmother knew how to get one, namely, from the local butcher. Also called blade steak, the flatiron cut is taken from the top blade (bone) side of a thickly cut (at least 4 inches) beef chuck (shoulder) roast. It's prized for pot roasting because it cooks up as tender as a tenderloin but happily simmers in the casserole for the long, slow cooking that a pot roast requires to develop its nature. There are still butchers who can cut one for you for that special pot-roast occasion if you call ahead. Without such a possibility, you can substitute cross rib roast, although chef McClasky would never do so, preferring not to make the dish until she has flatiron.

Pot Roast: Off-Broadway Productions

From culture to culture where there is beef served for the meal, there is almost always a special way to prepare it pot-roast style. The cut of meat, seasonings, and pot accompaniments vary. But basically it's a large cut of beef softened into goodness as it braises with flavorings. Following are three other pot-roast methods.

YANKEE. Instead of the flatiron cut, the whole chuck roast or a rump roast is used. Instead of pearl onions and fava beans, the meat is braised with lengths of carrot, onion quarters, and sliced potatoes to serve along with the meat.

JEWISH. This is a stew for both meat and dairy use. The flatiron cut is essential in the meat version. Along with the usual carrots and aromatics, dried fruit (prunes and apricots) is added, so the dish turns out a bit sweet.

SAUERBRATEN. A widely appreciated import from German cooking, it's made and served especially for family occasions. Rather than flatiron or chuck, the cut is often rump or brisket. The long cooking tenderizes the meat to the point that it practically shreds under your knife as you slice. The *sauer,* or sour part, is achieved by marinating the meat in spiced vinegar for several days. The meat is braised in the marinating liquid, which is sweetened with sugar and thickened with flour before serving. Sometimes ground gingersnaps are added for further thickening and flavor.

Elk or Venison Loin with Chokecherry Sauce

SERVES 6

"High in the mountains of Colorado, little can be grown in the garden. But outside the door of my log cabin are many woodsy wonders. Besides aspen leaves, blue spruce cuttings, and wildflowers to scent and decorate the house, there are sylvan treasures

for cooking: kinnikinnick to work into pemmican, pine sprigs to flavor olive oil, and, when you are lucky, chokecherries and juniper berries for a sauce that imparts altitudinous attitude to high mountain meats."

SUSANNA HOFFMAN (TELLURIDE, CO)

3 cups dry red wine
½ cup balsamic vinegar
1 medium onion, coarsely chopped
2 cloves garlic, minced
2 bay leaves, crumbled
4 large sprigs of fresh thyme or 1 teaspoon dried thyme
8 juniper berries
½ teaspoon salt
½ teaspoon black pepper
2½-pound loin of elk or venison
1 cup Chokecherries in Syrup (recipe follows)

1. Stir together the wine, vinegar, onion, garlic, bay leaves, thyme, juniper berries, salt, and pepper in a large nonreactive dish. Add the loin and turn to coat. Set aside in the refrigerator to marinate overnight, turning 3 or 4 times.

2. When ready to cook, remove the loin from the refrigerator to come to room temperature.

3. Prepare the chokecherry syrup.

4. Prepare a charcoal fire. When ready to cook, separate the coals into 2 piles with a space between them that is wide enough to position the loin so that it is not directly over the coals.

5. Lift the loin out of the marinade and place on the grill rack between the 2 piles of coals. Grill, turning once, until medium rare, 40 to 45 minutes. Transfer to a serving platter and set aside in a warm place for 10 minutes.

6. While the loin cooks, strain the marinade into a medium nonreactive saucepan. Add the chokecherries and their syrup and simmer briskly over medium-high heat until reduced and thickened into a sauce, about 45 minutes.

7. To serve, cut the loin into chops and arrange on the platter over the collected juices. Pour the sauce over the chops and serve.

OVEN-ROASTED ELK OR VENISON

You can also roast the loin, or other cuts of elk or venison, in the oven: Preheat the oven to 450°F. Brown the loin in a heavy skillet lightly greased with olive oil, about 10 minutes. Transfer to a roasting pan and reduce the oven heat to 375°F. Roast until medium rare, about 45 minutes, depending on the cut. Remove to a platter and continue with the recipe.

"The most common American wild cherry is the chokecherry, the Prunus virginiana. *It is found from Newfoundland to Georgia, and west to Nebraska and Texas. . . . The cherries are small, about the size of a pea, and usually quite astringent . . . chiefly valuable as jelly material."*

—Euell Gibbons, *Stalking the Wild Asparagus*

Chokecherries in Syrup

MAKES 1 CUP

2 cups wild chokecherries
1 cup sugar
½-inch piece cinnamon stick or dash of ground allspice
1 teaspoon fresh lemon juice

Combine all the ingredients and 1 cup water in a medium saucepan. Bring to a boil and simmer until thick enough to coat a spoon, 30 to 40 minutes, depending on the altitude.

Note: Sour cherries can be substituted for chokecherries or you can use chokecherry jelly. It is available in many mountain gift shops.

Swiss Chard Rolls with Elk Stuffing

MAKES 10 ROLLS

"Laramie is a small town on the high plains, 7,240 feet altitude, between the Laramie and Snowy mountain ranges. Needless to say, gardening is an adventure. We do grow tomatoes, tomatillos, carrots, beets, onions, peas, beans, squash, and most herbs. Our Brussels sprouts, broccoli, and Swiss chard crops were especially great this year. We've rigged up a pretty good cold frame that we cover the plants with until mid-June or so. As we say here at 7,200 feet, gardening builds character! My friends all hunt and give me elk, with some of which I dreamt up this recipe; you could substitute any lean ground meat."

DEB OLSON (LARAMIE, WY)

1 tablespoon olive oil plus some for greasing the baking dish
1 pound ground elk meat (see headnote)
1 small onion, chopped
4 cloves garlic, minced
2 cups cooked rice, any kind
2 tablespoons chopped fresh basil leaves
1 tablespoon chopped fresh oregano leaves
½ teaspoon salt
½ teaspoon black pepper
10 or so large Swiss chard leaves, ribs removed if large and tough (see page 221)
2 cups spicy tomato sauce (see page 296)
Freshly grated Parmesan or other hard cheese

1. Preheat the oven to 375°F. Lightly grease a 12 by 9-inch baking dish.

2. Heat the 1 tablespoon oil in a heavy skillet. Add the meat, onion, and garlic and sauté over medium-high heat until the meat is browned, about 8 minutes.

3. Stir in the rice, basil, oregano, salt, and pepper and remove from the heat. Let cool enough to handle.

4. Place some of the meat mixture on a chard leaf. Roll up the leaf, tucking in the ends if you like. Continue until all the leaves and meat are used. Place the rolls in the baking dish and spread the sauce over the top. Cover with foil and bake for 35 to 45 minutes, until the leaves are tender and the sauce is bubbling nicely.

5. Sprinkle with the freshly grated cheese and serve.

CHARD CHAT

The contributor explains that in her high-altitude, short-season garden, the ribs of the chard leaves usually do not develop past the supple stage. When she sometimes has chard with stiffer ribs, she cuts away the bottom part up to the point where the rib becomes rollable, taking care not to sever the leaf in half. It's much like removing the core part from a cabbage leaf when you want to make cabbage rolls.

Pork Sausage with Spinach and Provençal Herbs

MAKES ABOUT TEN 6-OUNCE PATTIES

Bruce Aidells, founder of Aidells Sausage Co., co-author of numerous cookbooks (The Complete Meat Cookbook)*, and widely recognized expert on the art of sausage making, advises that the sausage mix, though ready to use right away, benefits from an overnight stay in the refrigerator so the flavors can mellow and blend. He also suggests that for a taste variation, one that is also less caloric, you can replace part or all of the pork with chicken or turkey.*

BRUCE AIDELLS (KENSINGTON, CA)

3 pounds ground pork
1 pound spinach, washed, coarsely chopped, and blanched
3 tablespoons finely chopped shallots
1 tablespoon chopped fresh tarragon leaves
1 tablespoon chopped fresh thyme leaves
1 teaspoon chopped fresh rosemary leaves
1½ teaspoons chopped fresh sage leaves
¼ teaspoon ground nutmeg
3 teaspoons salt
⅓ cup kirsch or white wine

1. Place all the ingredients in a large bowl and mix well. Use right away or let stand in the refrigerator for several hours or up to 3 days. Can be frozen for up to 3 months.

2. When ready to cook, make patties and fry or grill them until cooked through, no longer pink in the center but not dry, 15 to 20 minutes. Serve right away.

The Many Faces of a Farce

One of the delights of a sausage blend, called *farce* in French cooking, is that it is malleable and lends itself to many forms, from links to patties to meatballs to meat loaf. Without kitchen equipment to stuff sausage casings, you can pat a sausage mix into shapes to fit whatever dish you are making.

For dinner: 6-ounce sausage patties are the right size.

For appetizers: 1½-ounce meatballs are about toothpick size.

For pasta sauces: Large meatballs, 2 to 3 ounces each, show up well over the pasta.

For poultry stuffing: The mix can be used in bulk as a perfect base for filling any bird.

For pâté, or fancy meat loaf: You can pat the sausage mix into a loaf pan, place a whole bay leaf in the center, lay a few strips of bacon over the top, and cook in a medium-low oven (325°F.) until the juices no longer run pink and the loaf is pulling away from the edges of the pan, 1½ to 2 hours.

For good-old-good meat loaf: Pat the sausage into a loaf pan, spread a thin layer of tomato sauce over the top, and cook as for pâté.

Jerk Pork

Serves 6

"While vacationing in Jamaica, my husband and I fell in love with the spicy-hot pork flavored with the habanero, or Scotch bonnet, chili pepper. The following spring, he (the gardener) planted many of the necessary ingredients—onions, thyme, and habanero peppers. Through trial and error, I (the cook) came up with an authentic-tasting recipe. You can adjust the heat by increasing or decreasing the amount of habanero. Also, removing the seeds, the hottest part of the pepper, decreases the heat; leaving them in increases it." When you're ready for another round of the Caribbean, use the feisty sauce for chicken pieces.

ERIKA AND KENNY BANALEWICZ (REHOBOTH, MA)

6 boneless center-cut pork chops

¾ cup Jerk Sauce (recipe follows)

1. Place the meat in a baking dish large enough to hold the pieces in one layer. Spread the sauce over the top and turn to coat the other side. Marinate in the refrigerator overnight. Remove and bring to room temperature before cooking.

2. Prepare a charcoal fire, or preheat the broiler.

3. Grill or broil the pork or chicken, turning once, until done as you like.

Jerk Sauce

MAKES 3/4 CUP

1 habanero chili, seeded or not and coarsely chopped
1 clove garlic, coarsely chopped
1 medium onion, coarsely chopped
1 teaspoon fresh thyme leaves
¼ to ½ teaspoon ground nutmeg, to taste
¼ teaspoon ground cinnamon
½ teaspoon salt
½ teaspoon black pepper
2 teaspoons brown sugar
4 tablespoons soy sauce
1 tablespoon cider vinegar
1 tablespoon vegetable oil

Place all the ingredients in a food processor and process until chopped as fine as possible. Use right away or store in the refrigerator for up to 1 week.

Marinades and Seasoning Pastes

Mike Tierney, co-founder and president of the esteemed Taft Street Winery in the Russian River region of Sonoma County, California, spends time cooking when he's not attending to business. His marinades and seasoning pastes offer uncomplicated ways to enhance summertime grills and leave the host chef free to enjoy the company and the wines being offered. He advises that "when putting together these marinades and pastes, relaxed entertaining is the key: you should feel free to add, delete, or improvise the herbs as you will." He offers, in addition, some wine selections both for the table and for enjoying around the grill (see page 226).

~ MIKE TIERNEY, TAFT STREET WINERY (SONOMA COUNTY, CA)

Lime-Garlic Marinade for Meats and Vegetables

MAKES ABOUT 1½ CUPS

½ cup olive oil
1 cup lime juice
2 tablespoons minced garlic
⅓ cup chopped fresh oregano leaves
1 teaspoon ground cumin

Whisk together all the ingredients in a small bowl. Use right away or store in the refrigerator for up to overnight. Especially good as a marinade for hearty meats in small cuts, such as flank steak, beef or lamb kabobs, or pork tenderloin, or as a quick pre-grill wash for sturdy vegetables such as potatoes, bell peppers, or eggplants.

Marinating Guidelines for Meat, Poultry, and Fish

For overnight marinating, choose a marinade that has little or no acidic ingredients, like citrus juice or wine, because the acid will pickle the meat so that it comes off the grill a little more flaccid than you had in mind. With a no- or low-acid marinade, meats and poultry can withstand, indeed benefit from, an overnight soak, in the fridge, of course. Fish, less dense and more porous than meats and poultry, will be well marinated in a few hours. If citrus juice or wine is a desired flavor, add it at the end, a few hours before grilling for meats and poultry, one hour for fish.

Thai-Style Herb Marinade for Poultry and Pork

MAKES ABOUT 1 CUP

¼ cup fresh basil leaves, any variety from Italian to Thai
¼ cup fresh mint leaves
¼ cup cilantro leaves
1 to 3 tablespoons minced garlic, to taste
1 small fresh chili pepper, such as serrano or Thai chili, seeded
1 tablespoon brown sugar
½ cup lime juice
2 tablespoons soy sauce
2 tablespoons fish sauce (see Note below)
2 tablespoons vegetable oil

Place all the ingredients in a food processor and blend to mix. Use right away or store in the refrigerator for up to overnight. Especially good for cut-up chicken, turkey pieces, or pork cutlets, chops, or loin roast.

Note: Fish sauce is available in Asian grocery stores, many supermarkeets, and health food stores.

Chili-Ginger Seasoning Paste for Fish Steaks

MAKES ABOUT ¾ CUP

2 tablespoons finely chopped small fresh chili pepper, such as serrano or Thai
2 tablespoons finely chopped fresh ginger
½ cup finely chopped cilantro leaves
3 tablespoons sesame oil
¼ cup vegetable oil
Salt and pepper, to taste

Combine all the ingredients in a small bowl. Use right away or store in the refrigerator for up to overnight. Especially good with tuna, swordfish, salmon, or halibut.

Lemon-Herb Seasoning Paste for Poultry, Rabbit, and Lamb

MAKES ABOUT 1 CUP

¼ cup minced garlic
¼ cup grated lemon zest
¼ cup finely chopped fresh parsley leaves
2 tablespoons finely chopped fresh thyme leaves
2 tablespoons finely chopped fresh rosemary leaves
2 tablespoons finely chopped fresh oregano leaves
½ cup olive oil

Combine all the ingredients in a small bowl. Use right away or store in the refrigerator for up to overnight. Especially good for halved chicken, bone-in turkey breasts, rabbit, and leg of lamb.

TIPPLING TIPS

An Everyday Guide to Wines

"Wine can accompany almost every dish, and grilled foods especially invite a glass of wine, beginning with keeping the chef company around the barbecue. I offer these easy suggestions and a few opinions for choosing among wines to accompany grilled foods."

WHITES

CHARDONNAY. There is an immense number from which to choose—Chardonnay is successfully grown all over the United States, as well as in Chile, Australia, France, and elsewhere. As a novice, begin by shopping the price. Way cheap is probably not way good. Very expensive often means pronounced oak flavors, which don't complement grilled foods. Try Chardonnay with grilled chicken legs seasoned with Thai-style marinade.

SAUVIGNON BLANC. For spicy, exotic foods, in particular Thai or other Pacific Rim dishes, this is the wine to have. Though not customary to serve with such cuisine—beer is more regular—if wine is your beverage of choice, select a sauvignon blanc. It cools the palate, stands up to the spice, and adds enjoyment to the meal without insisting on turning all attention to itself. Give it a go with grilled sea bass seasoned with the Chili-Ginger Paste.

ROSÉS

There are many delicious French rosé wines, from the rightfully esteemed Bandol to the more ordinary dry rosés found throughout the countryside. With a few notable exceptions, domestic wineries have not yet taken up the baton on this one. For the moment, it's best to stick with the rosés from southern Europe. Try one with grilled swordfish seasoned with the chili-ginger rub.

REDS

MERLOT. In part, since it is smooth textured and aromatic, Merlot has become to red wine what Chardonnay is to white wine—widely embraced, even ubiquitous. Bargain Merlots are harder to find than bargain Chardonnays. You are as likely to run across one as you are to find a Picasso at the flea market. However, shop around and you'll be rewarded. For the grill, add ginger, garlic, and cilantro to the lemon-herb paste for a butterflied leg of lamb.

SYRAH. I have a special love for Syrah, so much so that I am planting 600 vines in my front yard at the moment of this writing. The grapes turn into a spicy and full-bodied wine that is meant to be enjoyed with meat and game. For the grill, add crushed, toasted fennel seed, garlic, and ground cinnamon to the lime-garlic marinade to coat a pork loin.

ZINFANDEL. Among wine zealots—vintners, backyard barbecuers, and restaurateurs—Zinfandel wines provide endless opportunity for discussion. The wine has a rich and mysterious past, with historians still debating the grape's true ancestral ground. Whatever the academic outcome, the wine, now almost uniquely Californian, is made in numerous styles that range from fruity, almost Beaujolais-like, to blockbusters with high concentration of flavors. In any of the styles, a Zinfandel wine is always big. Try one of these "big boys" with a New York strip steak rubbed with a handful of fresh rosemary, garlic, salt, and pepper or to accompany other big meat tastes, such as grilled venison, wild duck, whole lamb, or suckling pig.

PINOT NOIR. Hands down, my favorite wine. The delicate perfume and soft headiness make this a wine I'll take anywhere. Yet, versatile as it is, I prefer to serve it with straightforward dishes so that its subtleties are not missed. It's great with salmon. Try it with a grilled salmon fillet seasoned with the chili-ginger mix.

—MIKE TIERNEY, TAFT STREET WINERY

vegetable sides:

seasonal borders for the plate

Vegetable side dishes of seasonal produce betoken the garden-to-table style. More than occasional whim, they signify a way of thinking about food and eating. Whether for the vegetarian or confirmed meat eater, no meal is complete unless embellished with a border of garden-fresh vegetables. With that in mind, this chapter focuses on the seasons and insofar as possible follows them in its organization. Many plants are anchored to a particular time of year and will grow only then—for instance, peas and asparagus in spring, tomatoes and eggplant in summer, apples, nuts, and Brussels sprouts in fall. Many others, refusing to be restricted to a single round of production, straddle the seasons. Onions, carrots, beets, broccoli, and citrus are available fresh and natural much of the year, if not from our own backyards, then from another close-by clime. Following are vegetable side dishes that characterize garden cooking. Each brings a taste of the garden to the meal; two or three together could easily make a satisfying plateful.

TOOLS *of the* TRADE

The Compost Pile

"Gardens love leftovers"

DEBORAH BISHOP (SAN FRANCISCO, CA)

If ever you've wished, as you prepare the vegetables for the meal, crack the eggs for a dish, replace the old coffee grounds with new ones for a fresh pot, that there was something to do with such classy "garbage," satisfy your mind and ease your conscience by turning all those peelings and parings and grounds into compost. Onerous as it may seem to keep from tossing them into a garbage bin and instead to separate the "good-for-compost" from the "not-good-for-compost" matter, this is the easy part. It's actually a simple formula.

Good for the compost

- Vegetable parings such as potato, carrot, beet peels, tomato skins, mushroom stems, too-old-for-the pot turnip tops, and so on.
- Egg shells, coffee grounds, tea leaves.
- Yard prunings, including tree trim, mown grass, raked leaves. If you want these to biodegrade in time to retill before the next decade, be sure to cut them into small pieces.

Not good for the compost

- Animal matter, including the chicken bones from last night's dinner. These call forth the creatures you don't want visiting your compost pile or your premises. Also, decomposing animal matter exudes a horrific smell to humans.
- Plastics, because these are not biodegradable in our lifetime, if ever. In the interim, they will clog the free flow of garden to house and back again which is the purpose of composting.

Design

Establishing the physical space and structure for composting takes a little planning. First, select a site handy to the garden and a little away from the house. Though in principle good compost doesn't smell, it does go through odoriferous periods during decomposition and you don't want the waft drifting into the house.

Depending on the size of your premises and your garden needs, you can set up:

- A spot in which to dump the good garbage, handy enough to the house that you have a mind to turn the heap from time to time as it biodegrades (see box on page 238).
- A series of three open bins. The first bin receives all the fresh garbage. There it rests until it is decomposed enough to turn with a pitchfork. Then it is forked over to a second bin by its side, where it rests some more to decompose further. So now the first bin is empty to receive a new round of ingredients. After a while, the contents of the second bin are pitched into the third bin to make room for what comes out of the first bin. From the third bin, what is now compost is forked into the garden and turned under to amend the soil. The process may sound complicated, but actually it's not. It does, however, require some space.
- A biostack composter that fits neatly into a small corner of the yard. Like a garden-size Chinese puzzle box or free-standing shelf system, its components stack, restack, and at the same time biodegrade the fill into compost almost without backbreaking effort on the part of the gardener. Well, there always is some work involved.

The good news is that, once set up, the compost pile, of whatever design you choose , will be a glory of your garden and a satisfaction to yourself as you pare and prune away, knowing all that's gone for the moment returns in a circle unbroken.

Glazed Green Onions

Serves 4

"We always have a garden with plenty of onions." In North Carolina and other mild-winter climates that allow fall planting, overwintering, and then a spring crop, the first onions are up in time for the vernal equinox. In those areas, the onion tenderlings for this dish are probably called spring onions, sometimes green onions. In cold-winter climates where the gardener must wait for spring to plant and into early summer to harvest, they are called scallions, sometimes green onions. Spring onions, green onions, or scallions, if they're not available from your garden, they are from the produce market. Swiftly glazed, they retain their color and add a bright spot on the plate. To serve them as a vegetable side dish rather than a side garnish, triple the recipe.

SUSIE TIMMONS
(WINSTON-SALEM, NC)

12 to 18 well-developed green onions (scallions), including tops, trimmed and cut into ¾-inch pieces
3 tablespoons butter or bacon grease
3 teaspoons sugar
½ cup water
Salt and pepper

1. Place all the ingredients in a skillet over medium heat. Simmer for 20 minutes, or until the liquid is gone and the onions are glossy.

2. Serve warm as a side dish garnish for meat or vegetables.

The Edible Allium: An All-Accommodating Lily

Alliums, otherwise known as the onion clan of the huge and wide-ranging lily family, provide beauty and imagination to any gardener's walk through the vegetable patch. Their leaves, standing upright, and their not-quite-open-yet flower heads mark the spots where, underground, they are growing to meet their promise of vegetable goodness for the kitchen. They also bring happiness to the cook. In all their stages, from tenderlings to flowering stalks to bulbs, and in all their varieties—chives, garlics, leeks, and globe onions—the alliums are edible from top to bottom. As an extra special goodness, their flowers add a long-lasting lilt to any bouquet.

Creamed Radishes

Serves 6

Seldom do radishes appear cooked in American cuisine. But here, following a Scandinavian preparation, the small turnip cousin is blanched just enough to soften the natural crunch and turned in a rich cream sauce to make an unusual, softly pink vegetable side dish.

LUCILLE ERGER (BELLE PLAINE, IA)

RADISH TOPS: SAVE OR TOSS? *Radish tops are edible and good. Mexican cooks would probably not think of tossing them into the compost, as is routinely done by North American cooks, unless they are old and bitter beyond salvation. Radish leaves should be used very young and tender, either raw in salads or briefly wilted, as in the creamed radishes. After that, well, maybe the compost bin is a good place for their salvation and eventual reincarnation as food for the soil.*

1 pound red radishes, preferably with tops
2 tablespoons butter
2 tablespoons all-purpose flour
½ teaspoon salt
⅛ teaspoon black or white pepper
½ cup heavy (whipping) cream
Radish leaves (optional garnish)

1. Trim the tops off the radishes, leaving a little of the green stem attached. Cut the radishes lengthwise in half and place in a medium pot with 1 cup of water. Bring to a boil and simmer over medium heat until pierceable but still firm, about 5 minutes. Drain, reserving the water, and set aside.

2. Melt the butter in a pot or sauté pan over medium heat. Add the flour and whisk to smooth. Stir in the salt, pepper, and reserved water. Bring to a boil and cook until thickened, about 1 minute. Whisk in the cream and continue cooking until thick again, 1 minute more.

3. Stir in the radishes and reheat. Serve warm, garnished with the radish leaves, if using.

Fava Bean Sauté

Serves 4 to 6

In tandem with young onions, another spring treat, fava beans provide a special dish for a new-season meal. If the favas are small and tender, they need not be peeled before sautéing. Anything larger than pea size, it's best to go the extra step and slip away the peel after blanching.

LYNN ALBERTI (FORT WORTH, TX)

6 pounds fresh fava beans, shelled
¼ cup olive oil
1 large clove garlic, minced
1 small onion, finely chopped
¼ teaspoon crushed red pepper
1½ teaspoons chopped fresh marjoram or ½ teaspoon dried marjoram
¼ teaspoon salt
⅛ teaspoon black pepper

1. Bring a large pot of water to a boil. Add the beans and cook over medium-high heat until the skins wither and begin to split, about 3 minutes. Drain and cool enough to handle. If the beans are small and tender, set aside. If they are large, slip them out of their skins before proceeding with the recipe.

2. Heat the oil in a large sauté pan over medium-high heat. Add the garlic, onion, and red pepper and cook, stirring occasionally, until the onion is soft but not browned, about 2 minutes. Stir in the beans, marjoram, salt, and pepper and continue cooking until heated through, about 1 minute more. Serve right away.

Fava: The Many Aspects of a Well-Traveled Bean

Fava beans are the only Old World bean to come our way fresh on a regular basis. That alone is enough to make them interesting. But, more important, they stand out as a consummate earth-to-table vegetable. Along with vetch and lentils, they have long been used as a fallow crop to replenish nitrogen in depleted, overfarmed soil. Their offering for the table is equally appreciated by cooks who know that, though the ultimate gain from a heavy weight of favas yields a small amount to eat and shelling and peeling them is a bit of a pain in the thumbs, their earthy, bittersweet flavor vivifies whatever dish they are included in. In the garden or on the table, favas have an inimitable way of bridging the ocean. They also are very pretty plants that rise high in the not-yet-warm spring sun, showing off their white-petaled, black-freckled faces to breathe the air of spring.

Elegant and Easy Sautéed Asparagus

SERVES 4

"Even though we have a short growing season in Maine, my husband and I enjoy gardening and cooking the fruits of our labor. We have a patch of asparagus—my favorite of all our veggies—that we planted several years ago. We also plant garlic in the fall to harvest in late summer and winterover in our cold cellar. When the asparagus, along with newly sprouted basil and the overwintered but still fresh garlic, appear together, this is the dish we cook." As befits the season's weather, the dish is excellent served at spring temperature—between chilly and warm. *For another asparagus laud to spring, see page 232.*

JACKIE DWINAL (BATH, ME)

1 to 2 tablespoons olive oil, enough to coat the bottom of the pan generously
1 pound asparagus, ends trimmed, stalks cut diagonally into 1- to 2-inch lengths (see Note below)
6 large cloves garlic, slivered
⅛ teaspoon salt
¼ teaspoon coarsely ground black pepper
2 to 3 tablespoons shredded fresh basil leaves

1. Heat the olive oil in a large sauté pan. Add the asparagus and garlic and sauté over medium heat until the asparagus is slightly wilted but still bright green and crisp, about 8 minutes.

2. Stir in the salt and pepper and transfer all to a serving dish. Sprinkle the shredded basil over the top and serve.

Note: If the asparagus stalks are thin, unpeeled 2-inch lengths work fine. If they are the fatter, lusher stalks from later in the season, you may want to peel them and cut them shorter, about 1-inch lengths, for ease of eating.

Asparagus Technique: Two Ways to Trim the Stalks

To trim asparagus when you are going to use whole stalks in a dish, hold a stalk and snap it at the point where it naturally gives easily. This results in eliminating the woody, tough end while keeping the tender top, the best part, for the dish.

For dishes that call for asparagus pieces, use a knife to cut the bottoms off at the point where the green ends and the yellow-brown begins. Discard the ends and cut the rest of each stalk into ¼- to 1-inch lengths, as the recipe calls for. This method results in more yield per pound, but sometimes it's nice to have longer lengths. You can always include the trim in a vegetable broth or add it to the compost pile.

Asparagus-Mushroom Flan

SERVES 4

"Having inherited my grandmother's asparagus beds, I am always trying new ways to enjoy those delicious stalks! Here is one I like to share with my best friends to celebrate the arrival of asparagus season."

PATRICIA KING (EDGEWATER, MD)

2 tablespoons butter
1 garlic clove, minced
1 large shallot, finely chopped
¼ teaspoon chopped fresh rosemary leaves
⅓ cup chopped fresh parsley leaves
2 ounces fresh shiitake mushrooms, trimmed and thinly sliced
1 pound asparagus, trimmed and cut into 1-inch pieces
1 cup heavy (whipping) cream
2 large eggs, lightly beaten
3 tablespoons grated Parmesan cheese

1. Preheat the oven to 350°F.

2. Melt the butter in a skillet. Add the garlic, shallot, rosemary, and parsley and stir over medium heat for 30 seconds, or until wilted. Add the shiitakes and asparagus and sauté for 2 minutes, or until wilted. Stir in the cream, bring to a boil, and remove from the heat. Set aside to cool slightly.

3. Stir in the eggs and Parmesan. Pour the mixture into 4 lightly greased 1-cup ramekins or one 1-quart soufflé dish. Place the ramekins in a baking dish filled with 1 inch of hot water and bake for 35 minutes, or until golden on top and a knife inserted in the center comes out clean. Serve warm.

Flavoring the Flan

A flan, basically a soft egg-and-cream custard, can coddle many savory flavors besides asparagus. Try the following.

FOR THE VEGETABLE: Broccoli, corn, green or globe onion, spinach or sorrel, zucchini

FOR THE MUSHROOM: Button, chanterelle, cremini, morel, oyster, porcini

FOR THE CHEESE: Aged Asiago, blue cheese such as Cambozola or Danish blue, cheddar, (orange or white as long as it's sharp), Jack, Gruyère, provolone

FOR THE HERB: Chervil, chive, cilantro, dill, tarragon, thyme

Or, for a pièce de résistance, use truffle, in which case omit any cheese, vegetable, or herb so the truffle can receive the attention it deserves.

Mrs. Ryan's Creamed Carrots

SERVES 8

Before butter and cream were banished from the dietetically righteous table, they were used with abandon to sweeten and enrich all manner of dishes. Not even counting the desserts and other sweets, cream sauces on everything from chicken to celery, creamed radishes, creamed peas and corn, and creamed carrots were regular meal treats. Though the admonition against an excess of butter and cream is not one to ignore, there are times such old-fashioned delights might once again be indulged for a moment, especially if the vegetable is fresh from the garden and there's company for dinner.

EDWARD CARERI (FREEPORT, NY)

8 tablespoons (1 stick) butter, melted
2 pounds carrots, scraped and julienned (see Note below)
4 medium onions, thinly sliced
3 tablespoons chopped fresh parsley leaves
1 teaspoon salt
1 teaspoon black pepper
¾ cup half-and-half

1. Preheat the oven to 350°F.

2. Combine the butter, carrots, onions, parsley, salt, pepper, and ½ cup of the half-and-half in a 13 by 9-inch baking dish. Toss to mix well.

3. Pour the remaining half-and-half over the top and bake for 50 to 60 minutes, or until the carrots are tender and the cream is thickened almost to curdling.

Note: The julienne blade of a food processor cuts the carrots just right.

Basically Carrots

Carrots are one of the five most-bought vegetables in the United States. They are also one of the most widely grown in home gardens because they are easy to plant by broadcasting; they sprout readily with a bit of watering; they seem to enjoy crowds, allowing other carrots and root crops to thrive alongside them as long as the soil is fairly loose and free draining. Once established, they wait patiently for months on end, without assuming a tough attitude, until the gardener comes to transport them to the kitchen. Not only that, they satisfy pretty much everyone at the table with the simplest of preparations, such as:

"Scrape and julienne as many carrots as you are cooking. Steam them until softened, about 2 minutes, then drain. Melt some butter, about 1 tablespoon per pound of carrots, and soften some sliced garlic to taste in the butter. Stir in the carrots and some chopped fresh herb, such as basil, thyme, or marjoram. Sauté until the carrots are cooked through but not browned, about 3 minutes. Serve right away."

—DEBBIE NESTLE (BLOOMFIELD HILLS, MI)

Baked Carrots in Horseradish Cream

SERVES 4

Carrots and horseradish have an affinity for each other both in the garden, where they successfully coexist side by side underground, and on the plate, where the pungent flavor of the one root complements the sweet flavor of the other. Wrapped together in a mayonnaise sauce that is pure Americana, they make a colorful side dish for fall through spring holidays.

LINDA REYNOLDS (RICHMOND, VA)

1 pound small carrots, scraped and cut in half lengthwise
¼ cup mayonnaise (see page 64)
¼ cup milk
¼ cup freshly grated horseradish (see box below)
Salt and pepper
¼ cup coarse bread crumbs, preferably homemade (see page 76), tossed with 1 teaspoon melted butter
Chopped fresh parsley leaves, for garnish (optional)

1. Preheat the oven to 350°F.

2. Place the carrots and enough water barely to cover in a saucepan. Bring to a boil and cook until fork tender, about 10 minutes. Drain, reserving ¼ cup of the liquid in the saucepan. Set the carrots aside.

3. Add the mayonnaise, milk, and horseradish to the saucepan and whisk to smooth. Season with salt and pepper to taste.

4. Spread the carrots in a 13 by 9-inch baking dish. Pour the sauce over the carrots and sprinkle the bread crumbs over the top. Bake until the topping is golden and toasted, about 6 minutes. Serve right away, while still warm, garnished with parsley leaves, if using.

Note: If the carrots are larger than small, cut them into 4-inch lengths, then slice them lengthwise into ½-inch-wide strips.

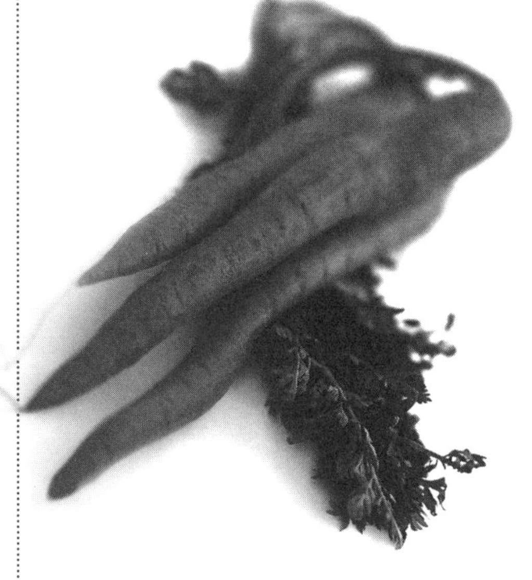

About Horseradish

Unless you truly love horseradish, you may wonder what would possess anyone to plant it in the garden. Once there, it is always there. Not that it bothers the other plants, but its invasive underground growth makes difficulties for the gardener each time a bed needs to be turned for a new planting. Every other six inches there's another of its wily tendrils trying to push forth to the sun and blocking the path of the shovel. On the other hand, once up, its expansive foliage provides pretty greenery and is a delight to anyone who keeps rabbits—horseradish leaves are one of their favorites. For the cook who does love the homely root for more than its symbolic Passover use, freshly grated horseradish eclipses any jarred product by far.

To grate fresh horseradish, peel it with a vegetable peeler or paring knife, then put it through a grinder fitted with the fine-hole blade. Or, more practically these days, process it in a food processor fitted with the finest blade you have, then mince it with a chef's knife. Or grate it on the medium-fine holes of a hand grater—this works but requires a lot of elbow grease for a small amount of horseradish.

Carrots Braised with Fennel

SERVES 4 TO 6

FENNEL WITH OTHER HERBS
If your fennel is not from the garden or a produce market that leaves some of the tops intact, you can substitute chopped fresh parsley for the garnish. Not much else will do, however. Fennel bulb does not take kindly to other herbs.

"I am enclosing a recipe I originally developed due to a 'garden problem.' I had a row of fennel that was about to be frozen by the first frost. It had not matured into bulbs at all—the plants were about 6 to 8 inches high, with about 2 inches of edible white (very tiny) bulbs at the base of each plant—and there was so much of it. Knowing they would not survive the frost, I harvested them, cut off the tops and roots, and sautéed them with carrots. Since that time this has been one of our favorite vegetable dishes."

LOUISE DIMANNO (HAMILTON SQUARE, NJ)

1 tablespoon butter
1 tablespoon olive oil
4 medium carrots, trimmed, scraped, and julienned (about 1 pound)
8 immature fennel stalks or 1 medium fennel bulb, trimmed and cut to same thickness as the carrots (about 6 ounces)
½ cup chicken broth, (see page 86)
⅓ cup white wine
¼ cup chopped fennel fronds (see left)

1. Heat the butter and oil together in a large sauté pan until the butter melts. Add the carrots and fennel and stir to coat. Cover the pan and cook over low heat for 10 minutes, or until the vegetables are wilted.

2. Add the broth and wine, raise the heat to medium, and cook, uncovered, for 10 minutes more, or until the liquid has evaporated and the vegetables are fork tender.

3. Transfer to a serving dish, sprinkle with the chopped fronds, and serve right away.

Fresh-off-the-Log Shiitake Mushrooms Sautéed with Garlic and Lemon

SERVES 4 TO 6

"We have been amazed at how many of our friends and acquaintances know and love the shiitake mushroom." That's perhaps because, whether for vegetarians or confirmed meat eaters, shiitakes fit into the repast. As a topping for pasta or polenta, these sautéed shiitakes make a meal of it. As a side with steaks or other beef or chicken dishes, they turn the plate into a grand occasion. Mounded on a lettuce leaf and garnished with a triad of crostini (see page 24), they provide an elegant and luxurious first course or luncheon dish.

MARY DYKES, BRIGHT FIELDS FARM (TA CENTER, WA)

- *¼ cup olive oil*
- *2 to 4 cloves garlic, finely chopped*
- *1 pound fresh shiitake mushrooms, stems trimmed off, caps cut into ½-inch slices*
- *2 teaspoons chopped lemon zest*
- *2 tablespoons fresh lemon juice*
- *½ cup chopped fresh parsley leaves*
- *½ teaspoon salt*

1. Heat the oil in a large sauté pan. Add the garlic and stir over medium-high heat until golden, about 30 seconds. Stir in the mushrooms and zest and continue cooking until the mushrooms have wilted a bit, about 2 minutes.

2. Add the lemon juice, parsley, and salt. Stir to mix and remove from the heat. Serve right away.

Growing Shiitakes

"Although shiitake mushrooms are typically grown on oak logs or in special indoor situations, we have been successful in propagating them on older logs, not oak, in the woods of our rainy Northwest acreage. The initial set-up was a lot of work, requiring the stacking of 16-foot-long logs five high on top of each other. Then we inoculated the logs with mushroom spawn. Six months later mushrooms began to appear, and we anticipate the logs will continue to produce mushrooms, without our tending, for at least five years." More simply, you can order shiitake growing kits from many garden catalogs. They produce a small crop, and it's fun to watch the mushrooms grow, though it takes a long time. Easiest of all, you can purchase fresh shiitakes at most produce markets and supermarkets these days.

—MARY DYKES

Simply Delectable Portobello Mushrooms

SERVES 2

"This year I grew garlic for the first time in my New Jersey seaside garden and was pleasantly surprised at how handsome the bold, strappy leaves are. I also grew portobello mushrooms from a kit purchased from a seed catalog. It was easy, fun, and satisfied that irresistible urge to grow something while waiting for spring." Our recipe testers found the mushrooms sautéed this way and served over buckwheat noodles also satisfied their appetite for a light meal.

NANCY MILANI (PHILADELPHIA, PA)

"Gardens were before gardeners, and but some hours after the earth."

—Thomas Browne, *The Gardens of Cyrus,* 1658

2 tablespoons olive oil
2 shallots, thinly sliced
2 cloves garlic, minced or pressed
2 portobello mushrooms, stems trimmed, sliced ⅛ inch thick (about 6 ounces each)
1 tablespoon balsamic vinegar
Pinch of salt
¼ teaspoon black pepper
1 tablespoon chopped fresh parsley leaves (optional)

1. Heat the oil in a large sauté pan. Add the shallots and garlic and sauté over medium-high heat until they release their fragrance, about 2 minutes. Add the mushrooms and continue sautéing until the mushrooms are soft but still hold their shape, about 10 minutes. Sprinkle in the vinegar, cover the pan, and cook 1 minute more.

2. Stir in the salt and pepper, sprinkle the parsley, if using, over the top, and serve right away.

From House to Garden: How to Pave the Way for Composting

Let's face it, no one is going to take the kitchen refuse to the compost pile on a daily basis. That realization alone may stop some from beginning. However, if the path from house to garden is divided into interim steps, it's not such a daunting proposition.

Begin by tagging a certain house-size garbage bucket "for compost only" and situate it where it can be enclosed, away from any pets who might find its contents a treat. That usually means in the cupboard under the kitchen sink. Then, if you have some acreage, or more than just a few square feet, between you and the garden, keep two buckets handy so there's plenty of room to collect the stuff until there's time to trundle it out to the compost bin.

Swiss Chard Artalie

Serves 6

In an unusual mix that combines chard and tomatoes, "a recipe I've adapted from one my wife's Italian grandmother used to make," there is also another cooking inspiration. It's that of infusing the oil for vegetable sautés with garlic and chili pepper gently warmed in the oil before adding the remaining ingredients. As well as in the recipe here, it works to turn out tasty dishes of many other vegetables, especially zucchini and broccoli.

BRENT BAILEY (MORGANTOWN, WV)

2 tablespoons olive oil
4 cloves garlic, minced
1 teaspoon finely chopped fresh red chili pepper (see Notes below)
2 large bunches red or green Swiss chard, coarsely chopped, washed, and drained (1½ pounds)
3 medium tomatoes, peeled, seeded, and coarsely chopped (about ¾ pound)
Salt and pepper

1. In a large sauté pan, heat the oil over medium heat. Add the garlic and chili pepper and cook, stirring frequently, until fragrant and lightly browned, 2 to 3 minutes.

2. Stir in the chard in batches, allowing each batch to wilt down a bit before adding more. Stir in the tomatoes, cover, and cook, stirring occasionally, until the chard is tender, about 15 minutes. Add salt and pepper to taste and serve right away.

Notes

• If you don't have a fresh red chili pepper, substitute a pinch of crushed red pepper along with a bit of minced red bell pepper, if possible, to keep the fresh vegetable taste.

• If making the dish with spring chard before garden tomatoes are ripe, good-quality canned ones, preferably from your own pantry (page 336), can be substituted.

Swiss Chard: Edible Color for the Garden and Kitchen

Leaf beet, another common name for Swiss chard, better describes its botanical category, namely, a type of beet grown for its leaves. There are several varieties of chard, with more or less savoyed leaves in a range of greens and stalks in a range of white to yellow, pink, red, and bright orange. A mixed grouping of the different varieties, all easy-to-grow edibles, makes a stunning display in borders or pots around and about the garden.

For kitchen use, there are some particulars:

Both the leaves and ribs of very young and tender chard, in all their colors, are best presented simply chopped, sautéed, together, and served up without much further ado, except maybe a splash of lemon and a drizzle of olive oil.

The white-ribbed variety is the most prized for the cook who wants the essence of chard. Young or old, its sweet ribs are treasured by Italian, French, and American cooks who strip away the leaves for another dish and braise the ribs as a separate vegetable.

For older chard with thicker ribs not of the white-stem variety, it is better to strip off the leaves, cook them only, and use the stems to replenish the compost pile.

TAMING THE BRASSICAS FOR THE TABLE

If you find the flavor of brassica (mustard family) greens a bit too strident, take a tip from Greek cooks and soften their pungence by blanching them in a large pot of boiling water for 10 to 20 minutes before further cooking. Drain briefly and proceed with the recipe. You will probably not have to add extra water during the second cooking.

Greens Sautéed with Garlic, Raisins, and Pine Nuts

SERVES 4 TO 6

"I have two young boys, a large garden, love for cooking, and no time. This recipe is tried and true and fairly simple." The combination of mustard family greens with raisins and pine nuts, which appears frequently on Mediterranean menus, is not only delicious but also unusual enough in American cooking to make the dish noteworthy.

MARY JANE SANGER (YORKLYN, DE)

2 large bunches hearty greens, such as mustard, turnip, kale, collard, or broccoli rabe, leaves only, shredded, washed, and drained (about 1½ pounds)
¼ cup (packed) raisins, black or golden
3 tablespoons olive oil
7 large cloves garlic, minced
½ cup pine nuts, lightly toasted (see box on page 135)
1 small red onion, very thinly sliced
¼ teaspoon salt
3 tablespoons balsamic vinegar

1. Bring ½ cup of water to a boil in a large nonreactive pot over medium-high heat. Gradually add the greens, stirring them down with each addition. When all the greens have been added and are well wilted, add the raisins, partially cover the pot, and reduce the heat to medium. Cook, stirring occasionally and adding more water if necessary, until the greens are very tender, about 20 minutes.

2. Meanwhile, combine the oil and garlic in a skillet and cook over medium heat until the garlic is soft, 3 to 4 minutes. Stir in the pine nuts, remove from the heat, and set aside.

3. In a small bowl, toss together the onion and salt and set aside.

4. When the greens are cooked, pour off any liquid remaining in the pot without draining thoroughly so the greens remain moist. Stir in the vinegar and garlic oil. Transfer to a serving dish, arrange the wilted onions over the top and serve right away.

Stir-Fried Kale and Spinach with Hazelnuts

SERVES 4

Kale and spinach work together as the yin and yang of leafy greens: the spinach is the soft and yielding, mild-flavored leaf; the stauncher kale brings a more assertive taste and texture to the pairing. The hazelnuts join the two in a combination you can serve hot for a vegetable dish, at room temperature like a warm salad, or chilled.

JOAN RANZINI (WAYNESBORO, VA)

½ cup hazelnuts
2 tablespoons olive oil
1 medium onion, chopped into ¼-inch pieces
4 large cloves garlic, minced
10 cups mixed thinly shredded kale and spinach leaves, washed, and drained but not dried (about 1 bunch each)
Salt and pepper

1. Toast the hazelnuts in an ungreased skillet over medium-high heat, stirring frequently, until the nuts are darkened in spots, 5 to 7 minutes. Cool enough to handle, coarsely chop, and set aside.

2. Heat the oil in a large sauté pan or wok. Stir in the onion and garlic and sauté over medium heat until translucent, about 5 minutes. Add the greens in batches, stirring them down after each addition, until all are in the pan. Stir-fry until tender, 8 to 12 minutes, depending on the age of the greens.

3. Stir in the hazelnuts and salt and pepper to taste. Toss gently and serve right away.

Variations

- Add a small splash of hazelnut oil when stirring in the hazelnuts at the end.
- Add a dash of orange or lemon juice when stirring in the hazelnuts.
- Garnish with orange or lemon zest.

TRICK *of the* TRADE

Preparing Leafy Greens for the Pan

Leafy greens of any variety always need to be well washed before cooking to rid them of dirt and any tiny garden creatures that may have been picked along with the greens. The most efficient way to do this is first to cut the greens whatever way the recipe calls for and then plunge them in plenty of water, not the other way around. Once in the water, give them a good swish and let the water come to rest so the debris falls to the bottom. Finally, lift the greens out of the water with your hands and transfer to a colander. Don't drain by pouring them along with the water into the colander or you will wind up with much of what you were trying to wash away still in the greens.

Unless the leaves are very sandy or mud-caked, as they can be in rainy seasons, this trick works well to get squeaky clean greens in one washing. It also works for lettuce and leeks.

Marmalade of Spring Greens

Makes about 1 cup

We might expect someday to see Paula Wolfert, award-winning cookbook author, on a Nova *or* National Geographic *special—one that features the food that nurtures the homes of the villages she has visited. A trekker par excellence, she travels far and wide to notice, record, and participate in the time-immemorial, daily activities of bringing food to the table. From the south of France (*The Cooking of South-West France*) across the eastern Mediterranean and on to the shores of Turkey (*Cooking of the Eastern Mediterranean*), the collecting and cooking of greens has been one of her favorite topics, which is, in fact, featured in her most recent volume,* Mediterranean Grains and Greens. *Here, in a recipe adapted from* Mostly Mediterranean, *she describes an unusual way with spring greens—cooked into a savory marmalade. The traditional use is to spread it lukewarm on thin rounds of baked or fried bread. She suggests that it also makes an excellent garnish for tuna carpaccio. And we've been known to use it as a vegetable side with meat, poultry, game, or a grain dish.*

PAULA WOLFERT (NEW YORK, NY; SAN FRANCISCO, CA)

Greens for Marmalade: Paula's Special Notes

Choosing the greens: There are two approaches—you can mix your greens or just use one type. But, in any case, avoid frozen spinach, which doesn't have enough taste.

Cooking the greens:

You can cook them in the microwave: Place in a microwave-safe dish. Sprinkle on a few drops of water if they're not still moist, cover the dish, and microwave on high until completely cooked, 4 to 15 minutes, depending on the type of green.

My way: "I prefer to cook greens by dropping them by handfuls into lots of boiling salted water (about ½ tablespoon of salt per quart of water), then keeping the water at a full boil throughout. According to my friend Jacques Chibois, the greens do not absorb the salt and the boiling 'sears' the leaves so that they can hold in all their nutrients."

2 pounds fresh spring greens such as spinach, escarole, Swiss chard

Salt

1 clove garlic, peeled and lightly crushed

2 tablespoons olive oil

4 flat anchovy fillets, drained and crushed with a fork

1½ teaspoons capers, preferably salted, rinsed and drained

¼ cup chopped kalamata olives

1½ tablespoons black or yellow raisins, soaked in warm water, drained dry, and chopped

⅛ teaspoon crushed red pepper, with a few seeds, or more to taste

1. Wash the greens until the water runs clear. Remove the stems, stalks, and any tough leaves, and drain.

2. Cook the greens in boiling salted water for 10 minutes, drain, refresh in cold water, and squeeze thoroughly.

3. Sauté the garlic in olive oil in a small skillet until lightly browned. Remove the garlic and discard. Add the greens and sauté, stirring, for 1 minute. Add the anchovies and capers and cook, still stirring, for 30 seconds more. Remove from the heat and allow to cool slightly.

4. Either by hand or in a food processor, finely chop the greens with the olives, raisins, and red pepper. Use right away, while still lukewarm, or cover and refrigerate for up to several hours.

GARDENING HINT

"If you have young children, skip the annuals! Plant herbs and perennials instead. These easy-to-grow plants need a lot less fussing and can weather curious hands and the occasional stray ball or Frisbee. Plus children love the sensory pleasures of hardy plants. Watch a child "pet" a lamb's ear leaf... smell a handful of mint ... pick a daisy... or taste a tiny rosemary leaf."

—VICTORIA ELLWOOD (COLUMBUS, OH)

Green Beans with Parsley-Pecan Pesto

SERVES 6 TO 8

A dish of green beans dressed with Parsley-Pecan Pesto gleams doubly green on the plate. Besides fresh beans, the pesto can also brighten lamb, chicken, pork, fish, potatoes, corn, and tomatoes, to name but a few.

BARBARA SCOTT-GOODMAN (NEW YORK, NY)

2 pounds young green beans, trimmed and left whole

1 cup Parsley-Pecan Pesto (recipe follows)

1. Bring a large pot of water to boil. Add the beans and cook over high heat until barely tender but still firm, 3 to 5 minutes. Drain in a colander and rinse under cool water. Set aside in the colander to drip dry or transfer to a cloth and pat dry.

2. Place the beans in a serving bowl, toss with the pesto sauce, and serve.

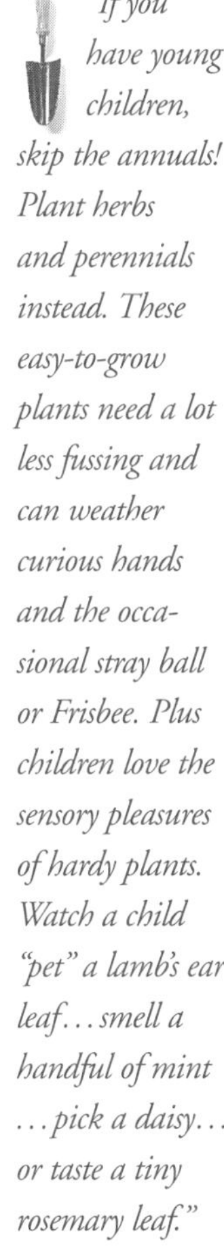

Parsley-Pecan Pesto

Makes 1 heaping cup

½ cup pecan halves
¾ cup (packed) fresh parsley leaves
¾ cup (packed) fresh basil leaves
2 cloves garlic, sliced
1 to 2 tablespoons fresh lemon juice
¾ cup olive oil
¼ teaspoon salt
¼ teaspoon freshly ground black pepper

Place the pecans, parsley, basil, garlic, and lemon juice in a food processor or blender and grind as fine as possible. Add the oil, salt, and pepper and continue processing until blended. Use right away or cover and refrigerate for up to 1 day. After that, flavor fades.

Storing Nuts

All nuts, hazelnuts, walnuts, and pecans especially, will eventually turn rancid if stored too long. To assure fresh-tasting nuts, store them in airtight containers. If the supply isn't used within a few months, transfer the nuts to the freezer. This works well to extend the shelf life of almonds and pine nuts. It does not work so well with hazelnuts, walnuts, and pecans, which tend to become soggy and still somewhat tired-tasting even when kept in the freezer. In general, it's a good policy to purchase small amounts of nuts at a time and from bulk bins so you can taste before buying. In any case, you should always taste the nuts before including them in a dish because rancid nuts can ruin the outcome beyond salvation.

Yellow Snap Beans Sautéed with Cracker Crumbs

Serves 4 to 6

"I remember fondly my grandmother, mother, and aunts cooking this dish. I and my daughter's family carry on the tradition. It's best when the beans are harvested before the seeds bulge within the pods so that you may leave them long." Lacking the delicately flavored yellow beans, you can use very small Blue Lake green beans or haricots verts for an equally excellent rendition of this dish.

KAY CHASE (CHESHIRE, MA)

CRUMBLING THE CRACKERS INTO CRUMBS
The best way to turn crackers into crumbs is to crush them with a rolling pin so that they are "crumbed" without being powdered. A food processor will make them too fine.

1 pound small yellow snap beans, trimmed and left whole
1 tablespoon butter
1 tablespoon olive oil
1 cup crushed saltine crackers (see left)

1. Bring a pot of water to a boil. Drop in the beans and cook over high heat until limp but still a little crunchy, 5 to 7 minutes. Drain and set aside to drip dry.

2. Place the butter and oil in a large sauté pan and heat until the butter melts. Add the beans and toss to coat. Add the crumbs, toss again, and cook over low heat, stirring from time to time, until the crumbs are golden and the beans are soft but not mushy, 8 to 10 minutes.

Note: It is important to sauté the beans slowly so that the crumbs turn golden without burning and the beans soften without wrinkling.

Romano Green Beans with Garlic, Lemon, Oregano, and Black Pepper

Serves 4 to 6

"In our small backyard garden we relish growing vegetables that are not readily available in the local markets. Among the heirloom tomatoes, pinkie-finger-size French cucumbers for cornichon pickles, and a lovely mix of lettuces (mesclun), one of our standout favorites is Italian Romano beans. Their bold flavor, long, flat shape, and rich green color make them a great addition to any summer meal."

FRANK AND JAYNI CAREY (LAWRENCE, KS)

1 pound green beans, preferably Romanos, cut diagonally in half
2 tablespoons olive oil
2 cloves garlic, minced
Big pinch of salt
1 teaspoon finely chopped fresh oregano leaves or ½ teaspoon dried oregano
¼ teaspoon freshly cracked black pepper (see right)
2 tablespoons fresh lemon juice

1. Bring a large pot of water to boil. Drop in the beans and cook over high heat until crisp-tender, 3 to 5 minutes, depending on the size and freshness of the beans. Drain and set aside.

2. In a large pot or sauté pan, heat the oil over medium heat. Stir in the garlic and salt and cook until the garlic is lightly golden, about 2 minutes.

3. Add the beans and stir to coat. Stir in the oregano, pepper, and lemon juice and continue cooking until the beans are heated through, about 3 minutes more. Serve right away.

CRACKED PEPPERCORNS
To match the hearty nature of the Romano beans and the not-at-all-shy-seasonings in this dish, you must smash, not grind, the black peppercorns so they are barely cracked open. It's another good use for that mallet (see page 162). Be sure to cover the peppercorns with a cloth or paper towel so they don't fly off the counter as you pound.

zucchini: the proverbial bounty

Whether you garden in a large plot, a backyard, or a few containers on the patio or deck, you've probably grown zucchini. Even if, for lack of space or time, only the thought of gardening must suffice, the grandiosity of a zucchini plant may have caught your eye in a neighbor's garden or in a glossy seed-catalog picture. The contributions to this volume testify to the ubiquitous appeal of zucchini. Why?

Of all the edible vegetable plants in the world, zucchini and its summer squash siblings are some of the most prolific. Indeed, their bounty is proverbial by summer's end.

Given a space with warmth and water, the plants will produce from early summer to early fall. They are particular about those two requirements and need to be located in the sun and given good watering. But they're not that choosy about the space. It can be a few feet of ground over which to spread, reaching farther and farther out as they grow. It can be a trellis or other thing to climb up on as the vine extends itself. It can be a container, which allows the plant to stretch over the edges.

Almost as soon as the zucchini plants begin producing, the harvesting can begin. The incomparable orange/yellow flowers that adorn the garden also entice picking for early summer treats of stuffed or fried squash blossoms. Then, beginning with the tiny, inch-long baby ones to the slightly paunchy, late-season ones, the zucchini fruit provide for the table in a way few other plants do. From the first tender sautés and quick grills to tasty casseroles, imaginatively stuffed entree delights, moist tea cakes, and onward all the way through pickling time, the zucchini plant keeps the cook dancing in the kitchen, devising ways to enjoy such a treasure. Following are several ways gardener cooks turn zucchini into creative vegetable side dishes.

Zucchini Rafts

Serves 4

"In my search for new ways to entertain both my kids and the thought of eating yet another zucchini, I came up with the zucchini raft. I skewer zucchini halves two or three astride, brush them with an oil and herb wash, and float them on the grill. This solves the summer 'zucchini thing' in a palatable, actually delicious, and delightful way." For a casual presentation, serve the rafts without removing the skewers. If there are those who might not be able to handle the pointy ends of the skewers safely, snip off the ends before placing on the table or remove the skewers altogether.

DEBBI BOHNET-NUTTALL (SAN JOSE, CA)

½ cup olive oil
2 tablespoons chopped fresh herbs, such as oregano, thyme, rosemary, basil, or a mixture
4 large cloves garlic, pressed
¼ to ½ teaspoon crushed red pepper
6 medium zucchini, halved lengthwise (about 2 pounds)
Freshly grated Parmesan cheese (optional)
Freshly ground black pepper (optional)

1. Prepare a charcoal fire.

2. Combine the oil, herbs, garlic, and red pepper to taste in a dish long enough to hold the zucchini halves without bending or breaking them. Add the zucchini halves and turn to coat all around. Set aside for at least 20 minutes, more if you have the time, turning several times.

3. Make the rafts by placing 3 zucchini halves, cut side down, on a counter. Holding them together with one hand, use the other hand and a gentle twisting motion to skewer through the halves crosswise about 2 inches in from the end. Place another skewer in the same way at the other end. Continue with the remaining zucchini halves. Return the zucchini rafts to the oil bath until ready to cook.

4. To cook, grill the rafts, beginning with the cut sides down, for 5 minutes. Turn the rafts over and continue grilling for 10 minutes more, until tender and nicely browned. Serve right away, sprinkled with the cheese, if using, and the black pepper, if using.

DON'T RAIN ON ME: A WATERING TIP FOR MANY VEGETABLES

The zucchini plant and all its cucurbit relatives dislike having their leaves wet. That means watering them around the ground only. Wet tops will result in mildew, weaken the plant, and reduce the output. This tip applies also to beans and peas, as well as tomatoes and many other summer vegetables. If you're unsure about others not listed, follow the guideline that underground vegetables don't mind wet heads. Otherwise, water the ground only.

Italian-Style Cucuzza Squash Sautéed with Tomatoes and Basil

SERVES 6 TO 8

"The cucuzza squash vine climbing up the trellis and fence line along the garden exhibits its yellow blossoms that soon yield long, light green squash. My grandmother, mother, aunts, and cousins have always grown this squash and prepared this dish—a true spring and summer favorite—which we serve as a vegetable side dish or over pasta." The freshness of the squash is the key. If you don't have a cucuzza squash vine, another type of zucchini will do as long as it was picked young and tender either from your garden or the farmers' market.

JODIE GLORIOSO (SHREVEPORT, LA)

3 tablespoons olive oil
1 medium to large onion, cut into ¼-inch dice
1 to 2 large cloves garlic, minced
7 to 8 medium tomatoes, peeled and very coarsely chopped, juices reserved (about 1¾ pounds)
1½ pounds cucuzza squash, peeled (optional) and chopped into ½-inch pieces
6 large leaves fresh basil, coarsely chopped
½ teaspoon salt
½ teaspoon black pepper
2 heaping tablespoons coarsely grated Parmesan cheese
Extra grated Parmesan cheese (optional)

1. Heat the oil in a large nonreactive pot. Add the onion and garlic and sauté over medium heat until translucent, about 8 minutes. Stir in the tomatoes and their juices and cook over low heat for 15 minutes.

White, Yellow, and Green; Round, Long, and Crooked: The Many Guises of Summer Squash

It's curious that, unlike tomatoes, roses, and runner beans, summer squashes have not been divided between everyday varieties and heirlooms, a tag that ipso facto elevates them above the ordinary. In the press at least, summer squashes are just summer squashes. Perhaps only an avid summer-squash cook would think the taste differences notable. The numerous colors and shapes, however, are remarkable. If ever you thought zucchini is just zucchini, vary the guise of those many summer squash dishes with:

- The long zucchini that is most familiar but now comes in colors from the usual dark green to golden yellow to the creamy white and faint green stripes of cucuzza, favored in Italian gardens.
- The roundish ones with scalloped edges, the pattypans, also known as cymlings, which now also come in colors from the usual pale green to golden and in round shapes without scalloped edges but prettily marked with striations of dark green and orange.
- The crooked ones, the other favorite, both for its stunning yellow color and also for its whimsical shape, bulbous at the bottom with a skinny neck that crooks around.

2. Add the squash, basil, salt, pepper, and Parmesan and continue cooking until the squash is very tender and the liquid is reduced and saucy, about 30 minutes.

3. Serve right away, accompanied by the extra Parmesan, if using.

Note: If the squashes are on the small side, you can cut them lengthwise into thin strips rather than peel and chop them. Remove the strips after 10 minutes in Step 2 and continue cooking the tomatoes for 20 minutes. Return the squash to the sauce before serving.

Sautéed Zucchini with Red Onion, Dill, and Aged Gouda

Serves 4 to 6

"Two years ago I planted two hills of zucchini and got more than we knew what to do with. This recipe was developed that year for a last-minute dinner party. Now it's a family favorite and we are looking forward to its coming for this year."

JOAN HOLMES (WESTMINISTER, MD)

¼ cup olive oil
1 large or 2 medium red onions, thinly sliced (1 pound)
1 tablespoon sliced garlic
6 medium zucchini, sliced ¼ inch thick (about 2 pounds)
1 tablespoon chopped fresh dill
½ teaspoon salt
½ teaspoon black pepper
3 tablespoons grated Parmesan cheese
1½ cups coarsely grated aged Gouda cheese

1. Preheat the broiler.

2. Heat the oil in a large cast-iron skillet. Add the onions and garlic and sauté until slightly wilted, about 3 minutes. Add the zucchini and sauté until crisp-tender.

3. Stir in the dill, salt, pepper, and Parmesan. Sprinkle the Gouda over the top and place the pan under the broiler until the cheese melts and turns slightly golden, about 4 minutes. Serve right away.

Golden Summer Squash with Dill and Chèvre

SERVES 4

"Every year I eagerly await the harvest of our summer squash; luckily, the plants are fast growers and usually prolific, although that first picking seems to take forever. This event always seems to coincide with the new shoots of volunteer dill that find their way all over our one-acre garden. These in combination with fresh chèvre from our own goat's milk is a dish worth waiting for." In place of your own fresh chèvre, you can substitute a good-quality soft chèvre that is mild enough not to overpower the delicacy of the squash.

BETH KOBE (COLUMBIA STATION, OH)

2 tablespoons olive oil
¾ cup thinly sliced onion
½ teaspoon mild paprika, preferably Hungarian
3 young yellow summer squash, cut into 4 by ½-inch strips (about 1 pound)
2 tablespoons chopped fresh dill
1½ tablespoons fresh lemon juice
⅓ cup soft chèvre cheese, at room temperature, thinned with milk to a yogurtlike consistency
Salt (optional)
1 tablespoon chopped fresh parsley leaves

1. Heat the oil in a large skillet. Add the onion and paprika and sauté until the onion is well wilted, about 5 minutes. Stir in the squash, dill, and lemon juice and sauté 1 minute more. Cover the pan and cook over low heat until the squash is barely tender, about 4 minutes.

2. Remove from the heat and stir in the chèvre. Taste and add salt if necessary. Sprinkle the parsley over the top and serve right away.

Note: Crookneck or yellow pattypan squash or golden zucchini may be used.

TRICK *of the* TRADE

Plastic Wrap for Keeping Cheese

How often has the cheese been bought and brought home, put in the refrigerator with all good intentions to star in tomorrow's dish or the next day's snack, and been forgotten? Maybe it's just a matter that you purchased too big a hunk. Professional chefs, eyeing the shelves in the walk-in refrigerator and evaluating the goods there, have come across the same consternation and have found a solution to such a dilemma. Thanks to that great modern product called plastic wrap, as long as you can remember to rewrap the cheese with a new sheet of plastic wrap every few days, the refrigerator life of the cheese will be extended far into the next week or month.

Summer Squash Baked with Cherry Tomatoes, Olives, and Fresh Thyme

Serves 6

As far north as southern Alaska, zucchini and tomatoes have found their way into the gardens even of that short-growing-season clime. The sun may not shine for many days of the year, but on the days it does, it's out all day and almost all night too. In that brief but intense time, gardeners, as everywhere, are challenged to come up with inspired uses for the zucchini and tomatoes while they're fresh and warm off the vine before putting them by for the winter. This is one such. Whimsically combining them with typical Mediterranean ingredients—olives, garlic, and fresh thyme (a welcome change from basil)—the cook, perhaps dreaming of warmer corners of the world, transports the diners there with this dish.

PHYLLIS WRIGHT (KETCHIKAN, AK)

- *¼ cup olive oil*
- *2 teaspoons finely chopped fresh thyme leaves*
- *1 to 2 tablespoons minced garlic*
- *1½ pounds green and yellow summer squash, such as zucchini, crookneck, pattypan, or scallopini, trimmed and sliced ½ inch thick*
- *2 cups cherry tomatoes, stemmed and halved*
- *12 good black olives, pitted and halved* *(see page 131)*
- *¼ cup crumbled feta cheese, preferably French, Greek, or Bulgarian (optional)*

1. Preheat the oven to 425°F.

2. Combine the oil, thyme, and garlic in an 8 by 12-inch baking dish. Add the squash, tomatoes, and olives and toss to coat. If using the feta, sprinkle it over the top. Bake for 20 to 25 minutes, or until the zucchini and tomatoes have thoroughly wilted down but still hold their shape.

3. Remove and cool enough to handle, then serve.

Zucchini Boats Filled with Herbs and Vegetables

"The garden is the poor man's apothecary."

—German saying

SERVES 4 TO 6

"I started early as I can remember helping my mother in the kitchen. Our family was large, and in preparing meals for a large family in those days, a vegetable garden was an indispensable food source. We grew almost every conceivable vegetable and plant. I learned early to appreciate my relationship to nature and the wonderful meals I could cook from the garden. These early childhood experiences influenced me so much that I later chose cooking as my career. I worked as a school chef for over 15 years cooking for a Children's Center in Los Angeles. Each day I prepared three meals a day for over one hundred children. These days I derive much pleasure in cultivating a small vegetable and herb garden in my backyard that also hosts one lemon and two fig trees. My grandchildren frequently assist my effort, and at the end of summer when the zucchini are almost out of hand, a dish we especially enjoy together is my stuffed zucchini."

NELLIE MARY HORNE (LOS ANGELES, CA)

2 large or 4 medium zucchini (about 1¼ pounds)
2 tablespoons olive oil
1 medium onion, finely chopped
4 cloves garlic, minced
6 medium celery ribs, trimmed and finely chopped
4 medium tomatoes, chopped into ¼-inch pieces (about 1 pound)
1 tablespoon chopped fresh parsley leaves
1 tablespoon chopped fresh basil leaves
1 tablespoon chopped fresh oregano leaves
2 tablespoons fresh lemon juice
1 teaspoon salt
½ teaspoon black pepper
½ cup grated sharp cheddar cheese
½ cup coarse bread crumbs, preferably homemade (see page 76)
2 tablespoons butter, melted
Fresh herb leaves, such as parsley, chives, or basil, for garnish

1. Preheat the oven to 375°F.

2. Cut the zucchini in half lengthwise. Hollow out the pulp, making sure not to pierce the shell. Brush the outsides of the shells with olive oil and set aside. Coarsely chop the pulp and transfer it to a large bowl.

3. Add the onion, garlic, celery, tomatoes, parsley, basil, oregano, lemon juice, salt, and pepper to the zucchini pulp and toss to mix.

4. Fill the zucchini shells with the vegetable mixture and place the shells on a baking sheet or in a dish large enough to hold them in one layer. Bake for 25 minutes, or until the shells are tender.

5. Sprinkle the cheddar and bread crumbs over the top. Drizzle the butter over the crumbs and continue baking for 10 minutes, or until golden brown. Garnish with the fresh herb leaves and serve right away.

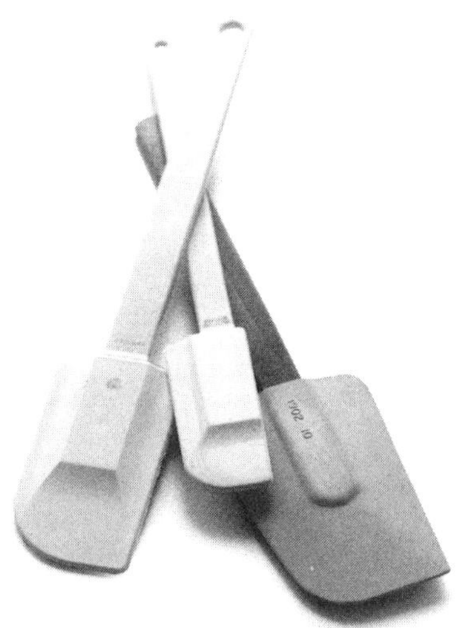

Tart and Creamy Spinach Filling for Summer Squash

MAKES ABOUT 1 CUP, ENOUGH TO FILL 2 LARGE OR 4 MEDIUM ZUCCHINI HALVES, SCOOPED OUT

1 large bunch spinach, leaves and tender stems only, coarsely chopped, washed, and drained (¾ pound)
4 tablespoons (½ stick) butter
¼ cup finely chopped onion
½ cup sour cream
1 teaspoon red wine vinegar
Salt

1. Wilt the spinach while still moist in an ungreased heavy sauté pan over medium-high heat or in a microwave bowl at high heat. Drain briefly in a colander, then squeeze dry. Set aside.

2. Melt the butter in a sauté pan over medium heat. Add the onion and stir until wilted, about 3 minutes. Add the spinach, sour cream, vinegar, and salt to taste. Stir to blend.

3. Use right away or store in the refrigerator for up to overnight.

Note: The contributor suggests using crookneck squash as the shell. Its yellow under the mottled-green, cream-colored filling makes a pretty picture.

—LIN JUCHHEIM (GRENADA, MS)

Hungarian Heritage Squash

SERVES 6

"A longtime favorite of our heritage, Hungarian squash soup is economical and satisfying, and very simple to prepare." Though called a soup in Hungarian, it's more familiarly described as a purée, suitable to use as you would mashed potatoes or soft polenta. The inclusion of fresh chili pepper is a little startling at first, but, when you think about it, paprika, another capsicum, is after all the *Hungarian spice.*

DAVID FERENCZI (BERLIN CENTER, OH)

2 tablespoons olive oil
1 tablespoon lard (see Note below)
1 large onion, finely chopped
2 yellow wax chili peppers, stemmed, deveined if hot, and finely chopped
8 medium zucchini, trimmed but not peeled, coarsely grated (about 2 pounds)
¼ cup chopped fresh dill
½ teaspoon sweet paprika, preferably Hungarian
½ teaspoon salt
Black pepper
¼ cup sour cream

1. Heat the oil and lard, if using, in a large nonreactive pot. Stir in the onion and chili peppers and cook over low heat until the onion is soft but not browned, about 10 minutes.

2. Add the zucchini, dill, paprika, salt, black pepper to taste, and ½ cup of water and stir to mix. Raise the heat for a minute, then cover and steam over low heat until the zucchini has collapsed almost into a purée, 15 to 20 minutes. Blend in the sour cream and serve right away.

Note: The lard is a traditional flavoring in Hungarian cuisine. If you prefer an all-vegetable or lower-calorie dish, substitute olive oil for the lard.

Southwestern Corn-and-Zucchini Sauté

SERVES 4 TO 6

"I lived in New Mexico for several years and prepare my own versions of many southwestern dishes. To this end, my primary gardening objectives are tomatoes and a variety of peppers. Throughout the summer, I harvest, roast, peel, and freeze fresh chili peppers, ensuring many dishes for winter warmth. This dish is a wonderful accompaniment to traditional Southwest dishes and also great with something as simple as black beans or baked chicken sprinkled with a bit of cumin."

~ JAMI BOETTCHER (NORMAN, OK)

A Brief History of Calabacitas: An American Specialty

In American cooking, *calabacitas* translates to corn and zucchini together. It's a combination to be revered because it offers two of the life-giving foods of the squash, corn, bean triad that sustained humans in lean times in the New World. Eventually there was some play in the kitchen: herbs and chilies for seasoning, the larger capsicums (bell peppers) were added for extra flavor. As with soul food everywhere, the dish, once released from its chains of abject necessity, became desired for the comfort it always gave.

2 tablespoons butter
1 large red bell pepper, stemmed, seeded, and coarsely chopped (about ¾ pound)
2 medium zucchini, trimmed, halved lengthwise, and sliced ¼ inch thick (about ¾ pound)
3 cloves garlic, minced
3 cups fresh corn kernels *(see page 122)*
½ cup chopped poblano chili pepper (see Note below)
1 teaspoon finely chopped fresh oregano leaves or ¼ teaspoon dried oregano
½ teaspoon ground cumin
½ teaspoon salt
½ teaspoon black pepper

1. Melt the butter in a large sauté pan. Add the bell pepper, zucchini, and garlic and sauté gently for 15 minutes, until the vegetables are just tender. Stir in the corn, chili pepper, oregano, cumin, salt, and black pepper.

2. Continue cooking until the corn is barely soft and the dish is heated through, about 5 minutes. Serve right away.

Note: If poblano chilies, also known as pasillas, are not available, the more common jalapeños make a fine substitute. They do have a higher heat level, however, so ¼ cup might do, depending on your heat tolerance.

Corn Storing Tip

"When you pick or buy corn on the cob, you are often not ready to use it right away, and even in a day it loses its sweetness. To save the special flavor of fresh-picked corn, trim the ends of the stalks, as you would flowers. Place the ears, either stripped or in the husks, trimmed ends down, in a deep container of water with a bit of sugar added. Place the container in a cool place. I've left corn this way for three days and it was still as fresh tasting and sweet as when first picked. I was told by a man from Phoenix who goes up to Prescott, Arizona, and brings home around two hundred ears for friends and family each year that it was a problem getting the corn delivered to all while still perfectly fresh until he heard about this. I hope others will be glad to hear of such a simple way to keep corn fresh."

—MARJORIE BROWN (BEAVERTON, OR)

Corn Grilled with Seasoned Butter

SERVES 4 TO 6

For those who swear corn must be grilled in the husk to be at its best, this method may come as an interesting surprise. The corn, wrapped in foil with butter and herbs, becomes perfumed with them, and they, held within the foil packet, melt into a seasoned butter to roll the ears in. The seasonings are open to a wide range of herb and spice innovations; the magic here is in the method.

M.J. WEBSTER (MISHAWAKA, IN)

8 tablespoons (1 stick) butter, softened
2 tablespoons minced fresh parsley leaves
2 tablespoons minced fresh chives
1 tablespoon minced fresh thyme leaves
½ teaspoon salt
¼ teaspoon cayenne, or to taste
8 ears fresh corn, husked and silks removed

1. Prepare a charcoal fire.

2. Place the butter, parsley, chives, thyme, salt, and cayenne in a small bowl and mix well.

3. Spread 1 tablespoon of the flavored butter over each ear of corn and wrap each individually in foil. Grill over medium-hot coals, turning frequently, for 12 to 15 minutes, or until the corn is tender. Unwrap and serve the corn in its butter right away.

Corncob Syrup

MAKES ABOUT 1 CUP

With American ingenuity and thriftiness, even the cob of corn, which could be seen as only an element for the compost pile, is instead put to further use. Besides drying and carving the cobs into pipes, you can boil them up into a tasty syrup. Perfect for pancakes, waffles, or oatmeal, it transforms corn fritters from a vegetable side dish into a quick dessert. ~ PEGGY MIKULENKA (KATY, TX)

6 medium corncobs, kernels scraped off for another use, cobs broken into chunks
1¼ cups (packed) dark brown sugar

1. Place the cobs and 4 cups of water in a large saucepan and bring to a boil. Cook briskly over medium-high heat for 30 to 45 minutes, until the liquid is reduced to about 2 cups.

2. Lift the cobs out of the liquid with a slotted spoon or wire strainer and discard. Add the sugar to the saucepan and bring to a boil again, stirring to make sure the sugar dissolves. Reduce the heat to maintain a brisk simmer without boiling over and cook until the liquid is reduced to about 1 cup and has the consistency of maple syrup, 10 to 20 minutes, depending on the dimensions of the pan.

3. Use right away, or cool and store in the refrigerator. Keeps indefinitely.

Corn Fritters

MAKES TWENTY-FOUR 2-INCH FRITTERS

"This recipe was derived from a very old Farmers' Almanac *that I found at an estate sale. It was really fun deciphering the ingredient amounts, written by teacup measurements, and making up our own version." Take care when frying the fritters; just like popcorn, the kernels pop and spew hot oil.*

~ JAN WHITE (TIGARD, OR)

2 cups fresh corn kernels, plus juices scraped from the cobs (see page 122)
½ cup milk
½ cup all-purpose flour
1 teaspoon baking powder
1 teaspoon salt
Black pepper
1 tablespoon butter, melted
2 eggs
Vegetable oil, for frying

1. Place all the ingredients except the oil in a medium bowl and blend well to make a wet batter. Set aside for 15 minutes, or until thickened a bit.

2. Heat ¼ inch of oil in a sauté pan until it begins to smoke. Drop heaping tablespoons of the batter into the oil to make as many fritters as will fit without crowding. Fry over medium-high heat, turning once, until golden on both sides, about 1 minute. Transfer to a paper towel and continue with another round until all the batter is used. Serve right away while warm and crisp.

Fritter Variations

Fritters are a recurring theme in many cuisines. Who doesn't like a fried goody, nuggets of chicken, catfish, or clam, patties of salmon, crab, potato, lentil? If you do, albeit only as a special treat these days, here are some variations on the classic American corn fritter.

IN THE BATTER
- Chopped fresh herbs, such as chives, thyme, parsley, or basil.
- Spices, such as nutmeg, mace, cayenne, or chili powder.
- Minced and blanched fresh vegetable, such as bell pepper (any color), peas, or green onion.

AS TOPPING OR GARNISH
- Melted butter, lemon wedges, maple syrup, Corncob Syrup (see box on page 256)

CORN ON THE COB WITH HUSKS
For those who remain convinced the husks are part and parcel of grilled corn, the foil-wrap technique can still be used to hold in the seasoned butter. Simply pull back the husks, remove the silks, spread on the butter, fold the husks back up, then wrap in foil.

Tostones: Crispy Fried Plantains

SERVES 6

"People in Puerto Rico have a somewhat narrow selection of homegrown produce. This is mainly due to the fact that very few fruits and vegetables can stay fresh for more than a few days in the tropical heat of the Caribbean. That explains why our staples consist

of rice, beans, roots, and the native fruits and vegetables that have adapted to the wilting climate. Traditionally, the freshest of fruits and vegetables are obtained from street side kiosks similar to the urban farmers' markets one finds in California. One of our favorite fresh staples is the plantain, especially the deep-fried green plantains called tostones. *At the kiosks, you can pick plantains right off the bunch* (racimo) *just as though off the tree. The secret to making the best* tostones *is to pick the largest and greenest plantains—the harder the plantain, the crunchier the* tostones *will be—and you must double fry the slices. They are usually served with rice and beans, moistened with the bean cooking liquor. They are also delicious as an accompaniment to roast pork."*

~ LOURDES LISBOA (OAKLAND, CA, VIA BAYAMON, PUERTO RICO)

4 plantains, as green and hard as you can find them (see Note below)
Salt
Vegetable oil, for frying

1. Make a slit from end to end in the peel of each plantain, taking care not to cut into the pulp. Peel the plantains (see box at left) and slice them into 1-inch-thick rounds.

2. Place the slices in warm salted water for 2 or 3 minutes. Drain and pat dry.

3. Fill a large frying pan half full of vegetable oil and heat over medium-high heat until a plantain slice dropped in sizzles.

4. Working in batches, fry as many plantain slices as will fit in one layer until they begin to turn golden. Remove and drain on paper towels.

5. On a cutting board, flatten each slice by covering with a plate and pressing down as hard as you can (the thinner the slices, the crunchier the *tostones*).

6. Fry the flattened slices as in Step 4 until golden brown and crispy. Remove to paper towels to drain as you go. Salt to taste and serve right away.

TRICKS *of the* TRADE

How to Peel a Plantain

The peels of plantains are thicker and tougher than banana peels and harder to remove. Here's a trick Caribbean cooks know to make it easier. Hold the plantain under warm running water. This helps loosen the peel enough that it can be pulled away without stressing your fingers.

Note: Plantains can be found at Latino markets and many grocery stores. The contributor notes that the "green plantains eventually ripen to a yellow color with black spots, and these *platanos maduros* may be substituted in the recipe, but bear in mind that they fry up sweet and tender soft, not crunchy.

Mosaic of Bell Peppers Sautéed with Caramelized Onion

Serves 6

Old World cooks have given New World cooks some of the most delightful ways to serve New World ingredients. Here, in a slow-cooked dish, starting with the onions and moving on to bell peppers, the natural sweetness of the vegetables is brought forth as they softly simmer into what some modern cooks like to call confit or jam. At the last moment, basil and mint are stirred in to supply a whiff of fresh air that keeps the concoction from cloying.

GLORIA PAGLIARINI (COVENTRY, RI)

2 tablespoons olive oil
1 medium onion, sliced into ⅛-inch-thick rounds
2 large red bell peppers, 2 large yellow bell peppers, and 1 large green bell pepper, all stemmed, seeded, and sliced into ¼-inch strips
½ teaspoon salt
½ teaspoon black pepper
2 tablespoons shredded fresh basil leaves
2 tablespoons shredded fresh mint leaves
2 tablespoons grated Parmesan cheese

1. Heat the oil in a large sauté pan. Add the onion and cook over low heat, stirring often, until light caramel in color, about 15 minutes.

2. Stir in the bell peppers, salt, and pepper. Raise the heat to medium and sauté, stirring often, until tender, about 25 minutes.

3. Transfer to a serving dish, add the basil and mint, and gently stir to mix. Sprinkle the cheese over the top and serve right away.

"It seems to me that the onion is the perfect garden vegetable. Onions are food for people; *they're not caterpillar food or raccoon dinner."*

—Abby Adams, *The Gardener's Gripe Book*

Mirella's Pimientos

Makes 6

"This dish is named for Mirella, the young Italian woman who cooked for us in Bonassola one summer. She served it with baked chicken and with Mediterranean fish, especially mackerel. It also goes well with cheese soufflé, zucchini frittata," or alongside almost any sandwich you may devise.

ELEANOR ROSS TAYLOR (CHARLOTTESVILLE, VA)

¼ cup olive oil
4 to 5 large pimientos or red bell peppers, stemmed, seeded, and cut into 1-inch-wide strips (2 to 2½ pounds)
5 tablespoons tomato paste
Big pinch of cayenne

Heat the oil in a large sauté pan. Add the peppers and sauté until soft, about 10 minutes. Stir in the tomato paste and cook gently until no longer moist, about 45 minutes. Stir in the cayenne and serve hot or cold.

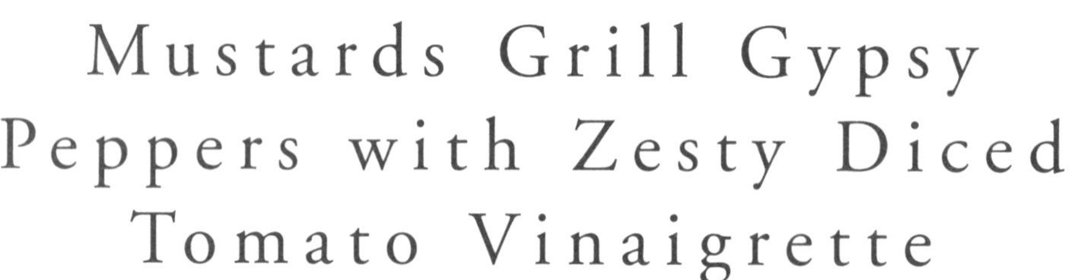

THE HIGH-SPIRITED GYPSY PEPPER

The gypsy pepper is a large sweet pepper, closely related to bell peppers but pointed at the tip, like pimientos, rather than box-shaped like bells. It's a variety that does particularly well in the Northwest, where the climate is not so conducive to growing other varieties of the sun-loving capsicum family. In lieu of gypsy peppers, you can use a large chili pepper, such as a poblano or Anaheim, or a medium-size bell pepper, preferably yellow.

Mustards Grill Gypsy Peppers with Zesty Diced Tomato Vinaigrette

Serves 6

Cindy Pawlcyn is the co-founder, executive chef, and culinary inspirer for the Real Restaurants, including Fog City Diner, Tra Vigne, Buckeye Roadhouse, Caffe Museo, and Mustards Grill, among others. Mustards is situated in the lovely Napa Valley, where each spring the wild mustards, fennel, and oxalis flower with such golden abandon that every orchard and vineyard as far as the eye can see is carpeted incandescent yellow. No wonder the yellow gypsy peppers inspired Chef Pawlcyn to create a dish featuring them for Mustards. Grill. She modestly suggests that the dish makes "a great appetizer or a nice focal point to a main course." Our recipe testers found it more than fine for a summer luncheon, singularly satisfying as only a plate of garden goodness under the sun can be. Chef Pawlcyn advises that "you may use other garden herbs if the mint and cilantro are unavailable and use any color or variety of tomatoes and chilies your garden may have for the vinaigrette," which, she enthuses, "is also fantastic served over fresh fish off the grill."

~ CINDY PAWLCYN (YOUNTVILLE,CA)

6 gypsy peppers
1 cup cooked basmati rice
½ cup golden raisins
2 tablespoons chopped fresh mint leaves
½ cup quality cream cheese, softened
⅔ cup crumbled feta cheese
1½ cups Zesty Diced Tomato Vinaigrette (recipe follows)
Sprigs of cilantro and mint for garnishing

1. Bring a large pot of water to a boil.

2. Slice the caps off the peppers and set aside. Remove the seeds and membranes from the center of the peppers. Drop the peppers into the boiling water and blanch until barely squeezable, 2 to 3 minutes. Drain and set aside until cool. Use right away or leave aside for up to several hours.

3. In a medium bowl, combine the rice, raisins, mint, cream cheese, and feta. Loosely stuff the peppers with the mixture, without packing tightly. Replace the caps, secure them with toothpicks, and set aside until ready to grill.

4. Prepare a charcoal fire.

Are You Ready?: Three and a Half Easy Steps to a Memorable Luncheon

As would a professional chef, you can divide the recipe into steps so that getting the dish from the kitchen to table is not a frenzy. Here are the clues:

STEP ONE. Using the same pot of boiling water, first blanch the tomatoes for peeling for the vinaigrette, then the peppers to wilt for stuffing. At the same time, in another pot, cook the rice. These preparations can be done up to a day in advance.

STEP TWO. Make the tomato vinaigrette and set aside. Combine the stuffing ingredients and fill the peppers. These preparations can be done several hours in advance.

STEP TWO AND A HALF. Start the grill 45 minutes to 1 hour before you would like to serve.

STEP THREE. When the fire is ready, spoon the tomato vinaigrette onto a serving platter or individual serving plates. Grill the peppers, place them on the platter or plates, and garnish as you wish. Without further ado, serve and enjoy your company.

"Tomatoes are the seductive vegetable—bright red, bursting with juice and flavor, fruitful to a fault. Had they been native not to Peru but to Asia Minor, a tomato—not an apple—surely would have caused our fall from grace."

—Barbara Damrosch, *The Garden Primer*

5. Grill the peppers, turning once or twice, until the peppers are singed on the outside and the cheese is melting inside.

6. While the peppers grill, spoon the tomato vinaigrette on a platter or on 6 individual plates, reserving a little for topping.

7. When done, set the grilled peppers on the vinaigrette, spoon a little extra vinaigrette on each pepper, and garnish with sprigs of cilantro and mint. Serve while still warm.

Note: While the peppers are fabulous singed over charcoal, they are also undeniably good cooked inside on a hot rock grill or under the broiler.

Zesty Diced Tomato Vinaigrette

MAKES ABOUT 1½ CUPS

3 medium tomatoes, peeled, seeded, and cut into ¼ inch dice (see page 72)
3 tablespoons minced red onion
Zest of 1 lime, finely chopped
Juice of 1 lime
¼ cup minced fresh cilantro leaves
3 to 4 serrano chilies, stemmed and minced
¼ cup olive oil
Salt and freshly ground black pepper

Combine all the ingredients in a medium bowl. Use right away or set aside at room temperature for up to several hours. May be stored in the refrigerator overnight.

Baked Herbed Tomatoes

SERVES 4

"Here is a simple recipe from one of the cooking classes I teach using herbs from my large herb garden." The recipe is uncomplicated and basic, it's true. At the same time it opens new horizons for having a warm but still fresh tomato side dish. See the box on page 263 for suggested variations.

PAT WINCHESTER (MCLEAN, VA)

2 large tomatoes, halved horizontally and seeded (about 10 ounces each)
½ cup finely chopped onion
½ teaspoon minced garlic
½ cup finely chopped fresh basil leaves
½ teaspoon chopped fresh thyme leaves
½ cup coarse bread crumbs, preferably homemade (see page 76)
1 tablespoon olive oil
Salt and pepper

1. Arrange the tomato halves, cut side down, on paper towels and leave to drain for about 1 hour.

2. Preheat the oven to 450°F.

3. Combine the remaining ingredients in a small bowl. Place the tomatoes, cut side up, in a baking dish and fill each half with the bread crumb mixture. Bake until the tomatoes are golden on top but still hold their shape, no more than 10 minutes. Serve right away or at room temperature.

Midterm Tomatoes

Once you've sated the lust for fresh off-the-vine tomatoes, eating them out of hand, still warm, as you visit the garden, and there's been enough of the carry-in, slice-for-the-table variations, and it's not quite time to think of putting by the rest, baked tomatoes provide many ideas for the interim. Halved, sprinkled, dolloped, curried, seasoned with this and that, baked tomatoes are another rendition of the never-ending glory of this most bounteous plant and a solution for "more tomatoes tonight." Some suggestions to vary the topping mix are:

FOR THE HERBS: Instead of basil and thyme, use chopped fresh bay leaf, tarragon, cilantro, or oregano combined with ⅓ cup fresh parsley.

FOR THE CRUNCH: Instead of bread crumbs, use ½ cup chopped pine nuts or blanched almonds.

INSTEAD OF THE CRUNCH: Omit the bread crumbs or nuts, and sprinkle ½ cup coarsely grated melting cheese, such as Jack or provolone, over the top of the onion-and-herb mixture.

FOR EXTRA SAUCE: Spoon sour cream over the tomatoes after they're seasoned and just before they're placed in the oven. It will turn into a golden topping you won't be able to resist.

Fried Green Tomatoes

SERVES 6

What American gardeners' cookbook would be complete without a recipe for fried green tomatoes? Since the movie of the same name, this humble favorite of southern cooking has assumed a certain aura of romanticism, if not downright cachet. One of the tastiest ways to use green tomatoes, frying offers immediate gratification, with no waiting for the pie to bake, the pickles to sour, or the relish to mellow.

EDNA GILES (THEODORE, AL)

1 large egg
½ cup milk
½ cup cornmeal
¼ cup all-purpose flour
Vegetable oil or shortening, for frying
3 large, firm green tomatoes, sliced ⅛ to ¼ inch thick
Salt

Baked Green Tomatoes

Green tomatoes can be baked any way you would red tomatoes (see page 262). They can also be simply seasoned with oregano, salt, pepper, and olive oil and baked at 450°F. until meltingly tender to use as a kind of savory jam condiment for any fish, meat, or poultry dish.

Other ways to use green tomatoes:

- Green Tomato Chutney (page 344).
- Green Tomato Relish (page 340).
- Sweet Green Tomato Pickle (page 329).

1. Mix the egg and milk together in a small bowl. In another bowl, combine the cornmeal and flour.

2. Heat about ½ inch oil or shortening in a large heavy skillet over medium-high heat. Dip each tomato slice in the egg-milk mixture, then in the cornmeal-flour mixture. Place as many slices as will fit without crowding in the skillet and fry, not too fast, until brown on both sides, 3 to 4 minutes altogether.

3. Transfer to a serving platter, sprinkle with salt to taste, and serve right away.

Variations

- Add a few tablespoons of bacon fat to the cooking oil for an authentic southern seasoning.
- Add a dash or two of cayenne to the flour mixture for extra punch.
- Serve with lemon wedges to squeeze on at the last minute for extra tang.

Eggplant Stuffed with Red Bell Peppers and Tomatoes

SERVES 4 TO 6

"My gardening 'career' began when I was about four years old, on the day I discovered those big seeds in the pods of sweet peas. Over the years, my avid interest in gardening spread from growing flowers to growing vegetables with sunflowers scattered throughout the rows (they add a zap of color and the birds love them). I love to create

recipes depending on what my crop of the moment might be, and I'm sending you this one, dubbed 'red boats' by its fans. It includes not only eggplant and bell pepper but also garden garlic and, of course, the ever-easy, ever-delightful garden herbs."

CHARMAINE RAWSTHORNE (STAMFORD, CT)

1 large globe eggplant (1 pound)
¾ cup olive oil
1 medium onion, finely chopped
½ teaspoon cayenne
½ teaspoon chili powder
2 large red bell peppers, stemmed, seeded, and finely chopped (about 1½ pounds)
2 small tomatoes, finely chopped (about 6 ounces)
2 to 4 cloves garlic, minced or pressed
½ cup tomato sauce (see page 293)
½ cup coarse bread crumbs, preferably homemade (see page 76)
½ teaspoon salt
Grated Parmesan cheese

1. Preheat the oven to 350°F. Lightly grease a baking sheet.

2. Cut the eggplant in half lengthwise. Carefully scoop out the pulp with a paring knife or metal spoon. Set the eggplant shells aside and coarsely chop the pulp.

3. Heat ½ cup of the oil in a large heavy skillet over high heat. Add the eggplant pulp and sauté until tender, about 5 minutes. Transfer to a large bowl and set aside.

4. Pour the remaining oil into the skillet and stir in the onion, cayenne, chili powder, red bell peppers, and tomatoes. Sauté until the bell pepper is softened but still brightly colored, 10 to 15 minutes. Stir in the garlic, tomato sauce, bread crumbs, and salt. Transfer to the bowl with the eggplant pulp, mix together, and set aside.

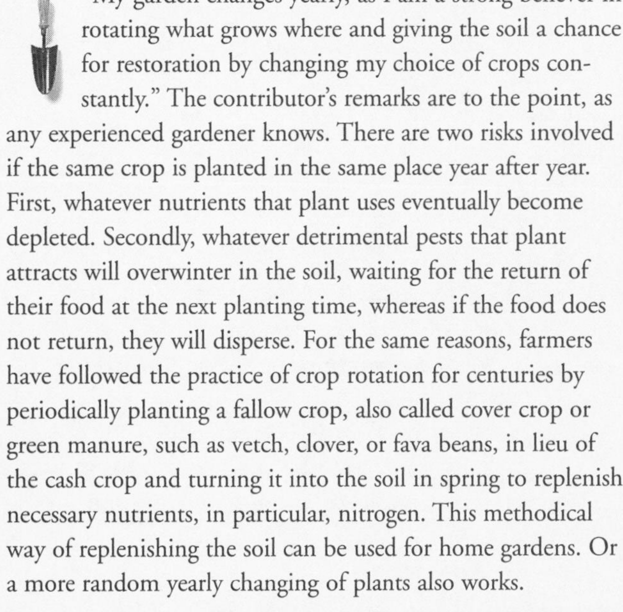

Rotating Crops: Good Garden Advice

"My garden changes yearly, as I am a strong believer in rotating what grows where and giving the soil a chance for restoration by changing my choice of crops constantly." The contributor's remarks are to the point, as any experienced gardener knows. There are two risks involved if the same crop is planted in the same place year after year. First, whatever nutrients that plant uses eventually become depleted. Secondly, whatever detrimental pests that plant attracts will overwinter in the soil, waiting for the return of their food at the next planting time, whereas if the food does not return, they will disperse. For the same reasons, farmers have followed the practice of crop rotation for centuries by periodically planting a fallow crop, also called cover crop or green manure, such as vetch, clover, or fava beans, in lieu of the cash crop and turning it into the soil in spring to replenish necessary nutrients, in particular, nitrogen. This methodical way of replenishing the soil can be used for home gardens. Or a more random yearly changing of plants also works.

—CHARMAINE RAWSTHORNE (STAMFORD, CT)

5. Fill the eggplant shells with the eggplant mixture. Place on the baking sheet and bake for 20 to 25 minutes, or until lightly browned.

6. Serve hot or at room temperature, accompanied with a bowl of freshly grated Parmesan.

Crisp Eggplant Rounds Baked with Bread Crumbs

Serves 2

"We have many eggplants in the garden and they're all ready at once. This is a great way to serve them. As the eggplants are baking, I go out to the garden and snip some basil and oregano. I usually top half with basil and half with oregano." The difference between the smaller Japanese eggplant and large globe eggplants is mainly one of size. Each will provide the appealing texture contrast between the crunchy bread crumbs and soft eggplant, so choose between them according to how many rounds you would like to dip and coat.

~ PAMELA RIEL (SOUTHBURY, CT)

APPETIZER-SIZE EGGPLANT ROUNDS

The crispy eggplant rounds also make a delightful appetizer. For this use, choose the Japanese eggplants so the rounds are bite size. Omit the tomato sauce, keep the cheese and herb topping, and serve with lemon wedges.

¼ cup olive oil
2 large eggs
¾ cup milk
2 to 3 Japanese eggplants or 1 medium globe eggplant (¾ pound)
2 cups coarse bread crumbs, preferably homemade (see page 76)
1 cup tomato sauce (see page 293), warmed
2 tablespoons grated Parmesan or romano cheese
1 tablespoon chopped fresh basil leaves
1 tablespoon chopped fresh oregano leaves

1. Preheat the oven to 400°F. Pour the oil onto a baking sheet.

2. Combine the eggs and milk in a medium bowl. Slice the eggplants into ¼-inch-thick rounds. Dip the rounds into the egg mixture, then coat each side with bread crumbs. Place the coated rounds on the baking sheet and turn so both sides are coated with the oil.

3. Bake for 10 to 12 minutes on each side, or until the bread crumbs are golden. Remove to a serving platter.

4. Top each round with a small dollop of the tomato sauce, then a sprinkle of the cheese, and finally a pinch of herb. Serve right away.

Asian Eggplants Marinated with Garlic, Ginger, and Sesame

Serves 6 to 8

"This is an interesting way to use garden eggplants in one of my favorite styles—Asian fusion cooking. Served with vegetable sushi or steamed vegetable dumplings and sake, the marinated and baked eggplant strips add up to a full meal."

~ LOIS RICHMAN (LYNBROOK, NY)

1-inch piece fresh ginger, peeled and minced
2 cloves garlic, minced
¼ cup rice wine vinegar
½ cup soy sauce
2 tablespoons sesame oil
7 to 8 Chinese or Japanese eggplants, trimmed and sliced lengthwise ⅛ inch thick (about 2 pounds)
2 tablespoons sesame seeds, toasted
3 tablespoons fresh cilantro leaves

1. Combine the ginger, garlic, vinegar, soy sauce, and oil in a glass or other nonreactive dish large enough to hold the eggplant pieces no more than 2 layers deep. Add the strips, turn to coat, and set aside to marinate for at least 30 minutes or up to 1 hour.

2. Preheat the oven to 400°F. Lightly grease 2 baking sheets.

3. Spread the eggplant pieces on the baking sheets, spreading them out so they don't overlap. Bake for 12 to 15 minutes, or until soft but still holding their shape.

The Global Bounty of Eggplants

Deep purple to the point of black, soft as lavender, white, even green; minuscule as a pea, huge as a desk-size globe of the world, wherever there's enough summer warmth to grow eggplants, they are part of the cuisine. One of the few edible nightshades from the Old World, they originated in the region of India and proliferated from Asia across Europe, up and down the Americas, and into the Pacific Rim. Cooks have met such generosity of presence with ideas of their own. Oil-laden as their reputation sometimes advertises, boiled up quick and skinny, wilted with salt and mustard, eggplants appear on the table in a wondrous number of sweet and savory ways. The only question is not whether, but how.

4. Transfer to a serving dish and garnish with the sesame seeds and cilantro. Serve right away while still warm, or at room temperature, or chilled.

Note: The eggplant strips can also be cooked under the broiler. They will take less time, about 8 minutes, and turn out a little browner.

Southern Ratatouille

SERVES 8

Timothy Murray, a principal writer for the Smith & Hawken catalog, grew up, one of eight children, on the farm in Virginia that his mother still tends. "My mom, Bunny Murray," he says, "gladly passes along her ratatouille recipe. She makes this in late summer when the garden vegetables are more than abundant. Fresh herbs could be added, but she prefers to let the flavors of the garden carry the show." The garden vegetables for this ratatouille include okra, a staple of southern cooking. See the box on this page for Bunny Murray's own delightful story of this dish.

BUNNY MURRAY (EARLYSVILLE, VA) AND TIMOTHY MURRAY (SAN FRANCISCO, CA)

Ratatouille: A Gardener Cook's Way with Summer Vegetables

"In the summer, with eight sons and their friends to feed on our Virginia cattle farm, I think I made as many trips out to our vegetable garden every day as I did to the grocery store. Overabundant zucchini, tomatoes, and okra became the basis for this ratatouille, a vegetable stew developed, no doubt, by a Frenchman with an overactive garden of his own. It makes a hearty companion to grilled chicken or steak, and because it simmers in its own juices, it doesn't require a lot of standing over the stove—a plus when the cook also had to serve as taxi driver, referee, and peace officer."

—BUNNY MURRAY

½ cup olive oil, or more if necessary
2 large onions, chopped into ¼-inch pieces
2 medium globe eggplants, peeled and cut into ¼-inch cubes
½ large green bell pepper, stemmed, seeded, and coarsely chopped
2 celery ribs, trimmed and coarsely chopped
1 small chili pepper, trimmed and finely chopped
3 garlic cloves, minced
6 fresh okra pods, sliced crosswise into ½-inch pieces
2 medium zucchinis, coarsely chopped
4 large tomatoes, peeled and coarsely chopped
12 mushrooms, stemmed and coarsely chopped
1 teaspoon salt
½ teaspoon black pepper

1. Heat the olive oil in a large stovetop casserole. Stir in the onions and eggplant and sauté over medium heat until the onions are translucent, about 3 minutes.

2. Add the green pepper, celery, chili pepper, and garlic and continue to sauté, stirring occasionally, until the celery is softened, about 3 minutes. Add more olive oil if necessary to keep the vegetables from scorching.

3. Add the okra, zucchinis, tomatoes, mushrooms, and salt and pepper to taste. Reduce the heat to low and continue cooking, stirring often, until the vegetables are tender and collapsed into a stew-like consistency, at least 30 minutes.

4. Remove from the heat and allow to cool and settle. Serve at room temperature or chilled, or reheat.

Pass-Along Recipes

Once it was over the fence; now it's over the fax, phone, and net. Does it matter? No, the spirit is still there and think of the ever-widening circle. Of course, you still have to get your own ingredients. Recipe testers, being used to French and Italian versions of such a dish, at the outset were a bit timid to try okra in the ratatouille. How come the mushrooms? However, with open minds and intrepid spirit, the dish was cooked up. Lo and behold, it was another inspirational pass-along, this time across the ocean. That's the joy of gardener cooks and plain old ordinary food lovers.

Country Okra Sauté with Fresh Tomatoes and Cornmeal

SERVES 8

"Many people are afraid to try okra because they've heard it's not very good. Try this—you'll be delightfully surprised." Almost like the Continental Divide that separates East from West or the Mason Dixon Line that divides North from South, the subject of okra clefts many a culinary gathering that might otherwise remain a happy unit. Some cannot live without it as a staple vegetable for deep-frying, stewing into gumbo, pickling, turning into relish, or sautéing into a side dish. Others, however, turn up their noses and walk away without so much as a sniff. Perhaps this dish, as claimed by the contributor, will bring accord to the divided okra camp.

ANN THRASH-TRUMBO (OTTUMWA, IA)

1 tablespoon olive or vegetable oil
4 medium onions, chopped into ¼-inch pieces (about 2 pounds)
1 pound very fresh okra, sliced into ½-inch thick rounds
¼ cup cornmeal
4 large tomatoes, coarsely chopped, juices reserved (about 2 pounds)
Salt and pepper

Who Owns Okra?

Okra, a member of the ancient mallow family, has traveled through eons far from its original home in the Nile Valley to establish itself around the world. Its botanical relatives include the large genus of hibiscus, beloved by tropical gardeners for their showy flowers. Also included is the common mallow, an edible weed that is respected both by foraging humans and also by butterflies looking to lay their eggs in a good spot. As a culinary plant, okra is adored by cooks in the Mediterranean, Africa, Asia, India, and North America. Sauté it, stew it, pickle it, and otherwise serve it up in one way or another. For instance, for a style that is:

AFRICAN: Sauté the okra with onions, garlic, and hot chili pepper.

GREEK: Stew it with dill, thyme, garlic, onion, and tomatoes or deep-fry it into fritters.

TURKISH: Stew it with sweet and hot peppers, coriander seeds, and garlic.

JAPANESE: Firm it in a bath of rice vinegar, then toss it with a tofu-sesame dressing, a miso-sake dressing, or a wasabe–soy sauce mixture.

INDIAN: Cook the okra in a sauté, stew, or curry and season it with a selection of exotic spices, such as fennel seeds, cumin, coriander, black mustard seeds, mango powder, turmeric.

SOUTHERN U.S.A.: Have the okra as gumbo stew, pickles (page 325), or a sauté (page 269).

1. Combine the oil and onion in a large, heavy skillet. Sauté over medium heat until beginning to wilt, about 3 minutes. Add the okra and a good splash of water, cover the skillet, and allow to steam for 5 minutes, or until the okra softens slightly.

2. Sprinkle the cornmeal over the okra mixture, but do not stir—stirring at this stage will make the dish gummy. Cover again and allow to steam 5 minutes more, adding a little extra water if necessary to keep the mixture from sticking to the bottom.

3. Add the chopped tomatoes, now stir gently, and bring the mixture to a simmer. Season with salt and pepper to taste and serve right away.

Roasted Vermillion Veggies with Mango-Basil Mayo

SERVES 12 TO 16

Sheila Lukins, co-founder of the Silver Palate store and recognized cookbook writer, most recently of The U.S.A. Cookbook, *offers here one of her best-loved garden-to-table recipes. "As summer's heat intensifies, the flavors and colors of my vegetable garden favorites—red bell peppers, tomatoes, and beets—follow suit. Roasting them enhances their natural sugars and further brightens their tastes. The lightness of a tropical mango mayonnaise spiked with fresh basil complements the forthright vegetables. For a beautiful presentation, I like to arrange the vegetables on a large colorful platter and garnish with nasturtium blossoms." The recipe is written with step-by-step instructions so that you can accomplish the dish in a reasonable, time-managed way, as the pros do. The ingredients may be proportionately reduced if you are serving fewer than the small crowd of 12 to 16. Then again, if you feel like having leftovers, make the whole batch and stockpile the extra in the refrigerator. The veggies will keep fresh for up to two days.*

SHEILA LUKINS (NEW YORK, NY)

8 medium beets, leaves trimmed off and reserved for another dish (about 3 pounds)
8 large tomatoes, cored and quartered (about 4 pounds)
4 medium red onions, peeled and quartered (about 2 pounds)
4 tablespoons olive oil
4 medium red bell peppers, stemmed, seeded, and halved (about 2 pounds)
2 cups Mango-Basil Mayonnaise (recipe follows)
2 tablespoons fresh lemon juice
Salt and pepper
½ cup fresh corn kernels, blanched and drained
3 green onions (scallions), trimmed and thinly sliced on the diagonal

1. Preheat the oven to 350°F.

2. Wrap the beets individually in aluminum foil. Place the foil packets in the oven and bake for 1 hour, or until easily squeezable when you pinch through the foil. Remove and set aside until cool enough to handle. Unwrap the packets and slip the skins off the beets. Cut into quarters and set aside.

3. Arrange the tomato and onion quarters in a nonreactive baking dish large enough to hold the pieces in one layer. Pour 2 tablespoons of the olive oil over the top and set the dish in the oven alongside the beets. Bake until the quarters are soft but remain in recognizable chunks, about 40 minutes. Remove and set aside.

4. Preheat the broiler.

5. Flatten the bell pepper halves by pressing them between the palms of your hands. Lay the halves, skin side up, in a single layer on a length of foil. Broil until the skins are charred and blistered, about 15 minutes. Remove and let rest to finish steaming, then peel them and cut in half again to make quarters. Set aside.

6. Prepare the mango mayonnaise.

7. To serve, arrange the pepper, beet, tomato, and onion pieces on a large decorative platter. Pour any collected juices over the top. Drizzle on the lemon juice and remaining 2 tablespoons olive oil and sprinkle with salt and pepper to taste. Finally, strew the corn kernels and scallion rounds over all and serve, accompanied with the mango mayonnaise.

Mango-Basil Mayonnaise

Makes 2 cups

2 ripe mangos, peeled, pulp pared away from the pits
2 tablespoons peeled Roasted Garlic (page 132)
½ cup mayonnaise (page 64)
¼ cup olive oil
Salt and pepper
½ cup shredded fresh basil leaves

1. Blend the mango pulp, garlic, and mayonnaise in a food processor. While the motor is still running, slowly add the olive oil until the mixture is smooth and pourable.

2. Transfer to a bowl and stir in salt and pepper to taste. Fold in the basil and serve right away or cover and refrigerate for up to 3 hours.

Mango Manipulations

Getting the pulp of a ripe mango off the pit is, no doubt about it, a messy operation. The pulp clings, as with almost no other fruit, to the pit. For puréeing or chopping, clumsy cuts don't matter because they'll become incorporated into the dish later.

For recipes that call for less soft, even green mangos, it's a neater job. Peel them, score them top to bottom lengthwise, and then around the middle. With that done, the sections should be easy to cut away from the pit in fairly neat pieces.

For enjoying mangos on their own, it's a good idea to have a supply of toothpicks or dental floss on hand. The mangos are fairly irresistible, but their strands do have a tendency to harbor in between the teeth.

Potato-Garlic Gratin

SERVES 6 TO 8

Potatoes seem to cry out for garlic. Whole, halved, slivered, coarsely chopped, finely chopped, minced, pressed, crushed, cooked, or raw cloves of the so-called stinking rose show up in potato dishes that have an equal number of variations in shape, other ingredients, and cooking method. In a spring gratin, "newly dug potatoes and big cloves of spring garlic combine into a comfort dish" just right for almost-warm days, still-cool nights, and dreams of the summer garden.

SONIA PETERSON (EDINA, MN)

Butter, for greasing baking dish
3 pounds Yukon Gold potatoes, scrubbed or peeled
3 cloves elephant garlic or 6 cloves regular garlic, finely chopped
1 cup heavy (whipping) cream
1 teaspoon salt
½ teaspoon white pepper

1. Preheat the oven to 350°F. Butter a 2-quart flameproof casserole or gratin dish.

2. Slice the potatoes 1⁄16 to ⅛ inch thick and layer them in the dish. Combine the garlic, cream, salt, and pepper in a small bowl. Pour the mixture over the potatoes, tilting the dish to distribute the cream evenly.

3. Place the dish on the stovetop and heat over low heat until warmed through. Transfer to the oven and bake until the cream is bubbling and the top is browned, 45 to 50 minutes. Cool for 10 minutes, then serve.

Scalloped Yukon Gold Potatoes on the Grill

SERVES 2 TO 3

For the hot days of summer's end, olive oil and lemon juice appropriately replace the tangy cream of spring scalloped potatoes. With these potatoes wrapped in a foil packet and cooked over the grill, "you have a tasty, somewhat gourmet dish with no pan to clean when finished and a nice, cool kitchen."

VIVIAN LEE (ST. LOUIS, MO)

THE COMPOST PILE AS A DUAL DELIGHT

"If you love baby potatoes I found this is the way to go. Cut a seed potato (I use red and Yukon gold) into thirds. Bury the potatoes into the back corners of your compost pile. After about two months, you can reach into the compost pile and harvest as many potatoes as you want for a meal and not disturb the rest of the plant."

—MICHAEL BONNET (MODESTO, CA)

1¼ pounds Yukon Gold potatoes, scrubbed and sliced as thin as possible (see Notes below)
1 medium Vidalia or other sweet onion, very thinly sliced
1 to 4 cloves garlic, chopped or slivered, to taste
¼ cup olive oil
Salt
⅓ cup torn basil leaves, preferably lemon basil
2 tablespoons fresh lemon juice

1. Prepare a charcoal fire.

2. On an 8-inch-square sheet of heavy-duty aluminum foil, layer the potatoes, onion, garlic, and basil, coating each layer with a little olive oil and dash of salt as you go. Pour the lemon juice over all and fold up the foil corner to corner to make a sealed packet.

3. Grill over a medium-hot fire for 30 to 40 minutes, or until the potatoes are cooked. Serve right away, in the foil packet if it's an informal meal or removed from the foil and transferred to a serving platter for a more formal meal.

Notes
• A food processor fitted with the slicing blade makes slicing the potatoes and onion an easy job.

• If you don't have heavy-duty aluminum foil handy, use a double layer of regular foil.

• The potato packet may also be baked in a 375°F. oven.

Instead of Yukons

Yukon Gold potatoes provide a soft, golden hue and just the right texture for mashed to sautéed to scalloped potatoes. Substitutes don't equal the natural butteriness of Yukon Golds, but there are some "insteads" that work. Very fresh red or white potatoes duplicate the firm texture; Idahos and other russets, though mealier, duplicate the easily mashed quality of Yukon Golds. For gratins, red or white potatoes work best; for scalloped potato dishes, choose russets.

New Potatoes Mashed with Garlic and Rosemary

SERVES 4 TO 6

In a mashed version of the always pleasing potato-and-garlic combination, the potatoes are of the waxy rather than russet type, so there are a couple of tricks to having them turn out fluffy: Once cooked, press the potatoes through a potato ricer or use a potato masher to mash them. Then quickly stir in the other ingredients without beating, or the whole mixture will become pasty and heavy.

MARY ANN WILLIAMS (SANDY, UT)

2 pounds red or white potatoes, peeled
2 sprigs of rosemary, rinsed
4 cloves garlic
4 tablespoons (½ stick) butter
½ cup heavy (whipping) cream
1 teaspoon chopped fresh rosemary leaves
½ teaspoon salt

1. Place the potatoes, rosemary sprigs, and 2 cloves of the garlic in a saucepan. Add water to cover, bring to a boil, and cook briskly over medium-high heat until the potatoes are fork tender, 30 to 40 minutes, depending on the size.

2. While the potatoes cook, combine the butter and cream in a small pan or microwave dish and heat until the butter melts. Mince the remaining 2 cloves garlic and add to the butter and cream. Set aside in a warm place.

3. Drain the potatoes and remove the rosemary sprigs and whole garlic cloves. Rice or mash the potatoes. Stir in the warm cream mixture, chopped rosemary, and salt. Serve right away.

Note: If the mashed and seasoned potatoes are too thick, thin the mixture with a little milk.

More Mashed Potatoes, Please

There's probably a different way to have mashed potatoes every day of the year. A few are:

- Use about 8 ounces sweet potato in place of 8 ounces of the red or white potatoes.
- Use 8 ounces celery root in place of 8 ounces of the red or white potatoes.
- Use russet potatoes in place of the red or white potatoes and stir in cooked kale to make Colcannon (see page 276).
- Use tarragon or dill instead of rosemary for cooking the potatoes.
- Use milk in place of the cream for a lighter dish.
- Garnish the potatoes with chopped fresh chives or a sprinkle of the herb used in cooking the potatoes.
- Pat leftover mashed potatoes into small cakes, dust them with flour, and fry until golden on both sides.

Colcannon

SERVES 8

"As an avid gardener of Irish ancestry, I think it fitting that my cooking contribution be a comfort food, traditionally served on November Eve, from my homeland. Whenever I serve colcannon, it is always all gone at meal's end. This tells me something ('this' being—it's quite good)!" The contributor does not explain what November Eve means, but she does explain that the name of the dish comes from cal, *for* colwort *or cabbage and greens, plus* ceannon, *for a small wooden vessel; put together they make colcannon. Though that etymological revelation doesn't exactly describe the potato part, perhaps that's a given in an Irish dish and not so noteworthy as the color green, which they are. The dish is served accompanied with steamed cabbage.*

SOPHIA GEOHEGAN (BOULDER, CO)

STEAMED CABBAGE
To make steamed cabbage, first shred and parboil it until wilted to make the leaves more manageable and also, some say, to "wash away" its gas-producing component. Drain and finish cooking until soft, using one of the vegetable steamers described in the box on page 281.

2 small bunches kale, stems cut off, leaves coarsely chopped, washed, and drained (1 pound)
2 medium-large leeks, trimmed, thinly sliced, and washed (about 1 pound)
⅔ cup half-and-half
3½ pounds russet potatoes, peeled and halved
Salt and pepper
8 tablespoons (1 stick) butter, melted
Steamed Cabbage (see left)

1. Place the kale in a large pot, add water to cover, and boil over medium heat until the kale is tender, about 30 minutes. Drain and set aside to drip dry.

2. Combine the leeks and half-and-half in a saucepan and simmer over medium heat until soft, about 10 minutes. Set aside.

3. Put the potatoes in a large saucepan, cover with water, and boil until fork tender, about 45 minutes. Drain and shake dry. Mash the potatoes with a potato ricer

Colcannon Art: Sculpting Mashed Potatoes

With an artistic flick of the wrist, assistant recipe tester Fernando Brito turns colcannon into a centerpiece for a special occasion.

"After transferring the colcannon to the serving dish (an ovenproof one), pat it into a cone shape. Using a fork, refine the shape by scoring the cone vertically all around to create a ridged effect. Make the well by pressing a small bowl into the center at the top. Remove the bowl and place the colcannon in a 350°F. oven for 25 minutes, or until the ridges are golden and the colcannon is piping hot. Pour in the warm melted butter and serve as described in the recipe."

—FERNANDO BRITO (BERKELEY, CA)

or masher or a pastry blender until fairly smooth. Stir in the kale, the leek-cream mixture, and salt and pepper to taste.

4. Mound the potatoes on a warm serving dish and make a well in the center of the mound. Pour the butter into the well and bring to the table. Spin the dish around once, then invite guests to serve themselves from the outside of the mound and ladle on butter to taste. Accompany with steamed cabbage.

Artichoke Supreme

SERVES 4

The artichoke, that edible thistle long prized on Mediterranean tables, started in this country as a regional hopeful, more or less stuck in Watsonville, California. It must have made the grade, because now it is shipped all over the nation. In sizes minuscule to gigantic, artichokes appear delectably marinated for an antipasti plate; subtly tucked into lamb stew; steamed and sauced; or boldly served as a separate side dish, as here.

CONNIE PETSCHEK (NEW CANAAN, CT)

4 medium-large artichokes, trimmed (see box on page 278)
1 tablespoon olive oil
1 large onion, finely chopped
2 medium tomatoes, finely chopped
1 tablespoon chopped fresh basil leaves
2 tablespoons butter
1 cup coarse bread crumbs, preferably homemade (see page 76)
Salt
Lemon wedges or lemon juice (optional)

1. Preheat the oven to 375°F. Lightly grease a baking dish large enough to hold the artichokes in one layer.

2. Half fill a large pot with water and bring to a boil. Add the artichokes, cover the pot, and cook briskly over medium-high heat until the leaves are tender at the base, 25 to 40 minutes depending on the size and age of the artichokes. Drain in a colander, very gently so as to keep the leaves intact. Turn the artichokes upside down to drip dry and cool slightly. Set aside.

RINSING AWAY THE PESTS

"To rid fresh vegetables of unwanted worms or bugs, wash them in a salt-water bath made of 1/4 cup salt in a sinkful of cool water. Drop the vegetables into the water and let them soak for 10 minutes or so. Rinse, drain, and continue with the recipe." This tip works especially well for artichokes that are susceptible to ants and aphids nestling into hard-to-get-at crevices.

—ANNALEE NESBIT (ELLIOTT CITY, MD)

3. Heat the oil in a medium sauté pan over medium-high heat. Add the onion and sauté for 5 minutes, until well wilted. Stir in the tomatoes and basil and continue cooking until the tomatoes wilt, about 4 minutes. Add the butter, stir the mixture until the butter melts, then stir in the bread crumbs. Season with salt to taste and set aside.

4. Place the artichokes, bottom down, in the baking dish. Spread the leaves of each artichoke slightly outward and spoon the bread-crumb mixture into the recesses of each. Bake until the filling is lightly toasted and the artichoke leaves are falling outward on their own, about 10 minutes.

5. Remove and cool. Serve warm or at room temperature with lemon wedges, if using. Or refrigerate overnight—they are delicious served chilled sprinkled with lemon juice.

Arti Art

To present large artichokes as prettily as possible and to save the diners from pricking their fingers on the thorny tips, the leaves need to be trimmed before cooking. If you are a very patient person, you can cut off the leaf tips one by one with scissors. Or you can do the job more quickly using a sharp knife to slice off the tips a row at a time working your way around the entire artichoke. The stems should also be trimmed off, flush with the bottoms, so the artichokes can stand upright for serving. After that, they are ready to boil or steam. The pot should be large enough to hold the artichokes in a single layer, and it should have a lid. The amount of water is not crucial as long as there is enough not to boil away before the artichokes are done. The water may be enhanced with lemon, herb, garlic, and/or oil. Some believe they add flavor. Others think it's a waste of ingredients, better used after the bath.

Once cooked, the artichokes should be drained very gently so they do not fall apart. They should be allowed to cool so they are not so fragile and can be handled, still gently, without too much risk of ruining their appearance. Then they can be filled, as in the recipe above or in a number of other ways. Some variations are:

- Use oregano or marjoram instead of basil.
- Add anchovy, garlic, and lemon zest to the stuffing.
- Replace half the bread crumbs with Italian sausage, cooked and crumbled.
- Replace all the bread crumbs with crabmeat or shrimp.
- Sprinkle Parmesan cheese over the top before baking.
- Omit the stuffing altogether, skip the baking step, and serve the artichokes warm with melted lemon butter or at room temperature with mayonnaise (page 64) or Aïoli (page 283) or Creole Aïoli (page 27) for dipping the leaves.

Turnips Braised with Peach Schnapps and Raspberry Vinegar

SERVES 8

We're not quite sure what led the contributor to create a dish featuring a vegetable he "always hated as a child." Perhaps a plethora, a main source for many gardener cook inspirations, here of turnips. Perhaps a visual epiphany when the beauty of newly pulled turnips with their green tops, lavender-tinged white bulbs, and still dirt-clad roots caused a turn of the head and new recognition. Perhaps a health article extolling the benefits of brassicas. Whatever the impetus, the turnips somehow came together with the flavors of peaches and raspberries in a dish the recipe testers enthusiastically described as "repeatable often."

MARTIN STRANSKY (PLAINVIEW, NY)

3 pounds turnips, peeled and sliced into ¼-inch-thick rounds
4 tablespoons olive oil
2 medium onions, halved and sliced ¼ inch thick
3 medium red bell peppers, stemmed, seeded, and cut into ¼-inch-wide strips
¾ cup peach schnapps
3 tablespoons Raspberry-Lemon Balm Infused Vinegar (see page 49)
¼ teaspoon salt
¼ teaspoon black pepper

1. Bring a large pot of water to a boil and blanch the turnip slices for 3 minutes. Drain and set aside to drip dry a minute.

2. Heat 2 tablespoons of the oil in a large sauté pan. Add the turnips and sauté over medium-high heat until tender but not collapsing, about 6 minutes. Transfer to a plate and set aside.

3. Heat the remaining 2 tablespoons oil in the same pan. Add the onions and sauté over medium-high heat until well

Turnips: A Two-Season Crop

Turnips are one of the few two-season crops. Like such root crops as beets, carrots, and onions, and above-ground crops like fava beans, artichokes and broccoli, turnips can be planted in spring the first minute after the last frost and harvested in 40 to 60 days. With successive plantings, you can have turnips throughout the summer and into the fall. In frost-free climates, turnip seeds can be sown again in fall to produce a winter crop.

In spring, tender turnip greens and young roots can be steamed together, lightly dressed with butter, salt, and pepper, and presented just as so. In the fall, the more robust greens can be cooked separately like other hearty greens, and the more developed roots braised or slawed (page 54).

wilted, about 6 minutes. Stir in the peppers and continue cooking until barely wilted, about 6 minutes more. Raise the heat to high, add the schnapps and vinegar, and cook until the liquid is reduced to a thick syrup, about 10 minutes.

4. Return the turnips to the pan and add the salt and pepper. Stir and cook 2 to 3 minutes more, until the turnips are heated through. Serve right away.

The Calling of Cauliflower

Cauliflower is loved by the gardener for the interim-season space it fills with its healthful offering for the table in a time not much else may be there. Besides, caterpillars like its flowers and leaves, and if you can plant enough to let them be, beautiful creamy-white butterflies will grace your garden with their fluttery beauty. Once in the kitchen, however, cauliflower may be lovely to look at, but what to do to liven it up for the table? In addition to steaming and dressing it with shallots, herbs, and butter, here are some other suggestions.

- Choose tiny heads, about 4 inches across, steam them whole to the al dente stage, and display them on an appetizer plate, either alongside a dip or splashed with lemon and olive oil. Score the head from the bottom so sections can be picked up to eat.
- Cook the cauliflower all the way to fork tender and purée it into a classy soup, called du Barry in French cooking. This entails nothing more than using enough liquid—water or chicken broth—to cover the florets by 2 inches. Once it is cooked and cooled, purée the mixture and thicken it with a butter roux (see page 188, Step 1), then stir in a little cream at the end. Just before serving, stir in lemon juice and salt to taste and garnish with a good sprinkle of chopped fresh chives.
- Make the cauliflower into the focus of a Moroccan couscous or sauté it with potatoes into an Indian gobi. In either of these dishes, the spices and surrounding vegetables lend extra flavor to the cauliflower, which returns the favor with a color, taste, texture, and aroma all its own.

"Cauliflower is nothing but cabbage with a college education."

—Mark Twain

Cauliflower Dressed with Shallot-Herb Butter

SERVES 6

The contributor succinctly states that this cauliflower dish is "a favorite way of giving a rather mild vegetable just the right fresh-from-my-garden seasoning." For other ways to accomplish the same end, see the box on this page.

JOANNE COOKE (WEST DES MOINES, IA)

1 medium head cauliflower, quartered, cored, and cut into florets (1½ to 2 pounds)
1 tablespoon minced shallot
1 tablespoon minced fresh chives
2 tablespoons finely chopped fresh parsley leaves
¼ teaspoon salt
¼ teaspoon black pepper
2 tablespoons butter, melted and warm
¼ cup grated Parmesan cheese

1. Steam or boil the cauliflower florets until barely tender, about 4 minutes. Drain and transfer to a serving bowl.

2. Add the shallot, chives, parsley, salt, and pepper and toss to mix. Pour in the butter and toss again. Sprinkle the cheese over the top and serve warm.

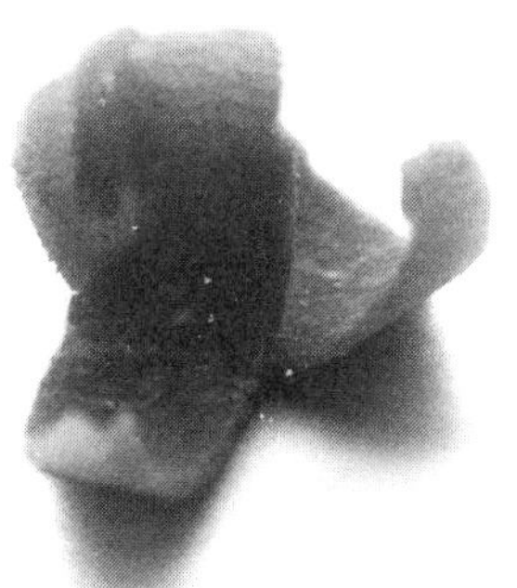

TOOLS *of the* TRADE

Vegetable Steamers

For any gardener cook who is keen on preserving the undiminished nutrition that is the reward of gardening labor and who is also always happy to have a quick-cook method, steam-cooking fulfills both intentions. Ways to go about it include:

VEGETABLE STEAMER STAND: a contraption, usually metal, that fits inside the pot and rests on legs that hold the vegetables out of the water.

WOK STEAMER: a bamboo-slatted round basket that sits above the water just inside the wok. It is used in conjunction with a snug-fitting bamboo lid to hold in the steam. The advantage of this type of steamer is that the baskets can be stacked two or three high so various vegetables can be separately steamed at the same time.

COLANDER IN A POT: a jury-rigged setup that works fine in a pinch as long as the colander has a stand to hold it out of the water and is small enough to fit completely inside the pot so steam doesn't escape through the top.

MICROWAVE: a modern convenience especially useful for quick vegetable steaming, since steam-cooking is the microwave's basic modus operandi.

Caramelized Roasted Parsnips

SERVES 6

Parsnips, a root vegetable typical of the cuisine of Middle Europe, are little thought of in American cooking where, except for some of those old favorite recipes passed along from family or neighbors, parsnips don't show up on the table. However, their culinary presence is preserved by gardeners who love getting to the root of the matter. Roasting parsnips to the caramelized stage is already unusual. Serving them over mashed potatoes, as the contributor suggests, turns them somewhat exalted, as humble vegetables go.

LINDA MAGEL (MANTECA, CA)

8 tablespoons (1 stick) butter, melted
2 tablespoons granulated sugar
2 tablespoons dark brown sugar
2 teaspoons minced garlic
½ teaspoon salt
½ teaspoon black pepper
3 pounds parsnips, peeled and cut into strips 6 inches long and ¼ inch wide
2 tablespoons chopped fresh chives
Mashed potatoes (optional, see page 274)

1. Preheat the oven to 350°F.

2. Mix the butter, granulated sugar, brown sugar, garlic, salt, and pepper in a roasting pan large enough to hold the parsnips in one layer. Add the parsnips and turn to coat. Cover the pan with foil.

3. Bake for 20 minutes. Remove the foil, stir, and continue baking, uncovered, for 20 to 30 minutes more, until the parsnips are fork tender and caramel color. Sprinkle the chives over the top and serve right away on top of the mashed potatoes, if using.

Parsnips: Delicious Duplicity

At first look, parsnips may seem unassuming, even uninteresting. But once they are tasted, the curtain of doubt is pulled aside to reveal a complexity of taste sensations. The first flavors call to mind celery, both the leaves, themselves reminiscent of lovage, and root celery. Cooking brings out a hint of sweet potato and a whisper of horseradish, two seasonal companions. Together, they add up to a parsnip, which might be better described as doubly duplicitous, a homely root that packs a lot of flavor in many pleasing ways.

Mélange of Root Vegetables Roasted with Fresh Thyme

Serves 4

A surprising cooking method is revealed within the instructions for this recipe. The vegetables, once prepared and cut to the prescribed sizes, all roast in the same pan for the same length of time. That means, once in the oven, the dish requires no other tending until the vegetables are done, some fork tender, some slightly caramelized. That alone would be enticement for the cook, but there's more: the mélange also delights the diners. With its familiar ingredients cooked in an unusual way, there's something for everyone. Also, the dish lends itself to further interpretation. Accompanied with a bowl of aïoli, it can anchor a casual party table (see box below).

DAVID BOLDUC (WARWICK, RI)

2 medium carrots, peeled and sliced into ¼-inch-thick rounds or strips (8 ounces)
2 parsnips, peeled and sliced into ¼-inch-thick rounds or strips (about 8 ounces)
1 large turnip, peeled and cut into 1-inch dice (about 8 ounces)
2 sweet potatoes, peeled and cut into 1-inch dice (about 1 pound)
2 white potatoes, peeled and cut into 1-inch dice (about 1½ pounds)
2 tablespoons fresh thyme leaves (see Note below)
2 tablespoons olive oil
1 tablespoon butter, melted
½ teaspoon salt
1 teaspoon cracked black pepper
2 tablespoons chopped fresh herb, such as parsley, dill, or chives, for garnish (optional)

1. Preheat the oven to 375°F.

2. Place all the vegetables in a large bowl. Add the thyme, oil, butter, salt, and pepper and toss to coat. Spread the vegetables on a baking sheet large enough to hold them without touching each other (or use 2 sheets). Roast for 45 minutes, or until all the vegetables are tender but still hold their shape.

3. Transfer the vegetables to a platter, sprinkle the herb, if using, over the top, and serve right away or at room temperature.

Note: Instead of fresh thyme, for this dish you could substitute another fresh, strong-flavored herb from the Mediterranean spectrum, such as rosemary, oregano, or marjoram.

Le Grand Aïoli

MAKES 1½ CUPS

No matter how drab, how ordinary or stodgy the elements of a dish may be, a crown of aïoli can transform them. The French have refined the concept to the point of naming it: le Grand Aïoli. The name is honestly come by. Root vegetables of all seasons, sprouts and stalks of spring, sparkling seafood from fresh or salty waters, can all be brought together under a cap of aïoli.

TO MAKE AÏOLI:

First soak 1 or 2 slices of crustless bread in some milk or water. When the bread is soft, squeeze out the liquid without wringing it bone dry. In a mortar and pestle, combine the soaked bread with 4 to 6 cloves of smashed garlic and pound them together until well mixed. Next begin to make a mayonnaise as directed on page 64. Add the bread-and-garlic mixture while swirling 2 egg yolks with 1 teaspoon lemon juice and 1 teaspoon mustard. Continue incorporating 1 cup oil until the mixture is the consistency of mayonnaise.

Note: You could, as some do, merely press the garlic straightaway into the mayonnaise. That will surely give you garlic mayonnaise; it will not give you aïoli.

If you live in a cold, early-winter climate where the garden gets shut down by October or so, the dried version of any of those herbs will work, especially if freshly home-dried.

Wild Rice with Walnuts and Apples

SERVES 8 TO 10

Nuts and fruit are natural flavor accompaniments for wild rice. The three together make a dish special enough to be the focus of the meal.

BARBARA PLATTS-COMEAU (PEMBROKE, NH)

Wild Rice: A Natural National Treasure

SERVES 8

Wild rice originally grew no other place in the world outside the marshes that once stretched from the Great Lakes down to the Gulf of Mexico. Today, the range of wild rice has diminished almost to the point of depletion, and it is foraged only around the Great Lakes. Yet so prized a crop eventually also became a commodity; enter cultivated wild rice. The cultivated version is more widely available, and the price is not too bad, particularly for a special occasion. But the genuine article remains, perhaps as nature intended, priceless, to be honored as it is eaten.

TO MAKE BASIC WILD RICE:

2 cups raw wild rice, rinsed
5 cups water

Put the rice and water in a heavy saucepan. Bring to a boil over medium-high heat, reduce the heat to a bare simmer, and cover the pot. Cook 50 minutes, or until the rice grains have opened and the water is absorbed. Turn off the heat and leave the pot on the burner to steam dry for at least 30 minutes or up to several hours.

Note: If the rice grains have not opened, they are not yet done. If they have opened but the water is not fully absorbed, drain the grains.

1 firm-fleshed apple, cored and cut into ¼-inch dice
1 cup coarsely chopped walnuts, toasted (see box on page 135)
1 celery rib, trimmed and thinly sliced
4 green onions (scallions), trimmed and thinly sliced
1 cup golden raisins
2 tablespoons finely chopped lemon zest
3 tablespoons fresh lemon juice
2 cloves garlic, minced or pressed
⅓ cup olive oil
½ teaspoon salt
½ teaspoon black pepper
1 recipe cooked Basic Wild Rice (see box on this page), at room temperature
2 tablespoons chopped fresh parsley leaves

1. Combine the apple, walnuts, celery, green onions, raisins, and lemon zest in a large bowl.

2. Combine the lemon juice, garlic, olive oil, salt, and pepper in a jar with a tight-fitting lid. Cap the jar and shake vigorously to mix. Pour half of the mixture over the apple mixture and toss well.

3. Place the cooked rice in a large bowl, add the apple mixture, and pour in the remaining lemon mixture. Toss and set aside at room temperature for at least 1 hour or up to 3 hours.

4. When ready to serve, sprinkle the parsley over the top.

Wild Rice with Fruit and Nuts, Continued

- Cook the rice with chicken stock instead of water.
- Substitute pecans for the walnuts and use orange zest and juice in place of the lemon zest and juice.
- Add chopped fresh mint to the rice mixture before tossing. The contributor adds, "The fresh mint I grow really makes this dish."

—JUDY YOUNG (SHAKER HEIGHTS, OH)

three out-of-the-ordinary dishes for the winter holidays

Seemingly too-fast-here and then never-ending, the winter holidays embrace Thanksgiving and Christmas as well as Hanukkah, Kwanzaa, and Ramadan. That pretty much covers the cold season, a time when sunny garden ingredients are absent. Fortunately, in such a diverse environment as ours, there are many options for embracing the season with dishes of grains, nuts, late-season produce, and dried fruits. Following are three such that fit into any winter feast and signify the artful style of contemporary American cooking.

Roasted Brussels Sprouts in Orange Sauce

SERVES 6

"Oh thrice and four times happy those who plant cabbages!"

—Rabelais

"When I was a child, my father cultivated a large vegetable garden; we grew up with the taste of just-picked vegetables. Preparation was simple, often only butter, salt, and pepper, until season's end when my mother tried more elaborate dishes. I am retired now and live in a city apartment, so for my fresh vegetables I patronize the seasonal farmers' markets. As a result, cooking, always a hobby of mine, has become more fun even though I depend on others to do the gardening for me. This Brussels sprouts recipe is a favorite in our family. Though many are turned off by the odor, a result of overcooking, roasting plus the orange flavor makes the vegetable appealing even to the most confirmed haters."

MARILOU ROBINSON (PORTLAND, OR)

1½ pounds Brussels sprouts
5 tablespoons olive oil
1 tablespoon butter
¼ cup orange juice concentrate
1 tablespoon balsamic vinegar
¼ teaspoon salt
½ teaspoon cracked black pepper
1½ tablespoons finely slivered orange zest, for garnish

1. Preheat the oven to 425°F.

2. Pull off any yellowing outer leaves, trim the stem ends, and cut a shallow X in the bottom of each of the Brussels sprouts. Place the sprouts in a baking dish, add 3 tablespoons of the oil, and turn to coat well. Bake for 15 minutes, turning once. Transfer to a serving bowl.

3. While the sprouts are baking, melt the butter in a small saucepan over medium heat. Stir in the juice concentrate, vinegar, salt, pepper, and remaining 2 tablespoons oil. Heat until warmed through but not boiling, about 5 minutes.

Transitions

There is an unsettling that occurs with the move from one season to the next, especially around the flurry of school's-in-again, garden tasks that need doing before frost sets, and then it's already winter-holiday-break time. Think of Brussels sprouts. Tiny cabbages—what they are, yet without the sweetness of their more full-headed cousins—they stand as a staunch vegetable icon to the changing season as the year turns chilly. Their roly-poly spheres appear on many winter holiday menus to the delight of some and the sneer of others. What's an icon to do? With a sparkly coating of orange sauce tanged with balsamic vinegar and peppered with freshly cracked, noticeably-there pieces of the spice, it can lead with a snappy step through the transition period and on to the next.

4. Pour over the sprouts, garnish with the orange zest, and serve hot.

Note: The dish may be prepared several hours in advance and briefly reheated (2 to 3 minutes) in the microwave.

The Multiple Layers of Citrus: Zest to Peel to Rind

Sometimes the peel of citrus fruit is the part to pare away and add to the compost pile because the pith is what the cook is after. But when the peel is a recipe ingredient, it is divided into three sections, each with a special texture, taste, and use. They are:

ZEST: The outermost layer, the colored part of the skin of the fruit. Most recipes call for zest because that's where the oils are. These imbue strong citrus flavor. To garner the zest, you can use a special tool called a zester to scrape the skin. As well as taking off the zest, the tool releases the desirable citrus oils in the process. This is a good way to go when you want the zest mostly for flavoring and not for visual effect. When larger pieces of zest are called for, use a vegetable peeler to pare away the zest without cutting into the white layer underneath. Then, depending on the recipe, use the pared pieces of zest without chopping further or use a knife to finely chop or shred the pieces.

PEEL: Includes the zest and the first, thin layer of white underneath. This part, a little bitter but not too much, is usually called for in recipes for jams, chutneys, and other dishes that are going to be significantly sweetened.

RIND: The whole outside down to the pith. Besides peeling to the pith, you can get the rind as a by-product of hand-juicing citrus. Either way, the rind is not to be tossed. Use it for candied citrus rind, marmalade, or a mint liqueur.

Acorn Squash Circles Filled with Spinach and Dried Cranberry Sauce

SERVES 8 TO 10

If ever you wanted to illuminate your winter holiday table, this dish provides a stunning presentation that all but eclipses the candles. After the visuals, there's also a taste won-

der: the cranberry sauce. Not of fresh berries but of dried cranberries, intensely condensed in flavor, combined with currants plumped with wine, and sweetened with maple syrup. It's a new delight for the American table.

~ DIANA LUCK (FARMINGTON, NM)

"After the strawberries and raspberries and blueberries, in fact just before the autumn frosts, come the cranberries. You will find them during September, round orange-red globes glowing amongst the moss and their own shiny leaves, in slight hollows of rocky terrain.

—Sylvia Boorman, *Wild Plums in Brandy—A Cookery Book of Wild Foods*

2 medium acorn squash (about $1\frac{1}{4}$ pounds each)
2 cups Dried Cranberry Sauce (recipe follows), warm
1 large bunch spinach, leaves only, washed, drained, and set aside to drip dry (about ¾ pound)

1. Cut the squash into 1-inch-thick rounds and scrape out the centers from each circle. Place the rounds in one layer in a vegetable steamer (page 281) and steam until soft but not mushy, 12 to 14 minutes.

2. Prepare the cranberry sauce and set aside.

3. Without removing the rounds from the steamer, layer enough spinach leaves across the center of each squash round to make a nest for the cranberry sauce (about 6 leaves per circle). Steam for 2 more minutes, just until the spinach wilts.

4. Transfer the rounds to a serving platter and set aside in a warm place. Continue with another batch until all the circles are steamed and spinached.

5. When ready to serve, spoon a tablespoon or so of the warm cranberry sauce in the center of the spinach bed in each round. Serve right away, accompanied with any extra cranberry sauce.

Dried Cranberry Sauce

MAKES ABOUT 2 CUPS

1 cup dried cranberries
⅓ cup dried currants, soaked in hot water for 10 minutes and drained
1 cup red wine
1 cup water
¼ cup maple syrup
½ teaspoon freshly grated nutmeg
1 teaspoon cornstarch

1. Combine all the ingredients except the cornstarch in a medium saucepan. Bring to a boil and simmer for 5 minutes.

2. Meanwhile, dissolve the cornstarch in 2 tablespoons of warm water. Whisk into the cranberry mixture and simmer for 5 minutes more, until thickened and cooked enough not to taste of the cornstarch.

3. Remove from the heat and cool until no longer boiling. Use right away. Can also be served at room temperature or chilled. Will keep in the refrigerator for up to 6 weeks.

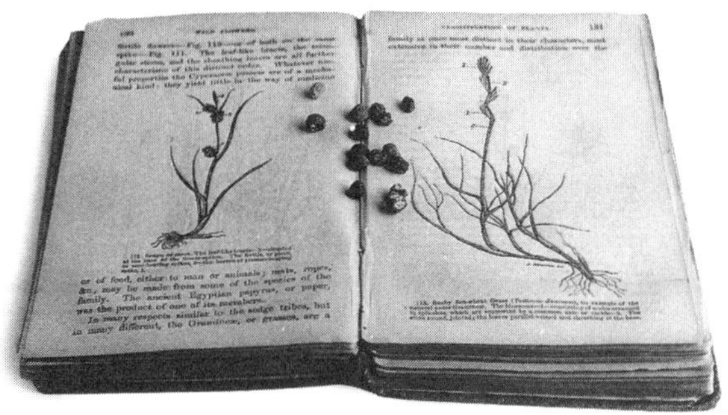

Holiday Apple and Onion Bake

SERVES 8

"My handwritten cookbook contains forty years of memories; buckwheat pancakes from my grandmother's Michigan farm and maple syrup from her 'sugarbush'; ethnic recipes from Chicago and Mexico City; Hopi recipes from Second Mesa. At age 70, my garden is much smaller. It still contains many of the herbs I love and nurture, and when the kitties and I go out to dig, I reach for my poacher's spade. Its handle, worn smooth, is just right for a little old lady." From her treasure chest of recipes and life experiences, the contributor passes along the following recipe.

JANET MAIN (NEWBURY PARK, CA)

Butter, for greasing baking pan
1½ pounds firm not-too-tart apples, such as Jonathan, Gravenstein, Granny Smith, Golden Delicious, or Fuji
1 large onion, sliced ⅜ inch thick and separated into rings (¾ to 1 pound)
¾ cup (packed) dark brown sugar
⅛ teaspoon salt
1½ cups coarse bread crumbs, preferably homemade (see page 76)
2 tablespoons butter, cut into small pieces

"There is a lovable quality about the actual tools. One feels so kindly to the thing that enables the hand to obey the brain. Moreover, one feels a good deal of respect for it; without it brain and hand would be helpless."

—Gertrude Jekyll

1. Preheat the oven to 300°F. Butter a 12 by 8-inch baking pan.

2. Arrange the apple slices in an overlapping layer in the baking pan. Top with a layer of the onion rings. Sprinkle the brown sugar and salt over the rings and top with the bread crumbs and bits of the butter. Cover with foil and place in the oven.

3. Bake for 3 hours, remove the foil, and continue baking for 30 minutes more, or until the juices are evaporated and the bread-crumb topping is browned. Cool slightly, then serve while still hot.

Wisdom for the Way with Tools

There's a Zen saying that goes: "Grasp the hoe by the smooth end of the handle." With her description of the well-worn, well-worked, well-loved, and well-respected poacher's spade, the contributor echoes the homily and extends its wisdom. It's a way of approaching the earth with gentle earnestness.

sauces, salsas, and pestos:

a bouquet of ways to dress the meal

Of all the ways cooking has changed in recent times, sauces are one of the most dramatic. Unlike the classic, luxurious reductions of eighteenth- and nineteenth-century European kitchens, which served the aristocracy in their own home palaces or the nouveaux riches in their fashionable new restaurants, today's sauces do not require a kitchen brigade to make sure each stage is just so. Ironically, this new, freer style takes its cues from other classics: the salsas of Mexico, pestos and quick pasta sauces from Italy, simplified reductions from the French *minceur* style. In this chapter are sauces that are light, fresh, not fussy, and quite feasible for making at home. They are sauces that reflect a heritage, recipes new immigrants brought to the United States and carry forth in their gardens and contemporary kitchens.

pasta sauces you can take almost anywhere

As the Italians might say, "It's the sauce that makes pasta basta." Following are pasta sauces from the main tradition of Italian cooking, fresh from the gardens of the New World. Each can top or envelop a plate of pasta, or a simple grain or potato, or a plainly cooked poultry offering for that matter, in a way that makes the dish quite plenty enough for a satisfying good meal.

TOOLS *of the* TRADE

For the Modern Saucier

At home or in a restaurant, for large buckets or small bowls, for many or for few, the sauce is the glory of any dish and the saucier is in charge of providing it. When that means you tonight, how to approach the challenge and the task? The home saucier has two easy tools to help. The trick is to use them both, one or the other or one after the other. They are:

CHEF'S KNIFE: This is the tool for fine-cutting ingredients that are to be showcased for their form as well as their taste. For example, the minced shallots for a mignonette sauce, the thinly sliced mushrooms for spreading over a steak or a bowl of polenta, the finely diced mango for a fruit salad.

The chef's knife is also the tool for cutting ingredients destined for the food processor into appropriate size pieces so that they can be finely chopped without being mashed. That means into about 1½-inch chunks for tomatoes and other soft, easily smashable ingredients; into about ½-inch chunks for crisper ingredients like peppers, onions, and other vegetables.

FOOD PROCESSOR: The food processor has undergone a stormy affair with cutting-edge professionals. It has also been quickly and eagerly accepted by home cooks. Embraced, rejected, and embraced again, the food processor is now standard equipment in most professional and virtually all home kitchens. That's because once its advantages are recognized and balanced against its drawbacks, there is no denying that this is a fine chopping machine.

There are brochures and videos geared to explaining how best to use your food processor—this blade for such and such, the other blade for so and so. And those are interesting. But in the final analysis, having the ingredients small enough or soft enough so that the standard blade can do the work is the point. This machine was made to chop.

Basic Quick-Cooked Tomato Sauce

Makes 7 cups

"As I looked in vain for a spaghetti sauce recipe that says, 'go to the garden and pick,' instead of 'open a can of,' I developed the recipe below from ingredients out of my own garden. Following that inspiration, our local garden club planted a perennial garden at a nursing home where, for the fun of it, we planted tomatoes and peppers among the flowers. The residents, most of whom had a garden at one time or another, now enjoy not only the flowers in bloom but also the bonus of tomatoes and peppers to eat." Whenever a recipe or whim calls for a fresh spaghetti sauce, you can reach for this one.

~ MARYJO BURKE (MONTICELLO, IN)

- *5 pounds tomatoes, peeled, seeded, and chopped, juices reserved*
- *1 large onion, finely chopped*
- *2 cloves garlic, minced or pressed*
- *1 small green bell pepper, seeded and finely chopped*
- *2 tablespoons chopped fresh basil leaves or 1 tablespoon dried basil*
- *1½ tablespoons chopped fresh oregano leaves or 2 teaspoons dried oregano*
- *2 tablespoons chopped fresh parsley leaves*
- *¼ teaspoon ground ginger*
- *¼ teaspoon ground allspice*
- *1½ tablespoons brown sugar*
- *½ teaspoon salt*
- *¼ teaspoon black pepper*
- *1½ tablespoons red wine vinegar*
- *½ cup tomato paste*

Place all the ingredients in a large nonreactive pot and stir to mix. Bring to a boil, reduce the heat, and simmer gently, stirring once or twice, for 45 minutes, or until the vegetables are soft. Use right away or cool and refrigerate for up to 1 week.

Note: For longer storage, the sauce may also be packed into sterilized jars and processed in a hot-water bath for 15 minutes (see pages 314–315). Or after cooling, it can be frozen.

ABOUT GARLIC POWDER

Garlic powder is an ingredient often called for in American cooking. There are those who eschew it because it is not a fresh ingredient. There are others, such as the famed chef Paul Prudhomme, who tout its power to wrestle the bite of fresh garlic into a supple balance easy on the tongue.

Tomato Sauce as an Ingredient

When a recipe calls for tomato sauce to mix into the dish rather than star as a topping, you can easily turn either of the basic tomato sauces into that ingredient. To do so, purée the sauce as fine as possible in a food processor for a chunky version. Put through a food mill for a smooth sauce.

Marinara Sauce

Makes 3 cups

"From a little village in the southern part of Italy known as Castiglione, to the new life in America, and then finally to settle in Harrisburg, Pennsylvania. These are the sentimental roots of my much revered recipe handed down through three generations. Coming from a long line of gardeners and cooks, we anticipate fresh tomato season as the best part of summer. One bite into the luscious red fruit sends me into the kitchen to start Marinara Sauce season."

BONNIE LEO (HARRISBURG, PA)

2 tablespoons olive oil
2 cloves garlic, minced
1½ pounds tomatoes, quartered
2 tablespoons chopped fresh basil leaves
2 teaspoons salt
1 teaspoon crushed red pepper
1 to 1½ tablespoons sugar, to taste
1 teaspoon garlic powder (see page 293)
½ cup Marsala wine

1. Heat the oil in a large sauté pan. Add the garlic and sauté over medium heat until golden, about 5 minutes.

2. Add the tomatoes and continue to sauté for 10 minutes, or until the skins start to separate from the pulp. Remove the skins with a fork as the tomatoes are cooking.

3. Add the basil, salt, crushed pepper, sugar, and garlic powder and stir to mix. Simmer for 10 minutes more, or until the mixture is a bit chunky with a consistency similar to chunky crushed tomatoes.

Classic Ways with an All-Purpose Tomato Sauce

The slow cooking and chunky texture of the Basic Long-Cooked Tomato Sauce (page 295) invite other elements that also require long simmering to blossom and develop flavor. With such additions, you can produce an even richer, more complex sauce. For instance:

- Add minced carrot, onion, celery, and perhaps some aromatics such as parsley, bay, or thyme when sautéing the garlic and let the mixture cook down until caramelized but not burned. Continue by adding the tomatoes and so on.
- Add not-too-finely chopped zucchini, eggplant, or mushrooms when sautéing the garlic. Cook long enough to soften, then continue with the recipe. This creates a sauce that is almost meaty, but still vegetarian.
- Add ground meat—beef, pork, veal, or a mixture—when sautéing the garlic and cook long enough to brown the meat and release its fat and juices. Continue with the recipe.

4. Stir in the Marsala and simmer for 15 minutes more, until thickened and saucy. Use right away. Or cool and store in the refrigerator for up to 5 days.

Basic Long-Cooked Tomato Sauce

MAKES 4 CUPS

"Here is my recipe devised about fourteen years ago after a trip to Italy, where we sampled so many fabulous tomato sauces. What an inspiration! As the crops mature in my husband's garden, I cook this in large batches and freeze the sauce to enjoy through our long Chicago winters."

MARY CAVALIER (KENILWORTH, IL)

- *¼ cup olive oil*
- *6 cloves garlic, coarsely chopped*
- *6 pounds large tomatoes, coarsely chopped, seeds and juices included*
- *1 cup coarsely shredded fresh basil leaves*
- *1 teaspoon salt*
- *1 tablespoon sugar (optional)*

1. Heat the oil in a large nonreactive pot. Add the garlic and sauté over low heat until soft but not browned, about 5 minutes.

2. Stir in the remaining ingredients, including the sugar, if using. Bring to a boil, reduce the heat to maintain a very slow simmer, and cook for 2 hours, stirring from time to time, until thick and richly colored.

3. Serve right away. Or cool and refrigerate for up to 3 weeks, or freeze for longer.

All the Way to Bologna

Once you've sautéed the garlic with the extra minced vegetables and herbs as described in the box on page 294, add ground meat at the end of sautéing the vegetables. Cook long enough to brown the meat and release its juices, then add the tomatoes and so on and continue with the recipe. You're most of the way there to the classic Bolognese sauce. All that's left is to add some cooking time, until the oil rises to the surface and the color of the sauce is a deep brown-red with overtones of copper. This requires extra time closely watching the pot at the end. For the extra added touch that defines a Bolognese and, some would say, elevates it above any other of its kind, stir in a tablespoon or two of milk at the end of the cooking time, just as you take the pot off the heat. This step works magically to bring together the liquids with the oils.

THE MESSAGE IN THE METHOD
The method of slow cooking, extended cooling, and slow cooking again has a dual advantage. It allows flavors to deepen over time and also frees the cook from having to attend the pot frequently, stirring often to avoid burning and sticking. It's a technique that can be applied to any long-cooking red sauce.

Spicy Tomato Sauce

MAKES 8 CUPS

"This is a sauce that develops its flavors slowly and will be better the longer it is allowed to sit. It is a bit spicy, good served on not-too-delicate noodles or over cheese ravioli, which cool the spicy bite of the sauce."

CHALLY SIMS (FAYETTEVILLE, AR)

2 dried ancho chilies
¼ cup olive oil
1 medium green bell pepper, stemmed, seeded, and finely chopped
1 medium onion, finely chopped
4 cloves garlic, minced
3 pounds Roma tomatoes, peeled and coarsely chopped into ½-inch pieces, juices reserved
1 tablespoon fresh thyme leaves
2 tablespoons chopped fresh parsley leaves
2 teaspoons chopped fresh rosemary leaves
2 tablespoons chopped fresh oregano leaves
½ teaspoon chili powder
1 teaspoon salt
1 teaspoon black pepper
1 tablespoon chopped fresh cilantro leaves
1 tablespoon honey
½ cup tomato paste

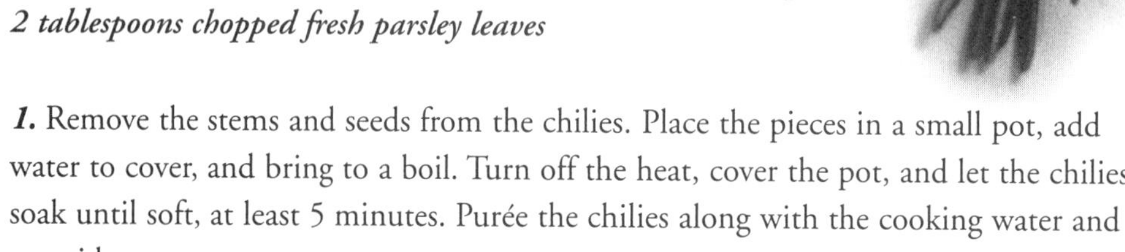

1. Remove the stems and seeds from the chilies. Place the pieces in a small pot, add water to cover, and bring to a boil. Turn off the heat, cover the pot, and let the chilies soak until soft, at least 5 minutes. Purée the chilies along with the cooking water and set aside.

2. Heat the olive oil in a large nonreactive pot. Add the bell pepper, onion, and garlic and sauté until wilted, about 3 minutes. Stir in the tomatoes, along with their juices, the thyme, parsley, rosemary, oregano, chili powder, salt, and pepper. Add enough water barely to cover the vegetables. Bring to a boil, reduce the heat to low, and cook, uncovered, for 1 hour, until the mixture has a saucy consistency and a brownish red color. Turn off the heat and let rest on the stove for at least 1 hour or up to 3 hours.

3. Stir in the cilantro, honey, and tomato paste and bring to a boil again. Reduce the heat and cook over low heat for 1 hour more, until the color has deepened and the sauce is thick but still chunky.

4. Use right away. Or, for best flavor, cool to room temperature and reheat just before serving. Will keep in the refrigerator for up to 5 days or freeze for longer storage.

Late-Summer Red and Yellow Pasta Sauce

Makes 1½ quarts

"The following is a simple recipe best made in mid- to late September with fresh ingredients from the garden or a farmers' market. It freezes well and can be brought out to stir memories of hot, sunny, abundant days and recall their warmth and savor."

INGRID DINTER (NEW YORK, NY)

2 large red bell peppers
2 large yellow bell peppers
2 large orange bell peppers
2 large red tomatoes
2 large yellow tomatoes
2 large orange tomatoes
¼ cup olive oil
1 large onion, finely chopped
5 cloves garlic, minced
1 cup (packed) chopped fresh parsley leaves
2 tablespoons chopped fresh basil leaves
1 teaspoon crushed red pepper
1 teaspoon salt

1. Stem, seed, and chop all the peppers into ½-inch chunks. Set aside. Peel the tomatoes and chop into ½-inch chunks. Set aside.

2. Heat the oil in a large sauté pan. Add the onion and garlic and sauté until translucent, about 5 minutes. Add the parsley, basil, and red pepper and stir to mix. Stir in the bell peppers and sauté until barely beginning to wilt. Add the tomatoes, mixing well, and cook until the oil rises to the top, about 10 minutes.

3. Reduce the heat to maintain a quiet simmer and cook, stirring occasionally, for 45 to 50 minutes more, until the peppers are very soft.

4. Stir in the salt and use right away or cool and store in the refrigerator for up to 1 week or freeze for longer storage.

The Ever-Changing Color of Peppers

As it turns out, the color of garden peppers, whether chili or bell, is determined more by the pepper's stage of ripeness than by varietal differences. That means, red chilies and red bell peppers are red because they've stayed longer on the plant, basking in the sun until their green turns from rosy to russet as they soak up the last of summer's rays. The color does indicate taste differences, but oddly divergent ones. For chilies, redder, riper means hotter; for bell peppers, redder means sweeter.

garden salsas across the nation

Salsas have swept the nation. They appear for breakfast, lunch, dinner, or snack. They strut in a parade that stretches from North to South, East to West, and everywhere in between. Without regard to ethnic background or present place of residence, people love salsas. To leave no doubt about their impact both culinarily and economically, you have only to consider the huge amount of shelf space salsas have claimed in almost all grocery stores. Such a phenomenon can be explained in many ways. The bottom line is: people like a bit of spice, a dash of difference, and a big soupçon of ease as they go about preparing the meal. Salsas meet all those requirements.

THE ESSENTIAL NATURE OF SALSA
Part of the appeal of fresh salsa is that it doesn't require oil of any sort, though sometimes cooks add it for a glossy touch. Those recipes are often quite delicious, but the oil is an embellishment that, if you are watching the calorie count, you can almost always omit.

Connecticut Salsa

MAKES ABOUT 3 CUPS

In case you're curious about how salsa also found its way to Connecticut, a state not known for its Latino population, the contributor explains, "My mother was Mexican, born in Mier in the state of Tamaulipas. A favorite recipe handed down from her family is for a salsa verde (green sauce) made with tomatillos, cilantro, garlic, and onions, all from the garden. It is delicious for breakfast next to scrambled eggs, for dinner served with chicken or pork, or as a taco topping." It is still a bit of a mystery about how her mother and the salsa got to Connecticut; it's clear, though, that tomatillos and cilantro now grow there and that the contributor carries on the family salsa tradition. This is a very mild sauce. If you prefer more spice, add some jalapeño when puréeing tomatillos.

NINA BLOOMER (GUILFORD, CT)

20 tomatillos (about 1¼ pounds)
⅔ to ¾ cup fresh cilantro leaves
4 cloves garlic
¼ cup olive or vegetable oil
2 medium onions, finely chopped
½ teaspoon salt

1. Bring a medium pot of water to boil. Peel the papery husks off the tomatillos and add the tomatillos to the water. Simmer until the tomatillos are soft, 8 to 10 minutes. Remove from the heat and cool in the water.

2. Lift the tomatillos out of the cooking liquid and transfer to a food processor. Add the cilantro and garlic and purée as fine as possible. Set aside.

3. Heat the oil in a sauté pan over low heat. Stir in the onions and cook slowly until slightly wilted and no longer sharp tasting, 1 to 2 minutes.

4. Add the tomatillo mixture and the salt, stir to mix, and bring to a boil. Remove from the heat right away and transfer to a bowl. Cool, then refrigerate until chilled so the flavors soften and blend.

5. Serve chilled, at room temperature, or reheated. This salsa will keep for up to 1 week in the refrigerator, but it should be used by then. It does not freeze well.

The Tomatillo: A Shy Member of the Nightshade Family

Tomatillos are part of the botanical family that includes tomatoes, potatoes, and eggplant. In flavor, however, they differ widely from the other nightshades. The taste and texture most closely resemble green tomatoes but with a softer, more glutinous pulp, a bit like okra, and a sharper taste. Like green tomatoes, they are almost never used raw. Instead, they are better suited as a mild thickening addition to Mexican and South American-style soups and stews or as the center of an unassertive green tomato salsa.

Conditions for Tomatillos to Thrive

Tomatillos are easy to grow anywhere tomatoes and eggplants do, namely, in a sunny spot in a warm garden that gets regular ground-level soaking (not overhead watering which wets the leaves, eventually resulting in mold and wilt that weaken the plant and reduce the crop). For tomatillos, as with tomatoes, once the plant has shown flowers, reduce watering. Once it sets fruit, water almost not at all, even resisting the impulse to provide a small drink in the heat of the summer. Remember that nightshades in general and tomatillos in particular are tenacious, drought tolerant, freely self-seeding, eternally recurring vines. As long as there is fruit on the vine and the leaves have not yellowed or browned beyond hope, stick to this plan and you will have the best, largest, and sweetest yield.

Maryland Salsa

MAKES 1½ CUPS

Seemingly out of nowhere, black beans appear on a Maryland table, in a salsa. It's as much a surprise as it is evidence of the presence this new American "dish" has established. This salsa in particular steps far wide of the normal range of such concoctions: it's a sauce, a topping, a condiment. Use it for dipping chips or for garnishing simply cooked chicken, fish, or rice dishes.

❧ GAYLE BAUER (BETHESDA, MD)

Nachos Tonight

Though our recipe testers dislike calling for canned ingredients, low-sodium, plain (not seasoned) canned black beans, drained, work just fine and are better than no beans at all for the salsa. Mounded on tortilla chips, covered with a blanket of soft cheese, and heated just to melting in a microwave, the combo makes nachos.

2 cups cooked black beans (see box at left)
1 small tomato, well chopped
1 tablespoon finely chopped onion
½ large jalapeño, stemmed and minced
2 green onions (scallions), trimmed and thinly sliced
1 small clove garlic, minced
2 tablespoons chopped fresh cilantro leaves
2 teaspoons chopped fresh oregano leaves or 1 teaspoon dried oregano
¼ teaspoon ground cumin
1 tablespoon olive oil
½ tablespoon red wine vinegar
½ tablespoon fresh lemon juice
Salt and pepper

Combine all the ingredients in a bowl and mix gently. Use right away or store in the refrigerator. Will keep for up to 1 week.

New Jersey Salsa

MAKES 3 CUPS

"From many years of outdoor and greenhouse gardening, some of the most rewarding garden experiences I have are the walks up and down garden paths throughout the growing season. Watching for the first bean sprout to appear, anticipating the first green tomato, intent on seeing the eventual crown of morning glories, invariably I find something, some little treasure: a bunch of baby greens and watercress for a salad, tarragon to season the fresh salmon for the grill. On such strolls, I've collected a mix of fresh vegetables that I make into a salsa I call stroll-through-the-garden salsa."

❧ TRICIA TREGO (FAR HILLS, NJ)

1 large Jersey tomato (see box below)
1 medium green tomato
1 medium green bell pepper
1 small red bell pepper
1 cayenne pepper
½ small onion
½ tablespoon chopped fresh parsley leaves
1 teaspoon chopped fresh tarragon leaves
½ tablespoon chopped fresh basil leaves
1 tablespoon chopped fresh chives
¼ teaspoon chili powder
¼ teaspoon salt
⅛ teaspoon black pepper
2 tablespoons tomato paste

1. Trim and coarsely chop the tomatoes, peppers, and onion either in a food processor or with a chef's knife, taking care to keep the pieces in ¼- to ½-inch chunks.

2. Place the chunks in a large bowl and add the remaining ingredients. Add 2 tablespoons water and stir to mix. Set aside in the refrigerator to chill and blend the flavors for at least 3 hours.

About Jersey . . .

Dubbed the Garden State, New Jersey holds within its boundaries some of the most prolific forests, meadows, streams, and fields in the nation. There are Jersey pines, muscovy ducks that grow best in Jersey, and Jersey tomatoes. Big, beefy, sweet and juicy, and plenty of them at the end of summer, they are the driving force for what became a Jersey salsa. The tomatoes alone are worth the trip to Jersey.

Indiana Salsa

MAKES 1 QUART

"Beefy tomatoes, green and yellow peppers both, and green onions, all garden fresh, make the best version of this salsa. Serve with tortilla chips, as a topping with chicken, or to spice up a salad."

BETSY SAJDAK (CARMEL, IN)

4 very large tomatoes, cut into ¼-inch dice (about 3 pounds)
1 small green bell pepper, stemmed, seeded, and cut into ¼-inch dice
1 small yellow bell pepper, stemmed, seeded, and cut into ¼-inch dice
1 jalapeño, stemmed, seeded, and minced
4 green onions (scallions), trimmed and finely chopped
2 tablespoons chopped fresh cilantro leaves
1 tablespoon fresh lime juice
½ teaspoon salt
Pinch of black pepper
1 tablespoon olive oil (optional)

Place all the ingredients in a large bowl, including the olive oil, if using. Stir gently and serve right away or chill first. Keeps in the refrigerator for up to 3 days.

Note: If a large, beefy tomato doesn't grow in your region, any not-too-watery, intensely sweet red tomato at the height of the season will do.

ON SEEDING CHILI PEPPERS

There's no need to remove the seeds from small chili peppers for casual dishes, such as salsas. For more formal presentations, when strips or dice are featured as a decorative as well as taste element, the seeds are removed to keep the look neat. Also, when making stuffed chilies (see page 8), the seeds need to be removed to make room for the filling. For larger chili peppers, pasillas (poblanos) or Anaheims, the seeds are always removed, as with bell peppers, for aesthetic reasons.

Nebraska Salsa

MAKES 2 QUARTS

In Nebraska, where the long winters bring a blanket of knee-deep snow that permits no gardening, the contributor has developed a means to keep some of the summer harvest until the land warms enough to plant again: "After mixing the salsa, I empty the contents into a strainer and let the liquid drain into a bowl. Then I put the salsa into a gallon jar to enjoy fresh and cook down the liquid for taco sauce."

TERRANCE PAVLIK (NORFOLK, NE)

8 medium tomatoes (about 2 pounds)
4 medium bell peppers, preferably an assortment of green, red, yellow, and purple, stemmed and seeded
1 to 3 jalapeños, stemmed and seeded, to taste
1 medium white onion
1 medium purple onion
6 cloves garlic
1 tablespoon crushed red pepper
1 teaspoon salt
Pinch of black pepper

1. Using a chef's knife or food processor, separately chop the tomatoes, bell peppers, jalapeños, onions, and garlic into ¼-inch pieces. Transfer the ingredients to a large bowl as you go. Add the crushed red pepper, salt, and pepper and stir to mix.

2. Transfer the mixture to a colander set over a large bowl and set aside to drain for a few minutes.

3. Serve the drained salsa right away, store in the refrigerator for up to 1 week, or freeze for longer.

4. Transfer the liquid collected in the bottom of the bowl to a small saucepan and cook over medium heat until thickened enough to make a taco sauce. Use right away, store in the refrigerator for up to 3 weeks, or freeze.

Note: The salsa may also be served without draining.

Iowa Salsa

MAKES 1 QUART

"I created this cooked salsa from trying other recipes and making up my own. Over several years, I've perfected it and now receive requests for the recipe from everyone who tries it. You can also make a fresh salsa with the same ingredients by leaving out the tomato paste and vinegar and skipping the cooking step." These words are testimony to the exuberance of a gardener cook who tests the standard, has fun innovating, and ultimately comes up with something that suits her own vision.

~ RITA SCOTT (MARION, IA)

15 Roma tomatoes (about 2½ pounds), peeled and coarsely chopped (see Note below)
1 medium onion, chopped into ¼-inch pieces
2 to 3 cloves garlic, minced
½ medium green bell pepper, stemmed, seeded, and chopped into ¼-inch pieces
2 Anaheim or poblano chilies, stemmed, seeded, and finely chopped
½ tablespoon chili powder
⅛ teaspoon celery seed
½ tablespoon pickling salt
¼ teaspoon black pepper
⅓ cup tomato paste (see box at right)
½ cup red wine vinegar
3 jalapeños, stemmed, seeded, and finely chopped (optional)

Tips on the Topic of Tomato Paste

While it might seem tomato paste is a matter of catch-as-catch-can to grab off the grocery shelf or stockpile in the cupboard, there are considerations to fuss over:

First, choose unseasoned tomato paste because the recipe will include other herbs and spices as the dish is made. This is easy: Read the label.

Second, and more important, consider the flavor-density level of the paste. In other words, what does it taste like? Brands vary a lot. Most desirable is a paste that is thick, almost heady with tomato flavor, and tastes like what you might have made yourself from summer garden tomatoes. This will, of course, take a bit of experimenting and comparing at home, since it would not be good form to take your can opener along and open the cans to taste test on the spot.

1. Place all the ingredients, including the jalapeños, if using, in a large heavy nonreactive pot. Bring to a boil and simmer for 10 minutes, or until the vegetables are wilted.

2. Remove and cool. Use right away or store in the refrigerator for up to 4 weeks. Or transfer to prepared jars, process in a hot-water bath for 25 minutes (see pages 314–315), and store for up to several months.

Note: If Romas are not available, substitute another kind of red, sweet tomato.

"Variety's the very spice of life."

—Voltaire

Georgia Salsa

MAKES 1 QUART

Out of Georgia, the salad-without-the-lettuce nature of salsa is highlighted. "Tomatoes, corn, and peppers freshly picked from the back garden and combined with balsamic vinegar, herbs, and oil make an incredibly easy and tasty accompaniment to grilled lamb, roasts, chicken, and seafood, especially shrimp." With balsamic vinegar and olive oil, it's a rendition of salsa that expands its versatility.

DUSTY HAVERTY (ATLANTA, GA)

1½ pounds tomatoes, seeded and chopped into ¼-inch pieces
1½ cups white or yellow corn kernels (about 2 ears)
2 medium bell peppers, one green and one yellow, stemmed, seeded, and cut into ¼-inch pieces
1 jalapeño, stemmed, seeded, and finely chopped
1 small white onion, finely chopped
2 teaspoons chopped fresh oregano leaves
2 teaspoons chopped fresh parsley leaves
1 tablespoon balsamic vinegar
1 tablespoon olive oil
½ teaspoon sugar
1 teaspoon salt
¼ teaspoon black pepper

Combine all the ingredients in a large bowl and mix gently. Let stand at room temperature for at least 1 hour before serving. May be stored in the refrigerator for up to 3 days.

Texas Salsa

MAKES ABOUT 3 CUPS

A colorful mix of summer fruit might have been called a fruit salad in former times. As salsa, piqued with ginger, ultra-freshened with mint, and moistened with a splash of Champagne, the fruit is ever so much more elegant. Whether alongside pancakes or French toast for breakfast, accompanying a simple grilled chicken breast for dinner, or garnishing a cooling sorbet for dessert, this salsa makes the most of seasonal, naturally sweet and tart fruit. "The amount of sugar needed depends on the ripeness of the fruit. It's best with sweet strawberries. Remember to choose mango by feel and smell, not by color."

AMY SELIG, YOUR PERSONAL CHEF (HOUSTON, TX)

2 ripe mangos, peeled and diced (see page 81)
10 to 12 large sweet strawberries, topped, hulled and sliced
6 ripe kiwis, peeled, quartered, and sliced
¾ cup blueberries
1 to 1½ tablespoons sugar, to taste
½ teaspoon grated fresh ginger
Splash of Champagne (see Note below)
8 fresh mint leaves

Combine all the ingredients except the mint in a large bowl, mixing very gently. Serve right away or within 1 hour, garnished with the mint leaves.

Note: If Champagne is not on the menu, substitute another not-too-dry white wine, such as a German Riesling, French Muscadet, or California Chablis.

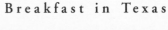

Breakfast in Texas

There was a time breakfast in Texas meant a vat of beans, platters of beef and sausage, big round tortillas to hold it all. Well, that was on the range. Perhaps there was a saucy salsa to perk up the fare. Years later, diced fresh fruit tinged with mint turned the salsa to the twentieth century. What might come next?

California Salsa

MAKES ABOUT 4 CUPS

Accenting the corn, highlighting the onions—both green onions and red onions—downplaying the chilies to none, keeping the cilantro, and adding balsamic vinegar, the contributor has created a salsa that's true to the airy spirit of California style. As well as for chips, it's a perfect accompaniment for grilled chicken, pork tenderloin, fish, or vegetables. Or, serve it on lettuce for a fat-free salad.

~ CRIS ENG (DANVILLE, CA)

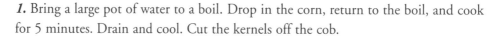

INSTEAD OF CILANTRO

Cilantro aficionados have a hard time understanding, but it's true: Many people find cilantro quite distasteful; for them, it leaves an unpleasant, kind of bitter, soapy taste in the mouth. However, the leafy green herb element is pretty much essential to fresh salsa. Rather than skipping it altogether, substitute another, such as chervil, dill, fennel, or parsley.

4 medium ears of corn
1 medium red onion, cut into ¼-inch dice
2 heaping cups cherry tomatoes, preferably a mix of red and yellow, stemmed and halved (about 2 baskets)
3 bunches green onions (scallions), trimmed and thinly sliced to make about 3 cups
½ cup chopped fresh cilantro leaves
2 tablespoons balsamic vinegar
2 teaspoons ground cumin
1 teaspoon salt
½ teaspoon black pepper

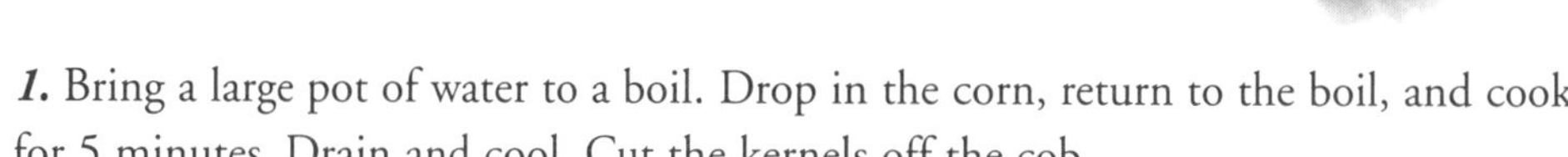

1. Bring a large pot of water to a boil. Drop in the corn, return to the boil, and cook for 5 minutes. Drain and cool. Cut the kernels off the cob.

2. Transfer the kernels to a bowl and add the remaining ingredients. Toss gently to mix and set aside at room temperature for 1 hour. Serve at room temperature or refrigerate for up to 3 days.

Oregon Salsa

MAKES 6 CUPS

"We grow Walla Walla onions, Roma tomatoes, cucumbers, and garlic to have this salsa on hand from July to November." The contributor calls the dish a salsa, but she notes that it's also good as a salad or side dish.

~ MARIANNE KEY (MEDFORD, OR)

1 large Walla Walla or other sweet onion, finely chopped
4 to 6 large Anaheim chilies, roasted, peeled, seeded, and chopped into ¼-inch pieces (see page 99; see Note below)
10 Roma, plum, or other small, ripe, red tomatoes, chopped into ¼-inch pieces (about 1½ pounds)
2 small cucumbers, peeled and chopped into ¼-inch pieces
12 black olives, pitted (see page 131)
2 large cloves garlic, minced
1 teaspoon salt
¼ teaspoon black pepper
¼ cup white wine vinegar
⅓ cup olive oil
½ cup pine nuts, toasted (see page 135)

1. Combine all the ingredients except the nuts in a large bowl. Refrigerate to chill thoroughly and allow the flavors to mingle, at least 2 hours, up to overnight.

2. Just before serving, add the pine nuts and toss gently.

Note: Anaheims are light green, elongated chili peppers with a very modest to no heat factor. They are the kind commonly available in cans, either whole or diced. Those will do, but the fresh ones, now conveniently available in supermarkets as well as ethnic markets, are a cut above. It's worth taking the trouble to roast and peel them.

The Sounds of Sweet Onions Growing

"Walla Walla" echoes a refrain from a Fifties pop song; catchy, repeatable, you might walk around all day trying to remember the rest of the words. Today the phrase refers to a kind of sweet globe onion, almost sweet enough to slice and eat raw and unadorned. You can often find Walla Wallas, three together, nicely bundled in net bags that keep them aerated and dry for freshness. They do not come cheap. Their competitors in the American beauty onion contest are Vidalias and Mauis, equally sweet and equally pricey. Each of the three has taken its name from its geographic location: Oregon for Walla Wallas, Georgia or Louisiana for the Vidalias, Hawaii for the Mauis. If you love onions, especially garden fresh, it's worth it to plant one or all of these, either from sets or seeds. Given enough space, they're no harder to raise than any other globe onion.

pestos around the year

The classic pesto, a specialty of the Italian region of Liguria, is a mix of basil, garlic, pine nuts, and olive oil pounded into a paste, with Parmesan and Romano cheeses stirred in at the end. Formerly the pounding was done with a mortar and pestle. Today a food processor facilitates the job, and, with this new ease, gardeners, cooks, and restaurateurs have devised many variations that keep the inherently delicious and versatile sauce available in all seasons. Following are classic and new pesto creations from contributors around the nation.

Classic Basil Pesto

MAKES ABOUT 3 CUPS

All adhere to the basic ingredients, though each has a certain preferred balance. More nuts, more cheese, more basil, you can vary as you will. In addition, all agree that of course fresh is best, but if you want the pleasure of basil in the winter, the pesto freezes just fine, so while you're at it, make plenty.

KAREN CADUFF (SALT LAKE CITY, UT), SUSAN PRIES (ALEXANDRIA, VA), CAROL TURRENTINE (ATLANTA, GA), JULIE GOELZ (PLAINFIELD, IL)

½ cup pine nuts
4 to 6 cloves garlic, to taste
4 cups shredded fresh basil leaves
1 cup olive oil
1 cup grated Parmesan or romano cheese, preferably a mix
Salt

Place the pine nuts, garlic, basil, and oil in a food processor and blend as fine as possible. Transfer the mixture to a medium bowl and stir in the cheese. Add salt to taste. Use right away or store in the refrigerator for up to 3 days.

Note: If freezing the pesto, don't add the cheese until ready to serve.

Growing the Ingredients for Basil Pesto

"GARLIC should be planted at the same time you plant tulips. Separate the cloves from the bulb, plant 2 inches deep and 4 to 6 inches apart. I sprinkle a little bone meal in the holes before planting. Next, use some mulch—leaves, straw, pine needles, etc. The garlic will sprout in the spring. When the green tops curl, cut off the top curl and use for salads. When the stalk is almost all yellow, dig the bulbs and hang in a dry airy spot for 2 to 3 weeks. Clean off the dry, loose soil before storing in open containers. With this preparation, you can keep garlic all winter.

"BASIL, which I start from seed because one small package of seed yields lots of basil for lots of projects. Basil hates cold so must be planted when the earth is warm (see page 309 for how to grow basil in winter). When gathering basil for pesto, I first hose down the plants so they are free of debris when I bring them in. For the pesto, I use only the leaves. I save the stalks, which I hang upside down to dry then throw them in the fireplace fire in winter for a nice aroma.

"PARSLEY, if you like it in your pesto, can be grown from inexpensive nursery seedlings or from seeds you sow yourself. Use only the leaves of Italian parsley. Caterpillars love parsley; you will have a caterpillar garden." The editors add a note to remember that those caterpillars will turn into butterflies to grace your garden from above so plant enough parsley for all to feast upon.

MARYJO BURKE (MONTICELLO, IN)

Arugula Lover's Pesto

MAKES 1 CUP

"In Oregon, basil is strictly a summer thing, but I wanted to have pesto year-round, so I set out to see if other greens could be substituted for basil and came up with this recipe. It has the potency and bite of arugula. If you want to tone it down, you can decrease the arugula and increase the parsley." You can also replace the walnuts with a milder-tasting nut, such as almonds or pine nuts.

ELIZABETH McLAGAN (PORTLAND, OR)

1 cup coarsely chopped arugula leaves
½ cup fresh parsley leaves
½ cup coarsely cut winter greens, such as mizuna, giant red mustard, or argentata
½ cup walnut halves or pieces
2 to 4 cloves garlic, to taste
1 to 2 jalapeños, stemmed, seeded, and coarsely chopped, to taste
½ teaspoon salt
½ cup Parmesan cheese
½ cup olive oil

1. Wash the arugula, parsley, and winter greens all together in a large bowl of water. Lift them out of the water and transfer to a colander. Set aside to drip dry a bit.

2. Pulverize the walnuts in a food processor. Add the remaining ingredients, including the still-moist greens, and process until minced as fine as possible. Use right away or store in the refrigerator for up to 1 week.

BASIL IN WINTER

To enjoy the effervescent taste and aroma of basil even when it's still cold out, follow this contributor's advice: "I grow basil indoors during winter. I start the seeds in a clear plastic seed-starting box using 3- to 4-inch containers filled with potting soil and a ¼-inch layer of sphagnum moss on top. Once the plants are growing, I place the box on a small table in front of a window and virtually watch them grow. In about one month, I can pick some leaves."

—NANCY SUTTON (SPRING HILL, FL)

Cilantro Pesto

MAKES 1½ CUPS

"With an abundant crop of cilantro every summer, I found that by substituting it for basil in the traditional pesto and adding one of my jalapeños, which also grow rampant, I could make a refreshing summer pasta dish."

KATHY LAFLEUR (RANCHO SANTA FE, CA)

4 cups cilantro leaves and tender stems
1 jalapeño, stemmed and cut up a bit
5 cloves garlic
½ cup pine nuts
¼ cup grated Parmesan
1 tablespoon fresh lime juice
1 teaspoon salt
½ teaspoon black pepper
½ cup olive oil

Place all the ingredients except the oil in a food processor and blend until almost smooth. Slowly add the oil and continue processing until well mixed but not puréed. Serve right away or store in the refrigerator for up to 5 days. Freeze for longer keeping.

Cilantro, Pesto Personality par Excellence

In addition to pasta, cilantro pesto lends itself to a wide variety of other applications. Use it to:

- Paint bruschetta or pizza before piling on the rest of the ingredients.
- Spread over bland fish, such as snapper or cod, either before or after cooking.
- Top rice or potatoes, baked, mashed or fried.
- Dollop on tacos or fajitas just before folding and eating. For this use, substituting *queso cotija* for the Parmesan is a nice touch.

Winter Pesto

MAKES 1¼ CUPS

"The sky (or the garden) is the limit for pesto variations. The principle stays the same; only the ingredients vary. This is what restaurants use when basil is not available." The spinach and watercress mix makes for a spunky yet still softly flavored pesto. Kale leaves lend a mustardy taste, or you can "add character to your winter pesto with one or two teaspoons of dried herbs, such as sage, thyme, marjoram, rosemary, or oregano." Be advised, the dried herbs should be used judiciously so that they add a whiff of flavor and not a sandy texture.

L.L. GROSS (PHILADELPHIA, PA)

2½ cups (packed) coarsely chopped mixed fresh greens, such as spinach, watercress, kale, or parsley
3 cloves garlic
¼ cup pine nuts
½ cup grated hard white cheese *(see box on page 311)*
1 tablespoon fresh lemon juice
½ cup olive oil
Salt

1. Place the greens, garlic, and nuts in a food processor and chop as fine as possible. Add the cheese, lemon juice, and oil. Continue processing until well blended.

2. Transfer the mixture to a bowl and stir in salt to taste. Serve right away or store in the refrigerator for up to 5 days. Freeze for longer keeping.

Sun-Dried Tomato Pesto

MAKES ABOUT ⅔ CUP

Precious as they are, turning sun- or oven-dried tomatoes into pesto is an extravagance to bestow on special guests for a special occasion. Unusual in that it has no nuts, this pesto is nonetheless rich and flavor-packed and a little goes a long way. The appetizer table is just the venue to let small amounts sparkle, for instance as a spot of red garnish on canapés, bruschetta, or crostini. Or, as the contributor suggests, as icing on a two-layer cream cheese torte with basil pesto as the filling in between. In fact, sun-dried tomato pesto in tandem with basil pesto is a heavenly combination you can extrapolate to other dishes, such as grilled boneless chicken breasts, seared tuna, and fried globe eggplant rounds. Or, use them together to garnish potato soup: tomato pesto on one side, basil on the other, make a swirl to have them meet without combining, and call yourself an artist.

LINDA HALE (VENTURA, CA)

Pesto Cheeses

The cheese for pesto can be the traditional Parmesan or Romano. It could also be another Italian hard cheese, such as aged Asiago, or the Greek dried ricotta called *mizithra,* or the Mexican *queso cotija.* All go well with green pestos, especially winter pesto and cilantro pesto, and each adds its own, different worth. The important thing is that the cheese be freshly grated, if not by you at home, then by your local deli or grocer.

1 cup (packed) dried tomatoes (see page 337)
4 cloves garlic
⅓ cup grated Parmesan
½ teaspoon sugar
½ teaspoon salt
¼ teaspoon black pepper
½ cup olive oil

1. If using oil-packed tomatoes, drain them, reserving the oil for later. If the tomatoes have not been packed in oil, soak them to soften in enough boiling water to cover for about 20 minutes, then drain.

2. Place the tomatoes and the rest of the ingredients in a food processor and process until well blended. Use right away or store in the refrigerator for up to 5 days.

Pesto Possibilities

Once you have the general idea of pesto, you can make up your own to suit many a garden offering. Try:

OREGANO in place of one-quarter of the basil plus parsley for the rest with pistachio nuts in place of the pine nuts.

RED BELL PEPPER, roasted, peeled, and puréed, in place of the basil with Asiago cheese in place of the Parmesan and romano cheeses.

SWEET POTATO, cooked and puréed, in place of the basil, but only half the amount with almonds in place of the pine nuts and a splash of red wine vinegar.

ROASTED GARLIC, using the recipe for Roasted Garlic Dressing (page 82), plus a handful of Parmesan or romano cheese.

In addition, see Parsley-Pecan Pesto (page 244).

pantry perks:

putting by the harvest

Whether you are bound by the elements to a short growing season or bask in the luxury of warmth and light almost throughout the year, at some point, any given crop comes to the end of its producing for the moment. Putting by is a way to enjoy out-of-season fruits and vegetables during the downtime. Without a personal garden, seasonal produce from the farmers' market or a roadside stand can be purchased in extra-large amounts for preserving and provide the same satisfaction as homegrown. If you're one of the few (it seems) who have no homegrown tomatoes, they are available by the bushel basket at any farmers' market at the end of summer. When strawberries are cheap, why not a flat or two for jam? When cucumbers are going begging, why not five or ten pounds for homemade pickles? In this chapter is a wealth of exquisite recipes for preserving garden goods, beginning with techniques and tips for those who haven't been doing so for several generations.

The Nitty-Gritty of Putting By

Depending on what you call your pantry—cupboard, refrigerator, or freezer—how much space it affords, and how much you are going to preserve, you can choose from among three basic techniques.

INSPECTING THE CONTAINERS

Do put a keen eye to the jars and caps you are using for canning. Cracked or nicked jars should not be used. Dented screw-band lids should not be used. Either of those conditions will result in a jar of preserves you will have to toss. That's cause for crying after the effort, so take care at the outset.

CANNING. The method that by far offers the longest-term keeping, it is also the most cumbersome and perhaps also the most unlikely for the modern cook. To simplify what may seem a rather complicated process and to make canning feasible, the recipes in this book are for those foods that require only a boiling-water bath to protect them against spoilage—foods high in acid, such as tomatoes and pickles, and cooked foods, such as jams, chutneys, and relishes. Low-acid foods and unbrined, uncooked foods that require a pressure canner to seal them safely do not have canning instructions given. If you decide to can your preserves:

Heatproof glass jars designed for home canning are essential. The lids must be sealable, which means the two-part screw-on kind. Both jars and lids must be washed in hot, soapy water, then rinsed in hot water. For the recipes in this book, the jars do not need to be sterilized, but they must be rinsed in hot water and left to sit in the hot water until ready to be filled. The lids, after rinsing, must be placed in a pot of water, brought to a boil, and set aside in the water until ready to use.

Use only the size jars described in the recipes. Larger jars won't be properly processed; smaller jars may be overprocessed. See also page 319 and page 323.

Fill the jars with warm preserves. Fill to within ½ inch of the top. This so-called headspace room is to allow for expansion during the water-bath processing (see box on page 315).

REFRIGERATING. Refrigerating the preserves is much easier than canning. The drawbacks are two: The preserves do not keep as long, in general about half the time than if canned. If you are putting by a large amount, there won't be room left in the refrigerator for other needs. Those two considerations aside, refrigerating is a good way to go for the modern cook who is probably not dealing with farm amounts of crop to put by or intending to hold the jars for longer than a few months. If you decide to stock your preserves in the refrigerator:

Glass jars are still preferable for two reasons: They more beautifully display what you've made. Plastic containers, though wonderful for short-term storage, tend to taint the flavor of the contents over time. The jars need not be heatproof, but they still must be properly cleaned. The dishwasher is suitable for this job.

The caps should be two-part screw-on lids or gasket-sealed as described for canning, though normal screw-on lids are also okay. The lids don't have to be boiled for this type storage, but they, too, must be properly cleaned—stick them in the dishwasher along with the jars.

Unlike for canning, the lids should be set in place only after the ingredients have cooled to room temperature. Then the jars can be refrigerated without further waiting.

The size of the jar is flexible. If you would like to view a grand amount on your own refrigerator shelf, use a half-gallon jar; if you are making Christmas gifts for all the neighbors and office workers, too, use half-pint jars.

FREEZING. A facile way to store many vegetables and fruits that previously required pressure-canner processing to hold over their season. Tomatoes, green beans, peas, corn kernels, parsnips, berries, persimmons, peach halves, all freeze beautifully. An added advantage is that for freezing, the product may be packaged in stackable containers, taking less space than for canning or refrigerating. A disadvantage is that freezer preserving is essentially a short-term method. Fruits, vegetables, even meats become "freezer burned" and lose savor within a few months. Also, unless you have a commercial premise with a wall of freezers, there are space considerations. That aside, if you decide to put by in the freezer:

Glass jars are subject to cracking and also take up far too much space. Instead, use plastic containers or freezer bags to package the ingredients. They stack more conveniently and are more easily shuffled about when looking for this or that in the icy realm.

Whether using plastic containers or freezer bags, make sure the ingredients are completely cool before packaging them.

If using plastic containers, leave ½ inch of headspace, as with filling jars for canning. If anything, freezing causes more expansion. If you pack the ingredients to the top, either the container will burst or else it will pop its lid and become freezer burned before you notice.

If using freezer bags, zipper bags are the way to go, especially for anything that has any liquid, such as berries or tomatoes. Pricey as such bags may be, the zip closure does guard against leakage. You can fill them, squeeze out the air, zip them up, set them in the freezer, and walk away until they're stiff. Then you can stack them to make more shelf space for the next round. Not only that, the bags are made of sturdy plastic that offers extra protection against freezer burn. Quite a modern convenience.

Hot-Water Bath

Canning pots are readily available in hardware stores and supermarkets, but you can also use any other large pot as long as it has a tight-fitting lid and a rack to set the jars upon so that they are held off the bottom of the pot. It must be deep enough to hold water to cover the jars by at least 1 inch.

When the jars are filled and capped and ready for processing, bring the water in the canning pot to a simmer. Place the jars on the rack and lower it into the pot. Make sure the jars are covered with water by at least one inch. Bring the water to a boil. Count the processing time as given in each recipe from the time the water comes to a boil, not from the time you set the jars in the pot.

If you are canning at an altitude higher than 1,000 feet above sea level, add one minute per extra 1,000 feet if the processing time given in the recipe is less than twenty minutes. If it is more than twenty minutes, add two minutes per extra 1,000 feet.

When the processing time is up, lift the jars out of the water bath, preferably with a jar lifter tool for ease and safety. Set the jars on a dish towel and leave at room temperature to cool for twelve hours. Don't be concerned if you hear an occasional snap; it's the sound of a lid sealing.

When the jars are cool, test the seal of each by pressing on the center of the lid. Any lids that spring back rather than remaining concave have not been properly sealed. These jars should be stored in the refrigerator and used before the others. The others you can store in a cool, dry, dark place for up to one year.

the basic elements for pickling

Pickling is a way of preserving foods with salt and/or vinegar. The produce is not necessarily cucumbers, nor is the flavor necessarily salty and sour, though that is the most common picture and taste that comes to mind from the word *pickle*. Sometimes salt alone is the preserving medium, as in the classic sauerkraut and kim chee pickles. Sometimes vinegar is blended with sugar for a sweet-and-sour taste, as in sweet pickled green tomatoes and garden mix pickles. Whether the outcome is to be salty and sour, sweet and sour, or just salt-preserved, the nature and quality of the salt and vinegar matter. Following are descriptions of what works best for each.

THE SALT: For pickling and canning, it is important to use a noniodized salt in order to keep the brine, meaning the pickling liquid, clear and fresh tasting. Kosher and pickling salt work equally well. Depending on your proclivities and what's available, you can choose between them. The differences are:

- Kosher salt comes in a slightly coarser texture and has a slightly softer taste.
- Pickling salt is finer in texture and a bit saltier in taste.

THE VINEGAR: For pickling, the important thing to keep in mind is that the vinegar must have at least 5 percent acidity for it to be a preserving medium. White distilled vinegar, apple cider vinegar, and malt vinegar are the usual choices. Sometimes a red or white wine vinegar or sherry vinegar may be selected as a matter of taste. That's okay as long as the acidity level is 5 percent or more or if the pickles are stored in the refrigerator.

Pickling Spices

While it's convenient to purchase premixed pickling spices, it's also fun to make your own and personalize the blend to your taste. Begin with a mix of allspice berries, bay leaves (crumbled), black peppercorns, cloves (whole), coriander seeds, mustard seeds, red chili peppers (dried and crumbled), and ground ginger in amounts to suit you.

For sour pickles, pickled meats, and meat stew seasoning, add one or all of: celery seed, dill seed, perhaps cinnamon.

For sweet pickles and pickled or spiced fruits, add one or all of: cardamom, mace, cinnamon, and replace the black peppercorns with white peppercorns.

Refrigerator Pickles

MAKES 1 HALF-GALLON

Refrigerator pickles are perhaps the easiest kind of pickle to make since they require no overnight soaking, daily crock skimming, or water-bath processing. The method is a quick and straightforward way to turn cucumbers into pickles. Following is a very special rendition of refrigerator pickles. With a perfect balance between sweet and sour, these crisp pickle chips resemble the classic bread-and-butter pickles, but with different spicing.

BETSY WOLLASTON (DARLINGTON, MD)

2 cups distilled white vinegar
1 cup sugar
¼ cup kosher or pickling salt
10 to 12 medium cucumbers, scrubbed and sliced ⅛ inch thick (about 2 pounds) (see Note below)
½ medium green bell pepper, seeded and sliced into ⅛-inch-wide strips
1 large white onion, thinly sliced
2 to 4 large cloves garlic, thinly sliced
1 tablespoon Pickling Spices (see page 316)
2 tablespoons dill seed

1. Prepare 1 half-gallon or 2 quart jars and lids for refrigerator canning as described on page 314.

2. Whisk together the vinegar, sugar, and salt in a medium bowl to dissolve the sugar. Set aside.

3. Layer the cucumbers, peppers, onion, garlic, spices, and dill in a half-gallon jar or divide between 2 quart jars. Pour in the vinegar mixture. It will not cover the vegetables at first but will as they release liquid as they cure. Cap the jar tightly and put in the refrigerator for 1 week, turning the jar upside down and shaking a bit once a day to keep the ingredients mixed.

4. Serve after 1 week or continue to store in the refrigerator for up to 6 months.

Note: Pickling cucumbers (Kirbys) are an excellent choice for this pickle because they are naturally crisp and small seeded. However, any crisp cucumber picked young enough to have small seeds will do.

Aren't Pickles Always in the Refrigerator?

Of course, the refrigerator is where you look when you want a pickle. But before there were modern refrigerators, a batch of refrigerator pickles might be limited to one jar, maybe two, so that they wouldn't take up all the room in the small ice box. Quick and easy as they are for home preserving, with today's commodious refrigerators, refrigerator pickles became a classic, eventually with many forms and many seasonings. You can vary them with different pickling spice blends or innovate with a little of this and a little of that from any of the other pickle recipes in this chapter.

Wild Child Dill Pickles

MAKES 2 QUARTS

The contributor, an artist and native Oklahoman proud of her Cherokee, Choctaw, and Irish descent, gardens in a rural southeastern corner of the state. She proclaims that "these dill pickles, made with ingredients grown in my garden, are unparalleled and can't be purchased anywhere." Who could resist trying? We did and agree.

DONNA SHAW, WILD CHILD DESIGNS (McALESTER, OK)

12 large pickling cucumbers, scrubbed (3 pounds)
6 to 8 large sprigs of fresh dill
1 clove garlic
1 dried red chili pepper
4 grape leaves (optional, see box below)
2 cups distilled white vinegar
¼ cup pickling salt

1. Prepare 2 quart jars and lids for canning as described on page 314.

2. Divide and tightly pack the cucumbers upright in the jars. Add equal amounts of the dill, garlic, chili pepper, and grape leaves, if using, to each jar. Set aside.

3. Combine 6 cups of water, the vinegar, and salt in a nonreactive saucepan. Bring to a boil, stir to dissolve the salt, and pour over the cucumbers. Seal and process in a hot-water bath for 15 minutes (see page 315). Or cool completely, cap the jar, and store in the refrigerator. Let stand for 2 weeks before using. Will keep for up to 6 months in the refrigerator, 1 year if processed.

Alum

In former times, alum was included in the pickling brines to ensure crisp pickles. These days, a grape leaf or two is thought to do the same job without adding the strange taste of alum. In lieu of fresh grape leaves, jarred will do. In lieu of either, don't bother. If your cucumbers are very fresh and your brine quite fine, you'll have crisp pickles.

Lithuanian Dill Pickles

MAKES 1 HALF-GALLON

In the home of her childhood, Chicago, Illinois, summer meant pickle making. It was a way her family, originally from the Lithuanian countryside, carried on tradition. Though they had no garden in their new home, cucumbers purchased firm and flavorful from the produce market preserved the cherished custom. Letting the pickles stand at room temperature is to begin the fermentation of the pickles. This can take anywhere from two days in warm weather up to four days in cool weather. Judge by "when you like their taste."

DANUTE NITECKI (BERKELEY, CA)

10 to 12 large pickling cucumbers, scrubbed (about 2½ pounds)
6 to 8 large sprigs of fresh dill
4 large cloves garlic, quartered
½ small onion, not cut
2 bay leaves
10 allspice berries
1 teaspoon mustard seeds
¼ cup distilled white vinegar
¼ cup pickling salt

1. Prepare 1 half-gallon jar and lid for refrigerator canning as described on page 314.

2. Tightly pack the cucumbers upright in the jar (see box below). Add the dill, garlic, onion, bay, allspice, and mustard seeds. Pour in the vinegar and set aside.

3. Combine 2 quarts of water and the salt in a saucepan and bring to a boil, stirring to dissolve the salt. While still boiling, pour the salt water into the jar to a level that covers the cucumbers by ¼ inch. Cover loosely with a piece of cloth or foil and set aside at room temperature for 2 to 4 days, depending on the weather (see headnote). Cap the jar and store in the refrigerator for 2 days so the flavors finish mellowing, then serve or continue to store in the refrigerator for up to 6 months.

FRESHNESS COUNTS

Whether from your garden or that of another, only unwrinkled, snappy fresh cucumbers will do. Out-of-season or too-long-off-the-vine produce results not only in soft pickles but also in less yield due to spoilage. The tip holds true for other produce—both fruits and vegetables—that are destined for pickling.

The Size of the Jar Counts

For this and other small batches of refrigerator canning pickles, using a half-gallon jar simplifies the measuring and packing. If you don't have such a size, you can pack the cucumbers into two quart jars and divide the remaining ingredients between them. If the pickles are to be processed, however, they must be packed into smaller jars, no larger than quart size, so that in the water bath they reach the proper temperature all the way through without the ones on the outside becoming cooked.

Crystal Pickles

MAKES 3 QUARTS

"This was my mother's recipe. I don't know how old it is. She died in 1989 at 94½ years of age. When I am no longer able to make pickles, no one in my family will carry on these pickles. I am sending them to your cookbook so that someone else will enjoy them as much as we have. They are wonderful, crisp, translucent pickles. I like to add some of the pickling solution to potato salad to spice it up a little. When pickles are gone from one jar, add small onions, carrot sticks, and such to the juice and refrigerate for more snacking." This is indeed an unusual recipe. Perusing pickle offerings in many cookbooks, from those devoted entirely to preserving to more expansive, all-inclusive tomes, we found no recipe exactly like this one. Thanks to the contributor, this treasure of American cookery is not relegated to the past.

CAROL SHEETS (CEDAR RAPIDS, IA)

2 cups pickling salt
25 large pickling cucumbers, scrubbed and left whole (about 6 pounds)
2 (2-inch) sticks of cinnamon
1 tablespoon whole cloves
½ teaspoon mace blade or ¼ teaspoon ground mace
1½ cups sugar
1 quart distilled white vinegar

1. *Day 1:* Combine 4 quarts of water and the salt in a large crock and stir to dissolve the salt. Add the cucumbers and cover with a plate small enough to fit inside the crock but large enough to cover the cucumbers and keep them under the liquid. Set aside in a cool place (see box at left) for 5 days.

2. *Day 6:* Drain and rinse the cucumbers, discarding the salt solution. Rinse out the crock. Slice the cucumbers into ¼- to ½-inch-thick rounds and return to the crock. Add enough plain water to cover the cucumbers and cover the crock again. Set aside in a cool place overnight.

What's Cool and What's Not for Pickle Making?

For pickle making, a cool place means one where the temperature is always less than 70°F. If you live where the outside temperature does not exceed that or you have a cellar that is always cooler, the initial soaking in the salt brine can be done there. Otherwise, place the crock in the refrigerator to keep the cucumbers from spoiling during the initial soaking and add some days for the first stage to be completed because the refrigerator environment will slow down the curing. For Steps 2 through 5, the temperature should be even cooler, less than 65°F. Again, unless there is such a place in your house, leave the cucumbers out in a place out of direct sun during the day, and put them in the refrigerator overnight for each of those steps. While taking them in and out of the refrigerator may seem a fuss, it's necessary to let them be in an unchilled place in order to cure properly.

3. *Day 7:* The next morning drain and rinse the cucumbers again, discarding the water. Rinse out the crock and return the cucumbers to it. Combine the cinnamon, cloves, mace, sugar, and vinegar in a large nonreactive saucepan and bring to a boil. Pour over the cucumbers right away. Cover with the plate as before and set aside in a cool place overnight.

4. *Day 8:* Drain the liquid into a nonreactive saucepan, leaving the cucumbers in the crock. Bring the liquid to a boil and pour over the cucumbers in the crock. Cover with the plate and set aside in a cool place overnight.

5. Prepare 3 quart or 6 pint jars and lids for canning as described on page 314.

6. *Day 9:* Drain the cucumbers, reserving the liquid in a sauce pan as in Step 4 (day 8). Transfer the cucumbers to quart or pint jars. Bring the liquid to a boil and pour over the cucumbers in the jars. Seal and process in a hot-water bath for 15 minutes (see page 315). Or cool, cap, and store in the refrigerator. Will keep for 6 months in the refrigerator, 1 year if processed.

Note: The recipe is obviously from an era when one pickled for the year, putting by both for family pleasure and for gift giving. For a smaller batch to store in the refrigerator, all the amounts can be halved or quartered without harming the outcome.

Preserved Children

"The origin and age of this hand-me-down recipe is unknown, but it is worth passing along."

Take 1 large field, half a dozen children, 2 or 3 dogs, a pinch of brook, and some pebbles.

Mix the children and dogs together well. Put them on the field, stirring constantly.

Pour the brook over the pebbles. Sprinkle the field with flowers. Spread over all a deep blue sky and bake in the sun.

When children are brown, set to cool in the bathtub.

—SKIP DAVIS (CLEARLAKE OAKS, CA)

Pickled Armenian Cucumbers

MAKES 4 PINTS

"My family were merchants, not farmers, in the Old World; for us that was Turkey. In the New World of California the garden became a way to keep the treasured foods of our heritage. In apron-size backyards, we grew tomatoes, peppers, eggplants, grapes, cucumbers. These plants, many in their actually native New World environment, thrived and gave us the produce for our beloved dishes. But the cucumbers, in the variety we prized, were not known in this new region. Their seeds, carried in pockets or pouches across many a sea, planted here, had to be collected at the end of each growing season so that there would be more next year. The favorite pickle of our family was a cucumber one, but it was

not authentic, or as good, without these special small-seeded, tender-skinned Armenian cucumbers. And so, as I moved from here to there in my career as a military officer, I always kept a packet of Armenian cucumber seeds to plant wherever my next garden was to be, just as my immigrant parents had. Eventually my wife took over the pickle making. Together, we passed the recipe on to our four daughters and would like to share it here."

~ HENRY JENANYAN (SUTTER CREEK, CA)

Preparing for Next Year's Crop

"To collect and ready Armenian cucumber seeds for the following year, select the straightest and fattest cucumber. Tie a rag around it so you remember not to pick it. Let it grow for the rest of the season—it will be big and yellow and soft, like a runaway squash. At the end of the season, pick the selected cucumber and split it lengthwise. Scoop out the seeds and, without washing them, spread them on newspaper in the sun. Every day or so, turn them over with a metal spatula. When they are completely dry, separate them from any clinging pulp. Put the seeds in a jar and seal until planting time next year. Plant in mounds, three to five per mound as you would for other cucumbers or summer squashes."

—HENRY JENANYAN

6 cups scrubbed and sliced Armenian cucumbers (see Note below)
4 cloves garlic
4 sprigs of fresh dill
3 cups distilled white vinegar
½ cup pickling salt

1. Prepare 4 pint jars and lids for canning as described on page 314.

2. Pack the cucumbers into the jars. Place 1 clove garlic and 1 dill sprig in each jar.

3. Boil together the vinegar, 1 cup of water, and salt for 10 minutes in a nonreactive saucepan. Pour over the cucumbers. Seal and process in a hot-water bath for 15 minutes (see page 315). Or cool, cap, and store in the refrigerator. Let stand for 2 weeks before using. Will keep for 6 months in the refrigerator, 1 year if processed.

Note: Armenian cucumbers are often available in produce markets. Also, the seeds to grow them are now available from many seed catalogs and garden stores.

Pickled Beets in Spiced Vinegar

MAKES 2 QUARTS

"I inherited this recipe from my wonderful mother. We grow our own beets. To harness the zucchinis from taking over the world and to preserve the beets too, we can them each separately to give as Christmas gifts." The spiced vinegar is one of the best parts of the recipe.

~ BEVERLY SHORT AND RICHARD STODDARD (GOLD BEACH, OR)

6 bunches beets (about 4 pounds)
2 cups Spiced Vinegar (recipe follows)

1. Cut the tops off the beets and set them aside for another use. Rinse the beets and place them in a large pot. Add water to cover by 1 inch and bring to a boil. Simmer briskly for 30 to 50 minutes, depending on the size of the beets, until a fork pierces easily to the center and the skins have begun to split. Drain and set aside until cool enough to handle.

2. Prepare 2 quart or 4 pint jars and lids for refrigerator canning as described on page 314.

3. Remove the skins from the beets with your fingers or a paring knife. Slice the beets into ⅛-inch-thick rounds and place in the pint jars (see box on this page).

4. Bring the spiced vinegar to a boil and pour over the beets. Cool to room temperature, then cap the jar and refrigerate for 36 hours before using. Will keep in the refrigerator for up to 6 months.

More About the Jars

If you are not processing the beet pickles, you can pack them into a half-gallon jar with no problem (see page 314). Full of the ruby beets and red red brine, it makes a pretty picture in your refrigerator and also presents glamorously on the table. Quart-size jars are perhaps more convenient for refrigerator storage because they can snuggle in between all those other pickled goods without demanding the kind of belly space a half-gallon jar does. Pint jars, more gift size, neatly stack in a corner of the refrigerator, out of the way until it's time for presents. (For even more about jar art, see box on page 319.)

Spiced Vinegar

Makes 2 cups

2 cups cider vinegar
¼ cup sugar
½ teaspoon kosher or pickling salt
1 tablespoon grated horseradish or 3-inch piece of horseradish root, scraped and cut in half
1 (1-inch) piece of cinnamon stick
½ teaspoon allspice berries
2 teaspoons mustard seeds
½ teaspoon whole cloves
1 teaspoon celery seeds

Combine all the ingredients in a nonreactive saucepan. Bring to a boil, stir to dissolve the sugar and salt, and remove from the heat. Strain and use according to the directions for the pickles you are making. Will keep in the refrigerator for up to 1 month.

Pickled Shallots

MAKES 2 PINTS

"Most of the homes in the village where I grew up near London, England, had vegetable gardens, as did ours. My mother pickled small onions, traditionally served with Sunday beef joint dinner. Over the years, I've modified the spices in the recipe to suit our tastes and use shallots instead of the small onions—we prefer their slightly sweeter taste. If malt vinegar is unavailable, substitute cider vinegar; the shallots will have a milder taste but will still be delicious."

JOHN S. KING (PORTLAND, OR)

1 pound shallots, peeled
1½ cups kosher or pickling salt
1 cup malt vinegar (see box below)
1 cup water
½ cup sugar
1 teaspoon ground ginger
1 teaspoon ground cloves
1 teaspoon Pickling Spices (see page 316)
1 teaspoon whole peppercorns
¼ teaspoon cayenne
1 teaspoon kosher or pickling salt

1. Place the shallots in a large bowl. Combine 2 quarts of water and 1½ cups salt in a saucepan. Heat until just beginning to boil, then pour over the shallots. Set aside at room temperature to soak overnight.

2. Prepare 2 pint jars and lids for canning as described on page 314.

3. Drain and rinse the shallots and pack them into the jars.

4. Place the remaining ingredients in a nonreactive saucepan and bring to a boil. Simmer gently for 15 minutes. Pour the vinegar mixture over the shallots. Seal and process in a hot-water bath for 15 minutes (see page 315). Or cool, cap, and store in the refrigerator. Let marinate for 1 week before using. Will keep for 6 months in the refrigerator, 1 year if processed.

Malt Vinegar

Malt vinegar is as British as apple cider vinegar is American. Made from malted grain, the same base as for the famed British ales, for vinegar making it is left to sour and then aged. Malt vinegar is more complexly flavored than apple cider vinegar, much as an ale compares to apple cider. Its deep golden-to-cordovan color is darker than apple cider vinegar. The British appreciate its special taste, fruity and grainy at the same time, for sprinkling on fish and chips, splashing on vegetables, and pickling. You can find malt vinegar in fancy supermarkets and gourmet food boutiques.

Pickled Okra

MAKES 4 PINTS

"The enclosed recipe makes good use of the bounty from my beach garden. The same method can also be used for asparagus, green beans, zucchini, yellow squash, cucumbers, and green tomato slices."

ISABEL COOPER (NAGS HEAD, NC)

2 pounds okra
4 small chili peppers
4 cloves garlic
4 sprigs of fresh dill
1 quart distilled white vinegar
½ cup pickling salt

1. Prepare 4 pint jars and lids for canning as described on page 314.

2. Pack the okra into the jars. Place 1 pepper, 1 clove garlic, and 1 dill sprig in each jar.

3. Boil together the vinegar, 1 cup of water, and salt in a nonreactive saucepan for 10 minutes, then pour over the okra. Seal and process in a hot-water bath for 15 minutes (see page 315). Or cool, cap, and store in the refrigerator. Let stand for 1 week before using. Will keep for up to 6 months in the refrigerator, 1 year if processed.

Okra's Okay If You Know How

If you are one who objects to okra's glutinous texture, you can follow the Greek technique of tossing it with vinegar before cooking. You can also follow the Japanese technique of presalting it before cooking. Both ways serve the same purpose of firming the pods and leeching out the mucilage that some find objectionable. Or you can make okra pickle, which accomplishes both the firming and flavoring in one fell swoop.

Pickled Cymling Squashes

MAKES 4 PINTS

"My husband and I are seniors, 76 and 74 years old. While traveling with Elderhostel in France last March, we noticed jars of tiny cymling squashes, also called pattypans, that were pickled. So we raised some in our garden this past summer.

When they were less than one inch in diameter, we picked and pickled them and they won both First Place Prize and a Special Awards ribbon in the Maryland State Fair. I am sending the recipe so that others may also pickle these darling little squashes."

BETSY HEDEMAN (RELAY, MD)

WORDS OF THE TRADE

Perusing old recipes from a 1920s cookbook, a Farmers' Almanac *from a similar era, or a family recipe-box card for preserves, you often run across the instruction to "grind" the ingredients. It means to chop enough so that the ingredients are smaller than diced but not so fine as minced.*

1 pound tiny cymling (pattypan) squashes
2 cups distilled white or cider vinegar
2 tablespoons Pickling Spices (see page 316)
2 large cloves garlic
2 large sprigs of fresh dill
¼ cup kosher or pickling salt
½ to ⅔ cup sugar, to taste

1. Prepare 4 pint jars and lids for canning as described on page 314.

2. Remove any blossoms from the squashes and set them aside for another dish. Rinse the squashes and pack them into the jars.

3. Combine the vinegar, 2 cups of water, the spices, garlic, dill sprigs, salt, and sugar in a large nonreactive pot. Bring to a boil and simmer for 15 minutes. Strain and pour over the squashes. Seal and process in a hot-water bath for 15 minutes (see page 315). Or cool completely, cap, and store in the refrigerator. Let stand for at least 4 weeks before serving. Will keep for up to 1 year.

Note: In lieu of baby pattypans, you can use baby zucchini. Larger pattypans halved or quartered will also do, but they won't be as "darling."

Lost Measures and Old Tunes

Like some old haunting melody, the measures by which people tolled the amount of dry goods and produce on the farms and kitchens of yesteryear reverberate still. These days, we take things in staccato rapido bites, and there's probably not much to do about reversing that trend. Yet there is a certain satisfaction in knowing what those sometimes grander flourishes, sometimes more delicate brushstrokes described. With the knowledge, if you are reading a recipe from former times, you can easily do the math to bring those calculations into your kitchen. From bushels to ounces, the rundown goes like this:

1 bushel equals 4 pecks
1 peck equals 4 gallons
1 gallon equals 2 quarts
1 quart equals 2 pints
1 pint equals 2 cups
1 cup equals 8 ounces
1 ounce equals about 1½ tablespoons
1 teacup equals about ¾ cup

One-Step Tarragon-Pickled Peppers

Makes 1 quart

These aptly named pickled peppers offer an unusual touch: tarragon used as a pickling herb. It's a standard for cornichons, the tiny cucumbers pickled in the French style, but a little out of the way for American pickles, especially those of peppers. Well, who knows what a gardener transplanted to a different garden might come up with. These are good. If you don't have fresh tarragon, you can substitute dried.

BARBARA RIEBEN (MEMPHIS, TN)

1 medium red bell pepper
1 medium green bell pepper
1 medium yellow bell pepper
1 medium onion, thinly sliced
2 cloves garlic, slivered
1 tablespoon fresh tarragon leaves or 1 teaspoon dried tarragon
1 tablespoon sugar
1 tablespoon kosher or pickling salt
1 cup distilled white vinegar

1. Prepare 1 quart jar and lid for refrigerator canning as described on page 314.

2. Stem, seed, and cut the peppers into ½-inch pieces or thin strips. Pack the peppers, onion, garlic, and tarragon into the jar.

3. Combine the sugar, salt, vinegar, and 2 cups of water in a nonreactive saucepan and bring to a boil over medium heat. Pour the mixture over the peppers and set aside to cool. Cool, cap the jar, and store in the refrigerator. Let stand 1 week before serving. Will keep for up to 3 months.

Bringing in the Seeds: Nasturtiums

Since once-in, never-out nasturtiums pop up in every corner of the garden, their multitudinous, freely dropped seeds might as well be gathered for the kitchen. A gardener cook takes the prize where it's found. The seeds can be used freshly gathered to lend their radishy bite to salads and pasta sauces. They can also be pickled, some say to make mock capers, which they don't. But they are quite nice in their own right.

To preserve nasturtium seeds:

1. Rinse the seeds and place them in a jar.

2. Combine ⅓ cup kosher or pickling salt and 1 cup water in a small pot to make a brine. Bring just to the boil, then pour over the seeds in the jar.

3. Let cool. Store in the refrigerator almost indefinitely. Since it's a very salty brine, it preserves for a long time.

4. To use, rinse or soak the seeds in clear water to take away the salty taste. Sprinkle on salads, stir into sauces, garnish crostini or bruschetta, have them in a small bowl by the side of a chop as a special pickle just by themselves.

Sweet Pickled Red Bell Peppers

Makes 2 quarts

"As beautiful in jars as it is delicious with almost anything, this preserve is the favorite from my garden in Oak Park, Illinois." Bounding beyond the contributor's somewhat modest comments, the editors and recipe testers add that the "almost anything" includes the special piece of swordfish for a fall occasion, the turkey, goose, or prime rib for your winter fête, the leg of lamb for a spring celebration, the chicken or vegetables for a sleepy summer meal while resting to think about collecting those peppers again.

JENNIFER SCHWAB (OAK PARK, IL)

8 large red bell peppers, seeded, and cut into 1 by ¼-inch julienne strips (about 4 pounds)
2 tablespoons kosher or pickling salt
3 cups sugar
2½ cups cider vinegar
1 (3-inch) piece of cinnamon stick
20 whole cloves

1. Place the peppers, 2 quarts of water, and salt in a large bowl and set aside to soak overnight.

2. Prepare 2 quart jars and lids for canning as described on page 314.

3. Place the sugar, vinegar, cinnamon, and cloves in a large non-reactive pot and bring to a boil. Cook over low heat until the sugar dissolves, 1 to 2 minutes. Drain and rinse the peppers and add them to the pot. Simmer until the peppers are tender, 15 to 20 minutes.

4. Pack in the jars. Seal and process in a hot-water bath for 15 minutes (see page 315). Or cool, cap, and store in the refrigerator. Will keep for up to 6 months in the refrigerator, 1 year if processed.

Toursi: Cooking Magic

Toursi, the pickle of the eastern Mediterranean, can be made of green bell peppers, green tomatoes, or cucumbers. For whichever vegetable, the simple brine remains pretty much the same. It includes salt, vinegar, and water in the proportions described in the Pickled Okra recipe on page 325. The seasonings can include some garlic, some fresh dill, sometimes a small hot pepper, but they don't vary much beyond that. Yet each vegetable produces a different taste. It's one of those magics of cooking

Sweet-and-Hot Garden Mix Pickles

Makes 4 quarts

Straight from the garden, cucumbers, squash, carrots, onions, and bell peppers are brought to the kitchen, sliced, and wilted in a sweet brine spiked with fresh hot chili peppers to make a pickle mix with a personality all its own, as much a relish as it is a pickle. "It's a very simple recipe and the vegetables come out crunchy like I like them."

NELDA MCMILLAN (NASHVILLE, AR)

4 cups peeled and coarsely cut (½-inch chunks) cucumbers (1 pound)
2 cups trimmed and sliced (½-inch-thick rounds) summer squash, preferably yellow for color (½ pound)
2 cups scraped and sliced (½-inch-thick rounds) carrots (½ pound)
1 cup sliced (¼-inch-thick) onions
1 cup seeded, and sliced (¼-inch-wide strips) red bell pepper
½ cup stemmed and thinly sliced jalapeños (3 peppers)
2 cups cider vinegar
2½ cups sugar
2 tablespoons kosher or pickling salt

1. Prepare 4 quart or 8 pint jars and lids for canning as described on page 314.

2. Pack the vegetables, distributing each kind evenly, into the jars.

3. Combine the vinegar, sugar, and salt in a nonreactive saucepan and bring to a boil. Pour over the vegetables. Seal and process in a hot-water bath for 15 minutes (see page 315). Or cool, cap, and store in the refrigerator. May be used the next day. Keeps for 6 months in the refrigerator, 1 year if processed.

Sweet Green Tomato Pickle

Makes 1 quart

"What do you do with all those green tomatoes at the end of the summer, after that first frost, and all you want to do is clean up the garden? You make this recipe, an almost instant sweet pickle, that was given to me by my friend Evie Fitzsimmons." The amount of sugar called for may at first seem excessive. It is a lot, but, combined with the

good helping of vinegar and aromatic spices, it saves otherwise expendable green tomatoes not only from the compost bin but also from being run-of-the-mill pickle. Serve this pickle with any meat (wild game, roast beef or lamb, crown roast of pork, turkey, goose) or grain (wild rice, barley, buckwheat groats) that comes to mind when designing a fall menu.

HELEN VOGT (PORT WASHINGTON, NY)

2 cups cider or distilled white vinegar
6 cups sugar
1 teaspoon ground cloves
1 teaspoon ground cinnamon
10 cups sliced (½-inch-thick) green tomatoes (about 20)

1. Prepare 1 quart or 2 pint jars and lids for canning as described on page 314.

2. Combine the vinegar, sugar, cloves, and cinnamon in a large nonreactive pot and bring to a boil. Cook for 1 minute, stirring to dissolve the sugar.

3. Add the tomato slices and continue cooking over medium-high heat until slightly wilted but still firm, about 5 minutes. Remove from the heat.

4. Transfer to the jar or jars, seal, and process in a hot-water bath for 15 minutes (see page 315). Or cool, cap, and store in the refrigerator. Will keep for 6 months in the refrigerator, 1 year if processed.

Green Tomatoes Everywhere

Sweet as it is, Sweet Green Tomato Pickle lends itself to other interpretations. For instance, you can think of it as:

A SPOON SWEET, a typical Greek welcoming offered to the guest in a special spoon filled with one piece of the preserved tomato and some of the syrup and accompanied by a demitasse cup of Turkish-style coffee.

CHUTNEY, the conserve adopted by cuisines far away from India's shores. Add whole almonds, raisins, sliced onions, and a few additional spices like cardamom, coriander, or black mustard seed to the pickle. See page 344 for another Green Tomato Chutney.

HARVEST PIE (Dorothy Winters, Derry, NH). To turn the pickle into a pie filling in the classic American style, combine Concord grapes, halved, with the green tomatoes, drained, in a pie crust. Sprinkle with flour and cover with a top crust. Bake as usual. You can also add a dash of vanilla extract, a traditional flavoring for green tomatoes.

# of angels, pinheads, and condiments

What's a relish, what's a chutney, are they both conserves? Maybe all are condiments because they're not salads or appetizers or vegetable sides or exactly sauce, though the distinctions are blurred. Like the question posed in philosphy 101 classes to open the mind and invite creativity—how many angels can dance on the head of a pin?—it's rhetorical. The answer is clear: either none or an infinite number or however many you say. In other words, as you call it. In this section, relishes and chutneys are presented as they are called by the contributors.

Sweet Bell Pepper and Onion Relish

MAKES 6 PINTS

"At the turn of the century, coal oil, snuff, and salt were the principal items on a grocery list. Country food was simple, but hearty and healthful, and sweet pepper relish made a daily appearance on many tables." With its mildly sweet flavor and fine texture, the relish also makes a noteworthy bread spread for a turkey sandwich or delightful replacement for sweet pickle relish on hot dogs.

BARBARA MITCHELL (HOUSTON, TX)

6 large green bell peppers, stemmed and seeded
6 large red bell peppers, stemmed and seeded
6 medium onions
4 cups boiling water
1 cup sugar
2 tablespoons kosher or pickling salt
½ teaspoon turmeric
2 cups cider vinegar

SEEDS TO HAVE HANDY IN THE PANTRY

Anise seed
Celery seed
Cumin seed
Dill seed
Fennel seed
Mustard seed
Poppy seed
Sesame seed

1. Chop the peppers and onions as fine as possible in a food processor. Transfer to a bowl and pour the boiling water over them. Let stand for 10 minutes.

2. Drain the peppers and onions. Combine them with the remaining ingredients in a large, heavy pot. Bring to a boil and cook briskly over medium-high heat for 20 minutes, or until thickened and reduced by one third.

3. Meanwhile, prepare 6 pint jars and lids for canning as described on page 314.

4. Transfer the mixture to the jars, seal, and process in a hot-water bath for 15 minutes (see page 315). Or cool, cap, and store in the refrigerator. Let stand for 24 hours before using. Will keep in the refrigerator for up to 3 months, 1 year if processed.

Spiced Celery, Onion, and Pepper Relish

MAKES 3 PINTS

The word spiced *in the recipe title refers not to chili heat but to the spices that flavor the relish. Based on fresh garden ingredients, it's a condiment for giving a lift to chicken, turky, or pork as well as, more classically, smearing on hot dogs or hamburgers.*

RUTH RICHMAN (WALTON, KY)

4 medium tomatoes, peeled, seeded, and coarsely chopped (about 1½ pound)
3½ cups finely chopped celery
3½ cups finely chopped onion (about 2 medium)
1½ cups finely chopped green bell pepper (1 large)
1 cup white sugar
1 cup (packed) dark brown sugar
3 tablespoons mustard seeds
1 teaspoon celery seeds
1 teaspoon mustard powder
1 teaspoon turmeric
2 tablespoons kosher or pickling salt
½ teaspoon hot pepper sauce
2 cups distilled white vinegar

1. Prepare 3 pint jars and lids for refrigerator canning as described on page 314.

2. Place the tomatoes in a large nonreactive saucepan and bring to a boil. Add the celery, onions, and green peppers, cover, and cook over medium-low heat until slightly softened, about 10 minutes. Drain and set aside.

3. Combine the remaining ingredients in the same pan and bring to a boil. Add the drained vegetables and simmer until the vegetables are soft and the liquid is reduced and saucy, about 15 minutes.

4. Transfer to the jars. Cool, cap, and store in the refrigerator. Let stand overnight before using.

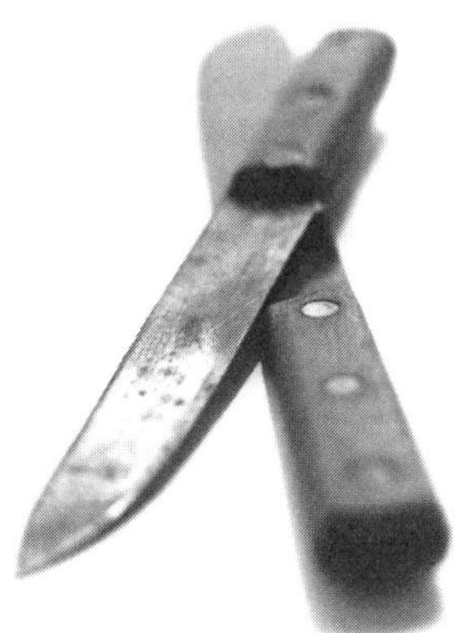

A Sauce of Commerce Home Again

The row upon row of chili sauces, from smooth to chunky, variously spiced, more or less sweet, that every grocery store displays give evidence to the popularity and salability of this staple condiment of American kitchens. While these commercial products afford convenience, the gardener cook may like to have a go at it with ingredients personally grown or freshly bought. With a yield of three pints (six half-pints), the Chili Sauce Relish recipe below provides enough for household hamburgers or fries for the year plus a bit to share, and that's a double reward.

Chili Sauce Relish

MAKES 3 PINTS

"Chili Sauce Relish is a great condiment for beef, pork, and poultry. I also love it over hamburgers and my husband loves it over mashed potatoes or as a snack by itself. Feel free to add more chili peppers if you like heat." (See also the following recipe, page 334.)" To retain the chunky home style of this sauce, the main vegetables should be chopped into ¼-inch pieces, not too much smaller or it will become refined beyond its station and not too much larger or it won't be a relish anymore.

MARY JANE WALLACE (STONINGTON, CT)

8 medium tomatoes, peeled, seeded, and chopped (2 pounds)
1 cup chopped celery
1 cup chopped onion
1 medium green bell pepper, stemmed, seeded, and chopped
1 medium red bell pepper, seeded and chopped
½ cup diced tart apple, such as Pippin
1 to 2 small chili peppers, such as jalapeño or serrano, stemmed and minced
¾ cup sugar
1 tablespoon kosher salt
½ tablespoon Pickling Spices (see box on page 316), tied in cheesecloth
¾ cup cider vinegar
3 tablespoons tomato paste

1. Combine the tomatoes, celery, onion, bell peppers, apple, chilies, sugar, and salt in a large, heavy nonreactive pot. Bring to a boil, lower the heat, and cook gently, stirring frequently, for 45 minutes, or until reduced by one-quarter and beginning to thicken. Add the spice bag and continue cooking for 50 minutes more, until reduced by half and thickened into a sauce.

2. Remove and discard the spice bag and stir in the vinegar and tomato paste. Continue cooking for 20 to 25 minutes, or until big bubbles rise from the bottom and the sauce is quite thick but not dry.

3. Meanwhile, prepare 3 pint jars and lids for canning as described on page 314.

4. Transfer the mixture to the jars. Seal and process in a hot-water bath for 15 minutes (see page 315). Or cool, cap, and store in the refrigerator. Let stand overnight before using. Will keep for up to 3 months in the refrigerator, 1 year if processed.

Chilies from Bush in the Garden to Sticks on the Grill to Bundle on the Wall

If you're one who grows chili peppers because you enjoy the thrill of the burn they so readily provide, yet have been overwhelmed by the abundance even one bush yields, here are a couple of ways to go:

When the chilies need picking but it's midseason and the plant is still producing, cut the pods off the bush with scissors so as not to harm the plant. Rinse and leave them whole and display in a basket so all can admire their colorful beauty. Within a few days, before they wilt, skewer them (see box on page 335) and place on the grill as you barbecue whatever meat and/or vegetables you are cooking for dinner.

When the bush has blossomed and fruited to fullness and the bed needs turning for the next round of planting, lift the entire plant out of the ground. A small pitchfork to loosen the soil around the plant helps free it so it can be pulled up by its roots without breaking its branches. Gently pull up the bush and brush away the dirt. Bundle the bush and tie it together with a length of raffia or ribbon. Wire will also do, but it's not so pretty.

Hang the bundle on the kitchen wall, over the mantel, or anywhere else you would like to express garden spirit as the season turns to winter.

Cayenne-Tomato Relish

MAKES 4 PINTS

Fresh cayenne peppers, the preferred hot capsicum in the South, are key to this hot and spicy relish. They render a favorite hamburger relish into finger-licking goodness. If fresh cayennes are not available, resist substituting ground cayenne. Instead, use two or three small chili peppers left on the plant long enough to turn red and extra spicy, and couple those with half a small red bell pepper so that the vegetable taste cayennes bring to the dish is not lost.

NONA TUNNELL (HORN LAKE, MS)

18 tomatoes, peeled, cored, and cut into quarters (5 to 6 pounds)
6 large onions, chopped into ¼-inch pieces
4 cayenne peppers, stemmed and finely chopped
¾ cup sugar
1 cup cider vinegar
1 tablespoon pickling salt
½ tablespoon black pepper

1. Combine all the ingredients in a large nonreactive pot. Bring to a boil, reduce the heat to low, and simmer, stirring from time to time, until thickened and bubbling up briskly from the bottom of the pot, 2 to 3 hours.

2. Meanwhile prepare 4 pint jars and lids for canning as described on page 314.

3. Remove the mixture from the heat and ladle into the jars. Seal and process in a hot-water bath for 20 minutes (see page 315). Or cool, cap, and store in the refrigerator. Let stand overnight before using. Will keep for 6 months in the refrigerator, 1 year if processed.

Note: For this and other long-cooking concoctions, especially those with tomatoes, it is important not to rush the process. That will surely result in burned goods.

TOOLS *and* TRICKS *of the* TRADE

Skewers and Skewering

For foods that won't twirl around the skewer as you turn them for even cooking, stringing them on a single skewer is fine. These include meat or fish chunks and whole small vegetables such as cherry tomatoes, boiler onions, and small chili peppers. Bamboo skewers of the ordinary sort you find in supermarkets are suitable.

For holding steady foods that will twirl as you turn the skewers, such as shrimp, lengths of eggplant or leeks, squares of peppers, and onion wedges, the double-skewer method, stringing the pieces on parallel skewers, is a good trick to know. It's a marvelous technique used by Japanese cooks for their grilled *dengaku* dishes. If possible, use the thinner, sharper-pointed skewers that are designed for this. They are available in Japanese food markets and gourmet kitchenware stores.

If you don't have the thinner bamboo skewers, use one of the regular kind and have handy a metal spatula to help turn them without the pieces slipping around.

Winterizing the Red Tomato Crop

From the time tomatoes were finally accepted as edible (not until about 1838) and then established as a cultivated crop in America, gardeners and cooks have been delighted with the hardy native vine and its bounty. Through time, innumerable shapes, colors, and tastes were hybridized to satisfy the horticultural curiosity for new cultivars and the culinary desire for new tastes. As a result, more and more ways had to be devised to make use of the output, which is especially prolific at the end of the season right before it's time to say good-bye to tomatoes until next summer. Following are several tomato preserving techniques to put by the last of the harvest and hold you over through the winter. They include options for freezing, canning, and drying offered by contributors from around the country.

CANNING

"These are so good and easy to can: Peel however many tomatoes you are preserving (see page 72). Cut them into quarters, cut out the cores, and lightly squeeze each piece to extract some of the juices and seeds. Place the tomatoes in a large nonreactive pot, bring to a boil, and simmer for 40 minutes, skimming off the foam from time to time. When the tomatoes are tender but still hold their shape and are no longer foamy, transfer them to prepared quart jars. Add 1 teaspoon salt to each jar. Seal and process in a hot-water bath for 45 minutes (see page 315)."

—MARTHA BRYANT (BAXTER, TN)

Called "Hunky Dunks" by the contributor, these tomatoes are cut up and seasoned before preserving. "Peel (see page 72) and very coarsely chop enough tomatoes to make 2 quarts. Transfer to a large nonreactive pot and set aside. Meanwhile, quarter and thinly slice a large lemon and boil the slices in 2 cups of water until tender but not soggy. Combine the lemon slices with the tomatoes and stir in 8 to 9 cups of sugar, to taste. Bring to a boil, reduce the heat, and simmer until just jelled, not too thick. Ladle into prepared jars while hot, seal, and process in a hot-water bath for 35 minutes (see page 315)."

—MINTA CLYDE (SONORA, CA)

For either of these recipes for canned tomatoes, you can store the jars in the refrigerator rather than processing them. Though it's not a cupboard that will hold as much as the old-fashioned pantry shelves in the cellar of childhood imagination, it will hold some jars and allow that wonderful feeling of having provisions: there are still jars of preserves; they're in the fridge.

FREEZING

"Using unblemished, fully ripe tomatoes, cut off about ⅜ inch from the stem end. Put in a freezer bag, pop the freezer bag into a brown grocery bag for extra protection, and place in the freezer. When ready to use, hold the frozen tomatoes under hot water for a few seconds. The skin will crack open and easily slip off. Then you can begin cooking them as usual. A gallon freezer bag holds about 25 plum tomatoes—just enough for a 'good-sized' pot of chili."

—KATHY BILLINGER (PERRY, MI)

Using the same freezing technique as described above, this contributor offers a different thawing method and a quick recipe that any cook will appreciate: "Make tomato soup on demand. Thaw the tomatoes at room temperature or in the microwave. Cook the tomatoes briefly with some minced onion that has been sautéed in butter or margarine and one or more cloves. Strain through a food mill and add salt, pepper, and sugar to taste. Serve as is, with a dollop of sour cream or some croutons as garnish."

—MARJORIE ZUCKER (NEW YORK, NY)

OVEN-DRYING

"Oven-drying tomatoes concentrates the flavor, adding a slightly smoky taste, and results in a texture somewhere between sun-dried tomatoes and fresh ones. Plum tomatoes and other small, dense-fleshed tomatoes work best. Line a large baking sheet with parchment paper. Cut the tomatoes in half and arrange, skin side down, on the parchment. Cook in a 250°F. oven for 2 hours, or until the tomatoes are shriveled but not blackened. Remove from the oven, peel away the parchment, and place the tomatoes on a plate if using right away or in a glass or plastic container if using later. Will keep for 1 to 2 weeks in the refrigerator. Use to make an elegant two-minute pasta sauce with chopped oven-dried tomato halves mixed with olive oil, crumbled goat cheese, and a good handful of an appropriate herb, such as basil, oregano, or parsley."

—STEPHANIE HARTMAN (NEW YORK, NY)

MICROWAVE DRYING

Tomatoes may also be dried in a microwave oven. The advantage is that the process is quick and results in a texture almost indistinguishable from long sun-drying. The disadvantage is that a microwave oven can accommodate only small batches at a time.

FOR ONE BATCH OF MICROWAVE DRIED TOMATOES:

Halve lengthwise 10 to 12 plum or other small tomatoes. Scoop out the seeds with a spoon or your fingers. Place as many halves, cut sides down, in a single layer on a microwave plate as will fit without touching each other. Microwave on high for 10 to 15 minutes, until collapsed. Remove and cool a few minutes, until no longer steaming hot. Pour off the collected juices and, with a metal spatula, turn over the halves, patting the pulp back into the centers. Microwave on high for 10 to 15 minutes more, until the tomatoes are dried out but still supple. Set aside without disturbing for 30 minutes, then transfer to a jar or plastic bag and store in the refrigerator for up to 2 months.

Either way the tomatoes have been dried, you can use them right away to make a dried-tomato pesto (page 311). Or, for a perfect and almost instantaneous crostini: slice some dried tomatoes, toss with a little olive oil and fresh oregano, and use to top a toasted bread round garnished with a few crumbles of feta cheese.

Gumbo Relish

MAKES 2 PINTS

Start with the idea of gumbo, the nationally recognized soup-stew of southern cooking. It often includes steak, chicken, sausage, or seafood; it is often okra-thickened (see box below). Subtract any meat, poultry, or seafood elements, add a soupçon of sugar and vinegar, and the gumbo turns into a table relish to embellish the very same meats and seafood that might have been cooked in the pot.

GENEVIEVE KRIPPENDORF (UNIVERSAL CITY, TX)

Okra by Another Name: How to Grow Gumbo

If the notion of gumbo seems murky—what is gumbo? what's in it? how can a gumbo be a relish?—the whole picture comes into focus when you know that gumbo is but another name for okra. At least, it started out that way. Originally, *gumbo* was the name of the vegetable, called by its African name, *ngombo.* That designation over time came to mean the name of the soup-stew the vegetable is most known for outside the American South. Today, most call the vegetable *okra* and the dish *gumbo.* If you like it, consider growing it. A single plant will yield enough for several okra dishes.

You can grow an okra bush in any sunny place that stays consistently warm during its growing season, spring to late summer. It doesn't mind its other conditions too much—a pot in the sun will do just fine, as long as the soil is rich and has good drainage. Okra does mind being transplanted, so sow seeds directly into the ground in spring when the earth begins to warm. As with all seedlings, keep moist until they germinate and feed once in spring. When established, weekly deep watering that soaks the entire root system will suffice.

When picking okra pods, wear gloves to protect your hands from their prickly surface hairs. To protect the plant from harm, use scissors to gather the pods rather than pulling them off the branches. Also, keep in mind, the fresher and smaller the okra, the less slimy and more tasty, so harvest while the pods are still no more than three inches long, which means every two or three days at the height of the season. Use the attractive, hibiscus-like flowers for garnishing.

1 tablespoon vegetable oil
1 medium onion, cut into ½-inch dice
2 cloves garlic, minced
1 jalapeño, stemmed and finely chopped
1 pound fresh okra, stemmed and cut into ½-inch-thick rounds
1 teaspoon salt
¼ teaspoon black pepper
5 medium tomatoes, peeled and coarsely chopped (1 to 1½ pounds)
¼ cup sugar
⅓ cup distilled white vinegar

1. Heat the oil in a large nonreactive saucepan. Add the onion, garlic, jalapeño, and okra and sauté over medium heat until slightly softened, about 5 minutes.

2. Stir in the salt, pepper, tomatoes, sugar, and vinegar and bring to a boil. Reduce the heat and boil gently until the okra is tender, about 20 minutes.

3. Meanwhile, prepare 2 pint jars and lids for refrigerator canning as described on page 314.

4. Transfer the mixture to the jars. Cool, cap, and store in the refrigerator. Let stand overnight before using. Will keep for up to 2 months.

Note: This relish is not a good candidate to process for extended keeping. Though its flavor is not particularly delicate, it does lose some if kept too long in the jar.

Middle Eastern-Style Zucchini Relish

MAKES 3 PINTS

In addition to its familiar relish seasonings—nutmeg, cloves, chili flakes—the exotic spice sumac lends a Middle Eastern tang to this distinctly American-style condiment that "is a delightful garnish for grilled meats as well as a flavorful addition to stews and sauces. I also like it on tortillas with shaved turkey." Its hot, sweet, and spicy flavors are also an excellent accompaniment to rich, gamy meats such as wild duck or venison.

~ JOANN STEIN (MADISON, WI)

8 cups peeled and chopped zucchini (¼-inch pieces) (about 4 pounds)
6 medium tomatoes, chopped into ½-inch chunks (about 1½ pounds)
1 medium onion, finely chopped
2 jalapeños, stemmed, seeded, and coarsely chopped
2 teaspoons crushed red pepper
1 tablespoon ground cloves
1 tablespoon ground nutmeg
1 tablespoon ground sumac
1½ tablespoons kosher or pickling salt
½ cup chopped fresh parsley leaves
2 cups sugar
1 cup cider vinegar

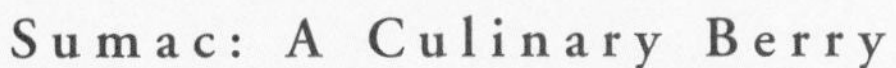

Sumac: A Culinary Berry

Sumac is an exotic spice used in Middle Eastern cooking from Turkey to Iran and not much elsewhere in the world. Despite its similar name, it is not at all the same plant that causes skin-distressing toxins and itching similar to those of poison ivy or poison oak. The culinary sumac produces red berries that are dried and powdered to lend a tang and a tint to grilled meats, poultry and vegetable stews, and yogurt sauces. Sumac is available in Middle Eastern markets and international food emporiums. There's not a true substitute. Its flowery perfume is incomparable, but a pinch of tamarind or of the Indian spice called *anardana* (dried and powdered pomegranate) can suggest its tongue-tingling flavor, and a beet leaf in the brine can offer a hint of its color.

1. Combine all the ingredients in a large, heavy, nonreactive pot and bring to a boil. Reduce the heat and simmer, stirring periodically, until reduced by half, about 1 hour 45 minutes.

2. Meanwhile, prepare 3 pint jars and lids for canning as described on page 314.

3. Transfer the mixture to the jars, seal, and process in a hot-water bath for 15 minutes (see page 315). Or cool, cap, and store in the refrigerator. Let stand overnight before using. Will keep for up to 3 months in the refrigerator, 1 year if processed.

Green Tomato Relish

MAKES 3 PINTS

"Montana summers are intense. The 120-day growing season explodes with a bang of bounty and then its end is equally abrupt and final. I always ripen some of the last zillion tomatoes inside so they don't go to waste. But they're just not like the real thing. This relish is a better thing to do with the last-of-summer green tomatoes."

LIBBY YOUNG (VICTOR, MT)

1 pound green tomatoes, finely chopped
1½ pounds onions, finely chopped
1½ pounds bell peppers, assorted colors if possible, finely chopped
1 large jalapeño, stemmed and finely chopped
2 tablespoons pickling salt
¾ cup sugar
1 cup distilled white vinegar
¾ teaspoon turmeric
2 tablespoons Pickling Spices (see page 316), tied in cheesecloth

1. Place the tomatoes, onions, bell peppers, jalapeño, and salt in a large bowl. Add water to cover and set aside to soak overnight at room temperature.

From Relish to Chowchow and Back to Piccalilli

You can transform the Green Tomato Relish into another savory classic, chowchow. To make chowchow:

Add some sliced pickling cucumbers, some cauliflower florets, and maybe some coarsely shredded green cabbage to the vegetables when you soak them overnight in Step 1 of the Green Tomato Relish recipe. Have ready a mix of ⅔ cup flour and 2 tablespoons mustard powder blended with 1 cup cider vinegar until smooth. When the brine ingredients have been combined and brought to a boil (Step 3), instead of adding the vegetables, stir in the flour and mustard paste and whisk until smooth. Then add the vegetables and continue with the recipe.

If you prefer the sweeter way with pickled vegetables, you can make piccalilli: Instead of green tomatoes, use cucumber slices and maybe some slices of celery in Step 1 of the Green Tomato Relish recipe. In Step 3, add 1 tablespoon mustard seed and 1 teaspoon celery seed to the sugar and vinegar mix before bringing to a boil. Continue with the recipe.

2. Next day, drain and rinse the vegetables. Set aside.

3. Prepare 3 pint jars and lids for canning as described on page 314.

4. Combine the sugar, vinegar, turmeric, and bag of pickling spices in a large nonreactive pot and bring to a boil. Add the drained vegetables and return to a boil. Remove from the heat immediately and ladle into the jars. Seal and process in a hot-water bath for 15 minutes (see page 315). Or cool, cap, and store in the refrigerator. Will keep in the refrigerator for 6 months, 1 year if processed.

pantry perks

TO SALT OR NOT TO SALT THE CHUTNEY?

Adding a touch of salt to a chutney is a particularly American gesture. In their lands of origin, chutneys take their flavor only from a complex blend of spices, sometimes with a bit of lemon or lime added rather than any salt. It's a matter of taste.

Fragrant Pear Chutney

MAKES 3 PINTS

"When my husband and I were first married, we lived in an 1850s farmhouse in Lincoln, Massachusetts. Outside our kitchen window was a very large pear tree—nearly three stories high, and quite productive. One of the ways we used its fruit was to make pear chutney, and one of our best ways to enjoy the chutney was on picnics. I remember making cream cheese, pear chutney, and ham sandwiches for summer concerts in a nearby meadow." The contributor never does say what kind of pear the towering tree yielded. For the recipe, any kind of pear will do, as long as it is firm, not mealy fleshed, and not overripe—just ripe enough to smell good. Anjou, Bartlett, and Comice are good choices.

TAMARA GODA (ALBUQUERQUE, NM)

2½ cups cider vinegar
5 medium fragrant pears, peeled and cored (about 3 pounds)
2 cups (packed) light brown sugar
1½ teaspoons ground ginger
1 teaspoon ground allspice
1 teaspoon ground cloves
1½ teaspoons salt (optional, see right)
1 medium green bell pepper, seeded and finely chopped
1 medium onion, finely chopped
½ cup golden raisins
2 teaspoons finely chopped lemon zest
3 tablespoons fresh lemon juice

1. Pour the vinegar into a large, nonreactive pot. Cut the pears into ½-inch chunks, dropping them into the vinegar as you go to prevent browning.

2. Stir in the brown sugar, ginger, allspice, cloves, and salt, if using, and bring to a boil. Reduce the heat and simmer for 10 minutes, until the pears are slightly softened.

3. Stir in the bell pepper, onion, raisins, lemon zest, and lemon juice and bring back to a boil. Reduce the heat and simmer, stirring frequently, until thick and golden, about 1 hour.

4. Meanwhile, prepare 3 pint jars and lids for canning as described on page 314.

5. Remove from the heat and ladle into the jars. Seal and process in a hot-water bath for 20 minutes (see page 315). Or cool, cap, and store in the refrigerator. Let mature for 1 month before using. Will keep in the refrigerator for up to 6 months, 1 year if processed.

Shopping the Spice Bazaar for Chutney Seasoning

Chutney making opens a world of possibilities for those who enjoy mixing and matching spices. An array to have on hand includes:

ALLSPICE, berry and/or ground

CARDAMOM, pods and/or seeds

CINNAMON, stick and/or ground

CLOVE, whole and/or ground

DRIED RED CHILI, pods, flakes, and/or ground

GINGER, fresh, ground, and/or candied

MACE, blade and/or ground

MUSTARD, seed and/or powder

NUTMEG, whole to grate and/or ground

PEPPERCORNS, black and white, whole and/or freshly ground

When seasoning the chutney, keep in mind some like the burst of flavor that comes from biting into a whole piece of spice. However, if you are concerned that could be a problem either for the aesthetics of the dish or the comfort of the diners, you can tie the spices in a cheesecloth bag to be removed before serving.

Cockholder Plum Chutney

MAKES 3 PINTS

"The recipe I am submitting is not one of my own, but that of a very dear friend who is a fantastic gardener and incredible cook as well. I knew that he, modest soul that he is, would never submit a recipe on his own, but I did manage to coerce him into writing this one down." As her story continues, we learn that "Washington state is famous

for its abundant apples. Less known, however, are the many other varieties of fruit trees that thrive here. It was the Italian plum tree in the Monet-like backyard of my modest mate that inspired his recipe for plum chutney." The chutney travels well from the dinner plate, where it serves as condiment for meat, poultry, or grain dishes, to the canapé tray, where it makes an unusual topping over shaved white cheddar cheese on a cracker or toast.

LOUISE SCULLY (SEATTLE, WA)

3 tablespoons olive oil
2 medium red onions, finely chopped (about 1¼ pounds)
1 tablespoon minced garlic
3 tablespoons coarsely grated fresh ginger
1 medium red bell pepper, stemmed, seeded, and finely chopped
⅔ cup cider vinegar
⅓ cup balsamic vinegar
½ cup granulated sugar
½ cup (packed) light brown sugar
2 teaspoons curry powder (see page 95)
½ teaspoon ground allspice
5 whole cloves
2 (3-inch) sticks of cinnamon
½ teaspoon cardamom seeds
1 teaspoon ground white pepper
¼ teaspoon crushed red pepper
6 cups pitted and very coarsely chopped plums, preferably Italian, juices reserved (see Note and box below)
½ cup dried currants

1. Heat the oil in a large, heavy, nonreactive pot. Add the onions and cook over medium heat, stirring occasionally, until wilted, about 6 minutes.

2. Stir in the garlic, ginger, and bell pepper and cook until softened, about 6 minutes more.

3. Add the cider vinegar, balsamic vinegar, granulated sugar, brown sugar, curry powder, allspice, cloves, cinnamon, cardamom, white pepper, and red pepper. Bring to a boil, lower the heat, and simmer, stirring occasionally, for 20 minutes, until the liquid is slightly reduced.

4. Add the plums and currants and continue simmering very gently, stirring frequently, until the plums are collapsing and the liquid is reduced enough to coat a spoon, 30 to 40 minutes.

5. Meanwhile, prepare 3 pint jars and lids for canning as described on page 314.

Peeling and Pitting Plums Pleasantly

The easiest way to peel and pit plums is to drop them into a pot of boiling water, bring back to the boil, and cook until the skins barely begin to split, 5 to 10 minutes, depending on the size of the plums and how many are in the pot. Drain and cool, then slip off the skins and pull out the pits. Be sure to catch the juices as you peel and pit; they're essential for the dish.

A microwave oven also works well. Rinse the plums, heap them into a large bowl, and microwave, covered, on high until the skins split. Cool, peel, and pit over a bowl to catch the juices. If the recipe does not call for peeled plums, let the skins fall into the bowl as you are pitting them.

6. Remove from the heat and remove the cinnamon sticks. Ladle into the jars, seal, and process in a hot-water bath for 15 minutes (see page 315). Or cool, cap, and store in the refrigerator. Let stand overnight before using. Will keep in the refrigerator for up to 6 months, 1 year if processed.

Note: Italian plums have a special sweetness all their own. However, any purple or red variety plums will do as long as they are naturally sweet, not mealy, and ripe.

WEIGHTS AND MEASURES
If you don't have a kitchen scale, you can ballpark the weight measurement called for, using the guideline "a pint's a pound the world around," more or less.

Green Tomato Chutney

MAKES 4 QUARTS

Horticulture editor for Country Living Gardener *magazine, author, and gardener, Ruth Rogers Clausen shares not only her recipe but also the story that surrounds it in true pass-along spirit. "This recipe was given to me by an older lady from Peterborough, Cambridgeshire. She had been making it for years to use the inevitable peck of still-green tomatoes hanging on the vine at the end of the season. It was intended to accompany cold meats and cheeses during the winter months and for me became a way to get together with an old friend for our once-a-year ritual of making this chutney as well as a huge batch of chili for freezing. We spend the entire morning making the chutney. Before embarking on the chili, we have a late lunch of toasted whole wheat bread and cheddar cheese sandwiches topped with the fresh-from-the-pot chutney and accompanied by a glass or two of sherry, all enjoyed in front of a roaring log fire. This is our special visiting and catching-up time with each other. Regrettably, it's all too short, so we won't say how often we actually get to the chili."*

RUTH ROGERS CLAUSEN (VALHALLA, NY)

2 pounds green tomatoes, rinsed and quartered
2 pounds tart green apples, such as Pippins, peeled, cored, and quartered
1 pound shallots, peeled
2 heads of garlic, peeled (20 to 24 cloves each)
6 fresh red chili peppers, stemmed and seeded
1-inch piece fresh ginger, coarsely chopped and tied in cheesecloth
½ pound golden raisins
1 pound Demerara or other crystal-form brown sugar
2½ cups distilled white or cider vinegar

1. Put the tomatoes, apples, shallots, garlic, and chilies through a mincer or finely chop in a food processor, taking care not to overchop them into a mush. Transfer to a nonreactive canning kettle or very large pot.

2. Add the ginger, raisins, sugar, and vinegar and slowly bring to a boil over medium heat, stirring from time to time. Lower the heat to maintain a gentle simmer and cook for 1 hour, or until all the ingredients are soft and the mixture has thickened into a loose syrup.

3. Meanwhile, prepare 4 quart jars and lids for canning as described on page 314.

4. Remove the ginger bag and ladle the chutney into the jars. Seal and process in a hot-water bath for 15 minutes (see page 315). Or cool, cap, and store in the refrigerator. Let mature for 1 month before using. Will keep up to 1 year if processed, 6 months in the refrigerator.

Quince-Ginger Chutney

Makes 1 pint

"I live on a property with two quince trees. Having never really heard of quince, much less eaten one, I was curious what I could do with them. When the trees produced almost three shopping bags worth of quinces, my work was cut out for me. This past fall, I put up 58 jars of quince jam! Quince with cranberry, quince with blueberry, and for a change of pace, this chutney, which I like serving with grilled chicken or pork."

DAVID ROSENTHAL (LAFAYETTE, CA)

2 cups peeled, cored, and chopped quince (2 medium quinces)
¼ cup golden raisins
¼ cup dark raisins
¼ cup candied ginger, slivered
¼ cup minced red onion
¼ cup minced red bell pepper
½ cup (packed) dark brown sugar
1 cup cider vinegar
¼ teaspoon ground cinnamon
¼ teaspoon cayenne
¼ teaspoon kosher or pickling salt (optional)

"When you would preserve your quinces white, you must not cover them in the boyling, and you must put halfe as much sugar more for the white as for the other. When you would have them red, you must cover them in the boyling."

—*A Book of Fruits and Flowers*, 1653

1. Combine all the ingredients in a large nonreactive pot. Bring slowly to a boil over medium-low heat. Reduce the heat to maintain a simmer and cook, stirring often, until the mixture thickens and the quinces are quite soft, about 30 minutes.

2. Meanwhile, prepare 1 pint jar and lid for refrigerator canning as described on page 314.

3. Ladle the chutney into the jar. Cool, cap, and store in the refrigerator.

Note: The recipe is written for a small, easy-to-manage amount; the chutney will keep for quite some time in the refrigerator. However, you can make more jars and process them for the pantry. Prepare the jars for canning as described on page 314. Fill and seal the jars and process in a hot-water bath for 15 minutes (see page 315).

When Is a Rose Not a Rose?

In a nutshell, the answer is when it's an apple or a quince. All are members of the wide-ranging Rosaceae family that gives so much to gardeners and cooks. It includes the ornamental roses so desirable in cultivated gardens, where they are often quite pampered. It also includes the more ambling, low-to-the-ground varieties that spread across untended landscape as far north as Nova Scotia and Scotland. That doesn't even begin to mention the brambles or the climbing ones that in a neglected garden grasp any wall or fence, just happy to ascend to the sun. When the rose's season is over and its hips, or fruits, are exposed to view, the noticing person can easily see the resemblance to its culinary relations, apples and quinces.

The quince member of this botanical family fruits in late fall only until frost, so you must catch it while you can. Also, the quince does not lend itself easily to kitchen preparation. Peeling a quince is not like peeling an apple. But the reward is great. Nothing matches the quince's flavor—one that reflects both its wild origins and domesticated garden status—and nothing resembles the delicate pink it imparts to any dish it is included in.

jellies and jams without pectin

When packaged pectin appeared on the market, it was a godsend for home canners. No more beginning from scratch, boiling up your own apples, letting the brew drip through a jelly bag overnight, then further reducing the liquid to gain a modest amount of the elixir, namely pectin, necessary for turning a batch of cooked fruit into jam or jelly. Eventually the quick-fix powdered or liquid pectin came to replace some of the fruit originally required to serve the same purpose. It's easy to see why. Now there could be jams and jellies with not so much fruit. Saves time; saves money; stretches output. There was, and remains, however, a drawback: Though the marvelous new products work well to set up jams and jellies in a thrice, they are sugar (dextrose) based and so interfere to some extent with the natural fruit flavors. Also, and more objectionable, most are laced with preservatives that are not necessary if you make jam or jelly the old-fashioned way.

Following are two recipes that offer formulaic examples of how to make jellies and jams without packaged pectin. They can be varied to accommodate the fruit you have.

Concord Grape Jelly

MAKES 1¾ CUPS PER POUND OF FRUIT

"I love to garden—first garden big enough to plow with a horse. Now it's about 4 feet by 20 feet." Though the size of this contributor's garden has diminished, apparently her enthusiasm for growing and cooking has not. The same method she offers in the following instructions for grape jelly may be applied to other fruits, such as raspberries, blueberries, and cherries. If you are worried about whether or not the fruit you are using contains enough pectin to set well, she offers a tip: add 2 cups grated apple, a natural source of pectin, to every 6 cups of fruit.

ROSEMARY HYMAN (HAWKEYE, IA)

"La vie est dure sans confiture."

—French saying

Concord grapes and sugar in equal amounts by volume

Lemon juice

1. Combine the Concord grapes and sugar in a large, heavy, nonreactive pot. Set over medium-low heat and slowly bring to a boil, stirring frequently. When beginning to boil, stir in the lemon juice, 1 tablespoon for every 3 pounds of fruit.

2. Continue cooking over medium-low heat, stirring frequently, until the mixture drips slowly from the spoon, 220°F. This will take anywhere from 25 to 85 minutes, depending on the amount you are making and the degree of ripeness of the fruit. Remove from the heat and let cool enough to handle.

3. Meanwhile, prepare jars and lids for refrigerator canning as described on page 314.

4. Put the grape mixture through a food mill to remove the skins and seeds, then ladle into jars. You can seal the jars with paraffin or cap them and store in the refrigerator. Jellies do not need processing.

Old-Fashioned Blackberry Jam

MAKES 1¾ CUPS PER POUND OF FRUIT

"This is the old-fashioned way to make the best jam you will ever taste. All it takes is berries and sugar. You can use any type of berry you choose; I like to use blackberries from my organic garden in the California desert. It's important to pick ripe fruit for flavor and include underripe fruit for the natural pectin that makes the jam firm."

Two Catsups: One Sweet and One Savory

"Enclosed you will find some recipe pages from a cookbook my great-grandmother and her six sisters contributed to. It was published in 1887. The recipes have been handed down and my sisters and I now have the tradition of gathering in the summer and trying to figure out how to make a recipe from *The Appleton CookBook* with goodies from our gardens."

GRAPE CATSUP

Mrs. Fuller, from *The Appleton CookBook,* written here as originally printed:

"5 pounds of grapes boiled and strained,
2½ pounds of sugar,
1 pint of vinegar,
1 tablespoonful of cinnamon,
1 tablespoonful of cloves,
1 tablespoonful of allspice,
1 tablespoonful of pepper,
1–2 tablespoonful of salt.

Boil till slightly thick. Excellent."

CUCUMBER CATSUP

Mrs. George W. White, from *The Appleton CookBook,* written here as originally printed.

"Take large green cucumbers, pare and grate them, put in a jelly bag and press dry. Take out of bag and add vinegar to make thin as catsup, season with salt and red pepper to taste. Fill your bottles and cork tightly. Requires no cooking."

—KIM McCREERY (ALEXANDRIA, VA)

The ratio of ripe to underripe fruit should be about three to one. This works just right for most berries, in particular, blackberries, which are high in pectin in any stage. For other berries or fruit that are not so full of natural pectin, you may need to up the sugar to an equal amount by weight (see Raspberry Jam, page 374).

~ JADE ALEXANDRA (VICTORVILLE, CA)

Blackberries, some ripe, some underripe
Sugar

1. Weigh the berries and place them in a heavy nonreactive pot. Add ¾ pound of sugar per pound of berries. Stir together and let stand at room temperature for 1 hour.

2. Bring to a slow boil over medium heat, stirring constantly to prevent scorching. Continue cooking, stirring occasionally, until the mixture falls from the spoon in a thin sheet as opposed to drips and reaches 222°F. on a candy thermometer, about 30 minutes.

3. Ladle into half-pint jars, cool, cap, and let stand overnight before serving. Or serve right away if you can't wait. Will keep in the refrigerator for up to 3 months.

Lime-Ginger Marmalade

MAKES 3 PINTS

"We live in a community called Lanikai. It's on a rather steep hill, so we grow veggies in pots, but in the ground bananas, papayas, lemons, oranges, and limes fare well. I recently worked up a recipe to use our seedless limes."

~ EVELYN BEAL (KAILUA, HI)

2 cups quartered and very thinly sliced limes
1 tablespoon (packed) coarsely grated fresh ginger
6 cups sugar

1. Place the limes and 5 cups of water in a large bowl. Cover and let stand at room temperature overnight.

pantry perks

NARRATIVE MEASURES

Sprinkle
Drizzle
Drop
Dollop
Pinch
Pugil

"Note, That by Parts is to be understood a Pugil; which is no more than one does usually take up between the Thumb and the two next Fingers. By Facsicule a reasonable full Grip, or Handful."

—John Evelyn, *Acetaria,* 1669

2. Next day, transfer the limes and liquid to a large, heavy, nonreactive pot. Add the ginger and bring to a boil. Reduce the heat and simmer until the lime pieces have softened, 5 to 10 minutes, depending on the age of the limes.

3. Stir in the sugar and bring to a boil again. Reduce the heat just enough to maintain a boil without the pot overflowing. Cook until the mixture heavily coats a spoon (230° to 235°F. on a candy thermometer), about 1 hour. Remove and cool until the boiling stops.

4. Meanwhile, prepare 3 pint jars and lids for canning as described on page 314.

5. While still hot, ladle into the jars. Seal and process in a hot-water bath for 15 minutes (see page 315). Or cool, cap, and store in the refrigerator. Keeps for up to 6 months in the refrigerator, 1 year if processed.

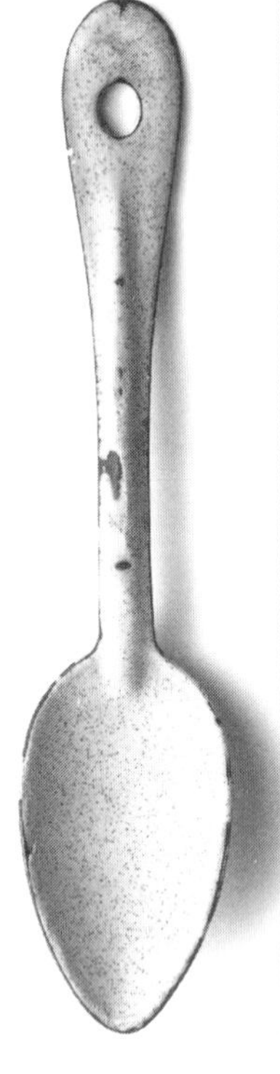

Tipsy Meyer Lemon Marmalade

MAKES 4 PINTS OR 8 HALF-PINTS

"Meyer lemons are a backyard fruit in California, pretty much unobtainable to someone in the East. Fortunately, my mother lives in California, and when the lemons are ripe, she sends me a box of them. Made from very ripe Meyers, this marmalade rivals the best Seville orange marmalade." Readers who live outside the prime Meyer lemon growing region and don't have a "mail order" connection, such as the contributor's mother, need not despair. The more widely available, "everyday" lemons, such as Eurekas or Lisbons, work perfectly well. They do take a bit longer to soften the rinds in the initial simmering.

~ BETH KELLY (SEWICKLEY, PA)

3 pounds very ripe Meyer lemons (12 to 15)
3 pounds sugar
3 ounces Scotch whisky (see page 351)

1. Scrub the lemons with a brush and place in a large nonreactive pot. Add water to cover and bring to a boil. Cover the pot and simmer until the skins pierce easily with a fork, 10 to 20 minutes, depending on the size and type of lemon. Drain and let cool enough to handle.

2. Cut off the stem end of each lemon, exposing a bit of the pulp. Squeeze the lemons into a strainer set over the same pot, reserving the rinds. Pick the seeds out of the strainer and add the pulp to the pot.

3. Slice the lemon skins lengthwise into halves or quarters, then crosswise as thinly as possible. Add to the pot with the strained juice and pulp.

4. Add the sugar and bring to a vigorous boil, stirring frequently to prevent scorching. Lower the heat and simmer until the mixture coats the back of spoon (222°F. on a candy thermometer), about 30 minutes.

5. Meanwhile, prepare 4 pint or 8 half-pint jars and lids for canning as described on page 314.

6. Add the Scotch, taking care to avoid the rising steam and spewing bubbles as the alcohol burns off. Simmer for 5 minutes more, or until the mixture settles down and returns to a marmalade consistency.

7. Ladle into the jars, seal, and process in a hot-water bath for 15 minutes (see page 315). Or cool, cap, and store in the refrigerator. Will keep in the refrigerator for up to 6 months, 1 year if processed.

ABOUT THE TIPSY PART
For those who enjoy the earthy, grainy flavor of Scotch whisky, a splash or so more will not make the marmalade too tipsy. You could, in a pinch, substitute another whisky, such as bourbon, though the outcome will not be so smooth. Other distilled liquors, such as brandy or rum, won't do at all; they are too heavy and heady for the marmalade.

Lemon Curd

MAKES 2 HALF-PINTS

How the classic Scottish lemon curd arrived perfectly intact and perfectly rendered in the dry desert of southern New Mexico is one of the wonders and glories of American cuisine, which brings together so many cultures in such surprising places. The contributor must have carried the recipe halfway round the world or else received it passed down through many generations. She doesn't say. She does advise to "Use on a daily basis as a breakfast spread for English muffins or toast, or dollop on scones for a teatime treat. For a special occasion, use to fill individual tart shells; for a very special occasion, decorate the tarts with crystallized violet petals." It also makes a filling for layered cakes or puff pastry shells.

OLGA BEZPALKO (SOCORRO, NM)

1 cup sugar
2 tablespoons finely chopped lemon zest
2 large eggs, lightly beaten
½ cup fresh lemon juice
8 tablespoons (1 stick) butter, at room temperature

PRIDE IN PRESERVING

"I do feel a sense of pride and joy when I open the pantry and see colorful jars of home-canned tart relishes, crisp pickles, sweet sliced peaches, tomatoes, jams, jellies. Canning and freezing is a tradition that has passed through four generations of my family. I started assisting my mother with canning tomatoes when I was about eight years old. Many other cooks and gardeners in our zone, which does not have the luxury of a long, warm growing season, pickle, can, and freeze the summer produce to capture the fresh tastes of fruits and vegetables and preserve them for later."

—JANE CALDWELL (PRIOR LAKE, MN)

1. Prepare 2 half-pint jars and lids for refrigerator canning as described on page 314.

2. Combine the sugar, zest, and eggs in a heavy, nonreactive saucepan. Stir until well blended and very smooth.

3. Add the lemon juice and butter and bring to a boil over medium-high heat, stirring constantly. Remove from the heat and pour into the jars. Cool to room temperature, then use right away or store in the refrigerator. Will keep for up to 3 months.

Plum and Rhubarb Fruit Spread

MAKES 2 PINTS

Plum and rhubarb, each a tart fruit, may not seem to invite each other's company. But when bound together with sugar, they bring out each other's best nature in a fine fruit spread. As the contributor rightly exclaims, "It's very good *on a nutty scone, shortbread, or as part of a peanut-butter sandwich."*

HEATHER HARGESHEIMER (SEATTLE, WA)

4½ to 5 pounds red plums, peeled, pitted, and coarsely chopped (see box on page 343)
2 large stalks rhubarb, cut into ¼-inch dice (about 1 pound)
1 cup sugar
3 tablespoons fresh lime juice

1. Preheat the oven to 375°F.

2. Combine all the ingredients in a large glass or ceramic baking dish and toss to mix. Place in the oven and cook until the juices are released, about 15 minutes.

3. Reduce the oven heat to 300°F. and continue to bake, stirring once or twice, until a spoonful of the fruit sets up immediately when dropped onto a chilled plate, 1½ to 2 hours, depending on the juiciness of the plums.

4. Meanwhile, prepare 2 pint jars and lids for canning as described on page 314.

5. Transfer the mixture to the jars, seal, and process in a hot-water bath for 15 minutes (see page 315). Or cool, cap, and store in the refrigerator. Will keep in the refrigerator for up to 6 months, 1 year if processed.

Using the Microwave for Preserving

For the modern home cook, the microwave oven is a dream appliance for preparing and processing foods. It's especially useful in jam and jelly making.

For Fruits

For peeling and pitting apricots, peaches, plums, and other stone fruits, a brief turn in the microwave will loosen their skins enough to slip off and soften the pulp enough to free it easily from the pit.

Once prepared, fruits from berries to cherries bubble up and thicken much more quickly in the microwave than on the stovetop and do so without generating a sticky pot to clean.

The microwave accommodates small amounts, so that if you see the perfect basket of strawberries and take a notion to make a pint of jam for the fridge, you can plunk the berries into a medium microwave bowl, sugar them to taste, and microwave on high to the consistency you would like with only one or two stirrings in the process.

The microwave oven's powers to preserve fruit by drying cannot be praised enough. Apricots, figs, grapes, and tomatoes can all be halved and microwave-dried in very little time. See page 337 for guidelines.

For Herbs and Mushrooms, Too

You can also use the microwave to dry herbs and mushrooms.

Herbs: Wash the sprigs or branches to rinse away any soil or bugs. Spin dry and lay them on a large microwave plate in a tight layer. Microwave on medium for 3 or so minutes, until looking crinkled. Let stand for 5 minutes. Strip off the leaves, transfer to an airtight jar, and store in the cupboard. Freshly dried herbs will keep longer than store-bought dried herbs, up to one year if tightly closed.

Mushrooms: Stem the mushrooms and make sure they are free of debris. For this purpose, you don't need to towel-wipe each one; a quick wash and shake-dry is okay. Slice the caps ¼ inch thick and spread them on a large microwave plate. Microwave for 13 minutes on medium, then for 12 to 14 minutes on high, until desiccated. Let stand until completely cooled to room temperature. Transfer to a paper or plastic bag or a *not* airtight container. Will keep in the cupboard for up to 6 months or in the freezer for longer in a resealable plastic bag.

Apple Butter

MAKES 4 TO 5 PINTS

Apple butter may be a familiar spread from childhood days when breakfast needed to be quick and healthful. A good layer of it over a piece of toast could serve to get you out the door in time for school. Or perhaps it was a special and desired treat, reserved for waffles or pancakes on the weekends, calmer times. With this recipe, the tradition is carried forth. The contributor explains, "During the summer months when the apples began ripening on our trees, my sons and I would pick buckets full and make pies, cobblers, and lots of apple butter. It's a great way to preserve that wonderful taste of fresh, hot apple pie after the summer bounty is gone."

PAMELA ROSS (CORTE MADERA, CA)

OVEN-BAKING FRUIT SPREADS *The technique of finishing the cooking of the apple purée in a slow oven after its stint on the stovetop frees the cook from having constantly to watch the pot to prevent sticking and burning. It's a method that can be used for other spreads and fruit butters as well.*

8 pounds apples, rinsed and quartered
3 pounds brown sugar
3 tablespoons ground cinnamon
2 teaspoons ground cloves
½ tablespoon ground allspice
1 teaspoon ground nutmeg

1. Place the apples in a large, nonreactive pot. Add water barely to cover, bring to a boil, and cook over low heat, stirring occasionally, until the apples are soft, about 1 hour. Remove from the heat and set aside to cool in the liquid.

2. When cool, drain the apples. Purée in batches in a food mill to remove the skins, seeds, and cores. You should have 16 cups of purée.

3. Add the remaining ingredients, adjusting the amounts if you have noticeably more or less of the apple purée, and mix well.

4. Preheat the oven to 350°F.

5. Spread the apple mixture into a nonreactive baking pan about 18 by 12 by 3 inches. Place in the oven and bake, stirring once or twice, until thickened and no longer soupy, at least 3 hours.

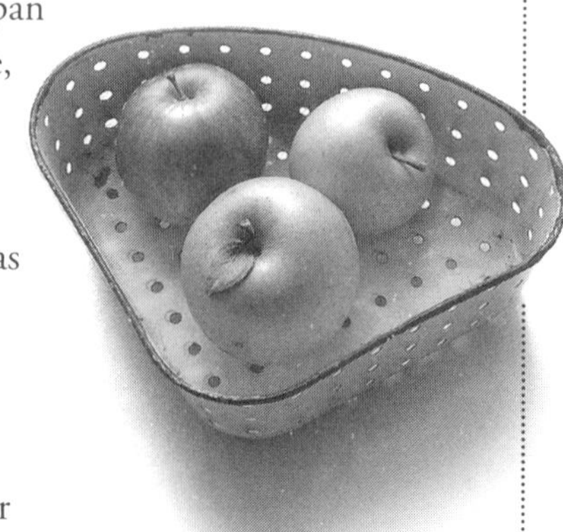

6. Meanwhile, prepare 5 pint jars and lids for canning as described on page 314.

7. Remove from the oven and ladle into the jars. (You may not completely fill the fifth jar. If so, refrigerate it and use it first.) Seal and process in a hot-water bath for

10 minutes (see page 315). Or cool, cap, and store in the refrigerator. Let stand for at least 6 weeks before using. Will keep in the refrigerator for up to 6 months, 1 year if processed.

Pear Honey

MAKES 2 PINTS

"I got this recipe from my cousin, Ruth Straw, and it was probably handed down from relatives from Maryland. It is very sweet, so spread it sparingly. To sieve the pears, the original recipe calls for using a dilver; I use a Foley's food mill." (See box below.)

JOSEPHINE ELSEN (WHEATON, IL)

6 large pears (about 3 pounds)
3½ to 5 cups sugar, to taste
2 tablespoons fresh lemon juice or cider vinegar

1. Quarter the pears without peeling them and place in a large, nonreactive pot (see box at right). Add 1 cup of water, bring to a boil, and simmer until very soft, about 15 minutes. Purée the pears along with the cooking liquid through a food mill. Transfer to a clean pot.

2. Mix the sugar and lemon juice into the pear purée. Bring to a boil over medium heat, then simmer briskly, stirring frequently, until the mixture is thickened and turned a pale golden honey color, about 15 minutes. Let stand overnight, stirring occasionally.

TOOLS *of the* TRADE

Dilvers, Food Mills, and Sieves

Sometimes it's important to cook fruit with the cores and peels to retain flavor and color, but then those need to be extracted before the dish is done. If you have a food mill, you can just press everything through it; the mill will press the pulp and juices through while keeping back the cores and peels. If you don't have a food mill, you can cook the pears, cool, then peel and core them, and purée the pulp in a food processor. Or you can follow the original recipe and press the pears, skins and all, through a finely meshed kitchen sieve, that is, a dilver.

"I could live in Paris only if I had a beautiful garden."

—Colette

3. Prepare 2 pint jars and lids for refrigerator canning as described on page 314.

4. Transfer the pear honey to the jars and store in the refrigerator. Will keep for up to 1 year.

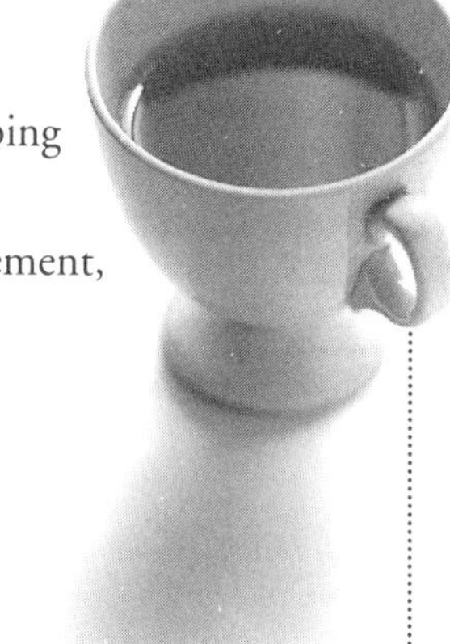

Note: This confection does not need to be processed for long keeping because it is essentially a sugar preparation that will last for a long time. However, it does need to be refrigerated because the fruit element, the pears, will eventually mold if left unrefrigerated.

the bakery:

quick picks for any time of day

Biscuits and breads; muffins and scones; cookies and crackers; pizza by the slice. Such is the fare you might imagine in a bakery of your dreams, one that fills the recurring need for a bite to eat any time of day. Walk in and you can choose a basket of buns for the morning coffee or afternoon tea; a can't-stop-to-talk snack to grab on the run; a baker's dozen of crackers for the appetizer table; rolls for the dinner table; crispy sweets to garnish the ice cream. If such a shop of wonders doesn't exist in your neighborhood, you can put your own hand to the matter and choose from the dream list of bakery goods in this chapter.

TOOLS *of the* TRADE

Pans for the Baker's Art

Once upon a time, an entire array of baking pans was part of the household kitchen. Each, with its specific name and shape, served a particular purpose. For those contemporary cooks who might not have a battery beyond the usual round cake or pie pan, here's a lexicon of the essential pans for the home cook who would like to expand baking horizons:

COOKIE SHEET/BAKING SHEET: In various sizes, always of metal so that the pan becomes quite hot and the ingredients cook from the bottom as well as the top.

JELLY-ROLL PAN: Like a baking sheet but with a rim 1 to 1½ inches high. Mainly used for shortbread pastry or a batter that needs to be contained at a certain height without overflowing the pan. Also useful for any cookie or baking sheet purpose.

LOAF PAN: A rectangular pan, usually 9 by 5 by 3 inches or 8 by 4 by 2¾ inches, either metal or tempered glass. A metal pan is perfect for cakelike quick breads, such as Papaya Tea Bread (page 377) or Tomato Spice Tea Bread (page 378) and also for yeast breads that need a supporting form to bake well. The glass pan is better suited to products for which the baking vessel should not get too hot, such as meat loaves, terrines, or custards.

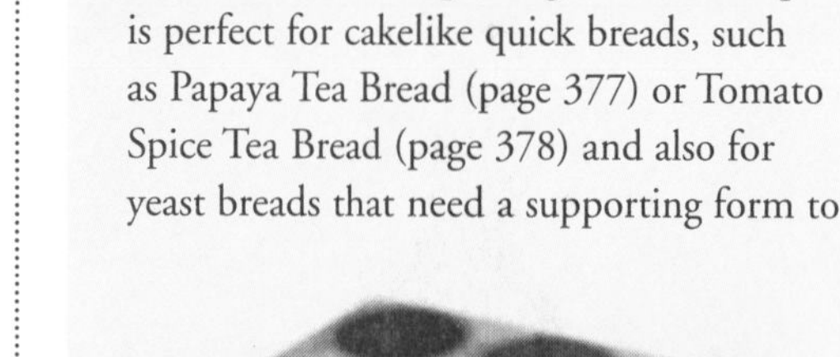

MUFFIN TIN: Metal baking pan with wells, ranging in number from 6 to 12. For making muffins, cupcakes, or popovers or turning any of the quick breads into individual servings. Also see page 383.

PIZZA PAN: The traditional size is 14 inches in diameter. Not absolutely essential but nice if you like your pizza round.

The Cooling Rack

Most bakers like to use a cooling rack, a metal or wood grid that sits high enough above the counter so that air circulates all around the baking pan. This allows the cookies, breads, cakes, or whatever to cool without becoming gluey or sticking to the bottom of the baking pan. If you don't have a cooling rack, you can easily improvise with a spoon or two set halfway under the pan so that the pan rests at a cock-eyed angle to the counter. You can also set the pan on two cans to elevate it above the counter. Either of these juryrigs serves the purpose.

Sweet Potato Biscuits

MAKES 12 BISCUITS

In these simple and tasty biscuits, the sweet potato supplies the sugar and a mix of flours supplies a pleasing grainy texture. The biscuits are best served warm, but they toast nicely too.

~ LARA PENNELL (IRVING, TX)

2 small sweet potatoes, peeled and diced (1 pound)
1 cup all-purpose flour
1 cup whole-wheat pastry flour
4 teaspoons baking powder
1 teaspoon salt
⅔ cup solid vegetable shortening
3 to 4 tablespoons milk

1. Preheat the oven to 400°F.

2. Bring a medium pot of water to boil. Add the sweet potatoes and cook until soft all the way through, about 10 minutes. Drain, mash, and set aside.

3. Mix the flours, baking powder, and salt in a large mixing bowl. Add the shortening and blend until crumbly. Add the mashed sweet potatoes and 3 tablespoons of the milk. Mix well, adding a little more milk if necessary to make a soft dough.

4. Transfer the dough to a floured surface and knead for 6 to 8 turns. Roll or pat the dough into a ¾-inch-thick disk. Cut into 12 rounds and transfer to an ungreased baking sheet.

5. Bake until very lightly browned, 12 to 15 minutes. Let rest a few minutes and serve hot.

Sweet Potatoes, Yams, and Then Again, Yams

In American cooking, especially that of the South, sweet potatoes are used morning to night, from biscuits to pies and numerous ways in between, including deep-fried sweet potato chips, puréed soups, cold nuggets in composed salads, and vegetable sides. Somewhere there must be a sweet potato ice cream. What about yams? There are a couple of distinctions to be made between the two.

The first is between sweet potatoes and American yams, which are botanical cousins, members of the nightshade family. The second is between New World sweet potatoes and yams and Old World yams, which are members of the grasses and lilies family. Though part of African and Asian, especially Japanese, cooking, they are hardly available here.

The major distinction between sweet potatoes and New World yams is texture: Sweet potatoes are mealy, similar to a russet potato; yams are more puddinglike, spoonable rather than forkable. As for appearance and taste, there are long, skinny sweet potatoes and wide, fat yams. There are sweet potatoes with a distinct orange hue and yams with a pallor. There are sweet potatoes sweeter than yams and vice versa. And grocers, not too interested in the academics of the topic, often mark them all yams.

How to choose for the dish at hand? The answer is, rely on the texture difference. For serving them like baked potatoes, either will do. For dishes in which it matters that the vegetables remain in discrete pieces, such as salads, fries, or layered casseroles, sweet potatoes are the first choice. For dishes that need a thoroughly mashed, smooth texture, such as pies and purées, yams are the way to go. For in-between dishes in which a bit of coarseness in the purée is desirable, such as mashed sweet potatoes or sweet potato biscuits, sweet potatoes are the choice, but yams will also do.

Blueberry-Sage Corn Muffins

MAKES 12 MUFFINS

"I love the scent and taste of sage. Although most people think of sage as a savory herb, it also tastes wonderful as an accent for fruits and sweets. This original corn muffin recipe proves the case."

JAN JACOBSON-JOHNSON (MADISON, WI)

1¼ cups all-purpose flour
¾ cup yellow cornmeal
¼ cup plus 1 tablespoon sugar
2 teaspoons baking powder
Pinch of salt
1 cup milk
¼ cup vegetable oil
1 large egg
¼ cup finely chopped fresh sage leaves or 2 tablespoons dried sage
2 cups fresh blueberries

Corn Cakes: Sweet and Round, Savory and Square

When it comes to corn cakes, there's not a lot of difference between corn muffins and corn bread except the muffins are usually sweeter. Otherwise, basically the same batter will get you either. To turn the Blueberry-Sage Corn Muffins into bread for savory use, such as corn bread for bruschetta (see page 22):

- Use only 1 tablespoon of the sugar.
- Use the sage or not and omit the blueberries altogether.
- Instead of a muffin tin, turn the batter into a lightly greased 8- or 9-inch square pan or a rectangular pan or baking dish of similar size.
- Continue with the recipe, cutting the cooked bread into whatever size pieces you would like.

1. Preheat the oven to 375°F. Lightly grease a 12-well muffin tin.

2. Mix together the flour, cornmeal, sugar, baking powder, and salt in a large bowl.

3. In another bowl, whisk together the milk, oil, egg, and sage. Add to the dry ingredients and mix thoroughly without beating. Fold in the blueberries.

4. Spoon the batter into the muffin tin and bake until the muffins spring back when pressed, and the tops are lightly golden, about 25 minutes. Cool enough to handle, then remove from the tin and cool on a rack. Serve warm.

Flowerpot Corn Muffins with Calendula Butter

MAKES 12 MUFFINS

"One morning at the Wildflower Inn my daughter was helping me prepare breakfast for our guests. We were baking mint-flavored muffins and I asked her to go to the herb garden and pick several sprigs of mint. She plucked, washed, and minced her gathering, and added it to the ready and waiting muffin batter. When the baking muffins began to waft their fragrance into the room, I commented that the mint smelled odd. We went to the garden and she pointed out the leaves she had chosen: two kinds of mint and a good handful of oregano. That day, we called the muffins Italian *mint muffins." The contributor concluded that "many good recipes are created in such a way, although next time we stuck to the original and used just mint." She then generously went on to share a multitude of flower-and-herb variations to spark your morning buns (see box at right).*

DONNA STONE, THE WILDFLOWER INN (FALMOUTH, MA)

¾ cup yellow cornmeal, preferably stone ground
1 cup all-purpose flour
¼ cup sugar
2 teaspoons baking powder
½ teaspoon baking soda
¾ teaspoon salt
1 cup sour cream
¼ cup milk
1 large egg, beaten
2 tablespoons butter, melted
2 cups edible flower petals, rinsed and patted dry
½ cup Calendula Butter (recipe follows)

1. Preheat the oven to 400°F. Lightly grease a 12-well muffin tin or an 8-inch square baking dish.

Flower Power: Edible Colors for the Gardener Cook

Dear to the heart of any gardener cook are edible flowers. More than for their individual distinctive but modest tastes, they are appreciated for the grand sweep they provide to any table presentation, bouquet to plate. Besides the herbs that are regularly collected for their flowers as well as leaves, plant for their own beauty and to pick for their petal garnishing possibilities:

- Calendula and its marigold look-alikes
- Chrysanthemum
- Citrus, all kinds
- Daylily
- Dianthus (carnation)
- English daisy
- Geranium
- Hibiscus
- Honeysuckle
- Nasturtium
- Pansy, Johnny-jump-up, and viola
- Rose
- Tuberous begonia
- Tulip

2. Combine the cornmeal, flour, sugar, baking powder, baking soda, and salt in a large bowl and stir to mix well.

3. In a separate bowl, whisk together the sour cream, milk, egg, and butter. Whisk this mixture into the cornmeal mixture to make a wet batter. Fold in the flower petals and let the batter rest for 10 minutes.

TOOLS *of the* TRADE

Glazed Pots from Garden to Kitchen

Considered duplicity is one of the marks of the gardener cook. For instance, a terra-cotta pot that might be thought to hold a seedling for the garden can also be the container for a kitchen muffin. For the seedling, the pot must have a drainage hole so the plant can be watered without drowning. For the muffin, the pot doesn't need a hole and, more important, it must be glazed so there is no adverse reaction between the batter and the surface of the pot. With glazed pots without a drainage holes the muffins bake to perfection.

4. Divide the batter evenly among the muffin wells. Bake for 20 to 25 minutes, or until the muffins turn golden around the edges and a knife inserted in the center comes out clean.

5. Meanwhile, prepare the calendula butter.

6. Remove, cool in the pan, then transfer to racks. Serve while still warm, accompanied by a pot of calendula butter.

Calendula Butter

MAKES ½ CUP

8 tablespoons (1 stick) butter, at room temperature

¼ cup calendula petals, rinsed and patted dry

Blend the ingredients together in a small bowl. Use right away or cover and refrigerate for up to 1 week.

Rosemary-Cheese Scones

MAKES 8 SCONES

"When my garden goes to sleep for winter, one plant stays awake to keep spring alive even in the coldest of days. Rosemary. Scones are a big part of our daily lives, so

it seemed only natural for rosemary to end up in the batter. These are particularly good split and filled with smoked turkey and avocado."

SWEETIE RUTTAN, COUNTRY PIE HERBS (DAYTON, WA)

3 cups all-purpose flour
5 teaspoons baking powder
1½ tablespoons finely chopped rosemary leaves
1 cup grated Monterey Jack cheese
½ teaspoon salt (optional)
⅔ cup solid vegetable shortening
1 tablespoon grainy mustard
1¼ cups milk
Extra flour, for kneading the dough

1. Preheat the oven to 425°F. Lightly grease a baking sheet.

2. Blend the flour, baking powder, rosemary, ¾ cup of the Monterey Jack, and the salt, if using, in a bowl. Add the shortening and mix until crumbly.

3. Whisk together the mustard and milk in a small bowl. Add to the flour mixture and blend with a fork to make a moist, biscuitlike dough.

4. Transfer the dough to a lightly floured surface and knead for 6 turns. Scoop the dough into a ball and cut the ball in half. Pat each half into a 6- to 7-inch round. Cut each round into 4 wedges to make a total of 8 scones.

5. Place the scones on the baking sheet. Brush the tops with a little water, then sprinkle with the remaining ½ cup cheese. Bake until very golden on top and a knife inserted in the center comes out clean, 18 to 20 minutes. Serve warm or at room temperature.

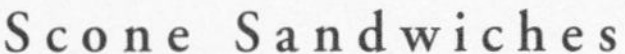

Scone Sandwiches

There's no telling where the sandwich will come to rest in the world. First there was an earl who couldn't be bothered to rise from his gaming table for a proper meal. Then there was an entire working class of people who couldn't return home or stop at a restaurant for midday sustenance. A sandwich became a solution, a satisfying one, at that. Eventually the croissant, epitome of simple, uncomplicated morning eating, was halved and its hollow shells filled with ham, cheese, salad. Bagels came to be spread with *schmeers* beyond any grandmother's ideas of what fits, and not only that, you have it in a café. Now scones are cut in half, filled with slices of meat and cheese, topped with something salady, and there's another sandwich.

There are special considerations for a scone sandwich. The filling must be minimal, just a hint of extra taste: one slice of smoked turkey topped with two thin slices of avocado; a slice of cheese topped with a tablespoon of jam; a slice of prosciutto topped with four sprigs of cilantro; some melted butter topped with cracked pepper.

Strawberry-Lemon Balm Scones

MAKES 8 SCONES

"Last summer I sold pastries at a farmers' market here in York, Maine. My biggest sellers were two scone variations flavored from my garden harvest: this one with my strawberries and lemon balm and another with anise hyssop." *In the making of so many scones for sale, the contributor learned a few tricks. She shares them in the box at left.*

CARLA ROLLINS (YORK, ME)

2⅔ cups all-purpose flour
3 tablespoons sugar
5 teaspoons baking powder
10 tablespoons (1¼ sticks) butter, cut into bits
½ cup sliced fresh strawberries tossed in a little flour
2 tablespoons chopped fresh lemon balm leaves
2 large eggs
1 cup buttermilk
Extra flour, for kneading the dough

1. Preheat the oven to 400°F. Lightly grease a baking sheet.

2. Blend the flour, sugar, and baking powder together in a bowl. Add the butter and mix until crumbly. Add the strawberries and lemon balm and blend lightly.

TRICKS *of the* TRADE

Scrumptious Scones

Recently scones have become the muffin of the hour. No longer reserved for tea, they have snuggled in beside, if not supplanted, buns and croissants for breakfast or midmorning coffee break. Well, why not? If the British have taken to a cup of coffee at teatime, Americans might as well enjoy a scone to start the day. Eager cooks have come up with variations probably not heard of before. Following are some professional tips for making scones with whatever elements you might choose to add.

FROM BETH HENSPERGER, bread-making expert and author of several bread-making cookbooks including *The Bread Bible:* "Knead the dough briefly, just four to six turns is usually enough for it to come together. This is not a vigorous technique as is called for in making yeast breads. Overworking the dough will result in a tough, chewy scone. When shaping the scones for baking, be equally light-handed and gently pat or roll the dough ½ to ¾ inch thick without pressing out the air. That way, you get a tender, high-rise scone."

FROM CONTRIBUTOR CARLA ROLLINS: "There are two tricks to scones: (1) don't handle the dough too much or it will become tough and (2) slice with a sharp knife so the layers don't flatten and become dense."

FROM OUR RECIPE TESTERS: "The amount of baking powder makes a big difference. There should be about 1 tablespoon for every 2 cups of flour. Sometimes 1 tablespoon baking powder is enough for up to 3 cups of flour, providing that there is another leavening agent, such as eggs, salt, or a mix of baking soda with an acid to activate it, and that added ingredients are not so heavy as to require double leavening to lift the dough as it cooks. More baking powder can be added to accommodate a particular recipe, but too much is not good. There is a cut-off point where more baking powder does indeed raise the dough a little higher but the end result tastes unpleasant on the tongue."

3. In another bowl, whisk together the eggs and buttermilk. Add all but 1 tablespoon to the flour mixture. Stir together with a wooden spoon.

4. Transfer the dough to a floured surface and knead for 4 to 6 turns. Cut the dough in half and pat each half into an oval about 10 inches long and 4 to 5 inches wide. Cut each oval first lengthwise and then crosswise to make 8 triangle-shaped scones.

5. Place the scones on the prepared baking sheet and brush the tops with the remaining buttermilk mixture. Bake until golden on top, 12 to 13 minutes. Serve warm or at room temperature.

Note: To make anise hyssop scones, replace the strawberries and lemon balm with 3 tablespoons chopped anise hyssop flowers.

A TASTE TREAT: SAVORY SCONES SWEETLY TOPPED
Consider serving savory scones with an extravagant spoonful of Strawberry Spoon Sauce (page 439) over the top.

Savory Sweet Marjoram Scones

MAKES 8 SCONES

"My mother introduced me to scones after we had lived in England for a short while. The first year that I had my own herb garden, I experimented cooking with them and came up with this recipe, a variation of my mother's basic scones. So tasty are they, a friend asked to serve them in her restaurant. So, without further ado, here is the recipe."

NAOMI THOMPSON (PAINESVILLE, OH)

2 cups all-purpose flour
2 teaspoons sugar
1 tablespoon baking powder
3 tablespoons chopped fresh sweet marjoram leaves
1 tablespoon freshly ground black pepper
8 tablespoons (1 stick) butter, at room temperature
1 large egg
¾ cup milk
Extra flour, for kneading the dough

A Surfeit of Scones

You can join the brigade of scone fanciers with variations of your own. Just for the fun of it, try making many and varying them by changing the:

HERBS: Instead of marjoram, use another sturdy, flavorful herb, such as oregano, rosemary, sage, savory, thyme.

CHEESE: Instead of Monterey Jack, use another tasty melting cheese, such as cheddar (orange or white as long as it's sharp), Gruyère or Emmenthal, Prince de Claverolle, kefalotyri, manchego, gouda, müenster, queso asadero.

In addition to any herb or cheese, add bits of dried fruit, such as apricots, cherries, currants, figs.

1. Preheat the oven to 450°F. Lightly grease a baking sheet.

2. Sift the flour, sugar, and baking powder into a large bowl. Add the marjoram and pepper and stir to mix. Cut in the butter and blend until the mixture is crumbly.

3. In a separate bowl, whisk together the egg and milk. Add to the flour mixture and stir to blend into a wet dough. With floured hands, knead the dough for 10 turns.

4. Divide the dough into golf-ball size pieces and arrange on the baking sheet without touching each other, like drop cookies. Press each ball into a ½-inch-thick round.

5. Bake for 12 to 14 minutes, or until cooked through and barely golden on top. Serve right away.

DROP SCONES

Drop scones are also traditional. Instead of patting out the dough and then cutting it into sections, divide the dough into small sections and then flatten them out. The result is a rounded, more biscuitlike shape. You can choose between the drop-and-pressed or pressed-and-cut methods described in the scone recipes included here.

Savory Cheese Crackers

MAKES ABOUT 3 DOZEN CRACKERS

Karen Frerichs grew up in Illinois and spent her youth journeying in Europe, New York, California, and New Mexico while continuing to earn a master's degree in education. A stairwell gardener, always ready to spend extra time on a good garden-to-table project, she was one of the major recipe testers for this volume. Also an accomplished baker, she developed these crackers especially for this volume. The dough can be made ahead and refrigerated or frozen until needed. Bake off a batch and serve them with a dish of olives (see page 3) for a quick and easy cocktail nibble.

KAREN FRERICHS (CHAMPAIGN, IL; SAN FRANCISCO, CA; SANTA FE, NM)

1 cup grated hard cheese, such as Parmesan, Romano, aged Asiago, or dry Jack
½ cup all-purpose flour
½ cup cornmeal
6 tablespoons (¾ stick) butter
¼ cup chopped fresh herbs, such as rosemary, thyme, marjoram, chives, or a mixture
Extra flour, for rolling out the dough

1. Combine the cheese, flour, cornmeal, and butter in a bowl or food processor and blend until a dough begins to form.

2. Mix in the herbs and form the dough into 2 or 3 balls. Wrap in plastic wrap and refrigerate until well chilled, at least 30 minutes, or freeze until needed. Bring the dough to room temperature before proceeding.

3. When ready to bake, preheat the oven to 400°F.

4. On a floured surface, roll out the dough, 1 ball at a time, to ⅛ inch thick. Cut with a cookie cutter or use the point of a knife to make free-form rectangles, diamonds, triangles, hearts, or whatever else you'd like. Transfer to an ungreased baking sheet and bake for 7 to 8 minutes, or until browned around the edges.

5. Serve right away or cool and store in an airtight container for up to 2 weeks.

A Stairwell Garden

"I live in a city apartment but have fantasies of living in the country with a garden for flowers and herbs. While I dream of this change, I have found a way to ease the wait. Over the years, I've accumulated many window boxes, which I hang at different levels over the railings of my back stairwell. The upper level, most exposed to the sun, is a Mediterranean microcosm with rosemary, oregano, marjoram, lavender, and several kinds of thyme. Next come the arugula, parsley, and sage, then basil interplanted with marigolds to protect it from too much sun. Farther down are several mint plants, including lemon balm. Interspersed are scented geraniums—rose, lemon, lime, ginger, and tutti-frutti—as well as trails of purple lobelia and white alyssum for color. A potted fig tree, a recent addition, reigns at the very top and is doing beautifully. This lush and fragrant garden within arm's reach of my back door is a great source of pleasure that gives me so much satisfaction I'll always want something like it, whether I move to the country or not."

—KAREN FRERICHS

Oregano Breadsticks

MAKES ABOUT 12 BREADSTICKS

Mark Miller, restaurateur (Coyote Cafe, Santa Fe, NM, and Las Vegas, NV; Red Sage, Washington DC) and author of numerous cookbooks, is a little hard to pin down as to one activity or place of residence. The ingredients and cooking style of the American Southwest imbue his artistic and practical endeavors, that is, when he's not thinking of cooking in Thailand, another place that has captured his imagination. In this recipe, he focuses on an uncomplicated way to feature an herb native to the landscape he adores. "Wild oregano, somewhat more pungent than the Italian or Greek variety, grows along the arroyos and washes of the semiarid high desert of the Southwest. It's an herb that exudes a particular aroma that reminds one of the high chaparral and the open range. Like many other wild herbs, wild oregano was traditionally used for teas and medicinal purposes by the Native Americans of Mexico and the Southwest, and was passed down through the early Hispanic culture to modern times. There are still shops in Santa Fe that carry such remedial dried herbs. When baking these breadsticks, make sure they thoroughly dry out and become crisp. If necessary, lower the oven heat and cook them a little longer. They are ideal with barbecued foods."

MARK MILLER (SANTA FE, NM)

½ cup warm, not hot, water
1 teaspoon active dry yeast
1 tablespoon olive oil
1½ cups all-purpose flour
1 teaspoon sugar
1½ teaspoons salt
2 tablespoons chopped fresh oregano leaves or 1 tablespoon dried
Extra flour, for kneading the dough

1. Pour the water into a large mixing bowl. Sprinkle the yeast over the water, add the oil, and without mixing, let sit for 1 minute.

2. Add the flour, sugar, and salt to the bowl. Mix with a dough hook or knead by hand until the mixture turns into an elastic dough.

3. Add the oregano and mix for 30 seconds more, until well blended. Cover loosely with a cloth and set aside in a warm place for 1 hour, until doubled in bulk.

4. Preheat the oven to 400°F.

5. Punch down the dough and transfer it to a well-floured surface. Divide into 12 equal pieces and, one by one, roll each piece between the palms of your hands into a pencil-thick length about 18 inches long. Set each on an ungreased baking sheet, 1 to 2 inches apart.

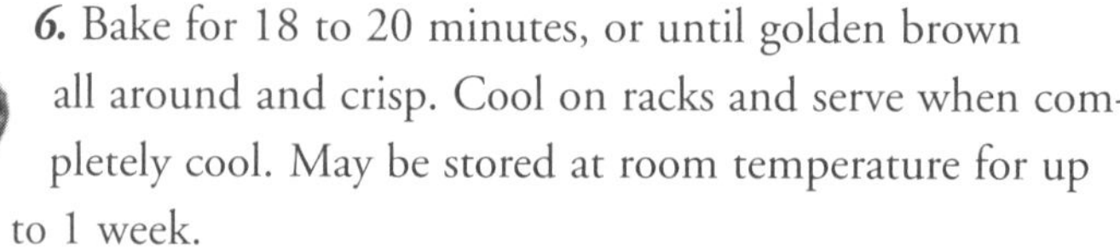

6. Bake for 18 to 20 minutes, or until golden brown all around and crisp. Cool on racks and serve when completely cool. May be stored at room temperature for up to 1 week.

Sage Cheese Crisps

MAKES ABOUT 30 CRISPS

Emelie Tolley, co-author of Herbs *and* Cooking with Herbs, *among many other books, likes to combine herbs and spices in a way that magically calls forth the best possibilities of a dish. For her specialty Moroccan dishes, she gathers a bagful of North African spices and mixes them into an exotic blend (see box below) to use as a rub for grilled lamb or other meats. Other times, in moments when simplifying is revivifying, she selects one seasoning ingredient, for instance, fresh sage leaves, and combines it with cheddar cheese in a crisp cracker that makes you wish you had a factory nearby to supply as much as you want. She suggests that for variation, you can omit the sage and instead roll the dough in coarsely cracked pepper or toasted sesame seeds before slicing and baking.*

EMELIE TOLLEY (BRIDGEHAMPTON, NY)

8 ounces sharp cheddar cheese, either white or orange, coarsely grated
1 cup (2 sticks) butter, at room temperature
1½ cups all-purpose flour
½ teaspoon salt
Dash of hot pepper sauce
3 tablespoons chopped fresh sage leaves

1. Place all the ingredients except the sage in a food processor. Blend until thoroughly mixed, then pulse in the sage.

2. Transfer the dough to the refrigerator; then chill until stiff and shape into two 7-inch-long rolls. Wrap the rolls in plastic wrap and chill again until firm enough to slice neatly, at least several hours or up to overnight. Or freeze the dough until ready to use.

3. Preheat the oven to 350°F.

Ras el Hanout

MAKES 1 TABLESPOON

What cook is not enamored of spice mixes? Herbes de Provence (page 180), Pickling Spices (page 316), Cajun Spice (page 189), curry powders (page 95) all trigger culinary creativity and open new seasoning horizons. Ras el hanout is another. It's a Moroccan blend you can almost smell as you read down the list of ingredients and remember or imagine the enticing aromas issuing from the spice vendors' stalls in a North African marketplace. To make ras el hanout, combine:

1 teaspoon ground cinnamon
½ teaspoon freshly ground black pepper
½ teaspoon freshly ground white pepper
½ teaspoon freshly grated nutmeg
¼ teaspoon ground cloves
¼ teaspoon ground cardamom

4. Cut the chilled dough rolls into ¼-inch-thick slices and place them on ungreased cookie sheets about ½ inch apart.

5. Bake for 15 minutes, or until the edges of the crisps are lightly browned. Remove and cool on racks. Serve or store in an airtight container for up to several weeks.

Lemon Balm Cookies

MAKES 2 TO 4 DOZEN COOKIES, DEPENDING ON THE SIZE

"Lemon balm is a symbol of sympathy and gentleness. It is an easy-to-grow perennial native to southern Europe. I use cuttings of lemon balm with my flowers, as its textured leaves are so pretty in bouquets and, when rubbed, give a delightful lemony scent. I also add sprigs to my sun tea, add it to potpourris," and make lemon balm cookies.

JULIENE BRAMER (GREENE, IA)

Sweet Melissa

Lemon balm, *Melissa officinalis,* is an attractive member of the mint family. It is called sweet both for its prettiness and for the blessing it provides all around the house and garden.

IN THE GARDEN, it aids plant propagation by being a strong attractor of bees. Hence, its botanical name, *Melissa,* from the Greek word for bee.

FOR MEDICINAL USE, a tea of lemon balm is reputed to relieve any number of ailments, from indigestion, flatulence, and nausea to various nervous conditions, including melancholia and insomnia. A rub of its fresh leaves is said to be a quick remedy for insect bites.

IN THE KITCHEN, its distinctly lemon-flavored leaves can be used much like, or in place of, lemon to flavor stuffings, fruit salads, beverages, and ice creams.

FOR DECORATING THE HOUSE, don't forget to add it to floral arrangements or place it in small vases to put round and about any ledge or sill that might "want" a bit of natural refreshing.

8 tablespoons (1 stick) butter, at room temperature
½ cup sugar
1 egg, lightly beaten
2 cups all-purpose flour
¼ cup lemon balm leaves, finely chopped

1. Cream together the butter and sugar until a little fluffy. Add the egg, flour, and lemon balm and mix until still slightly crumbly but firm enough to gather into a dough ball. Wrap the dough in plastic wrap and press all around to smooth. Refrigerate for at least 1 hour or up to overnight.

2. When ready to bake, preheat the oven to 350°F. Take the dough out of the refrigerator to come back to room temperature.

3. Divide the dough into 3 portions. One portion at a time, roll out the dough between 2 sheets of plastic wrap ⅛ to ¼ inch thick. Peel away the plastic wrap and cut the dough into whatever cookie shapes you like.

4. Transfer the cookie shapes to ungreased baking sheets and bake until golden around the edges and firm but not hard. Cool slightly. Serve or cool completely and store in an airtight container for up to 2 weeks.

Grandma Jean's Herb Cookies

MAKES ABOUT 5 DOZEN COOKIES

Don't be fooled by the homey name; these cookies are everything a cookie can be: The dough is simple to make and easy to roll and slice; it bakes up buttery, crisp, and sweet but not too sweet; and it has an exotic flavoring—a generous helping of chopped fresh herbs. The contributor offers a selection of herbs to choose from: lemon balm, mint, rosemary, or thyme are good first choices. Anise hyssop, lime geranium, or another of the culinary geraniums can also lend their own unusual and surprising taste and turn a traditional refrigerator cookie into a perfect accompaniment to any sorbet.

PAMELA SLIPKO (PLANO, TX)

⅓ cup chopped fresh herbs (see headnote)
1 teaspoon vanilla extract
1 cup (2 sticks) butter, at room temperature
⅔ cup sugar
1 large egg
2⅓ cups all-purpose flour
¼ teaspoon salt
Extra flour, for rolling out the dough

Modern Ways with Old Recipes: Refrigerator Cookie Options

Refrigerator cookies open new horizons for the organized cook who likes to divide the recipe into manageable steps. For instance:

SHORTEST:: Refrigerate the dough, then proceed with cutting and baking the cookies in a few hours.

FOR LONGER: Take your time and leave the well-wrapped dough logs in the refrigerator overnight, even for two days, then cut and bake. Be sure to allow time for the dough to come to room temperature before cutting so that the knife can press easily through the dough log.

FOR EVEN LONGER: Freeze the well-wrapped dough logs for up to 2 months. Before proceeding, defrost the logs. Then cut them into cookies, and bake as in the recipe.

1. Combine the herbs and vanilla in a small bowl and press with the back of a spoon to release the herb flavors and infuse the vanilla. Set aside.

2. Cream together the butter and sugar in a large bowl, beating until the mixture is light and fluffy. Add the egg and the herb mixture and beat well.

3. Gradually beat in the flour and salt, mixing well after each addition, until blended into a moist dough. Gather the dough into a ball, cover the bowl with plastic wrap, and refrigerate until firm, at least 1 hour or up to overnight.

4. When ready to bake, preheat the oven to 350°F. Remove the dough from the refrigerator to soften a bit.

5. Roll out the dough on a lightly floured surface until ⅛ inch thick. Cut into 2-inch rounds and place ½ inch apart, on ungreased baking sheets. Bake until lightly browned, 8 to 10 minutes.

6. Transfer the cookies to a wire rack to cool. Use when cool or store in an airtight container for up to 2 weeks.

Bakers' Magic with Cookie Swirls

In case you've ever wondered how those neat flat disks of cookies got swirled into multicolored rolls or pinwheels, the trick is now revealed. It's easy to duplicate. Here's the technique, plus some suggestions for how to have fun with it.

Make the dough for herb cookies and divide it into two or three parts. Roll out each part ⅛ inch thick.

Spread any filling you choose—jam, fruit purée, chocolate, ground nuts, fresh herbs softened in a little butter—across the dough. With floured fingers, roll each piece of dough into a cylinder about 2 inches in diameter. Wrap in plastic wrap and refrigerate.

When ready to bake, unwrap the rolls and slice into ¼-inch-thick rounds. Place flat side down and bake. The cookies will be swirled from the center to the edges, like pinwheels.

Best-Ever Sugar Cookies with Homemade Raspberry Jam Centers

Makes about 30 cookies

"In the Wisconsin of my childhood, wild raspberries ripened in August. They were our biggest berry crop of the year, although areas of high yield shifted with returning forest growth. There were famous years for the old pasture, for the meadow on the way to the lake, and so on. On one memorable occasion, my father spotted a glorious raspberry patch while fishing near a clearing Grandma remembered from logging days. Off went about eight of us to pick, empty lard cans with wire handles strung through our belts. The sound

of the plump fruit as it drummed the empty buckets soon stilled; it was replaced with approving exclamations as the fruit levels rapidly rose. Grandma Follstad was a master of all kinds of cookies, but everyone's favorites were the fine, thin sugar cookies with a wild raspberry jam–filled pocket at the center. These are they."

ROBERT LAMBERT (LARKSPUR, CA, VIA WI)

⅔ cup Raspberry Jam (recipe follows)
1 cup (2 sticks) butter, at room temperature
1½ cups sugar
1 large egg
1 teaspoon vanilla extract
3 cups all-purpose flour
½ teaspoon baking soda
½ teaspoon salt
Extra flour, for rolling out the dough
Extra sugar, for sprinkling over the cookies

1. Prepare the jam and set aside 1 jar to cool.

2. Combine the butter and sugar in a large bowl and beat until light and fluffy. Beat in the egg and vanilla.

3. Sift the flour, baking soda, and salt into the bowl. Beat until the mixture comes together into a dough that pulls away from the sides of the bowl. Turn the dough onto a lightly floured surface, pat it out even, and cut in half.

4. One half at a time, roll out the dough into a 16-inch square. With a cookie cutter or sharp knife, cut rounds out of the dough, about 30 from each half.

5. Place about 1 teaspoon of the jam in the center of half the rounds. Moisten the dough around the jam on each round and top with another round. Gently press the top and bottom rounds together to seal them and enclose without pressing into the center. Place the cookies on ungreased baking sheets and set aside while heating the oven.

6. Preheat the oven to 350°F.

7. Sprinkle the cookies with sugar and bake just until they begin to turn golden around the edges, 10 to 12 minutes. Transfer to a rack and cool enough to handle. Serve right away or store in an airtight container for up to 1 month.

Raspberry Jam

Makes about 6 half-pints

5 cups fresh raspberries

5 cups sugar

1. Inspect the raspberries and discard any that are beginning to mold. Gently rinse away any debris. Place the berries in a large, heavy pot or jelly kettle and stir them with a wooden spoon to break them up a bit and release their juices.

2. Add the sugar and stir well. Bring to a full boil over high heat, stirring from time to time, then reduce the heat to medium-high. Continue to stir and boil for 3 to 5 minutes, or until the mixture dribbles, not runs, off a spoon.

3. Remove from the heat and allow the boiling to subside. Skim off any foam and, while still hot, ladle into jars prepared to be processed in a hot-water bath for 10 minutes (see page 315). Or cool completely and store in the refrigerator for up to several months.

Notes

• Though frozen berries can be used for many purposes, they will not work here; fresh raspberries are essential for this recipe.

• Don't worry too much about the "dribble or run" guideline in Step 2. The timing is precise for turning out a jam with a consistency that works for filling sugar cookies or smoothing over toast, "just barely thick enough to stand in the jar, not so firm that it's carvable like Jell-O."

Biscotti

Makes 24 to 36 cookies

It is somewhat remarkable to note that in this wildly popular, originally Italian, dipping cookie, the pine nuts and anise seed are natives of both Europe and America. Biscotti, meaning twice-baked to describe the way they're made, have become one of the fanciest cookies in town. They store well in airtight containers; in fact, flavors mature over time.

~ JACQUELINE CASCIOLA (BRADENTON, FL)

1 cup (2 sticks) butter, softened
1 cup sugar
3 large eggs
2 teaspoons vanilla extract
3 cups all-purpose flour
1½ teaspoons baking powder
3 tablespoons anise seeds
¾ cup pine nuts, toasted (see page 135)
Flour, for shaping the dough

1. Preheat the oven to 325°F.

2. Mix together the butter and sugar in a large bowl. Add the eggs, one at a time, mixing thoroughly after each. Stir in the vanilla.

3. In a small bowl, stir together the flour and baking powder until well blended. Gradually add to the butter mixture. Add the anise seeds and pine nuts, stirring until they are well distributed throughout the dough.

4. Divide the dough into 3 equal parts. On a floured surface and with floured hands, shape each into a log about 3 inches in diameter and 10 to 12 inches long. Place the logs on ungreased baking sheets, leaving 2 to 3 inches between them, and bake for 25 to 30 minutes, or until golden brown. Remove and cool thoroughly, at least 20 minutes.

5. Cut the logs on the diagonal into ½- to ¾-inch-thick slices. Place the slices on the baking sheets and bake 5 to 8 minutes per side, until dry and lightly toasted. Remove and cool. Use right away or store in airtight containers for up to several months.

Biscotti: A Cookie That Travels from Cradle to Grave

Traditionally served with red wine for dipping, or espresso or liqueur for sipping alongside, biscotti also serve, like mandelbrot or melba toast, as baby teethers or milk toast. Pulverized, they enhance cakes or pie crusts. However you would like to serve or use them, they are amenable to a wide variety of flavorings. Here are some suggestions for ways to have fun with biscotti.

IN THE BATTER

Nuts: Almonds or hazelnuts (filberts) in place of the pine nuts.

Seeds: Fennel seed or peppercorns in place of the anise seed.

Herbs: In addition to the other ingredients, lavender flowers or fresh thyme (especially if serving with red wine).

Fruit: In addition to the other ingredients, zest of lemon or orange; candied lemon, orange, citron, or angelica; dried cranberries, cherries, currants, or golden raisins.

Extracts: Almond or anise extract in place of the vanilla.

Liquid: In addition to the other ingredients a splash of lemon juice, brandy, anisette, or espresso.

OUTSIDE

Coat one side or dip one end of each biscotti into chocolate.

Everyone's Favorite Lemon Shortbread Squares

MAKES ABOUT 3 DOZEN 1½-INCH SQUARES

"When I came to California from New England, I was thrilled to have citrus trees that produced fruit all year. I began experimenting with recipes that used both juice and zest and could be frozen. These lemon squares, a version of a sweet popular on Christmas dessert tables back East, were devised from a mixture of several old recipes." Less sweet and more lemony than some and with a crust more like a cookie than a cake, the lemon squares are perfect as they come. For a bonus, the shortbread pastry makes a fine cookie on its own.

SYLVIA WALLACE (SANTEE, CA)

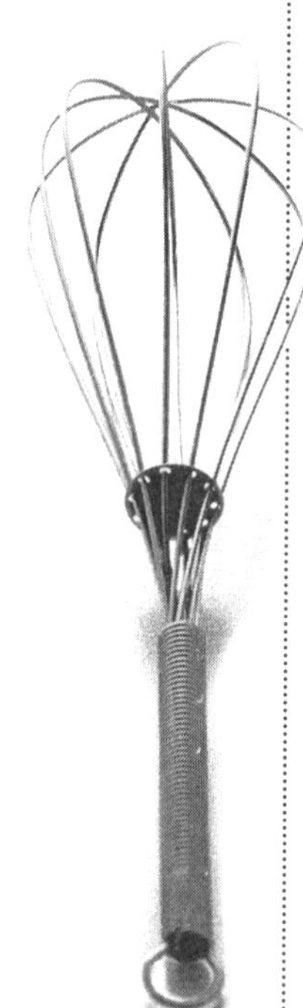

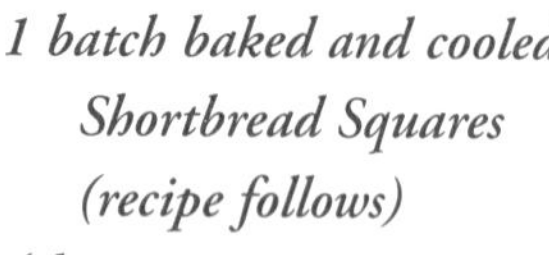

1 batch baked and cooled Shortbread Squares (recipe follows)
4 large eggs
2 cups granulated sugar
¼ cup all-purpose flour
1 teaspoon baking powder
1 tablespoon finely chopped lemon zest
½ cup fresh lemon juice
Confectioners' sugar, for dusting the tops of the squares

1. Preheat the oven to 350°F.

2. Prepare the shortbread and set aside to cool.

3. Crack the eggs into a large bowl and beat well. Add the sugar, flour, baking powder, lemon zest and juice and whisk to mix. Pour over the shortbread, spreading evenly, and bake until golden on top, 20 to 25 minutes. Remove and cool in the pan.

4. When cool, sift confectioners' sugar over the top, cut into squares, and serve.

Shortbread Squares

MAKES ABOUT 3 DOZEN 1½-INCH SHORTBREAD SQUARES

2 cups sifted all-purpose flour
½ cup sugar
1 cup (2 sticks) butter, at room temperature

1. Preheat the oven to 350°F.

2. Combine the flour and sugar in a large bowl. Cut the butter into the bowl and mix with your fingers or a pastry blender until the mixture forms a finely crumbed dough.

3. Spread the dough on an ungreased 15 by 10-inch jelly-roll pan, pressing and patting it out until it evenly covers the pan. If using for lemon squares, bake until lightly browned, 15 to 20 minutes. If using for shortbread, continue baking until the center is cooked through and the bottom is golden, about 5 minutes longer. Remove and set aside to cool.

4. If using for lemon squares, continue with the recipe. If using for shortbread, cut into squares the size you'd like. As shortbread, the squares can be used as soon as cool or stored in an airtight container for up to 1 week.

"Should I,
after tea
and cakes
and ices,
Have the
strength to
force the
moment to
its crisis?"

—T. S. Eliot,
"The Love Song of
J. Alfred Prufrock"

Papaya Tea Bread

MAKES TWO 8 BY 4-INCH LOAVES

"Our garden is an orchard and farm designed with the help of Clifton Dodge, Rachel Kattlove, their helpers, and the Smith & Hawken tools they insisted on using to bring my dream to reality. Today, it's not only a vision of loveliness but a learning tool for guests and gardening enthusiasts alike. We grow coffee trees, guava, citrus, inga, passion fruit, sweet potato, pineapple, pepino, loquat, kumquat, mango, macadamias, roses, native Hawaiian medicinal and herb plants, flowers, and much more, including, of course, papayas to make this 'onolicius' bread."

~ SUSAN KAUAI, KULA VIEW BED AND BREAKFAST FARM (KULA, HI)

2 medium very ripe papayas (2 pounds)
¾ cup sugar
8 tablespoons (1 stick) butter or margarine, at room temperature
2 large eggs
1½ cups all-purpose flour
1 teaspoon baking soda
¼ teaspoon baking powder
½ teaspoon salt
½ teaspoon ground cinnamon
½ teaspoon ground allspice
½ teaspoon ground ginger
½ cup raisins
¼ cup chopped walnuts

1. Preheat the oven to 325°F. Lightly grease two 8 by 4- inch loaf pans.

2. Cut the papayas in half and remove the seeds. Scoop the pulp into a bowl and mash it with a fork. Set aside.

3. Place the sugar and butter in a large mixing bowl and beat until light and fluffy. Add the eggs and beat to mix well. Add the papaya and mix again.

4. Sift the flour, baking soda, baking powder, salt, cinnamon, allspice, and ginger into the bowl. Beat until smooth. Stir in the raisins and walnuts.

5. Pour the mixture into the prepared loaf pans and bake until golden on top and a knife inserted in the center comes out clean, about 50 minutes. Remove and cool until firm to the touch, 1 to 2 hours. Unmold, slice, and serve. Will keep wrapped in plastic for up to 1 week.

Tomato Spice Tea Bread

MAKES ONE 9 BY 5-INCH LOAF

The spice here refers not to chili but to a generous helping of cinnamon in the batter. The tomato in the title does refer to tomatoes, puréed and used as the liquid element in the batter. The tomatoes also color the bread an unexpected and quite appealing reddish brown. As the contributor notes, "It's a different way to deal with an abundance of tomatoes. Toasted and buttered, it's a wonderful breakfast bread; sliced and served plain, it's excellent for afternoon tea."

MARTHA SCOTT (FORT SCOTT, KS)

2 cups all-purpose flour
1 tablespoon baking powder
½ teaspoon salt
1 teaspoon ground cinnamon
⅓ cup vegetable oil
½ cup granulated sugar
½ cup (packed) dark brown sugar
2 large eggs
1 pound tomatoes, peeled, seeded, and puréed to make 1 cup
¼ cup sliced unblanched almonds

1. Preheat the oven to 350°F. Butter and flour a 9 by 5-inch loaf pan.

2. Combine the flour, baking powder, salt, and cinnamon in a bowl, mix well, and set aside.

3. Combine the oil, granulated sugar, brown sugar, and eggs in a large bowl and beat with an electric mixer until fluffy, about 3 minutes. Beat in the puréed tomato. Gradually add the flour mixture, blending well after each addition, to make a wet batter.

4. Pour the batter into the loaf pan, sprinkle the almonds over the top, and bake for 50 to 60 minutes, or until a knife inserted in the center comes out clean. Transfer the pan to a rack to cool for 5 minutes, then remove the bread from the pan and continue to cool it on the rack until room temperature.

5. The bread may be sliced and served right away or wrapped in plastic and stored at room temperature for up to 3 days, in the refrigerator for up to 1 week.

TOOLS *of the* TRADE

Mixing Devices for Quick Breads

As implied by their description, quick breads should be quick, especially in the making. That means, first, no waiting time required for the yeast to rise. Second, they should be mixed easily, no extra time spent kneading. The quick breads in this section—papaya, tomato spice, rose geranium, apple harvest, and black walnut—meet the first requirement in their recipe ingredients. For the second, the mechanics of the matter, you can use:

A HAND-HELD ELECTRIC MIXER: This is the quickest and easiest mixing device for quick breads. You may need to stand and hold it a few minutes to cream the butter and sugar, but it does a fine job and is a whiz to clean and store away.

A STURDY WIRE WHISK AND AN EVEN STURDIER ARM: This combination also does a fine job. Remember to hold your arm high and bent and have the bowl on a counter at about waist level so your wrist can turn without stress on the elbow. You can also sit and hold the bowl between your knees to gain the same position. With this setup, expect to spend a bit more time to get to the fluffy stage of creaming butter and sugar.

Rose Geranium Tea Cake

MAKES TWO 9 BY 5-INCH LOAVES

This is a lovely, classic pound cake, even textured and subtly flavored with just the right amount of flowery herb. "The rose geranium leaves can be substituted with any sweet herb leaves. I have used pineapple sage, orange mint, and lemon verbena. I have also substituted calendula petals and called it Marigold Cake. You may also want to try lemongrass, melissa (lemon balm), pineapple mint, spearmint, or lemon thyme. Just make sure you have one to two tablespoons of the chopped herb." One thing is certain, the contributor has a great good time with her pound cake recipe and feels quite free to innovate with dif-

ferent herbs according to what is available and the whim of the day. Baking the cake in two loaf pans works well to ensure the loaves come out cooked through but still moist on the outside. If you'd like a larger cake, use a tube or bundt pan.

LELA KHAN (CARROLLTON, TX)

1 cup (2 sticks) butter, at room temperature
2 cups sugar
1 large egg
1 cup milk
3 cups all-purpose flour
2 teaspoons baking powder
1 teaspoon salt
1½ tablespoons rose geranium leaves, finely chopped (see box on this page)

1. Preheat the oven to 350°F. Lightly grease two 9 by 5-inch loaf pans.

2. Cream together the butter and sugar in a large bowl. Add the egg and milk and beat well. Add the flour, baking powder, and salt and beat well. Stir in the rose geranium leaves.

3. Spoon the mixture into the loaf pans, dividing evenly. Bake for 55 to 60 minutes, or until a knife inserted in the center comes out clean.

4. Remove, cool, and serve at room temperature. Will keep, wrapped in plastic wrap, stored at room temperature for up to 3 days.

About Culinary Geraniums

Geraniums, the gaily-colored flowers of bed borders, rock gardens, and window boxes from Mexico to Austria, also have a place in the kitchen garden. In mild-winter climates, their nearly evergreen leaves provide verdance for most of the year. Their attractive flowers bloom from early summer to fall. Cut and placed in small vases, the leaves and flowers provide long-lasting mini bouquets to scent the bathroom, decorate the desk, or stand ready on the kitchen windowsill, there for plucking to perfume cakes, biscuits, puddings, and sweet sauces. For kitchen use, choosing among them is a bit like being in a 30-flavor ice cream shop. What shall it be today? Rose, lemon, lime, nutmeg, peppermint . . .

Black Walnut Coffee Cake

MAKES ONE 13 BY 9-INCH CAKE

"The first fall my husband and I were retired and moved into our summer home, I eagerly awaited the time for the black walnuts from our three trees to conveniently fall to the ground so I could gather them. But, day after day, all I found were empty nutshells. One morning I took my coffee out to the deck and, looking toward the walnut trees, saw a squirrel climb up and knock down a nut. He scurried down the tree, found the nut,

quickly hid it, and started over again. After watching him a few minutes, I decided he had enough of the nuts and I should have the rest. As he knocked one down, I ran and picked it before he could get down the tree. Not finding the nut on the ground, he ran back up the tree to knock down another. By the time he gave up, I had enough nuts for my cake. However, I think the squirrel had the last laugh. Do you know how hard it is to open the shells of black walnuts? This recipe is one passed on from my husband's family. If you can't find black walnuts, you can use regular English walnuts." This cake has a dense texture with a fine crumb and is rich enough to serve on its own. For a more elaborate presentation, you could accompany it with a bowl of freshly sliced peaches or one of crème fraîche.

ELAINE BARTLETT (BARNSTABLE, MA)

1 cup (2 sticks) butter
¼ teaspoon salt
2 cups sugar
4 large eggs
3 cups sifted all-purpose flour
1 cup buttermilk
¼ teaspoon baking soda
1 teaspoon vanilla extract
1 teaspoon lemon extract
1 cup walnuts, chopped small but not fine

1. Preheat the oven to 300°F. Lightly grease a 13 by 9-inch baking dish.

2. Cream together the butter, salt, and sugar in a large bowl. Add the eggs, one at a time, beating well after each.

3. Add the flour alternately with the buttermilk in 3 batches. Before adding the last part of the buttermilk, stir the baking soda into it and add them together. Stir in the vanilla and lemon extracts, then the walnuts.

4. Pour into the baking dish and bake for 60 minutes, or until a knife inserted in the middle comes out clean. Remove and cool for 10 minutes, then remove from the pan. Slice and serve.

The Black Walnut from Shore to Shining Shore

The black walnut is an American nut tree, native in both West and East. Not surprisingly, it takes on a somewhat different form in each place. In the West, where it grows along the Pacific seaboard from Mexico to northern California and inland to Arizona, it is a large shrub or small tree, from 30 feet to 80 feet or so. In the East, where it ranges from Vermont to Illinois, it attains a more grandiose stature with a height of 100 feet or more. There, it provides a canopy for humans to rest under and take shade in the heat of summer; high branches for birds to nest; plenty of produce for squirrels and humans alike; and eventually, probably its most treasured offering, wood for fine furnishings.

The black walnut is not commercially grown. For those who have a tree, or the favor of a friend who does, its nuts are prized for their extra richness, which exceeds that of the English walnut, a native of Asia and Europe, now widely grown in California. As the contributor notes, however, the meat of the black walnut is hard to get to; the squirrels may help bring the nuts to the ground; after that, it's you and your hammer to the task.

Apple Harvest Coffee Cake

MAKES ONE 13 BY 9-INCH CAKE

Flavors reminiscent of apple pie but in an easily sliceable cake invite you to take a break in the day, perhaps sit down and gossip awhile over a cup of coffee, perhaps put up your feet and ponder what you'll do with the rest of those apples waiting their turn in the kitchen.

JENNIE FOX (ORCHARD LAKE, MI)

8 tablespoons (1 stick) butter, at room temperature
1½ cups sugar
3 large eggs
2 cups all-purpose flour
2 teaspoons baking powder
¼ teaspoon salt
1 teaspoon ground cinnamon
¼ teaspoon ground nutmeg
2 tablespoons brandy
1 teaspoon vanilla extract
½ cup walnuts, toasted and coarsely chopped *(see page 135)*
4 large soft-pulp baking apples, such as Gravenstein or Jonathan, peeled, cored, and chopped into ¼- to ½-inch pieces (about 1½ pounds)
1 teaspoon ground cinnamon mixed with 2 teaspoons sugar, to sprinkle over the top of the cake
2 cups Crème Fraîche (optional, see box below)

1. Preheat the oven to 350°F. Lightly grease a 13 by 9-inch baking dish.

2. Cream the butter and sugar together in a large bowl until almost smooth. Add the eggs and continue beating until the mixture is light and fluffy.

3. Sift in the flour, baking powder, salt, cinnamon, and nutmeg and beat until blended. Stir in the brandy, vanilla, walnuts, and apples.

4. Spoon the batter into the baking dish and bake for 50 to 60 minutes, or until a knife inserted in the middle of the cake comes out clean.

Crème Fraîche

MAKES 3 CUPS

Crème fraîche straddles the fence between sour cream and heavy whipping cream. It is used in many cuisines in which a mildly fermented thickened cream is appreciated either as an ingredient for a dish or as a garnish. There's no mystery to it. You can make it at home in the kitchen in a day or day and a half.

Stir together 3 cups heavy (whipping) cream and 1 tablespoon buttermilk in a glass jar or heavy plastic container. Cover with plastic wrap and let stand at room temperature until slightly thickened and mildly tart, 24 to 36 hours. Use right away or store in the refrigerator for up to 1 week. If the crème fraîche turns out a bit thicker than you want for a particular recipe, thin it with a little fresh cream.

5. Remove from the oven and cool for 10 minutes. Invert the pan and gently pry the cake onto a large platter. While it is still warm, sprinkle the cinnamon-and-sugar mixture over the top of the cake. Slice and serve right away or at room temperature. Accompany with a bowl of crème fraîche, if desired.

Dill-Parmesan Popovers

MAKES 12 POPOVERS

Diana Murphy is editor of Country Living Gardener *magazine and author of* Country Living Picnics and Porch Suppers. *She loves to cook with fresh herbs from her garden. As a favorite example she offers these dill-infused popovers, "crunchy on the outside and moist in the middle," and suggests serving them hot from the oven with soups, salads, or your favorite Sunday roast. Hot-from-the-oven is a good tip: popovers do not wait. Their tenderness is of the moment; after that, they become rubbery. Catching them just right, you'll be eternally seduced by their almost vaporous texture that somehow also transports a full-blown taste. As you mix together the ingredients, don't be daunted when the batter becomes thinner and thinner, especially with the final addition of water.*

DIANA MURPHY (NEW YORK, NY)

1 cup all-purpose flour
½ teaspoon salt
¼ teaspoon black pepper
1 tablespoon chopped fresh dill
¼ cup grated Parmesan cheese
⅔ cup milk
2 large eggs, beaten
2 tablespoons butter

1. Preheat the oven to 425°F.

2. Combine the flour, salt, pepper, dill, and cheese in a bowl. Beat in the milk, then the eggs, and finally ½ cup water, mixing until large bubbles form.

3. Cut the butter into 12 pieces and place one piece in each cup of a 12-well muffin pan. Place the pan in the oven for 1 minute, just until the butter melts. Remove the pan from the oven, ladle the batter into the wells, filling them two-thirds full, and return the pan to the oven. Bake for 15 minutes, then turn the oven temperature down to 375°F.

4. Continue baking for 20 minutes more, or until the popovers

MUFFIN PANS
Muffin pans come in various sizes. Standard tins have either six or twelve cups, called wells, which hold one-half or one-third of batter. For popovers, the wells should be half-cup size because the batter rises high as it cooks and in shallower cups you will have spillover that might still be tasty, fun to call oven art, but a big mess to clean up.

are golden brown all across the top and beginning to pop over their cups. Remove, lift out the popovers, and serve right away.

Note: The batter can be refrigerated after Step 2 for up to several hours. Allow to come to room temperature again and whisk well before proceeding with the recipe.

Cousin Gert's Herbed Refrigerator Rolls

MAKES ABOUT 3 DOZEN ROLLS

In the Fifties, when baking ingredients had once again become available, fresh rolls accompanied by a bowl of iced butter were part of the fine dining experience. These rolls are in that style, which still serves well when you'd like to greet your guests with a welcoming basket of warm buns. A special note for those on a low-sodium diet: the rolls are salt-free.

JEFF STELMACH (SAN FRANCISCO, CA)

1 cup lukewarm water
1 package active dry yeast
2 large eggs
8 tablespoons (1 stick) butter, melted
4 cups all-purpose flour
⅓ to ½ cup sugar
1½ to 2 tablespoons finely chopped fresh herbs, such as fennel, rosemary, basil, oregano

1. Pour the water into a large bowl and sprinkle the yeast over the top. Set aside for 15 minutes, or until bubbly.

2. Whisk together the eggs and butter and set aside. In a separate bowl, mix together the flour, sugar, and herbs and set aside.

3. Stirring all the while, alternately add some of the flour mixture and then some of the egg mixture to the dissolved yeast until you have a wet dough. Cover and let stand in the refrigerator until well chilled, at least several hours or up to overnight.

4. When thoroughly chilled, divide the dough into 4 parts. Roll or press out each part ½ inch thick and cut into any shape desired, using a biscuit cutter to cut out rounds, for example, or a knife to cut out triangles to bend into crescents.

5. Place the dough shapes on ungreased baking sheets, cover with a cloth, and set aside in a warm place to rise until doubled in bulk. 1½ to 2 hours.

6. Toward the end of the rising period, preheat the oven to 350°F.

7. Bake until golden on top and cooked through, about 15 minutes. Serve right away, while still warm.

Sage-Onion Focaccia

MAKES ONE 12-INCH FOCACCIA

"My style of cooking is mainly vegetarian and I love to use seasonal produce to inspire me. Although our growing season is relatively short here on the Maine coast, I can purchase fresh from some of the local farms that manage to have goods to market as early as mid-May. These keep me supplied until my own garden starts to yield. With the fresh young sage leaves and summer onions, picnics and focaccia come to mind."

KAREN TURNER (SOUTH PORTLAND, ME)

STORING FOCACCIA

Focaccia may be stored overnight wrapped in plastic wrap. After that, it is best to store it in the freezer for up to several days and reheat before serving.

- *1 cup warm water*
- *1 teaspoon (about 1½ packages) active dry yeast*
- *2 teaspoons sugar*
- *2 tablespoons olive oil*
- *2 teaspoons salt*
- *1 medium onion, finely chopped*
- *2 tablespoons chopped fresh sage leaves*
- *⅓ cup grated Parmesan cheese*
- *1 cup semolina flour*
- *2½ cups all-purpose flour*
- *Extra olive oil, for coating the rising dough, greasing the baking pan, and brushing the focaccia*
- *Extra flour, for rolling out the focaccia*
- *Cornmeal, for dusting the baking pan*

1. Combine the water, yeast, and sugar in a large bowl. Set aside for 5 minutes, until bubbly.

2. Add the oil, salt, onion, sage, Parmesan, semolina flour, and ½ cup of the all-purpose flour to the bowl. Mix until well blended but still wet, about 3 minutes.

Focaccia Plain and Fancy

With an inviting round of focaccia dough patted out, ready to bake, and shining its dimpled face at you, you may be drawn to focaccia fancies. For instance, before baking, you could tuck into each dimple:

- a pitted black olive
- a cherry tomato half
- a pinch of lemon zest, parsley, and garlic, finely chopped and mixed together
- a pinch of finely chopped sun-dried tomato tossed with fresh basil
- an almond
- a pinch of chopped anchovy fillet mixed with capers and oregano
- a walnut half from the Rosemary-Roasted Walnuts (page 3)
- a strawberry from the Strawberry Spoon Sauce (page 439)

3. Gradually add the remaining all-purpose flour and beat until the mixture gathers into a dough ball. Place the ball on a floured board and knead for 5 minutes, adding more flour to keep from sticking. Or use the dough hook of an electric mixer and knead for 2 to 3 minutes, or until the dough is smooth and elastic.

4. Coat the dough ball with a little olive oil and return it to the bowl. Cover and let rise in a warm place until doubled in bulk, 1½ to 2½ hours.

5. Lightly grease a 12 by 12-inch or larger sheet pan or pizza pan. Sprinkle a light coating of cornmeal over the pan.

6. Transfer the dough to a floured surface and roll it out into a disc 10 to 12 inches in diameter and ½ inch thick. Place the disc on the pan and, with your fingertips, dimple it deeply. Cover and set aside to rise again for 30 minutes.

7. Preheat the oven to 400°F.

8. Bake for 10 minutes, spraying the oven with water 3 times to create steam. Continue baking undisturbed for 10 to 15 minutes more, or until golden around the edges. Remove and cool to room temperature, then slice and serve.

Wheat Germ: Why, Why Not?

Wheat germ, the embryo of the wheat berry, is separated out when the wheat flour is refined to make white flour. It is not, however, merely a by-product of the refining process. Wheat germ is one of the few complete, not animal-based sources of protein. (Soybeans are another.) If you can get past the too-healthy-for-me image—wheat in all its aspects is, after all, the staff of life—you might find it also tastes good. Included in doughs and batters for baking, it improves flavor as well as nutritional value. Sprinkled on yogurt, cereal, salads, or into orange juice, it adds a pleasing grassy taste to the dish.

Carrot Bread

MAKES ONE 9 BY 5-INCH LOAF

"I love to bake yeast breads. Not only do they make the house smell good, but the feeling of live dough as it permeates the premises is very satisfying. One year when I was invited to a Halloween dinner, once again the bread supplier for this group, I decided to make an orange bread. Carrots, one of the most orange vegetables, were in my garden pots and so I dug up a few and coupled them with orange juice for extra liquid and orange-tinted sweetness. One of my favorite spices is cardamom, a flavor that blends easily with citrus. Eventually the carrot bread became one of my most requested recipes."

NATALIE SPIEGAL (PORT ANGELES, WA)

1 package active dry yeast
½ cup fresh orange juice, warmed (see Note below)
1 tablespoon peanut or other vegetable oil
1 cup all-purpose flour
2 tablespoons honey
1 teaspoon ground cardamom
1 teaspon salt
2 large eggs, well beaten
1 cup coarsely grated carrot
2 cups wheat germ (see box on page 386)
Extra flour, for kneading the dough

1. Sprinkle the yeast over the orange juice in a large bowl. Let rest until bubbly, about 15 minutes. Lightly grease a 9 by 5-inch loaf pan.

2. Add the oil, flour, honey, cardamom, and salt and beat until smooth. Add the eggs, carrot, and wheat germ and beat to a smooth but still wet dough.

3. In the bowl or on a lightly floured surface, knead the dough with floured hands for 5 minutes, or until it gathers easily into a nonsticky ball.

4. Transfer the dough to the loaf pan and pat to fill the pan in a loaf shape. Cover and set aside in a warm place until risen to the top of the pan, 1 to 1½ hours.

5. Preheat the oven to 200°F.

6. Place the loaf in the oven and bake for 20 minutes. Increase the oven heat to 250°F. and continue baking for 15 minutes more. Raise the oven heat once again, this time to 350°F., and continue baking for 20 to 25 minutes, or until the bread pulls away from the sides of the pan and a knife inserted in the center comes out clean. Transfer the pan to a rack and let rest for 10 minutes.

7. Remove the loaf from the pan. Place the loaf back on the rack, to cool until set enough to slice.

8. Slice and serve while still warm or wrap the loaf in foil and store at room temperature until ready to serve. It will keep in the foil at room temperature for up to 2 days.

Note: Warm orange juice is unusual. Here it's to replace the warm water that usually is the medium for proofing the yeast, and so it should be a little warmer than room temperature. A few seconds in the microwave will do the trick.

Carrots from Pillar to Post and into the Pan

"Since we live on a heavily wooded property right on the Straits of San Juan de Fuca, my vegetable gardening is limited to species that can be grown in pots so they can easily be moved several times a day to follow the path of the sun and resist the wind. I've found that carrots and potatoes do well grown this way. As long as we are willing to move the pots daily, sometimes twice a day, they yield provender for my kitchen, especially for one of my favorite breads." Those are the words of a dedicated gardener cook who, for the love of fresh food, will attend to growing despite the burdens it imposes in order to have fresh harvest for the kitchen.

—NATALIE SPIEGAL

Russian Cheese-Filled Skillet Bread

MAKES TWO 8-INCH ROUND LOAVES

"The crisp flavor of fresh chives contrasted with the tang of blue cheese is a real palate pleaser." It's also a cook's delight to have a savory quick bread—a little resting time but no rising necessary—that can be cooked on the stovetop. "Serve as an accompaniment for soup or salad," or cut into thin slices and have for breakfast or tea.

BRENDA JOHNSTON (NEWBURYPORT, MA)

"The garden, then, is a finite place in which a gardener (or several gardeners) has created, working with or against nature, a plot whose [sic] intention is to provide pleasure; possibly in the form of beauty, possibly in the form of cabbages—and possibly beautiful cabbages. And nature? Nature is what wins in the end."

—Abby Adams, *The Gardener's Gripe Book*

3 tablespoons vegetable oil
1¾ cups all-purpose flour
1 tablespoon cornstarch
¾ teaspoon baking soda
¼ teaspoon salt
2 tablespoons chopped fresh chives
¾ cup plain yogurt
1 egg, beaten
5 ounces feta cheese
3 ounces blue cheese, such as Roquefort, Cambozola, or Danish blue
½ teaspoon cracked black peppercorns
Extra flour, for forming the loaves

1. In a large bowl, blend together the oil and 3 tablespoons of the flour until smooth. Add the cornstarch, baking soda, salt, chives, yogurt, and remaining flour. Mix to blend well, cover, and set aside to rest for 1 hour.

2. While the dough rests, mix together the egg, feta, blue cheese, and peppercorns. Divide into 2 balls and set aside.

3. When the dough is ready, divide it in half. With floured hands, form one half into a loose ball and press one cheese ball into the center. Fold together the dough to enclose the cheese, pinching the edges of the dough to seal.

4. Place the cheese-filled dough ball on a floured surface. With your hands, flatten the ball into an 8-inch round loaf. Set aside and continue with the second dough ball.

5. Lightly grease a large heavy skillet and warm it over medium heat. Place one of the loaves in the skillet, partially cover, and cook over medium-low heat, turning once every 5 to 8 minutes, for 30 to 40 minutes, or until browned on both sides and a knife inserted in the center comes out clean. Remove and continue with the second loaf. Serve warm or at room temperature.

Note: Watch the skillet closely and adjust the heat often to avoid scorching.

Cabbage-Beef Buns

MAKES 16 BUNS

These are fun buns. The buns alone, not stuffed, are fine. The filling can travel to pirogis, empanadas, or almost any other hand pie you'd like to have.

~ OTTIE JOHNSON (CROSBY, ND)

¼ cup warm water
1 package active dry yeast
1 cup milk
2 tablespoons solid vegetable shortening
2 tablespoons sugar
1 large egg, beaten
3½ cups all-purpose flour
¾ teaspoon salt
4 cups Cabbage-Beef Filling (recipe follows)

1. Pour the warm water into a large mixing bowl and sprinkle the yeast over the top. Set aside for 15 minutes, until bubbly.

2. Combine the milk, shortening, and sugar in a small saucepan. Heat until beginning to bubble around the edges but not yet boiling. Remove from the heat and set aside to cool to room temperature.

3. Combine the flour and salt. Stir the egg into the yeast. Add the flour mixture alternately with the milk mixture, incorporating well after each addition, until you have a stiff but sticky dough. Knead the dough in the bowl by hand or by machine (see right) for 15 turns, incorporating any flour remaining on the bottom or clinging around the edges, until somewhat smooth and no longer sticky. Cover the bowl with a cloth and set aside in a warm place until doubled in bulk, 1½ to 2½ hours.

4. Meanwhile, make the filling.

5. When ready to bake, preheat the oven to 400°F. Lightly grease a baking sheet.

6. Divide the dough into 16 portions. One at a time, press or roll a portion into a square or round about ⅛ inch thick and 5 inches across. Place 2 heaping tablespoons of the cabbage filling in the middle of the dough. Fold over the dough edge to edge to enclose the filling in whatever shape seems easiest. Pinch the edges together to seal, transfer to the baking sheet, and continue until all the buns are filled. If necessary, use another baking sheet so the buns don't touch each other.

7. Bake for 14 to 16 minutes, or until golden all around. Serve right away or at room temperature.

THE MECHANICAL POSSIBILITIES OF DOUGH MAKING

For this and other stiff doughs that need kneading, an electric mixer or wooden spoon works well for the first few additions of flour. After that, when the dough becomes too stiff to mix, it's easiest to finish incorporating the flour with your hands before kneading the dough. Or if you have a stand mixer with a dough hook attachment, let it do the job from the final mixing all the way through the kneading stage.

Cabbage-Beef Filling

MAKES ABOUT 4 CUPS

2 cups thinly shredded cabbage
¾ cup finely chopped onion
¾ pound lean ground beef
1 tablespoon oil, for greasing the skillet
½ teaspoon salt
½ teaspoon black pepper
1 tablespoon chopped fresh dill or 1½ teaspoons dried dillweed (optional)

1. Bring a medium pot of water to boil. Add the cabbage and onion and simmer briskly until crisp-tender, about 5 minutes. Drain and set aside to cool and drip dry.

2. Brown the beef in a lightly greased skillet over medium heat until no longer pink, 8 to 10 minutes. Pour off any grease, transfer the beef to a medium bowl, and let cool enough to handle.

3. Crumble any large chunks of the beef, add the cabbage mixture and the remaining ingredients, and mix well. Use right away or store in the refrigerator for up to 2 days.

Cabbage All Around

This type of cabbage filling is used in a broad spectrum of cuisines from Germany to Poland to Russia, in numerous variations. Some possibilities are:

THE SPICING: Parsley, thyme, or caraway in place of or in conjunction with the dill.

THE BEEF: Add a small bit of fried bacon or salt pork, raisins, or mushrooms.

MEAT-FREE FILLING: Increase the cabbage and onion and replace the beef with 1 cup of diced cooked potato or cooked rice.

three pizzas and a crust

From different coasts and different gardens, the following three recipes show how fresh ingredients and a toasty crust bring together garden and kitchen in a time-tested way that meets practically any food need at practically any moment. It's called pizza. From traditional to innovative, these explore the possibilities for this variable food.

Criscione Pizza

MAKES ONE 14-INCH PIZZA

"My husband and I, modern-day pioneers, moved from Chicago to a small rural town, Halsey, Oregon. This recipe combines the magic of Chicago-style pizza with the zesty vegetables from our Oregon garden." The best part of this pizza is the homemade crust. Of course, the garden toppings are also wonderful. On third thought, maybe the best part of this pizza is its unfussy ease.

ANICIA CRISCIONE (HALSEY, OR)

One Pizza Crust (recipe follows)
Oil and semolina flour or cornmeal, for preparing the pizza pan
½ cup Marinara Sauce (see page 294)
1 large tomato, sliced ¼ inch thick
½ onion, thinly sliced
½ green bell pepper, thinly sliced
1 tablespoon roughly torn fresh basil leaves
½ cup grated pepper Jack cheese (see Note below)

1. Prepare the crust.

2. Preheat the oven to 450°F. Lightly oil a pizza pan and sprinkle it with semolina flour or cornmeal.

3. Press the pizza dough into the prepared pan. Spread the sauce over the dough and arrange the remaining ingredients over the sauce, ending with the cheese as a blanket covering all.

4. Bake for 20 minutes, or until the crust is cooked through and the cheese is golden. Remove and serve right away.

Note: Pepper Jack cheese is a recent arrival on the "cheeses for everyday" market. It's bland, like other Jack cheeses, but its dots of finely chopped chili pepper carry a bit of extra punch. Most kids like it.

Pizza Crust

MAKES ONE 14-INCH CRUST

⅔ cup warm water
1½ teaspoons (about ½ package) active dry yeast
1¾ cups all-purpose flour
½ teaspoon sugar
½ teaspoon salt
1 tablespoon olive oil

1. Pour the water into a small bowl, sprinkle the yeast over the top, and set aside in a warm place to proof until the mixture is beginning to bubble, 10 to 15 minutes.

2. Combine the flour, sugar, and salt in a large bowl and stir to mix. Set aside.

3. Make a well in the center of the flour mixture. Pour in the yeast mixture and the oil and mix together by hand. Turn the dough onto a floured board and knead for 10 minutes, or until smooth, shiny, and elastic.

4. Lightly oil a clean bowl, place the dough in the bowl, and turn to coat it with the oil. Cover the bowl with a cloth and set it aside in a warm place to rise until doubled, about 30 minutes.

5. When doubled, punch down the dough and roll it out on a lightly floured surface into a 14-inch round. Press the round into a lightly oiled pizza pan and use right away.

Note: After rising, the dough may be punched down, wrapped in plastic wrap, and stored in the refrigerator for up to 2 days. Bring it to room temperature before using.

TOOLS *of the* TRADE

Rolling Pins

For those who like to bake, a rolling pin is a personal matter. In fact, some may have a selection to suit different jobs. The best rolling pins are of a hard wood, evenly balanced, just the right length and heft to fit in your hands. It might have handles with ball bearings so that when you roll back and forth there is no stress on your elbow joints. On the other hand, it might have tapered ends that allow quick and easy movements for rolling out delicate doughs. It might also be a short length of broomstick or a wine bottle set on its side—both work in a pinch.

Zucchini, Sausage, and Fontinella Pizza

MAKES ONE 14-INCH PIZZA

After all the sautéing, casseroling, stuffing, and pickling, when there's still a bit of zucchini that shouldn't go to waste, slice it thin, fry it up with some sausage, moisten with cream, spread the mixture on a pizza crust, and bake away. Not low-cal, it's true, but a thin slice will do for a snack, two slices for a meal.

DONNA LUKACS (GRAND RAPIDS, MI)

One Pizza Crust (see page 391)
½ pound sweet Italian sausage, removed from casing
3 tablespoons olive oil
3 medium zucchini, sliced into thin 1½-inch-long sticks (about 2 pounds)
3 cloves garlic, minced or pressed
Salt
¾ cup heavy (whipping) cream
8 ounces Fontinella cheese, grated
Extra olive oil, for brushing the pizza dough
2 teaspoons chopped fresh oregano leaves or ¾ teaspoon dried oregano
1 teaspoon black pepper

1. Prepare the crust.

2. Preheat the oven to 450°F.

3. Sauté the sausage in a heavy skillet over medium heat, crumbling it to break up any chunks, until cooked through, about 10 minutes. Transfer the sausage to a plate, pour off the grease, and wipe out the skillet.

4. Add the olive oil to the skillet and heat until beginning to smoke. Add the zucchini, garlic, and salt to taste and sauté over medium heat until the zucchini is crisp-tender, about 7 minutes.

5. Return the sausage to the skillet, pour in the cream, and bring to a boil. Stir in half of the cheese and immediately remove the skillet from the heat. Set aside.

6. Brush the pizza dough with a thin film of oil. Spoon the sausage-and-zucchini mixture over the dough and sprinkle on the oregano and pepper. Top with the remaining cheese and bake for 12 to 15 minutes, until the cheese is bubbling and golden. Cool slightly, slice, and serve.

Phyllo Forgiveness

Phyllo is a most merciful pastry. First of all, it comes already made and packaged, available in the freezer section of most supermarkets. Second, it lends itself to all kinds of savory and sweet concoctions, from pizzas to pastries, even if you are a novice. A little ragged here, a little bunched up there, the phyllo still crisps beautifully and tastes good. The only trick is to keep the phyllo sheets covered with a damp cloth as you build the layers so that they don't become too dry and brittle to handle.

Rosie's Tomato Phyllo Pizza

MAKES ONE 15 BY 10-INCH PIZZA

"After ten years of gardening and ten years of catering, this year for the first time my husband and I grew heirloom tomatoes from seed. So it only seems right that I send you a recipe, named after

one of my former partners, that shows off tomatoes to great advantage. It is especially beautiful with Old Flames and Brandywines alternated on top."

LINDA OLSON (MADISON, WI)

5 sun-dried tomatoes
1 cup fresh parsley leaves
4 cloves garlic, cut up a bit
1 teaspoon fresh oregano leaves or ½ teaspoon dried oregano
1 teaspoon fresh thyme leaves or ¼ teaspoon dried thyme
1 cup coarsely chopped onion
1 cup coarsely grated mozzarella cheese
1 cup freshly grated Parmesan cheese
7 sheets frozen phyllo dough, thawed
Olive oil, for brushing on the phyllo
1 pound (3 to 4) vine-ripened tomatoes
Fresh thyme sprigs, for garnish (optional)

1. Preheat the oven to 375°F. Lightly grease the bottom of a 15 by 10-inch baking sheet.

2. Place the dried tomatoes, parsley, garlic, oregano, thyme, and onion in a food processor and chop as fine as possible. Set aside.

3. Combine the mozzarella and ¼ cup of the Parmesan in a bowl. Set aside.

4. Place 1 sheet of phyllo on the baking sheet and brush it lightly with oil, going all the way to the edges. (Keep a damp towel over the rest of the phyllo to prevent drying out as you work.) Sprinkle 1 heaping tablespoon of the remaining Parmesan over the sheet of phyllo. Place another sheet over the first, brush it with oil, and sprinkle with Parmesan. Continue until all 7 sheets of phyllo are used.

5. Spread the tomato mixture over the last layer of phyllo. Arrange the tomato slices over the top and sprinkle the cheese mixture overall. Fold up the edges of the phyllo to make a nice edging and brush lightly with a little more oil.

6. Place the phyllo pizza in the oven and bake until it is very golden and crisp around the edges and the cheese topping is bubbling, about 30 minutes.

7. Remove and cut into sections as large or small as you desire. Garnish each piece with a small thyme sprig, if using, and serve.

In addition to the recipes in this chapter, you can find other baked savories in this book. They include:

Tri-Color Sweet Pepper Quiche (page 169)
Sweet Onion Tart (page 171)
Tomato, Basil, and Cheese Pie (page 172)
Kale Pie (page 174)
Tomato Zucchini Tart in a Potato Crust (page 173)
Garlic-Parmesan Crackers (page 109)

sweets:

dulcet inspirations from garden gleanings

Since the time it was refined enough to melt into candy, sweeten doughs, and turn a bitter brew palatable, sugar has enjoyed a most esteemed place around the world. From apothecary shelves to kitchen cupboard to dining-room hutch, sugar became part and parcel of parties around the world. This chapter begins with a hospitality sweet of sugared and herbed fresh figs to greet guests as they enter your home. It ends with another hospitality treat of green almonds suspended in syrup, this time offered to wish guests well on their way home. In between are many dulcet concoctions—cakes, pies, puddings, and poached fruits—to satisfy any sweet tooth in fresh, garden ways.

Hospitality Figs with Cinnamon, Anise, and Fresh Bay Leaves

MAKES 24 FIG SANDWICHES

"I am a potter living and working on the Greek island of Paros. The recipe that I would like to share with you is one taught to me by my Greek mother-in-law, Evdoxia Ghikas. It was a tradition in her family and one she learned from her mother, who was from the island of Naxos. Fig trees are abundant here on Paros and all over the countryside in the Greek islands. When there are more figs than one can handle, the next best thing is a dried fig in winter. We always offer a few, with a small glass of locally made grappa, as a hospitality treat."

MONIQUE MAILLOUX, STUDIO YRIA (PAROS ISLAND, GREECE)

24 fully ripe green figs, any variety with sweet pulp
1 tablespoon ground cinnamon
1 teaspoon anise seeds
24 whole blanched almonds
Bay leaves, preferably fresh (see Note below)

Bringing in the Figs

"The best figs to use are kalamata or calimyrna. Both are small, green fruit with a light brandy-colored pulp. They are best gathered just as they are turning brown and the overripe ones fall into your hands upon touching. Figs can also be collected from the ground around the tree, as long as they have not yet rotted." When fully ripe, figs are naturally sweet and need no extra sugar to make a dulcet treat. In fact, they are so sweet, the refreshing aromas of anise seed and fresh bay are welcome.

—MONIQUE MAILLOUX

1. Rinse the figs and set them on a rack in the sun to dry. Leave for at least a day or up to 1 week, until they begin to wilt but are not dried out.

2. When ready to prepare, heat the oven to 250°F. Mix together the cinnamon and anise seeds on a plate and set aside.

3. Snip the stems off the figs and pull them open from the bottom, leaving them in one piece. Dip the inside of the opened-out figs in the cinnamon mix to coat lightly. Place an almond in the center of one side and fold the fig closed to make a sandwich. Press in the palm of your hands to compact slightly and place the fig sandwich on an ungreased cookie sheet. Continue until all the figs have been sandwiched, arranging them on the cookie sheet without overlapping.

4. Bake until a toasty golden color, about 1 hour. Remove from the oven and layer them in a ceramic or glass bowl or canister. Let stand at room temperature overnight.

5. Next day, tuck 3 to 4 bay leaves between each layer and press down to compact the layers. Set aside in a cool place for 2 days, then serve. Or, if you can resist eating them, store in the refrigerator for the winter.

Note: The amount of bay leaves depends on whether or not they are fresh or dried. Fresh, they have a less pungent effect and you can use large whole leaves in quantity. Dried, the amount should be more modest and only small leaves selected

TOOLS *of the* TRADE

Pans for the Pastry Chef's Art

If you love to make cakes and pies, you may be willing to allot a noticeable portion of cupboard space to a variety of pans to suit the shape of the cake or tart or pie. A good basic selection includes:

TUBE PAN: Round and high-sided with a tube so that the cake comes out round with a hole in the middle. Good for cakes or coffee cakes that benefit from heat in the center so that they bake up tender throughout, not done on the outside and wet in the middle. A special shape is needed for angel food cake. Also good for making molded dishes, such as aspics or mousses.

BUNDT PAN: Like a tube pan, only with fluted outer edge so that the cake has a scalloped form. Excellent for presentations that require a fancier touch.

SPRINGFORM PAN: A round cake pan with a high edge (ring) and removable bottom. The sides can be loosened and removed.

DEEP-DISH PIE PAN: Round like a regular pie tin but deeper for cooking cobblers and crisps, either slant sided or straight sided. Also useful for savory pies.

REMOVABLE-BOTTOM TART PAN: Similar to a regular pie tin, except that the bottom can be lifted out of the ring for serving. Essential for dishes, such as French tarts, that are more attractive and more easily served if free of the pan.

MULTIPLE-PURPOSE BAKING PANS: Many sizes, including a 9-inch square, 9-inch round, 13 by 9-inch baking pan, plus a 9 by 5-inch loaf pan, are inexpensive and handy to have for brownies, layer cakes, and pound cakes.

Black Raspberry and Beet Brownies with Chocolate-Sour Cream Topping

MAKES 18 APPROXIMATELY 2-INCH SQUARES

If ever there were a gardener's brownie, this would be it. The contributor, a member of the Empire State Chef's Association of The American Culinary Federation, created the

recipe for an annual harvest dinner to benefit a regional moveable feast program. It was also entered in the New York State Chocolate Festival (1995), where it won second place. Not content with just chocolate and sugar, the contributor stirred puréed beets into the batter and swirled black raspberry jam over the top to create an almost Tintoretto picture of a brownie, cordovan red from top to bottom, moist, and cakey. Why add the beets? Well, the color is not the same without them; they add a garden flavor that would be lost without them; they help moisturize the batter. Go the extra step and coat the brownies with the chocolate glaze. For a less elaborate affair, omit the coating.

~ DONNA WENZEL (CANAAN, NY)

Oil, for greasing the baking pan
4 ounces unsweetened chocolate
8 tablespoons (1 stick) butter, at room temperature
4 small trimmed beets, cooked, peeled, and puréed (about ½ pound)
¾ cup black raspberry jam
2 large eggs
¼ teaspoon salt
1½ cups sugar
1 teaspoon vanilla extract
1 cup all-purpose flour
½ cup Chocolate-Sour Cream Topping (optional, recipe follows)

1. Preheat the oven to 350°F. Lightly grease a 13 by 9-inch pan.

2. Place the chocolate and butter in a saucepan or microwave bowl and heat until melted. Add the beets and ¼ cup of the jam and whisk to smooth. Set aside.

3. Crack the eggs into a large bowl, add the salt, and beat until foamy. Add the sugar and vanilla and whisk until blended. Whisk in the chocolate-beet mixture, add the flour, and continue whisking until blended into a batter. Pour the batter into the baking pan.

4. Gently melt the remaining ½ cup jam without boiling it and drizzle over the top of the batter. Use a knife to make a swirled pattern, lightly cutting through the batter. Bake for 25 to 30 minutes, or until a knife inserted in the center comes out almost clean.

5. Prepare the topping if using.

6. Remove and cool the brownies. Spread the chocolate topping, if using, over the top. Cut into squares and serve at room temperature. Will keep, wrapped in foil, in the refrigerator for up to 5 days.

Chocolate-Sour Cream Topping

MAKES 1/2 CUP

5 ounces semisweet chocolate, melted
⅓ cup sour cream
1 teaspoon vanilla extract

Combine all the ingredients in a small bowl and whisk to smooth. Use right away.

Zucchini Blondies

MAKES NINE 3-INCH SQUARES

Using up an excess may have been the impetus for including zucchini in these blondies. The fortuitous outcome is that the zucchini adds just the needed moisture to the somewhat stiff batter to keep the blondies light as they bake.

JESSICA KURTZMAN (GREENVILLE, RI)

Oil, for greasing the baking pan
5 tablespoons butter, melted with 1 tablespoon water
1 cup (packed) dark brown sugar
1 large egg
1 teaspoon vanilla extract
1 cup all-purpose flour
1 teaspoon baking powder
⅛ teaspoon baking soda
½ teaspoon salt
1 medium zucchini, peeled and chopped into ¼-inch pieces (6 ounces)
½ cup coarsely chopped walnuts or pecans
⅓ cup chocolate or butterscotch chips

1. Preheat the oven to 350°F. Lightly grease a 9-inch square baking pan.

2. Pour the melted butter into a large mixing bowl. Add the brown sugar and

When's It Done? Brownies and Cakes Aren't the Same

Many recipes use the knife-inserted-in-the-center guideline for judging when baked goods are done. Brownies and blondies, which are moister than cakes, should be removed from the oven when a knife inserted in the center comes out with a little bit of almost-dry batter clinging to it.

Using the press-in-the-center guideline, cakes are done when a gentle press pops back up right away. Brownies and blondies are done when they hold an indent. After that, they're overdone.

mix well. Crack the egg into the bowl, add the vanilla, and beat until blended.

3. Sift the flour, baking powder, baking soda, and salt into the bowl and stir to mix. Add the zucchini and nuts and stir to mix into a stiff batter.

4. Spread the batter in the baking pan and sprinkle the chips over the top. Bake for 30 minutes, or until a knife inserted in the center comes out almost clean but still a little batter coated (see the box on page 399).

5. Remove, cool enough to handle, and slice into squares. Serve warm or at room temperature. Will keep, covered, for 3 days at room temperature. Or wrap individually and freeze for longer storage.

Lemon-Herb Tea Cake with Lemon Glaze

MAKES ONE 9 BY 5-INCH LOAF

With its lemon glaze and multiple serving possibilities, this delicate cake fits into many aspects of the day. In particular, it "becomes an impressive dessert, especially if garnished with fresh pansies. The real secret to a successful outcome is to take the time to encase the loaf in the glaze—this provides a lovely initial zing and seals in moisture." The contributor goes on to share another secret: "I use whichever of the lemon herbs are presently in my garden. I personally favor the balm and verbena." Our recipe testers included a bit of lemon thyme and lemon geranium in the cake and glaze both. It was a delightfully lemony, but not puckery, outcome.

ELIZA CICCOTI (GILLETT, PA)

Butter and flour, for the pan
¾ cup milk
2 to 3 tablespoons chopped fresh lemon herb leaves, such as lemon balm, lemon verbena, lemon thyme, or lemon geranium
8 tablespoons (1 stick) butter, at room temperature
1 cup sugar
2 large eggs
2 cups all-purpose flour
2 teaspoons baking powder
¼ teaspoon salt
1 tablespoon finely chopped lemon zest
1 cup Lemon Glaze (recipe follows)

1. Preheat the oven to 325°F. Butter and flour a 9 by 5-inch loaf pan.

2. Combine the milk and herbs in a small saucepan and bring to a boil. Remove from the heat, cover, and set aside to steep for at least 5 minutes or up to 30 minutes.

3. Place the butter in a large mixing bowl and beat until soft and fluffy. Add the sugar and eggs and mix well. Whisk in half of the herb-milk mixture. Add the flour, baking powder, and salt and whisk until blended. Stir in the remaining herb-milk mixture and lemon zest and pour the batter into the loaf pan.

4. Bake for 50 to 60 minutes, until a toothpick inserted in the center of the loaf comes out clean. Remove and set the pan on a rack to cool for about 10 minutes.

5. Prepare the glaze.

6. When the loaf is slightly cooled but still warm, drizzle the glaze over it while still in the pan. Set aside for 30 minutes while the loaf absorbs the glaze and the glaze becomes half set.

7. Invert the loaf onto a serving platter, using a small spatula or table knife to prod it out if necessary. Slowly drizzle the glaze remaining in the pan over the loaf, allowing it to run down the sides.

8. To serve, cut into thin slices. For an added touch of garnish, see the headnote. Will keep, loosely covered (see right), for up to 3 days at room temperature.

STORING CAKES
An old-fashioned cake dome is a perfect way to store cakes. You can simulate one with a plastic wrap tent using toothpicks to hold the wrap above the cake.

Lemon Glaze

MAKES ABOUT 1 CUP

2 cups confectioners' sugar
¼ cup fresh lemon juice
1 teaspoon finely chopped lemon herb (optional)

Combine the sugar, lemon juice, and herb, if using, in a bowl. Set aside until ready to use, but not so long that it is no longer liquid and beginning to crystallize.

Apple-Flavored Winter Squash Cake with Apple Cider Glaze

SERVES 10 TO 12

Mashed winter squash is one of the surprises in this cake. The apple flavor, which comes from apple cider rather than chopped fresh apples, is another. The two, laced together with ground ginger along with the more predictable spices, make for a simple, and somewhat different, seasonal cake.

MARION PENNINGTON (LONDON, KY)

Butter and flour, for the pan
8 tablespoons (1 stick) butter, at room temperature
1½ cups sugar
2 large eggs
1½ cups cooked and mashed winter squash, such as butternut, or acorn
½ cup apple cider
1¾ cups all-purpose flour
1 teaspoon baking soda
¼ teaspoon salt
½ teaspoon ground cinnamon
½ teaspoon ground nutmeg
¼ teaspoon ground cloves
¼ teaspoon ground ginger
1 cup Apple Cider Glaze (recipe follows)

1. Preheat the oven to 350°F. Butter and flour a 9- to 10-inch tube or bundt pan.

2. In a large bowl, beat the butter until fluffy. Slowly beat in the sugar until mixed. Add the eggs, one at a time, beating after each addition. Add the squash and apple cider and beat until well mixed.

3. Sift together the flour, baking soda, salt, cinnamon, nutmeg, cloves, and ginger. Add to the creamed mixture in 3 batches, beating well after each addition.

4. Pour into the pan and bake for 45 minutes, or until a knife inserted in the center comes out clean. Remove and cool for 10 minutes, then turn the cake out onto a wire rack to cool completely.

5. Prepare the glaze.

6. Drizzle the glaze over the cake and let set to firm. Slice and serve. Will keep, loosely covered, for up to 3 days at room temperature.

PUTTING THE ALPHABET TO GOOD USE

If you arrange your spices in alphabetical order in the cupboard, you save an immense amount of time and headache rooting about to find what is needed for the recipe. You also have an orderly rank from which to choose spices that might be desirable, though not yet determined, for the dish you are making up on the spot.

Apple Cider Glaze

MAKES ABOUT 1 CUP

1½ cups confectioners' sugar

¼ cup apple cider

Sift the sugar into a small bowl. Add the cider and whisk until smooth. Use right away, while still pourable and not yet crystallized.

Sweet Potato Pound Cake with Citrus Glaze

SERVES 12 TO 16

Though sweet potato might suggest a dense texture, this cake turns out light and tender. The sweet potato tints the cake a beautiful deep golden, and the citrus glaze adds an orange- and yellow-dotted shine. It's altogether an impressive presentation to end a casual fall or winter meal.

HAZEL ANDERSON (NORTH WILKESBORO, NC)

Butter and flour, for the pan
2 pounds sweet potatoes
3 cups all-purpose flour
¼ teaspoon salt
2 teaspoons baking powder
1 teaspoon baking soda
½ teaspoon ground nutmeg
1 teaspoon ground cinnamon
1 cup (2 sticks) butter, at room temperature
2 cups sugar
4 large eggs
1 teaspoon vanilla extract
½ cup coarsely chopped pecans
½ cup unsweetened coconut flakes, finely chopped (see Note below)
1 cup Citrus Glaze (recipe follows)

1. Preheat the oven to 325°F. Butter and flour a 9- to 10-inch tube or bundt pan.

2. Peel the sweet potatoes and cut them into 1-inch chunks. Place in a pot and add water to cover by 1 inch. Bring to a boil and cook until the potatoes are soft all the way through, about 20 minutes. Drain and purée. Set aside.

3. Combine the flour, salt, baking powder, baking soda, nutmeg, and cinnamon in a bowl and stir to mix well. Set aside.

4. Cream together the butter and sugar in a large bowl. Add the sweet potatoes and beat until light and fluffy. Add the eggs, one at a time, beating well after each addition. Stir in the vanilla.

5. Add the flour mixture 1 cup at a time, incorporating well after each addition, to make a stiff batter. Stir in the pecans and coconut and spoon the batter into the pan.

6. Bake for 1 hour and 30 minutes, or until a knife inserted in the center comes out clean.

7. Prepare the glaze.

8. Remove the cake from the oven and cool for 10 minutes. Invert the pan and gently pry the cake onto a large platter. While it is still warm, slowly drizzle the glaze over the top and around the edges, spooning up any that pools around the edges and drizzling it over the top again. Set aside for a few minutes to allow the glaze to soak into the cake as it continues to cool.

9. Slice and serve. Will keep, loosely covered, for up to 3 days at room temperature.

Note: For the best flavor in the cake, it's important to use *unsweetened* coconut flakes, which are available in natural food stores and produce markets. The more usual, presweetened flakes have lost much of their coconut flavor in processing and are too fine, anyway.

Citrus Glaze

MAKES ABOUT 1 CUP

2 cups confectioners' sugar
1½ tablespoons finely chopped orange zest
1 tablespoon finely chopped lemon zest
¼ cup fresh lemon juice or a mixture of fresh lemon and orange juice

Sift the sugar into a bowl. Add the zests and juice and stir until the sugar is dissolved and the mixture is smooth enough to glaze a cake. Use right away or set aside at room temperature for up to 30 minutes, but not longer or the glaze will crystallize and not coat the cake evenly.

Chocolate-Zucchini Cake Frosted with Chocolate Chips

MAKES ONE 13 BY 9-INCH CAKE

In this vegetable-moistened cake, modest amounts of cocoa and chocolate provide a discernible chocolate flavor without weighing down the cake's delicacy. Also interesting is the use of clabbered milk (see box below). It's an old-fashioned way to add a mildly tart flavor and ensure a tender crumb in cakes and other baked products.

SONYA COLLETT (YANKTON, SD)

Butter, for the pan
8 tablespoons (1 stick) butter
½ cup vegetable oil
1¾ cups sugar
2 large eggs
1 teaspoon vanilla extract
½ cup clabbered milk (see box below)
2½ cups all-purpose flour
½ teaspoon baking powder
1 teaspoon baking soda
½ teaspoon salt
¼ cup unsweetened cocoa powder
½ teaspoon ground cinnamon
½ teaspoon ground cloves
2 cups finely chopped zucchini
¼ cup chocolate chips
1 cup sour cream whisked with 2 tablespoons confectioners' sugar (optional)
Edible flowers, for garnish (optional, see box on page 361)

1. Preheat the oven to 325°F. Lightly butter a 13 by 9-inch baking pan.

2. Cream the butter, oil, and sugar in a large bowl. Add the eggs, vanilla, and clabbered milk and beat well.

3. Combine the flour, baking powder, baking soda, salt, cocoa, cinnamon, and cloves. Stir into the batter, then add the zucchini, mixing well each time. Pour into the baking pan and sprinkle the chocolate chips over the top. Bake

The Science of Clabbered Milk

Clabbered milk is a cultured milk product, much like buttermilk, sour cream, crème fraîche, and yogurt. To make it, milk is deliberately and carefully soured naturally to add a tart flavor to cakes, pancakes, and sauces. With virtually all the milk available today pasteurized, which prevents good souring before going bad, savvy cooks have found a simple way to sour (clabber) milk for baking and sauce making:

Combine 1 tablespoon of white vinegar and 1 cup of milk and allow to sit at room temperature for 5 minutes, or until it begins to curdle, or clabber. Use right away.

for 40 to 45 minutes, or until a knife inserted in the center comes out clean.

4. Remove from the oven, cool slightly, then slice and serve. If using the sour cream, place a dollop on each plate and prop an edible flower or two, if using, in the center. Will keep, covered, for up to 5 days in the refrigerator.

WASHING VEGETABLES AND FRUITS

A dream scene for any gardener cook is to have a deep sink at the back door supplied with running water so the veggies and fruits picked from the yard can be rinsed before being brought to the kitchen. In any case, it's a good idea to rinse produce, organic or not, to wash away bugs and other debris before cooking.

Zucchini-Carrot Cake with Cream Cheese Frosting

MAKES ONE 9-INCH SQUARE CAKE

From the carrots to the Cream Cheese Frosting, this is a classic of American quick cakes. Combining the carrots with zucchini, however, is a bit different. Some cooks may ponder the value of this difference; gardeners will say hallelujah because there go some more zucchini.

LUCY SPERFSLAGE (CENTRAL CITY, IA)

Butter, for the pan
2 large eggs
1 cup sugar
⅔ cup vegetable oil
1¼ cups all-purpose flour
1 teaspoon baking soda
½ teaspoon salt
1 teaspoon ground cinnamon
1 cup grated zucchini
½ cup grated carrots
½ cup raisins
½ cup chopped walnuts
1½ cups Cream Cheese Frosting (recipe follows), at room temperature

1. Preheat the oven to 350°F. Lightly butter a 9-inch square baking pan.

2. Beat the eggs with the sugar in a large bowl until the mixture is frothy, then beat in the oil.

3. Sift the flour, baking powder, salt, and cinnamon into the bowl and beat until well mixed.

4. Add the zucchini, carrots, raisins, and walnuts and stir to mix into a stiff batter. Spoon the batter into the baking pan

and bake for 35 minutes, or until a knife inserted in the center comes out clean. Cool on a rack.

5. Prepare the frosting.

6. When cool, spread the frosting as thick as you'd like over the top of cake. Slice and serve. Will keep, covered, for up to 5 days in the refrigerator.

Cream Cheese Frosting

MAKES ABOUT 1½ CUPS

3 ounces cream cheese, softened
1 tablespoon butter, at room temperature
1 cup confectioners' sugar
1 teaspoon vanilla extract

Beat together the cheese and butter in a medium bowl. Add the sugar and vanilla and beat until smooth. Use right away, while still spreadable.

Rosemary Layer Cake with Rosemary-Cream Cheese Frosting

MAKES ONE 9-INCH 3-LAYER CAKE

Though a bold combination, the flavors of lemon, coconut, pecans, and rosemary subtly blend into a light, moist cake. Grandly layered three tiers high, it's a creation fit for special occasions. More extravagantly still, you can use Lemon Curd (page 351) as filling between the layers and the rosemary frosting for the top.

LORA SHERIDAN (WINSTON-SALEM, NC)

Butter and flour, for the pans
1¾ cups sugar
8 tablespoons (1 stick) butter, at room temperature
½ cup vegetable oil
5 large eggs, separated
1 tablespoon chopped fresh rosemary
2 tablespoons finely chopped lemon zest
¼ cup fresh lemon juice
1 teaspoon baking soda
1 cup buttermilk
2 cups all-purpose flour, sifted
1 teaspoon vanilla extract
1 cup unsweetened coconut flakes (see Note on page 404)
½ cup coarsely chopped pecans
3 cups Rosemary-Cream Cheese Frosting (recipe follows)
Extra coconut flakes and/or rosemary sprigs, for garnish (optional)

1. Preheat the oven to 325°F. Butter and flour three 9-inch cake pans.

2. In a large bowl, cream together the sugar, butter, and oil until light and fluffy. Add the egg yolks, rosemary, lemon zest, and lemon juice and beat until well blended.

3. Stir the baking soda into the buttermilk. Add the flour to the sugar mixture alternately with the buttermilk mixture, stirring after each addition. Add the vanilla, coconut flakes, and pecans and mix well to make a loose batter.

4. In a small bowl, beat the egg whites until soft peaks form. Fold into the batter, mixing gently until no streaks remain. Pour the batter into the prepared pans, dividing evenly. Bake for 25 to 30 minutes, or until the edges pull away from the sides of the pans and a knife inserted in the centers comes out clean.

5. Cool on racks for 10 minutes, then turn the cakes onto greased racks and set aside to cool completely.

6. Prepare the frosting.

7. To assemble the cake, place one layer on a serving platter and spread one-third of the frosting over the top. Place the second layer on top of the frosting, coat it, and repeat with the third layer, spreading the remaining frosting over the top. Garnish with fresh rosemary sprigs and/or coconut flakes, if desired. Slice and serve.

Rosemary-Cream Cheese Frosting

MAKES ABOUT 3 CUPS

6 ounces cream cheese, at room temperature
8 tablespoons (1 stick) butter, at room temperature
1 teaspoon vanilla extract
1 tablespoon chopped fresh rosemary
2 teaspoons finely chopped lemon zest
2 cups confectioners' sugar, sifted

Cream together the cheese and butter until light and fluffy. Beat in the vanilla, rosemary, and zest. Gradually add the sugar, beating well after each addition. Use right away or within 1 hour, while still soft enough to spread.

tarts, pies, crisps, and cobblers

There are cake lovers and there are pie lovers. In cakes the garden elements—herbs, fruits, nuts—are subtly revealed. In tarts, pies, crisps, and cobblers, there is a turnaround and the garden elements—a bowlful of fruit, neatly arranged or mounded not so neatly, cooked or not; a spread of jam; or a sweet vegetable purée—become the feature. If you're looking to make a dessert that is undoubtedly garden inspired and are not so inclined to whip up a cake, this section offers a number of pielike delicacies.

Lindsey's Almond Tart

Makes one 9-inch tart

Lindsey Shere, presently a partner in the Downtown Bakery and Creamery in Healdsburg, California, was the acclaimed pastry chef at Chez Panisse Restaurant in Berkeley, California, from day one until she retired in 1997. In all that time, twenty-six years, and through each evolution of the restaurant, her almond tart was rarely off the menu. It remains still a house specialty. Lindsey advises that this tart is best eaten with the fingers; it is too hard to cut easily with a fork. For the same reason, it makes an excellent picnic dessert; it is virtually indestructible!

LINDSEY SHERE (HEALDSBURG, CA)

Short Pastry Crust (recipe follows)
¾ cup heavy (whipping) cream
¾ cup sugar
1 teaspoon Grand Marnier or other orange liqueur
2 or 3 drops almond extract
1 cup sliced unblanched almonds

1. Prepare the crust, freezing it for at least 30 minutes before baking.

2. Preheat the oven to 375°F.

3. Prick the bottom of the crust in several places with a fork. Bake until golden brown all over and cooked through, about 25 minutes. Set aside.

4. Combine the cream, sugar, Grand Marnier, and almond extract in a large saucepan. Heat, stirring occasionally, until the mixture comes to a rolling boil and bubbles thickly. Remove from the heat, stir in the almonds, and set aside for 15 minutes.

5. Raise the oven temperature to 400°F. and place a length of foil on the bottom of the oven in case the tart bubbles over.

6. Pour the filling into the shell, making sure the almonds float evenly throughout the mixture. Bake for 30 to 35 minutes, or until the top is a creamy caramel color.

7. Cool on a rack, loosening the sides of the tart pan every few minutes until set, 5 to 10 minutes. Lift the tart out of the ring and return to the rack to cool completely. Serve right away.

Note: It is important to let the tart cool and set for 5 to 10 minutes before lifting it out of the ring or the sides will collapse.

Lindsey's Short Pastry Crust

MAKES ONE 9-INCH TART SHELL

1 cup all-purpose flour
1 tablespoon sugar
¼ teaspoon salt
8 tablespoons (1 stick) unsalted butter, at room temperature
½ teaspoon vanilla extract

1. Mix the flour, sugar, and salt in a medium bowl. Cut the butter into ½-inch slices and work it into the flour mixture with your hands or a pastry blender until the butter is mostly in cornmeal-size pieces and the mixture is beginning to hold together.

2. Combine 1 tablespoon water and the vanilla and work it into the flour mixture just until the mixture is blended and holds together when pressed. Gather it into a ball and wrap in plastic wrap. Let rest for 30 minutes, then use right away, store in the refrigerator for up to 2 days, or wrap in foil and freeze for up to 1 month.

3. When ready to use, use your fingers to press the pastry evenly into a 9-inch removable-bottom tart pan. Wrap the shell in foil and set in the freezer for 30 minutes or up to overnight before baking.

Crusts You Can Trust

The shortening for your pie crust dough is a matter of personal preference. There are those who insist on butter and nothing but butter. Some favor liquid vegetable shortening; others swear by solid vegetable shortening as the only way to achieve a tender crust. Still others opt for margarine. In this book, the entire range of shortening options is covered and you can choose among the following perfect crusts to suit yourself:

Cheddar Cheese Pie Dough (page 418)
Easy Tart Crust (page 170)
Flaky Cream Cheese Pie Crust (page 416)
Potato Crust (page 174)
Lindsey's Short Pastry Crust (page 411)
Vegetable Oil Pie Crust (page 414)
Walnut Crust (page 413)

Penny's Pear Tart with a Walnut Crust

MAKES ONE 11-INCH TART

Ceramist and painter Penny Brogden, also an earnest and enthusiastic gardener, maintains gardens in Berkeley and in Napa, California. As if that weren't enough, she is also an accomplished cook with many years of professional experience, including recipe testing for this volume. "After years of gardening, the miracles never lessen. The colors and tastes of each season are never tiresome. Pear tart means fall. Walnuts mean fall, if I can get them away from the squirrels. When the pears show a luscious yellow tinged with red starting to take over the green, I think pear tart. It's funny how I don't think of this all year until I see a pear drop from the tree. At the same time, late October, the red starts creeping over the shiny green peppers. Having caught my eye, they suggest roasted peppers, and there looking straight at me is dinner—fennel and sweet red pepper over buckwheat noodles (see box below), pear tart for dessert." The pear trees on Penny's properties are so old, the name of their variety has been lost in family history, but she suggests Comice, Anjou, or Bartlett as good choices for the tart. The crust is very unusual. There is very little flour, which turns out a shell reminiscent of Middle Eastern pastries.

PENNY BROGDEN (BERKELEY AND NAPA, CA)

Walnut Crust (recipe follows)
6 to 8 ripe but still firm pears, rinsed, cored, and cut into ¼-inch-thick slices
2 tablespoons whole wheat flour (see Note below)
2 tablespoons dark brown sugar
1 tablespoon finely chopped lemon zest, preferably Meyer
2 tablespoons fresh lemon juice, preferably Meyer
¼ teaspoon ground cinnamon
Butter, for dotting top of the tart before baking (optional)
1 cup Crème Fraîche (see box on page 382)

1. Prepare the crust.

2. Preheat the oven to 375°F

3. Place the pears, flour, brown sugar, lemon zest, lemon juice, and cinnamon in a bowl and toss gently to mix.

4. Arrange the pear slices in concentric circles over the crust, starting from the outer edge. Dot the top with butter, if using, and bake for 30 minutes, or until browned and bubbly.

5. Serve warm or cold, accompanied by crème fraîche.

Note: All-purpose flour is okay for both the filling and the crust if you don't have whole wheat flour on hand.

An Easy Fall Menu: Fennel and Sweet Red Pepper Bake

SERVES 6

If you have been tantalized by Penny's fall garden menu and would like to make the vegetable bake to top buckwheat noodles, here's how.

¼ cup olive oil
6 tiny fennel bulbs, trimmed and cut lengthwise or crosswise into ⅜-inch-thick slices (1¾ pounds)
2 to 3 large red bell peppers, seeded and cut lengthwise into ¾-inch-wide strips
2 lemons, preferably Meyer, cut into ⅜-inch-thick slices
¼ teaspoon salt
½ teaspoon black pepper

1. Preheat the oven to 375°F.

2. Pour the olive oil into a 13 by 9-inch baking dish. Add the remaining ingredients and toss to mix. Bake until the vegetables start to caramelize, 45 minutes to 1 hour. Serve over buckwheat noodles or as a separate vegetable side dish, garnished with a few fennel fronds if you have them.

Walnut Crust

MAKES ONE 11-INCH CRUST

2 cups walnut halves or pieces, finely chopped but not pulverized
½ cup whole wheat flour
2 tablespoons dark brown sugar
¼ teaspoon ground cinnamon
5 tablespoons cold water
Butter, for greasing the pan

1. Combine the walnuts, flour, brown sugar, and cinnamon in a bowl. Add the water and mix with a fork until the mixture holds together but is not sticky.

2. Lightly butter an 11-inch removable-bottom tart pan. Spread the walnut mixture in the pan, and with the heel of your hand, press it to cover the bottom and sides. Use right away; this crust doesn't store well.

MAKING A PRETTY TART WITH NOT-SO-PERFECT PIECES

"If some of the pear slices break apart, I make one circle with the good slices and pile the rest in the middle, like a pear flower. Sometimes I make applesauce and spread a thin layer of that across the crust before arranging the pear slices on top."

—PENNY BROGDEN

Strawberry-Rhubarb Pie

MAKES ONE 9-INCH COVERED PIE

"My husband and I live in the Blue Mountains of Pennsylvania. We have a large stocked pond and every year a large vegetable and herb garden. Our grown children are scattered from Seattle to Houston, Atlanta, and Philadelphia, and when they visit, there is always a request for Strawberry-Rhubarb Pie." The crust is very easy to work with, malleable, not crumbly, and the technique of rolling out the dough between wax paper sheets ensures a smooth, easy-to-move top and bottom.

GEORGA LANG (NEW TRAPOLI, PA)

Vegetable Oil Pie Crust (recipe follows)
4 large stalks rhubarb, cut crosswise into ½-inch-wide pieces (about 1½ pounds)
2 pints strawberries, hulled and sliced
1⅓ cups sugar
½ cup plus 1 tablespoon all-purpose flour
2½ tablespoons minute tapioca (see box on page 414)
½ teaspoon finely chopped orange zest
½ teaspoon ground cinnamon
¼ teaspoon ground nutmeg
2 tablespoons butter
1 small egg, beaten
1 tablespoon sugar, for sprinkling on top

1. Prepare the crust.

2. Preheat the oven to 425° F.

3. Place the rhubarb and strawberries in a bowl, toss to mix, and set aside. In another bowl, combine the 1⅓ cups sugar, flour, tapioca, orange zest, cinnamon, and nutmeg and set aside.

4. Peel away the wax paper from the larger pastry round and place it in a 9-inch pie pan. Place the fruit mixture over the pastry and spread the dry ingredients over the top of the fruit. Dot with the butter and place the second crust over the top. Trim and crimp the edges. Paint the top crust with the beaten egg and sprinkle the 1 tablespoon sugar over the top. Make 3 or 4 slashes in the top of the crust to allow steam to escape.

5. Bake for 40 to 50 minutes, or until the filling bubbles up through the slashes and the top is golden.

6. Cool on a rack. Slice and serve warm or at room temperature.

Minute Tapioca

Minute tapioca is not to be confused with tapioca pudding mix. Minute tapioca comes in boxes of tiny granules called "prills," which are quick cooking and serve to thicken sauces, puddings, and fruit fillings. It works in the same way, but not in the same amount nor in the same resulting texture, as flour or cornstarch. As a thickener, it lends a somewhat grainy, often desirable, texture to the dish.

Vegetable Oil Pie Crust

Makes two 9-inch crusts

2⅔ cups all-purpose flour
Pinch of salt
⅔ cup vegetable oil
⅓ cup milk

Place the flour, salt, oil, and milk in a medium bowl and mix with your hands, 2 forks, or a pastry blender until you can gather the mixture into a smooth ball. Divide the ball into 2 almost equal parts. Roll out each part between 2 pieces of wax paper to make rounds about 11 inches in diameter. Use right away or set aside at room temperature for up to 2 or 3 hours.

Note: You can make the pastry crust up to a day in advance. To store, wrap the rolled-out dough, still in its wax paper, in plastic wrap and refrigerate. Bring the dough back to room temperature before using.

Churrant Pie in a Flaky Cream Cheese Crust

MAKES ONE 9-INCH PIE

*Cookbook author (*The Pie and Pastry Bible*) Rose Levy Beranbaum kindly shares her cherry and fresh red currant (churrant) pie recipe, which clearly tickled her imagination as she developed it. "Fresh currants, tart and tiny bright red globes, come into season in early July at the same time as sour cherries do. Stuffed into cherries, they keep the cherries full and plump and seem to give more cherry taste without imparting a flavor of their own. My original goal was to find a way to keep the cherries plump as they are in food photos—of course stylists use pits to achieve this effect! Although many people will find the idea of stuffing cherries with currants too tedious to consider, those lucky ones who try will be amply rewarded. No one will ever guess what the mysterious enhancer is or why this cherry pie has so much extra flavor and texture." The recipe also includes her professional tips for creating a lattice pie covering (see box on page 417).*

ROSE LEVY BERANBAUM (NEW YORK, NY)

Flaky Cream Cheese Pie Crust (recipe follows)
1 cup sugar
2 tablespoons plus 2½ teaspoons cornstarch
Salt
¼ cup fresh red currants, stemmed, washed, and dried (see Notes below)
1½ pounds fresh sour cherries, pitted, juices reserved (see box below)
¼ teaspoon almond extract
1 large egg yolk mixed with 1 teaspoon heavy (whipping) cream, for glaze (optional)

1. Prepare the crust.

2. Remove the larger piece of dough from the refrigerator and let sit for about 10 minutes, until it is soft enough to roll out. Using 2 sheets of plastic wrap sprinkled with flour, roll the pastry ⅛ inch thick and large enough to cut a 13-inch round. Cut the round and transfer it to a 9-inch pie pan. Fold the dough under so that it is flush with the edge of the pan. Cover with plastic, and refrigerate for at least 30 minutes but not longer than 3 hours.

3. Place the oven rack on the lowest level and place a baking stone or baking sheet on it. Preheat the oven to 425°F.

TOOLS *of the* TRADE

Pitting Cherries

"A large, heavy hairpin is the ideal cherry pitter. Insert the looped end into the stem end; hook it around the pit, and pull it out, taking care not to rupture the cherries."

—ROSE LEVY BERANBAUM

4. Stir together the sugar, cornstarch, and salt in a bowl. Stuff a currant into each cherry. Add the cherries to the sugar mixture along with any juice and the almond extract and gently stir. Set aside for at least 10 minutes. Stir again and transfer the mixture to the pie shell.

5. Roll the remaining, smaller piece of dough into a 10½ by 8-inch oval. Cut lengthwise into ten ¾-inch-wide strips. Cover the top of pie in a lattice pattern.

6. Set the pie on the baking stone or sheet and bake for 15 minutes. Cover the edges with foil and continue baking until bubbling thickly all over and the center is slightly puffed, 25 to 35 minutes. Transfer to a rack and let cool for at least 3 hours before serving. May be stored, uncovered, at room temperature for 2 days.

Notes

- If whole fresh currants are not available, you can make an all-cherry pie. Reduce the sugar by 2 tablespoons and the cornstarch by 1 teaspoon to 2 tablespoons plus 1½ teaspoons to allow for the different balance of sugars without the currants.
- If the lattice starts to become too dark toward the last 10 minutes of baking, lightly cover the pie with a piece of foil with a vent hole in the center.

Flaky Cream Cheese Pie Crust

MAKES ENOUGH FOR ONE 9-INCH LATTICE PIE

8 tablespoons (1 stick) unsalted butter, cold
1⅓ cups pastry flour or bleached all-purpose flour
⅛ teaspoon salt
⅛ teaspoon baking powder
3 ounces cream cheese, cold
1½ tablespoons ice water
½ tablespoon cider vinegar

1. Cut the butter into ¾-inch bits. Wrap in plastic wrap and freeze until solid.

2. Place the flour, salt, and baking powder in a reclosable gallon-size freezer bag and place in the freezer for at least 30 minutes.

3. Place the ingredients from the bag in a food processor and process a few seconds to combine. Add the cream cheese and process until the mixture resembles coarse meal, about 20 seconds. Add the frozen butter and process until all the butter bits are no larger than the size of peas. Add the water and vinegar and process until most of the butter is reduced to the size of small peas. The mixture will be in particles and will not hold together. Spoon it back into the freezer bag.

4. Holding the bag closed, knead and press the mixture from the outside of the bag until it holds together and feels slightly stretchy when pulled. Divide the dough into two-thirds and one-third portions, wrap each portion in plastic wrap, flatten it, and refrigerate for at least 45 minutes, preferably overnight. Will keep refrigerated for up to 2 days, frozen for 3 months.

Weaving a Lattice Pie Covering

To create a woven lattice pie covering, roll out the dough into an oval 1⁄16 inch thick. Cut into ¾-inch-wide strips and arrange half the strips, evenly, spaced parallel to each other across the top of the pie. Gently curve back every other strip a little past the center and place another strip perpendicularly across all the strips. Uncurve the strips so that they lie flat on top of the perpendicular strip. Working in the same direction, curve back those strips that were not curved back the first time. Lay a second perpendicular strip on top and uncurve the strips. Continue in this manner with a third perpendicular strip, curving back the strips that were not curved back the second time. Apply the remaining strips to the other side of the pie, starting near the center and working out toward the edge.

—ROSE LEVY BERANBAUM

Braeburn Apple and Cheddar Cheese Pie

MAKES ONE 9-INCH COVERED PIE

Sweet-tart, red-green, crunchy Braeburn apples provide a perfect filling for apple pie. Similar to Golden Delicious and Granny Smith apples, both of which grow in the same zones, Braeburns hold up under cooking and soften without collapsing. Laced with cheddar cheese, snuggled between a top and bottom crust that includes a little more of the cheese for accent, the apple mixture fulfills a dream of the *perfect all-American apple pie. Serve with vanilla ice cream on the side if you'd like it à la mode.*

AMY FALK (HOUSTON, TX)

"It is one of the anomalies of garden sentiment that he who shares his apples with the canker worm is reckoned a poor excuse for a gardener, while the gardener who shares his cherries with the birds, is credited with an ear for music and a poetic soul. True, birds, unlike, say, tent caterpillars, toil not neither do they spin. They do not actually disfigure the tree: it is presentable both before and after the catastrophe. They do, at times, sing, but then, canker worms can be melodious."

—Ian Jackson

Cheddar Cheese Pie dough (recipe follows)
5 to 6 cups Braeburn or other sweet-tart apples, such as Golden Delicious or Granny Smith
½ cup sugar
½ cup coarsely grated extra-sharp white cheddar cheese
¼ teaspoon ground cinnamon
¼ teaspoon ground nutmeg
1 tablespoon all-purpose flour
Extra sugar, for sprinkling on top after baking

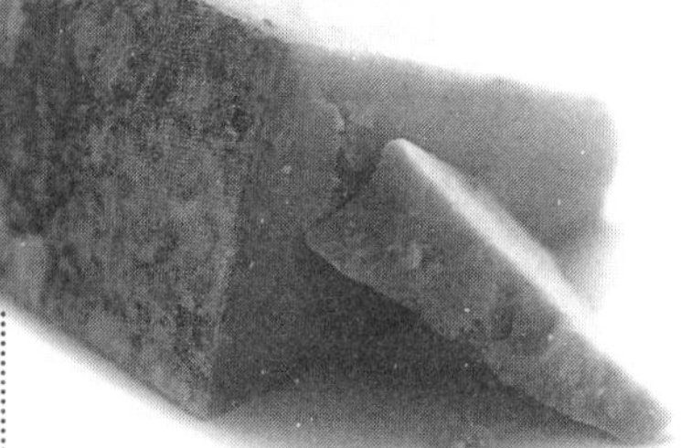

1. Prepare the pie dough.

2. Preheat the oven to 375°F.

3. Place all the remaining ingredients except the extra sugar in a bowl and toss to mix. Set aside.

4. Divide the dough unevenly in half. On a lightly floured board, roll out the larger half of the dough into a 12-inch round and place in a 9-inch pie pan, arranging so that it overhangs evenly all around. Put the filling into the pan, mounding it a bit in the center. Roll out the second half of the dough and place it over the filling to make a covered pie. Using a little water if necessary, crimp the top and bottom crusts together around the edge of the pie to seal in a decorative way.

5. Make several slits in the top crust to allow steam to escape. Bake for 1 hour, or until the top is speckled golden and bubbles are beginning to rise up through the slits. Remove and sprinkle a little sugar over the top. Cool on a rack. Slice and serve.

Cheddar Cheese Pie Dough

MAKES 2 PIE CRUSTS

1¼ cups all-purpose flour
¼ teaspoon salt
5 tablespoons unsalted butter, softened to room temperature
1 tablespoon solid vegetable shortening
½ cup coarsely grated extra-sharp white cheddar cheese
2 to 3 tablespoons cold water

1. Mix together the flour and salt in a large bowl. Add the butter, shortening, and cheese and mix with a pastry blender or your fingers until the mixture is crumbly.

Work in the cold water, starting with 2 tablespoons and adding the extra tablespoon if necessary, until the mixture is moist enough to gather into a ball.

2. You can use the dough right away. Or wrap it in plastic wrap and refrigerate for up to 3 days or freeze for up to 1 week.

Italian Plum Pie Crisp

SERVES 6 TO 8

Sometimes called prunes because they dry so well for keeping, Italian plums, which this contributor gathers from the two trees on her property in northern coastal Oregon, also make a perfect jam or jelly. "But you can only make so much plum jelly. This beautiful pie is a wonderful way to use the bounty." It's easy to make, and with a pie crust underneath and crisplike topping, it's innovative. If Italian plums are not available, you can substitute almost any other variety of dark-colored, not green, plum. Adjust the sugar to match the sweetness or tartness of the fruit.

CAROL ROSE (MILWAUKIE, OR)

One 9-inch ready-to-bake pie crust (see Notes below)
1 cup sugar
1 cup all-purpose flour
1 tablespoon cornstarch
¼ teaspoon salt
½ teaspoon ground cinnamon
¼ teaspoon ground nutmeg
4 cups pitted and quartered Italian plums (see Notes below)
1 tablespoon fresh lemon juice
2 tablespoons butter, melted
6 tablespoons (¾ stick) butter, at room temperature

1. Preheat the oven to 425°F.

2. Bake the pie crust until it begins to brown, 10 to 12 minutes. Set aside.

3. Combine ½ cup of the sugar, ¼ cup of the flour, the cornstarch, salt, cinnamon, and nutmeg in a large bowl. Stir to mix. Add the plums, lemon juice, and 2 tablespoons melted butter. Stir to mix and set aside.

4. Combine the remaining ½ cup sugar, remaining ¾ cup flour, and 6 tablespoons butter in a small bowl and mix until crumbly.

5. Pour the plum mixture into the crust. Sprinkle the topping over the plums. Bake for 10 minutes, reduce the heat to 350°F., and continue baking for 20 to 30 minutes, or until bubbling and browned on the top.

6. Cool slightly, then serve.

Notes

• Any of the pie crust variations listed on page 411 will suit this pie just fine. No prepared crust out of the freezer section of your grocery store will suit it at all.

• If using plums that are larger than the smallish Italian plums, that is, more than about 1 inch in diameter, cut them into sixths or eighths.

Blueberry Kuchen

MAKES ONE 9-INCH KUCHEN

In German, kuchen *means cake, and when the word is used in English, it also means cake. Usually. But in American cookery, liberties are sometimes taken with the dough, which is not at all cakelike, rather more like a cookie crust. This blueberry delight stretches the libertarian notion even further, so that a crust-bottomed, fruit-filled, crisp-topped, and fresh-fruit-garnished concoction becomes an American rendition of what the contributor describes as a kuchen, and "the rave of summer." Since the crust is almost a cookie, a spring-form pan or removable-bottom tart pan is essential so the kuchen can be removed from the pan and sliced without crumbling.*

STEPHANIE JUTILA (CLOQUET, MN)

1 cup plus 2 tablespoons all-purpose flour
⅔ cup plus 2 tablespoons sugar
⅛ teaspoon ground cinnamon
⅛ teaspoon salt
8 tablespoons (1 stick) butter, at room temperature
1½ to 2 tablespoons cider vinegar
5 cups blueberries (see box on page 421)

1. Preheat the oven to 400° F.

2. Mix together 2 tablespoons of the flour, ⅔ cup of the sugar, and the cinnamon in a small bowl. Set aside for the topping.

3. Combine the remaining 1 cup flour, remaining 2 tablespoons sugar, and the salt in a large bowl. Cut in the butter with your fingers or a pastry blender until the mixture is evenly crumbly. Add the vinegar and gather together into a dough ball.

4. Transfer the dough to a 9-inch springform or tart pan with a removable bottom. Pat and press the dough evenly across the bottom and about ¾ inch up the sides of the pan.

5. Spread 3 cups of the blueberries over the bottom of the crust, then sprinkle the topping over the berries. Bake for 50 to 60 minutes, or until the berries are bubbling and jamlike and the top is golden.

6. Remove from the oven and immediately arrange the remaining blueberries over the top. Set aside to cool.

7. When cool, remove the outer ring from the pan, slice the kuchen, and serve.

Berries: To Freeze or Not to Freeze?

Unlike Hamlet's dilemma, there's no doubt here: fresh berries are always best, but, for storing, berries of all kinds take well to freezing. As long as the fruit is freshly picked and tightly wrapped to prevent freezer burn, it defrosts with much of its original sparkle intact. So if you have a bounty, freezing is a good way to keep berries awhile. If you have an irresistible hunger for a certain berry dish, such as the Blueberry Kuchen, and it's the very beginning of the season when the cost of fresh fruit is still shockingly high, use mostly frozen berries for the filling and purchase a small basket of fresh berries to use as a garnish for the top.

Blueberry Bonanza with Cornmeal Topping

SERVES 6 TO 8

"From my childhood blueberry-picking days, I remember the camaraderie of young and old among the blueberry bushes quietly tending to the work at hand, interrupted only by nature noises and earthy aromas. Back home with the harvest, I remember blueberry muffins, pies, cobblers, and mostly my grandmother's Blueberry Bonanza coming straight from the oven. To this day, its taste and color evoke a rich, starry night enjoying this fruit of our day's outing."

~ JUDY ROGERS (BREWSTER, MA)

3 to 4 cups fresh blueberries (see box on page 421)
½ cup sugar
1 tablespoon fresh lemon juice
½ cup yellow cornmeal
¾ cup all-purpose flour
1½ teaspoons baking powder
½ teaspoon salt
½ cup plain yogurt or milk
3 tablespoons butter, melted
1 large egg, lightly beaten
Ice cream, frozen yogurt, or Crème Fraîche (optional, see box on page 382)

1. Preheat the oven to 425°F.

2. Place the blueberries in a 9-inch square baking dish. Add ¼ cup of the sugar and the lemon juice and toss to mix.

3. Mix together the cornmeal, flour, baking powder, salt, and remaining ¼ cup of sugar in a large bowl. Add the yogurt, butter, and egg and stir briefly until blended.

4. In 1 tablespoon amounts, drop small mounds of the cornmeal mixture over the top of the blueberries. Bake until the topping is golden brown, 20 to 25 minutes. Remove and cool enough to handle, then serve warm or at room temperature, topped with the cream garnish of your choice, if using.

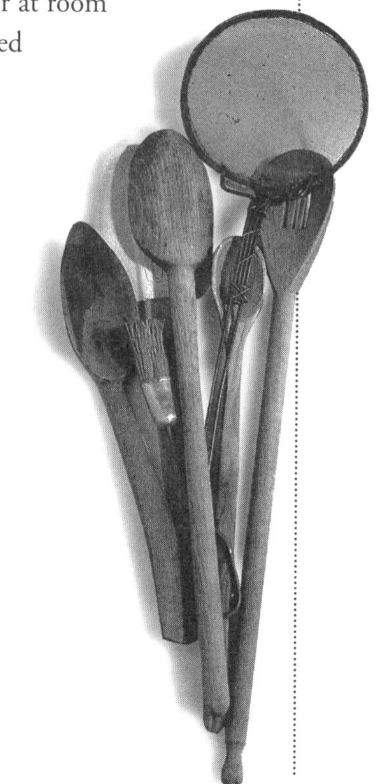

Blueberry Nostalgia: A Story

"When I was a child, blueberry picking was a ladies' day outing. The day was chosen when my mother, her sisters, and my great aunts agreed it was the perfect day. They'd all don their aprons with the widest pockets and tie their broadest hats under their chins. Their attire also included their everyday sturdy black shoes, rolled-down thick hose, and neatly pressed housedresses that wouldn't mind a blueberry stain or two. High-bush berries meant berry pails made of coffee cans with a nail hole on each side and a string laced through the middle and slung around the neck so that both hands remained free. Low-bush berry picking meant sitting on the ground, often in the midst of many prickly branches that sometimes hid cantankerous creatures. (On one otherwise perfect picking day for low-bush berries, at age five, in positioning myself this way, I sat on a hornets' nest. Of course, the event successfully ended our outing for that day.)

"It is said that Native Americans held blueberries in high esteem, that the Great Spirit sent 'star berries' to relieve the hunger of children during a famine. Fresh, smoked, or dried, berries were a staple food, used in soups, stews, and rubbed into meats. Tea from their roots was used as a relaxant during childbirth."

—JUDY ROGERS

Apple-Fennel Crisp with Pine Nut Topping

SERVES 6 TO 8

"In August, fennel flowers fill the driest corner of the garden with yellow lace and the smell of licorice. In September, the flowers go to seed—just in time for apple season. I cut the seedheads while they are still plump and let them dry in a bowl in the kitchen so I can continue to enjoy the scent. Then I bake."

ARIEL SWARTLEY (LOS ANGELES, CA)

Butter, for the baking dish
2 teaspoons fennel seeds
3 pounds firm, sweet-tart apples, such as Gravenstein, Granny Smith, Gala, or Braeburn, quartered, cored, and thinly sliced
1/8 teaspoon crushed mace blade
1 cup sugar
3/4 cup all-purpose flour
1/8 teaspoon salt
1/4 cup pine nuts, toasted (see Note below and page 135)
6 tablespoons (3/4 stick) butter, at room temperature, cut up
Heavy (whipping) cream or ice cream, for garnish (optional)

1. Preheat the oven to 350°F. Lightly butter a 2½-quart ceramic or glass baking dish.

2. Toast the fennel seeds in the oven, an ungreased skillet on the stovetop, or a microwave oven until beginning to brown, about 1 minute. Remove and let cool enough to handle. Crush in a mortar and pestle or in a spice grinder.

3. Place the apples, mace, fennel seeds, and ½ cup of the sugar in the baking dish and stir to mix.

4. Combine the remaining ½ cup of sugar, flour, salt, pine nuts, and butter in a medium bowl and mix with your fingers until crumbly. Sprinkle over the apples.

5. Bake until the apples are tender and the topping is golden brown, about 1 hour, depending on the type of apple.

6. Cool slightly, then serve warm, accompanied with cream or ice cream, if using.

Note: You can toast the fennel seeds and pine nuts in the oven at the same time; be sure to keep them separate.

Strawberry-Rhubarb Crisp with Pecan Topping

SERVES 8 TO 10

"I enjoy gardening and cooking with a passion and always look forward to spring when I can pick rhubarb from the garden for this crisp." With oats and pecans in the topping, what might be just another rendition of the classic strawberries and rhubarb combination becomes a reminder of the Kentucky landscape. As a culinary bonus, the topping can be transposed to many other crisps.

JEAUNE HADL (LEXINGTON, KY)

Pecan Topping (recipe follows)
1 pound rhubarb stalks, trimmed and cut into ½-inch pieces (about 4 cups)
4 cups strawberries, hulled and halved
½ cup sugar
1 tablespoon cornstarch
2 tablespoons fresh orange juice

1. Prepare the topping.

2. Preheat the oven to 400°F.

3. Combine the rhubarb, strawberries, sugar, cornstarch, and orange juice in a large bowl. Transfer to an ungreased 13 by 9-inch baking dish and dot the topping over the fruit mixture. Bake for 35 to 40 minutes, or until the topping is golden brown.

4. Cool slightly and serve.

Pecan Topping

MAKES 3 TO 3½ CUPS

1½ cups all-purpose flour
1 cup old-fashioned (rolled) oats
1 cup (packed) dark brown sugar
1 cup (2 sticks) butter, at room temperature
1 cup coarsely chopped pecans

Place the flour, oats, and sugar in a large bowl and stir to mix. Add the butter and mix with your fingers or a pastry blender until moist clumps form. Mix in the pecans and use right away.

Apple Impromptu with Praline Topping

SERVES 10 TO 12

Amateur lepidopterist, naturalist, and published writer on these subjects, the contributor is also well versed in the foods of the world. She offers this recipe, along with a toast to share around the table. "How enticing, the lateness, intimacy, and elegance of the supper where this was the last dish served at an occasion arranged in honor of my high school graduation and valedictory address by a good friend of my mother, my former scout mistress, during the last year our family lived in Social Circle, Georgia. I remember gratefully what I received, and I propose a toast to gracious generosity everywhere and those whose work sets forth good food: May they sit in comfort with good company, enjoying the fruits of their labor."

BARBARA DEUTSCH (SAN FRANCISCO, CA, VIA SOCIAL CIRCLE, GA)

Butter, for the baking dish
3 pounds apples, quartered, cored, and very thinly sliced (see Note below)
1 cup sugar
1 teaspoon crushed cardamom seed
½ teaspoon ground cinnamon
1 teaspoon finely chopped lemon zest
2 large eggs
2 tablespoons butter, at room temperature
2 teaspoons vanilla extract
1 cup all-purpose flour
1 teaspoon baking powder
¼ teaspoon salt
2 cups coarsely chopped pecans
2 cups heavy (whipping) cream lightly whipped (optional)

1. Preheat the oven to 400°F. Generously butter a 13 by 9-inch baking dish.

2. Place the apple slices in the baking dish and toss with ½ cup of the sugar, the cardamom, cinnamon, and lemon zest. Cover and bake for 15 to 20 minutes, or until the apples are tender but still hold their shape. Remove and set aside.

3. Lightly beat the eggs in a bowl. Add the butter, vanilla, and remaining ½ cup sugar and cream together. Sift the flour, baking powder, and salt into the bowl. Add the pecans and mix until blended.

4. Drop silver dollar-size pats of the pecan mixture on top of the apples, arranging the pats so they are just touching but not overlapping. Bake until the topping is golden and the juices are bubbling up, 25 to 30 minutes.

5. Cool slightly, then serve while still warm, accompanied by the whipped cream, if using.

Note: If the apples are tender-skinned, such as red Gravensteins or Braeburns, there's no need to peel them. If they are thick-skinned, such as Pippins, Granny Smiths, or Winesaps, it's better to pare away the peels so they cook up tender.

Variations

- Rather than bake the apples, poach them in a little butter and red wine before assembling the dish.
- Vary the spices with ground allspice, nutmeg, or cloves in addition to or in place of the cinnamon and cardamom.
- Use almond extract in place of the vanilla extract.
- Substitute almonds for the pecans; although the almonds will, strictly speaking, not make a praline topping, it will still be good.
- Instead of whipped cream, serve with Crème Fraîche (see box on page 382) or vanilla ice cream.

Upside-Down Peach Shortcake with Biscuit Topping

SERVES 8 TO 10

"Though I garden, I am more enthusiastic about cooking, baking, and developing new recipes. My neighbors, however, are avid gardeners and I reap the harvest of their efforts. The appeal of this recipe, which came to me from my mother, is the ease with which it can be made and its flexibility. I have included nectarines, plums, rhubarb, strawberries, or apples as alternates to the peaches." The biscuitlike topping can be baked on its own for a classic strawberry shortcake, but since it was peaches that day and the biscuit was on top instead of underneath, our recipe testers dubbed this recipe upside-down peach shortcake.

RUTH TILLMAN (LOUISVILLE, KY)

"The Bartons End orchards started when Thomas planted apples, pears, quinces, and cherries. It was quite common to have to wait ten or twenty years before one got a crop from a big standard apple or cherry tree. Moreover, when the orchard was producing, the fruit might be stolen. Thomas Barton took the view that, even if the interval between planting and cropping were long,

(continued on next page)

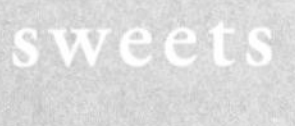

Biscuit Topping (recipe follows)
Butter, for the baking dish
6 to 8 cups peeled, pitted, and sliced peaches
2 tablespoons cornstarch
½ to ¾ teaspoon ground cinnamon, to taste
⅛ teaspoon salt
1 to 2 cups sugar, to taste and depending on the sweetness of the fruit
1 cup heavy (whipping) cream, whipped until soft peaks form (optional)

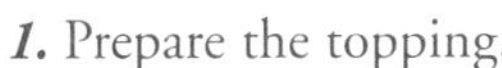

1. Prepare the topping.

2. Preheat the oven to 375°F. Lightly butter a 13 by 9-inch baking dish.

3. Combine the peaches, cornstarch, cinnamon, salt, and sugar in a nonreactive saucepan and stir to mix. Cook over medium heat, stirring frequently, until the sugar melts and the mixture begins to thicken, 3 to 5 minutes. Transfer to the baking dish.

4. In 1 tablespoon amounts, drop the biscuit topping over the peaches. Bake for 30 minutes, until the topping is lightly browned and cooked through. Remove and let cool.

5. When cool, slice and serve, accompanied by the whipped cream, if using.

Biscuit Topping

MAKES ENOUGH TOPPING FOR A 13 BY 9-INCH COBBLER OR NINE 2½-INCH BISCUITS

1½ cups all-purpose flour
½ cup sugar
½ teaspoon salt
2 teaspoons baking powder
¼ teaspoon baking soda
4 tablespoons butter, at room temperature
1 cup plain yogurt or ½ cup milk
2 teaspoons vanilla extract (optional)

1. Blend the flour, sugar, salt, baking powder, and baking soda in a bowl. Cut in the butter, blending until the mixture is crumbly. Add the yogurt and the vanilla, if using, and stir just until mixed into a wet dough. Use right away or set aside at room temperature for up to 30 minutes.

2. To use as a topping, drop tablespoon-size dollops over the fruit just before baking.

3. To use as a biscuit under fresh fruit, divide the dough into 9 portions. Pat each into a round about ½ inch thick. Place the rounds on an ungreased cookie sheet and bake in a 425°F. oven for 12 to 15 minutes, or until lightly golden on top and cooked through. Remove and cool, then use as desired.

(continued from previous page)

one was adding to the value of the farm and planting for one's children. . . . As to the theft, there were two remedies: one was to have a pair of mastiffs roaming the area and the other, possibly more important, recourse was to be generous with one's fruit when it finally arrived."

—George Ordish, *The Living Garden*

Sweet Potato Crunch

SERVES 8 TO 10

"Sweet potato tubers are usually harvested in mid-October in the Deep South. They are easily stored in a cool, dry bin and keep almost as well as other potatoes. They never seem to linger around our house because of this fabulous recipe." It's no wonder. This is a sweet potato pie without the crust, instead with a crunchy pecan topping, a lot like toffee that is a kind of heaven for butter and brown sugar lovers.

MIKE RAWL (JACKSONVILLE, FL)

Butter, for the baking dish
2 large eggs
1 cup sugar
3 cups cooked and mashed sweet potatoes
8 tablespoons (1 stick) butter, melted
1 teaspoon vanilla extract
⅓ cup all-purpose flour
1 cup (packed) light brown sugar
6 tablespoons (¾ stick) butter, at room temperature
1 cup finely chopped pecans

1. Preheat the oven to 350°F. Lightly butter a 9-inch square baking dish or a 10-inch deep-dish pie pan.

2. Crack the eggs into a large bowl and beat lightly. Add the sugar and beat until blended. Beat in the mashed sweet potatoes, then the melted butter and vanilla. Pour into the baking dish.

3. Combine the flour and brown sugar in a small bowl. Cut in the butter and mix until crumbly. Stir in the chopped pecans and spread over the sweet potato mixture.

4. Bake for 40 to 45 minutes, or until firm and a knife inserted in the center comes out clean. Cool completely, then slice and serve.

fruit for dessert

Fruit in season is a special prize from the gardener who has pruned, watered, fed, and, in any other way required, tended its growing. At first not much needs doing beyond collecting and enjoying the fruit on the spot. A bit later, however, when there's more from the tree or bramble or bush than can possibly be consumed out of hand, enter the cook. In the kitchen, the fruit is transformed into an end-of-meal delight. By then, of course, the dish may include some kitchen embellishments not found in the garden. Praise the gardener; praise the cook.

Fresh Figs and Raspberries with Mint-Infused Ganache

SERVES 6 TO 8

Alice Medrich, founder of Cocolat chocolate stores and cookbook author, has made her fame with her exquisite, fanciful chocolate concoctions. For this garden cooking book, she offers a dessert of fresh fruit cozily tucked in a blanket of ganache. She explains, "Chocolate melted with fresh cream is called ganache. For the infusion, fresh peppermint with bright green leaves, rather than the rusty-edged spearmint, is what we are looking for here. Toss out all prior notions about mint-flavored chocolate. Use a very nice quality chocolate and expect a revelation. Serve this simple but sophisticated dessert in rustic earthenware bowls or your best stemmed crystal. Some might be inclined to gild the lily with a little bitty dollop of whipped cream."

ALICE MEDRICH (BERKELEY, CA)

FIG INSPIRATIONS

Fruit to please the palate.
Leaves to bed the plate and wrap the sausage.
Clothes for Adam and Eve.

¾ cup heavy (whipping) cream
⅓ cup chopped fresh peppermint leaves
6 ounces quality bittersweet or semisweet chocolate, finely chopped
12 ripe fresh figs, quartered
¾ cup fresh raspberries
⅓ cup slivered or sliced almonds, toasted (see page 135)
6 to 8 good-looking small peppermint sprigs, for garnish

1. Combine the cream and chopped mint in a small saucepan and bring to a boil. Remove from the heat, cover the pot, and allow the mint to steep in the cream for 5 minutes.

2. Place the chocolate in a bowl and set a strainer over it. When the cream has steeped, pour it through the strainer, pressing gently on the mint to extract all the cream. Discard the mint.

3. Gently stir the cream-and-chocolate mixture until it is perfectly smooth and all the chocolate is melted. Let cool just until the consistency of a thick sauce.

4. Spoon about 2 tablespoons of the sauce into 6 to 8 individual bowls. Scatter the figs and raspberries over the sauce. Drizzle the remaining sauce over the fruit. Sprinkle with the toasted almonds, garnish with the mint sprigs, and serve.

Note: You can cool the ganache completely and rewarm it very gently in its pan set over another pan of barely simmering water.

Stuffed Fig Variation: Cut figs into halves instead of quarters. Cool the ganache to a soft, spreadable consistency. Spread a mound of the ganache on the cut surface of each fig and sprinkle with toasted almonds.

Poached Peaches with Vanilla Custard and Wild Blackberries

Serves 4 to 8

There Are Peaches, and Then There Are Peaches

For the poached peaches, Dori doesn't specify the variety of peach, though she does say in her cookbook that many kinds of both freestone and cling peaches are part of the farm crop, and that she prefers the freestones for their more flavorful flesh. In addition, freestone peaches are easily pulled away from the pit into neat halves.

Dori Sanders, novelist (Clover, Her Own Place) *and cookbook writer* (Dori Sanders' Country Cooking) *grew up on the family's peach plantation near York, South Carolina. To this day, she does most of her writing in the winter so that in the growing season she can take care of the family farm and peach stand. In this recipe, as in her writing, she weaves the skill, craft, and art of her various activities into a whole that opens horizons perhaps not expected from the title. "I've been trying to understand why anyone would want a poached peach recipe since to poach simply means to cook in a hot liquid that is kept below boiling. For sure in my day, it was common cooking for farm women. With ovens crammed full of baking bread, potatoes, and so on, stovetop cooking was necessary. Sometimes when my mother wanted to make something sweet for dinner and didn't have extra butter, she'd poach a big kettle of peach halves, then slice or cut them into pieces. If there was a block of ice in the ice house, she'd make a thin custard sauce—something she nearly always had the ingredients for—lightly chill it, and spoon it over the peaches before serving. I am almost certain this recipe and the idea to serve poached peach halves filled with vanilla custard came from my Aunt Vestula." Cook Sanders recommends that each person be served two peach halves; for a somewhat less extravagant but equally satisfying portion, one custard-filled half per person is still a good helping.*

DORI SANDERS (YORK, SC)

2½ cups Vanilla Custard, chilled (recipe follows)
3 tablespoons honey
½ teaspoon ground allspice
4 ripe but still firm peaches, peeled, halved lengthwise, and pitted (see box on page 430)
1 cup wild blackberries, rinsed and gently patted dry (see Note below)

1. Prepare the custard and refrigerate until chilled.

2. Bring 2 quarts of water, the honey, and allspice to a boil in a large saucepan. Add the peach halves and reduce the heat to maintain a simmer. Cook, uncovered, until tender, 5 to 7 minutes. Drain, place the peaches in a shallow dish, and refrigerate until chilled.

3. To serve, spoon the custard into the chilled peach halves and top with the blackberries.

Note: If you don't have wild blackberries, or the deer and birds have got to them before you went picking, you can substitute raspberries, blueberries, or another summer berry.

Vanilla Custard

MAKES 2½ CUPS

2 cups milk
3 medium egg yolks
¾ cup sugar
1 teaspoon vanilla extract

1. Bring the milk just to the boil in a medium saucepan. Remove from the heat and set aside to cool.

THICKENING THE CUSTARD

For any kind of custard, pudding, or egg-thickened cooked sauce, there are two ways to go. The less risky is to use a double boiler. That way, the ingredients never get so hot the eggs scramble in the blink of an eye. The trickier way to go is to set the saucepan directly over medium-low heat and be ready to lift it off the heat from time to time when the mixture even hints at getting too hot. This requires a bit of expertise, but with practice it works and is more direct.

2. In a medium bowl, beat the egg yolks until light and lemon-colored. Add the sugar in 3 batches, beating after each addition. Continue beating until well blended, then slowly add the milk.

3. Pour the mixture into a nonreactive saucepan or double boiler over slowly boiling water. Cook over medium-low heat, stirring constantly, until the mixture thickens and coats the spoon (see page 431).

4. Stir in the vanilla and use right away or pour into a bowl and chill.

Note: For another crème anglaise-type custard sauce, see page 441.

Peach Dessert Salad

SERVES 6 TO 8

From "a city gardener in downtown Philadelphia with only a roof deck for my plants, flowers, herbs" comes a most refreshing concoction of sweetened fruits highlighted with fresh mint. It's for after dinner, "perfect for summertime, especially after a large or heavy meal."

LYNDA CONNELLY (PHILADELPHIA, PA)

2 pounds ripe peaches, peeled and thinly sliced
4 very firm kiwis, peeled and thinly sliced
1 cup fresh orange juice
¼ cup fresh lemon juice
2 tablespoons sugar
1 tablespoon shredded fresh mint leaves

1. Place all the ingredients in a large bowl and gently stir to mix. Cover and refrigerate long enough to chill, up to several hours.

2. Spoon the fruit and juices into individual bowls and serve.

Sun and Shadows and Mint on the Roof

Mint of any sort is a good candidate for rooftop container gardening—there's sun and shade both, enough of each to make the mint happy as the day turns. Sun enough from overhead to make it perky. Shade enough from the eaves of the roof, a clothesline of laundry flapping in the breeze, shadows cast over the roof by neighboring buildings to protect it from leaf burning or wilting. With adequate water provided by the doting rooftop gardener, the mint thrives in its pot. An added advantage is that the container, whether on the rooftop or on the patio, tames mint's invasive tendency so the gardener does not constantly have to pull it back from overcrowding its neighbors in the ground.

garden-inspired cooldowns

When it's time to wipe your brow, take a rest, and relish an icy spoonful of release from the labors of a hot day in the garden, a sorbet is just right. With some berries or herbs and a recipe on hand to turn those ingredients into a spirited cooldown, you can be prepared for that moment. Following are three offerings from contributors who must have had the same notion on a summer afternoon.

How Deep the Freeze, How Smooth the Ice?

The answer depends on what version of flavored ice you are making. Beginning with a fruit purée or herb-infused simple syrup, you can turn out a sherbet, sorbet, granita, or slush. Following is a description of each and how to attain it.

SHERBET: Puréed fruit or herb-infused simple syrup, either egg or cream thickened. Smooth as ice cream; should be frozen all the way through.

SORBET: Frozen through like sherbet but not egg enriched; with or without cream (with cream leads back to sherbet; without tends toward granita).

GRANITA: Also called ice; without dairy and frozen almost but not quite through. For granitas, the mixture is broken up from time to time as it freezes so that it comes out with a finely granulated texture. Ice cream makers won't do for making this kind of ice. A touch of alcohol, such as tequila or vodka, besides adding a bit of flavor, also helps keep the ice from freezing solid.

SLUSH: Basically a sweetened fruit purée that is partially frozen. An ice cream maker will do to begin the freezing. Then, while still half liquid, the mixture is whisked to homogenize it, and it is served as a smooth liquid ice, usually with a straw.

Beyond all those, there are snow cones, smoothies, and slurpies, the cooldowns popular at summer carnivals and fairs and at fast food stores. These are mostly finely crushed ice flavored with a fruit syrup, rather than a fruit purée. They come in a range of flavors and are usually served with both a straw and a spoon.

Marion Berry Sorbet

Makes 3 cups

"Though I do not have marion berries in my small garden, I make a trip to Sauvie Island to pick them, usually in early July. Their intense berry flavor and iridescent purple-red color are experiences no one should miss." If you don't live in the Northwest, you probably can't get fresh marion berries. However, they are available frozen, and frozen will do for sorbet. You can also substitute another variety of blackberry, such as loganberries, boysenberries, or olallies.

MOLLY BROWN (PORTLAND, OR)

⅔ cup sugar
⅓ cup light corn syrup
2 tablespoons fresh lemon juice (optional)
2 cups marion berries, rinsed

1. In a small saucepan, combine ⅔ cup water, the sugar, corn syrup, and lemon juice, if using. Stir over medium heat until the sugar dissolves. Remove and cool.

2. Purée the berries in a food processor (see Notes below), stir in the sugar mixture, and freeze in an ice cream maker according to the manufacturer's instructions. Will keep in the freezer for up to 2 weeks.

Notes

• The optional lemon juice is to help keep the color bright. It's not important for flavor or texture, and the sorbet is fine with or without it.

• If you would like a smooth sorbet, purée the berries in a food processor, then press through a strainer to remove the seeds. Or pass them through a food mill straightaway.

The Lowdown on Sorbet and Ice Cream Makers

Small, refrigerant-filled, cylinder-type ice cream makers that require no salt or ice are a useful tool for most home sorbet and ice cream making. The drawback is that they are small and don't do quite the whole job if making sorbet for more than four. You can solve that by making the sorbet or ice cream in batches, transferring each to another (freezer) container as you go. Transfer your sorbet to a plastic tub and let the freezer finish up on its own.

Thyme-Infused Lemon Sorbet

MAKES 3 CUPS

"I like desserts that contain savory elements and I prefer sorbet to ice cream. Lemon and thyme are two of my favorite flavors. I created this sorbet especially for a refreshing conclusion to a summer meal. The inspiration comes from my raised beds, mere yearlings still at this moment, especially the one devoted to herbs that sits just outside our kitchen door." One of the recipe testers remarked that it's interesting to find out how much herb it takes to get a distinctive herb flavor in such a dish, and goes on to note that this recipe has done it. So don't be intimidated by the amount of herb called for—sometimes that's what it takes.

KATHRYN WALSH (DORCHESTER, MA)

1½ cups sugar
3 to 4 tablespoons chopped lemon zest, to taste
¾ cup fresh lemon juice
3 to 4 cups very coarsely chopped fresh thyme

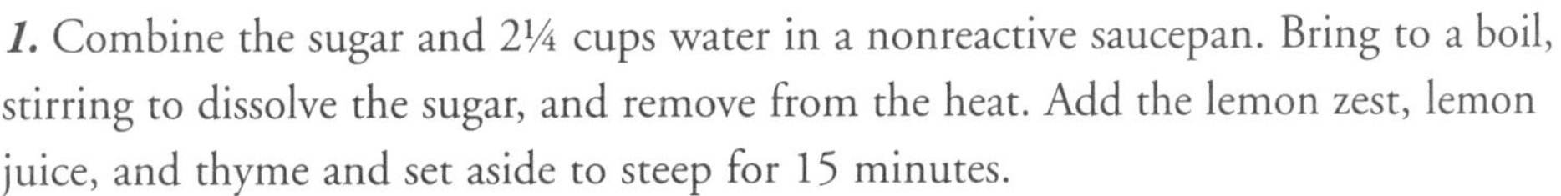

1. Combine the sugar and 2¼ cups water in a nonreactive saucepan. Bring to a boil, stirring to dissolve the sugar, and remove from the heat. Add the lemon zest, lemon juice, and thyme and set aside to steep for 15 minutes.

2. Strain and chill the liquid, then freeze in an ice cream maker according to the manufacturer's instructions.

3. Serve right away or store in the freezer for up to 10 days.

Note: If you would like to keep flecks of the lemon zest in the sorbet, don't chop the thyme. Leave it in sprigs and tie the sprigs in a bundle. That way, you can remove the thyme from the infusion, leaving the zest and freezing the mix without straining.

Fashioning Other Herbaceous Lemon Sorbets

The lemon flavoring of a simple sorbet leaves the cook freedom to innovate by replacing the thyme with another edible, aromatic herb. Particularly good in combination with lemon are the blossoms or flowers of chamomile, acacia, angelica, lavender, caraway, and chrysanthemum.

> *"To make Snow: Take a quart of thick Creame, and five or six whites of Eggs, a saucer full of sugar finely beaten, and as much Rose water, beat them all together, and always as it riseth take it out with a spoon, then take a loaf of Bread, cut away the crust, set it in a platter, and a great rose-mary bush in the middle of it, then lay you Snow with a Spoon upon the Rosemary, and so serve it."*
>
> —*A Book of Fruits and Flowers*, 1653

Cracked Peppercorn and Buttermilk Sorbet with Lemon Thyme

MAKES 1½ QUARTS

In a wild innovation that runs true to American style, Chef Kennedy has concocted a sorbet based on buttermilk and speckled with black peppercorns. The buttermilk makes the sorbet opaque, more like ice cream in appearance, but one taste and you know it's clearly a sorbet, refreshingly light and lemony, with a punch from the pepper. The peppercorns should not be too coarsely cracked.

KEVIN KENNEDY, CHEF, GREENWOOD INN (PORTLAND, OR)

4 cups buttermilk
1½ cups light corn syrup
½ cup sugar
1 tablespoon lemon thyme leaves
1 teaspoon cracked black pepper
1½ teaspoons finely chopped lemon zest
½ cup fresh lemon juice

1. Combine all the ingredients in a large bowl and mix until the sugar is dissolved. Freeze in an ice cream maker according to the manufacturer's instructions.

2. Serve right away or store in the freezer for up to 10 days.

Sugar on Snow over Maple Squash Conserve

SERVES 8

One of Vermont's renowned natural gifts paired with one of its widely cultivated vegetables in a garden-meets-kitchen conserve stretches far beyond state boundaries in a sweet winter embrace. As the contributor explains, "Sugar on snow is a Vermont tradition. In spring, when the maple sap is being cooked down over wood fires to make maple syrup, ladles full of boiling syrup are poured over dishes filled with fresh snow. The syrup instantly hardens, forming a rich candy that tastes wonderful with the cold, airy mouthfuls of snow. The 'snow' in this recipe is vanilla ice cream, and around here, we prefer Ben & Jerry's World's Best Vanilla."

DEBORAH KRASNER (PUTNEY, VT)

½ cup maple syrup, preferably Grade B dark (see box on this page)
2 cups Maple Squash Conserve (recipe follows)
8 scoops vanilla ice cream

1. Boil the syrup in a nonstick pan until bubbles form and it beads off a wooden spoon. Set aside, keep warm, and bring to a boil again just before serving.

2. Spoon about ¼ cup of the conserve into 8 individual bowls. Add a scoop of vanilla ice cream. Ladle the boiling syrup over the top and serve right away.

Maple Syrup Secrets from Where They Know

For Vermonters, the preferred maple syrup is the one commercially classified as Grade B. Though that may call up memories of report cards where you didn't quite make it to the A, in this case the down-one-notch, B grade is more desirable. Darker brown and less refined than the lighter-colored, more lightly flavored, and more expensive Grade A maple syrup, Grade B retains the taste and spirit of the sugar maples from whence it comes.

Maple Squash Conserve

MAKES 2 CUPS

½ to 2 pounds Red Kuri, acorn, butternut, or other orange-fleshed winter squash (see box on page 438)
½ cup maple syrup, preferably Grade B
1 tablespoon butter
1 tablespoon finely chopped orange zest
1 tablespoon Triple Sec or other orange liqueur

1. Preheat the oven to 375°F.

2. Cut the squash in half. Scoop out the seeds and fibers, scraping the surface of the pulp clean. Place the squash halves, cut side down, in a baking dish filled with 1 inch of water. Bake until the skin is easily pierced with a fork and the pulp is also fork tender, 45 minutes to 1 hour. Remove and set aside to cool.

3. When cool enough to handle, scoop out the pulp. In a food processor or blender, purée it with the maple syrup until smooth.

4. Melt the butter in a nonstick pan. Add the squash purée and cook down over low heat, stirring as necessary, until reduced by half. This will take from 30 to 45 minutes, depending on the water content of the squash you are using.

5. Add the zest and liqueur and cook for 5 minutes more. Remove from the heat and use right away or cool and store in the refrigerator for up to 5 days.

Winter Squashes in a Winter Wonderland

"Vermont's climate is perfect for growing hard-skinned winter squash, from well-known varieties such as sugar pumpkin, acorn, and butternut, to less well-known ones like Red Kuri. Although all these squashes are similar in flavor, they vary in water content enormously. In particular, butternuts and Kuris are dry and take less time to cook down than other varieties, yet yield a rich, chestnutlike texture. The squash conserve can be made with any kind of winter squash, but adjust the cooking-down time accordingly."

—DEBORAH KRASNER

Variations: You don't need to save the conserve for dessert. Have it:

- for breakfast on top of pancakes, with the extra maple syrup.
- alongside Thanksgiving turkey, without the extra maple syrup.
- over rice, with the extra maple syrup for a healthful snack or interim meal reminiscent of rice pudding or Chinese jook.

dessert sauces and condiments

"What's sauce for the goose is sauce for the gander."

—American saying

Sometimes when the cake or pie asks for more decoration, when the ice cream needs a bit of dressing up, a sweet sauce can meet the call in just the right way. With textures smooth as silk, nubby as chenille, pillowy as clouds scudding across the sky and colors to choose form, the following sauce recipes offer choices for however you'd like to dollop, douse, or dose your dessert.

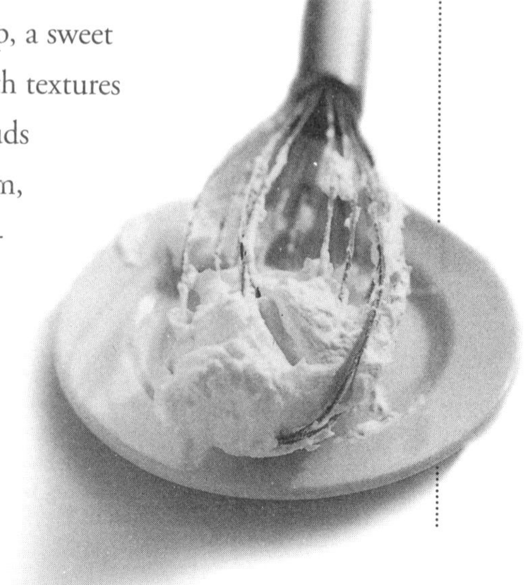

Strawberry Spoon Sauce

Makes 2½ cups

"Strawberry Point received its name from the wild strawberries that used to grow here. Though they are no longer plentiful, we still celebrate Strawberry Days every June with many strawberry preparations. I received this particular recipe from my mother-in-law fifty years ago. It does not need any extras, and it is quick and easy—the berries plump and thicken by standing overnight. You should never do more than one quart of strawberries at a time." With a consistency more like syrup than jam, but with whole fruit, this sauce closely resembles sunshine strawberries (see box on page 440) and a Greek-style spoon sweet, which is served in a hospitality spoon along with a small cup of coffee or tea. Over ice cream, plain pound or sponge cake, rice pudding, waffles, pancakes, a sweet biscuit, swirled into plain yogurt—its pleasures go on and on.

CHARLOTTE FLIEHLER
(STRAWBERRY POINT, IA)

4 cups whole strawberries, hulled and rinsed
2 tablespoons fresh lemon juice
4 cups sugar

1. Place the strawberries and lemon juice in a large nonreactive pot. Slowly bring to a boil over medium-low heat.

2. Add the sugar, stir gently to mix, and bring to a boil again. Reduce the heat to maintain a steady boil without boiling over the pot and cook for 8 minutes.

Spoon Sauce Subtleties

Some recipes can be doubled, tripled, halved, or quartered without effect on the outcome. It's just more or less; do the math and you're there. Others, however, don't come out the way they're meant to with straightforward adding and subtracting. Such is this strawberry spoon sauce. If you try to make a huge amount, more than the recipe calls for, the strawberries will render so much liquid in the initial stage that, even with more sugar, the short cooking time that is essential to this preparation will not work. You will have to cook the strawberry mixture into another, not necessarily undesirable, state—that is, strawberry jam, not strawberry spoon sauce.

3. Remove from the heat and pour into a crock or heat proof glass bowl. Let stand for 24 hours, stirring occasionally to plump the berries and make sure the sugar remains evenly distributed throughout the mixture.

4. Use right away or transfer to jars, cap (see page 314), and store in the refrigerator. Will keep for up to 3 months.

Solar Strawberry Topping

"As a gardener, spending as much time as possible outdoors is my greatest passion. To grow my own fruits and vegetables under the sun and to harvest them under the sun ideally means the end result has been or can be cooked under the sun."

Strawberry Spoon Sauce is remarkably similar to the sunshine strawberries that some of our recipe testers remembered from Girl Scout days. Here's how to make them.

Choose ripe red strawberries. Overripe will not do, nor will underripe. Hull, rinse, and pat dry the berries. Slice them in half and measure how much you have.

Place the berries in a clear glass dish. For every 2 cups strawberries, add 1 cup of sugar and ½ lemon, sliced. Stir gently, cover the dish with plastic wrap, and set aside on a counter that receives direct sunlight for 5 hours or so.

Transfer to a nonreactive pot and remove the lemon slices. Bring to a boil over medium-high heat, stirring all the time. Lower the heat to maintain a brisk simmer, skim off the froth, and cook for 8 minutes, or until the liquid is syrupy. Or cook a little longer for a thicker, more jamlike consistency. Cool and use right away or transfer to glass jars and store in the refrigerator.

—WANDA ROWE (MIAMI, FL)

Strawberry-Rhubarb Sauce

MAKES 2½ TO 3 CUPS

"I've been a gardening cook and a cooking gardener for more than thirty years now. One of my favorites was always and still is Strawberry-Rhubarb Sauce. Rhubarb is one of the hardiest plants in any garden, and strawberries are the perfect flavor complement. The recipe is so simple it hardly qualifies as a recipe, but in a hurry-up society, something this quick and easy can be rewarding to make and provide a touch of nostalgia." The sauce is a versatile breakfast, lunch, and dinner sauce. Use it on pound cake, angel food cake, waffles, or pancakes. It's also a delicious accompaniment to pork or game dishes or, southern style, for rice.

LUCILLE WENDELL (SOUTH HOLLAND, IL)

1 pound rhubarb stalks, trimmed and cut into ½-inch pieces (about 4 cups)

2 cups strawberries, hulled, rinsed, and halved

1 cup sugar

3 tablespoons water

1. Combine all the ingredients in a nonreactive saucepan and bring to a boil over medium heat. Reduce the heat to medium-low, cover the pan, and cook, stirring frequently, until the rhubarb is tender, about 20 minutes.

2. Remove and cool. Use right away or chill first. Will keep in the refrigerator for up to 2 weeks or freeze for longer storage.

Variations

- For a less sweet sauce, increase the rhubarb to 5 cups per 1 cup of sugar.
- Add orange, either zest or juice concentrate, more or less to suit your taste.

The Ruddy Rhubarb

Botanically speaking, rhubarb is a leafy stalk and so belongs to the realm of vegetables. But culinarily, it belongs to the realm of fruit. It is sometimes described as "red celery" for its resemblance to that other leafy stalk or, more poetically, as "the harbinger of spring" because it is one of the first "fruits" to appear after frost. Its nickname, "pie plant," aptly describes its use in the kitchen, where the stalk (not the leaf, which is toxic) is employed as filling for pies and crisps or as an ingredient in mixed jams and dessert sauces paired with ginger, orange, angelica, or its most common companion, strawberry.

Lavender Cream

MAKES 1½ CUPS

Lavender is mostly thought of and used as a scent for soaps, for sachets in the lingerie drawer, and for pillowcase wrapped bouquets tucked under the pillow to encourage sweet dreams. Yet the cook, ever curious about the kitchen use of any garden edible, also leans toward lavender's potential for the pot. For this purpose, the blossoms are selected—the leaves being too pungent—and used in herb rubs, especially those destined for lamb; brewed into a calming tea; or, as here, infused into an aromatic crème anglaise–type dessert sauce. Serve it as a sauce for berries, chocolate cake, plain pound cake, or sponge cake. Or spoon it into small bowls and accompany with cookies.

PAM BACKUS (VALDERS, WI)

1 cup heavy (whipping) cream
1 cup milk
¼ cup honey
⅓ cup sugar
Pinch of salt
Blossoms from 10 sprigs of lavender
4 extra-large egg yolks

1. Combine the cream, milk, honey, sugar, salt, and lavender in the top of a double boiler. Set over simmering water and cook, stirring occasionally, until beginning to thicken, about 10 minutes.

Lavender from Creature to Creature

Lavender lends it stalwart, aromatic, hardy beauty to many living things. Let go in a wide-open meadow, a stand of it will grow thick and high as a hedge and yield a crop of cuttings enough for the gardener to contemplate commerce. In the herb bed of the garden, it stretches its multihued purple spikes up to the sky, or at least three feet high, as it seeks its spot in the sun above the other plants. Or, with attentive pruning, it happily lies lower to the ground to provide a border around a sunny flower bed. In any of these situations, the sight and scent of lavender, from top to bottom, invites creatures of many kinds. The nectar of its blossoms attracts pollinating bees and hungry butterflies. Its upright stems suggest a natural loom for spiders to weave a web. Its thick undergrowth serves as an umbrella for cats to nap under, sheltered from the heat of the day and mostly safe from intrusion—except from the gardener cook, who is foraging for lavender cuttings. As the cat yawns, stretches, and ponders whether or not to move, as the bees and butterflies scurry away while the spiders are not to be budged, the gardener cuts some of the plant, flower and stem both, taking care not to disturb the other minuscule inhabitants of such a generous plant. The cuttings go to the kitchen; the flying creatures return; the cat goes wherever a cat goes.

2. Lightly beat the egg yolks in a bowl. Whisk in half the warm cream mixture. Whisk this mixture back into the double boiler. Continue cooking over the simmering water, stirring from time to time, until the mixture thickens enough to coat the spoon, about 10 minutes more.

3. Strain the cream mixture into a clean bowl. Cool to room temperature, stirring occasionally, and chill. Serve as described in the headnote.

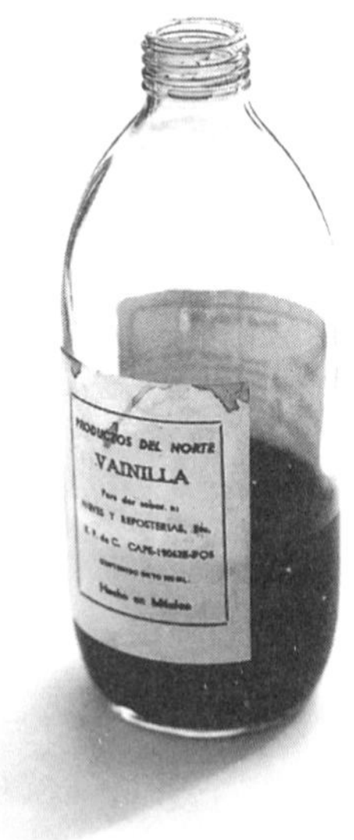

Swedish Cream

SERVES 8 TO 10

"My friend Judy Pucci gave me this recipe twenty-seven years ago when our husbands were both low-on-the-totem-pole employees at the College of William and Mary and we were neighbors in college housing. Since then, we've both left college housing and she has left Williamsburg, but I've gotten miles and miles from her recipe. Dozens of student visitors, as well as our own family members, have been treated to this delicacy when the strawberries are in season. Smiles abound whenever I serve it." With a consistency

thicker and stiffer than whipped cream and not quite as dense as a pudding, Swedish Cream need not be served only at strawberry time. It invites a pile of almost any kind of berry on top, or some sliced peaches underneath, or Swedish-Style Candied Pecans (recipe follows) on the side.

MARY LIZ SADLER (WILLIAMSBURG, VA)

1 cup sugar
¾ tablespoon (1 envelope) unflavored gelatin
2⅓ cups half-and-half
2 cups sour cream
1 teaspoon vanilla extract

1. Combine the sugar and gelatin in a medium saucepan. Add the half-and-half and heat gently, stirring constantly but gently, and taking care not to boil the mixture, until the sugar and gelatin dissolve, 3 to 5 minutes.

2. Transfer the mixture to a medium bowl. Cover and chill until thickened, about 2 hours.

3. Add the sour cream and vanilla to the chilled mixture. Whisk to smooth and chill again until well set, at least 2 to 3 hours, preferably overnight.

4. To serve, spoon the cream into individual dessert bowls and garnish as described in the headnote.

THE SOURCE

The original source of the Swedish Cream recipe seems to be the Snowbird Mountain Lodge in North Carolina's Nantahal National Forest. Beginning with lodge owners Eleanor and Jim Burbank, the recipe has been generously passed along until it reached this volume via our contributor. To serve the cream as they do at the lodge, combine 10 ounces frozen raspberries with 1½ cups red currant jelly and 1½ teaspoons cornstarch in a small saucepan. Bring to a boil, then simmer until clear and slightly thickened. Strain and chill until ready to serve.

Swedish-Style Candied Pecans

MAKES 4 CUPS

For these candied pecans, "it helps to have a friend with a pecan grove (ours is on Mobile Bay in Point Clear, Alabama) and a young person to help pick them up." Lacking such a situation, you can purchase pecan halves and turn them into a treat everyone likes—toasty, flavored nuts.

SUSAN TIPLER (BIRMINGHAM, AL)

8 tablespoons (1 stick) butter (see Notes below)
2 egg whites
1 cup sugar
4 cups pecan halves

1. Preheat the oven to 325°F.

2. Place the butter in a large metal baking pan. When the oven is warm enough, place in the oven until the butter melts. Remove and set aside.

3. In a large bowl, beat the egg whites until soft peaks form. Add the sugar and continue beating until stiff peaks form. Fold the pecans in with a rubber spatula or wooden spoon, gently mixing until they are well coated.

4. Spread as many coated pecans on the baking sheet as will fit in one uncrowded layer. Bake for 30 minutes, stirring and turning every 7 to 10 minutes, until the coating is golden. Remove to paper toweling and continue with another batch until all the pecans are baked.

TENDER MEANS:
Young and soft.
Cooked just right.
Taking care.
Money, when it's legal.

5. Serve right away or store in an airtight container for up to 3 months.

Notes

• If you are using sweet butter, add a tiny pinch of salt along with the sugar when beating the egg whites.

• A 15 by 10-inch jelly roll pan works well for this recipe. A regular cookie sheet also does the job. It's important for the pan to be metal and to do as many batches as necessary so the pecans are baked in one layer—otherwise, they bind into clusters and the individual nuts are not thoroughly coated.

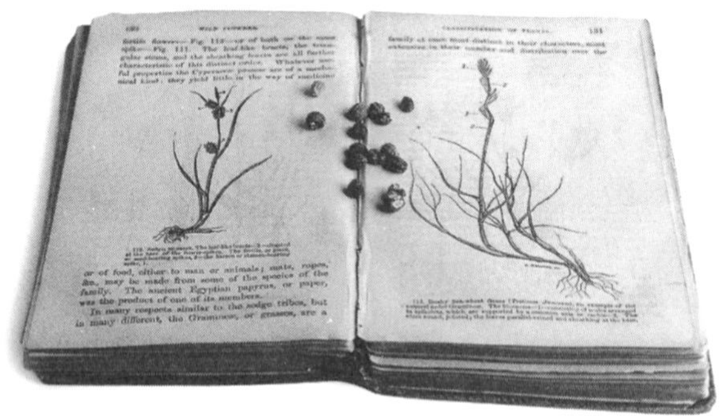

Candied Angelica

MAKES ABOUT 3 CUPS

"My college major was medieval art, so I have a fondness for keeping ancient plant traditions alive. One of my favorite 'medieval' herbs is angelica—that lime-green plant that grows seven feet high and more and produces a cloud of white flowers. One of the old traditions I've carried forward is candying the stem of the plant in summer when it's in its prime." When candied, the sturdy, stringy stems soften enough to accept the sugar

syrup, then, as they dry, firm up again into a toothsome bite that makes a special addition to fruit cakes or Biscotti (page 374) or garnish for frosted cakes, ice creams, and sorbets. Or they may disappear as just plain candy.

ALICE SHARIE-REVELSKI (CHICAGO, IL)

4 cups cut angelica stems (1½-inch lengths)
2 cups sugar
Sugar, for sprinkling

1. Place the angelica in a pot and add water to cover. Bring to a boil, then reduce the heat and simmer until the stems soften and turn a darker green. Drain, discard the water, and set aside.

2. Combine the sugar and ⅔ cup water in the same pot and bring to a boil. Reduce the heat just enough to maintain a brisk boil without overflowing and cook until the liquid is syrupy, 8 to 10 minutes. Remove from the heat, add the angelica, and set aside at room temperature overnight.

3. The next day, lift the angelica out of the syrup with a slotted spoon and transfer it to a plate. Bring the syrup to a boil and cook for 1 minute. Return the angelica to the pot and set aside at room temperature for another night. Repeat the process 2 more times.

4. On the fourth day, after boiling the syrup and stirring in the angelica pieces, lift them out of the syrup and transfer to a rack. Reserve any remaining syrup for another use.

5. Sprinkle the angelica with sugar and set aside in a cool, airy place to dry completely. This will take 3 to 5 days, depending on the weather.

6. When dry, use right away or store in an airtight container. Will keep fresh and supple for up to 6 months.

Angelica: An Angel for the Garden and Kitchen

Herbalists have long extolled angelica's medicinal virtues. In fact, it is told that in the Middle Ages, a monk received a visionary revelation from an angel that this herb would bring about a cure for the plague, and that's how angelica got its name, *Angelica archangelica.* Gardeners appreciate angelica's yellow-green foliage, dainty white flowers, and generous height that can brighten and nicely fill a partially shaded spot. Cooks are intrigued by its property of turning from the taste of generic "greenery" to an indescribable and seductive flavor of flowers, gardens, and gentle days when cooked. All parts of the plant are edible. The stems can be candied and used as described. Not candied, the stems can be used fresh to flavor stewed fruit, especially rhubarb, whose tartness is softened by the angelica, or to infuse custards, dessert creams, rice puddings, and eaux de vie. The leaves, seeds, and root are used fresh or dried for ointments, herbal baths, and soothing teas.

ONE FOR THE ROAD

Green Almond Hospitality Treat to End the Meal

Gary Jenanyan, executive chef for the Robert Mondavi winery Great Chefs Program, now operates his own firm, Gary Jenanyan and Associates, Culinary Consulting and Design, in Oakville, California. Though he travels widely for his food consulting and kitchen design business, the fertile valleys of northern California are still home.

"For those who grew up in Sacramento, California, when it harbored pockets of country yet afforded the convenience of city, backyards full of produce for the table were a given of life. On our property, not so large as a farm but bigger than a *potager,* we grew enough vegetables and fruits to supply lots for the daily table in summer and a bit to put aside for the nongrowing season. Each year, the first excitement over the coming bounty occurred in spring when the almond trees had set fruit but not matured. Some of the green almonds had to be culled in order to make room and allow energy for the tree to continue on to its true destiny in life—full-grown almonds. I have queried my mother about this activity, the particulars of which I don't clearly remember; but I do remember eating the raw, slightly sweet, not at all bitter, creamy white, soft, skinless kernels. Probably I was sneaking the goods from the counter as she was preparing them for a more civilized use. She first soaked them in a lime solution, which in those days was thought necessary to ensure crispness. Then she made a simple syrup of 2 parts sugar to 1 part water. The young almonds were simmered in this for a while, 30 minutes or so. Then the brew was flavored with stick cinnamon and whole cloves and simmered a bit more, until the syrup had reduced enough to drip off the spoon with a noticeable time interval between drops. At this point a dash of lemon juice was stirred in and the concoction simmered another 30 minutes or so, or until the almonds hung suspended in the syrup. As the mixture—spread out on a plate—cooled and dried, the sugar adhered, enrobing each individual nut in a crunchy coat wrapped around a creamy core. These were served as a sort of after-dinner sweet with the coffee. I can still see those crystalline confections. But mostly, when I stand under an almond tree, I remember the taste of the ones purloined as my mother prepared for the guests."

—GARY JENANYAN
(NAPA VALLEY, CA)

contributors index

contributors index

H

I

J

K

L

M

N

O

P

index

D

I

J

K

L

M

N

Q

R

S

W

Y

Z